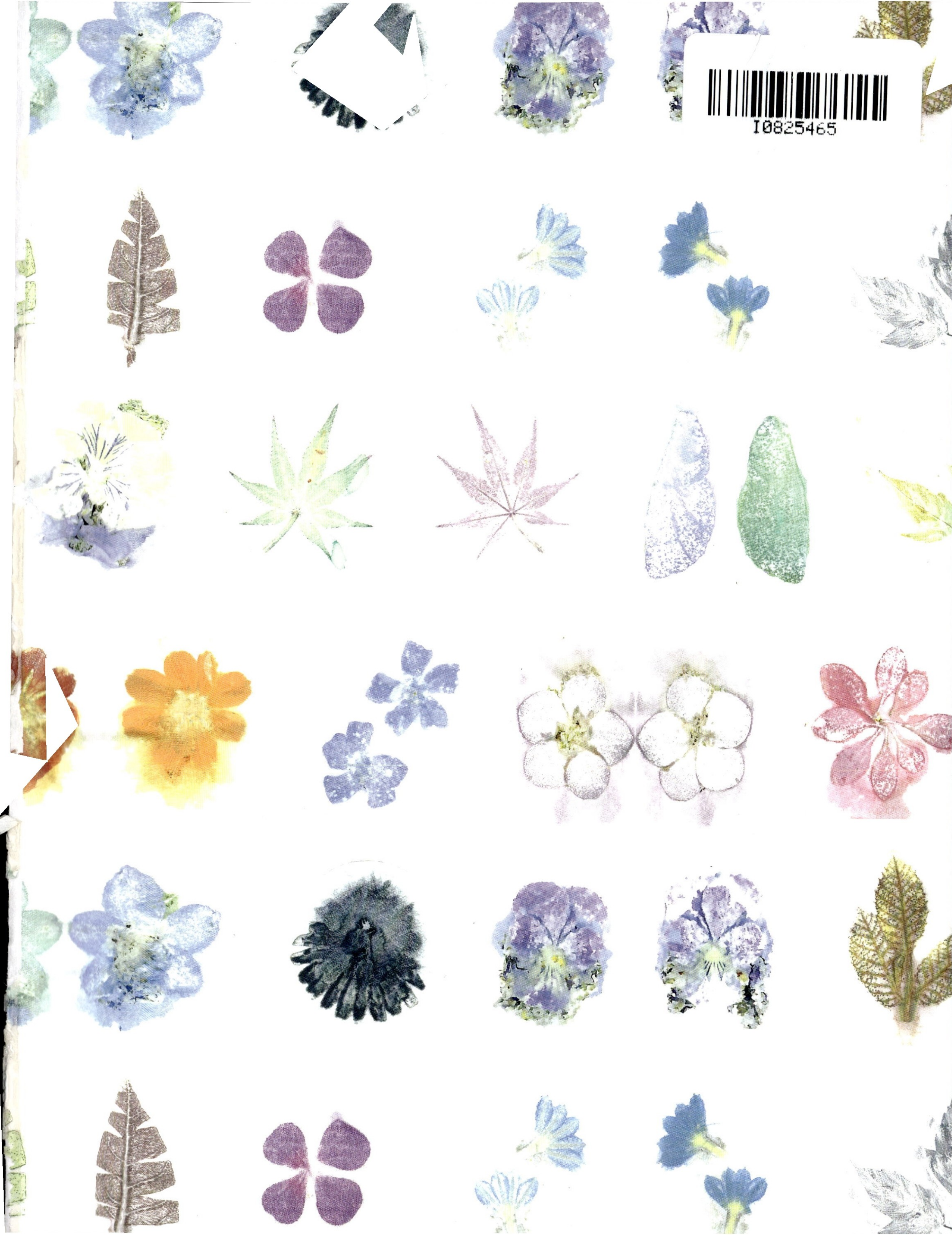
I0825465

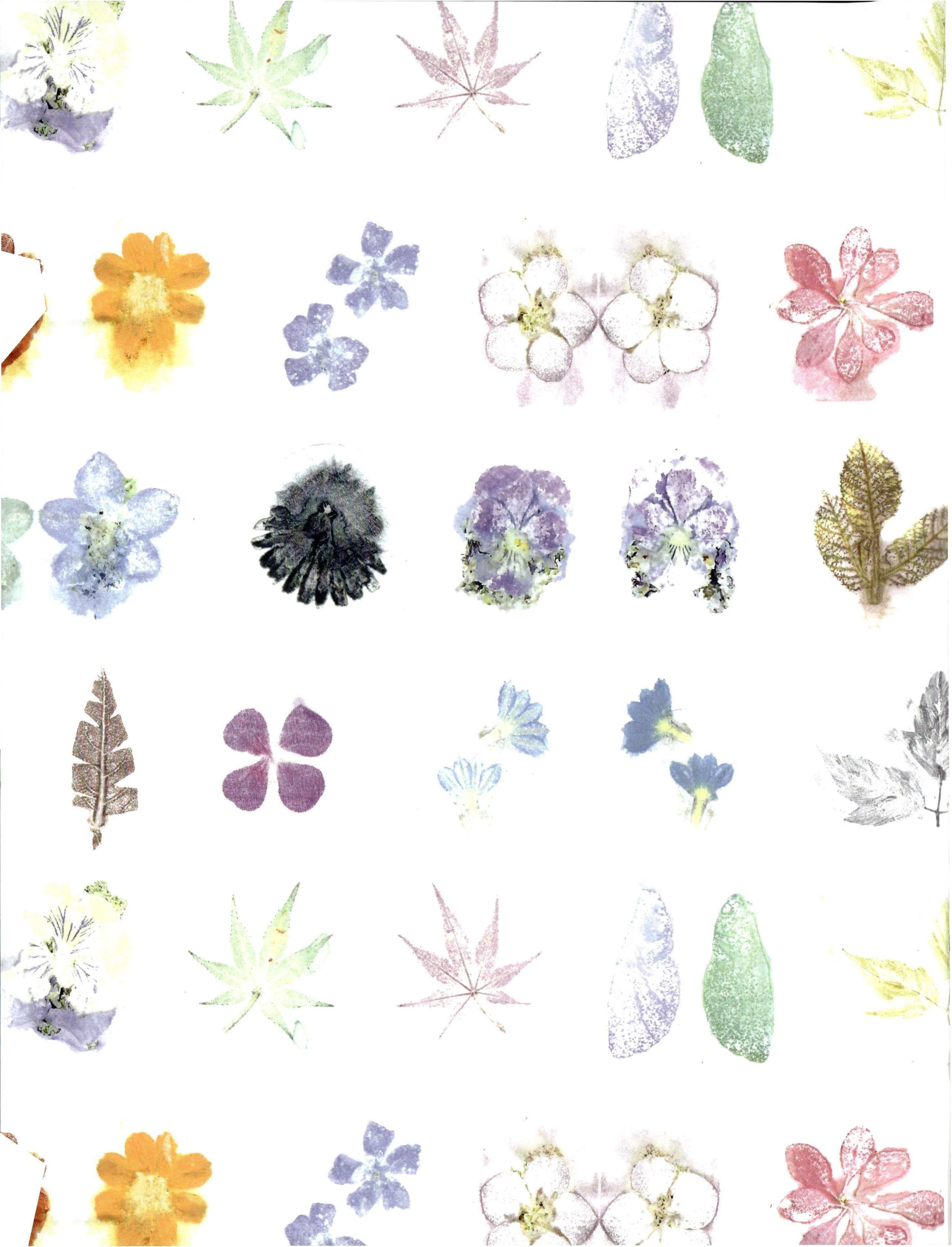

1000 Botanical Colors

Make Your Own Dyes, Paints, Inks, Stains, and Pottery Paints from 250 Plants

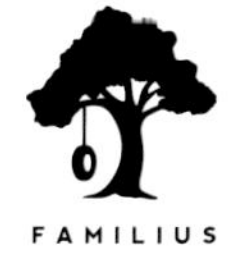

Published by Familius LLC, www.familius.com
PO Box 1130, Sanger, CA 93657

Familius books are available at special discounts for bulk purchases, whether for sales promotions or for family or corporate use.
For more information, contact Familius Sales at orders@familius.com.

Library of Congress Control Number: 2025936680

Print ISBN 9798893960600
Ebook ISBN 9798893960853

Printed in China

Edited by Peg Sandkam and Gretchen Picklesimer Kinney
Cover design by Carlos Mireles-Guerrero and Brooke Jorden
Book design by Mara Harris and Brooke Jorden

10 9 8 7 6 5 4 3 2 1

First Edition

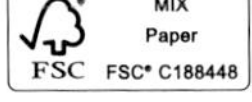

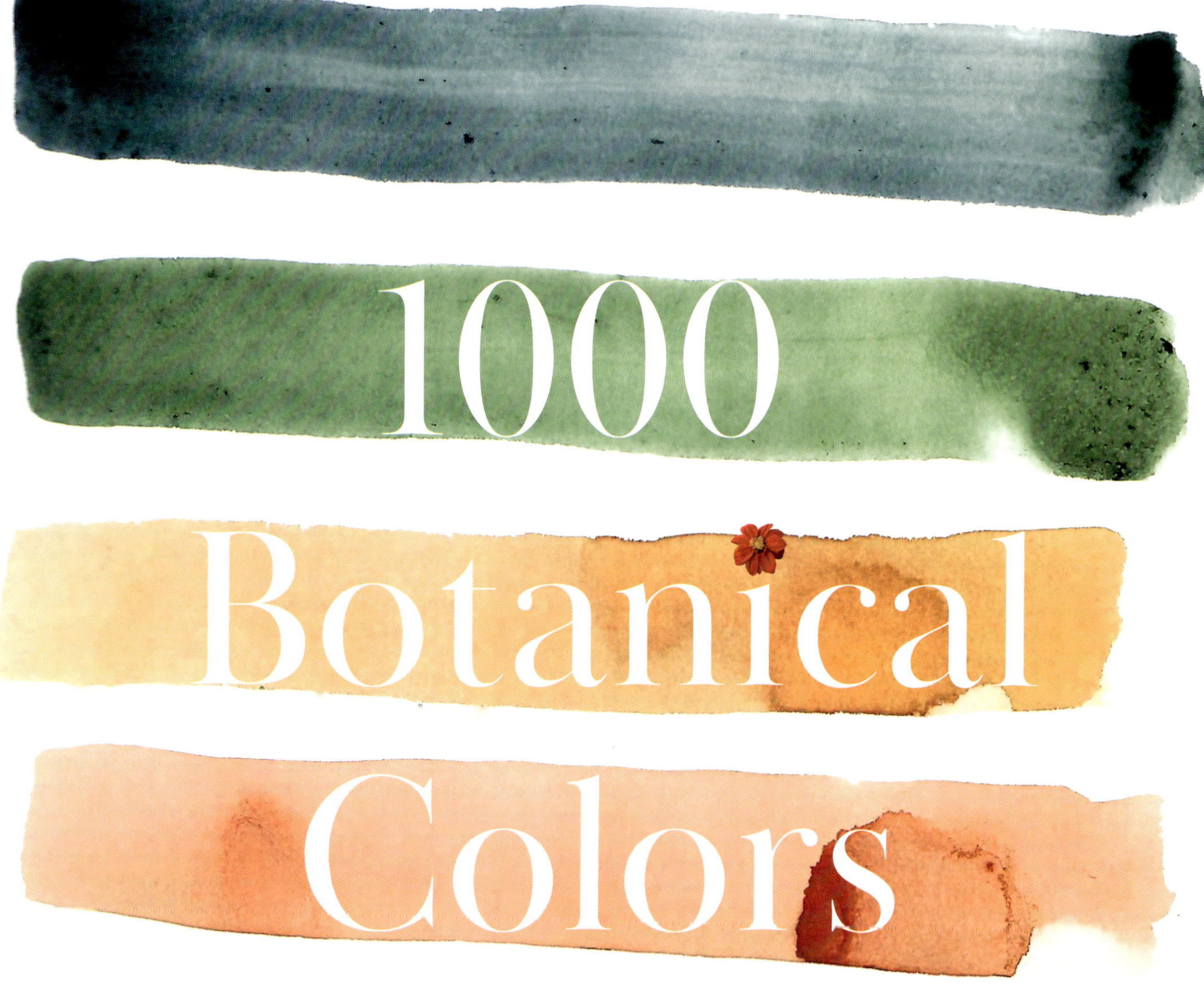

1000 Botanical Colors

Make Your Own Dyes, Paints, Inks, Stains, and Pottery Paints from 250 Plants

Caleb Warnock

Contents

Learning the Basics

Mordants

Fabric Dye Methods

Paper Dye Methods

Homemade Ingredients

Homemade Inks

Homemade Paints

Homemade Stains

Homemade Pastes

Homemade Crayons and Sculpting Materials

Homemade Glairs

Putting This Book Into Practice

Botanical Color Swatches by Plant Type

Color Blocks and Botanical Art

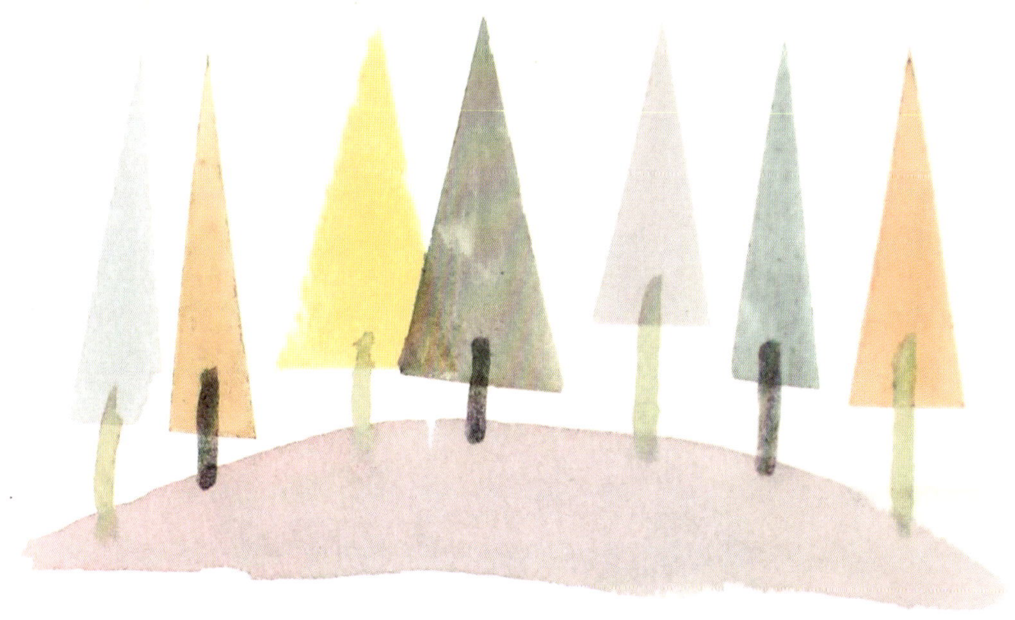

Forest scene made with various botanical watercolors and masking tape used to block out the tree shapes on paper.

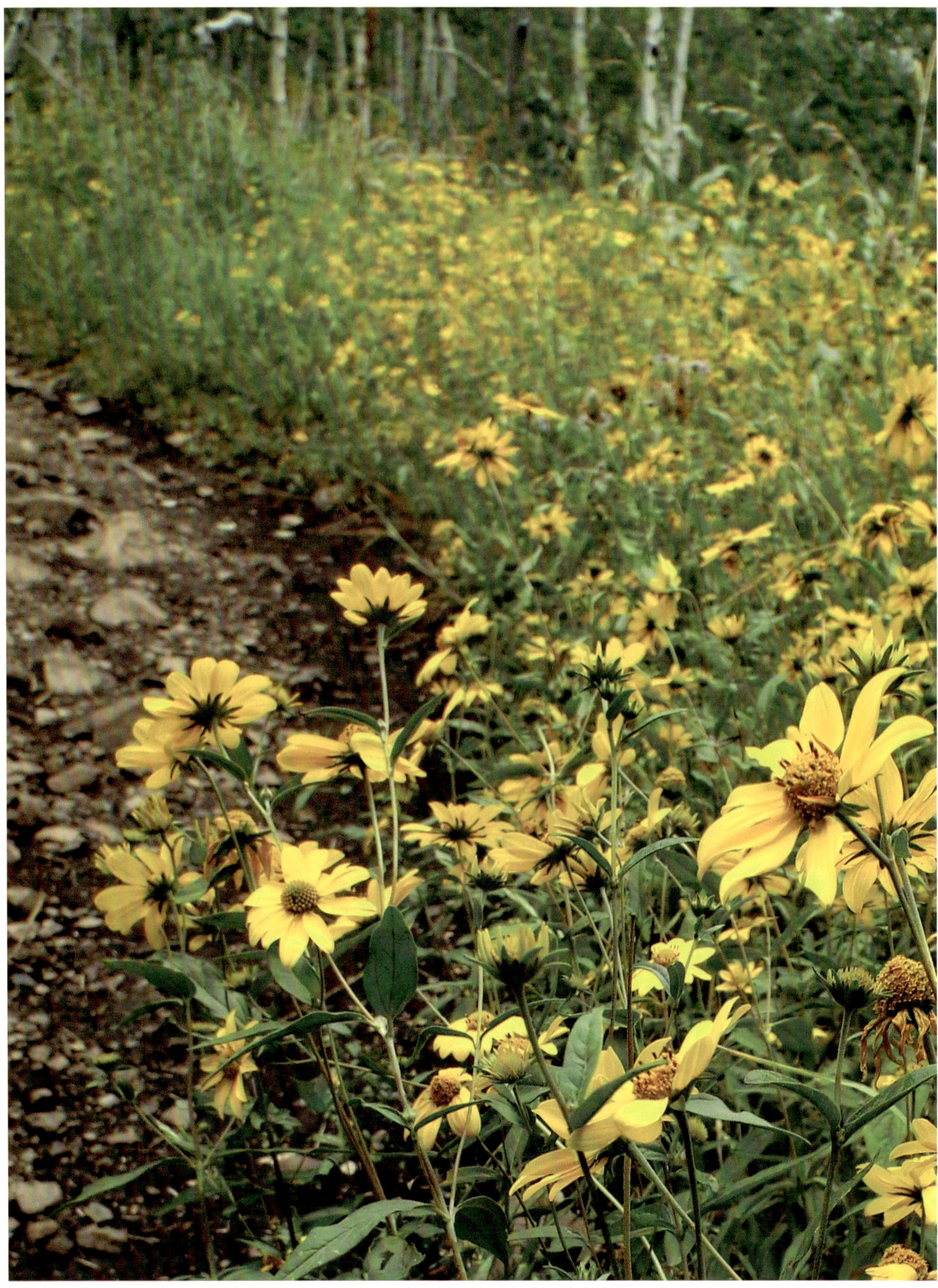

Dedication

This book is dedicated to my great-grandmother Eleanor Jane Ashby Nielson, who died five days before my fifth birthday. I still vividly remember her immaculate garden of roses and flowers—a wonder in the desert. I honestly thought she was magic. Thank you for teaching me to be fascinated by flowers.

I do not exaggerate when I say that on many days, every single plate, cup, and bowl in our house was being used to make botanical paints, pigments, and dyes. So, if you enjoy this book, the person to thank is my wife, Charmayne. She allowed this massive disruption to our kitchen FOR FIVE YEARS. The only complaint I ever heard from her was in frustration because she could not find a bowl for lunch: "I think I will buy my own bowls and hide them from you." We ended up buying dozens more bowls. This book is only possible because of her generosity of spirit. As I write this, she is headed up the canyon, by herself, to get me a single thimbleberry to test with a particular mordant to help me meet a deadline. She is very much looking forward to getting her kitchen back. Thank you for taking me on. This book is also dedicated to you. I love you.

Gratitude

One day when I needed bougainvillea and the nearest was eight hundred miles away, my son-in-law happened to be getting on a plane to Portland in his relentless pursuit of his beloved Los Angeles Dodgers. I asked him if he would bring me some petals. Instead, he flew home with a potted bougainvillea on his lap. That plant is still growing in my greenhouse. Thank you, Johnny Walker.

He, Chelsie, and their beloved, miraculous son, Vin, have acted as travel agents for my wife and me, traveling probably more than ten thousand miles with us to make this book possible. When I needed to go to Hawaii to cook plants, they had tickets and hotel rooms for the five of us in less than twenty-four hours. When I needed to go to the deep desert in Arizona and the Sea of Cortez in Mexico, they flew with us and then chauffeured us. They've taken us to Oregon so many times, to Maine, to Massachusetts, to Iowa—and Spain, Portugal, Morocco, the Netherlands. One of my favorite memories with one-year-old Vin is the day he, my wife, and I all stood around our mulberry bushes gobbling the juicy berries as fast as we could. Vin could not get enough. He is a bright light.

One day Ariel Buckner Lott drove herself and our grandkids from Montana to Oregon to go camping. When I asked her to get me some salmonberries and mail them to me, she did not hesitate. Thank you for your kindness—and for picking the right husband in Trent. I love you all. And thanks for three grandchildren who printed flowers on T-shirts at our kitchen table with such gusto!

When I needed boysenberries, Amberlee Buckner Saunders let her "faux pa"—as she likes to call me—raid her garden. Thank you for taking care of the zoo while we travel, for working at ReStore with me on those difficult days, for two remarkable grandsons, and for traveling with us. We're all "faux" now! You have my heart. As I write this, Mike Saunders, your husband, is standing in our kitchen telling me he is going to make stuffed mushrooms, especially for me, and peach cobbler from our peaches for us all for dinner at your house, if I will stop writing long enough to eat. So I will see you this evening!

To all thirteen of our grandkids who spend time in the garden and in nature with us, I am so happy to be with you. Special thank you to Xander, Cora, Ada, and Gwen for all the work you have done in the garden over the years, to Xander for helping me build greenhouses, and to Ada for getting on the roof to install the roofing and for helping me build the koi pond! You've all saved my aching back! You bring me happiness. You are hard workers.

Kathleen Baer is my close friend and, when I need her, my assistant. Kathleen has spent so much time working with me in our home and garden. Kathleen scanned hundreds of paint samples and dye swatches for this book. She has helped me seed and keep alive thousands of plants. She has run so many errands, organized so many tasks, corrected so many of my mistakes, cleaned up my messes, and made my seed business, SeedRenaissance.com, possible. I am forever grateful.

One day I forlornly mentioned that this book would have to be without poke berry colors because my deadline was days away and my bushes had nary a flower. My great friend Linda Quackenbush Turner got on the phone with her friends and family in Virginia and they picked ripe poke berries and mailed them to me. She arranged this as a surprise and would not even let me pay for shipping. She also handed me greater celandine out of her garden one sunny summer afternoon so it could appear in this book. Linda is a spiritual giant and a great supporter and loves Mother Nature and wants a clean earth for all of us.

Both Kathleen and Linda are members of my beloved gardening club, along with Judy Ball, Melody Rush, Cathy Dobrusky, Rochelle Wise, and Zach Miller. You make gardening fun! Judy, you give so much and work so hard. Melody, you've helped so many people with their nutrition. Thank you for caring. Cathy, you are generous and a hard worker and the best pie maker in America. Zach, you are too nice to all of us. Thank you for being my friend.

To everyone in the neighborhood, my town, and around the world who let me take flowers and plants, thank you. This book is richer because of you.

To my publisher, Christopher Robbins (yes, his real name!), thank you for being the kindest and most trustworthy man in all of publishing. Thank you for making my author-life a happy one. Thank you to Editorial Director Brooke Jordan for long patience, total kindness, and cheerfulness. We all know you do all the hard work. To everyone at Familius Publishing and Hachette who make my books possible, deep gratitude.

Finally, to you, my beloved readers. I do all of this for you. Thank you for coming on the journey with me for all these years.

—Caleb Warnock

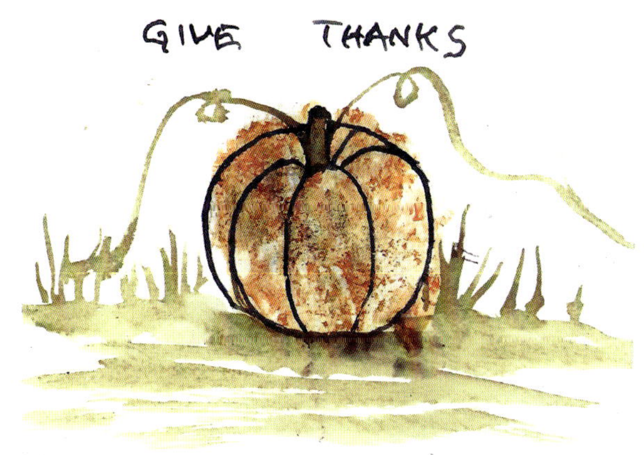

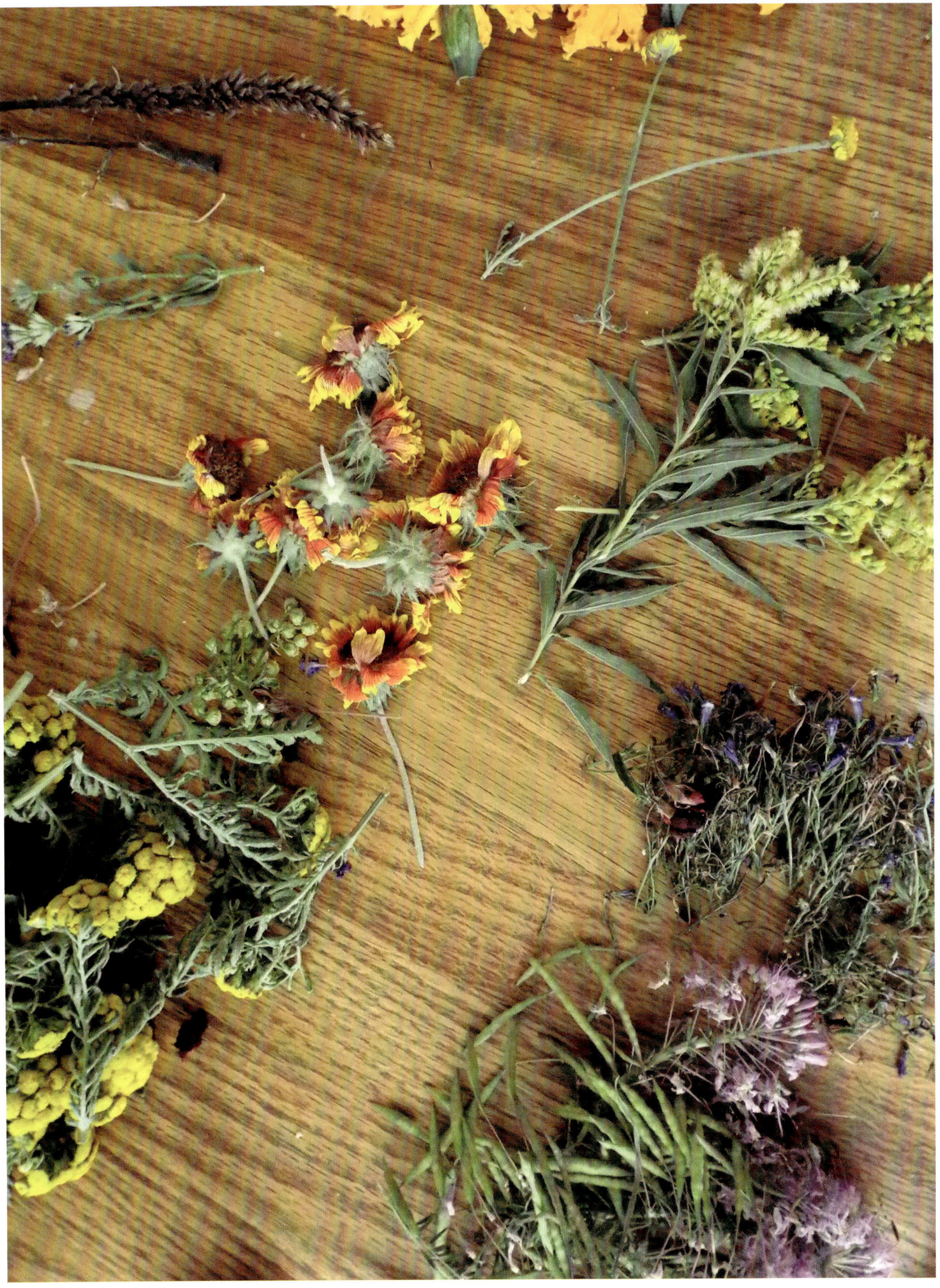

Introduction

Welcome to a world of forgotten botanical colors. Learn to make 100% natural pigments from scratch, just as it's been done for thousands of years. You'll use petals, roots, bark, stems, fruit, leaves, mushrooms and more to make colors like you've never seen before. We start with simple hot and cold dye techniques, then convert dyes into pigments and paints, stains and inks. Every color is possible from easy yellows, browns, reds, pinks, and purples, to less common oranges, and blacks, to the rarest colors—blues and whites.

You can use your homemade colors to dye wool, silk, cotton, and linen, to make powder or glaze pigments for storage, and to make watercolor, gouache, tempera, oils, stains and inks, for use on paper, fiber, canvas, wood, metal, glass, stone and more.

Relax while you join me in using petals to make paint, leaves to make prints, bark and nut hulls to make wood stains. We will use blooms to make colorful air dry clay, and weeds to make kiln paint for pottery. We'll return to nature by turning trees into ink, cactus into pigment, aloes into dye, and berries into art.

To create this book, I spent five years making every single paint, pigment and dye sample on these pages, by hand and from scratch, using only natural ingredients. Every recipe has been tested and tested again. As with all my books, I wanted to write this text because there is a huge need for a true dictionary of botanical colors, with lots of pictures. In this book, at last we have a single convenient source to find out which plant, mixed with which mordant, in which recipe, makes which color, and how those colors vary on paper, canvas, fabric, soap, clay, cloth, and more.

This book is just plain fun. Is there anything more calming and pleasurable than walking through nature—or your own garden or local park—to collect flowers and leaves to make sun prints, watercolors, milk paint, oil paint, pebble crafts, or dyed shirts, scarves and bags? When stress looms large, loosen up by mulling the petals of a single rose, or berries, into a handful of astonishing paints. Or turn tomato leaves to artist's ink, or blueberries into stamping ink, or carrots into ink for botanical prints.

You will never see an acorn, an avocado pit, an eggshell, or backyard clay in the same way again. Once you get into this new habit, you will see the ingredients for colors and art and dyes everywhere you look, every day of the year. If you're like me, you will be on vacation thousands of miles from home and beg your family to pull over the car so you can grab a sample of petals or twigs or clay. You will be able to treasure botanical journals of your travels and happy memories with prints and impressions from Mother Nature. If you are not careful, you will draw curious onlookers who want to watch you do mordant tests on the hiking trail, and finger-pressed prints on the beach. You can warm the house in winter by dyeing shirts, and entertain the kids or grandkids by turning frozen berries into fingerpaint, radishes into paper dolls and spinach into holiday crafts.

You are only limited by your imagination.

And not for nothing, everyone benefits when we work hand in hand with Mother Nature. This book offers a unique and fascinating path to connect yourself, your family, and those you love, firmly to the earth that mothers us all.

Uniting with the natural world is a hands-on experience.

For example, this morning, as I write this in August, my garden club met at my house at 8 a.m. for garden charcuterie. I served fresh-picked blackberries, carrots, snap beans, gooseberries, beets, a rainbow of heirloom tomatoes, and homemade stevia grape juice. Several of them had driven over an hour to be here, and everyone was hungry because we were about to get our hands in the dirt. After breakfast, we filled pots and planted them with autumn garden vegetable seeds—cauliflower, carrots, lettuce, zucchini, spinach, fava beans, pak choi—for everyone to take home. Because I own a seed company (SeedRenaissance.com) the seeds were not hard to come by. Next we examined two prototypes we are building of a solar dehydrator for preserving fruits and vegetables. I had painted these wooden contraptions with handmade, completely natural black paint--made from grape vines—to help the sun gather heat. Then the club toured my autumn garden and greenhouses, and I talked about dyeing fabric with homemade edamame milk, gave a report on managing wasp nests without chemicals, discussed building more cold frames and garden boxes as a group, and invited them to pick all the gooseberries, Egyptian walking onions, and garlic they wanted. At noon, we sat at the kitchen table to taste and judge three scratch-made salad dressings on a bed of greens, jicama spread with peanut butter, and pecan flour crepes with blackberry filling. We love our potluck lunches.

As we made a priority list of projects, talk turned, as it always does, to how we can make things with nontoxic, natural technologies that have been used for all of human history. We talked about making milk glue, botanical dyes, and recycling cedar wood for garden boxes. One of our group members wondered why it is so hard to find the things we want, like completely natural, nontoxic, exterior-grade wood glue. Such glue used to be sold in every store, and has been used for hundreds of years. Today, you can't buy it for love nor money. We talked about natural methods for preemergent weed control, for wood stain, for making waterproof fabric. Why is it so vexing to find any living memory of methods that were common and widespread even 70 years ago?

"Because of 'Better Living Through Chemistry,'" said one of our members. "The whole world has bought into that completely."

She was referring to an advertising slogan that debuted in 1935 from DuPont. For decades, that slogan became synonymous with progress and new technology. As an ad campaign, it has perhaps never been surpassed. Hundreds of millions of people were convinced to give up the "old" ways in a fever dream of plastic, gasoline, petroleum fertilizer, synthetics and now, chemicals that never biodegrade.

For the first time in history, the human race was creating "forever pollution" that cannot be cleaned up, recalled, fixed, taken back or undone.

Of course, this discussion is reductive. Chemistry has improved everyone's lives. I don't have a problem with progress or better living—after all, I'm writing this book on my laptop! We need innovation, a healthy economy, and good jobs. But almost a century ago, at the same time we fell in love with better living through chemistry, we also made a decision in the halls of Congress, in state legislatures, and in the courts, that those companies bringing us progress would have little responsibility for the associated toxic waste. Making synthetic paint or synthetic fabric dye, just to give two examples, creates massive amounts of leftover chemical waste. In the US, we "solved" our Cancer Alley crisis by passing laws that force manufacturers to move to poorer countries. Now we get the same goods and services, but we leave all the "forever pollution" in the poorest nations of the world. We justify this by saying it benefits their economy to swallow our poison pill.

And it certainly has worked. Forcing our toxic waste to move abroad has improved American air and water. Good for us. Right?

Other consequences of our chemical romance have not been as easy to "solve." Yes, the toxic heavy metal waste from the dye that colors our jeans is now dumped in rivers out of sight, out of mind. The same with the residues from manufacturing paint. But the actual paint itself quietly degrades into our landscape. You put up the cutest, most photogenic white picket fence in your garden. But in a few years, that fence has faded and flaked and must be repainted. What happened to the paint that flaked away? The microscopic dust of old paint—containing xylene, formaldehyde, acetone, toluene, heavy metals and more—is now the dust mixing in our gardens and soil.

While this book is fun, and the arts and crafts are relaxing, we can also take pride in the fact that everything in this book is clean—for our air, water and soil, for the animals, the oceans, the children, and their parents. Clean for the generations to come. Botanical paints, pigments, and dyes have a real impact on human and planetary health. And that is worth celebrating—by making a botanical print, or a quick card, or by dyeing a shirt. This book will teach you how.

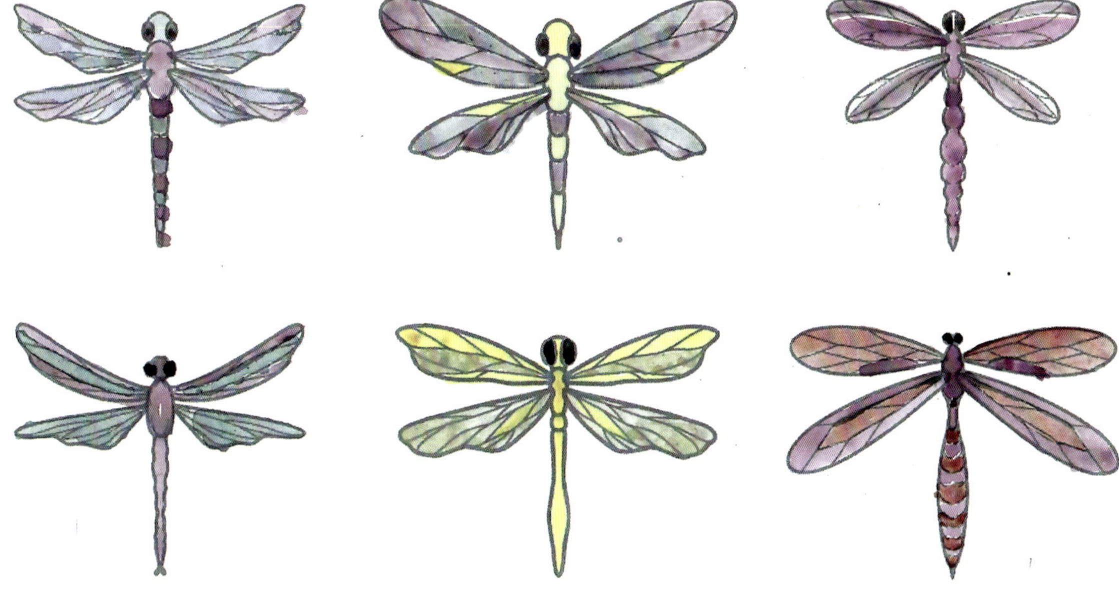

Learning the Basics

The History of Synthetic Dyes

In 1856, William Henry Perkin was an eighteen-year-old chemistry student at the Royal College of Chemistry in London, England. He went home for the Easter holiday with homework: to use the colorless oil of coal tar, called aniline, to experiment with developing a synthetic quinine, which was needed to treat malaria. To do this, Perkin set up a rudimentary laboratory at home. When he added potassium dichromate, the oil turned purple. (Potassium dichromate is a carcinogen that also damages the kidneys and liver.) While recording the results of his experiment, Perkin left purple fingerprints on his notebook pages, still visible today on display at the Science and Industry Museum in England. Perkin knew immediately he had created a dye. He tested it on a piece of silk, which dyed purple. Calling his discovery "mauveine," he took out a patent in August 1856. It made him wealthy and completely changed how dyes and colors are created to this day.[1]

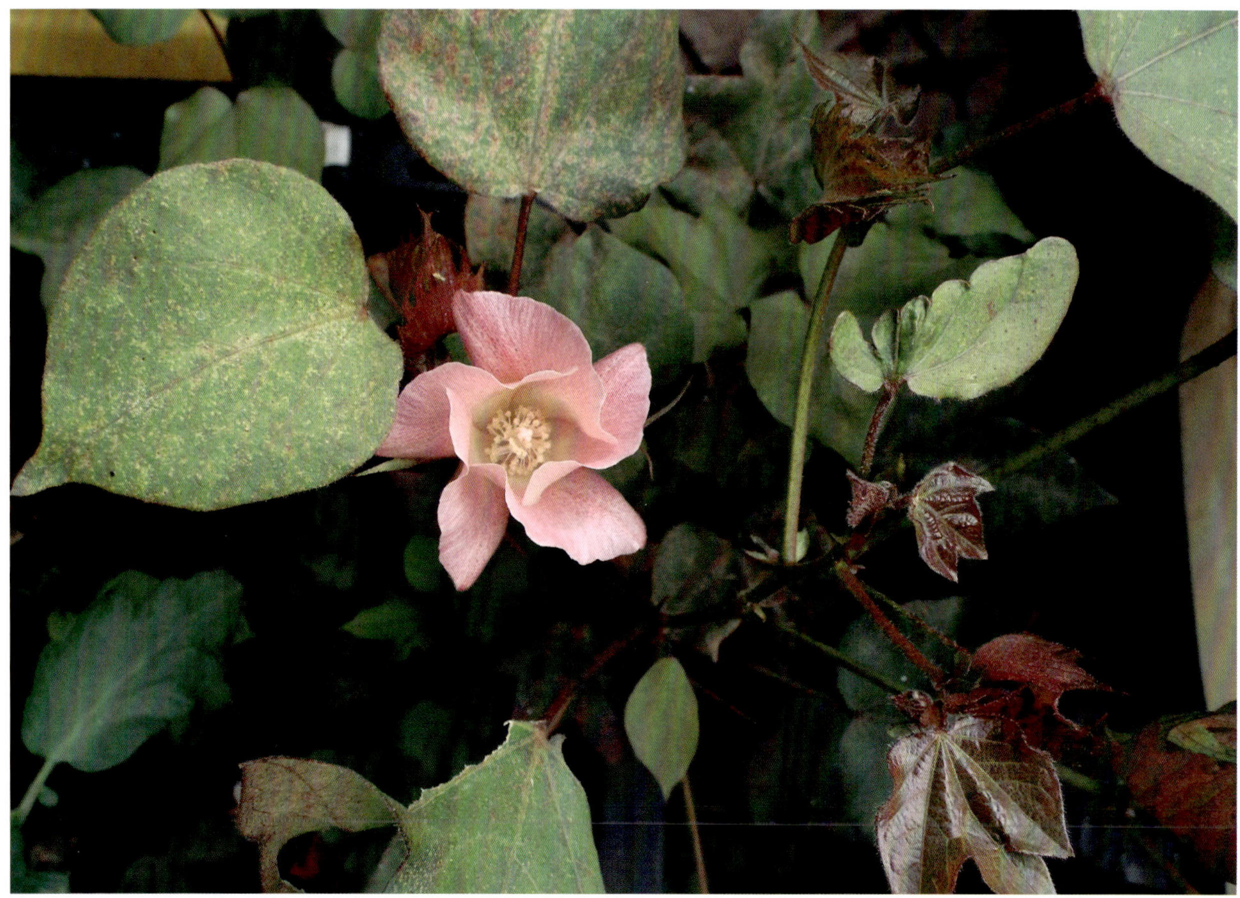

pink cotton flower

Eco-Printing: Playing with Plants, Connecting with Nature

When plants and botanical paints and dyes are used to print on fabric or paper, or make art or clothing, the process is called "eco-printing." Eco-prints are one of the great joys of life for people like me who love to make art from botany. There are a lot of us. Eco-printing has become popular online, with many people making videos about their process and experiments.

Here are some examples:

- Use botanical paint on the back of a leaf and then print that leaf onto paper.
- Use a spoon, hammer, your fingers, or a die-cut machine to print a leaf or a flower onto fabric.
- Layer flowers or even rusty metal pieces onto fabric, roll the fabric tightly, and steam the roll to create prints.
- Finger-press found flowers into a small notebook to document a vacation, a journey, or the seasons of your favorite wild places.

These are just four examples. But eco-prints are only limited by our imagination! In this book, I've listed fifty possible creative projects for adults, and another fifty for children. Many of these projects can be considered eco-printing.

The word "eco-print" was coined by artist India Flint of Australia in her 2010 book *Eco Colour: Botanical Dyes for Beautiful Textiles*. In 2022, Flint described her work in an essay at WomenCreate.com as "using ecologically sustainable contact print processes from plants and found objects." The purpose of her art, she said, is to immerse herself in nature by "paying deep attention to wherever I happen to be, gathering thought and experience, imagery and marks, as well as harvesting materials for making. I try to step lightly on the land while being nourished by it."

Beautifully said.

Eco-prints can be pressed flowers preserved on paper by all-natural decoupage paste (see page 85). Or a wax-resist print of a leaf on paper washed with botanical watercolor. Or making color block "quilts" by rubbing fresh petals and leaves onto masked patterns on paper. And everything in between.

The goal is to disconnect—from the stress and pressure of the modern world, from the now-massive and influential (and sometimes depressing) news and trends from the digital world. Then we can return to things that are real and tangible and timeless—flowers, leaves, trees, gardens, vegetables, meadows—time with family and friends in nature. Eco-printing allows me to really examine what is around me and how we can help each other. I can plant the flowers and they give me not only beauty for the eye, but also paint and pigment and dye. I can collect the leaves and they give me not only greenery and fruit from their branches, but also colors to make art. Perhaps more important, eco-printing is maybe one last way that kids and families alike can really connect to the earth while having fun. If kids and parents and cousins and grandparents are walking, gathering, and making with the flowers and plants the world has to offer us, they are also not online. They are exploring their earth, connecting with something that does not demand money in exchange for beauty or experience.

As India Flint said, making prints from nature allows us to pay deep attention to and be deeply touched by the soil and living things that give us life and everything we have. That is the goal of this book. We must more often leave behind the rush and discord of the grumpy and increasingly dangerous modern world. Think of how a child's life is changed if they study and play in nature.

How to Steal Flowers— from Yourself and Others

Once when I was teaching a class on botanical eco-printing, one of the students said, "I can see myself getting quite addicted to this. I'm going to need a lot more flowers."

Indeed.

I've pressed, cooked, or dried thousands of flowers, leaves, barks, and roots. I grow a lot of flowers, but none of us can grow everything. We all need to borrow what we can from friends, neighbors, and Mother Nature. Here are tips and tricks to getting the botanical colors you need to have fun with this book.

1 **Least visible.** Whether harvesting from your own yard, a friend's yard, or Mother Nature's yard, always take what is least visible. I have found that my wife is more amenable to me "stealing" flowers from our yard if the plant appears untouched after I've harvested. I take from the back side of the plant, from the least visible spot. For example, when I took lilacs this spring, I took them from the center of the bush, choosing the flowers that were most hidden by the foliage. When I took tulips, I cut one tulip per clump and took the flower that was least visible and closest to the ground. When I take things from nature or neighbors, I do the same. I always try to make it as hard as possible for the naked eye to tell that I've been taking flowers.

2 **Dying petals.** We keep orchids in our kitchen and in the greenhouses. My wife has a special purple orchid right now that she has given pride of place in the entry to our home. When I wanted to see how it would eco-print, I knew I could not cut off a flower without risking marital hellfire. So I waited patiently until one of the blossoms wilted and fell to the ground, not dried yet. This way, my wife was happy and I got to print all the orchid flowers I wanted. I just had to be patient.

3 **Local plants.** To make all the samples in this book, I needed access to far more plants than I could grow. So I asked friends and neighbors and used social media groups to ask total strangers—and everyone was happy to help. On Facebook, I am a member of my local Buy Nothing group. When I needed a specific flower—red hot poker, for example—I went online and asked. My friends brought me plants, and I was already notorious for taking divisions or cuttings from the yards of everyone I know. Dozens of my property consultation clients have given me divisions of their flowers and trees. When asking others for flowers, I am careful to explain rules one and two, so they know I'm not just going to clear-cut all the color from their yard. If they are with me when I harvest, I ask them to pick which blossoms I take.

4 **Greenhouse sale.** My favorite local plant nursery has a clearance sale every autumn and puts hundreds of annuals and perennials on sale for a dollar apiece. I got a couple dozen of the samples in this book from those sales. Find the clearance sales in your area. And if you love flowers but don't have your own geothermal greenhouse yet, let me design one for you as part of a property consultation. You will love it!

5 **Weddings and funerals.** People spend a lot of money on blooms for weddings and funerals, but they often end up in the trash. Ask to take some! You can also make this request of strangers on social media groups, like a local Buy Nothing group, where it is pretty common for people to offer wedding flowers after the wedding.

6 **Memorial holidays.** This past Mother's Day, my wife and I went to the cemetery to place fresh iris blossoms from our backyard on the grave of my mother-in-law. The whole cemetery was awash in fresh flowers. This is also true on Father's Day, Memorial Day, and Veterans Day—and there are fresh flowers in smaller numbers on graves almost every unfrozen day of the year (we live at 5,200 feet elevation). These flowers are collected by cemetery employees and thrown away. Ask your cemetery if you can have flowers they are throwing out.

7 Travel ready. I always keep a pair of garden clippers, a trowel, and a box of sandwich bags in my truck. Because I travel a lot doing property consultations, I often stop to collect things from the side of the road, from friends in the area, and from my clients. For example, because I make both paint and pottery paint from natural clays, I am always on the lookout for a good roadside clay bed. I have taken small clay samples of different colors from hundreds of miles around where I live. The colors range from red to pink to orange to white. I'm still looking for really good green, gray, and black clays. The holy grail of clay is blue. I always have my eye out. My wife is very patient when I suddenly veer off the road to scoop up a fun color. If I'm not in my vehicle because we have traveled by plane, for example, I always keep a sandwich bag in my pocket for collecting clay, seeds, or flowers. (Be careful though: You can't bring clay, seeds, or flowers across international borders.)

8 Plant your own. Of course! If you have a balcony, plant a grow-box or pots. If you have a porch, you've got space for flowers. A sunny window? That will work! Or a garden of any size or flower beds around your home. If you don't own a home, find a friend, family member, or neighbor who will let you do some gardening on their property, or get the landlord's permission to put pots of flowers near the entry. I have a renter friend who grows her whole vegetable garden in pots this way. You can also borrow a garden—people who once had large gardens but now are too old to keep it all up will welcome your help and friendship! You can also offer to adopt a flower bed at City Hall or the local cemetery or church.

9 School flower beds. If I had my way, every school would have an "Adopt-A-Flower Bed" program. Each class in the school would get one flower bed on the property to tend. Parent volunteers would coordinate with the teachers to provide plants and seeds. This is a great way for parents or grandparents to make a difference at school. And then you can teach the kids how to make eco-prints and grow a few edible flowers to taste too! Hint: Kids and adults love borage flowers, which taste like cucumbers! Nasturtiums are tasty if you love arugula! Violets and columbines are sweet to the taste and plant themselves year after year! I was eating violets in my garden this morning! Larkspurs are the most beautiful blue color, make great dye and paint, and plant themselves year after year.

10 Bonus! What NOT to take. Never take from protected lands, such as national parks. Some collecting of limited seasonal material may be allowed in your local national forest—for example, our national forest allows collecting wild berries—but always ask first or look up the rules online. Call your local forest ranger office if needed. Never take things that are rare or from limited populations. Never take more than 1 or 2 percent of the total flowers from a roadside patch because local insects and animals also use the flowers, and the flowers need a vigorous breeding population for long-term health. If you don't own the property, ask permission before harvesting, of course. And just because something is growing on public property doesn't mean you can harvest it. Once I wanted some walnuts to make dye. A few blocks from my home was a sidewalk lined with walnut trees. The trees were encroaching on the walkway, which is technically illegal, so I thought I could help myself. The homeowner loudly disagreed with me when they saw what I was doing. He said to me, in a very yell-y voice, "If you had knocked and asked first, that would have been one thing, but to take without asking is not right!" He was correct, and I repented.

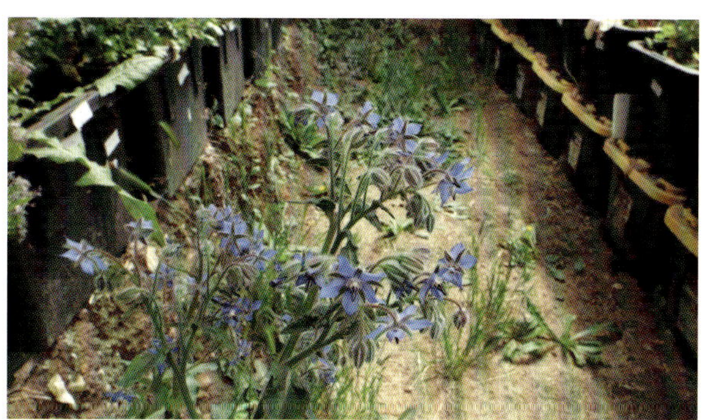

Essential Tips for Making Botanical Paints and Dyes

- The more water you add, the more diluted the color becomes. The more water you put in, the more work and time required to remove it to strengthen the color. For example, when you are cooking a small batch of berries or petals, use just enough water to cover your material. If you are mulling fresh flower petals without cooking them, use only drops of water.

- When you are boiling a huge pot of berries, leaves, or petals in preparation for dyeing a shirt, you will need a large amount of botanical material to start, which means you will need a lot of water. But you will get a stronger color by letting the pot boil to evaporate water for an hour or two. However, you must retain enough water to get your garment in the dye with enough space to move around freely.

- All paints and stains work best when applied in thin layers and allowed to dry completely between coats. If you put a second layer on too soon, it will begin to lift the first layer when you brush it on, especially on wood, metal, or glass. If you look carefully at some of my samples on wood in this book, you can see where I rushed and this happened. Sigh.

- Don't burn yourself. Making paint sometimes involves boiling water. Be careful, and don't let your kids or grandkids around dangerous elements, including boiling water or bags of chemicals like urea, iron powder, or vinegar of copper. Some things, though they are natural, require respect and adult supervision. Don't get hurt while having fun.

- Allow yourself to fail your way to success. As in all aspects of life, success is based on layers of failure. Each failure teaches you how not to proceed. This is useful information. Successful people use failure as a step forward.

- Keep notes. Write down what you put in every batch so you know afterward whether those ingredients and processes worked or not. The tiniest addition and subtraction can make a huge difference. I can't tell you how many times I've had to add another drop or two of water or binder or another flake or two of a dried ingredient. In a week, you will love the result, but you will be frustrated when you want to make it again and you forgot to write down exactly how you did it!

- Do not layer different paint recipes. If you do, the different layers may flake or bubble—even if the recipes are only one ingredient different. The paint layers make look great for a day or two, but a week later you see the paint is flaking off.

- If you dry the paint too fast, in heat above 85 degrees, or in direct sunlight, you also might experience bubbling and flaking paint.

- Over time, decide what is worth investing in. Invest in a good glass muller set early on. As you go, you will want to buy some alum, some good quality paper, maybe some ascorbic acid, maybe some citric acid. Start with things you get cheap and free, and as you get more serious, gift yourself small amounts of good brushes or ingredients as needed. This does not need to be expensive. Most of what you do should be very inexpensive indeed.

- Don't expect botanical and natural ingredients to behave, or be as consistent, as petroleum-based commercially prepared paints, which are mordanted with harsh chemicals. As one of my students recently put it, one of the joys of using botanical materials is that they are never fully controllable or predictable. She said this because she and another student were sharing a desk and a muller to make a batch of paint, but when each student painted the exact same paint on different grades of paper, the paint turned different colors. Because this student was a professional bookbinder, she knew immediately why this had happened—because all paper is coated with a liquid sizing, and the expensive paper she brought had different sizing on it than the cheaper paper her partner was using. The result was two completely different colors because the different sizings mordanted the paint differently. This is indeed one of the joys of the botanical journey—there are a lot of surprises and magic moments along the way. I told the class, after we discussed what had just happened to this batch of paint, that three times I have been able to make cobalt blue from woad seeds, but all other attempts at that color have always ended in failure. As I was teaching, I was wearing a shirt dyed with citric acid and red rose petals and vinegar of copper. Despite several attempts, I've never managed to get a dye vat to capture that mixture of red, green, and blue again. And the worst of all, I told them, are the flowers of Russian sage. I swear you get a different result from those flowers every day of the year, whether fresh or dried. Occasionally they make stunning blue or turquoise, but you can repeat the exact recipe from the flowers of the same bush the next day and get nothing even close! We forget that, as living chemical factories, the molecular makeup of every plant, animal, and human being actually changes every minute of every day.

Pressing Fresh Flowers and Leaves

QUICK MICROWAVE METHOD

Flowers and leaves

2 ceramic plates with relatively flat bottoms

Paper towels

1. Gather and trim your flowers and leaves. Get the cleanest, best-quality plant material you can without missing pieces, insect damage, or sun damage. Plant material should be picked at its prime.

2. Line one plate with a paper towel and top place leaves or flowers on top so they don't touch each other; cover with a second paper towel. Put the second plate on top of the paper towels and microwave the stacked plates and material for about 45 seconds. Do not overcook the material or it will crumble when you remove it from the plates.

3. Let the plates cool for a minute or two before removing them from the microwave. Carefully unstack the plates and remove your flowers and leaves. Set them on a flat surface, away from direct sunlight, to finish cooling. They are now ready to use to make sun prints, crumble for making paint or pigment, or store for later use.

SUN METHOD

Flowers and leaves

2 sheets of copy paper

Baking sheet

Sheet of glass

1. Gather and trim your flowers and leaves. Get the cleanest, best-quality plant material you can, without missing pieces, insect damage, or sun damage. Plant material should be picked at its prime.

2. Between two sheets of copy paper, place leaves and flowers in a single layer so they don't touch. Put the stack of papers on a large baking sheet.

3. Cover with a sheet of glass and set in direct, strong sunlight. After a few minutes, if you see moisture building up on the glass, add another sheet of paper on top of the material under the glass. Leave in the sun for up to a day. Avoid doing this on windy days.

BOOK METHOD

Flowers and leaves

Heavy book

1. Gather and trim your flowers and leaves. Get the cleanest, best-quality plant material you can, without missing pieces, insect damage, or sun damage. Plant material should be picked at its prime.

2. Place your material between the pages of a heavy book and leave it for weeks or years. If you are like me, you will find the leaves that you collected with your four-year-old nephew a quarter century ago, realize he now has his own four-year-old, and be sad about how old you are. Set these feelings aside and move on.

How to Use a Glass Muller

A glass muller set is like a flat version of a mortar and pestle used to grind herbs or ingredients in the kitchen. A muller set is essential for making homemade paint, and versions of this have been used for thousands of years. It is a true ancient technology that is just as relevant today. A set includes a handheld muller and a plate of tempered glass called a "slab."

The key to happy mulling is to use <u>tiny batches</u>. When I teach classes on botanical paints, pigments, and dyes, the number one problem students have is trying to mull batches that are too large. The larger your batch is, the longer it takes and the harder it is to mull.

The ideal batch on a muller plate should be no more than half a teaspoon of your paint base, and less than a teaspoon with all your ingredients included. The wider your handheld muller is, the faster you will make paint. A good batch should take no more than thirty seconds to prepare once your ingredients are on the slab. Having mulled thousands of batches of paint, I can tell you from experience that it is <u>much faster</u> to mull several tiny batches than it is to try and mull one large batch.

A common mistake is thinking that you need to use pressure to mull the paint. The weight of the handheld glass does most of the work, and you should never apply more than medium pressure to the glass. Figuring this out just takes experience. When I teach my class at the University of Utah, I tell the students not to use too much pressure, but then they use too little. And if I say nothing, they use too much. It is possible to break the glass slab from too much downward pressure. So it is important to use small to medium pressure, usually less pressure in the beginning and a little more pressure toward the end of the mulling process.

While mulling wet ingredients is most common, it is not uncommon for me to also mull dry ingredients. Yesterday, as I write this, I was showing my students how to mull my dried mixture of kaolin clay and vinegar of copper into permanent indigo fabric paint. A long time ago, I mixed vinegar of copper with kaolin clay and cooked them together so I would have a quick and ready-to-use copper base for various recipes of blue. But this means that, to mull the paint, I first had to mull a small chunk of hardened clay into a liquid base (edamame milk, in the case of fabric paint). When mulling such hard dry chunks, even though they are small, the key is to go slow and start with small pressure, working up to medium pressure. Turning the muller in a circle helps to immediately break down the dry material. This method is true whether the dry material is clay-based, dried flower petals, fresh flower petals, or even shavings of Osage orange wood. Let the muller do most of the grinding. Don't press too hard. Take your time.

Once you have begun to force your ingredients to mix on the muller plate, your ingredients will begin to spread into a circle. You will need to use a spatula once or twice in the process to scrap everything back to the center. Mulling several times is the key to making a smooth, thoroughly mixed paint, ink, or stain. The thinner your mix is on the slab, the smoother it will be. When finished, scrap your paint back to the center and use the spatula to move it to a palette or just use it fresh off the slab.

If you are mulling your paint and it begins to thicken but there are still lumps in it or specks of pigment, you need to add more water and mull more.

My students often ask how you know when the mulled paint is finished and ready to use. One of the best signs is that the muller begins to suction to the glass. If you can lift your muller and the glass slab comes with it, even momentarily, that is a good sign that your paint is nearly finished. Another sign: when you scrap the paint into one spot, it stays where you put it and does not run away. Another sign: your paint looks like paint. It has the thickness and smoothness that you want. If you are unsure, brush a bit of your paint onto paper to see if it needs any further mulling. If you see the paint is uneven, or there are specks of pigment, then mull more. By testing on paper, you can also see if you have achieved the saturation of color you want. If the color is too pale, you can still mull in more botanical pigment.

When mulling fresh petals, berries, or leaves into a base paint for tinting, too much pulp always causes cracking and flaking.

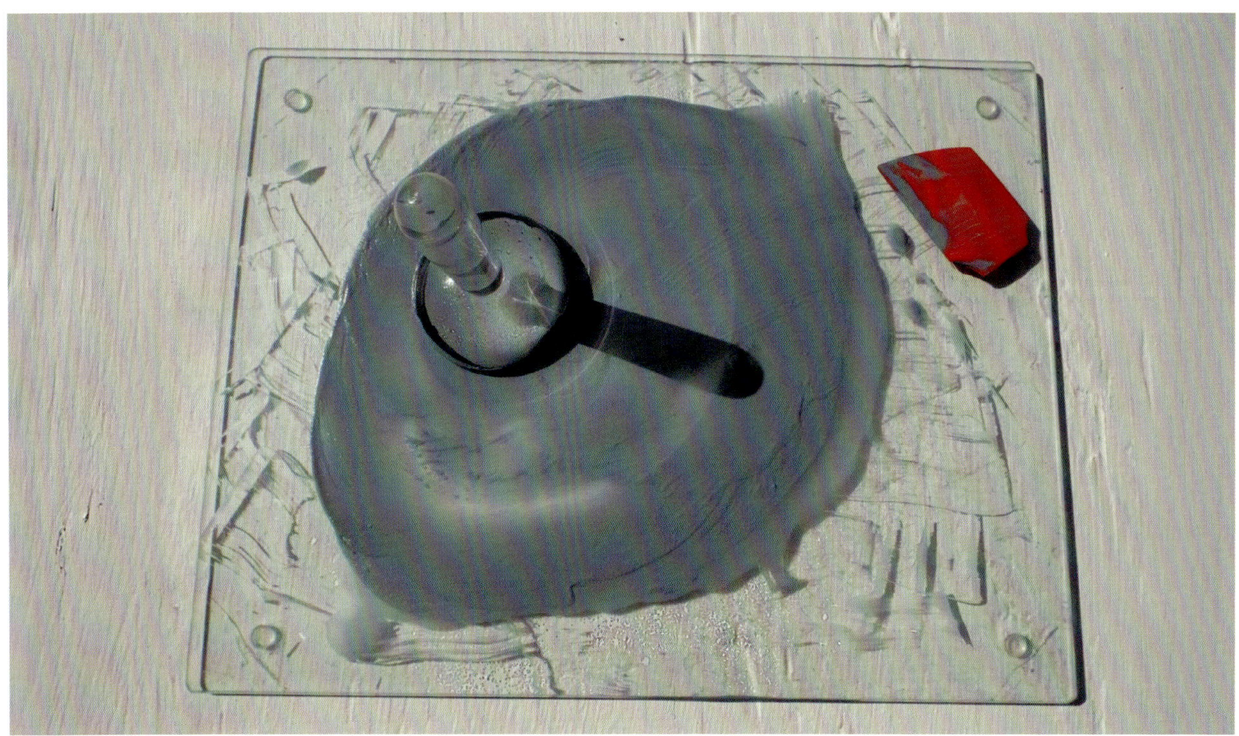

If you get interrupted and need to step away from your mulled paint, of any kind, it will need to be covered to keep it from drying out. I use a spatula to gather my paint into one spot and then I put an upside-down cup over the paint. It will keep for several hours this way. You may need to spritz it with water when you return.

To clean your muller and slab between batches, wash with soap in the sink or wipe with a wet cotton cloth. When you do wash your slab, be careful not to drop the glass in the sink! Glass is slippery when wet.

To clean the muller and plate after making oil or tempera paints, use homemade foaming hand soap with hot water and then rinse. (Okay, if you don't have homemade soap yet, you can use store-bought. I'll allow it, ha ha!)

If you are mulling fresh petals or other botanical material and it is taking too long, or some stubborn pieces are not grinding down, here are some options. First, always mull the petals or other material alone with a few drops of water first, before adding other ingredients. Other ingredients, especially alkali ingredients, may make the mixture too slippery for effective grinding, so you want to get the plant material ground up first. Still not grinding down? Add a tiny bit of sea salt. Use less water until most of the grinding is done. If necessary, after trying all other suggestions, increase the alkalinity by adding a tiny bit of washing soda to help break down the material. And sometimes, plant parts are just stubborn. Use tweezers to remove those parts.

Practice makes perfect. After a few batches, you will find that mulling becomes quick and intuitive and even relaxing and meditative. It is always fascinating to watch the magic of ingredients becoming paint before your eyes. When teaching my classes, I love to show the students the "alchemy" of using mordants to change paint colors instantly on the glass. Yesterday, as I write this, I had my sixteen students gathered around me at the front of the class and they oohed and ahhed as they watched me instantly turn nonfat yogurt paint base with Oregon grape berry juice from bright red to bright green on the slab simply by mulling the ingredients together. Then they all went to their desks and repeated the magic on their own slab. Lots of fun!

Making Pigment

FROM FRESH FLOWER PETALS

The advantage of making pigment from fresh petals is that you can achieve colors not possible using heat. It is also the fastest, easiest method of making art pigment.

Choose clean petals and remove them from the flower. Some flowers, like *Bidens* species (tickseed), make stronger colors if you keep the center of the flower, but most flowers make better paint with the petals alone.

Mull the petals in drops of water on a muller slab until they fully disintegrate. This usually takes less than a minute. If they do not fully disintegrate in a timely manner, add a bit more water, mull a bit more, and then strain this liquid through an inexpensive piece of craft felt (available at the $1.25 store) or old cotton cloth to sieve out any remaining botanical matter. The more water you add when making this pigment, the more dilute the color, so avoid adding too much water. This liquid can be used as watercolor paint or added to most recipes in this book as pigment.

FROM DRIED FLOWER PETALS

Choose clean petals and remove them from the flower. Allow them to air dry or dry them using the microwave method for pressing flowers in this book (see page 15). When fully dried, crumble them with your fingers and then mull them in drops of water on a muller slab until they fully disintegrate. If they do not fully disintegrate in a timely manner, add a bit more water, mull a bit more, and then strain this liquid through an inexpensive piece of craft felt or old thin cotton cloth to sieve out any remaining botanical matter. The more water you add when making this pigment, the more dilute the color, so avoid adding too much water. This liquid can be used as watercolor paint or added to most recipes in this book as pigment. The advantage of making pigment from dried petals is that you can achieve colors not possible when cooking flowers and you can have flowers and botanical material stored for use any time of year.

Making Paint

FROM FRESH FLOWER PETALS

Choose clean petals and remove them from the flower. Mull one or two into half a teaspoon of any of the paint recipes in this book instead of using another pigment. Choose only material that is thin and easily disintegrates when mulled, which will take some experience. As a general rule, thin petals and leaves that are not waxy work best. The paint base may modify (meaning it may act as a mordant on) the color of the petals, depending on the pH of the recipe and the petals. The advantage of making paint from fresh petals is that you can achieve colors not possible using heated pigments. It is also the fastest, easiest method of making artist paint.

FROM DRIED FLOWER PETALS

Choose clean petals and remove them from the flower. Allow them to air dry or dry them using the microwave method for pressing flowers in this book (see page 15). When fully dried, crumble them with your fingers and then mull them into any of the paint base recipes in this book instead of using another pigment. Choose only material that is thin and easily disintegrates when mulled, which will take some experience. As a general rule, thin petals and leaves that are not waxy work best.

Juicing Fresh Flowers or Leaves

Choose clean botanical material. Wash or rinse as necessary. Add the material, and enough water to cover it, to a food processor or blender. Process the material. Remove the material from the processor and allow the liquid to drain into a bowl through a sieve like a piece of craft felt or thin cotton kitchen towel. This juice can be used fresh as pigment for paint recipes in this book or allowed to air dry on a plate or bowl to be rehydrated later for use as pigment. Always label your material so you know what it is later.

Powdering Dried Flowers or Leaves

Choose clean botanical material. Wash or rinse as necessary. Air dry the material. Process the dry material in a coffee grinder. Remove the material from the processor, and sieve. Dry material powdered in a coffee grinder (or even a mortar and pestle, if you are living your best nonelectric life) can be used immediately or stored for later use.

Number of Drops in Fractions of a Teaspoon

100 drops	1 teaspoon
50 drops	½ teaspoon
25 drops	¼ teaspoon
12 drops	⅛ teaspoon
6 drops	1⁄16 teaspoon
3 drops	1⁄32 teaspoon

Recipes Using Parts Instead of Measurements

Recipes listing "parts" make it easy to scale the size of a recipe up or down. For example, if a paint recipe calls for 5 drops of this and 10 drops of that, and you need to make a gallon of paint, it would take forever to measure out the ingredients needed for a gallon using drops. But recipes using parts can be easily scaled to fit the size of your project. If the recipe calls for 1 part of this and 5 parts of that, you simply decide what measure is one part. For example, one part might be a drop, a cup, a gallon, a milliliter, a handful, a bucketful, a scoop. The recipe will still work because a recipe of "parts" is based on ratios, not specific measurements.

Natural-Resist Dyeing Methods

Making a natural resist allows you to coat some areas of fabric or fiber to prevent the dye from touching those areas, which creates patterns or pictures. The following natural resist methods have been used for millennia:

1. Best resist. The best-quality resist is made by adding one part hydrated lime and one part starch, like white flour, to two parts water to form a smooth paste. Because the lime is alkaline, the dye changes colors where it touches the resist, but that does not affect the fabric because the resist will be washed off later.

2. Starch resist. Stir together equal parts starch and water until the paste is smooth (common white flour works well, but the starch of potatoes, rice, or soybeans also works). This wet paste can be applied with a brush, spatula, or palette knife over a reusable stencil or a one-time-use homemade stencil.

3. Wax resist, applied before or after dyeing. This method is expensive and messy, but it works if you want to try it. Apply wax to areas of the material you don't want dyed. Then dip or otherwise dye the material, dry, and scrap off the wax for reuse. You could also dye your material and then apply wax to desired areas and dye the material again to create new patterns. Any unwanted wax residue can be removed by applying rubbing alcohol to the wax.

RESIST APPLICATIONS

- Hand paint the resist as desired.

- Stamp the resist. This usually works best when you apply the resist to the stamp with a brush in a thin, even coat and then stamp with even pressure. I have had good luck with wooden craft materials like leaves or holiday-themed items.

- Stencils. Reusable stencils are available at craft stores, or homemade stencils can be made by using a razor knife to cut into craft paper. Common printer paper will work, but a slightly thicker paper—labeled premium copy paper—works better. You can also cut designs into stickers or packing labels applied to fabric. When using a stencil, hold it carefully while you scrape on a thin layer of resist (if the stencil moves, the image will be ruined). Remove the stencil carefully. Allow the resist to dry (if I'm in a hurry, I use a blow-dryer) and then paint or dip your material with dye. Dry and then rub the material together under cold water to remove the starch resist and rinse as normal.
- Crackle. Paint your fabric with resist and then allow it to dry completely. Scrunch up the fabric to crack the dried resist, then dip bath and wash off the resist to reveal crackle patterns of dye.

All-Natural Glitter and Glitter Paint

Adding vermiculite to paint or the decoupage paste recipe in this book (see page 85) makes all-natural glitter. Vermiculite flakes are a form of volcanic rock that have been heated to pop like popcorn. They are widely used in garden soil and can be purchased at any garden store. For artist-quality vermiculite, Kremer Pigmente and other suppliers sell various grades of vermiculite. You can also use clear or gold mica flakes, also available online. Beware so-called "biodegradable glitter" or "bio glitter" sold online. Most of it is natural mica that has been dyed with synthetic dyes. Crushed sea salt, table salt, or Epsom salt can also be sprinkled onto paint, but do not mix into paint—like you would mica or vermiculite—otherwise it will dissolve.

Smalt Glitter

Historically, crushed glass (clear or tinted) was used to make commercial signs by adding the glass on top of wooden signs painted with oil paint. The paint adhered to the glass, and the glass not only drew the eye, but also made the signs reliably weatherproof. Genius. Smalt glass is a type of glass that is easy to crush and can still be used in the same way, or it can be used on its own as a pigment.

Smalt glass is not like plate or craft glass. It is actually made by adding a mineral carbonate, like potassium carbonate, to the glass to make the glass frothy, bubbly, and weak, and thus easily crushed. Smalt glass chunks actually look more like lava stone than glass. Smalt glass can be purchased from Kremer Pigmente and a few other suppliers online.

Artists today use smalt glass glitter or even crumbled windshield glass adhered to oil paint to make small or large glitter. I have swept crumbled windshield glass off the road for the same purpose and keep a supply of it. You can also buy non-smalt "diamond dust" and "diamond flakes"—both made of glass—as natural art glitter, for adult use only. Look for it online.

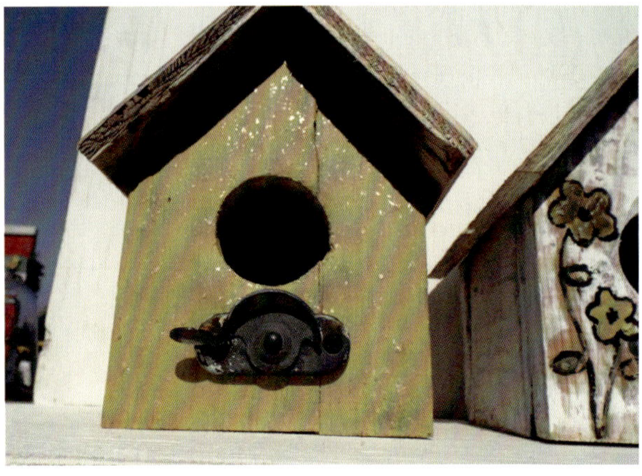

Natural Botanical Watercolor Binders

Binders are added to watercolor for two reasons: (1) to increase "flow," which is the ability of the paint to move smoothly on the paper, and (2) to increase adhesion to the paper—or said in plain language, to make the paint stick better to the paper.

If you look online for how to make natural watercolor paints, the popular recipe is to combine honey with gum arabic and other ingredients like soap, essential oils, or vegetable glycerin. And that recipe works fine, but the ingredients are expensive and unnecessary. I also worry that adding honey to paint, even in tiny amounts, will attract bugs or mildew.

There are natural botanical binders that work equally as well and cost nothing. I will say that for most dried watercolors, made as explained in this book, no binder is needed. They often work and adhere perfectly when applied just with soft water. Some even flow on the paper just fine. However, the flow of some pigments is improved by using one of the following natural binders. I make all of these fresh, without any cooking.

1. Aloe. Aloe contains a natural chemical called aloin that can be an irritant and must be "washed" to be removed. To do this, cut a fresh leaf of aloe and stand the cut leaf in a cup of water and leave it for at least 30 minutes. Change the water and repeat. Cut the leaf into pieces, place in a blender, and barely cover with soft water. Blend for about 20 seconds. Strain. The strained liquid can be used immediately as the "water" for your dried homemade botanical watercolors or you can set it aside and let the leaf residue settle before using, but this settling takes a couple days. Keeps up to two weeks, or longer if refrigerated.
2. Soapwort. Cut a single stalk of soapwort. It does not matter if the plant has flowered, is in flower, or is past flowering. The soapwort may also be used dried from fresh. Cut the stem in pieces to fit in the blender. Barely cover with soft water. Blend 20–30 seconds. Strain. The strained liquid can be used immediately as the "water" for your dried homemade botanical watercolors, or you can set it aside and let the leaf residue settle for a few hours. Keeps up to two weeks, or longer if refrigerated.
3. White cosmos petals. Use only white petals, without the center of the flower or sepals, picked fresh. Place the petals in the blender and barely cover with soft water. Blend for 20 seconds. Strain. The strained liquid can be used immediately as the "water" for your dried homemade botanical watercolors. Keeps only for two to three days, or longer if refrigerated. This liquid will slowly turn pale brown, but that has not affected the color of my watercolors.
4. White bindweed petals. Used as white cosmos petals, above. Sometimes I do half white cosmos petals and half white bindweed petals, which also works nicely. Bindweed liquid will also slowly turn pale brown. (I feel I should be awarded a Nobel Prize for finding a great use for one of the most obnoxious weeds in the garden, ha ha.)
5. Fig sap. Fig trees release a white sap when you pick the fruit or a leaf. This sap makes an excellent binder that has been used for centuries, at least.

Essential Tips for Dyeing Fabric

Some botanical dyes work best with some kinds of fabrics and not others. Silk and wool are protein fibers, while cotton and linen are cellulose fibers. Cellulose and protein respond differently to different mordants and dyes. When trying to determine whether a particular dye is right for your fabric, there is no substitute for making a small batch as a dye sample.

I usually add my mordants right into my dyes and I have good success with this method, but most people seem to want to mordant their fabric before dyeing or after. I don't dye (or wear) expensive fabrics like silk except when making dye samples, so I don't worry too much about ruining anything. If you have a garment to dye that is precious or expensive, make extensive samples before you proceed to make sure you know exactly what your plant for dyes and mordants must be.

There has lately been a lot of interest in new yarns and fabrics made of bamboo, but what I have found is that most of them also contain synthetic fibers. When I tried to dye bamboo yarn that promised to be 100 percent natural, it fell apart in the dye vat.

When dyeing, some mordants act as fixative for dyes to make them more permanent. Some mordants act as modifiers, meaning they change the dye color. Many act as both, depending on the botanical material being used. The best way to know is to try a sample.

Mixing mordants is another frontier of dyeing that can bring fascinating results. I've mixed as many as seven or eight mordants with a single dye. Using two or three mordants is not uncommon. You won't know what the result will be until you try it!

When using synthetic dye, you always rinse after you dip a garment. This is not good advice for botanical dyes, unless you want to make the color paler on purpose. Once a garment, fabric, or yarn has been dyed, I suggest you avoid the temptation to rinse it unless you have to. I suggest you first dry and then heat-set your dye. Other dyers disagree and think you should rinse the garment immediately. The strongest dye is heat-set before being rinsed or washed. Allow the garment to air dry if possible. Some people then heat it in the dryer (which I think potentially could leave stains in your dryer), by ironing (which can leave stains on your iron, so use a cloth barrier), or carefully in the microwave, which is my favorite method because I am impatient. Put the garment in the microwave for 30 seconds at a time, removing it each time to allow it to steam, and then putting it back in the microwave and heating again. I repeat this pattern for several minutes. Heat setting can help increase the longevity of your dye in some cases, but in other cases, dye is just fragile no matter what you do to it.

Some dyes are strongest, brightest, or most permanent in soft water and others in hard water. Some people add eggshell or calcium to their water in tiny amounts to darken shades, like madder root. Once again, making a sample is your best friend.

Cleaning Botanically Dyed Fabrics and Fibers

Once your fabric is dyed to your liking, I strongly suggest you forevermore wash it only with soapwort soap or another pH-neutral soap. Common laundry detergent, which is strongly alkaline, usually strips away most if not all botanical dyes, or at least grays and dulls them. The more you wash them, the more they are washed away. To avoid this, purchase pH-neutral soap, available online, and hand-wash your materials in cold water. You may also wash them in cold water without any soap.

Historically, dyed fabrics were washed with soapwort (*Saponaria officinalis*). This is a naturally pH-neutral liquid soap that is quick and easy to make. In days gone by, stocks of this plant, fresh or dried, were pulverized by roughly grinding the material with stones. The crushed plant was added to cold water and immediately turned soapy.

You can put a single stem of soapwort—with or without flowers, fresh or dried—into a blender with a quart of cold, soft water, such as rainwater. Simply blending will create the soap. You can then strain this liquid and put it in your washing machine as the pH-neutral laundry soap, then rinse and dry as normal. (You can also just put a stem of soapwort directly into the washing machine and the churning will create the soap—but then you would have a plant stem in your wash.) It also makes a good binder for botanical paint.

Soapwort seeds are available at SeedRenaissance.com.

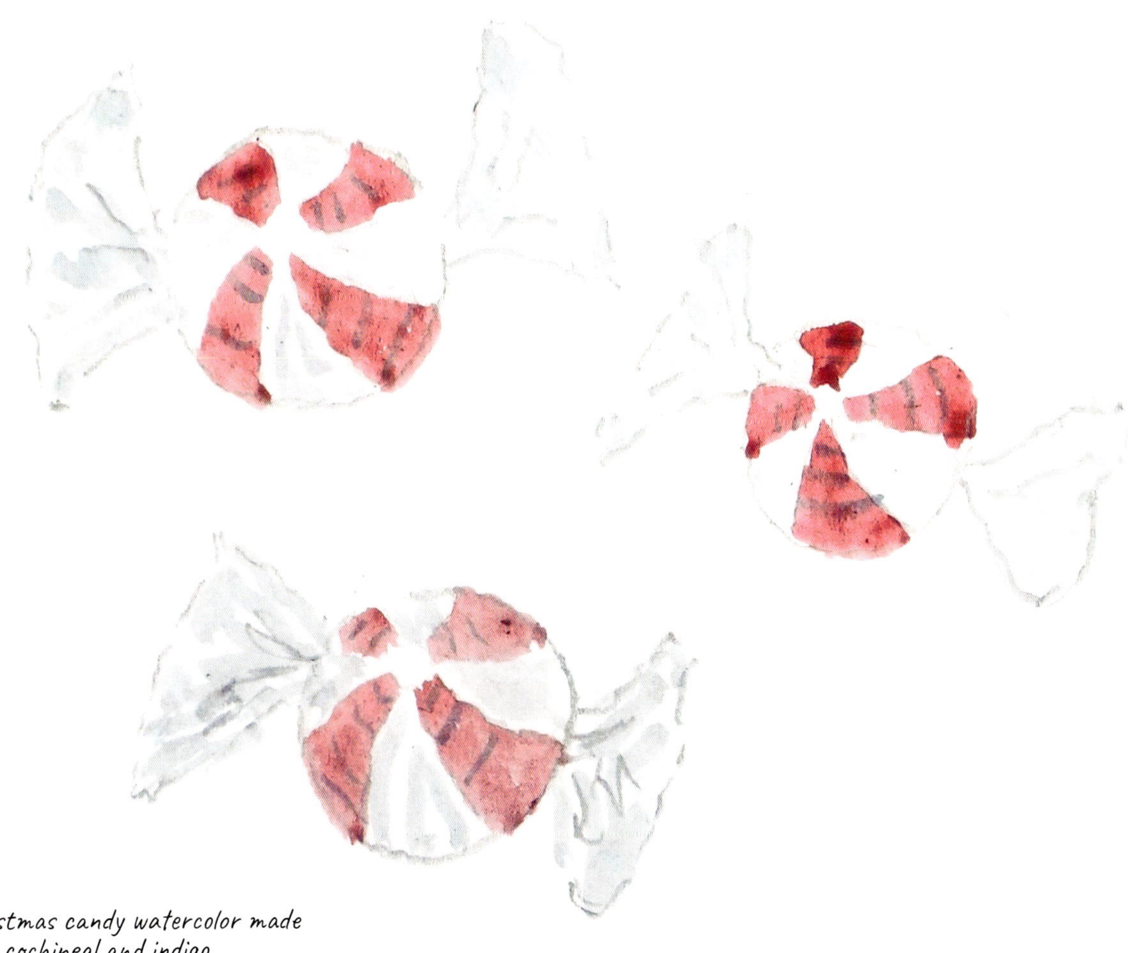

Christmas candy watercolor made from cochineal and indigo

Mordants

Mordants for Base Pigments and Paints

Mordants make it possible to make up to a dozen colors and even more hues from a single flower or plant. Most botanical paints and pigments include mordants. Mordants are natural ingredients (natural chemicals) that change botanical colors or help make colors more resistant to fading from light or washing. Mordants create new colors or hues of colors or make colors more permanent on paper, wood, fabric, canvas, metal, or glass. In this book, the paint and pigment recipes do not tell you to include mordants because mordants may not be necessary for the paint or pigment you are trying to achieve; but in most cases, mordants are used to achieve colors not possible in any other way. This is why I have included so many swatches of mordanted botanical colors in this book, to make it easier for you, the reader, to know what is possible. Mordants almost always improve paints and pigments.

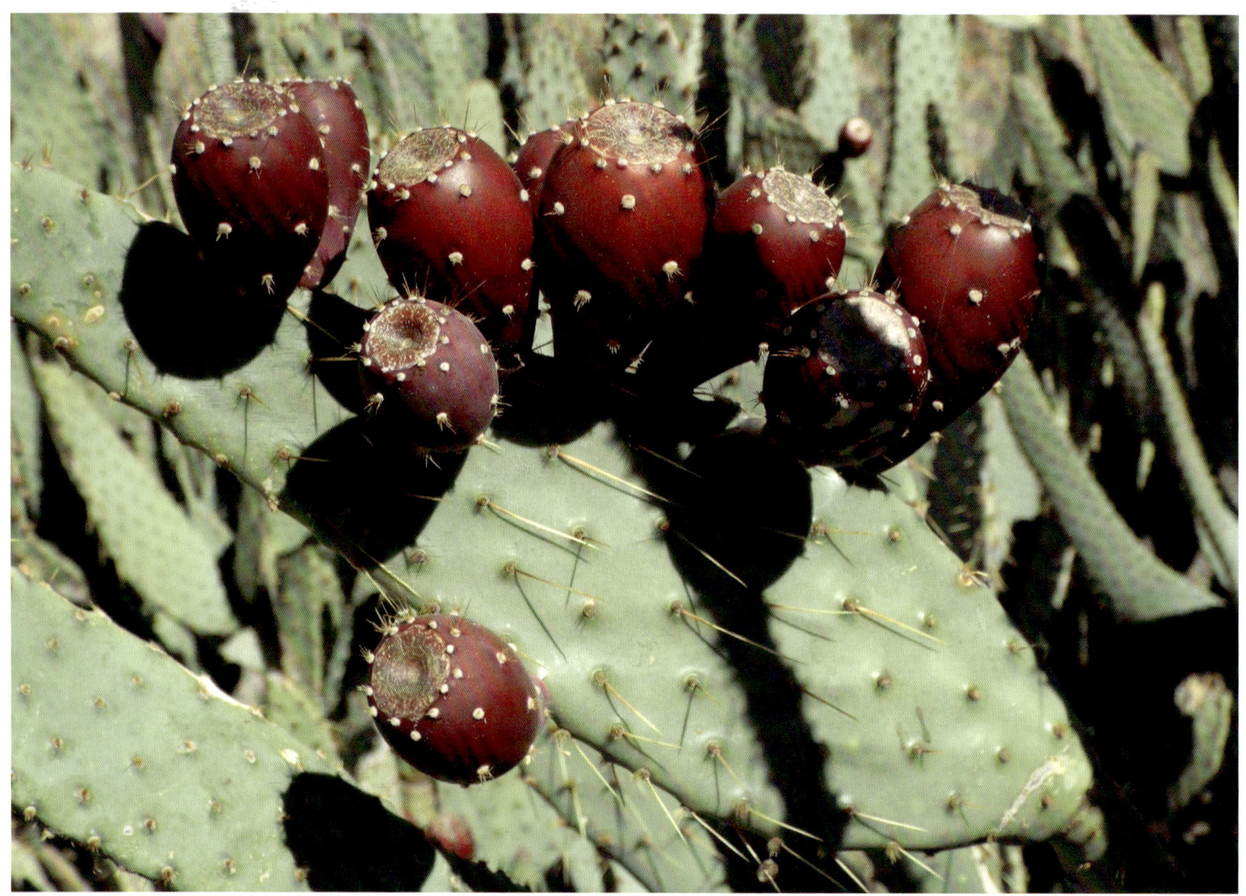

Notes on Adding a Mordant to Paint or Dye

You can add mordants at any stage of making paint, pigment, or dye, but if there are still botanical materials in your batch (like petals or leaves), they can absorb some of the mordant before you sieve them out. For this reason, I mostly add mordant after sieving.

Some mordants will change color in cold liquid, but most will only give their best color if added to boiling liquid or if boiled after being added to your base pigment. There are exceptions and mordants do help in paints and pigments made with fresh, uncooked petals and leaves. Add mordants in tiny amounts to see what color appears. For example, if you have boiled a cup of water down to about half a cup of base pigment, you need only use a tiny pinch of baking soda, alum, or iron—less than the equivalent of a half of a drop!

I keep my powdered and liquid mordants in glass baby-food jars and I teach my students to always pour them into the lid of the jar first and then pour any excess from the lid back into the jar. Never, never pour directly from the jar into your liquid base pigment because there is a strong likelihood you will overpour. Too much or too little mordant will affect the color and often damage or ruin the color.

With practice and experience you will be able to better intuitively know what amounts of mordant are needed in a batch of paint or dye. Because mordants react differently to every single plant, there is no simple recipe to follow except this: You can always add more, but you can never take away what you've already added. So always start with small amounts.

Some Mordants are Astonishingly Toxic

If you are wearing clothes right now that contain colors of blue, green, red, orange, purple, black, or white, those colors were almost surely made of synthetic dye mordanted with chrome, cobalt, tin, zinc, stannic chloride, tungsten, or titanium. These are all natural elements of the earth, but when combined with dye, they create a toxic waste that has to be disposed of somewhere. In poor countries around the world, they are often dumped directly into rivers or the ocean after being used to dye fabric, where they kill fish and poison water supplies and sicken people and animals downstream. There is beginning to be a huge pushback around the world against these practices, but the sad truth is, until we switch to using biodegradable mordants, the clothes we wear, the paints we use, and the colorful labels we package with all leave behind a legacy of toxic waste. The burden of that waste almost always falls to the poorest people on earth.

Common Mordants

Almost any substance with a pH that is not neutral, and even some neutrals, are a potential mordant. Experimenting to see what natural, nontoxic, biodegradable mordants are possible is half the fun!

Here are some common mordants to get you started.

ALUM

Action: Helps make many botanical colors stronger, sometimes brighter, and always more permanent. Alum is a critical ingredient in making alum lake pigments.

Amount: A tiny pinch, equivalent to about a half drop, per tablespoon of glaze base pigment, or up to 2 tablespoons per gallon of non-glaze dye bath, but I advise starting with two teaspoons.

Available in the spice aisle of the grocery store.

pH: varies from 5.5 to 6.5

What is sold as alum in stores can actually be three different chemical formulations: Potassium aluminum sulfate is the most common, followed by sodium aluminum sulfate. The third, aluminum sulfate, is not sold in grocery stores but is used in gardening to correct soil pH and in papermaking. The ancient Egyptian people gathered it from dried desert lake beds, where it still forms naturally, and used it for paint, dye, mummification, and deodorant, to name a few uses. Some modern people who want to live close to the earth get nervous about the use of aluminum in food, but most fresh vegetables naturally contain aluminum, which is necessary for the health of plants, animals, and humans. I consider it absolutely safe and appropriate for use in natural botanical colors.

AMMONIA

Action: A strong alkaline that often saddens colors (makes them gray or darker) and destroys some yellows, oranges, and reds. Also sometimes used to extract blue from woad plants.

Amount: Mix 1 drop with a tablespoon of water and then use drops of this water as a mordant for muller batches. Mix drops of ammonia directly into larger batches of dye, up to 1 to 2 teaspoons per gallon if needed, but I advise starting with a quarter teaspoon per gallon.

Available in the cleaning aisle of the grocery store.

pH: 11 to 13, depending on concentration.

Ammonia stinks, is not good to breathe, and is volatile and dangerous when mixed with other chemicals. I won't use it in the house. Nor chlorine bleach either. I keep tripping on this soapbox of mine.

BAKING SODA

Action: Often creates stronger yellows and browns. Can destroy some oranges, pinks, and reds. Its exact action varies for every plant material.

Amount: Use about 1 drop per tablespoon of glaze base pigment, or up to half a cup per gallon of dye that has not been reduced (for example, a dye bath for dyeing a shirt).

Available at the grocery store.

pH: 9 (twenty times more alkaline than neutral water with a pH of 7, by way of comparison)

Baking soda is food-safe and has been made for thousands of years from the ash of certain plants. The purpose of baking soda in cooking is to add an alkaline (base) to the acidic food ingredients to create a bubbling reaction, which in turn creates loft and fluffiness in food like biscuits, making them tastier. In paint and pigment, the alkaline pH of baking soda creates a chemical reaction, which creates new chemical structures, which reflect light differently, which in turn appears to be a different color to the human eye. Fascinating, right? Did you know that all "color" that you and I see is actually just a different reflection of wavelength? When wavelengths of light absorb or reflect slightly differently off different molecular materials, we call this shift "color." Now you know.

CALCIUM CHLORIDE

Action: Makes some botanical dyes more permanent and brighter or stronger. Helps some botanical dyes to penetrate deeper into cellulose fibers (cotton, linen, bamboo).

Amount: A single granule or a dust of powder in a muller batch, up to a quarter cup per gallon of dye bath if your dye bath needs calcium.

Available in the canning aisle of the grocery store. Sold by Ball as "Pickle Crisp," but also available from other brands.

pH: 8 to 9, depending on concentration

CITRIC ACID

Action: Brightens and intensifies many reds and some pinks and oranges. Destroys many yellows.

Amount: Use a tiny pinch of grains, roughly eyeball equivalent of a quarter of a drop per tablespoon of glaze base pigment, or up to 2 tablespoons per gallon of non-glaze dye bath, but I advise starting with a teaspoon. Adding too little can be fixed, but adding too much can ruin a dye bath.

Available in the canning aisle of the grocery store.

pH: 3 but depends on concentration in water.

I'm sure I'm not the first to discover the power of food-grade citric acid as a mordant, but I discovered it by accident. I was teaching my first semester Botanical Paints, Pigments, and Dyes class at the University of Utah and I happened to have a new truck. In my old truck, I didn't care too much if a bit of vinegar leaked, but I did not want anything leaking in my new truck. I stood in the kitchen trying to think if there was a powder equivalent to a jar of vinegar—and remembered I had citric acid powder for canning. In class, when I added it to fresh red rose petals that I was mulling, they turned cherry red, something that had never happened with vinegar. I was astonished. I've since used citric acid widely on red colors with great results in paint, stains, and dye baths. If you look online and in books, citric acid is almost never mentioned as a mordant, but it works great. I have only experimented a little with replacing citric acid powder with lemon or lime juice, but so far they seem to have the same effect.

CREAM OF TARTAR

Action: Brightens some botanical colors, especially reds and some oranges and pinks, especially when used with alum or citric acid. Shifts or stabilizes some colors and makes them more permanent.

Amount: A tiny pinch, equivalent to about a half drop, per tablespoon of glaze base pigment, or up to 2 tablespoons per gallon of non-glaze dye bath, but I advise starting with two teaspoons.

Available in the baking or spice aisle of the grocery store.

pH: 3.5

Cream of tartar is called "tartaric acid" or "potassium bitartrate" in chemistry. See the recipe in this book for making homemade cream of tartar from grapes (see page 52).

GLAUBER'S SALT

Action: Makes some colors more permanent and some colors stronger. Makes dyes slower to penetrate and thus more even on fabric. Makes higher quality tie-dye and shibori by slowing dye penetration.

Amount: A small pinch, equivalent to 2–3 drops, per tablespoon of glaze base pigment, or up to a cup per gallon of non-glaze dye bath, but I advise starting with a quarter cup.

Available online and, rarely, in large hardware stores.

pH: 7 (neutral)

Discovered in Austria in spring water in 1625 by apothecary Johann Rudolf Glauber (1604–1670), who was experimenting with using minerals to color glass in hopes of finding the mythical philosopher's stone. Occurs naturally along the rim of saline springs and pools. Glauber's salt revolutionized glassmaking because it lowers the melting point of the ingredients of glass without compromising the quality of the glass and opened the way for possible advances in making colored glass. It has also been a popular herbal (mineral) tonic for centuries.

GLYCERIN/VEGETABLE GLYCERIN

Action: Preserves some botanical colors, strengthens some colors, is an excellent binder for botanical colors, and used to make dyed flowers look natural. Slows drying time of paint, which enables artists to work their canvas longer. Glycerin has a special affinity for calcium when forming paints and dyes, creating a strong and useful paint base.

Amount: Use only 1 to 2 drops in a muller batch of paint or the paint will take forever to dry. If you use the right amount, it will dry within hours, especially in paints using eggshell, baking soda, or hydrated lime (all forms of calcium). Use roughly a tablespoon per gallon in a dye bath if needed, but it is rarely used for this purpose.

Available in pharmacies and health-food stores and online.

pH: 6 (ten times more acidic than neutral water, by way of comparison)

If you've ever made homemade liquid soap (which I make by the gallon), then you've made homemade glycerin. Homemade liquid soap is about half glycerin (the difference between homemade liquid and bar soap is potassium lye versus sodium lye). Commercial glycerin is made from mixing vegetable oil with lye and extracting the glycerin portion.

HYDRATED LIME

Action: A strong alkali that readily bonds with calcium to make milk paint and dyes that are resistant to fading in sunlight.

Amount: A tiny pinch, equivalent to about a half drop, per tablespoon of glaze base pigment, or up to 2 tablespoons per gallon of non-glaze dye bath, but I advise starting with two teaspoons.

Available at hardware stores and garden centers.

pH: 12.4 (fifty-four times more alkaline than neutral water, by way of comparison)

Hydrated lime is a form of calcium and is made by heating limestone (natural calcium carbonate stone) to about 1,800 degrees in a process called "calcination." After being calcined by heat, limestone instantly turns to dust when added to water—an invaluable trait for humans who did not have electricity or gasoline to grind stone. Today, hydrated lime is the primary ingredient in concrete and, thus, the (literal) foundation of modern society. Calcined limestone that has not been slaked in water is called "quicklime" and is not safe to breathe because it can form concrete in the lungs. Hydrated lime, however, is slightly safer to breathe because it does not react as readily to moisture, having already been soaked in water to change its chemical state and then dried. When using hydrated lime for dye and paint, avoid breathing the dust. For instructions on how I make hydrated lime in my backyard—the way civilizations have done for millennia—see the recipe in this book (see page 53).

IODIZED TABLE SALT

Action: Helps smooth and unify dye color. Helps some fibers, like cotton and paper, to accept the dye more deeply into the fiber. Useful in applications where you don't want alkaline sea salt because it may shift the color of your dye. The trace amount of iodine can help some botanical pigments be more permanent because iodine has a negative electrical charge, while table salt alone has a neutral electrical charge.

Amount: A tiny pinch, equivalent to about a half drop, per tablespoon of glaze base pigment, or up to a cup per gallon of non-glaze dye bath, but I advise starting with a quarter cup or less.

Available in grocery stores.

pH: 7 (neutral)

Whenever I have an unruly paint on the muller slab, I often mull in a few grains of salt, which immediately helps thin and smooth the paint, increasing flow and decreasing viscosity.

LIQUID CASTILE SOAP

Action: An alkaline color modifier and binder for some botanical paints. Putting a drop of liquid soap in a liquid botanical pigment will instantly change some colors, which is always magical for students and grandkids.

Amount: Mix 1 drop of liquid soap with a tablespoon of water and then use drops of this water as a mordant or as a binder ingredient. Mix drops of liquid soap directly into larger batches of dye, up to 1 to 2 teaspoons per gallon if needed, but I advise starting with a quarter teaspoon per gallon. The concentration of castile soap sold in stores is usually watery because real soap will continue to thicken and coagulate over time. Because store-bought castile is thin, you may need to add more. Of course, use only the dye-free kind for dyeing.

Available in grocery stores in the cleaning aisle or make your own at home from olive oil and lye, as has been done for millennia. I recommend Catherine Failor's book *Making Natural Liquid Soaps*.

pH: 9 to 11, depending on concentration.

Most soap, both bar and liquid, sold in stores is not soap at all but is classified chemically as "detergent," meaning it is just a mixture of chemicals that saponify. Real soap only has three ingredients: water, oil, and wood ash lye. Castile soap is real soap and making your own at home is easy.

OXALIC ACID

Action: A strong acid that brightens some colors, especially reds and some purples. Destroys some yellows and oranges. If it makes a color stronger or brighter, it usually also makes it more permanent and lightfast.

Amount: The equivalent of 1 to 2 drops per tablespoon of water and then use 1 to 2 drops of this solution in a muller batch, or use directly in a dye bath, up to roughly a teaspoon per gallon.

Available in powder form online and from beekeeping suppliers. Available naturally as a tea extract of oxalis, which grows in many irrigated lawns and looks like a four-leaf clover and has a strong lemon flavor. Also found in tea of sorrel and dock plants or field bindweed, so you can make revenge tea from your bindweed to use in dyeing! Also the active ingredient in the popular Bar Keepers Friend used to clean stainless steel.

pH: 1 to 4, depending on concentration.

Oxalic acid is naturally present in many vegetables and berries. Beekeepers use oxalic acid to naturally control mites in beehives by smoking the hive with a vaporized form of it in the spring before adding honey supers, but it doesn't work very well in my experience. Sigh. However, some beekeepers swear by it.

POTASSIUM BICARBONATE

Action: An alkali that can be used to make blue dye from red rose petals and to make blues, purples, and grays from other red botanical materials. Shockingly, the blue dye from red rose petals makes excellent permanent blue dye on cotton that has even withstood washing in laundry detergent.

Amount: A drop or less in a tablespoon of pigment. I have found that potassium bicarbonate can change colors from gray to blue to black or even purple with even the smallest changes in amount, so start with a tiny dusting and add more as desired.

Available in powder form online and from some restaurant supply stores.

pH: 8.3, depending on concentration

Potassium bicarbonate is widely used in place of baking soda in some commercial bakery recipes.

SEA SALT

Action: Helps to make some colors more permanent, especially on paper and cotton. Helps to make color more even and smooth, especially in some botanical paints. Helps increase grinding action of botanical material on a grinding slab.

Amount: A tiny pinch, equivalent to about a half drop, per tablespoon of glaze base pigment, or up to a cup per gallon of non-glaze dye bath, but I advise starting with a quarter cup or less.

Available at the grocery store.

pH: 10 (thirty times more alkaline than table salt)

Salt rarely creates an immediate change of color as a modifier and is instead used more as a mordant to fix and unify color.

TANNINS

Action: Makes some colors more permanent to weather, water, laundry detergent, and light. Saddens most colors (makes them darker or more gray). Significantly strengthens the action of some mordants on cellulose fabrics (cotton, linen, bamboo).

Amount: One drop for a muller batch, up to 2 tablespoons per gallon of dye bath. However, the amount of tannins in natural sources varies widely and you may need to adjust, so always start with a small amount because you can always add more.

Available widely in nature. Maple leaves, acorns, and oak leaves, rhubarb, grape leaves, black tea, and avocado pits are a few examples.

pH: approximately 6 depending on concentration.

UREA POWDER

Action: Urea powder is used to make some milk paints stronger and more resistant to weather, water, and light. However, if you get urea milk paint on your clothes, it may never come out—nor out of the container you mixed it in. Also used sometimes to alkalinize a woad dye vat.

Amount: 1 to 2 percent of the weight of hydrated lime in a milk paint recipe, which is a tiny dust of urea powder in a muller paint and maybe a quarter teaspoon in quart of paint.

Available online.

pH: about 6, depending on water and concentration

For a long time I thought urea and ammonia were interchangeable in making paints and pigments, but I was wrong. Historically, urea was made by allowing human urine to ferment for about a week, and, for dyeing purposes, there is a whole historical rabbit hole about whose urine you could use. Some dyers used only the urine of young girls, while others used only the urine of young boys. Sometimes the gender of the urine dictated the color of dye it should be used with. Some Native American tribes are documented as being adamant about using only the urine of virginal girls who had arrived at puberty. There are many centuries of folklore and tradition about urine and dyeing. To avoid wading into all that, today we just buy urea powder online, ha ha. Urea is what is in that bag of petrochemical fertilizer you put on your lawn and garden. Today, urea is not made from urine. Instead, we make it from natural gas. Don't get me started on how that has created wars and geopolitical suffering around the world—all so that we can have unnaturally green lawns. (And I'm stepping off my soap box—almost.) Every action has a consequence. (And I'm off now.)

VINEGAR (ANY TYPE)

Action: Often brightens and strengthens botanical colors, which is why it is added to those Easter egg dye tablets you use with your kids. The vinegar mordants the dye color on the calcium eggshell. Vinegar destroys about half of all botanical red, orange, and yellow dyes. Vinegar is also a fixative for many dyes, making them more permanent. This is why vinegar can be mixed with almost any botanical pigment that it doesn't destroy to make a simple wood stain.

Amount: Use about 1 drop per tablespoon of glaze base pigment, or up to half a cup per gallon of non-glaze dye bath, but I advise starting with a quarter cup or less. Adding too little can be fixed, but adding too much can ruin a dye bath.

Available at the grocery store or look online to learn how to make your own from various fruits.

pH: 2.5 (forty-five times more acidic than neutral water, by way of comparison, and roughly the same pH as the acid in your stomach)

Colored vinegars may affect the color of your dye as colors mix. Vinegar of 5 percent is food-safe and has been made since time immemorial by allowing sugary fruits to ferment in water. Vinegar is the biodegraded state of alcohol, so in nature and in factories, decaying sugary liqueurs become alcohol and then biodegrade to become vinegar. In factories, that vinegar is then heated to kill the mother bacteria that created it, filtered, and added to distilled water to achieve a uniform percent of acid. Distilled white vinegar is made differently, as a distillation of petroleum oil by-products to create pure acetic acid, which is then added to distilled water to create a uniform percent of acid. Food-grade vinegar is required to be less than 5 percent acetic acid by law.

VINEGAR OF COPPER

Action: Creates blue and black colors and makes colors more permanent. Used for all human history to make kiln-able black paint for pottery.

Amount: 1 to 2 drops mixed in a quarter cup of water to form water of copper will mordant many, many batches of paint. Copper is only needed in the tiniest amounts as a mordant. The water of copper that I use as a mordant has only the faintest blue coloring and looks like plain water in passing, that's how little copper is needed.

Not sold in stores, to my knowledge, but is widely used throughout human history and easy to make (see page 58). In modern times, it has largely been replaced by powdered sulfate of copper, which I avoid because it is dangerous and unnecessary for my uses.

pH: 5

Called "cupric acetate" in chemistry. Also widely used in herbal medicine, even though it is not an herb, and in fruit orchards and gardens to treat fungal and bacterial infections and pests. Some people who want to live close to the earth get nervous about using copper in dye and paint, but various forms of copper are widely sold and used as supplements taken orally. In addition, almost all vegetables and fruits contain natural copper and some are rich in copper, including salad greens, mushrooms, beans, peas, squash, and more. Copper in the right amounts is important to the health of soil, plants, animals, and humans. While I agree that certain forms of copper made using harsh chemicals should be avoided and create toxic waste, small-batch cupric acetate is not among those, and I consider it absolutely safe and acceptable when used correctly and with respect. I have kept a batch of vinegar of copper for many years; it is a striking and beautiful blue color and irreplaceable to me in its uses.

VINEGAR OF IRON

Action: Makes rust and terracotta reds, yellows, silvers, grays, and blacks. Saddens all colors by making them more gray or dark. A critical ingredient through all human history in making permanent paints, dyes, pigments, stains, and kiln-able pottery paints.

Amount: 1 to 2 drops mixed in a quarter cup of water to form water of iron will mordant many, many batches of paint. Iron is only needed in the tiniest amounts as a mordant and using too much will instantly make colors too dark. In addition, using too much iron mordant on fabric will slowly eat holes in the fabric. Too much iron will also stain your pots and pans, your fingers, your clothes, everything. My grandparents lived in a very rural town with bright red soil because of high natural iron content and my grandmother was always unhappy that her white socks were stained permanently red when she gardened. What some people call "stained socks," other people call "dyed socks," ha ha! (Dear reader, you must keep me from these tangents! Shoo me on to the next paragraph!)

Available online or make your own with the recipe in this book (see page 59).

pH: varies from 5 to 8

Called "iron acetate" or "ferric acetate" in chemistry.

VITAMIN C (ASCORBIC ACID)

Action: Brightens and makes more permanent some yellows and reds and is miraculous in intensifying and preserving some orange colors, like marigold petals.

Amount: A tiny dust of ascorbic acid for a muller batch, up to 1 to 2 teaspoons or even tablespoons as needed in a dye bath.

Available in the canning aisle of the grocery store. Sold by Ball as "Fruit Fresh" powder for canning but also available from other brands. I haven't tried using vitamin C tablets, just because I have ascorbic acid already for canning and making jam and jellies, but they probably work too.

pH: 1 to 2, depending on concentration

Ascorbic acid is a widely used food preservative, especially in cases when you want to avoid browning or oxidizing food colors. Ascorbic acid is added to peaches and nectarines when you want to cut them up and freeze them as pie filling, for instance, so the fruit doesn't slowly brown and degrade in the freezer. It's added to canned fruit and jams and jellies for the same reason.

WASHING SODA/SODA ASH

Action: A strong alkali often used in creating blue and green from woad plants. Not used often in dyeing but is an ingredient in almost all laundry detergent. Washing soda is made by heating baking soda.

Amount: 1 to 2 tablespoons per gallon of dye bath.

Available in the laundry aisle of the grocery store or see the recipe in this book (see page 59).

pH: 11

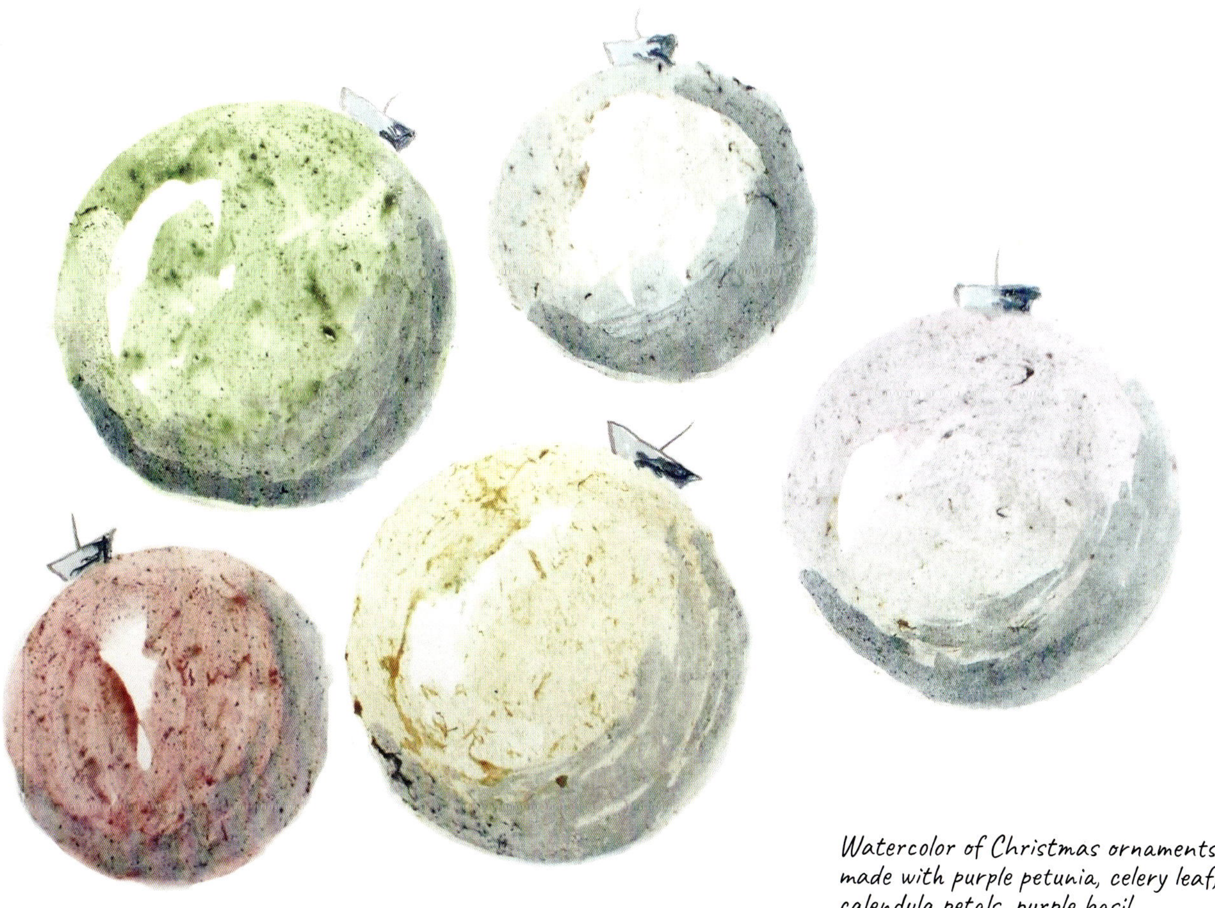

Watercolor of Christmas ornaments made with purple petunia, celery leaf, calendula petals, purple basil

Fabric Dye Methods

Dyeing by Fabric Type

Most synthetic fabrics will not accept natural dyes. Blends of natural and synthetic materials also give poor results. Cotton, wool, silk, and linen are the most widely used natural fabrics. Each has its own requirements, which vary by plant, mordant or mordant blends, dye temperature, length of time in the dye bath, pH of the dye bath, and color saturation of the dye bath. Because of all these variables, you should test a piece of your desired material before committing to any dye process. One dye process may make a beautiful result on cotton but a terrible result on wool, or a beautiful result on silk and a terrible result on linen. Rare is the dye vat that works excellently on all natural fibers. For a beginner's guide, refer to the fabric dye swatches in this book.

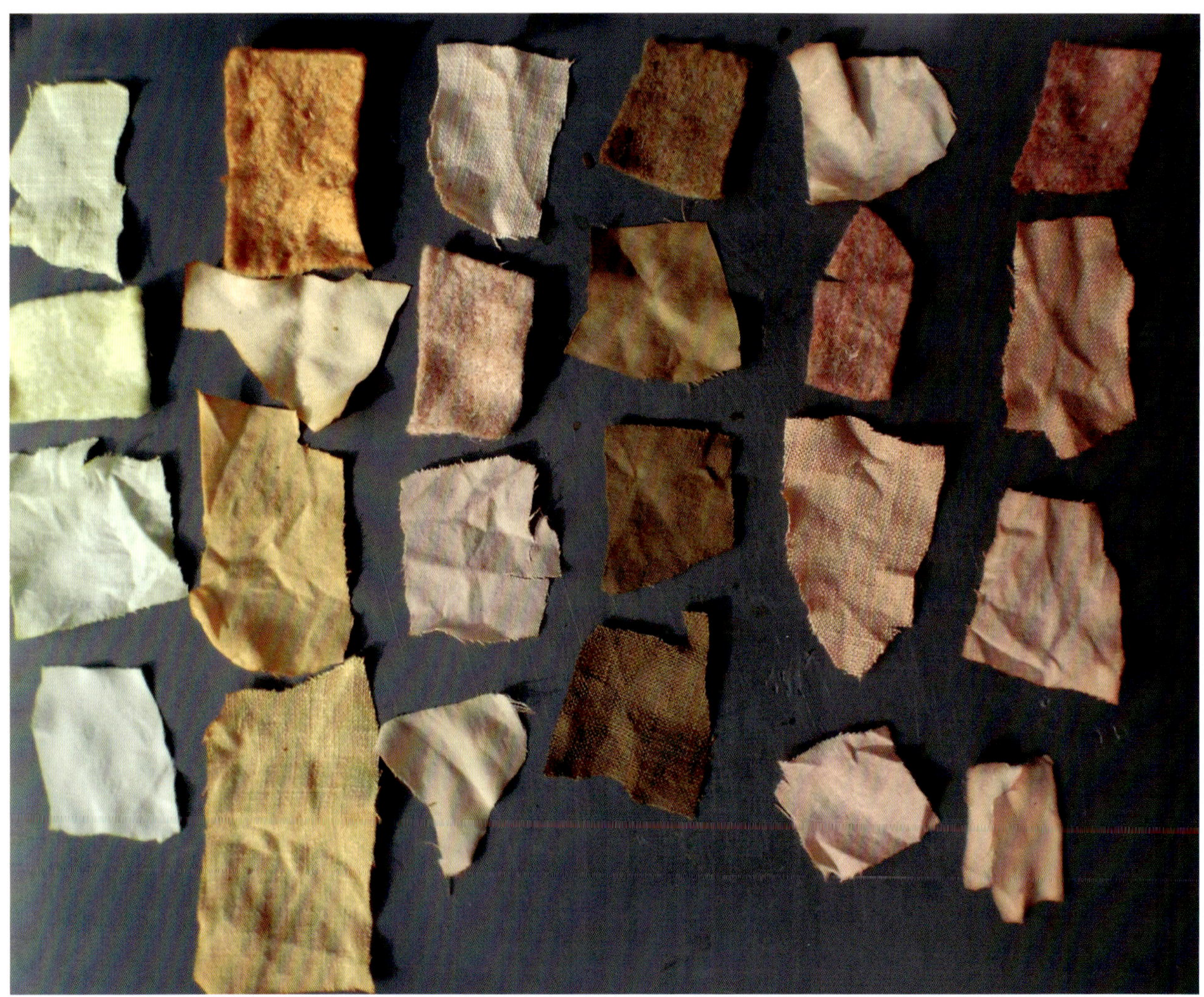

WOF Measurements for Fabric Dye Mordants

If you hang out in the world of fabric dyeing for very long at all, you will begin to see a lot of dye recipes that refer to measuring mordants like vinegar, salt, or alum by "percent WOF," which stands for a percentage of "weight of fabric." For example, if you have a cotton shirt you want to dye, a recipe may say you need to add an amount of alum equaling 15 percent of the weight of your fabric. So if your fabric weighs a pound, which is 453 grams, then you would need to measure out 68 grams of alum powder to add to your dye bath as mordant or add to water so you can boil the shirt in the alum water to premordant the fabric.

I know serious dyers won't like this answer, but I don't ever get involved in WOF measurements.

To some people, using gram scales and measuring with exactness makes them feel like they are in a laboratory doing chemistry like when they were in college and it is nostalgic good fun for them. But left-brained people like me hate WOF measurements. We are the people who never measure when we cook food. We are the people who can easily and accurately eye a teaspoon or a cup measurement of anything. So when I dye, I add mordant based on my years of experience and not by WOF from someone else's recipe.

In addition, WOF measurements require dyeing in distilled water. Distilled water is a modern invention and was never available to be purchased in all of history. I always use soft water when dyeing, never distilled water, because it is not historical and it is expensive. But when using WOF measurements, the only way to be accurate is to use distilled water because even a tenth of a percent change in pH changes the amount of mordant you need.

In my opinion, there is no need for such anxiety. Dyeing should be fun and intuitive and the worst that can happen if you don't get it quite right is that you get to do it again. Most of us are doing this as a pleasant pastime. We don't need WOF measurements.

SCOURING

All fabrics should be cleaned before dyeing in a process called "scouring." If the material you want to dye is not expensive and will be for home or craft use, people simply wash their fiber, fabric, or garment in the washing machine with regular laundry detergent and allow the machine to rinse as usual.

I want to emphasize that if you are just dying for practice, fun, or experimentation, scouring is not necessary, and I often skip this step. But for new material that has not been previously dyed, scouring is necessary to achieve the highest dye quality. This is because commercially prepared fabrics and fibers (and even art paper) are usually treated with a liquid called "size." Size helps the color of the material to be uniform, the material feed smoothly through industrial machinery, and ensure even uptake of dye, ink, or paint.

In addition, natural fibers have natural dust and grease and naturally uneven texture and color. Many natural materials come pre-bleached, but it is possible to get some raw materials, like raw linen. To complicate matters more, residues of bleach, grease, and dust can be left behind from industrial processes, even if the material is raw and unsized.

For all these reasons, when you want the best-quality dye result, fabrics, fibers, and garments should be scoured before dyeing. Scouring water is made by adding 2 tablespoons of washing soda per gallon of water. Washing soda can be purchased, or you can make your own, like I do, by spreading baking soda in an even layer on a cookie sheet and baking at 200 or 250 degrees for an hour. After the baked soda is cooled, it can be stored indefinitely in a jar.

To scour the material, boil the material in soapy water (laundry soap works well), often for 30 to 60 minutes, in soapy water and then rinse in clean water. Some dyers repeat this process just to be sure, especially if the material is expensive or important. Scouring can be critical to the quality of the finished product. Raw products, such as raw linen, may surprise you by how dark they are because we are used to seeing industrially bleached and prepared fabrics. If you use raw materials, you will need to repeatedly scour the material until the scour water comes clean after boiling. Because the washing soda water is alkaline, the material must then be completely rinsed to remove all washing soda residue, otherwise the washing soda will act as a mordant when the dye is applied.

BLEACHING

Scoured materials may be naturally bleached by soaking or boiling material in a mixture of ⅛ cup lemon juice to 1 gallon of water, making up as many gallons as needed. A stronger natural bleach is made by adding an equal amount of hydrogen peroxide to the lemon juice. (The strongest bleaching effect comes when you take this hydrogen peroxide–soaked material and hang it in strong summer sunlight for a couple days.) Alternatively, you could wash the material in your washing machine on the small load setting by adding ½ cup of lemon juice and no detergent.

Raw linen is especially difficult to bleach. The linen dye swatches you see in this book were scoured four times and then bleached in lemon juice, hydrogen peroxide, and sunlight four times, a process that took a couple of weeks.

Historically, before lemon juice was widely available, people used a very earthy method indeed. First, they gathered human urine and allowed the urine to "stale" for about a week, which allowed the urea to ferment and create ammonia. This natural ammonia was then used to soak or wash the fabric or fiber. Natural discolorations when then spot-treated with more homemade ammonia. The material was then cleaned, soaked, and washed in a solution of homemade lye—made from a process of steeping and straining wood ashes—then sour milk was either added to the lye or the garment was rinsed and then soaked in the sour milk, and finally the garment sun-bleached and then rinsed. Historically, to get really white fiber or fabric, this process was repeated up to eighteen times! There are many variations of this process. I have not tried any of the urine–lye–sour milk processes. Thank goodness for the lemons I grow in my greenhouses here at 5,200 feet above sea level!

Dip-Dyeing

Oh, dip-dyeing. Sigh. Dipping a fabric or yarn in dye is fraught. The mere action of boiling can often make a dye leave streaks or blotches on fabric. Not to mention it can be dangerous. For sure you will need tongs, and you should never dip-dye with kids or pets around. Or on hot summer days, because boiling really heats up a house (save it for winter). The real problem with dip-dyeing is that boiling water causes fabric to float, and exposure to air can cause immediate and permanent streaks in fresh dye. You can try to put a stone or a plate in the boiling dye vat to weigh down the fabric, but then you can get streaks or blotches where that touched the fabric.

I say skip the dip when the water is boiling. Instead, boil the water, dye material, and mordants. Then strain the dye bath slowly and carefully—it can be easy to burn yourself with steam alone, not to mention the boiling water. If you don't strain the bath, leaving botanical material in the dye can cause many problems—streaks, blotches, and inadvertent imprints on the fabric, not to mention sticks, petals, and leaves getting stuck in your fabric. Once the dye is strained, if it is still steaming strongly, then you can dip your fabric with tongs. If you are careful, you can even put a plate or a stone on the fabric to keep it from floating up, with a smaller chance this will leave blotches. If the dye is strong, you may only need to dip and immediately remove the garment.

If the dye is weak, you may want to save the dye bath and then air dry or carefully microwave to heat-set the garment, then bring your dye back to boiling, then dip again. If using a microwave to heat-set between dips, it is so easy to scorch the fabric. However, some light scorching can create interesting tie-dye effects. The only way to avoid scorching in the microwave is to wad up the wet fabric, place it on a plate or bowl, microwave for 30 seconds, then remove the garment, unwad it, let it cool for several minutes, and repeat several times. It does not have to be totally dry in the microwave to be heat-set because the microwave can get the fabric quite hot. Once the fabric is nearly dry, you can dip it again. If you do not at least dry the garment, and preferably heat-set it between dips, you can often dip all you want, or soak the garment in the dye for as long as you want, and may never get a deeper color. However, with some botanical dyes, soaking can create a deeper color. But in my experience, most of the time it does nothing unless you dry and heat-set between dips.

Dip-dying is the fastest, easiest method to dye fabric. To me, this is a great method for clothes you will wear around the house.

OPTION 1: WITHOUT MORDANT

Generally speaking, you get best results if you have a large amount of dye for the garment, fabric, or fiber to "swim" in. This is because material that is not freely "swimming" in the dye pot, meaning it does not have a lot of room, tends to have streaks when finished. Packing the material in the pot in too little water causes these streaks. The often-recommended amount of dye is 4 gallons per pound of fabric. This required an enormous amount of botanical material to create a strong color, which is why I often use less dye when I am experimenting or just dyeing shirts for fun or to wear around the house.

To start, boil botanical material as long as needed to achieve dye. Botanical material may be fresh or dried but cannot be contaminated with dirt. Sieve. If desired, boil again to reduce water to intensify color, but keep in mind the volume requirements. Turn off the heat. Thoroughly soaking the material in clear water before dyeing will give a more evenly dispersed dye. Slowly dip the garment in the hot dye bath. Allow to soak for up to an hour. If the garment touches air at the top of the pot, streaks and marks will result. Some people may like this result, many will not. To avoid this result, weigh down the garment, but keep in mind that the weight (I often use a ceramic plate) can also cause streaks if any air is trapped under the weight. If you try to boil while the garment is in the dye pot, you will get streaks due to air exposure, so it is important to make sure the dye has stopped boiling before adding your material. Even allowing the garment to touch air for a mere moment will result in uneven dyeing. I strongly suggest you practice first on scrap fabric.

To get a stronger color, after dyeing, allow the garment to fully dry without rinsing by hanging the garment outside. (Some dyers choose to rinse between dips to keep the color even. Experiment to see which method you prefer.) Once dry, create a fresh dye bath of the same material and dye the whole garment again. I sometimes re-dye a garment up to four times to get a deep color.

OPTION 2: PREMORDANT

Premordanting your fabric is recommended to get a less streaky and more evenly colored result. Boil water in the amount necessary for your garment (4 gallons per pound of fabric is recommended). When the water is boiling, add the mordant you desire, but no dye material, and stir. Boil for several minutes and stir intermittently to disperse. Add your garment and boil for 20 to 30 minutes. Remove your garment and dry it completely, usually by hanging outside. When dry, dip-dye following the instructions in option one.

OPTION 3: POST-MORDANT

Follow the steps in option one. Once the material is dyed, you can paint on different mordants with brushes, dip in mordant solution, stamp on mordant, or squeegee on mordant. In Japan, for example, when working with delicate and expensive kimono silks, fabric is botanically dyed and a thin paste (made by boiling 1–2 teaspoons of rice flour per cup of soft water) is applied to a board. The fabric is then stretched out on the board to keep it flat. A mordant is either painted on, stenciled on, or brushed over the whole fabric, depending on the effect intended. The fabric is then allowed to dry on the board, water is applied to get the fabric off the board, and the fabric is rinsed.

Hand-Painted Dye

Dyes can be painted on fabric with brushes or any implement that creates a pleasing texture. Dyes may be hot or cold. Fine art scenes or loose and natural patterns can be painted.

Hikizome

Hikizome is a Japanese method where fabric, often expensive kimono silk, is stretched in the air like a hammock, using wooden ribs to keep the material taut. The silk is wetted and the dye is applied with large brushes, creating a watercolor wash effect. The fabric air dries and is then steamed to fix the colors. Resist paste is sometimes used to keep colors from interacting.

Shibori

Shibori is a more sophisticated Japanese version of tie-dye that uses origami-style folding, and sometimes stitching, to create a pattern on the fabric before dipping or painting with dye. Dyes may be hot or cold. Accordion folds are an easy way to start. Or you can fold fabric in quarters until you can't, or you can make a long accordion fold and then fold that up in repeating triangles. Ironing each fold makes the folds crisp but is not necessary. Hold together with strings, stitches, binder clips, or woodworking clips.

There are endless patterns possible with shibori, but honeycomb shibori is one of my favorites. One advantage of this type of dying is that it uses at least half the amount of dye per garment, depending on your pattern. Take a shirt or a piece of fabric and lay it out flat. At the bottom of the fabric, lay out a piece of string that is about 3 inches longer than the fabric on both sides. Roll the fabric around this string. Your fabric now looks like a long tube with string hanging out both ends. Bring the ends together to form a horseshoe. Hold the strings together and push the fabric down to form a scrunch shape. Tie the string to make the "scrunch" as tight as you can. Dip the material in your dye bath. After dipping, untie the string and lay out the shirt to reveal the honeycomb pattern. Dry the shirt and then clean using cold water or pH neutral soap.

You could also create this pattern as a stringless version: Roll the fabric around a rolling pin or piece of pipe or cardboard tube. Attach it to the tube with rubber bands (or string or ribbon) and then slide the whole thing down onto itself tightly, making a scrunchy shape. Dip to dye (or use far less dye by painting or spraying with dye), unfold, dry, and clean. Wherever you start the roll is where you will get the least dye. For example, if you start rolling at the bottom of a T-shirt and roll up to the top before scrunching the shirt, the resulting honeycomb will be dyed heavily at the top of the shirt and be less and less pronounced toward the bottom. To make a cross-hatch, roll the shirt or fabric diagonally on the tube so the corner of the shirt looks like a check mark at the top of the tube.

Solar Dye

QUICK METHOD

Bring water, botanical dye material, and mordants, if any, to a boil. The amount you need will depend on the amount of fabric you want to dye, the absorbency of that fabric, the saturation of color you desire, and the size of your vessel. Place your garment or yarn in a glass jar or bowl. Once boiling, pour the dye bath into the jar or bowl carefully. Leave the water to steep for a day or longer. I often use this method when making dye samples.

COLD METHOD

This method uses no boiling water, which some people prefer for safety or ecological reasons because it can be done without electricity. Simply add water, botanical material, mordants (if any), and fabric, yarn, or your garment to a clear glass jar and leave it in bright sun for days or weeks. Just don't leave it so long that it goes moldy, because that can ruin your fabric. Most people leave it about a week. The amount you need will depend on the amount of fabric you want to dye, the absorbency of that fabric, the saturation of color you desire, and the size of your vessel.

Tie-Dye

The point of tie-dye is to create unusual and fun patterns by tying, clamping, or knotting the fabric to make it harder for dye to penetrate some areas. The material is then dipped or sometimes painted with dye. After being rinsed, knots, clamps, and ties are removed to reveal a pattern. Any creative way you can think of to manipulate the fabric to create a pattern works. Some people make circles by pushing a marble into the fabric and securing it with a rubber band. There are endless ideas online.

You could simply tie a garment into knots: Take a shirt, fold the sleeves in, then fold in half repeatedly until you can't. Then tie the shirt in knots. You may only be able to get one or two knots, which is fine. Then dip the shirt in botanical dye (which could be hot or cold). The knots slow penetration of the dye so it does not reach all parts of the fabric.

The problem with botanical dye is that it saturates faster than synthetic dyes, which use chemicals to slow saturation. Luckily, we can use a natural chemical to do the same: Glauber's salt, a mineral that forms on the edges of saltwater springs. Also called "mirabilite," it can be purchased online. Glauber's salt can also make the color more permanent. It may also sadden the dye, which we fight by adding citric acid, cream of tartar, or both. Add 2 tablespoons of Glauber's salt per gallon of dye bath and, if needed, 1 tablespoon of citric acid or cream of tartar. As always, test a scrap of fabric first. Even with this addition, I recommend you just quickly dip the fabric and remove it. You can always dip again, but if the whole garment is saturated too fast, the tie-dye effect is ruined. Don't let it soak.

Paper Dye Methods

Dyeing Paper

First, use masking tape to secure your paper to a flat surface, like a cutting or art board. Paint or spray on botanical dye, making the dye as deep or pale as you wish. If you are going to use the paper for journaling, for example, you'll want light colors, but if you're dyeing paper for collage, you may want deeper colors. Once you have applied dye, if you want the color deeper, add more dye while the paper is shiny with water but not overly wet. If you want colors lighter, you can sponge off extra dye at the shiny stage or add more water to dilute the color, though this will create a pattern. Do not dry paper in the sun, which can cause the masking tape to bond with the paper, making it impossible to remove cleanly. Remove the tape once dry.

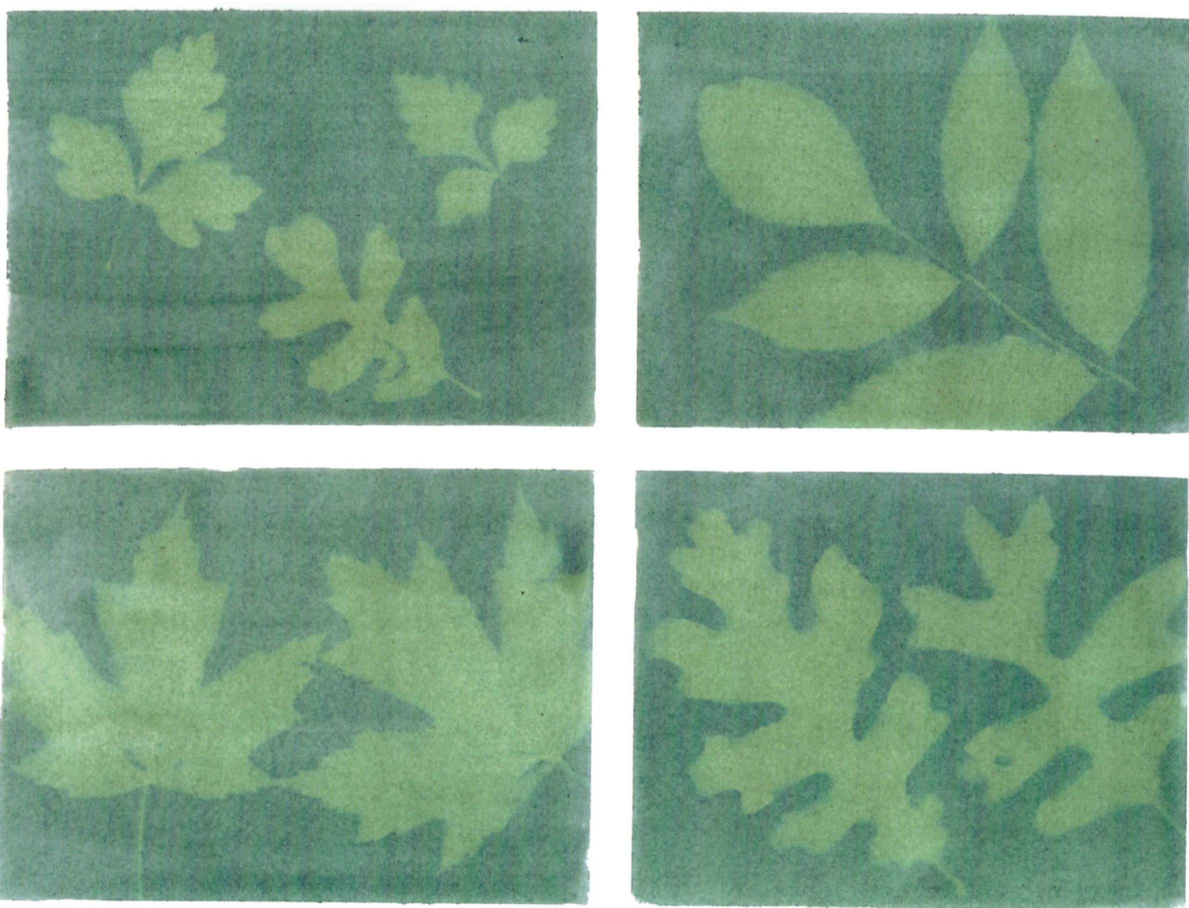

Botanical Sun Prints

CABBAGE METHOD

It can be surprisingly hard to find leaves and flowers that make a good botanical print. Serrated leaves work best, like maples and oaks. Leaves that will just print a blob shape do not work well. Flowers need to be trimmed to make them more two-dimensional.

The fastest way to ruin a sun print is by using fresh leaves and flowers. Because the moisture of fresh leaves and flowers can ruin the botanical ink, you should use dried leaves and flowers. Dry your materials using one of the three methods listed in this book (see page 15).

While traditional sun prints are made by the sun fading the ink around the image to reveal a positive image of the dried plants, this method actually does the opposite.

Red cabbage

½ cup water

Pinch of baking soda

Mixed media paper

A large baking sheet

Dried leaves and flowers

A sheet of glass smaller than the baking sheet

1. Boil a slice of red cabbage in water for 6–10 minutes.
2. Eat the cabbage; leave the liquid dye.
3. Add baking soda to the dye liquid and cook it again to near-glaze stage.
4. Use this to paint your paper, then allow the paper to dry completely.
5. Lay your dried paper on the baking sheet. Carefully arrange your dried leaves and flowers and carefully cover with the glass. Lay this out in full sun somewhere where your dog can't ruin it, the wind can't ruin it, the grandkids can't ruin it . . . Good luck with all that.
6. Leave it in bright sun for several hours. After about 15 minutes, you will see that the lime green paint you made from the red cabbage mordanted with baking soda is now beginning to darken. Over time, it will become more of a forest green.

SPIRULINA METHOD

Blue spirulina powder is available online. Ascorbic acid is found online or in the canning aisle of the grocery store and is sometimes called "Fruit Fresh."

It was shockingly difficult to find botanical pigments that would fade fast enough in sunlight to make sun prints. If you find another botanical pigment that works well, let me know! You can find my email address at SeedRenaissance.com. (While you are there, order some excellent seeds for dye plants and veggies! Shameless plug!)

This method has the fun element of looking like traditional cyanotype sun prints without any of the harsh chemicals or expense!

1 teaspoon blue spirulina powder

¼ teaspoon ascorbic acid

1 cup water

Mixed media paper

A large baking sheet

Dried leaves and flowers

A sheet of glass smaller than the baking sheet

1. Mix the blue spirulina powder and ascorbic acid with water; boil for 6–10 minutes.
2. Use this blue ink to paint your paper, then allow the paper to dry completely.
3. Lay your dried paper on the baking sheet. Carefully arrange your dried leaves and flowers and carefully cover with the glass. Leave this in bright sun for several hours. The ink will fade in the sun, revealing a print of your leaves and flowers.

Homemade Ingredients

Alum Acetate

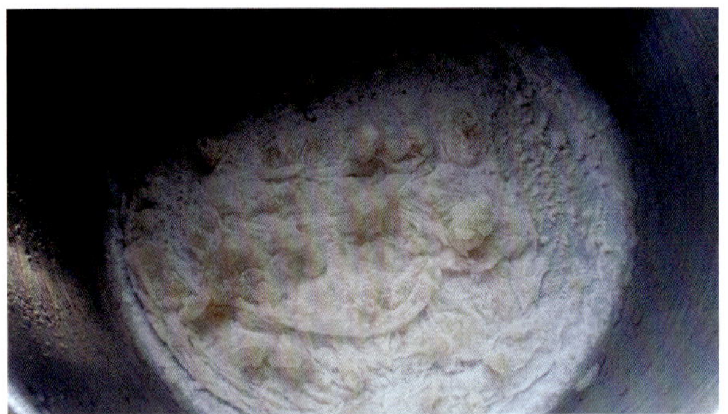

A premordant or mordant used on cellulose fibers (paper, cotton, and linen) to make dye more permanent. I also add this powder to dye baths and liquid base pigments sometimes as a mordant instead of a premordant.

1 cup white vinegar

1 tablespoon baking soda

1 tablespoon alum

1. Slowly mix the vinegar and baking soda. There will be a lot of foaming, so mix in a large bowl.
2. When the vinegar turns clear, boil the vinegar dry. At the very end of boiling, move the pot on and off the heat to control the evaporation. In the last seconds, crystals will form from the last of the liquid.
3. When the crystals form, turn off the heat and let the pan dry overnight.
4. The next day, scrap the powder crystals from the pan and add a tablespoon of alum powder. Mix the powders.
5. When you want to use this powder, use a measure equaling 5 to 10 percent of the weight of the fiber (WOF) you wish to dye. Add that amount of powder to a boiling water bath with enough water to let the fiber move freely.
6. Boil the fiber in this mordanted water for 30 minutes and then remove to dry.
7. Once dry, you can dye the fiber as normal.

Casein Powder

Casein powder is an ingredient in some versions of milk paint.

Prepared quark (any amount)

1. Take any amount of prepared quark and spread it in a thin layer on a lined cookie sheet. Dry at room temperature until completely dry. Powder in a food processor or blender (it will sound like you are blending rocks; be careful not to overheat the machine). You can also stone grind it; I use a stone mano and metate to grind paint pigments, dried plants, and casein powder. Do not try to mull dried cottage cheese that has not been powdered. You may break the glass.

Cream of Tartar

I add this for those of us who are really "extra" and love to make our own stuff. Cream of tartar can be purchased in the spice aisle of the grocery store or online and is inexpensive. But if you like to bottle your own homemade grape juice, like we do, you can easily make your own powdered cream of tartar.

This only works when you bottle whole grapes. If you bottle the steamed juice of grapes, the tartaric acid stays in the juice and rarely crystallizes. Tartaric acid crystals also form in some wines. Cream of tartar is a useful mordant, often used with citric acid or vinegar to help brighten red colors and make them more permanent.

Whole purple grapes (only purple grapes seem to make tartar)

Glass quart jar

⅛ cup sugar (optional)

Water

1. Wash the grapes and put them in the jar until it is ¾ full. (If you want to add sugar, do so now.) Fill the jar with water, seal, and water bath as normal for

canning juice. If you are new to canning juice at your elevation, consult with your local Extension Service for help.

2. After sitting for about six months, you can open the jar, strain out the grapes and feed them to the chickens or the grandkids, and drink the juice.
3. In about every other jar, you will find a lump of crystallized tartaric acid has formed in the bottom of the jar. Rinse this lump and allow it to air dry.
4. Grind the lump in a mortar and pestle and now you have cream of tartar powder! Store in a cupboard.

Edamame Milk

For a small batch:

8–10 fresh or frozen edamame beans

½ cup water

For a large batch:

½ cup fresh or frozen edamame beans

1 quart water

1. Blend the beans and water in a blender until completely smooth.
2. Strain the milk through a thin cotton cloth or felt. Edamame milk lasts less than a day in the heat, but stays good for several days when refrigerated.

Ground Eggshell Powder

Ingredient in some paint versions.

LARGE BATCH

Eggshells of 12 white eggs

1. Boil eggshells for at least 20 minutes.
2. Drain the water and rinse the shells.
3. Put the shells, with fresh water, into a blender and blend until smooth.
4. Allow the eggshell powder to settle in the blender for a few minutes and then carefully dump the water while retaining the eggshell powder.
5. Add new water and blend and drain again.
6. Repeat a third time.
7. When the water is clear of all egg residue after blending, drain the water and allow the eggshell dust to air dry on a plate or cookie sheet. Store in a sealed bag or jar with lid when completely dry.

SMALL BATCH

Eggshell of 1 white egg

1. Crush the eggshell and boil in a bowl of water in the microwave for 4–6 minutes.
2. Drain the water and rinse the shells.
3. Grind the shells in fresh water with a mortar and pestle or in a jar with a stick blender.
4. Allow the shell to settle, drain the water, rinse, and repeat grinding and draining until the water is clear of all residual egg residue. Take the wet eggshell powder and use it in a mulled batch of eggshell paint.

Hydrated Lime

Okay, I know that including this recipe is really, really extra, as the youth say, but since I do actually make my own hydrated lime—and you can, too (and civilizations have been making it for at least 5,000 years)—I might as well tell you how. Just in case you are as "out there" as I am (as my friend's spouse put it gently).

Just to be clear, hydrated lime has nothing to do with limes from the grocery store. "Lime" is simply a nickname for "limestone," which is a natural form of calcium. This (sometimes) soft rock is made of calcium carbonate, which is the same thing that stalagmites and stalactites in caves are made of. Hydrated lime is also the major ingredient in concrete.

To make homemade lime, you will need a kiln of bricks or mud bricks. My kiln is made of concrete bricks I got for free from people giving them away online. (Ask in your local Buy Nothing group on Facebook.) I gather soft limestone from the desert. Limestone is found in most of the world and is made of up fossilized shells and geological calcium debris. I "bake" it in my kiln by building a fire on top of the limestone hot enough to cover the limestone with red hot coals. (Having a simple kiln makes this much easier to accomplish, as opposed to an open fire, which is why all civilizations have made kilns of some kind.) For those who wish to use an infrared thermometer, a minimum temperature of 1500 degrees and a maximum temperature of 2000 degrees is required. I just know that if I bury it in hot coals, preferably from hardwoods, it will get hot enough.

You will know you have made lime if you can then pour water on the baked limestone and it immediately melts into dust. Pouring water on it is what makes it "hydrated." Mixing water with lime is called "slaking" the lime. You dry the slaked lime to make hydrated lime. Lime that has not been slaked and dried is called "quicklime" and you should avoid it because it is dangerously dehydrating.

To be clear, hydrated lime is also dehydrating and you should not breath the dust, but breathing the dust of quicklime basically immediately begins to form concrete in your lungs, so always pour water on your kilned limestone.

The dried slaked powder is stored in airtight containers because if water or humidity gets to it—you guessed it—it forms concrete. Hydrated lime is absolutely required for making milk paint, is a powerful mordant, and is important because any color mordanted with lime is likely to be exterior grade, meaning it will be resistant to damage from ultraviolet light. This is why I always include a mordant of lime in my basic mordant swatch tests. Then I always know which colors I can use to make in milk paint.

Lake Pigment Powders

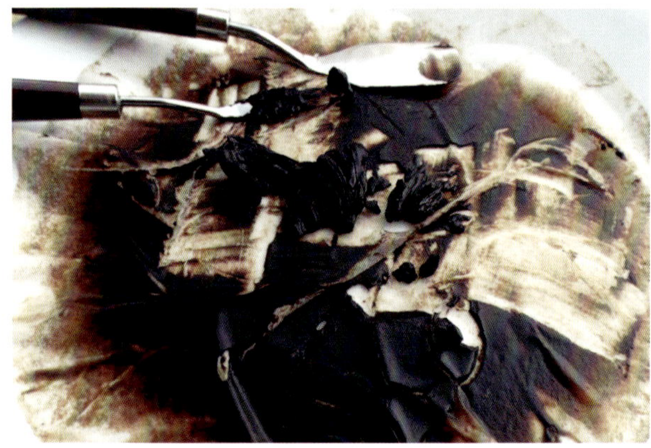

Lake pigments are created as a way of turning liquid dye into a dry powder that can be stored for later use.

POWDER OF ALUM

2 cups hot liquid base pigment in a quart glass mason jar

2 ½ teaspoons alum powder

1 teaspoon soda ash (see page 59)

1. Liquid base pigment should be brought to a boil and then removed from heat.
2. Stir alum into the hot liquid and bring to a boil again for a few seconds. Remove from the heat.
3. Slowly stir in the soda ash, which will create quite a bit of foam. Do not let the jar foam over. Stir down the foam.
4. Once completely mixed, and the foam has begun to reduce, allow this mixture to sit and cool for hours or overnight. The pigment will slowly begin to settle to the bottom of the jar. In some cases, the water will become clear as the pigment settles out.
5. Once pigment has settled, pour the liquid into a coffee filter or a piece of felt or silk to sieve. When only wet pigment remains, scrape the pigment onto a piece of glass, like the glass from a thrift store picture frame. This wet pigment can be used immediately if desired.

6. To dry for storage, spread the pigment into a roughly even layer and allow it to air dry. When completely dry, it can be stored in a resealable bag or lidded jar for later use. (Some people dry the pigment on the coffee filter that strained it, which works, too, but is much harder to get all the pigment off once it is dry.)

POWDER OF BAKING SODA AND CREAM OF TARTAR

Cream of tartar is available in the grocery spice aisle. The tartar in this recipe helps bring the baking soda closer to neutral. This lake pigment works especially well with paint recipes containing liquid pine as an ingredient.

Flowers or other botanical matter, about a cup.

Water, enough to cover the botanical material in the cooking pot.

1 teaspoon baking soda

¼ teaspoon cream of tartar

1. Cover flowers or other botanical matter with water and simmer until color is released (about 6–10 minutes for many flowers and leaves).
2. Strain the liquid and discard the botanical remnants.
3. Add baking soda and cream of tartar to your liquid pigment and then boil the liquid to nearly dry, stirring as the water evaporates.
4. Allow this pigment to cool completely before storing in a resealable bag or jar.

POWDER OF EDAMAME

Unsweetened, nonfat soy milk may be substituted for edamame milk. This can be made at home by soaking dried soybeans overnight, then blending until completely smooth and straining through a thin cotton cloth or felt.

Petals, leaves, or other botanical matter; it is hard to boil amounts smaller than a cup so start with a cup or more

Edamame milk (see page 53), enough to cover the botanical material in the cooking pot

1. Boil petals, leaves, or other botanical matter in edamame milk. When the milk is colored to your liking (6–10 minutes for many petals and leaves), strain and discard the botanical material.
2. Put the strained liquid back into the bowl or pan and boil down to near-glaze stage.
3. Scrape this liquid onto a piece of glass or a ceramic or glass plate. Allow the pigment to air dry completely.
4. When dry, scrape it up and store in a resealable bag or jar.

POWDER OF HYDRATED LIME

1 cup water

1 tablespoon hydrated lime

Flowers or other botanical matter, up to a cup depending on color saturation desired.

1. Mix together the water and hydrated lime.
2. Cover flowers or other botanical matter with water mixture and simmer until color is released (about 6–10 minutes for many flowers and leaves).
3. Strain the liquid and discard the botanical remnants.
4. Boil the liquid to nearly dry. Allow this pigment to cool completely before storing in a resealable bag or jar.

POWDER OF WHITE KAOLIN CLAY

White kaolin clay is available online and in health and beauty stores. You can experiment with using other white clay, even wild clay. Use only clay that is still white or nearly white when mixed with water. Because every natural class is molecularly different, using wild clay will be an experiment!

Flowers or other botanical matter, about 1 cup

Water to cover the botanical material in the cooking pot

1 tablespoon white kaolin clay

1. Cover flowers or other botanical matter with water and simmer until color is released (about 6–10 minutes for many flowers and leaves).
2. Strain the liquid and discard the botanical remnants.
3. Add kaolin clay to your liquid pigment and then boil the liquid to nearly dry, stirring as the water evaporates.
4. Allow this pigment to cool completely before storing in a resealable bag or jar.

Liquid Base Pigment

This base pigment can be used fresh as ink, watercolor paint, or dye. Or it can be allowed to air dry in a bowl or cup and stored for later use; spritz with water to rehydrate dried material. (Don't forget to label your material immediately or you will forget what you made!)

¼ cup (ish) fresh plant material of your choice or ⅛ cup dried

½ to 1 cup soft or distilled water (you want pH neutral or slightly acidic water, not hard water)

STOVETOP

1. Put plant material in a heavy-bottom saucepan and cover with water. The higher the ratio of water to plant material, the longer it will take to reduce the color, so only use as much water as necessary.

2. Boil for ten minutes; if the liquid in the pan is to your liking, sieve it in a tea strainer (available at the $1.25 store) or through a piece of craft felt or a thin kitchen towel. (About 90 percent of plant material is ready after ten minutes; however, barks and roots may take much longer. Be careful not to allow the liquid color to boil dry though! Add more water, if needed, in small amounts.)

3. To achieve depth of color, put the strained liquid back in the pan and boil again until you have removed as much water as possible. I always try to get my pigments as near a glaze as possible, having removed about 99 percent of the water. This is because you can always lighten a color, but you can never darken it once the cooking is finished.

MICROWAVE

1. Put plant material in a white glass bowl that is wide and shallow. Do not use clear or colored bowls because it will make it difficult to see the true color and monitor the progress of what you are cooking. Do not use a drinking cup or tall and skinny container because the liquid will boil over the cup while cooking. A white glass Corelle cereal bowl (or similar) works best because it allows you to see the true depth of color as the liquid reduces. You can use white ceramic bowls, but they take longer to heat and are more likely to burn your fingers when handling them. The higher the ratio of water to plant material, the longer it will take to reduce the color, so only use as much water as necessary.

2. Boil in the microwave for six to ten minutes, checking it every two minutes and then every thirty seconds near the end of the process. If you scorch the liquid, it will ruin the color.

3. When the color of the liquid in the pan is to your liking, sieve it in a tea strainer or through a thin cotton cloth or craft felt. (About 90 percent of plant material is ready after six to ten minutes; however, if longer is needed, make sure you don't boil the bowl dry or it may shatter. Add more water, if needed, in small amounts after the hot bowl has cooled. Do not add cold water to a hot glass bowl or it may shatter.)

4. To achieve depth of color, put this liquid back in the bowl and boil again until you have removed as much water as possible. The deepest color is called "glaze" and there is about ten to fifteen seconds of microwave boiling between a perfect glaze and a ruined, dried-out bowl of color, so keep your eye on the bowl and stop the microwave frequently as the water evaporates near the end of the process.

Liquid Gum Arabic

There is a dirty little secret in the art world that no one talks about—the harsh chemicals added to every commercial jar of liquid gum arabic. When you make your own liquid gum arabic, you quickly realize that it goes moldy after a few days, especially on warm days. It even goes moldy quickly when stored in the fridge. So how is the commercially prepared liquid gum arabic not going rotten? The answer: toxic preservatives. One of the most common is sodium benzoate, but there are dozens of similar preservatives. According to the US National Library of Medicine, sodium benzoate "was found to cause mutagenic effects, generate oxidative stress, disrupt hormones, and reduce fertility" in humans.[2] So no, we won't be using that.

[2] https://www.ncbi.nlm.nih.gov/pmc/articles/PMC9003278/

⅓ teaspoon gum arabic powder

¼ cup soft or pH-neutral water, hotter than blood temperature (the temperature you can touch it without it feeling hot) but below boiling (about 130 degrees is great)

1. Sprinkle the gum arabic powder into the hot water. Resist the temptation to stir it!
2. Let it thicken for about a half hour, then you can stir it. If you stir it too soon, the only thing that will happen is clumps of gum will stick to your utensil.

Liquid Pine

Food-grade methylcellulose, which I call liquid pine when it is mixed with water, is made by extracting cellulose from pine wood with alcohol. Non-food-grade uses harsh chemicals instead of alcohol and should be avoided.

¼ teaspoon food-grade methylcellulose powder (available online)

⅓ cup cold water

1. In a small jar with a lid, sprinkle powder onto cold water. (Resist the temptation to stir because most of the powder would stick to your spoon.) Close the jar and shake occasionally while allowing it to sit for several hours, until you cannot see the powder and the water has returned to being completely clear. This liquid should be thicker than water but not a gel. If a gel forms, add a tablespoon or two of water.
2. Store in a lidded jar. Stores for months but will go moldy if contaminated with any botanical paint residue, so always use clean utensils or brushes in this jar.

Prepared Egg Yolk

Make sure you don't get any of the yolk sac into the paint!

1 egg

Paper towel

1. Carefully crack open an egg and separate out the white. (You can use the white to make glair!)
2. Place the whole, unbroken yolk on the edge of the paper towel, and then fold the paper towel in half over it.
3. Hold this over a cup or bowl at an angle and then use a knife to pierce the sac. Allow the yolk to slowly run into the bowl. The sac will stay on the paper towel. Then discard the paper towel.

Quark

Quark is an ingredient in some versions of milk paint.

COTTAGE CHEESE VERSION

You can use any percentage of milk fat cottage cheese because all cottage cheese is made from nonfat milk. The milk fat percentages listed on the container are achieved by adding cream, and you will rinse away all the cream, so the percent milk fat is irrelevant to making quark. This is an excellent way to use up that cottage cheese forgotten in the back of your fridge!

1 container cottage cheese

1. Rinse cottage cheese with hot tap water until the rinse water is completely clear.
2. Strain cottage cheese through a sieve.

MILK VERSION

You can speed up this process by warming the milk (not warmer than blood temperature) on the stove or in the microwave before stirring in the vinegar.

½ gallon room-temperature nonfat milk

⅛ cup white vinegar

1. Stir together milk and vinegar. Allow to sit until the milk has separated into curds and whey, which may take 30 minutes to several hours depending on room temperature.
2. Strain curds and whey. Discard whey (or use it to boil pasta; delicious!). Rinse curds completely in warm water.

Vinegar of Copper

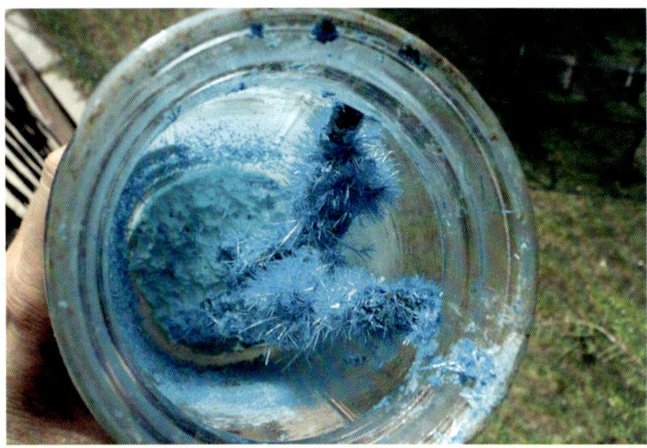

Vinegar of copper has been used by humans for as long as human history and has endless uses. It is extremely important in (external) herbal medicine and is a power ingredient in homemade dormant oil to stave off fungal infections in fruit trees and landscape trees. For our purposes in this book, it is an invaluable mordant for making blue and black colors, and it is critical for making kiln-able pottery paint. Natural copper oxides are found all over the world; I have a collection of them that I've gathered (legally) from the desert near my home. Where I live in the Rocky Mountains, it is still possible to find veins of natural copper oxides in road cuts.

I've used a piece of copper water pipe taken from our basement during a remodel, but you can find copper wire and other objects at thrift stores and Habitat for Humanity ReStores, or you can buy new copper screws or wire at any hardware store. You want real copper, not something just coated in copper, so avoid pennies.

While this concoction has been called "vinegar of copper" for centuries, today most people refer to it by its proper chemical name, "cupric acetate."

Any piece of copper

1 cup white distilled vinegar

1 cup water

Quart glass mason jar

1 cup hydrogen peroxide (optional)

1. Put the piece of copper, vinegar, and water in the mason jar. A chemical reaction will begin to happen, so leave the lid off the jar for two days to let gases escape. If you put a lid on the jar while this reaction is active, the jar will build up pressure and explode.

2. If you want to make vinegar of copper faster, add a cup of hydrogen peroxide. This makes the reaction speed up.

3. After a couple days, put the lid on the jar and store the jar in a cupboard. Within hours or days, the vinegar will begin to turn blue. Within about a week (sometimes longer), blue crystals of copper oxide will begin to form on any part of the copper above the waterline of vinegar. You can scrape off the soft crystals and use them to make paint all on their own or use the blue liquid as a mordant.

4. If you keep the jar closed and shake it every once in a while, it will just keep growing copper crystals for years to come. My jar has been going for years, and I've only once added about half a cup of water to it.

Quark mulled with blue crystals of vinegar of copper and a tiny dusting of borax and hydrated lime

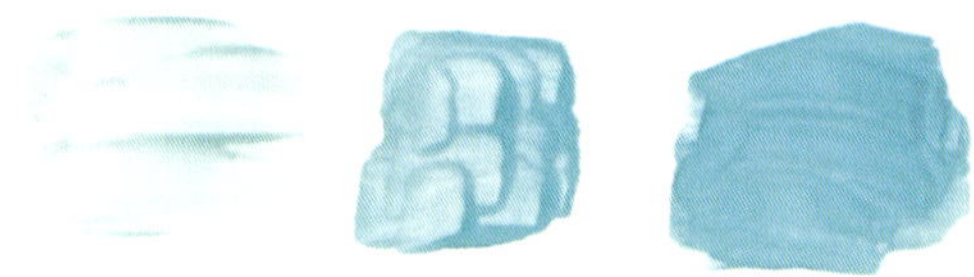

Glair mulled with increasing amounts of crystals of vinegar of copper

Crystals of vinegar of copper mulled with glycerin and water

Twice the crystals of vinegar of copper, compared to above, mulled with glycerin and water

Vinegar of Iron

Iron is a useful mordant for making colors more permanent, especially when exposed to sunlight or laundry. But iron saddens almost every color it mordants. "Saddening" is an old dyer's term meaning a mordant that makes a color darker or more brown, black, or gray, thus making the color "sad." But sad colors can be useful, especially in moody and ethereal art. I don't generally like sad colors on clothes, but that is just me. Some dyers sadden all their dye to make the colors more "earthy." To each their own. I put mine on a shelf in a shed or greenhouse and forget about it for a couple months.

It is important to note that you should not use plain vinegar of iron as paint or to dye fabric because it will slowly eat through the fabric or paper. Also, iron quickly damages linen, silk, and wool and, even as mordant, must be used sparingly—if at all—with those fabrics. Also, I can tell you from experience that vinegar of iron stains permanently. My dye pots will attest to that!

Note: Different iron oxides, of which vinegar of iron is one, make different rust colors ranging from orange to black, grey, yellow and red. In chemistry, these are called "iron(I)," "iron(II)," and "iron(III)." Each oxide is a different chemical composition. The recipe above is likely to make black or gray but also sometimes makes red, depending on the kind of iron used.

Rusty nails or any rusty scrap of iron

Quart glass mason jar

1–2 cups white distilled vinegar

1. Put the rusty nails or rusty scrap of iron and vinegar into the mason jar.
2. Leave the lid off the jar and wait a few weeks. (The rusting reaction of iron and vinegar off-gases while the reaction is active, so it is important the lid is off and the jar is placed in a well-ventilated area.)

Washing Soda/Soda Ash

Washing soda, also called "soda ash," used to be cheap but has now become expensive and hard to find in the laundry aisle of the grocery store. Over the past decade, the price of commercial washing soda has more than doubled—to the chagrin of those of us who always make our own laundry soap and have been doing so for decades. So now I make my own washing soda, which is cheap and easy.

Baking soda has a pH of 8.3, but the simple act of baking your baking soda turns the sodium bicarbonate into sodium carbonate, which increases the pH to 11.4. This strong alkaline pH is invaluable for doing laundry and for mordanting some botanical colors, especially woad.

Baking soda has been made for millennia by burning certain plants to ash, but that is another story and another recipe for another book, coming soon, of course.

1 box baking soda

1. Spread the baking soda over a cookie sheet in a roughly even layer and bake at 250 degrees for an hour.
2. Let it cool and store it in an airtight container.

Homemade Inks

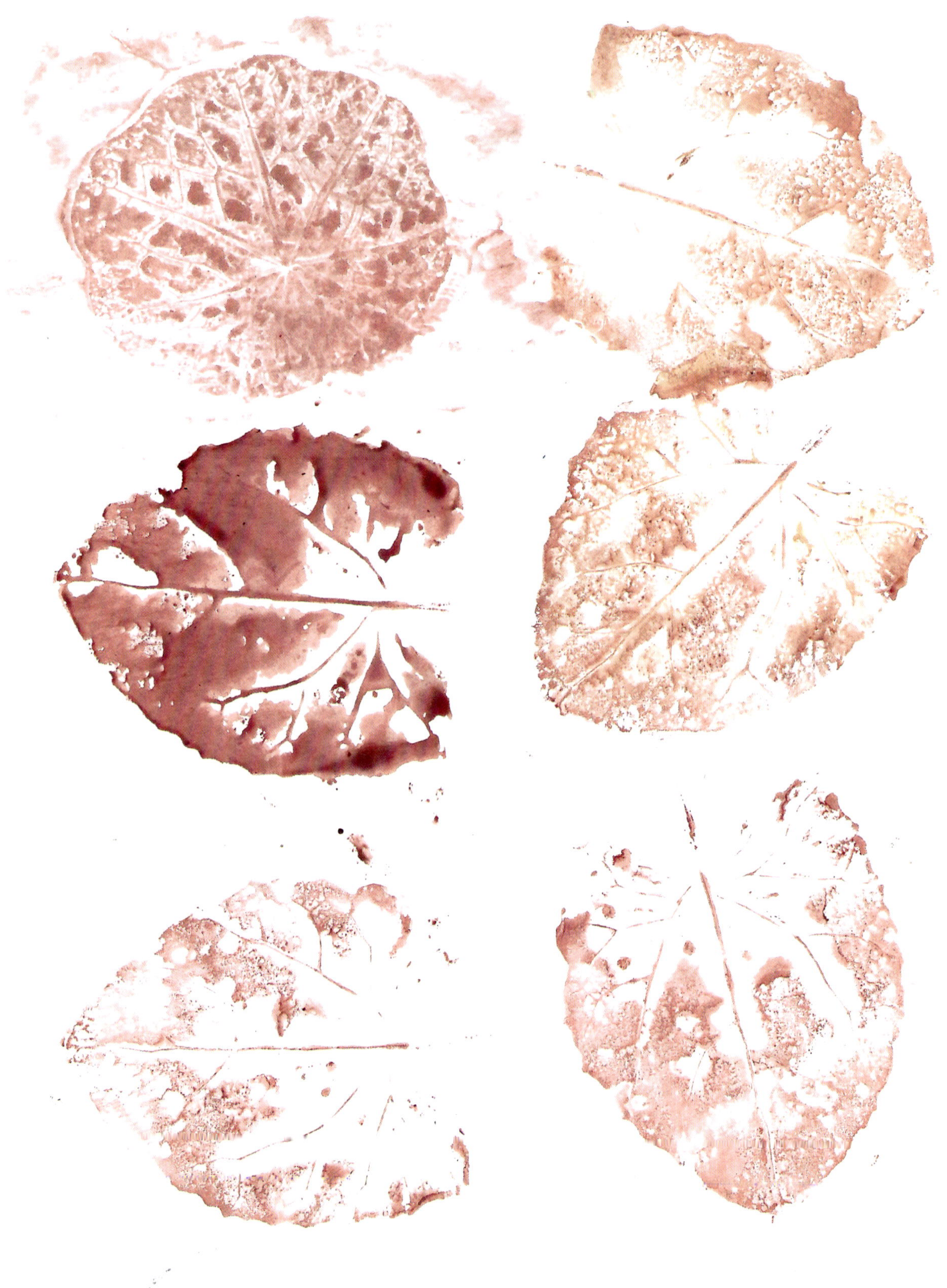

Ink for Stamping

Add water as desired to a liquid base pigment, fresh or dried. If the pigment is at true glaze stage (slightly thick) or is dried, it will need a little more water than a fresh pigment.

Make sure the pigment is clear, strong, and without lumps or specks. If it is not perfect, filter it through a piece of felt.

Using any flat lid that will hold liquid, cut a piece of felt to fit the lid. Pour just enough pigment in to dampen the felt; this will be your do-it-yourself stamp pad. Even being careful, I sometimes found that I had lumps and specks of pigment that would appear on top of the felt after I poured on the stamping ink. When this happened, I simply turned the felt over.

Stamping works best on a flat, firm surface; I recommend putting both your stamp pad and the paper you want to stamp on the glass mulling plate. If the ink is too thick, add water by drops.

Thinner paper takes stamping better than thicker paper.

It is also possible to use a drop or two of liquid gum arabic in this recipe, but not if you intend to store the wet ink. I have tested this recipe both with and without gum arabic and it actually seemed to me that adding gum made it a little harder to get a good stamp.

Historic "Fine Red" Ink

1 tablespoon hot water

¼ teaspoon powdered cochineal

¼ teaspoon ammonia

1 drop liquid gum arabic

1. Shake ingredients together in a jar and let this mixture sit in sunlight for at least a week.
2. Strain the ink through craft felt and it is ready to use.

Historic Green of Tartar Ink

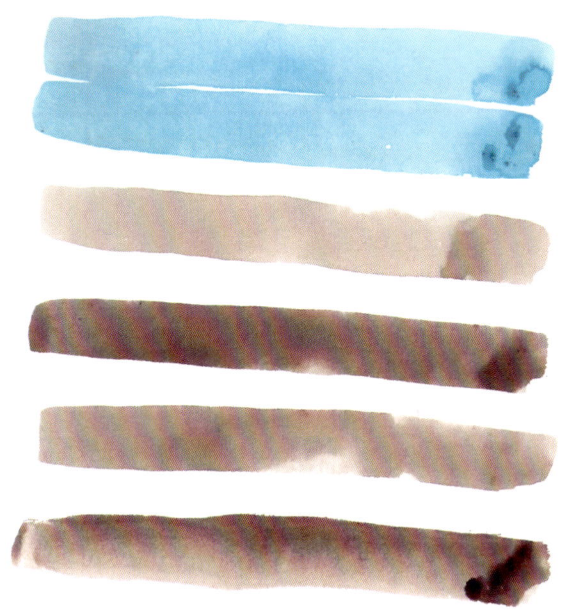

2 tablespoons vinegar of copper, strained through craft felt to remove copper solids

1 tablespoon cream of tartar

½ cup water

½ teaspoon liquid gum arabic

1. Mix vinegar of copper, cream of tartar, and water together.
2. Boil until reduced by half.
3. Filter through craft felt. Add gum arabic and heat again on low heat (so you don't overcook it) until reduced to one tablespoon. Check often if using a microwave.
4. Filter again. Let cool and it is ready to use. This ink darkens a little as it dries on paper. Store in a lidded jar.

Historic King of Purples

1 tablespoon logwood shavings

½ cup water

¼ teaspoon vinegar of copper

1 tablespoon alum

1 teaspoon liquid gum arabic

1. Add the logwood shavings and water to a saucepan and boil. Reduce down to 2 tablespoons of strained liquid.
2. Add the vinegar of copper, alum, and gum arabic to the strained liquid. Mix together and let sit for about a week before using.

From Berries or Petals

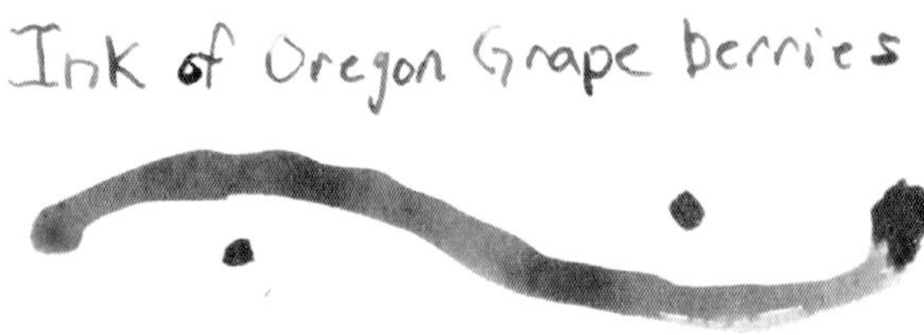

This recipe makes excellent, dark ink with great flow.

While they, too, make good ink, you don't have to use grocery store berries like raspberries or blackberries. Berries of Cotoneaster, Oregon grape, pokeweed, Virginia creeper, and other non-sweet berries also make good ink.

1 cup berries

1 cup water

1 teaspoon table salt

1 teaspoon vinegar (any type)

1 teaspoon liquid gum arabic

1. Place the berries in a saucepan and smash.
2. Add the water and boil to reduce by half, then strain.
3. Add salt and vinegar and reduce by half again.
4. Add gum arabic and stir.
5. Test the ink. If the color is not strong enough, reduce until you like the color. This ink keeps for a few days at room temperature and longer in the fridge.

From Marigolds

¼ cup fresh marigold petals, or ⅛ cup dried

1 cup water

⅛ teaspoon ascorbic acid (optional, but makes a brighter orange ink)

¼ teaspoon table salt

¼ teaspoon alum

¼ teaspoon liquid gum arabic

1. Combine petals, water and ascorbic acid. Bring this mixture to steaming but not boiling on the stove in a pan with no lid. Steam until reduced to ¼ cup.
2. Add salt, alum, and gum. Bring mixture back to steaming on the stove and reduce to 2 tablespoons.
3. Strain and cool. This ink lasts about six weeks if not kept in the fridge.

From Nuts

This makes brown ink. You can add vinegar of iron or particles of iron oxide with the alum and baking soda to make black ink.

1 walnut (or similar nut) with the hull

1 cup water

1 pinch of alum

1 pinch of baking soda

1. Crush the hull and boil in the water until reduced by half.
2. Add alum and baking soda and reduce by at least half again.
3. Test the color to see if it is dark enough.

From Oak Galls

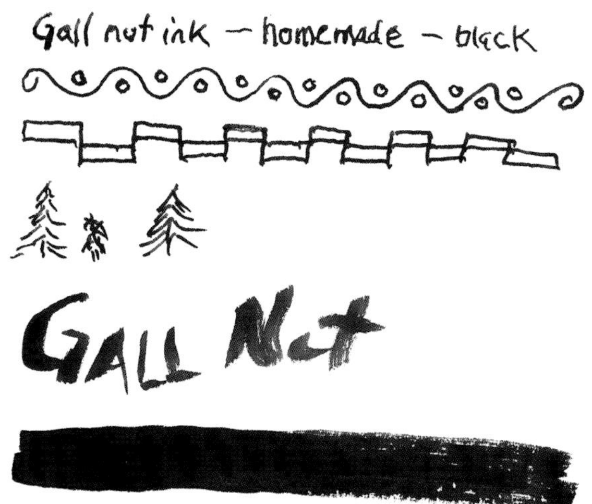

Don't spill this ink; it is permanent, waterproof, and sunproof!

If you are gathering your own oak galls, they must be tan in color and not black. They are usually ripe in September where we live.

After drying for 24 hours, this ink is both waterproof and UV-resistant. Counterintuitively, the less ink you use, the more waterproof it is. Paper only absorbs so much ink and only ink bonded with the paper is waterproof. I can tell you from experience that if you pour water on the ink, the base writing will be waterproof even if you scrub the paper, but excess ink will become soluble and wash away. The lettering below will remain intact. So use less ink for best results.

¼ cup water

5 grams of oak galls (powder or small pieces) (about 1 ¼ teaspoons)

1 gram of ferrous sulfate or iron oxide powder (about ¼ teaspoon)

¼ teaspoon liquid gum arabic

1. Mix water and gall powder in a clear glass jar. Let this mixture stand in the sun for a couple of bright days and then strain.
2. Add remaining ingredients to this liquid and let it stand in the sun for at least a week, then it is ready to use.

Invisible

1 tablespoon lemon juice

Dash of salt

1. Mix lemon juice and salt together and heat for 30 seconds in the microwave.
2. Use the ink to write a note on white paper and then let the paper dry. You can speed the drying in the microwave.
3. When dry, heat the paper on a lightbulb or with an iron to reveal the ink.

Homemade Paints

All-Natural Fabric Paint

For cotton fabric.

Note 1: Guar gum is the natural gum dietary fiber of the beans of the guar plant, *Cyamopsis tetragonoloba*. Gum tragacanth is the bark resin of the tragacanth shrub, *Astragalus gummifer*. Sodium alginate is an extract of several kelp and algae species. All three are used to thicken foods and for art, crafts, and other purposes.

Note 2: Some brands of parchment paper are apparently made with PFAS forever chemicals; avoid those brands.

Edamame milk (see page 53)

1 tablespoon liquid or dried botanical glaze pigment

A pinch of guar gum or sodium alginate powder

Parchment paper

1. Paint edamame milk onto an area of a garment you want to print, stencil, or paint, or dip the entire garment, if desired.
2. Dry the fabric completely by microwaving it in 30-second intervals, refolding the garment each time, being careful not to scorch any spot on the garment. Once the garment is fairly dry, you can finish drying it in the sun or iron it dry between sheets of parchment paper. The fabric must be completely dry before proceeding.
3. Heat your liquid botanical glaze. Add guar gum or sodium alginate powder to pigment. Liquid must be hot before you add the gum or alginate. Stir this together and allow to thicken as it cools. Use this paint to hand-paint or stencil on your fabric.
4. Dry the painted shirt in the microwave, with an iron, or in the hot sun. Heat helps set the pigment in the fabric.
5. Wash the fabric or garment with regular laundry soap. This will remove the mordant of edamame milk and reveal the finished painting or stenciling, which is now fused to the fabric.

Baking Soda Paint

This paint is transparent and slow to dry on wood and paper.

Fresh, liquid, or dried botanical pigment

1 drop liquid gum arabic

2 drops liquid pine (see page 57)

⅛ teaspoon cream of tartar

⅛ teaspoon baking soda

Dusting of salt

1. If you are using fresh botanical material, first mull together with some drops of water to grind it up.
2. Mull all ingredients together until smooth.

Best Gouache

This paint works well when used on paper.

6 drops of soft water

6 drops of liquid gum arabic

3 drops of honey

1 drop of glycerin or homemade soap concentrate

Fresh, liquid, or dried botanical pigment

1 to 2 parts kaolin clay or eggshell powder

1. Add ingredients to a mulling slab.
2. Mull everything together until smooth.

Best Small-Batch Milk Paint Base

This makes a great flat white paint that dries quickly and smoothly.

1 tablespoon quark

1 drop of borax

2 teaspoons hot water

1 teaspoon hydrated lime

2–3 parts slaked eggshell powder, hydrated lime, or chalk (optional)

1. Mull quark to smash it (alternatively, you can push it through a strainer, but this wastes quark).
2. Mull together quark, borax, water, and hydrated lime. If you are looking to make a white paint, you could also mull in eggshell powder, hydrated lime, or chalk.
3. Let sit for 5–15 minutes until thick. Stir before using because chalk, hydrated lime, or eggshell may settle.

Best Tempera Gouache

The difference between watercolor and gouache is calcium carbonate (powdered eggshell or seashells) or clay. Gouache is opaque; watercolor is translucent.

Yolk Tempera Base Paint (see page 77)

White kaolin clay

1. To the Yolk Tempera Base Paint, add small touches of clay until you like the consistency. Only add tiny amounts; you can always add more, but too much ruins the paint color.

Bright White Glair Gesso (White or Tinted)

This paint can be used to prepare canvases or as a white paint. However, the lime in this gesso mordants some colors. This paint appears somewhat transparent when wet but dries opaque. Also, with less mulling, you can use this as a very thin whitewash under or over other paints. With more mulling, you get a creamier, thicker gesso. You can add pigments to this to make a color, but they will be pastels because there is so much lime in it.

For white gesso:

1 teaspoon glair

1 teaspoon slaked (wet) hydrated lime

Pinch of sea salt

Water, as needed

For tinted gesso:

1 teaspoon glair

½ teaspoon slaked (wet) hydrated lime

Pinch of sea salt

Fresh, liquid, or dried botanical pigments

Water, as needed

1. Whether you are making white or tinted gesso, add all relevant ingredients to a mulling slab.
2. Mull everything together.

Edamame Paint

Creates a thin, transparent paint on paper.

Several drops of edamame milk (see page 53)

Fresh, liquid, or dried botanical pigment

1. Add edamame milk and pigment to a mulling slab.
2. Mull everything together until completely smooth.

Eggless Tempera Paint

⅛ teaspoon glair

3 drops liquid gum arabic

Fresh, liquid, or dried botanical pigment

Tiny dusting of salt

Water, as needed

1. Add all the ingredients to a mulling slab.
2. Mull everything together until smooth and the paint begins to thicken.

Eggshell Milk Paint

When liquid pine is added to glair, it begins to coagulate; this goes away as you mull the paint.

1 drop liquid pine

Ground eggshell

Casein powder

Glair

1. Add liquid pine and roughly equal parts ground eggshell, casein powder, and glair to a mulling slab.
2. Mull everything together.

Eggshell Semitransparent Gesso (White or Tinted)

Mixing water with glair makes a stronger paint.

For white gesso:

½ teaspoon glair

½ teaspoon (or less) ground white eggshell

Pinch of salt

Water, as needed

For tinted gesso:

½ teaspoon glair

½ teaspoon (or less) ground white eggshell

Pinch of salt

Water, as needed

Botanical base pigment

1. Whether you are making white or tinted gesso, add all relevant ingredients to a mulling slab.
2. Mull everything together. Mulling eggshells takes longer than mulling other paints. The longer you mull this recipe, the thicker it will become, and to use it as semitransparent gesso (to add light and layers to your art), you will want it thinner.

Eggshell White Pine Paint

This paint is matte and slightly textured. It appears translucent when applied but dries opaque.

Mixing water with glair makes a stronger paint.

½ teaspoon glair

½ teaspoon (or less) ground white eggshell

½ teaspoon (or more) hydrated lime powder

1 drop liquid pine

Dusting of salt

Water, as needed

1. Add all ingredients to a mulling slab.
2. Mull everything together. The more you mull, the finer the paint will be. The more hydrated lime you add, the whiter and more opaque the paint will be.

Exterior Swedish Flour Paint

The key to making a great Swedish flour paint is to pretend you are making a perfect, lump-free gravy for Sunday dinner, not too thick, not too thin—a skill few people have anymore. Luckily, my grandma Wilhelmina "Billie" Nielson taught me how in her kitchen.

This recipe can be doubled or quadrupled, dries translucent, and is traditionally for wood, but it also works on paper and canvas.

A little bit of this paint goes a long way. It goes on transparent but dries semiopaque and really brings out the grain in wood.

Whoever created this paint recipe, centuries ago, should be reanimated and given an award because it is wonderful to have a durable, weather-resistant exterior paint option beyond milk paint. Not that there's anything wrong with milk paint, but options are nice. This paint is a double winner because it is cheap, easy, and quick to make.

Please note that this may be one of the few recipes in this book that cannot—repeat, **cannot**—be made in the microwave. If this paint turns out lumpy, it is ruined, and cooking flour and water on high heat in the microwave is always, always going to turn into lumps. I've tried and tried to make a microwave version of this paint for you, to no avail. You really just have to use the stove.

One more note. The oil in this recipe really makes a difference in the color. If you use turmeric powder as your pigment and use linseed oil, you will get a bright yellow paint. If you use the same pigment with walnut oil, you get a less bright but still nice yellow color. So choose your oil according to the hue of paint you desire. Sunflower and safflower oils should also make brighter colors, but not as bright as linseed.

¾ cup cold water

2 teaspoons white flour

Liquid or dry pigment as desired (start with ¼ teaspoon)

2 teaspoons linseed, walnut, sunflower, or other botanical drying oil

1. In a small saucepan, whisk together cold water and flour. You really are going to need a whisk for this recipe. Without a whisk, I wouldn't attempt it.
2. Once incorporated, turn on the heat to medium-low. Whisk while you slowly bring this to a slow, low boil. It will froth for a couple minutes while you whisk, then suddenly the froth will start to "volcano" and threaten to overtop the pan. Turn off the heat.
3. Whisk the froth down. Add the oil and whisk to incorporate. Add the pigment and whisk to incorporate. Turn the heat back on.
4. Whisk while you bring the whole mixture back to a low, slow boil. Once it starts to boil, turn the heat down almost to low. Keep whisking for about 10 minutes. When the paint is shiny and just beginning to thicken in the pan, it is done.
5. Turn off the heat and continue to whisk for a minute so the paint does not form a skin. Apply the paint hot or cool, but it is best applied while warm.

Gum Arabic Paint

There is debate in the art world about whether adding natural gums to base pigments makes ink or watercolor paint. The answer is yes, and no. Any base color thickened with gum can be used as ink. But traditional "ink" is made of oak galls and does not use any gum thickener. Because base pigment can be used by itself, the only time you need to add gum arabic or any other natural gum thickener is if you need a thicker or smoother color. At that point you call it "watercolor paint," "ink," "gum paint," or make up some name. It doesn't matter what we call it, as long as it works. I will say that I rarely add gums to my base paint simply because they are not necessary. But they do create a smoother paint with better flow in some cases, which gives you, as an artist, more control of the paint.

The best and cheapest way is to simply make a small fresh batch of liquid gum when you need it (see page 56) or to use gum arabic powder directly in a mulled batch of paint without making it into a liquid first. The powder stores for years.

For liquid base pigment:

Making a gum arabic pigment can preserve some colors that are fleeting.

½ teaspoon gum arabic powder

½ cup liquid base pigment

¼ teaspoon liquid nano silver (optional)

1. Stir together gum arabic powder and liquid base pigment.
2. Cook in the microwave or on the stovetop until heated enough that the gum dissolves (about 30 seconds in the microwave) or you can just add the gum to the hot liquid base immediately after making the base.
3. If you are not going to use the gum arabic paint immediately, mix in the liquid nano silver. This is because gum arabic, as well as botanical inks, will go moldy after a few days, especially in hot weather.

For mulling paint:

Drop or less of gum arabic powder

Paint ingredients

1. Add the gum arabic powder to the paint ingredients on your muller slab.
2. Mull everything together.

Historic Red Pottery Paint

This paint is black if you omit the iron rust.

1 teaspoon Wild Botanical Pottery Paint using sunflowers *(see page 74)*

1 teaspoon iron rust (or other powder kiln-fast colorant)

⅛ teaspoon tree resin crystals

¼ teaspoon clay

1. Grind or mull the ingredients together to form a paste using a stone or glass muller until a thick paste is created, about 2–3 minutes.
2. Paint onto bisque to achieve a flat color or greenware to create a painted look that stays on top of the clay. If painted on greenware, do not polish painted areas.

Honey Paint

This paint works well for use on paper.

6 drops of soft water

6 drops of liquid gum arabic

3 drops of honey

1 drop of glycerin or homemade soap concentrate

Fresh, liquid, or dried botanical pigment

1. Add ingredients to a mulling slab.
2. Mull everything together until smooth.

Micellar Milk Paint (White or Tinted)

For white paint:

¼ cup water

Tiny pinch of borax

2 teaspoons micellar casein

3 teaspoons hydrated lime

For tinted paint:

¼ cup water

Tiny pinch of borax

2 teaspoons micellar casein

1 teaspoon hydrated lime

Liquid or powdered botanical pigment

1. Whether you are making white or tinted paint, mix all relevant ingredients in a bowl.
2. Let the paint sit 30 minutes and mix again before using.

Nonfat Milk Paint

1 cup nonfat milk

⅓ cup hydrated lime

⅛ teaspoon borax

1. Stir together all ingredients.
2. Wait 30 minutes and stir well.
3. Mull and use immediately or wait overnight and then stir well to use as unmulled paint.

Nonfat Plain Yogurt Paint (White or Tinted)

This paint is foamy; to defoam the paint, stir in a drop of homemade or castile soap.

Don't panic! This paint may look white when it is ready to apply, but when it is brushed on, it is transparent. It will dry opaque like regular paint.

For white paint:

¼ teaspoon borax

1 teaspoon warm water

1 cup nonfat plain yogurt

8–10 tablespoons hydrated lime powder

For tinted paint:

¼ teaspoon borax

1 teaspoon warm water

1 cup nonfat plain yogurt

3 tablespoons hydrated lime powder

Botanical pigment

1. Whether you are making white or tinted paint, dissolve borax in warm water and then allow to cool.
2. Whisk together the borax-water, yogurt, and hydrated lime powder (the proper amount for white or tinted paint).
3. If you are making tinted paint, whisk in the pigment to achieve desired color.
4. Whisk every 5 minutes for 15 minutes.
5. Apply paint and let it dry. You can apply a second coat for a stronger whitewash. If ambient temperature is above 80 degrees, the paint will crack as it dries.

Oil Paint

Note: Making oil paint requires drying oil. Olive oil is not a drying oil. Linseed oil is a strongly yellowing oil, meaning it will slowly change some botanical colors. For example, when linseed oil is used to make botanical oil paint, most blues become green and many greens become yellow over about a month. Walnut oil is less yellowing than linseed but can sadden or brown some colors; however, it is widely used and loved by many artists. Sunflower oil and safflower oil are my favorites because they are the least yellowing. Poppy seed oil is also non-yellowing but is expensive and difficult to get. Many artists use the drying oil that best matches the color mood they hope to achieve. I like brighter colors in my art, so I use sunflower and safflower, but many traditional artists like a darker more traditional, more realistic palette and walnut works well for that.

Base pigment

Water, as needed

Glair

Drying oil (e.g., sunflower oil, walnut oil, or linseed oil)

1. Add base pigment, water, and equal parts glair and drying oil to a mulling slab.
2. Mull everything together until thick, about 30 seconds.

Pottery Paints

These paints withstand scrubbing, meaning they become a permanent part of the clay after being fired in a wood-fired kiln or even if fired correctly in a pit fire.

BLACK

¼ teaspoon liquor of vinegar of copper (liquor is the "thick" sludgy vinegar at the bottom of the jar)

⅛ teaspoon clay (same clay used to make the pot you wish to paint)

A pinhead of crushable pine tree resin per 1–2 teaspoons of paint (not the gooey resin on the bark but the crusty flaky crushable resin found on the bark)

¼ teaspoon vinegar of iron

Water of copper, as needed

1. Mull all ingredients together, using drops of water of copper to thin the paint as needed.
2. Apply this paint to bisque pottery and then fire in a kiln.

PEACH BLUSH

I almost hesitate to include this recipe because the success of the recipe may depend on the type of clay you add to it, but it is such a beautiful pottery paint that I think you should at least try it if you are into wild clay pottery.

⅛ teaspoon Wild Botanical Pottery Paint using wild tansy mustard (see page 74)

⅛ teaspoon vinegar of iron

A pinhead of crushable pine tree resin per 1–2 teaspoons of paint (not the gooey resin on the bark but the crusty flaky crushable resin found on the bark)

¼ teaspoon wild brown ball clay

1. Mull all ingredients together.
2. Apply this paint to bisque pottery and then fire in a kiln.

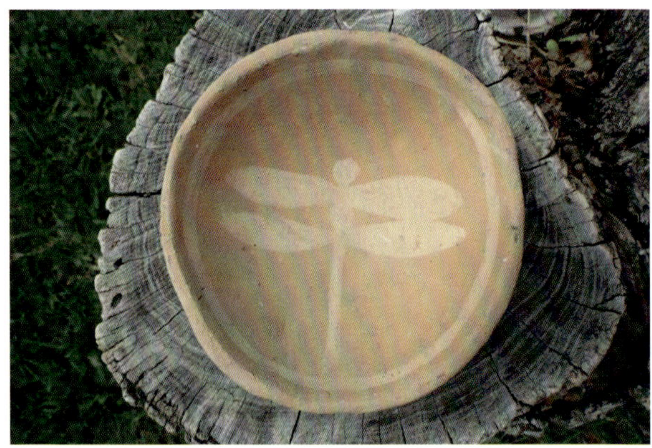

WILD BOTANICAL

These paints come out brown, brown-black, gray, or black after being fired, depending on temperature, clay, burnishing, and thickness. If you want to be sure these paints come out black and not brown or gray, add liquor of copper, iron oxide, or powdered manganese at the mulling stage.

Mesquite sap does not need to be thick or fully dried to store, but it should be reduced by boiling until it is oily. Mesquite sap paint does not need any additives. It is applied to bisque pottery and then fired briefly on coals until shiny.

Over-firing will dull any of these botanical pottery paints.

Quite a bit of one of the following botanical material

- Wild sunflower plants (*Helianthus annuus*), picked green before or while flowering. You can include all parts of the plant.
- Wild tansy mustard (*Descurainia pinnata*), picked green or in flower. You can include all parts of the plant.
- Rocky Mountain beeplant (*Cleome serrulata*), although I suspect any *Cleome* species will work. You can include all parts of the plant.
- Cactus fruit (*Opuntia* and other species).
- Yucca fruit (several species).
- Beans or sap-coated bark of the mesquite tree (*Neltuma glandulosa*, also called *Prosopis glandulosa*). The sap makes a shinier paint than the beans of this tree.

Water

Strainer

1. Pack your botanical material in a large pot.
2. Add enough water to cover the botanical material and boil for at least 1 hour, if not 2.
3. Strain out the material and then continue to boil the liquid until almost all water is gone and the paint becomes thick, almost syrup, but be sure not to scorch the paint.
4. Allow the paint to air dry and become solid in a bowl or jar. It can be stored for years and rehydrated by spritzing with water.
5. Paints from all of the plants above except the sap of mesquite are mixed with equal parts clay and a speck of flakey pine resin, then mulled or worked in a mortar and pestle until smooth and fully incorporated. Applied in a single coat, this paint can be applied when pottery is fully dried but often bonds more deeply into the clay when applied at the leather-hard stage and then lightly burnished, traditionally with a smooth stone.

Powdered Milk Mulled Oil Paint

This paint is semi-gloss and slow to dry.

½ teaspoon nonfat powdered milk

⅛ teaspoon hydrated lime

2 drops of walnut oil or drying oil

Tiny dusting of borax

Drops of water, as needed

1. Add all ingredients to a mulling slab.
2. Mull everything together

Powdered Milk Mulled Paint

This paint is opaque and matte.

½ teaspoon nonfat powdered milk

⅛ teaspoon hydrated lime

Tiny dusting of borax

Drops of water, as needed

1. Add all ingredients to a mulling slab.
2. Mull everything together.

Quark Oil Paint (White or Tinted)

Best applied in thin layers. This paint is somewhat transparent. Makes about 2 cups of paint.

The order of this recipe is important. Adding ingredients out of order may ruin the paint.

For white paint:

1 ½ cups cottage cheese quark

⅔ cup water

Glass mason jar

⅓ teaspoon borax

1 cup hydrated lime

1 teaspoon walnut or other drying oil

For tinted paint:

1 ½ cups cottage cheese quark

⅔ cup water

Glass mason jar

⅓ teaspoon borax

¼ cup hydrated lime

1 teaspoon walnut or other drying oil

Dried or liquid botanical pigment

1. Whether you are making white or tinted paint, add the quark and water to the mason jar and blend until smooth.
2. Add borax and blend again. At this point, the paint will be thick.
3. Add hydrated lime (the proper amount for white or tinted paint) a little at a time, blending as you go. When you first add the hydrated lime, the paint will go quite thin; it will thicken as you blend in the remaining hydrated lime.
4. Blend in drying oil.
5. If you are making tinted paint, blend in the pigment to achieve desired color.
6. When all ingredients are blended and smooth, let the paint sit for 30 minutes and then blend again. It is now ready to use.

Quark Paint (White or Tinted)

Best applied in thin layers. Makes about 2 cups of paint; recipe can be halved.

The order of this recipe is important. Adding ingredients out of order may ruin the paint.

For white paint:

1 ½ cups cottage cheese quark

⅔ cup water

Glass mason jar

⅓ teaspoon borax

1 cup hydrated lime

For tinted paint:

1 ½ cups cottage cheese quark

⅔ cup water

Glass mason jar

⅓ teaspoon borax

¼ cup hydrated lime

Dried or liquid botanical pigment

1. Whether you are making white or tinted paint, add the quark and water to the mason jar and blend until smooth.
2. Add borax and blend again. At this point, the paint will be thick.
3. Add hydrated lime (the proper amount for white or tinted paint) a little at a time, blending as you go. When you first add the hydrated lime, the paint will go quite thin; it will thicken as you blend in the remaining hydrated lime.
4. If you are making tinted paint, blend in the botanical pigment to achieve desired color.
5. When all ingredients are blended and smooth, let the paint sit for 30 minutes and then blend again. It is now ready to use.

Vine Black

Vine black is made by charring grape vines until they crumble to char dust.

1. Take clippings of fresh or dead grape vines. Place them in a metal or wood-fired ceramic container. Some people use a soup can or a metal box leftover from breath mints. I do a larger batch in a large metal food can.
2. Cut the vines so they fit entirely inside the container. Then, inside a firepit, turn the can upside down so the vine pieces are completely covered by the can.
3. Then light a wood fire over and around the can and burn enough wood so that the container is covered in coals. Let cool completely, which may take a full 24 hours.

4. Carefully remove the ashes and coals from around the can. Tip the can on its side carefully and collect the charred remains of the vine.
5. Some or all of the vines may collapse into char dust. Those that don't can be easily and gently crushed with a rock or brick.
6. Gather the char dust for storage and use on its own or in a recipe in this book.

Vinegar Tempera

This paint is slow to dry and works better on paper than wood. The vinegar in this recipe will mordant some colors.

1 part soft water

1 drop of white vinegar per teaspoon of water

1 part prepared egg yolk

Fresh, liquid, or dried botanical pigment

1. Add ingredients to a mulling slab.
2. Mull everything together until thick.

Weather-Resistant Nonfat Milk Paint (White or Tinted)

For white paint:

1 cup nonfat milk

⅓ cup hydrated lime

⅛ teaspoon borax

2 tablespoons walnut oil

For tinted paint:

1 cup nonfat milk

2 tablespoons hydrated lime

⅛ teaspoon borax

2 tablespoons walnut oil (or drying oil of choice)

Botanical pigment

1. Whether you are making white or tinted paint, stir together all relevant ingredients.
2. Stir occasionally over the next 12 hours as the paint slowly thickens.
3. Use immediately for mulled paint or wait overnight and then use as unmulled paint.

White Pine Paint

This paint is excellent on wood.

2 drops liquid pine

¼ teaspoon hydrated lime

⅛ teaspoon water

2 drops of glycerin

1. Add ingredients to a mulling slab.
2. Mull everything together.

Yolk Tempera Base Paint

This paint is slow to dry.

1–2 parts water

1 part prepared egg yolk

Fresh, liquid, or tried botanical pigment

1. Add all ingredients to a mulling slab.
2. Mull everything together until smooth and the paint begins to thicken, about 30 seconds.

Homemade Stains

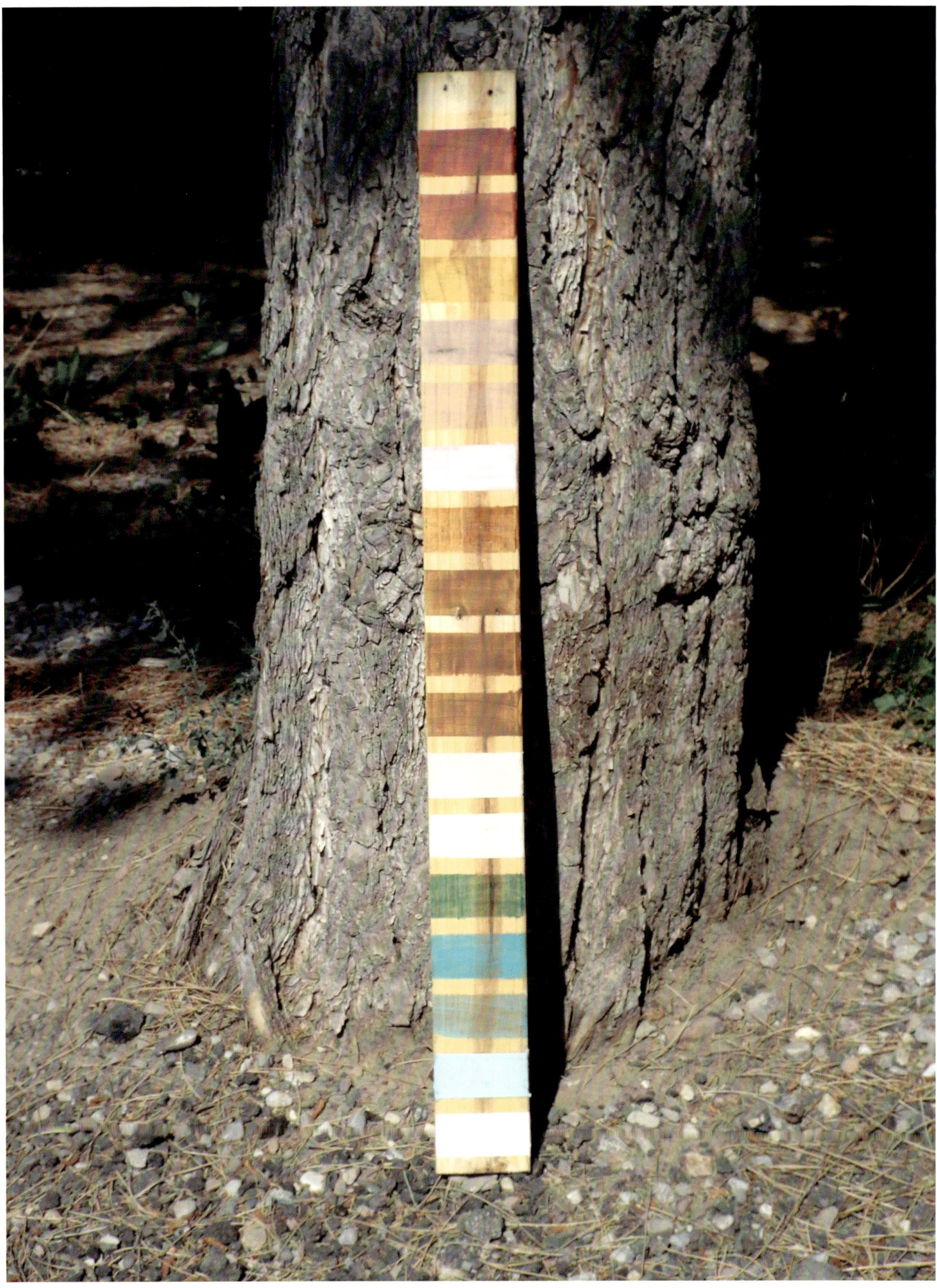

Natural Brown Stain for Wood

This stain brings out the highlights of wood grain.

Note: Walnut makes a darker stain, while acorns make the lightest stain.

Green acorns, whole walnuts or walnut hulls, hickory nut hulls, or pecan hulls

Water

1. Boil nuts or hulls in enough water to cover them for at least 10 minutes and up to 1 hour, depending on the amount of water you are using and the saturation of color you desire.
2. Strain the liquid.
3. Boil the strained liquid to nearly a glaze.
4. Apply this liquid directly onto wood with a cloth or brush.

Natural Brown Oil Stain for Wood

This recipe dramatically brings out the wood grain but is slow to dry. This is excellent for protecting wooden garden boxes, birdhouses, or bird feeders.

1 drop of walnut oil

1 teaspoon Natural Brown Stain for Wood (see previous column)

1. Add walnut oil to stain and mix well.

Natural Brown Vinegar Stain for Wood

This recipe is slightly redder than the recipe above. Vinegar stain is also purported to resist weather.

1 drop of vinegar

1 teaspoon Natural Brown Stain for Wood (see previous column)

1. Add vinegar to stain and mix well.

Homemade Pastes

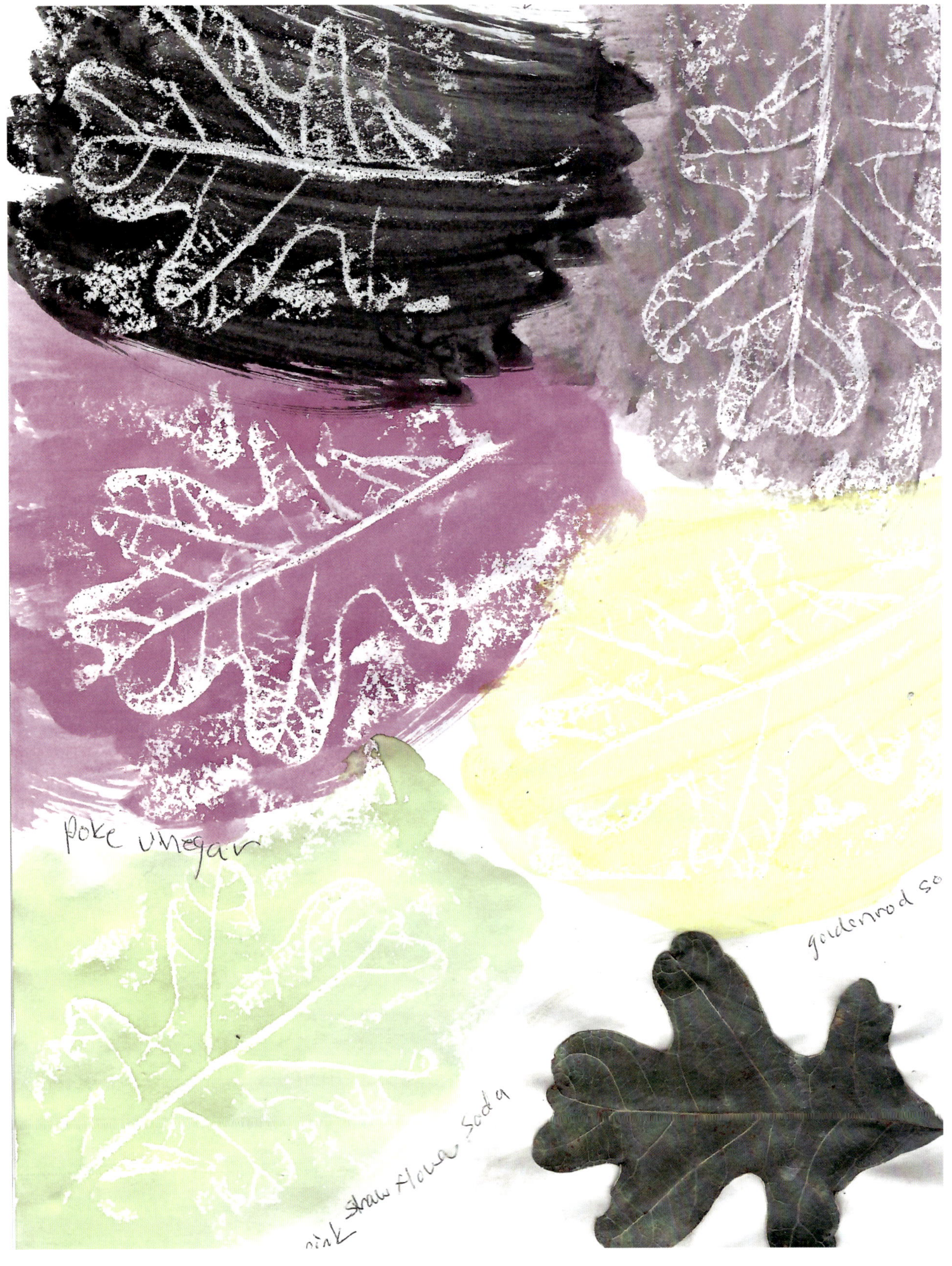
poke vinegar
goldenrod so
pink straw flower soda

All-Natural Decoupage Paste

Decoupage paste works best on mixed media or thicker paper. Dries clear.

⅓ cup white flour

⅓ cup white sugar

1 cup water

1 teaspoon vegetable glycerin or vegetable oil

1 teaspoon white vinegar (preservative)

1. Bring ingredients to a low boil, whisking, until the mixture thickens, which happens quickly. Remove from heat and let it cool.
2. Once cool, store in a lidded jar. Use within a couple days or refrigerate for a couple weeks or more. You can add drops of water if you need to thin this paste.

Traditional Rice Glue and Paint Binder

This glue has been used since time immemorial in Japan, where I used to live. You can substitute any white simple starch if you don't want to powder rice. White flour works but the glue is thicker and doesn't last as long or hold as well. Potato starch or cornstarch also works. Some people add a drop of honey to this glue.

Note: To make your own rice flour, put white rice in a blender, coffee grinder, or food processor to powder.

1 teaspoon rice flour

⅓ cup cold water

1. Stir rice flour into water until completely dissolved.
2. Bring to a boil for 1 minute on the stove or in the microwave.
3. When cooled, this paste can be used as glue for paper crafts or as a paint binder.

Homemade Crayons and Sculpting Materials

Lake Pigment Beeswax Crayons

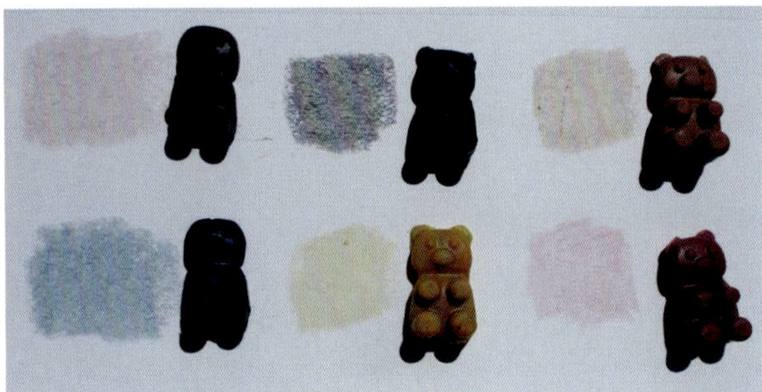

Wax can only be tinted with oil-soluble pigment. Therefore, it is best to start out making small crayons as you test your botanical pigments. I use a gummy bear silicone candy mold.

Tips for making crayons:

- For softer crayons, increase the amount of cocoa butter to ½ part.
- Making crayons is not an activity for kids because hot wax can burn; caution is necessary.
- When stirring the melted ingredients together, the bowl will be very hot. Have a hot pad ready. Stir slowly and carefully.
- When mulling pigment into oil to make crayons, a mulled oil that is completely free of pigment specks is only necessary for artist-quality crayons. If you're simply making crayons for the kids or grandkids, you don't have to worry about specks of pigment in the oil.
- Don't be stuck in thinking that crayons must be the shape of commercial crayons. Kids love to color with crayons of all shapes and sizes!

Make sure you use strong pigment and saturated color. I used about twelve cochineals to make red, dried marigold petals ground in a coffee grinder to make yellow (you can add ascorbic acid for orange), indigo extract powder to make blue, and vine black to make black. Turmeric also works well in oil.

½ teaspoon food-grade clear drying oil, like safflower, walnut, linseed, or sunflower oil

⅛ teaspoon dry powdered lake pigment (see page 54)

1 teaspoon beeswax

¼ teaspoon cocoa butter, shea butter, or coconut oil (any soft butter that is also hard when cold)

One silicone mold

1. To start, pour drying oil on a muller plate. Add powdered pigment and mull until the oil is clear and there are no specks or lumps of pigment. The pigment will likely thicken, which is okay; don't be tempted to add more oil, as this will only dilute the color of the finished crayon.
2. Use a spatula to scrape the color into a small white ceramic or glass bowl (clear or colored bowls make it difficult to see and judge the color mixture). Add beeswax and butter or coconut oil, then melt in 30-second intervals in the microwave or in a double boiler on the stove. Stir with the spatula to mix. (Not all pigments are compatible with oil, and you won't know whether any particular botanical pigment will work until you've tried it. If your pigment will not stay suspended in the oil but drops to the bottom of the oil within a few seconds, that pigment is not going to work and your batch is ruined.)
3. When the wax is melted and well-mixed, pour it into your mold and set aside. Immediately use paper towels to wipe off the spatula and wipe out the bowl or it will harden and be very difficult to remove. You must clean the muller plate between each color batch. The mulling plate is cleaned by oil pulling: add a few drops of oil to the plate after completing a mulled oil and then wiping the clean oil off the plate with a paper towel. Because oil and water don't mix, you want to avoid washing the plate until you are all done mulling all your colors of oils. Depending on the volume of your mold, your crayons will likely set up and be ready to use in as few as 10 minutes. If they are not, you can put them in the fridge to hurry the hardening process.

Flower Petal Beeswax Crayons

Because saturated pigment is needed to make strong crayon colors, try using petals with saturated color, like amaryllis, geranium, or gladiolus. Petals without saturated color will make pastel crayons.

Certain non-waxy leaves, like mint leaves, can be used instead of petals if desired. If you need more clay pigment base for the size of crayon you are making, double the recipe as needed.

⅛ teaspoon white kaolin clay

Dried or fresh flower petals of choice, as needed

Water

Lake Pigment Beeswax Crayons (see page 88)

1. Place clay and petals on a glass muller plate. If using dried petals, crumble them with your fingers or, if you have enough, grind them first in a coffee grinder.
2. Add 4–6 drops of water to the clay and petals and begin to mull. Add a drop or two of water as necessary and continue to mull until the petals have completely disintegrated. Mull until you have a thick paste free of chunks or specks of petals (about 1–2 minutes).
3. Using a spatula, clean the pigment paste from the muller plate and smear it into the bottom of a bowl. Microwave for about 30 seconds to evaporate out the water. Do not overcook the paste or it will be difficult to mull into oil.
4. Mix this dried paste into the Lake Pigment Beeswax Crayons recipe.

Natural Clay Beeswax Crayons

Natural so-called "wild clay" around the world can be found in a startling variety of colors, including white, black, blue, green, red, orange, yellow, brown, and I even found some purple clay in the desert near my home recently. I keep an eye out for unique clay wherever I travel, but if you don't want to gather your own, you can buy natural colored clay online or in some craft stores. Clay mulled in oil makes an excellent pigment for crayons.

Once you have your clay, use it in place of lake pigment in the Lake Pigment Beeswax Crayons recipe (see page 88).

Beeswax-Tinted Sculpting Wax

To make sculpting wax, start with the Lake Pigment Beeswax Crayons recipe (see page 88), but only use ⅕ teaspoon cocoa or shea butter (do not use coconut oil for this recipe).

Note: This recipe is for artist's sculpting wax. If you want sculpting wax for kids to play with, use one of the crayon recipes with ¼ part butter. Sculpting wax should be harder than crayons, but for kids, you want it a little softer than the artist's version.

All-Natural, Air-Dried Clay (White or Tinted)

LARGE BATCH (WHITE OR TINTED)

This recipe makes enough to do one child's handprint in a circle or square, or to make small craft projects.

- Raspberries make lavender dough.
- Blueberries make turquoise dough.
- Blackberries make purple dough.
- A single cochineal with a dust of citric acid and alum makes rosy pink. Use double for red.
- Goldenrod liquid base pigment makes yellow.

For white clay:

⅓ cup water

¼ cup baking soda

¼ cup salt

¼ cup cornstarch

For tinted clay:

⅓ cup plus 2 tablespoons water

¼ cup berries or flower petals

¼ cup baking soda

¼ cup salt

¼ cup cornstarch

1. If you are making tinted clay, add the relevant amount of water and berries or flower petals to a small saucepot; boil on the stovetop for at least 2 minutes, until the water has good color; and strain through a coffee filter back into the saucepot.
2. If you are making white clay, add the relevant amount of water to a small saucepot.
3. To the saucepot, stir in baking soda, salt (to prevent cracking), and cornstarch until there are no lumps.
4. Turn on heat to medium-low and stir with a fork constantly. This begins to form dough before it begins to boil. As soon as the dough begins to form a ball, turn off the heat.
5. Allow the dough to cool about 10 minutes before handling.

SMALL BATCH (TINTED)

I created this recipe to make it possible to make small batches for the grandkids, each of a different color, without spending too much money on ingredients.

2 tablespoons botanically dyed water

2 tablespoons plus 2 teaspoons baking soda

1 ⅓ tablespoons cornstarch

1. Add botanically dyed water, baking soda, and cornstarch to a cereal bowl.
2. Microwave for 30 seconds.
3. Stir until the dough forms a ball in the bowl and then cool until safe to handle.
4. Knead the dough to make it more uniform. If the dough seems dry, knead in water, one drop at a time. Be careful because too much water will ruin the dough.

Clay Pigments

Used fresh or dried as a pigment medium for paints and stains.

You can experiment using colored clays to make these pigments too, but any color but white will add a darker hue to your pigment. You can also use clay by itself in small amounts as pigment. For example, you can use white clay and hydrated lime to make white paint. Or you make some great paints by using naturally colored wild clays, which I collect whenever I find them in nature. Or you can simply add small amounts of clay to most paint recipes as a binder or to make the color more opaque.

White clay (kaolin or wild)

Botanical matter (Fresh or dried petals or leaves, etc.) or prepared botanical base pigment

1. Take roughly equal amounts of clay and botanical matter or prepared botanical base pigment. If you use dried material, add water by drops as needed.
2. Mull the clay and material together until smooth and free of lumps.
3. You can use this immediately as a pigment in a paint recipe, or you can scrap this off your muller slab and allow it to air dry, then store it in a plastic bag or jar for later use. Don't forget to label it!

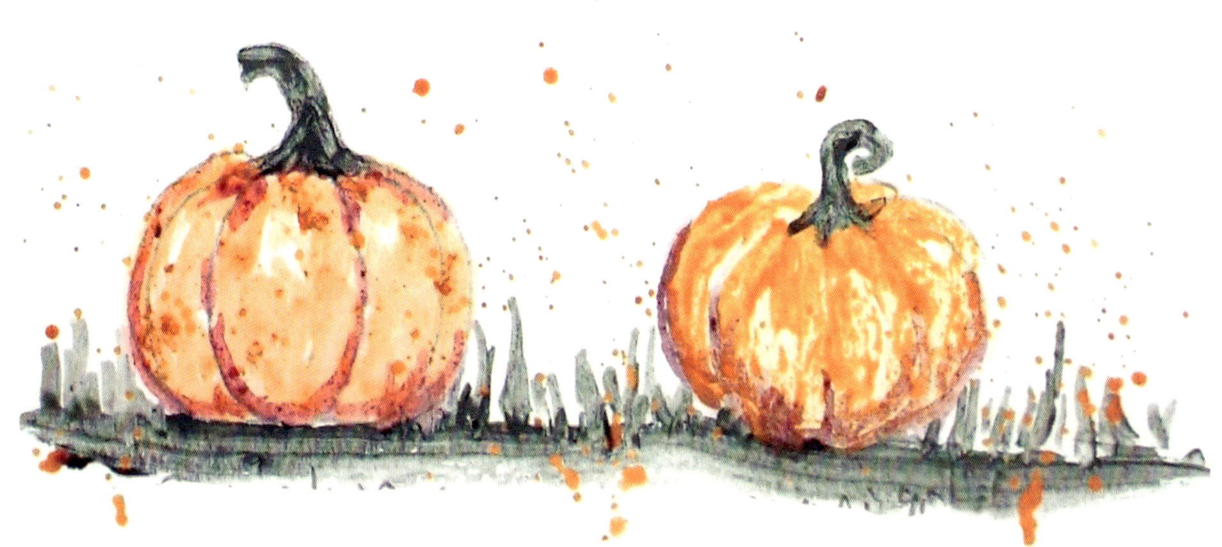

Pumpkins painted with mulled pumpkin skin (left) and mulled marigold petals (right)

Homemade Glairs

Glair (Egg White Paint Binder)

Glair is a critical paint binder. Before we dive into this recipe, let's pause to talk about the "ick" factor. *There is none.* I can't tell you how many times my students and friends have pulled faces when they learn about glair. Some even shudder and say "that's gross!" Fermented egg whites! Eww!

But experience is our best teacher. They are confusing fermented eggs with fermented egg whites. Fermented egg whites (glair) have only a *very faint* earthy smell when liquid and *zero smell* when dried as an ingredient in paint.

So calm yourself, gird up your britches, and get into the mindset of your ancestors. If you have ever been to a museum, you have seen many paintings made with glair. Did they stink? They did not. You can do this.

1 or more eggs (I usually do 6–12 eggs in a batch)

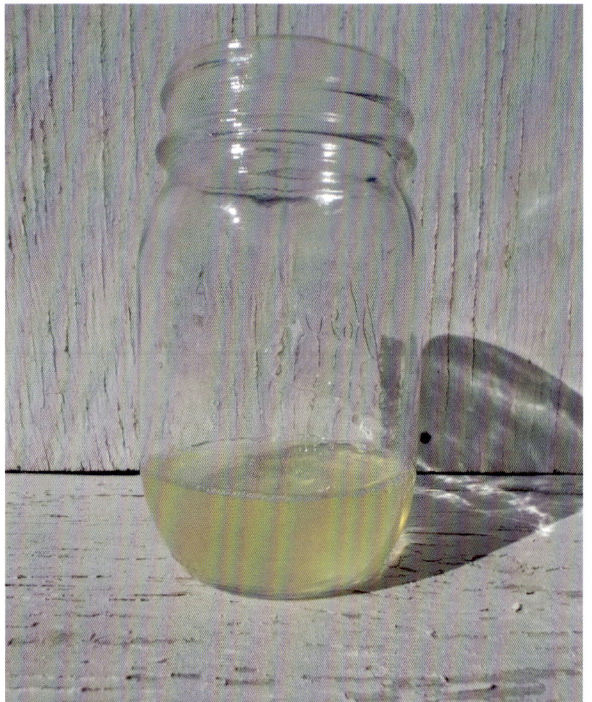

1. Carefully crack open the egg(s) and separate the white from the yoke. Discard the yolk (or mix it in with your dog's food). It is essential that you do not get even the smallest amount of yolk. No yolk or shell should be present in the egg white.
2. Froth the egg whites with a fork in a bowl or jar for about 30 seconds, just until it starts to become frothy. Do not overwork. Allow this frothy egg white to sit at room temperature in an open jar or bowl for at least a day, but preferably a week. No, it does not smell. Remove the foam after a day or two.
3. After a week, it can be stored for up to a year at room temperature in a sealed jar. But glair is always used with water when making paint, so when you are ready to use it, combine the prepared glair and water using a 1:1 ratio. Please note, once you add water, it goes bad after about six months and begins to smell and darken. Dispose of it at this point.
4. If you are really (unduly) terrified of it spoiling (again, you are misinformed), then you can store it in the fridge, but it can only be used for paint at room temperature (cold glair congeals), which is why no artist in the world stores their glair in the fridge. And yes, plenty of modern artists use glair, chief among them are the restorers at all major museums. Glair is used in many different versions of paint, from simply adding glair to base pigment, up to using it in oil paint and milk paint.

Glair Casein Clay Paint

Excellent semiopaque milk paint for wood, paper, canvas, and metal.

Micellar casein is available online.

Paint made with casein cannot be rehydrated for later use, so make only small batches for immediate use.

1 part glair

1 part micellar casein powder or quark

½ part white kaolin clay (or less, depending on desired opacity)

Wet or dry botanical pigment

Water, as needed

1. Add all ingredients to a mulling slab.
2. Mull everything together. Expect to mull about twice as long if using quark instead of micellar casein.

Glair Casein Paint

Excellent semitransparent milk paint for wood, paper, canvas, metal, and glass. Almost like a stain for wood.

Micellar casein is available online.

Paint made with casein cannot be rehydrated for later use, so make only small batches for immediate use.

1 part glair

1 part micellar casein powder or quark

Wet or dry botanical pigment

Water, as needed

1. Add all ingredients to a mulling slab.
2. Mull everything together. Expect to mull about twice as long if using quark instead of micellar casein.

Glair Eggshell Pine Paint for Tinting

⅛ teaspoon eggshell powder

⅛ teaspoon glair

1 drop liquid pine

Fresh, liquid, or dried botanical pigment

Water, as needed

1. Add all ingredients to a mulling slab.
2. Mull everything together until smooth and the paint begins to thicken.

Glair Milk Pine Paint

When liquid pine is added to glair, it begins to coagulate. This goes away as you mull the paint.

⅛ teaspoon casein or quark

⅛ teaspoon hydrated lime

⅛ teaspoon glair

1–2 drops liquid pine

Botanical pigment

1. Add all ingredients to a mulling slab.
2. Mull everything together.

Glair Oil Paint

Dries semitransparent.

2 drops drying oil (walnut, sunflower, safflower, linseed, etc.)

4 drops glair

Fresh liquid or dried botanical pigment

Water, as needed

1. Add drying oil to glair and mull together with pigment.
2. Add water by drops as needed for mulling (adding water makes this a stronger paint).

Simple Glair Paint

This paint is translucent. Because glair coagulates when heated, be sure the pigment is room temperature.

Room-temperature fresh or dry pigment

Glair

1. Mull together equal parts pigment and glair.
2. If a different color is desired, add more pigment or glair.

Thick Glair Paint (White or Tinted)

This paint can be used to create texture effects. If using casein, please note that casein paints cannot be rehydrated for later use. This paint appears somewhat transparent when wet but dries opaque. Also, hydrated lime in this recipe also acts as a mordant and changes some colors. Kaolin makes a white that mordants fewer colors but will still change the colors of some base pigments.

Some notes on ingredients: Please be sure to use sea salt and not table salt, which contains iodine. Do not use botanical material; we need to use liquid or dry base botanical pigment. Hydrated lime is available at hardware stores; be sure you are getting hydrated lime, not quicklime. Add water as needed when mulling.

For white glair:

1 teaspoon glair

⅛ teaspoon sea salt

¼ teaspoon casein powder, white kaolin clay, or half and half

2 teaspoons hydrated lime

For tinted glair:

1 teaspoon glair

⅛ teaspoon sea salt

¼ teaspoon casein powder, white kaolin clay, or half and half

Botanical pigment

1 teaspoon hydrated lime

1. Whether you are making white or tinted glair, add all relevant ingredients to a mulling slab.
2. Mull everything together.

Thin Glair Paint (White or Tinted)

This paint is used when a thinner, more translucent paint is desired. This paint appears somewhat transparent when wet but dries opaque. Also, the hydrated lime in this recipe acts as a mordant and changes some colors. Kaolin makes a better white that mordants fewer colors but will still change the colors of some base pigments.

For white glair:

1 teaspoon glair

¾ teaspoon hydrated lime

Pinch of table salt (which makes a thinner paint than sea salt)

⅛ teaspoon casein powder, white kaolin clay, or half and half

For tinted glair:

1 teaspoon glair

¾ teaspoon hydrated lime

Pinch of table salt (which makes a thinner paint than sea salt)

⅛ teaspoon casein powder, white kaolin clay, or half and half

½ teaspoon fresh or botanical pigment

1. Whether you are making white or tinted glair, add all relevant ingredients to a mulling slab.
2. Mull everything together.

Tinted Glair "Acrylic"

This paint appears somewhat transparent when wet but dries opaque.

1 cup water

1 tablespoon hydrated lime

1 cup flowers or other botanical matter

¼ teaspoon room-temperature glair

1. Mix together the water and hydrated lime.
2. Add the flowers or other botanical matter to a bowl and cover with the hydrated lime water.
3. Simmer until color is released.
4. Strain and then boil the liquid to nearly dry.
5. <u>Allow this pigment to cool completely because if you use hot pigment with glair, the glair will be ruined.</u>
6. Add glair to ⅛ teaspoon of dry pigment and mull until the paint begins to thicken. If it becomes too thick, add a drop of glair and some water. Use fresh or store for later use.

Tinted Glair "Acrylic" with Liquid Pine

This paint is more transparent than tinted glair "acrylic."

1 cup water

½ tablespoon hydrated lime

1 cup flowers or other botanical matter

¼ teaspoon room-temperature glair

1 drop liquid pine

1. Mix together the water and hydrated lime.
2. Add the flowers or other botanical matter to a bowl and cover with the hydrated lime water.
3. Simmer until color is released.
4. Strain and then boil the liquid to nearly dry.
5. <u>Allow this pigment to cool completely because if you use hot pigment with glair, the glair will be ruined.</u>
6. Add glair and liquid pine to ⅛ teaspoon of dry pigment and mull until the paint begins to thicken. If it becomes too thick, add a drop of glair and some water. Use fresh or store for later use.

Yolk Glair Pine Tempera

2 drops of glair

1–2 drops of liquid pine

1 drop of prepared egg yolk

Fresh, liquid, or dried botanical pigment

1. Add ingredients to a mulling slab.
2. Mull everything together until thick, about 30 seconds.

Yolk Glair Tempera

Fresh, liquid, or dried botanical pigment

2 parts glair

1 part prepared egg yolk

1. Add ingredients to a mulling slab.
2. Mull everything together until thick, about 30 seconds.

Putting This Book Into Practice

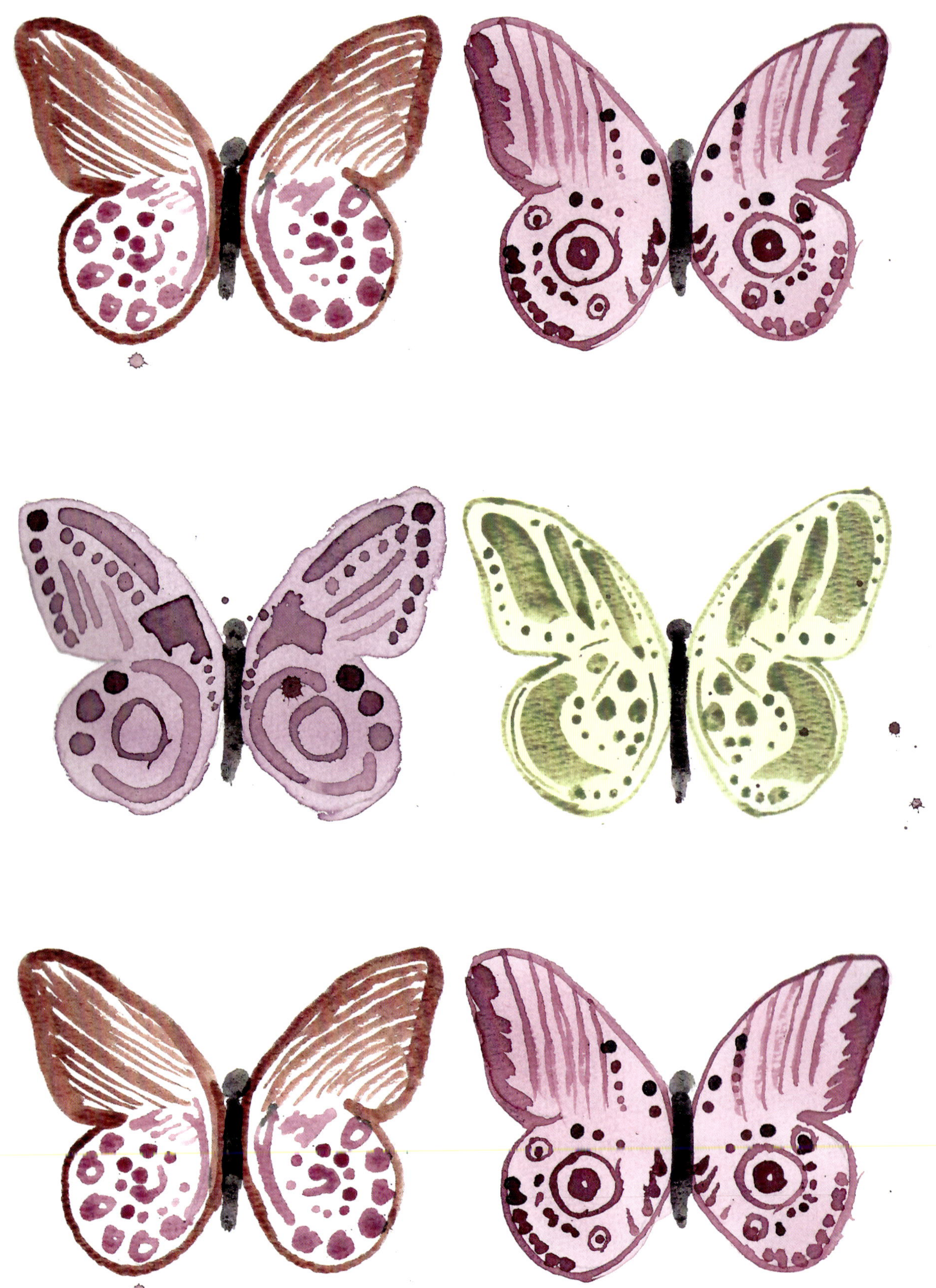

Natural Food Colorings

All edible plants, like rose petals, can be used as food coloring if they are clean and have not been sprayed with chemicals. Pomegranates, blueberries, nasturtium flowers, calendula petals, raspberries, blackberries, spirulina, turmeric, cherries, spinach, beets, saffron, cacao, dandelion flowers, blood oranges, paprika, annatto, cranberries, spinach, purple sweet potatoes, parsley, cinnamon, and purple cabbage are some of the best foods for use as natural food coloring. Mordants can be used to adjust the colors if they are food grade. This lemonade recipe is an example how easy—and delicious—natural food coloring can be.

Kids and grandkids love to help with this recipe. You can use lemons, but our family always prefers limes. Enjoy!

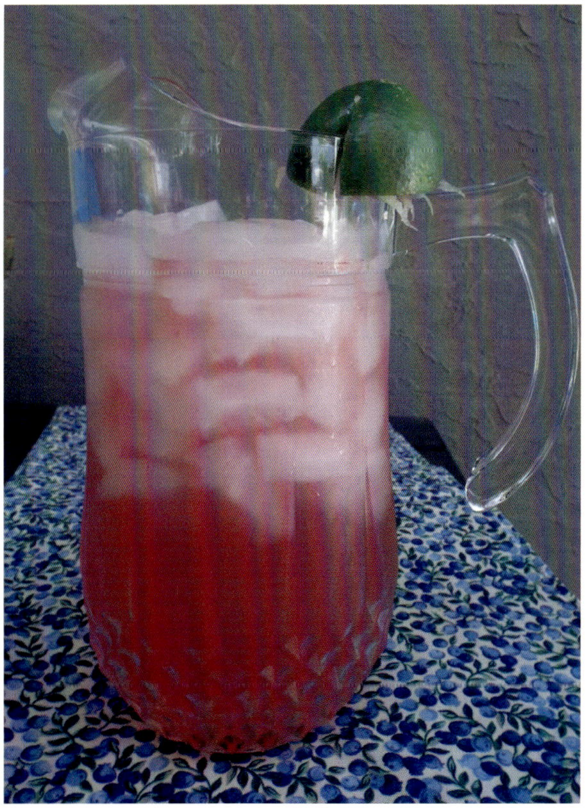

Handful of red rose petals

3 cups water

1 quart ice

Juice of 5–10 limes or lemons, to taste (I use 5)

2 quarts cold water

Liquid stevia, to taste

1. Place petals in water and boil or microwave for at least 5 minutes to release the color. (For a darker color, strain and boil another 5 minutes.)
2. Meanwhile, place ice in a gallon pitcher. Add juice and cold water. Stir in the rose petal liquid and watch it instantly change color to pink.
3. Add stevia to taste and serve.

Spice Rack Paints

Did you know that you can make paint by using most of the spices in your kitchen? Mull them into one of the recipes in this book. (And the paint usually smells great too—at least until it dries.) Parsley makes a bright green. Powdered cloves, cinnamon, or cocoa powder make brown. Turmeric makes yellow, or red with baking soda as a mordant. Try mustard powder, thyme, paprika, basil, marjoram, oregano—why not experiment with all the spices!

Homemade Spray Paint

Liquid botanical base pigment that is not a glaze can be used in a spray bottle. You want the paint to be a somewhat strong color, but you don't want it glaze-thick or it won't be sprayable. Strain the pigment through craft felt or a coffee filter to make sure there are no specks of botanical matter to clog the sprayer. I like to use the small craft spray bottles from the $1.25 store, the kind you push down on the top instead of squeezing a trigger handle. These small bottles give you more control over the spray.

50 Ways to Use this Book (for Adults)

1 **One Plant, Many Colors.** How many distinct colors can you make, using mordants, with the petals of a single red rose, or a slice of beetroot, a leaf of cabbage, or the berries of a single bush?

2 **One Plant, One Painting.** Create a full landscape painting using only the mordanted colors of one plant.

3 **Color Walking.** How many botanical colors can you collect on one walk, or hike, or in a city park?

4 **Colors in Time.** Keep a 12-month journal showing every botanical color sample you obtain for each month of the year and where you collected them.

5 **Their Yard, Their Card.** Surprise a loved one with a thank you card made entirely from botanical colors from their own yard or garden or city.

6 **Yule Blooms.** Create Christmas art using only your poinsettia or perhaps a Christmas cactus or Christmas-blooming red amaryllis flowers.

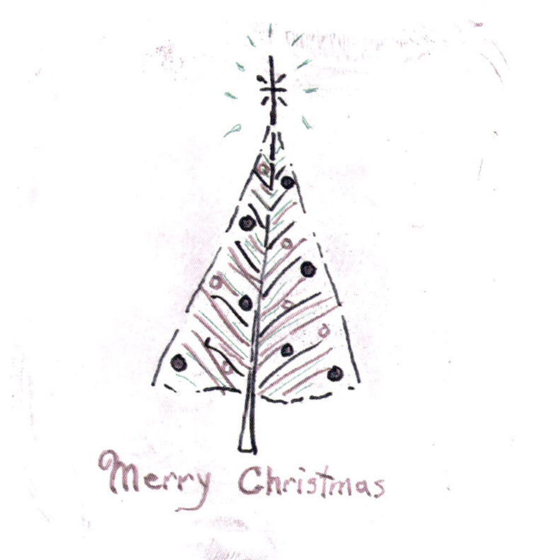

7 **Lunch Coloring.** Have a dye brunch with a couple friends. Invite them to join you for finger foods like berries and nuts and vegetables-- and then use the leftovers to make botanical colors for dyeing scarves or paper crafts or holiday wrapping paper or get-well cards for a mutual friend.

8 **Revenge Paint.** Make revenge art in your backyard by pulling weeds to see how many different colors or prints you can make from whatever uninvited plants are invading your property.

9 **Adulting Is Overrated.** Buy or print coloring pages for adults, then use botanical colors to fill up your pages. If the kids get to color, and take naps, so do we!

10 **Print the Sky.** Find the ten most interesting leaves you can use to make botanical sunprints. You might be surprised about how hard it is to find really great leaves to print! Hint: look for serrated leaves, like Japanese maples.

11 **Scout the Ground.** Collect fallen petals and flowers from a park or cemetery or other public space to see how many inks you can make at home.

12 **Remember When.** Ask your mother or grandmother or daughter or someone you love what their favorite flowers were when they were a child, and why. Then collect these flowers to make a simple painting of their childhood home or some evocative childhood memory.

13 **St. Flowers Day.** Send your grandmother or mother a Valentine's Day card made entirely from home-crafted botanical colors. If they have passed, leave a card on their grave or simply display the card in their memory. You may not know it, but your grandma wants a Valentine card from you!

14 **Memento Mori.** One of the most special botanical memories I have is taking clay, dirt and leaves from the cemeteries where my most beloved are buried. I remember them every time I make paint or ink or any project using these items. I keep them in jars labeled with the name of the cemetery or the grave where I collected them.

15 **Healing Art.** Collect pebbles from or near the cemetery or grave of a loved one and then take those home to paint them with botanical colors from your own yard, or the deceased person's home, or their favorite flower or food. You can keep these on a window seal or in a garden pot as a reminder of that person, or you can return to the cemetery and place them on that person's grave. This can be a useful way to process grief.

16 **Meow and Wow.** Make a paw print using botanical ink or paint of your favorite pet, or the pet of someone you are close to. Be sure to clean their paw afterward. Or simply make the common image of a paw print instead of an actual print.

17 **Pocket Paints.** Recycle the palette of an inexpensive watercolor set. Wash out the remnants of the original paints, and fill it with your own botanical colors. Put them in wet and allow them to dry for later use.

18 **Vintage Advantage.** Print coloring pages for adults or traceable images or historic line drawings on mixed media paper and use botanical watercolors to fill them in. By searching online, you can find beautiful vintage line drawings to fill in, or modern images too. Thousands are available for free. I purchase inexpensive books of mixed media paper, cut them to the common printer size, and print one sheet at a time.

19 **Flattened Flowers.** Using local clay, or the air dry clay recipe in this book, or purchased clay, roll the clay into flat sheets and use botanical matter to make prints. Try maple leaves, poppy seed pods and stems, any leaf with pronounced veins, or leaves with unique shapes, like geranium leaves, or rosemary, or maple seed pods, or juniper fronds. Anything that will make a clear image can be used. You can use cookie cutters to cut shapes before or after printing, or just cut circles or ovals or rectangles. Once you have pressed the material into the clay to create the image, allow it to dry slowly and completely, then use botanical or pottery kiln paints from this book to paint in the images. Real clay with real pottery botanical pottery paint can be fired for display or made into tiles. Searching out the leaves or twigs or seed pods to press is half the fun. If something doesn't work well, simply reuse the clay before it dries.

20 **Leaf Mold.** Using local clay, purchased clay or the air dry clay recipe in this book, roll out a quarter-inch slab. Lay a leaf on the slab. Use a toothpick or similar tool to trace and then cut out the shape of the leaf. Allow the clay to dry a little (called leather-hard stage) and then use a bowl as a mold to shape clay leaves into a bowl. Allow the clay to dry in the mold. Once dry, you can paint the clay if desired. By the way, your great-grandparents would get the joke of the title of this challenge. In their day, composted leaves were called leaf mold.

21 **Rice the Leaf.** Collect brightly colored autumn leaves and apply them to paper with one of the glue recipes in the book (see page 85). You can display anything from a single perfect leaf to groups of leaves, to shapes made from leaves. You can cut leaves and use them as the medium for collage.

22 **Tree Stencils.** Use fresh or flat dried leaves to carefully outline on mixed media or watercolor paper, and then use botanical watercolors or gouache or inks from this book to fill in the shapes, creating your own unique leaf art for display.

23 **Leaf Your Mark.** Using fresh or dried leaves, paint the underside (the side with the most pronounced veins) with botanical paints, then print those images on paper. You can use your fingers, an art brayer, or even the back of a spoon to print the images. Or you can paint around the leaf to create the negative image of the leaf and then use the leaf to print that negative space. You can also print leaves on fabric for making throw pillows, cotton bags, T-shirts, or scarves.

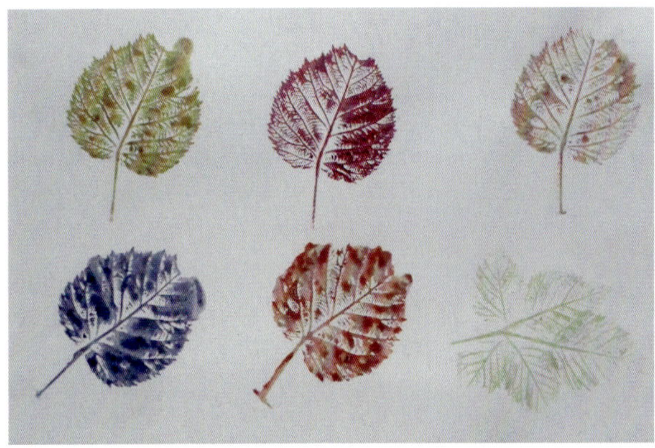

24 **Nature Creature.** Use botanical paints to create creatures or people for display by drawing faces or applying homemade eyes on dried leaves. Or paint a leaf or twig in white paint, dry, and then paint on faces or eyes.

25 **Slow Slither.** Speaking of creatures, I happened to see online that some people create "slow" garden art by using pebbles to make a cheerful "garden snake" over time. They find a sort of large arrow-shaped rock and paint it with eyes to be the head, and then add hand-painted pebbles over time, to make the snake longer and longer. I'm looking forward to doing this. This is a great activity to do while streaming a show or keeping grandkids occupied. You can display your creature-creation alongside your sidewalk or garden path, but it would also be a fun way to brighten up a little-used corner of your garden. I have fossils, geodes, agates, shells, miniatures, little statues, and art hidden all over my gardens for me to look at while I take garden walks.

26 **Nature's Gift.** Thanks to social media, it has become trendy to make pebble crafts, painted shells, wood slices, or any homemade painted craft with a nature theme and leave them along trails, paths, and sidewalks, from the deep forest to the concrete canyons of skyscrapers. These are meant as surprise gifts for strangers, adults or children. When you use botanical paint, you rest easy knowing your art is truly in tune with nature.

27 **Framing the Light.** Take an inexpensive picture frame with glass or plastic and use the decoupage recipe or natural glue recipes from this book (see page 85) to apply real or paper-crafted leaves to the glass. Put the glass back into the frame and hang it in a window for a homemade stained glass effect.

28 **Ring in the Wreath.** Outline real leaves to create art of a leaf wreath and then use botanical paints from this book to color in the wreath.

29 **Circle the Season.** The possibilities for wreath art are endless. Make a wreath of stones decoupaged with real leaves (see decoupage paste recipe on page 85) to put around a botanically colored homemade holiday candle. Decoupage real leaves to make a wreath for the front door. Or real leaves on paper as seasonal decor. Or eco-print leaves to make a paper wreath. Or use the microwave method to flatten and dry leaves, then gloss them with all-natural decoupage paste, then attach them to a wreath form that has first been wrapped in fabric dyed from the same leaves. If you are really crafty and patient, you can make a gradient wreath starting with yellow leaves at the top, changing to orange, red, green, and brown as you circle down the wreath form. Then teach this as a class and make some extra holiday money.

30 **Willow You Wreath Me?** Make a willow wreath form and then wrap it with botanically dyed fabric or use the fabric to attach real branches and boughs. If you have a jig saw, you can cut a wreath from scrap lumber and dye it with acorn stain before decorating it. Or wrap it with a rainbow of botanically dyed yarns. I could keep going. I'll stop now.

31 **Petiole Pattern.** Find the largest leaves you can and dry them using the instructions in this book (see page 15). Once dry, use white botanical paint to create geometric patterns on the leaves. These leaves make great displays. You can also use the white paint to write notes to someone on a giant leaf or as primer to cover the leaf, allow it to dry, and then paint art using the leaf as your canvas.

32 **Candle the Leaf.** Use the wax-resist technique in this book (see page 19) to make leaf prints on paper for display, napkins for Thanksgiving dinner, paper "stained glass" for the windows, holiday cards, or to brighten up your journal—or just as an excuse to get together with a friend.

33 **Pebbles in Bloom.** Decoupage single leaves or flower petals to pebbles, then coat them again and use them as a display in the home, the garden, or a fairy garden. Leave them under your child's pillow as a gift from the Garden Sprites on special occasions—or no occasion. Or you can do a really large version of this project to leave under the pillow of your spouse when they are being disagreeable. Kidding!

34 **Caring Garden.** Nursing homes are always, always looking for volunteers to brighten the day of those they care for. Take a resident for a walk in the nursing home garden and pick a few things to make any of these crafts. Or better yet, volunteer to help residents plant and maintain a simple dye and eco-print garden at the nursing home.

35 **Insects to Love.** Cut leaves and petals to create or eco-print print images of butterflies, moths, dragonflies, or other creatures. Glue the images to paper with the glue recipes in this book (see page 85) or use the leaves to create outlines of the creatures that can then be filled in with paints from this book.

36 **Sliced Tree.** Create intricate or simple art on wood slices using the paints in this book. You might paint on the natural wood, either rough or sanded, or you might use black or white paint as a background to paint on.

37 **Hammer Flowers.** Use a rubber mallet, available at the $1.25 store, to gently hammer flowers onto paper. Use these images as display art or cut them out to use in making paper crafts.

38 **Hammered Cloth.** Take the same rubber mallet (you can also gently use real hammers) to print flowers on white cotton shirts, inexpensive cotton tote bags, or scarves. You can also use the back of a spoon.

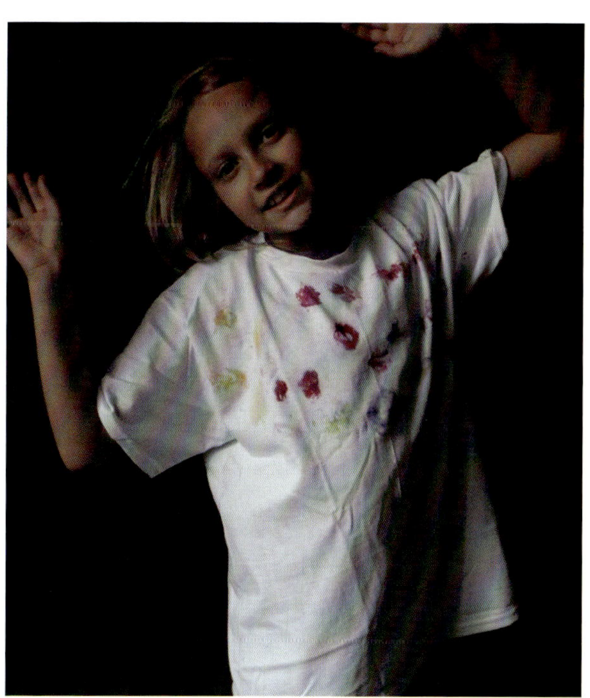

39 **Got Steam?** Here is a real challenge. I know it is very popular in the online world of botanical crafts to make steam prints using fresh flowers. To do this, pick flowers, place them on a clean white shirt, then roll the shirt and steam it for at least 10 minutes. Here is the challenge: to find a better way. I've made plenty of steam prints, and they are always a dull, out-of-focus mess when they are dried. I don't think they are worth the trouble, and when I teach botanical printing at the University of Utah, I don't even touch on this subject because I think these are not great prints. I have not found a good method for making crisp steam prints with flowers, so I challenge you, my readers. Can you invent a better steam print?

40 **Sealed with a Flower.** Remember four hundred years ago when we all stamped our hand-written correspondence (see oak gall ink recipe on page 65) with a wax seal to zhuzh up the written word? No? Me either. Well, wax seals have been making a comeback in the world of stationary. You can make your own using one of the botanically tinted crayon recipes in this book (see pages 88–89). Use a candle to melt the crayon onto your envelope and then stamp it. You can use many things as makeshift wax stamps: jewelry, a fingerprint, an actual ink stamp, a coin, a veiny leaf, a fossil, a shell, a piece of bark. Anything that will print a picture or texture.

41 **Actually Sealed with a Flower.** One of the latest old medieval fashions to be revived is to actually place dried flowers in your wax to seal an envelope. To do this, you must use small blossoms and dry them in advance (see microwave pressing instructions on page 15). Have your dried flowers and tweezers prepared before you melt the wax because you only have a moment to apply your dried flowers. You can apply these by hand on every invitation to a wedding! Just kidding. The bridesmaids can do that. Or the in-laws.

42 **Flower Inside the Lines.** Make crayons for the kids. See the crayon recipes in this book (see pages 88–89). Let them help you choose the plant material, perhaps on a garden walk. Then they can color flowers with flowers!

43 **Layered Crayons.** When I was teaching Waldorf elementary school, some of the most fun I ever had in long, boring staff training meetings was making layered crayon art. Did you know that crayons don't really mix? Because of this, you can layer them to make textures and patterns. For example, if you carefully color a yellow over a red, you can make orange. Then, again being careful, you can scrape away the yellow layer from the orange to reveal the red underneath. This allows you to make all kinds of fun patterns, borders, and pictures.

44 **Rainbow the Crayon.** Another fun homemade crayon project is to make a rainbow crayon from botanical tints. A rainbow crayon is one crayon with several distinct colors, like a colored pencil with multi-colored lead. You can make your own by pouring complimentary or opposing colors into the mold when you make crayons, one layer at a time. Or you can take the single-color crayons you've already made, cut off a piece with a butterknife, warm the pieces in your hands, and force them together to create a new crayon.

45 **What a Relief.** Use the all-natural air-dry clay recipe in this book (see page 89) to fill a chocolate or craft mold to create a bas relief. Once dry, you can use botanical paints to paint the relief. If you make small bas reliefs, you can even affix them to sealing wax as decoration for your fancy wax-sealed envelopes.

46 **Botanical Relief.** You can also make great three-dimensional art to paint or use plain by making your own mold, similar to a chocolate mold. First, find a flower or plant you want to mold, like dried poppy stem or stem of wild rye. Imprint them in air-dry clay (see page 89) and let the imprint harden slowly. Then fill that mold with actual clay or melted wax to make the bas relief. Hang the relief as decor. You can also use slip clay to create the bas relief.

47 **Flower Catcher.** Create a suncatcher of real flowers. Use a piece of glass or plastic from a thrift store frame. Use decoupage paste (see page 85) to attach flowers to it and set it on a window sill to illuminate Mother Nature's art.

48 **Print the Negative.** Find or print a simple silhouette of some object, like the outline of a rooster, mushroom, dinosaur, flower, bird, butterfly, or shark. Cut out the image. Then center the cutout on a piece of paper or wood and carefully paint over the image. When you lift away the image, the negative of the image is revealed. This is a simple way to create holiday art or theme decor for your home. For even more "vibes," as the youth say, once the paint is dry, you can use sandpaper to give it an antique look—or if you are really crafty, you can first apply a botanically tinted layer of paint, with white paint on top, and then sand it to reveal the layers. You could do a negative of a rooster for your kitchen, a pumpkin for your porch, or a bunny for Easter.

49 **Fresh Quilt.** Make botanical "quilt" art as you've seen in this book (see pages 362–367). Use masking tape to create a color block pattern and then fill in each block by using a fresh petal or leaf to print that one block. To make the pattern, I use a piece of masking tape on the back of another piece of masking tape, leaving only the edges sticky. I then put masking tape on the edge of the paper and put the tape that only sticks on the edges as my spacer, then I put down another row of tape, then move my spacer, then another row of tape and so on. I repeat this process in the opposite direction. Then I use petals and leaves to print each available square. When those squares are totally dry, I take off the masking tape and tape over the colored squares. This allows me to now paint in the squares that were covered. In this way, you can fill an entire piece of art paper with distinct blocks of botanical color, as if you are making a quilt. This is one of my favorite ways to enjoy botanical paints.

50 **To Please the Robot Overlords.** Here is a very modern idea for using thousand-year-old paint techniques: Use artificial intelligence to generate a black and white line drawing of whatever whimsical, ethereal, vintage, or atmospheric theme you can think of. Then print the image on mixed media paper and use your homemade paints to bring it to life. This kind of art is an excellent way to keep our AI robot overlords distracted so they can't take over the world.

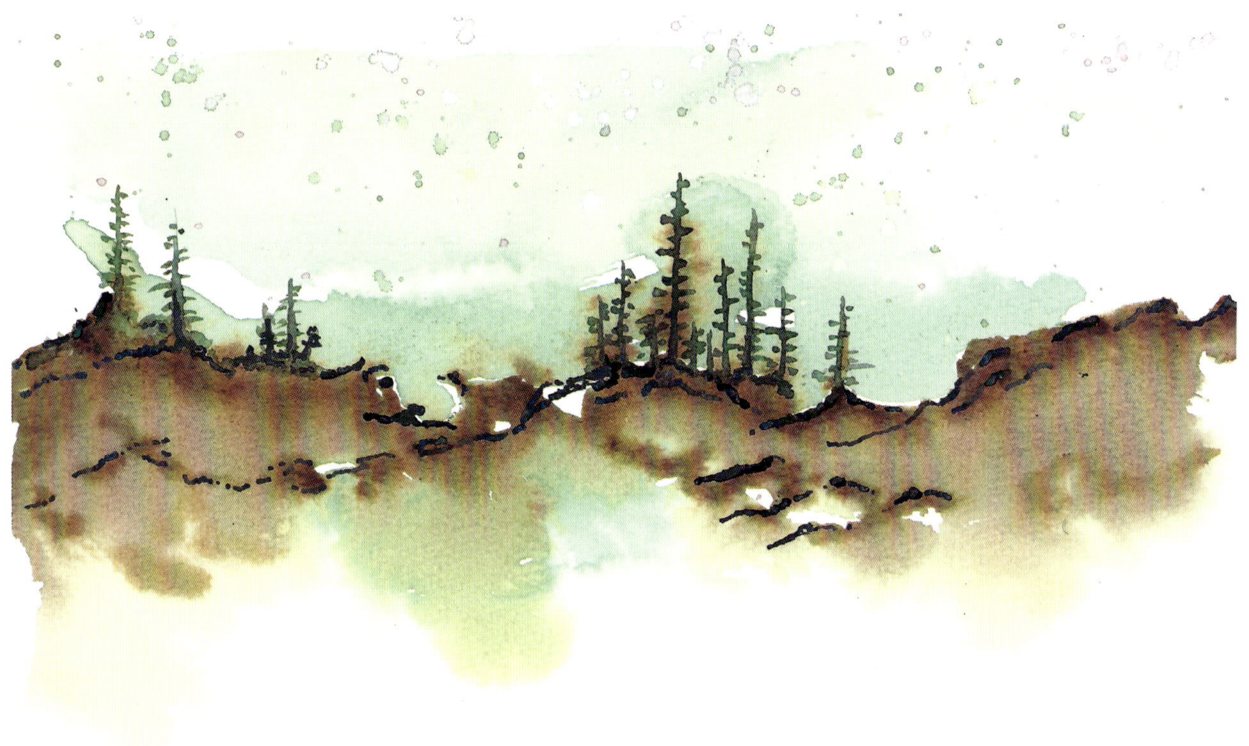

50 Ways to Use this Book (for Kids, with Supervision)

1 **Brush Game.** Give your kids (or grandkids) two or three minutes (kids love a deadline game) to scavenge for the most unusual household items to use as "brushes" for making art, shapes, or prints. For example, they can use the end of a pen to make dots from botanical paints, celery as a moon-shaped stamp, or the cap of a bottle to print circles. Encourage them to look for ordinary, everyday items that can be used to make unusual shapes and textures. Then let them paint with your botanical paints.

2 **Veggie Prints.** This can be a fun idea for a birthday party or just a quiet afternoon at home. From the garden or grocery store, get a rutabaga, turnip, parsnip, carrot, cabbage, celery, radish, lettuce—whatever you want. Because most kids are never exposed to vegetables beyond carrots, have them try to guess what each vegetable is, one at a time. Then let them taste a sample. Then let them use butter knives to carve shapes from these vegetables for printing. For example, they can cut a radish in half to print a circle or cut it into a square to print a house. Give each child a piece of paper and have them first print a border around the paper by cutting circles, squares, rectangles, triangles, unusual shapes, or natural shapes into the vegetables. Then use these as stamps. They can create a scene inside the border.

3 **Herb Prints.** The same idea as above can be done without any vegetable carving by using herbs. Let the kids taste mint, lavender, lemon balm, parsley, dill, thyme. Then they can apply paint to the greens with a paint brush and use the greens to print the herbs and label them. Or they can use the botanical spray paint in this book (see page 101) to print the negative images of leaves or herbs.

4 **Ink Stamps.** Using the stamping ink recipe in this book (see page 63), let the kids make their own stamp pads and inks and then stamp up a storm with stamps from the thrift store, borrowed from your crafty neighbor, or found in your local Buy Nothing group.

5 **Smash Flowers.** Using the back of a spoon, let kids print fresh flowers onto shirts, totes, scarves, paper cards, display paper, or preprinted paper wreath outlines. Kids love to print flowers!

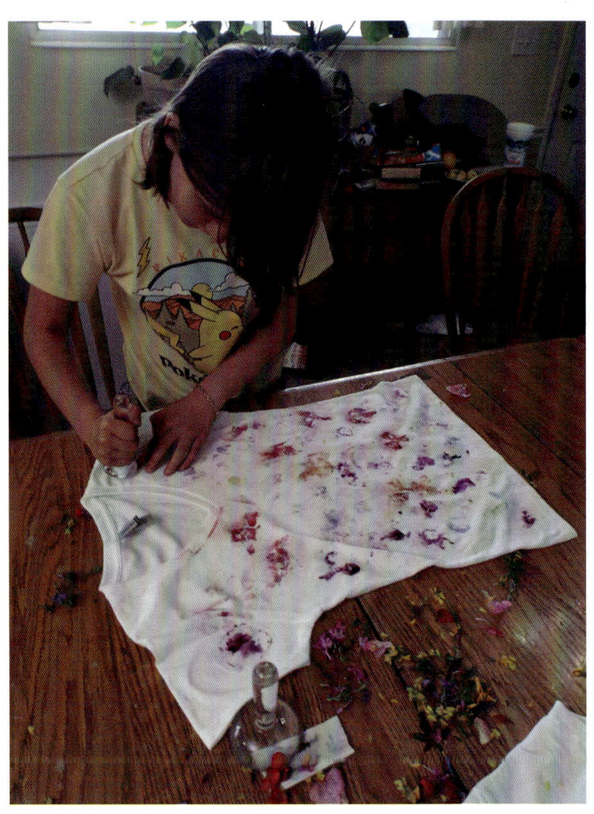

6 Leaf Peepers. When my nieces and nephews were young, my cousins and I would go out to collect autumn leaves with the kids each year. We'd have a campfire lunch or s'mores and everyone would gather leaves of all colors. The kids can press some and use others fresh to print positive and negative images. While gathering leaves, they can also gather flowers to make the ink or paint and acorns and walnuts to make ink.

7 Flat Flowers. Children love to "press" flowers in the microwave (see page 15). They can immediately use those flowers for decoupage crafts, rice glue crafts, or flour glue. They can make cards, collage, jewelry, or paper flower crowns or they can decorate jars or pebbles. They can use a flower to make a character to create a story or as scenery for a story.

8 Mint Plates. Because the decoupage paste in this book (see page 85) is made of all edible ingredients, you can use it to make some fun projects. For example, let children pick tea herbs from the garden, like spearmint, peppermint, anise hyssop, fennel seeds, or lemon balm. Help them make tea. While the tea is cooling, let them decoupage the tea herbs on tea plates. They can sweeten the tea with honey or stevia leaves and then serve it on the plates they decorated.

9 Flowery Thanks. Using the all-natural decoupage paste recipe in this book (see page 85), use fresh leaves and petals to create thank-you cards or seasonal display cards.

10 Royal Heads. Use strips of paper to create headbands or crowns for kids. Use the rice glue recipe in this book (see page 85) to decorate those crowns with either real or paper-crafted leaves.

11 Found Beads. Drill holes in acorns with the caps removed for the kids (use a clamp or pliers to hold the acorns as you drill them). Make botanical paint (with or without the kids, depending on age) and allow them to turn the acorns into painted beads. Once dried, use string to create necklaces or bracelets. You can also use shells; walnuts; large seeds (such as Job's tears); dried beans, peas, or fava beans; poppy seed heads; or wood slices from thin branches, or find other creative "beads" in nature. If you're good with a drill or Dremel tool, you could also use pebbles. Or make beads from the air-dry clay recipe in this book (see page 89).

12 Face It. On a sheet of art paper, have kids draw and then paint sets of eyes in all shapes, colors, and expressions. Challenge them to create happy eyes, crazy eyes, goofy eyes, silly eyes, surprised eyes. Then cut out the eyes and apply them to pebbles, leaves, or twigs using the natural glue recipes in this book (see page 85), creating fun creatures and characters.

13 Printable Pages. The internet is rife with free coloring sheets you can print for kids of many ages. Type "coloring sheet" and the theme or type you want and print the pictures. Our grandkids have done hundreds of these. Help them make botanical paint to use on the sheets or make the paint for them beforehand. Botanical watercolors work great for this, and the coloring sheets can be printed on regular copy paper. We also save scratch paper and print on the back side.

14 Double Bubble. Add a bit of dish soap and water to a botanical color and let your kids make bubble art on paper using a straw. Or let them use an old toothbrush to splatter paint (hint: do this outside).

15 Easter Dye. Make Easter eggs using only homemade botanical colors, such as raspberries, lettuce, grass, tulip petals, weeds, parsley, or turmeric. If you are really brave, volunteer to help their whole class do this at school.

16 Temporary Tattoos. If your littles are like our grandkids, temporary tattoos are all the rage. A botanical version is easy—just use a real rubber stamp with botanical stamping ink. I get my stamps at the thrift store. Use a botanical watercolor paint or add gum arabic to make ink. I find it best to paint the ink onto the glass muller plate and then stamp into the ink. It is also fun to let the kids or grandkids choose their own stamp at the thrift store and have them pick the flowers to be made into the ink.

17 Pressed Garden. Have the kids pick flowers and then microwave-press them. Using the rice glue recipe in this book (see page 85), glue the pressed flower to paper and have the kids draw on stems and leaves to create their own garden.

18 Spooky Help. Here is an idea for which I should be awarded a Nobel Prize: How to get the kids (or grandkids) to help you remove rocks from the garden without a single complaint! I think that sentence deserves two exclamation marks!! Kids love to put eyes on things. Have them each make twenty pairs of two-dimensional "googly eyes" on paper using botanical paint, like white milk paint or vine black paint (see pages 70 and 76). They can make cartoon eyes or whatever eyes they want. Then they can cut out the eyes with appropriate scissors. Then take them to the garden to gather twenty rocks or pebbles they think look like "creepy creatures." They wash their rocks, blow dry or towel dry them, and then use rice glue or the decoupage recipes in this book (see page 85) to turn their rocks into eyeball creatures. Use these creatures to line the sidewalk or porch for Halloween. Extra smart parents and grandparents will have them do pebble Easter eggs with eyes (or just paint egg-shaped rocks), birthday party rocks—pebbles for every occasion until your garden is free of pebbles! You're welcome.

19 Magic Flowers. Kids can make color-changing flower prints while learning about pH. Have the children press fresh rose petals onto white paper with their fingers, the back of a spoon, or a die-cut machine. Then paint or spray mordant onto the pressed image to watch it instantly change color. For example, pressing red rose petals and then spraying the print with a pinch of baking soda in 1/4 cup warm water will turn the petal prints green. Citric acid water or lemon or lime juice in water at the same ratio will turn them brighter red. Alum will turn them purple. This is a great way for kids to experiment with the concept of pH. Bidens flowers are another type that change color well. Or slice the end off a beet as a stamp and then spray the prints with mordants to watch them change color. If your "stamp" runs dry, slice off a bit more.

20 Painted Flowers. White Shasta daisies, white yarrow, and white hollyhocks are a few of the options for fresh white flowers that can be painted. You can even turn a Shasta flower into a rainbow of petals or add glitter using the all-natural glitter paint recipe in this book (see page 20). Then the painted flowers can be displayed fresh.

21 Body Double. Get butcher paper and, working together, have the kids lay out paper larger than their body, taping paper together if needed. Then one child lies on the paper while another traces them. Then the kids paint their outlined body with botanical paints. They can also decoupage flowers for the eyes, make patterns for clothes, or use stamps. Then they cut out their body double and tape it to their bedroom door or to cardboard to make it stand up.

22 Flower Child. This is a simpler version of Body Double. Have the kids draw or trace their own head, life sized. Have them add hair by adding flowers, petals, and leaves with either the rice glue or all-natural decoupage recipe found in this book (see page 85). They can paint in eyes and features with botanical paints.

23 Edible Food Paint. Kids and adults of all ages may enjoy painting food with edible paints. Divide unsweetened condensed milk into small bowls and tine each bowl with a different edible botanical pigment, like the juice of raspberries, blueberries, spinach, or turmeric. (Using unsweetened condensed milk encourages the kids to actually paint instead of just eating the paint, but you can also use the sweetened version.) Be sure to shake or stir the condensed milk because it does settle and separate in the can over time. Allow the kids to use the paints on sugar cookies, marshmallows, blondie bars, or—for a real treat—on white sweet potato toast (simply cut sweet potatoes into 1/4-inch slices and toast the slices). Or have them paint on thin slices of raw jicama or use the edible pigment to make paint from a light-colored nut butter, like cashew or almond butter. You can use edible food paint to color white chocolate, frosting, or cream cheese; make "art paper" from thin sheets of white chocolate; or paint saltine crackers or graham crackers. They could paint the graham crackers and the marshmallows and then make s'mores. So many foods to paint, so little time!

24 Gummy Treats. Kids love to make gummy candy and there are myriad simple recipes online. Gummy candy can be naturally flavored and tinted with the juice of berries. Also, making elderberry gummies is a great way for kids and adults to prime their natural defenses when they get a cold. My company, SeedRenaissance.com, ships live elderberry bushes each spring, starting around mid-April to May.

25 Colored Sanding Sugar. Sanding sugar, which is larger and crunchier than normal sugar, can be naturally colored by spraying it with an edible berry juice using the spray paint recipe from this book (see page 101). Don't overspray or it will melt. Use the sanding sugar to decorate sugar cookies with cream cheese frosting. It works even better to warm (but not melt) the sugar in a microwave first so the spray paint dries quickly.

26 Glitter Salt. Rock salt can be dyed the same way as sanding sugar and then used to make "glitter" art by sprinkling or pressing it onto the decoupage paste recipe in this book (see page 85). If rock salt is too big, it can be crushed as desired.

27 Bathtub Paint. Mix 1 teaspoon cornstarch or 1/2 teaspoon of kaolin clay into 1/8 cup castile biodegradable liquid soap to thicken the soap, then color the soap with an edible botanical color. You can put multiple colors in an ice cube tray or in plastic cups. Give the kids brushes, cotton swabs, or cotton balls, depending on age, and let them paint the tub and themselves before washing it all away. On a hot summer day, they can paint themselves outside and then run through the sprinkler! Be sure to tell them not to eat the soap, of course.

28 Cloud Cakes. Make or buy mini angel food cakes. Whip heavy cream and supervise the kids while they color the cream with edible juices of berries or fruits or with dyed sanding sugar. This is a fun birthday activity. Technically, you could just skip the cakes and let the kids eat the cream . . .

29 Foam Wars. Kids are always looking for great backyard summer games. Well, here is one for the brave parents. Pour one can of aquafaba (drained liquid from canned garbanzo beans) into a bowl, and add 1/8 teaspoon cream of tartar, and whip with a mixer. You will want one recipe per child. Then let each child color their foam with a unique edible food color, like beet juice, berry juice, or boiled cabbage dye. Outside, they throw their color of foam on each of the other players. It's like paintball but with foam! When you get hit with someone's foam, you have to freeze in place until the "it" person hits you with their foam to activate you again.

30 Scratch and Sniff. Make the rice glue recipe in this book (see page 85) and divide it into small batches of about 1 tablespoon. To each tablespoon, add a natural color and scent, like rose petal citric acid watercolor pigment and lemon essential oil to make pink lemonade or mint oil with mulled mint leaves for a green color. The kids can paint with these or even paint on label paper to make stickers. Once dried, these make great scratch and sniff paints.

31 Easter Decoupage. Use the decoupage paste recipe in this book (see page 85) to let kids decorate hollowed-out eggs, wood blocks, wood craft cut-outs, or papier-mâché shapes with fresh or dried petals.

32 Flowers for Readers. Have the kids choose a flower to microwave-press. Cut bookmarks from paper and use decoupage glue (see page 85) to add the flower to the bookmark. This works especially well with flowers that actually become flat when pressed, like phlox, pansies, violets, and larkspur. If you don't have these, have them press individual petals instead of whole flowers. Of course, they can also press bookmarks with a die-cut machine or the back of a spoon or gently hammer flowers onto paper with a rubber mallet. They can also make botanical paint to simply color bookmarks or dye paper by spraying or using a paint brush and then cutting out a bookmark.

33 Flower Flags. A great way to introduce kids about ten and up to sewing is to have them make hammer flower flags. Have them cut a "flag" about 4 inches by 7 inches. They can also cut a pennant shape if they wish. Show them how to fold under and down the top inch and sew it down to create the rod pocket. Then hammer flowers onto the flag. They can use a twig for the rod and hang the twig on the wall with string, or just use string through the rod pocket. Once they master sewing flags, it's not far for them to sew a small drawstring bag, purse, or collection bag they could then print with flowers.

34 Flower Cards. Hammer flower cards are especially great for Mother's Day and Father's Day. Don't forget that grandparents need cards too! The grandparents are most important. We all know it. Especially grandpas.

35 Friendship Hearts. Cut a heart from botanically painted or printed paper and then cut that heart into two friendship hearts. Let them choose who to give the second half to. For older kids, this can be done with the air-dry clay recipe in this book (see page 89).

36 Kindness Coins. Encourage kindness and gratitude in kids by having them make kindness coins on pebbles, wood slices, or even leaves. They can paint the words "thank you" or just paint a favorite flower, animal, or any image. Then when someone does something nice for them without being asked, they can give that person the kindness coin as a gift and explain how they can pass the coin along to the next person. Don't use pebbles if the kids are young enough to be throwers.

37 Trading Flowers. One great way to encourage kids to get to know the natural world around them is to help them create botanical trading cards. After cutting out paper cards, they can decorate those cards with botanical eco-prints, sun prints, or paint them with botanical paint. Each card should represent a different plant or flower, kind of like flash cards about plants. Label each card. Older kids can add the botanical Latin name of the plant. Once made, they can trade these cards with each other and collect them.

38 Trading Seeds. Use rice glue or the decoupage paste recipe (see page 85) to glue seeds onto rice paper, craft paper, homemade paper, scratch paper, recycled paper, or even copy paper. Cut out trading cards, botanical shapes, or traced cookie cutter shapes. If each child makes multiples of only one kind of seed, then the cards can be traded. The cards are labeled and planted directly in the garden. Another fun twist is to use botanical watercolors to paint the cards before gluing on the seeds.

39 Funny Money. Have kids print flowers onto paper, cut each flower into a coin shape, and use these as money to trade or spend at a homemade family craft store.

40 Paper Beads. Have the kids paint a sheet of paper with botanical colors. Cut the dried paper into long, thin triangle strips, then spread natural glue or decoupage paste from this book (see page 85) on the unpainted side of the paper. Roll the paper around a pen, pencil, or paintbrush handle to form a bead. Removing the handle creates the hole in the center of the bead. Once dry, these can then be coated with decoupage paste, dried again, and then strung on string to make necklaces and bracelets, hair ties, or earrings. Pay extra attention to getting the tip of the triangle to stay flat to the bead. The wider you make the beads, the fewer beads you will need to string a bracelet or necklace.

41 Painted Jack-o'-Lanterns. Painting pumpkins instead of carving them has become increasingly popular at Halloween, but it always gets up my dander just a smidge because I could always take a carved pumpkin and compost it or feed it to my horse after Halloween—but not when it's covered in plastic-based paint. Botanical paints solve this problem! To paint on pumpkins (or as they did historically, on turnips) use botanical oil paint, milk paint, or tempera recipes from this book (see pages 73, 70, and 97).

42 **Wax Resist.** Put a leaf upside down under paper that is thin, like copy paper. The more pronounced the ribs on the leaf, the better the print will be. Maple leaves make great prints. Show the kids how to create a rubbing of the leaf on the paper using a clear wax candle or crayon like those that come with the Easter egg kits. (I don't recommend using a white crayon because the wax is too hard). Don't let the paper or leaf move while you rub it with wax—this can take some practice. Then paint the paper with botanical watercolors to reveal the print.

43 **Invisible Made Visible.** Once kids discover they can make "invisible" art with wax rubbings, then they realize they can make wax rubbings of everything—the sidewalk, coins, the bottoms of their shoes, tree trunks, wood planks, fabric, stencils. Anything with a texture can be turned into wax rubbing art. Let the kids go crazy. Adults like me love to do this too. You can also do this method on fabric, like shirts, bags, and scarves.

44 **Play Dishes.** Let kids make plates and tea plates from the air-dry clay recipe in this book (see page 89). Using a butter knife to cut the shapes, they can make teacups by using the bottom half of a small apple to mold the clay around. They can botanically color the clay or paint the clay dishes after they are dry. They can even make pots, pans, spoons, and forks.

45 **For the Birds.** Make and paint a wooden bird feeder using milk paint. Or buy a birdhouse kit at a craft store to paint. Or use the botanical wood stain recipes in this book (see page 81).

46 **Map of Memories.** Have the kids paint a map of your state and mark all the places of significant memories using a small eco-print of a leaf or flower. Remembering family trips together this way is especially fun for younger kids. Of course, they will want to go back again.

47 **Family Tree.** Have kids draw or paint your family tree and print the names with homemade ink or paint. You could make botanical ink from a significant plant or tree, like flowers from grandma's garden or leaves from the tree with the swing. This makes a great gift. You can also do a fingerprint in botanical ink from each member of your immediate family. Sometimes I sign my art with a fingerprint of botanical ink.

48 **Carved Pottery.** Have the kids make a pinch pot using the air-dry clay recipe in this book (see page 89). Allow the pot to dry to leather-hard stage, where it can be handled without breaking but is not fully dry. Have them paint the pot with a botanical color and then carve away the paint with a butter knife or pumpkin carving tools to make designs in the clay.

49 **Ice Art.** Help kids make botanical dye and then freeze it in ice cube trays. Once frozen, you can dye shirts or fabric by placing the ice on the fabric or crushing the ice and allowing natural patterns to form as the ice melts. You can also do this on watercolor paper if you tape down the paper.

50 **Cob Dolls.** Here is a real historical throwback. My own grandmother used to make corncob and hollyhock dolls with her granddaughters. Botanical colors have been used for a long time to dye or paint corncob dolls. Look online for instructions.

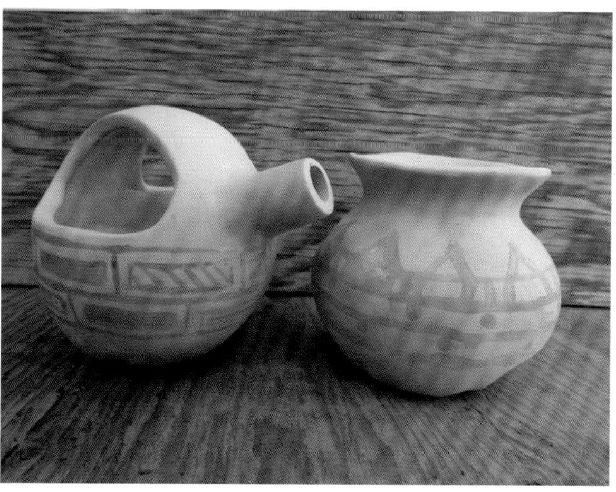

Botanical Color Swatches by Plant Type

QUERCUS SPECIES

Acorns and Oaks

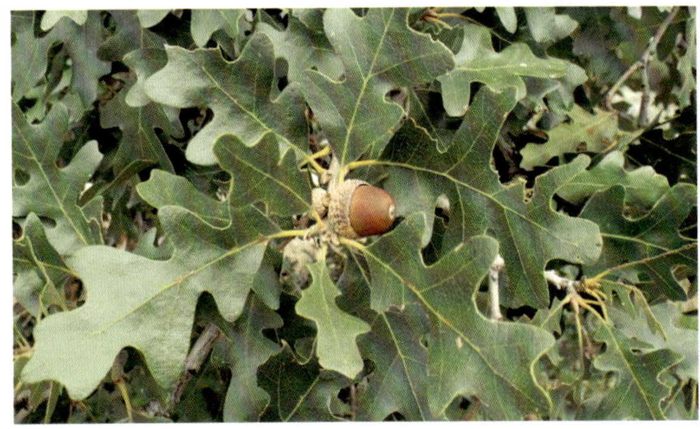

COLORS CREATED brown, black

PARTS USED FOR PIGMENT acorns, leaves, bark, galls

PLANT TYPE trees or shrubs, depending on species

HARDINESS ZONE varies by species

1. Simmer for 10 minutes to make pigment or dye Strain.
2. Simmer again to reduce liquid to desired color strength.

Notes: Acorns can be boiled with or without caps. Green acorns make a darker pigment. Oak galls are used to make the millennia-old indelible ink recipe in this book (see page 65), which is waterproof and highly sun-resistant. Oak leaves make especially good eco-prints because of their high tannin juices.

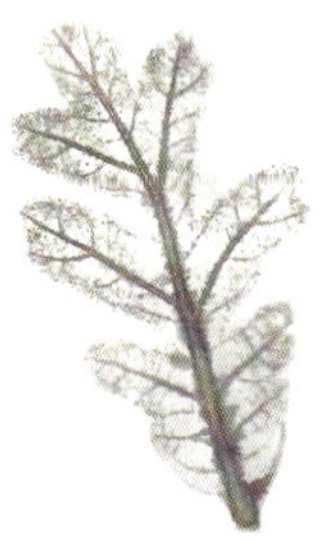

BROWN ACORN

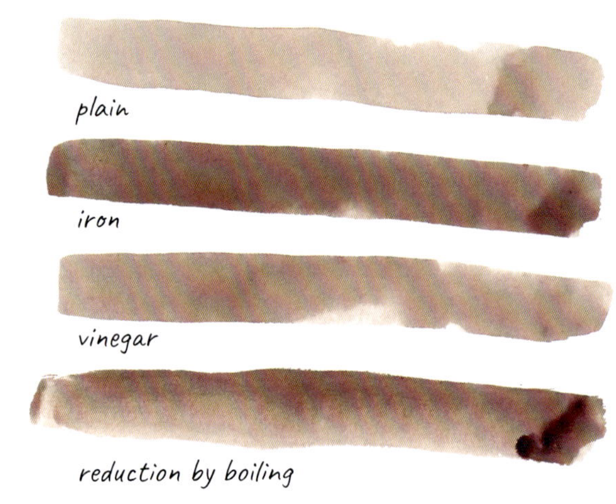

OAK ACORN

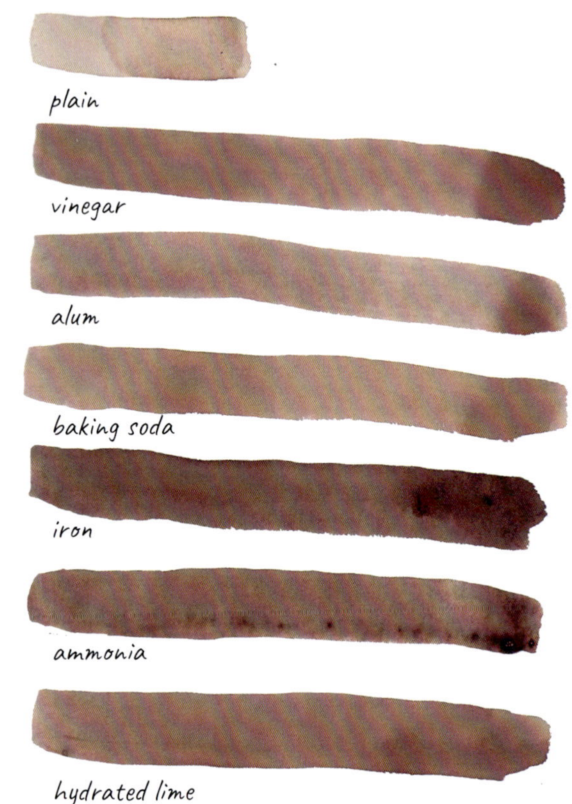

SPATHODEA CAMPANULATA

African Tulip Tree

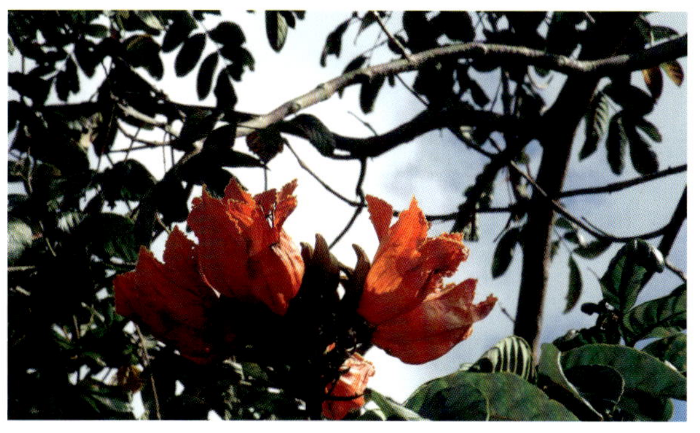

COLORS CREATED	tan, pink with citric acid, yellow with baking soda
PARTS USED FOR PIGMENT	red flowers
PLANT TYPE	tree
HARDINESS ZONE	varies by cultivar

1. Simmer for 10 minutes to make pigment or dye. Strain.
2. Simmer again to reduce liquid to desired color strength.

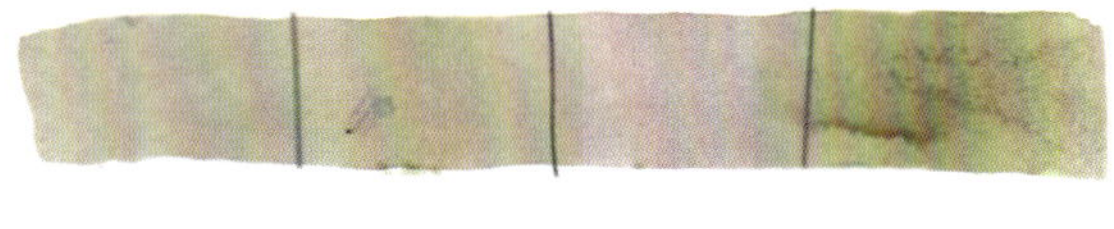

Agapanthus Species

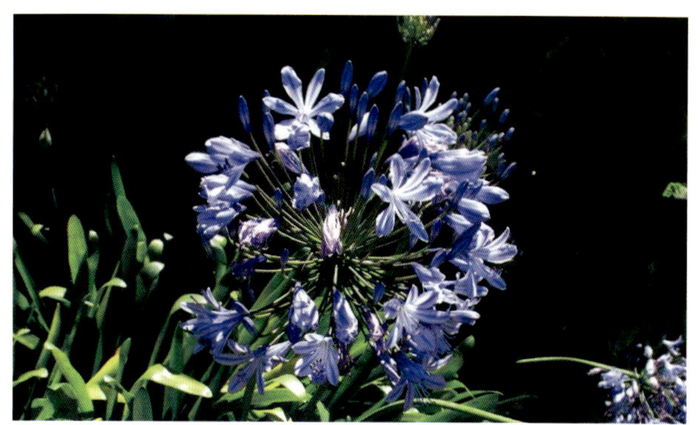

COLORS CREATED	blue, yellow with baking soda
PARTS USED FOR PIGMENT	petals
PLANT TYPE	varies by species
HARDINESS ZONE	varies by species

1. Simmer for 10 minutes to make pigment or dye. Strain.
2. Simmer again to reduce liquid to desired color strength.

AGRIMONIA EUPATORIA

Agrimony

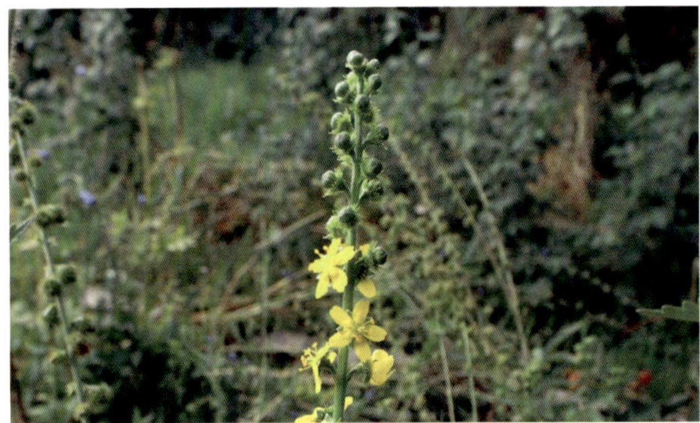

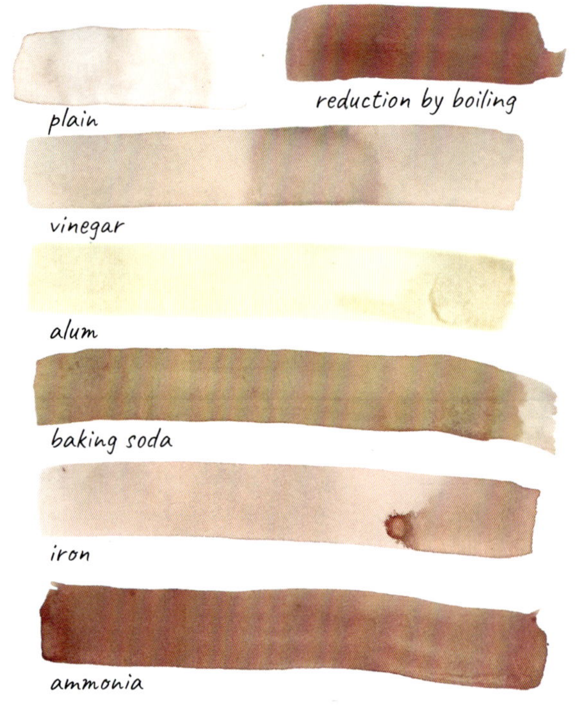

COLORS CREATED	brown, red, yellow
PARTS USED FOR PIGMENT	spikes of yellow flowers
PLANT TYPE	perennial
HARDINESS ZONE	5–9
SEEDING	Plant directly outside in spring or autumn. Seeds available at SeedRenaissance.com.

1. Simmer for 10 minutes to make pigment or dye. Strain.
2. Simmer again to reduce liquid to desired color strength.

LOBULARIA MARITIMA

Alyssum

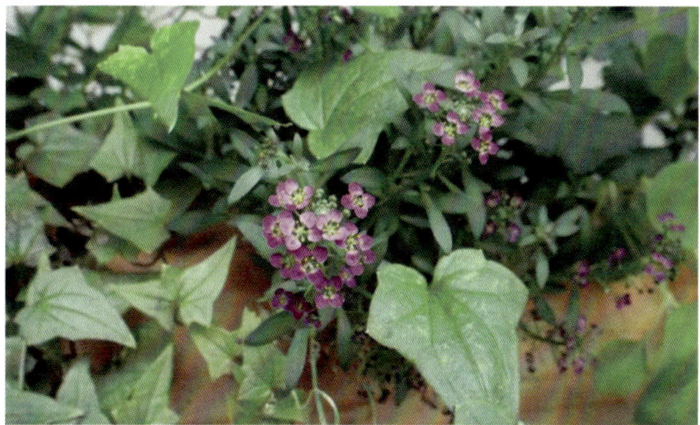

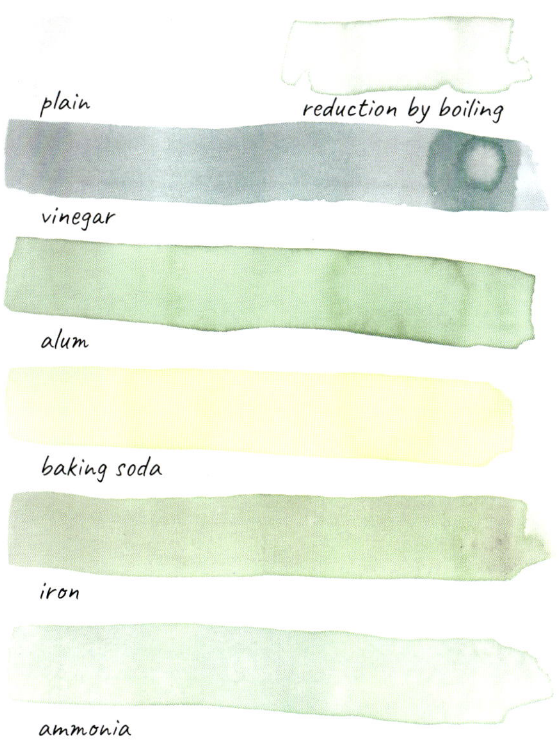

COLORS CREATED	turquoise with vinegar; green with alum, iron, and ammonia; yellow with baking soda
PARTS USED FOR PIGMENT	purple flowers
PLANT TYPE	annual
HARDINESS ZONE	varies by species and cultivar

1. It is not necessary to remove the tiny flowers from their stems. Simmer the flowering stems for 15 minutes to make pigment and dye. The flowers of purple alyssum, when used fresh and uncooked, make a good blue pigment and eco-print.

Notes: Often grown as a landscape annual, although it is perennial in my geothermal greenhouse.

Aloe Species

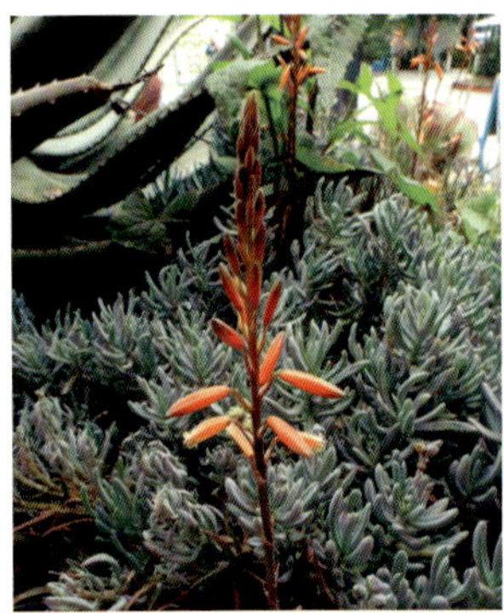

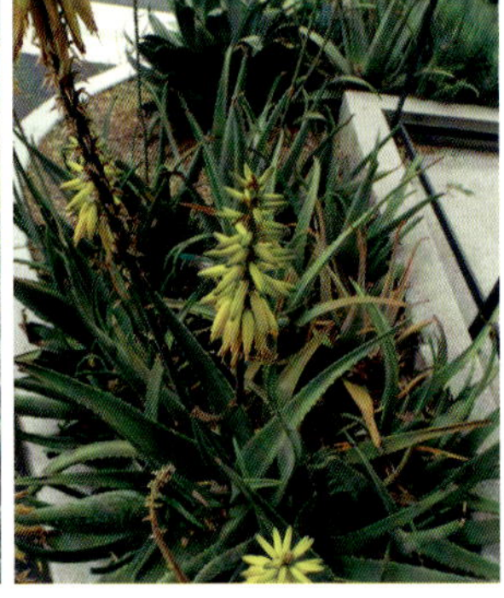

AMMONIA SOLAR

linen

cotton

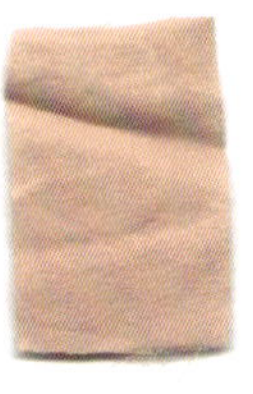

silk

wool

citric acid

yellow aloe flower

COLORS CREATED	red, yellow
PARTS USED FOR PIGMENT	leaves, flowers
PLANT TYPE	perennial succulent
HARDINESS ZONE	varies widely by species and cultivar
GROWING	Live plants are planted outside in warm winter zones, kept in greenhouses like mine, or kept as houseplants in cold zones.

1. The green leaves make red solar dye when washed of their aloin. To remove the aloin juice from the stem (which is not the aloe part of the juice), cut the stem into pieces and soak it in water for 15 minutes.
2. Change the water and then repeat. You can then blend up the stems in water and put them in the sun for several days to create red dye. The yellow and orange flowers make yellow and orange when pressed fresh and uncooked.

Amaryllis Species

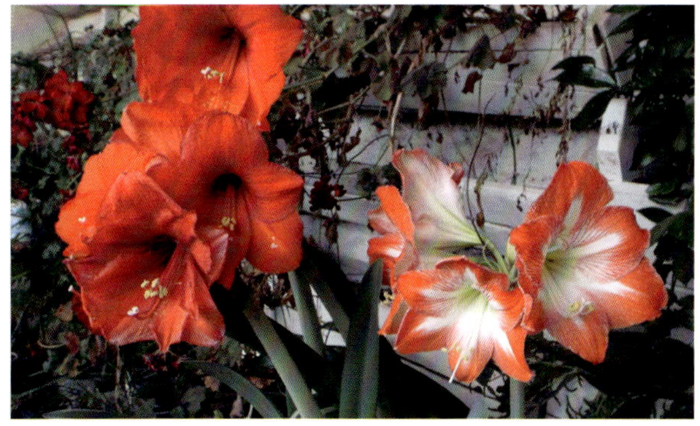

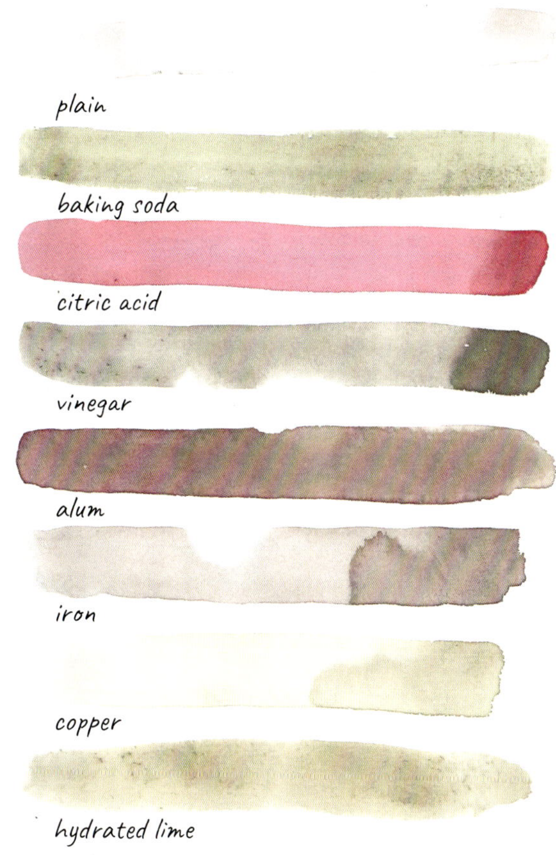

COLORS CREATED	red with citric acid, alum
PARTS USED FOR PIGMENT	flowers
PLANT TYPE	bulb
HARDINESS ZONE	tropical
GROWING	Widely forced as a Christmas flower, these huge stunners bloom in late June in my geothermal greenhouses where they live year-round.

1. Even a tiny bit of one of these huge flowers makes a lot of rich, deep pigment when used fresh. Flowers are gooey when pressed and can easily get pigment everywhere and temporarily stain fingers.

Notes: At least thirty years ago, I dried the blooms after growing them for Christmas and then framed and displayed them for years. Even dried, they were as big as dinner plates and retained their red hues.

MALUS PUMILA

Apple Tree

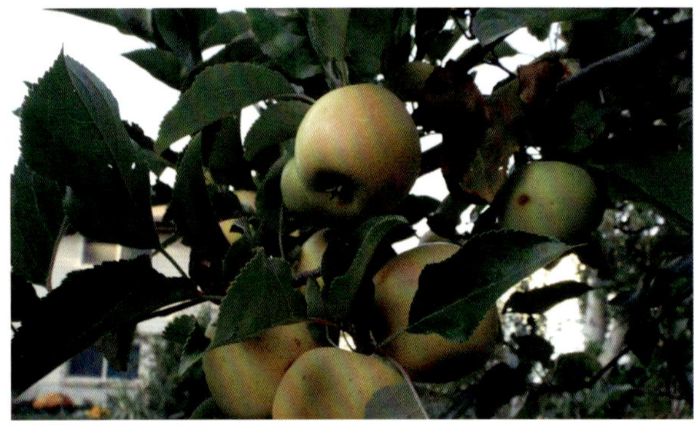

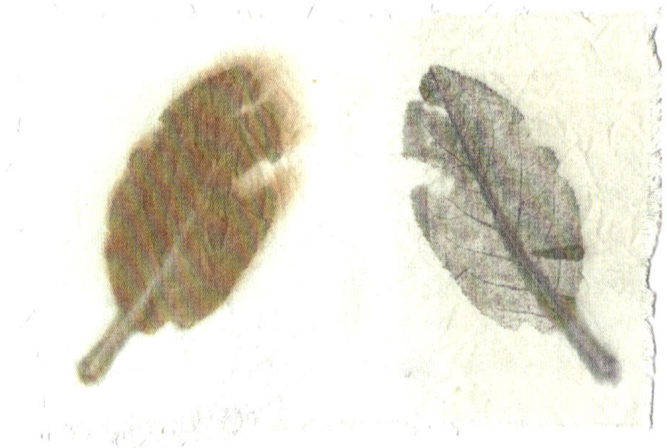

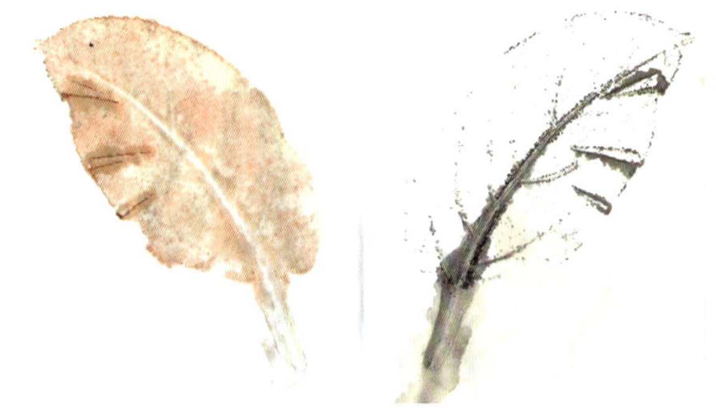

COLORS CREATED	green from leaves, brown from bark or twigs
PARTS USED FOR PIGMENT	tree leaves
PLANT TYPE	perennial tree
HARDINESS ZONE	varies widely by cultivar

1. Fresh leaves are used because pigment is degraded in dried leaves.

Notes: Leaves make one of the best well-defined eco-prints and respond well to mordants of iron or copper.

ARONIA SPECIES

Aronia Berries

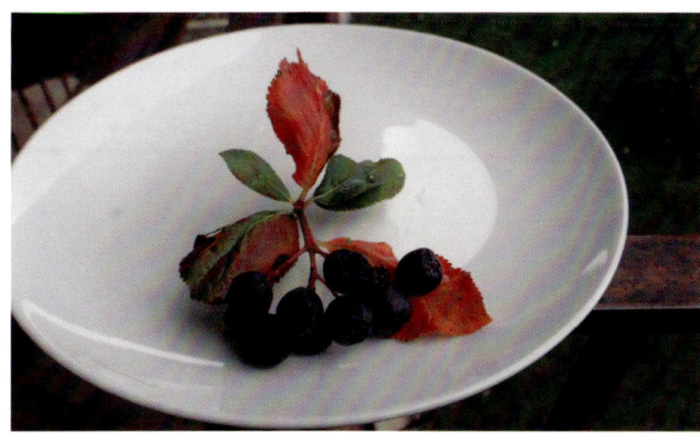

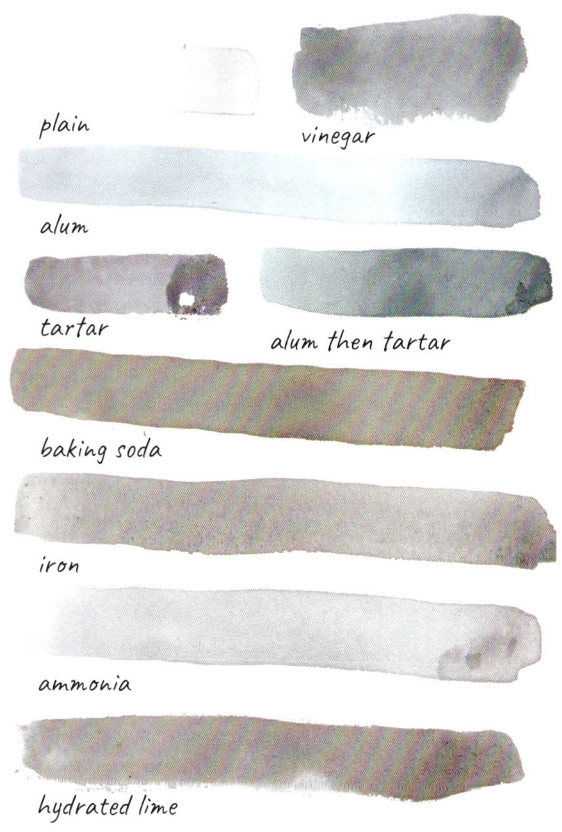

COLORS CREATED	blue with alum; purple with cream of tartar; green with alum and cream of tartar; blue-gray with vinegar; brown with baking soda, iron, or hydrated lime; gray with ammonia
PARTS USED FOR PIGMENT	berries, leaves
PLANT TYPE	Aronia berries are a cold-hardy cultivated backyard berry
HARDINESS ZONE	3–8

1. Simmer mashed berries for 10 minutes to make pigment or dye. Strain.
2. Simmer again to reduce liquid to desired color strength.

Notes: These tasty berries are not grown as widely as they should be. They look and taste somewhat like blueberries but grow easily in drier and more alkaline soils, like my garden in the Rocky Mountains.

BALSAMORHIZA SAGITTATE

Arrowleaf Balsamroot

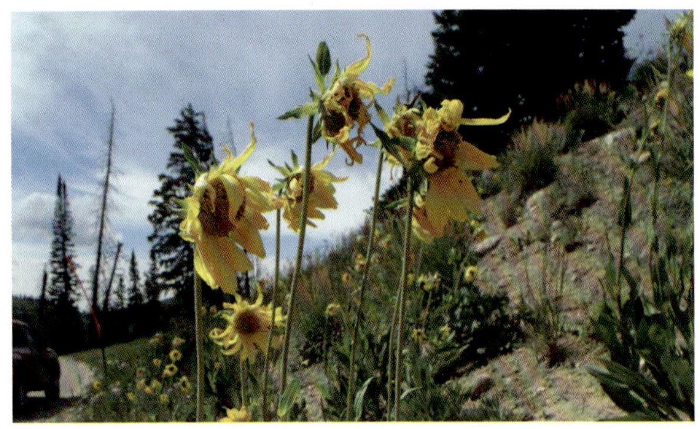

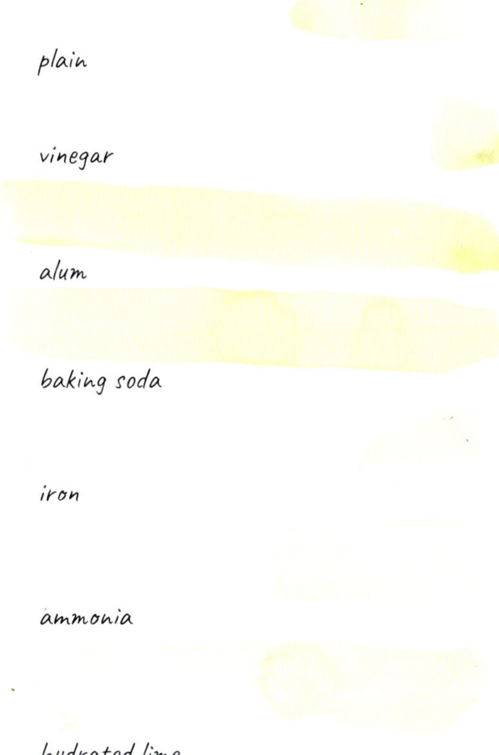

COLORS CREATED	yellow with alum or baking soda
PARTS USED FOR PIGMENT	flowers
PLANT TYPE	annual (roots may be perennial)
HARDINESS ZONE	3–10

1. Simmer for 30 minutes to make pigment or dye. Strain.
2. Simmer again to reduce liquid to desired color strength.

Notes: These massive spring bloomers bring thousands of hikers to our hometown after the snows melt. There is a hike near our home where it is very popular to take selfies in front of the tens of thousands of these blooms covering the hillsides. While they herald spring, they don't last long.

Artemisia Species

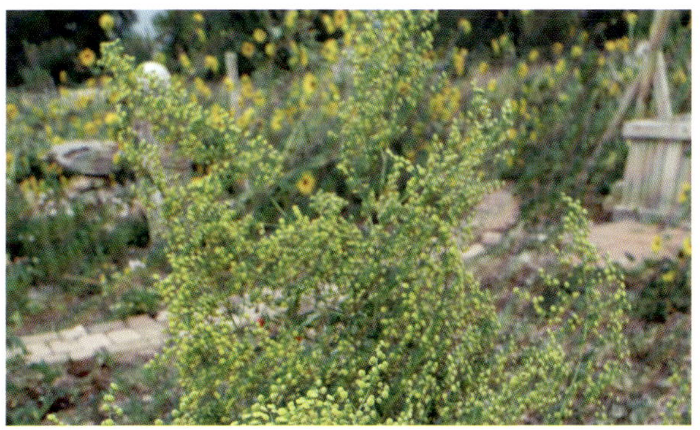

ARTEMISIA ANNUA

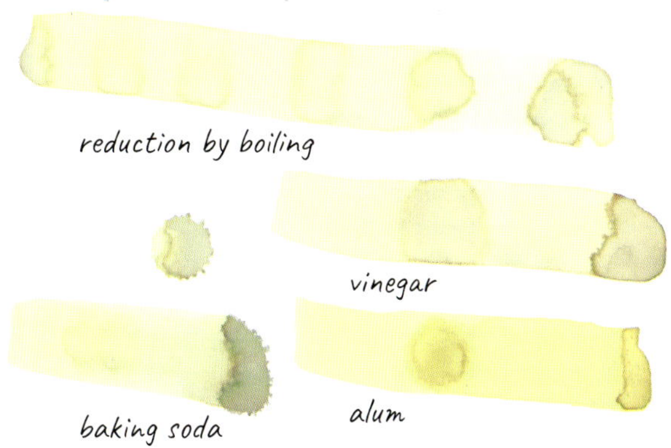

ARTEMISIA VULGARIS

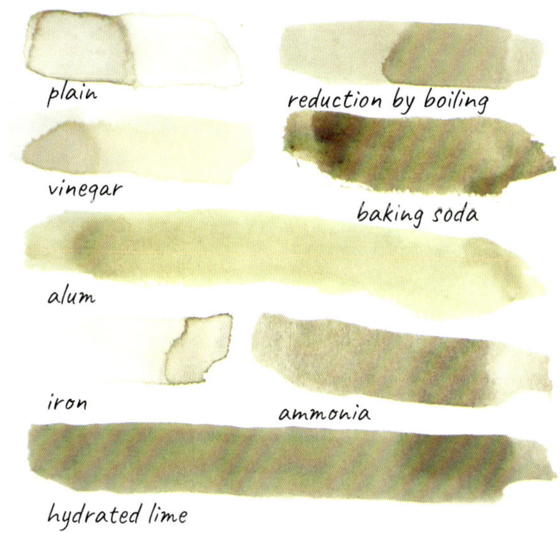

COLORS CREATED	yellow with alum (from Sweet Annie, *Artemisia annua*), brown with all mordants (from mugwort, *Artemisia vulgaris*)
PARTS USED FOR PIGMENT	flowering stems with leaves
PLANT TYPE	Sweet Annie is annual; mugwort and other bush types like sagebrush are perennial
HARDINESS ZONE	varies by species
SEEDING	Seeds available at SeedRenaissance.com.

1. Simmer for 10 minutes to make pigment or dye. Strain.
2. Simmer again to reduce liquid to desired color strength.

Notes: Mugwort tea has long been used by native peoples in wild clay to improve the quality of clay for pottery, including lowering the temperature of vitrification in the kiln. Sweet Annie is a critically important medicinal herb, as are other artemisia species.

CYNARA CARDUNCULUS

Artichoke & Cardoon

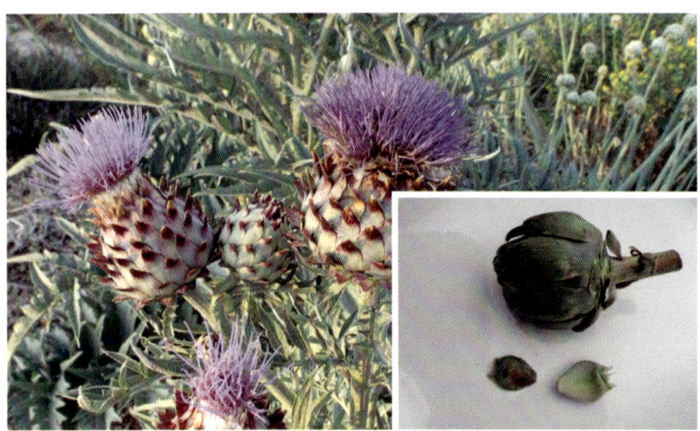

COLORS CREATED	green (from artichoke petals), yellow (from cardoon)
PLANT TYPE	perennial
HARDINESS ZONE	Artichokes are hardy only to zone 7. Cardoon is hardy to zone 5 if you don't clear away the frost-killed leaves, which act as a protective winter blanket for the roots.
SEEDING	Seeds available at SeedRenaissance.com.

1. Simmer for 10 minutes to make pigment or dye. Strain.
2. Simmer again to reduce liquid to desired color strength.

Notes: Making green pigment is an especially good use for the leftovers when eating artichoke for dinner. The dried flower heads of cardoon, after they have gone to seed, are all I use with flint and steel to start fires; the fluff of the dried flowers is extremely flammable. Beyond being good to eat, flowering cardoon is used as a showy centerpiece in high-end garden urns. The plants are dramatic and drought tolerant.

ARTICHOKE PETALS

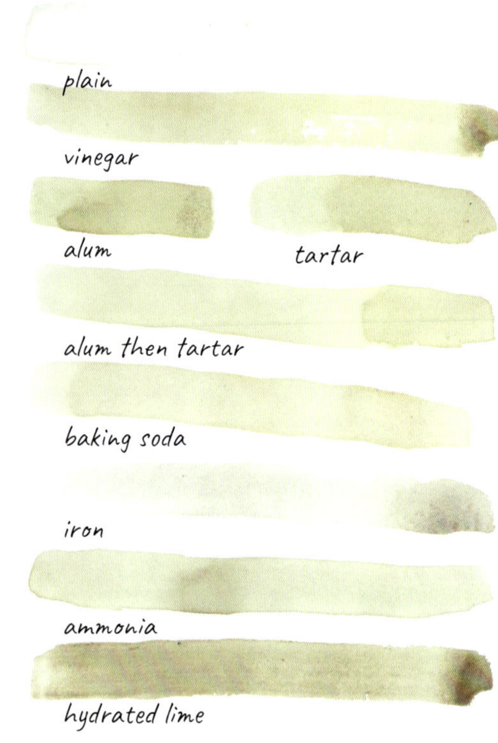

CARDOON

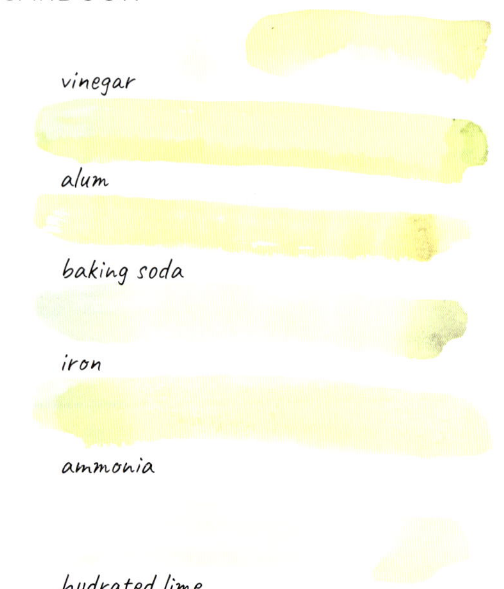

ASPARAGUS OFFICINALIS

Asparagus

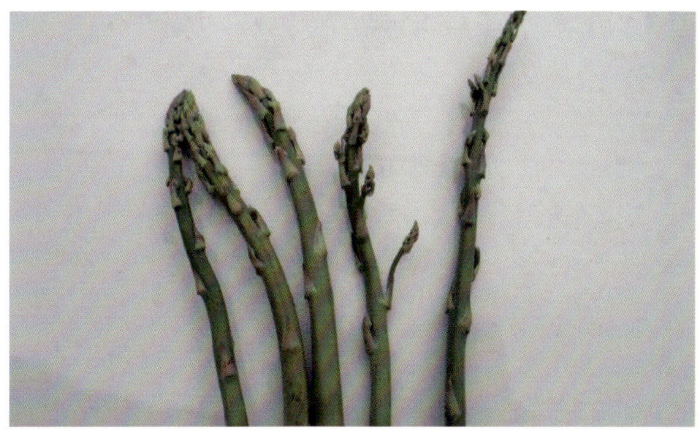

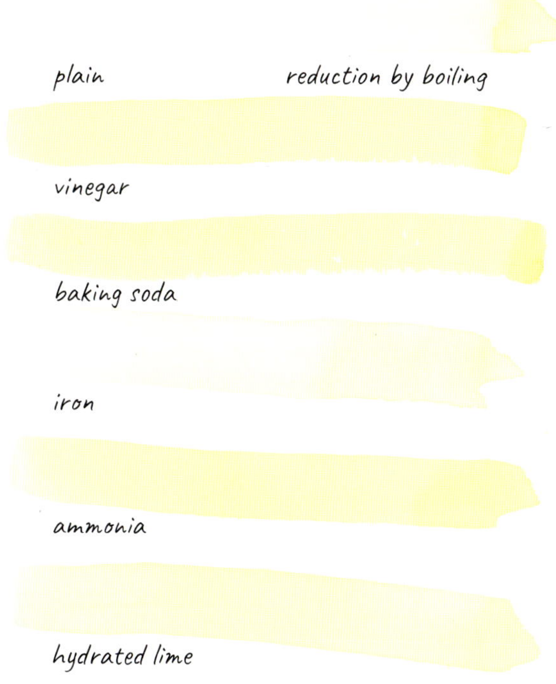

COLORS CREATED	yellow
PARTS USED FOR PIGMENT	stalks
PLANT TYPE	perennial
HARDINESS ZONE	3
SEEDING	Seeds available at SeedRenaissance.com

1. Simmer for 10 minutes to make pigment or dye. Strain.
2. Simmer again to reduce liquid to desired color strength.

Notes: Making color is an excellent use for the woody stumps of asparagus that you trim off before serving for dinner.

Aster Species

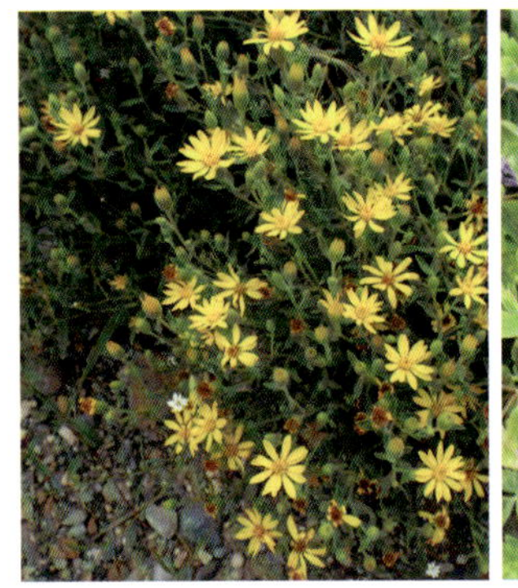
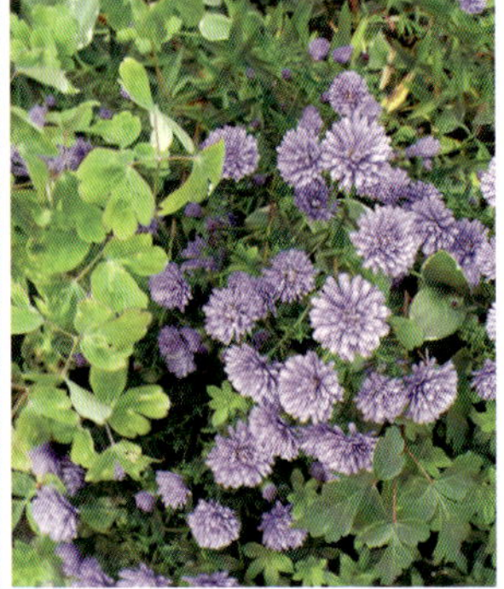

COLORS CREATED	yellow, tan
PARTS USED FOR PIGMENT	flowers
PLANT TYPE	perennial
HARDINESS ZONE	varies by species

1. Simmer for 10 minutes to make pigment or dye. Strain.
2. Simmer again to reduce liquid to desired color strength.

ALPINE GOLDEN ASTER

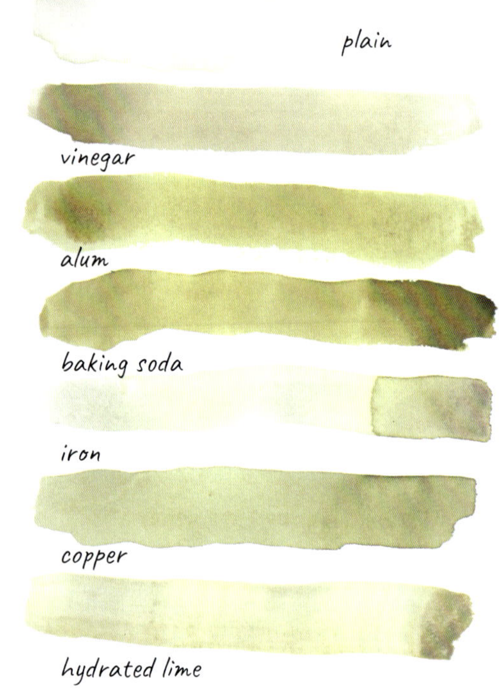

PURPLE ASTER AUTUMN BLOOMS

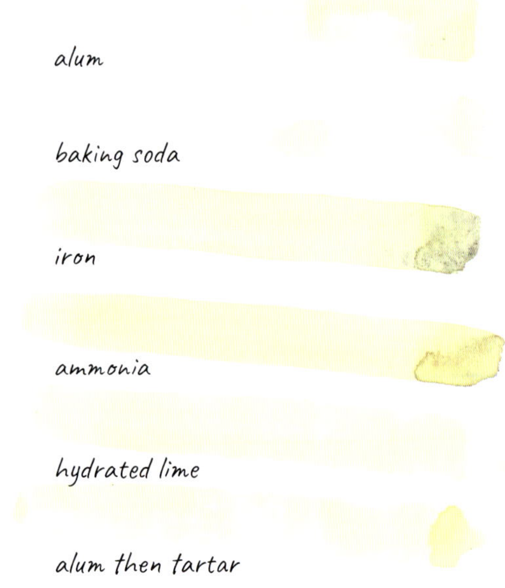

PERSEA AMERICANA

Avocado

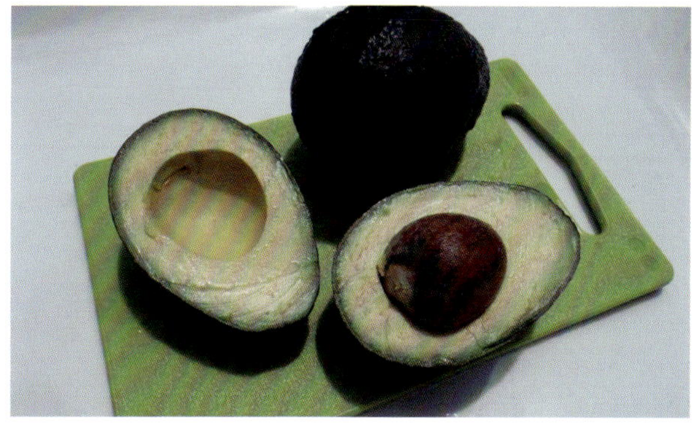

COLORS CREATED	red, pink, brown
PARTS USED FOR PIGMENT	pits
PLANT TYPE	perennial tree
HARDINESS ZONE	tropical

1. Whole pits are boiled, with or without the skin. The interior of the pit gives more color If It is chopped. Pits can be re-boiled several times to create the same dye with little or no loss of color.

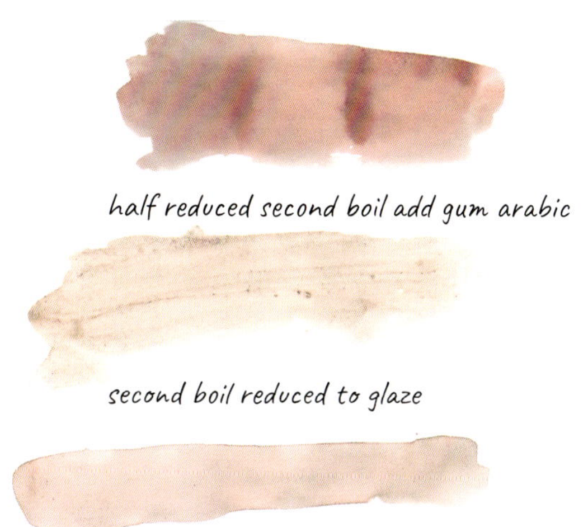

half reduced second boil add gum arabic

second boil reduced to glaze

third boil

BOILED AVOCADO

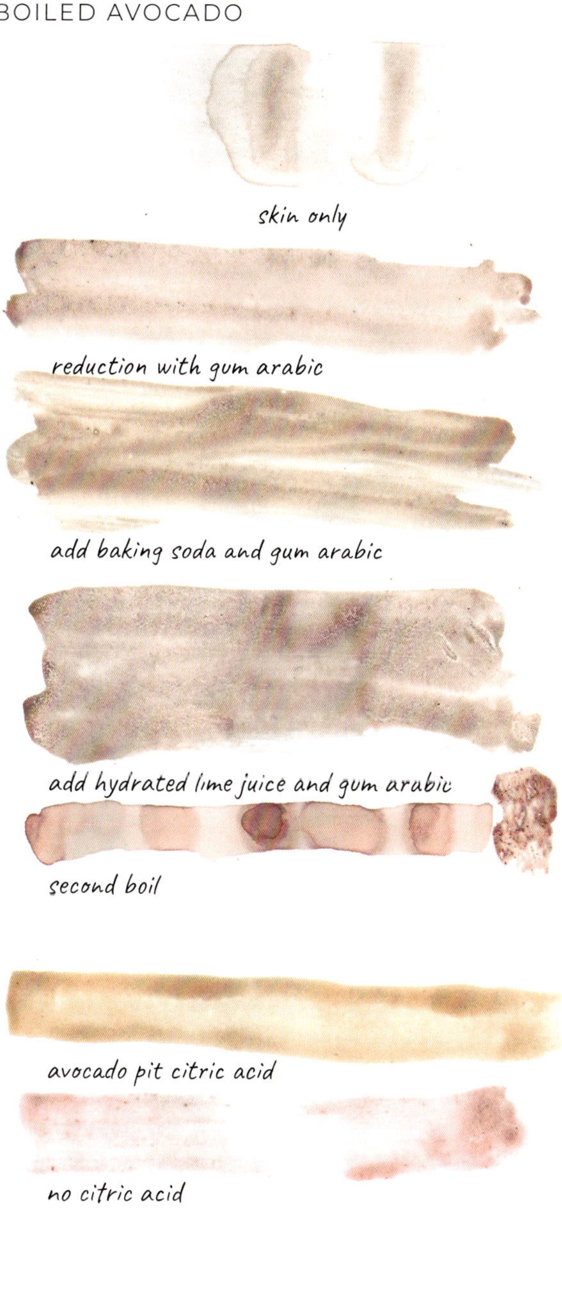

skin only

reduction with gum arabic

add baking soda and gum arabic

add hydrated lime juice and gum arabic

second boil

avocado pit citric acid

no citric acid

PLATYCODON GRANDIFLORAS

Balloon Flower

COLORS CREATED	blue
PARTS USED FOR PIGMENT	fresh blue flowers
PLANT TYPE	perennial
HARDINESS ZONE	3
SEEDING	Seeds available at SeedRenaissance.com.

1. Fresh petals are pressed or mulled to make blue pigment.

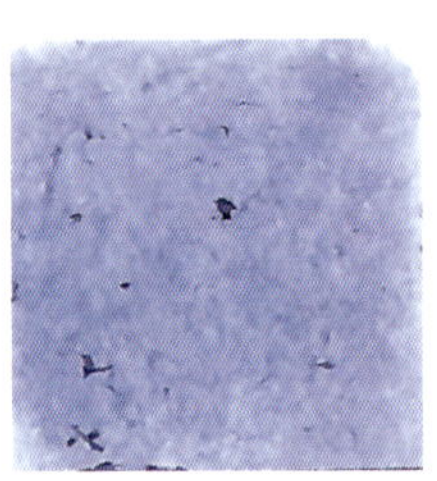

BERBERIS THUNBERGIA

Barberry

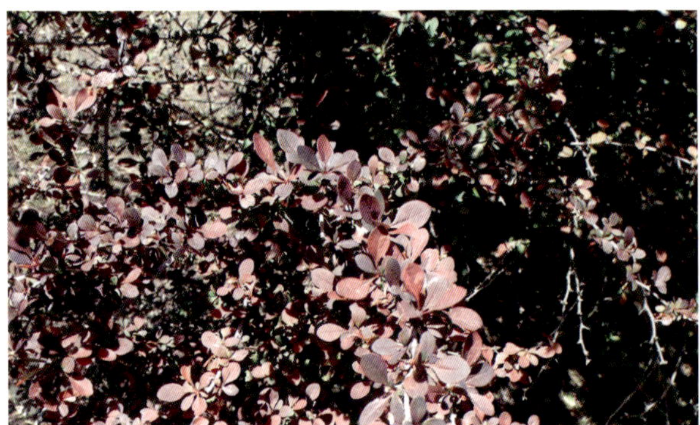

COLORS CREATED	red, green
PARTS USED FOR PIGMENT	leaves
PLANT TYPE	perennial shrub
HARDINESS ZONE	4

1. Simmer for 10 minutes to make pigment or dye. Strain.
2. Simmer again to reduce liquid to desired color strength. Fresh leaves make bright red eco-prints that turn green when mordanted with diluted vinegar of copper.

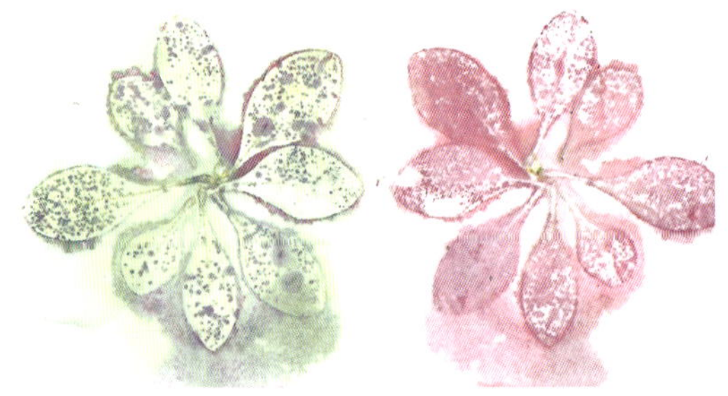

OCIMUM BASILICUM

Basil

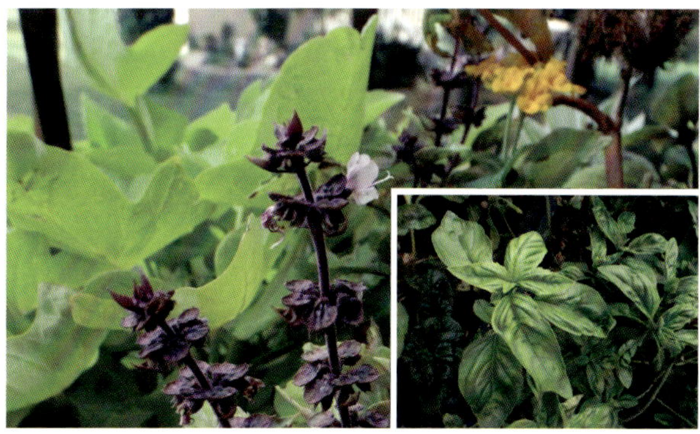

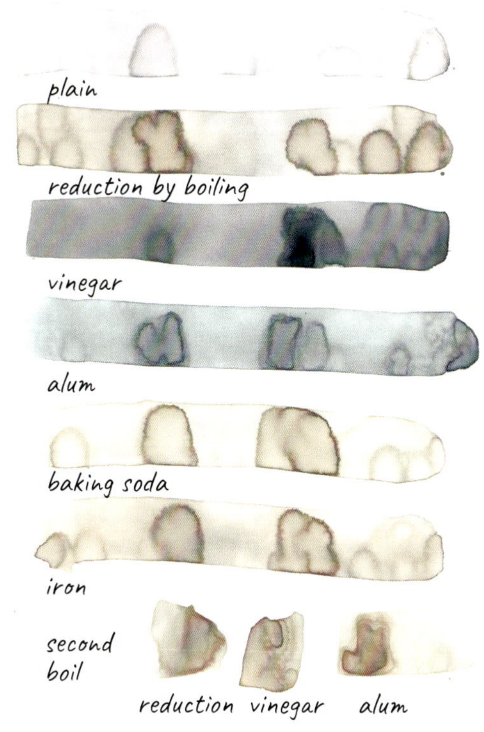

COLORS CREATED	brown, purple, turquoise, gray
PARTS USED FOR PIGMENT	leaves, stems
PLANT TYPE	annual
SEEDING	Plant directly outside in spring. Seeds available at SeedRenaissance.com.

1. Cook purple leaves for 30 minutes, strain, and reduce with further boiling. Fresh leaves make brown.

BASIL SEED STEMS

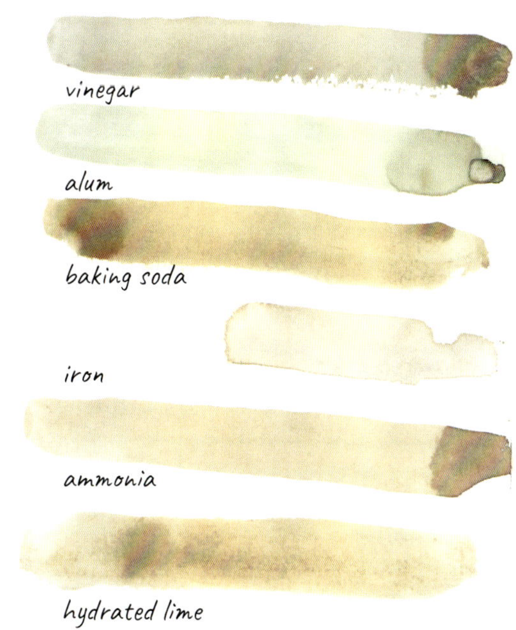

PHASEOLUS VULGARIS

Beans

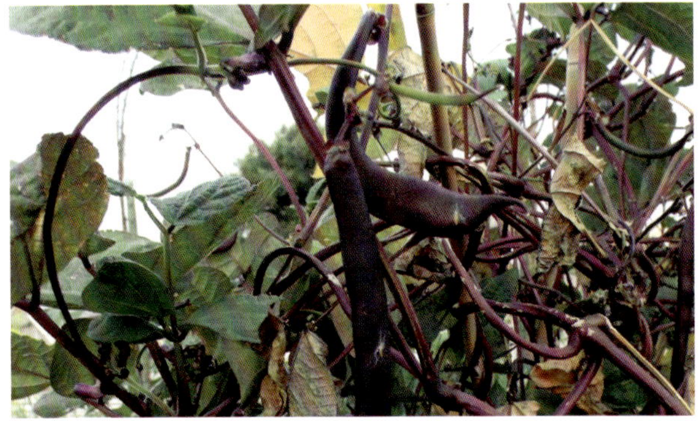

COLORS CREATED	brown (from fresh leaves or cooked black beans), yellow with a vinegar of copper mordant (from cooked purple snap beans), and blue (if you are righteous)
PARTS USED FOR PIGMENT	dry beans or fresh leaves
PLANT TYPE	annual
SEEDING	Plant directly outside in spring or autumn. Seeds available at SeedRenaissance.com.

PURPLE BEANS

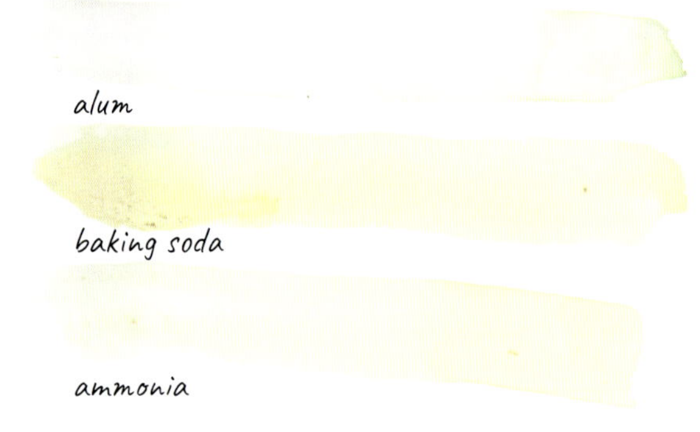

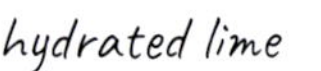

1. Simmer leaves or snap beans for 10 minutes to create certain pigments or dyes. Simmer dried beans for hours to be disappointed because they do not make blue.

Notes: Black beans are supposed to create blue dye with an alkaline mordant. While many people seem to accomplish this, I have tried and tried and only get ugly, soupy brown pigments. I've tried canned beans and dried black beans from various stores, and even my black tepary beans from SeedRenaissance, with no luck. When people do achieve blue, the color is reportedly quite unstable and fades to gray over time anyway. Still, I am ashamed (not too badly) to bring you this book with no blue from black beans. It wasn't for lack of trying!

CANNED BLACK BEANS

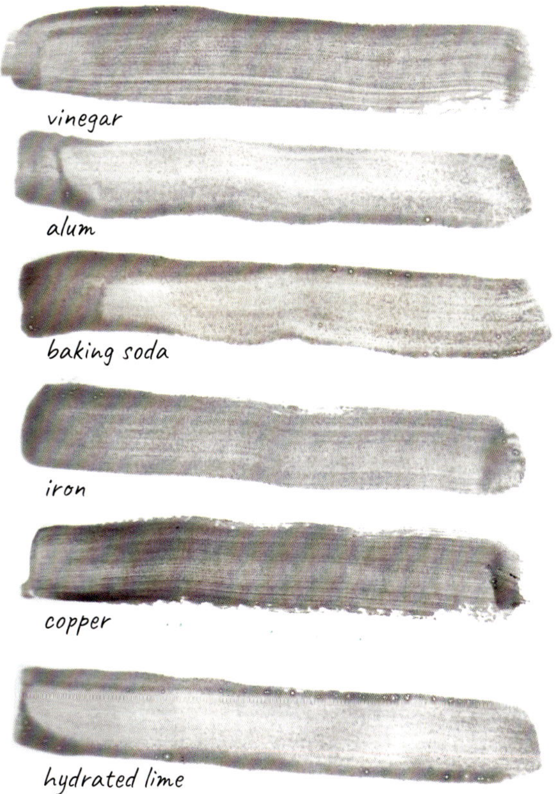

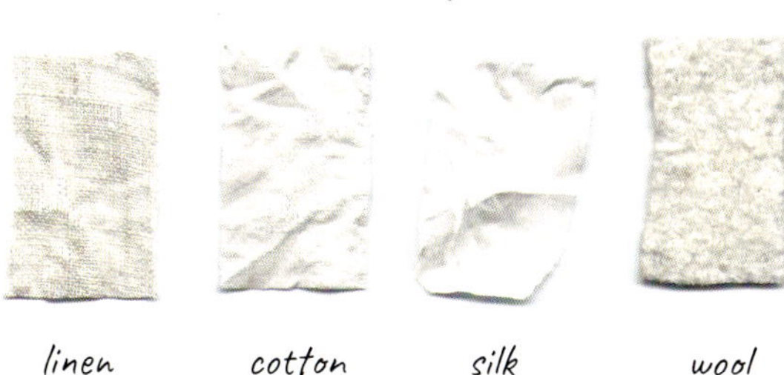

BLACK BEANS

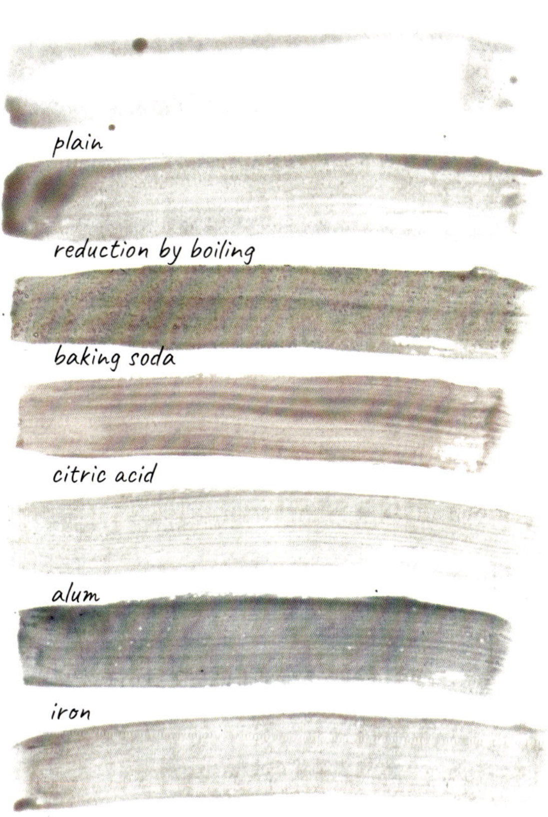

BETA VULGARIS

Beets

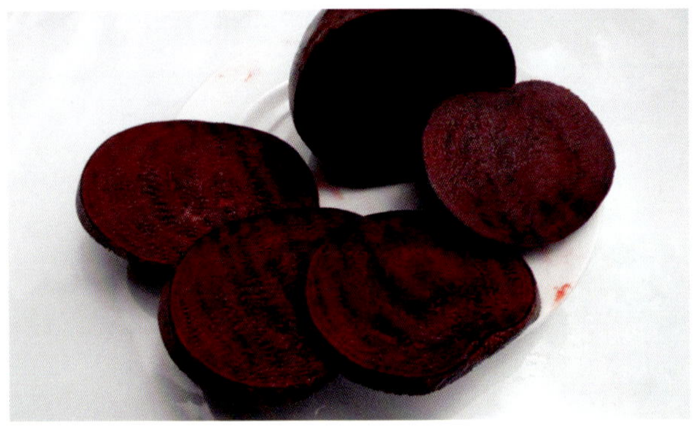

COLORS CREATED	red, pink, orange
PARTS USED FOR PIGMENT	root
PLANT TYPE	biennial
HARDINESS ZONE	2
SEEDING	Plant directly outside in spring. Seeds available at SeedRenaissance.com.

1. Chop root and add just enough water to cover. Boil at least 10 minutes, then strain out the beet root.
2. Intensify the color by reducing the liquid at a steaming, not boiling, temperature. Boiling can over process and permanently darken the color. Finished color can be made lighter or darker depending on amount of water and pigment mixed together. Orange is created by adding vinegar mordant. Pink is created by boiling the strained root a second time in new water.

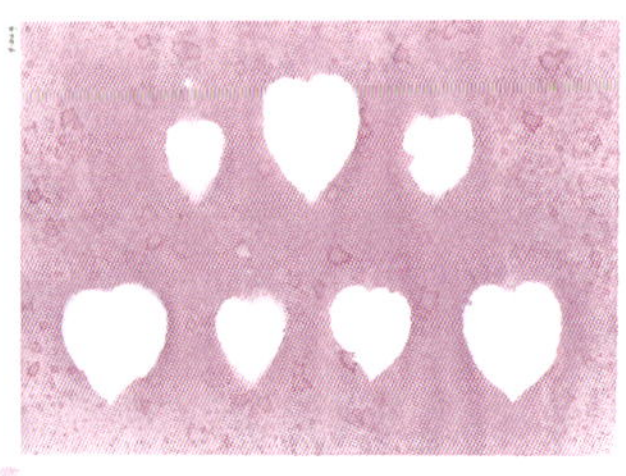

BEETROOT POWDER

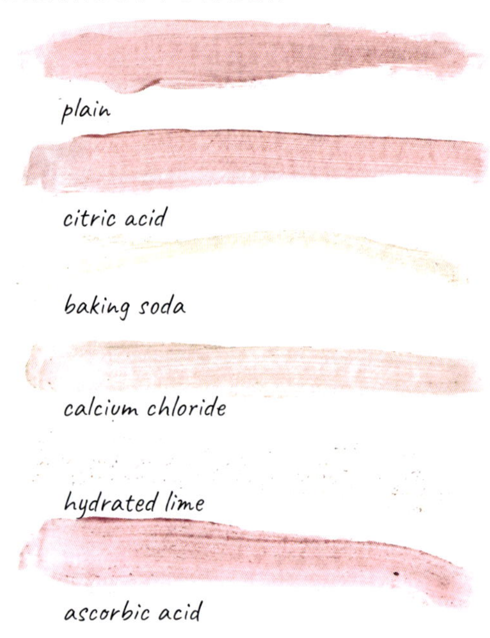

RED BEETROOT

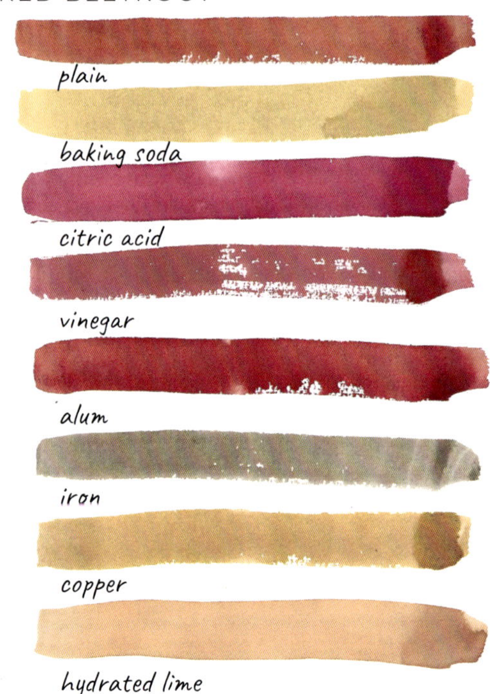

Begonia Species

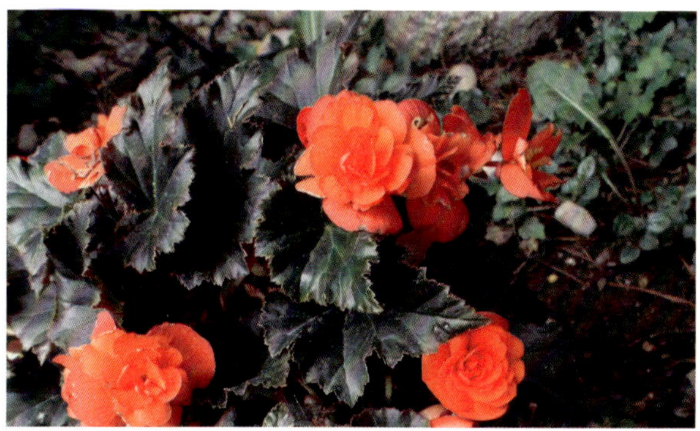

RED BEGONIA

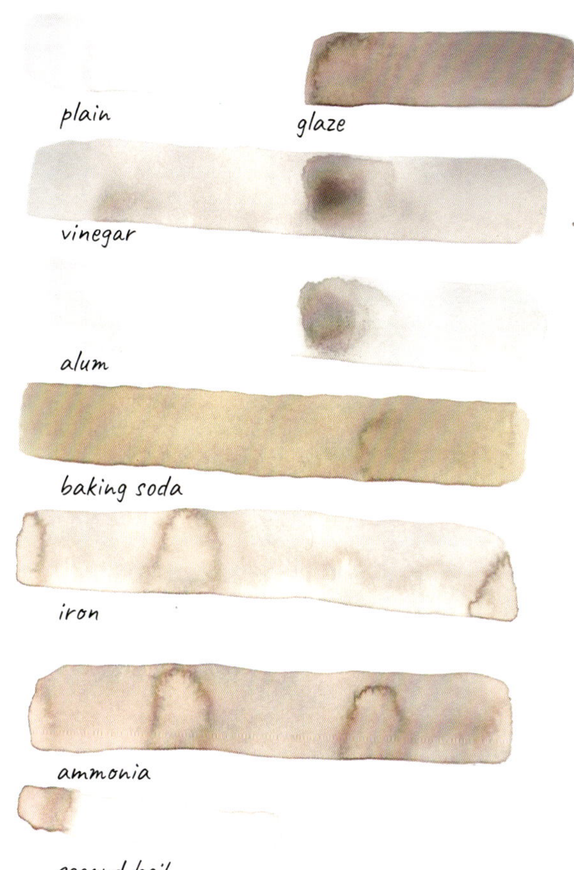

COLORS CREATED	muddy reds and browns
PARTS USED FOR PIGMENT	petals only (no sepals)
HARDINESS ZONE	9

1. Simmer for 10 minutes to make pigment or dye. Strain.
2. Simmer again to reduce liquid to desired color strength.

Notes: Disappointing colors from such show-off flowers. Boo!

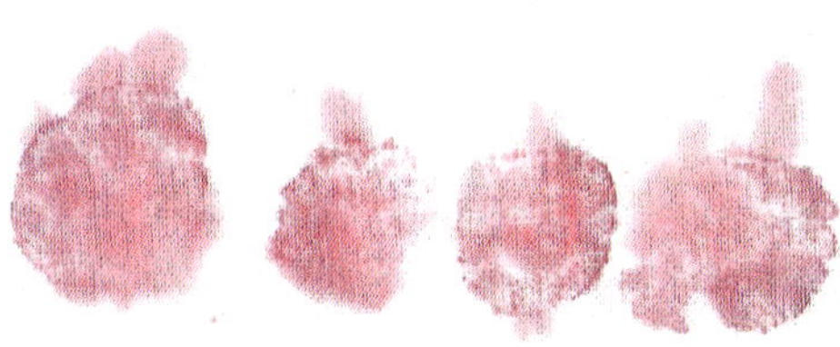

Bidens Species

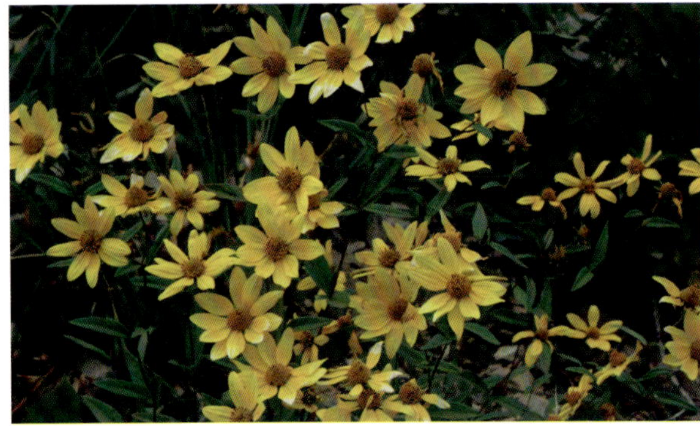

COLORS CREATED	grapefruit, pink, coral, red, yellow
PARTS USED FOR PIGMENT	yellow petals only (no sepals)
PLANT TYPE	annual

1. Simmer for 10 minutes to make pigment or dye. Strain.
2. Simmer again to reduce liquid to desired color strength.

Notes: There are many species of *Bidens* flower in the wild and domesticated for sale, and they probably all make these interesting colors. One of my students dyed her linen pants with bidens and they came out golden and almost shiny. Purple stem beggarticks appeared wild in one of my garden paths a few years ago and I was so excited, I've let it take over the path. They all make fun colors, fresh or cooked.

APACHE BEGGARTICKS

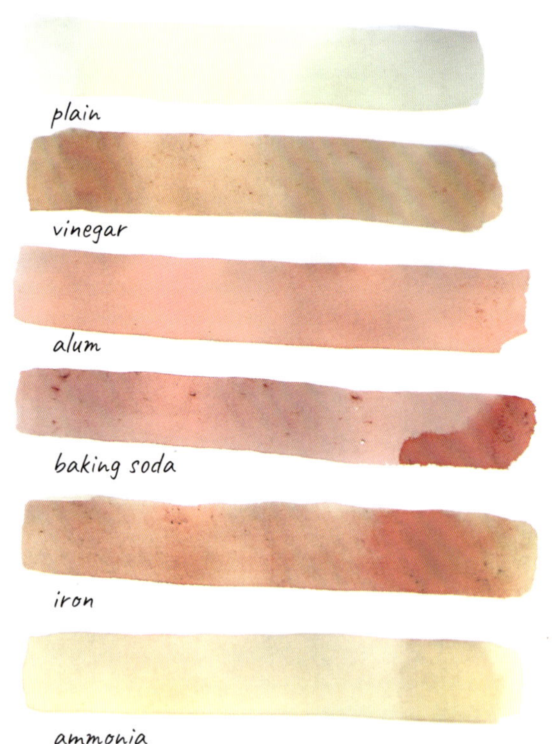

WILD BIDENS WHOLE FLOWERS

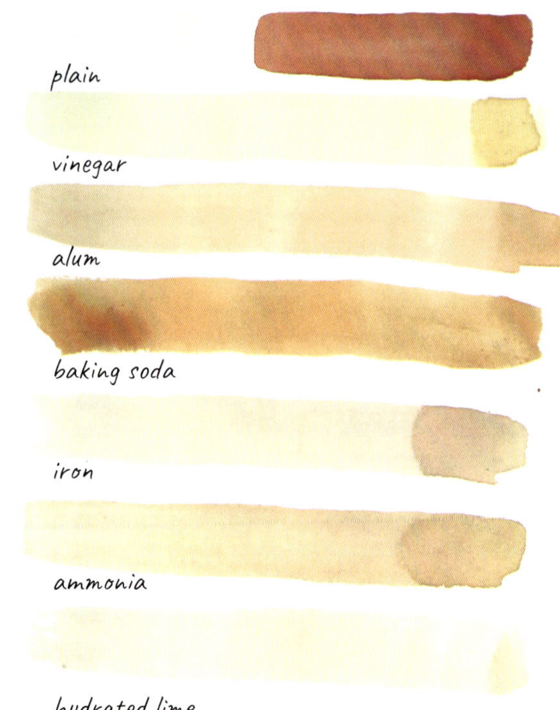

TICKSEED

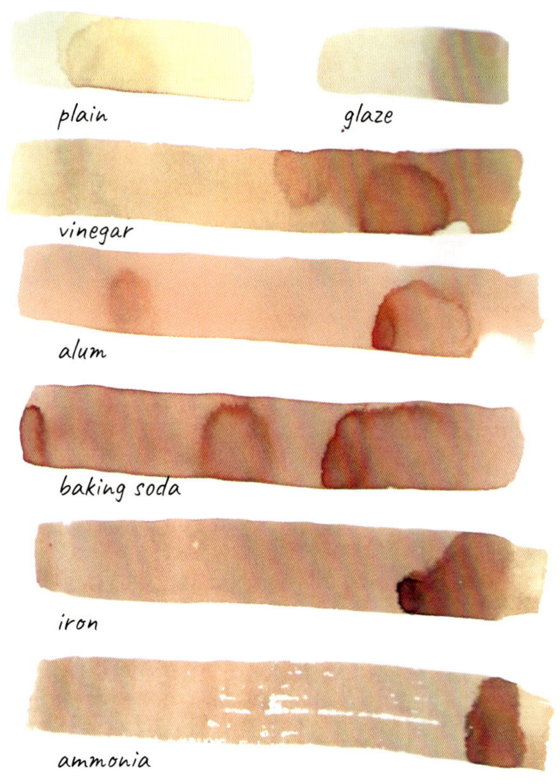

PURPLE STEM BEGGARTICKS

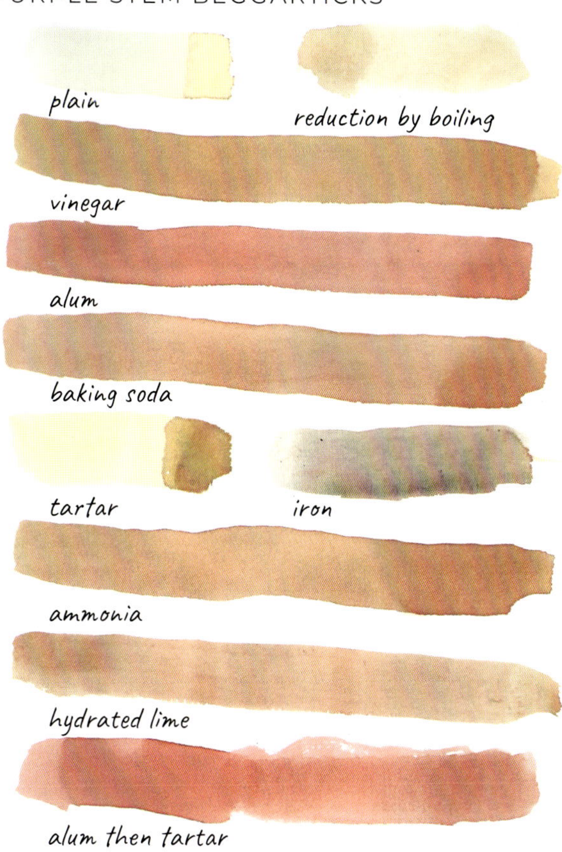

FRESH TICKSEED

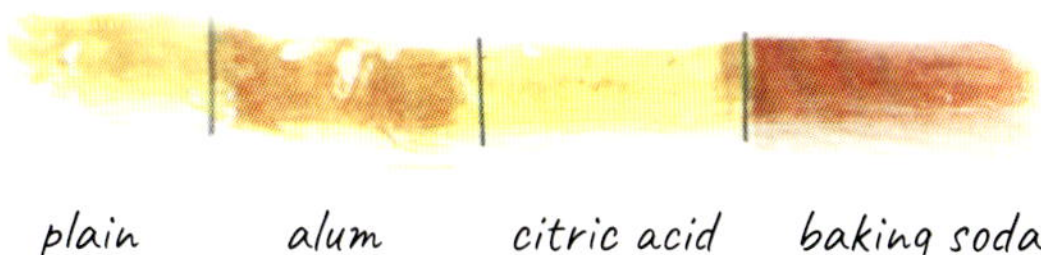

TICKSEED PAINT SAMPLES

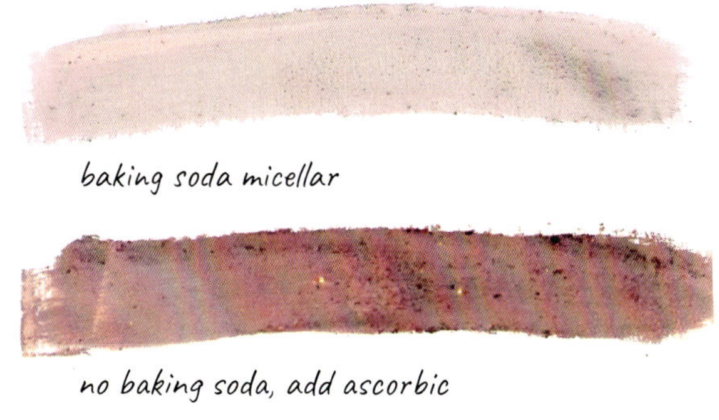

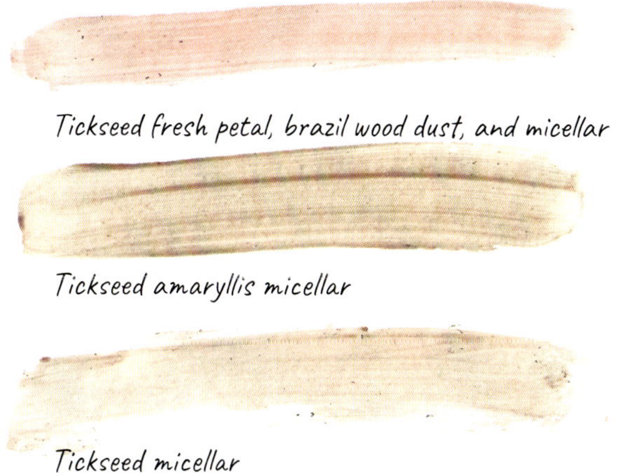

STRELITZIA REGINAE

Bird of Paradise

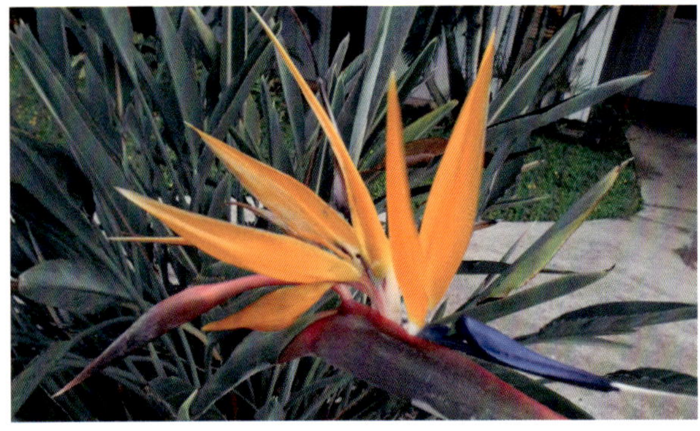

plain alum citric acid baking soda

COLORS CREATED	red, pink
PARTS USED FOR PIGMENT	orange sepal
PLANT TYPE	tropical

1. Best used as fresh petals.

Notes: Unfortunately, my tests of the blue portions of the flower failed to give any color, even with mordants. The fresh orange petals give orange pigment, but it is destroyed if cooked.

RUDBECKIA SPECIES

Black-Eyed Susan

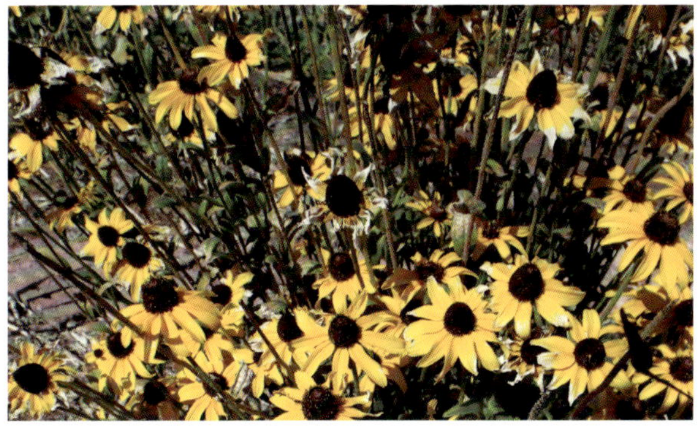

PETALS ONLY

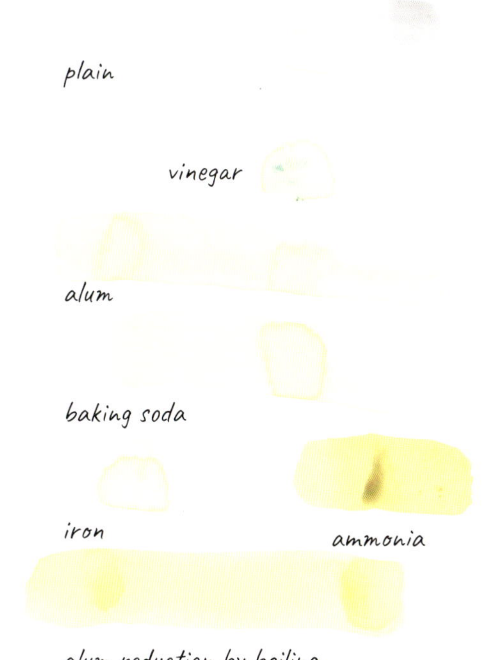

COLORS CREATED	yellow and green with alum, brown with baking soda
PARTS USED FOR PIGMENT	whole flower head to make green; yellow petals only to make yellow
PLANT TYPE	perennial
HARDINESS ZONE	3
SEEDING	Seeds available at SeedRenaissance.com.

1. Simmer for 15 minutes to make pigment or dye. Strain.
2. Simmer again to reduce liquid to desired color strength.

WHOLE HEAD

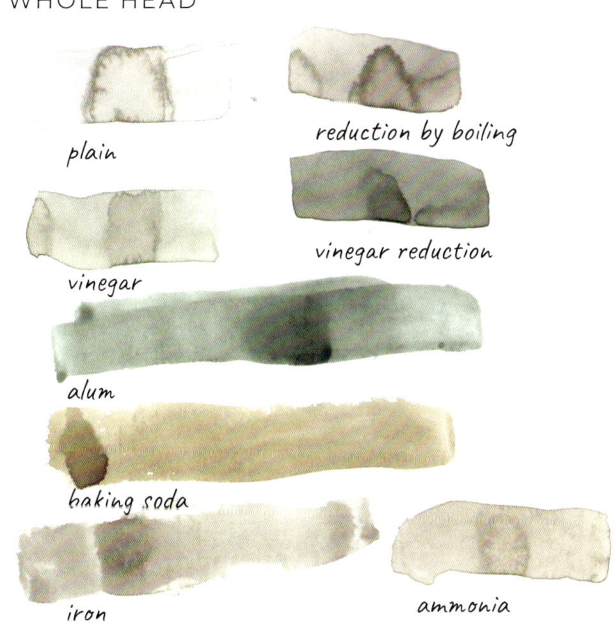

RUBUS ALLEGHANIENSIS

Blackberries

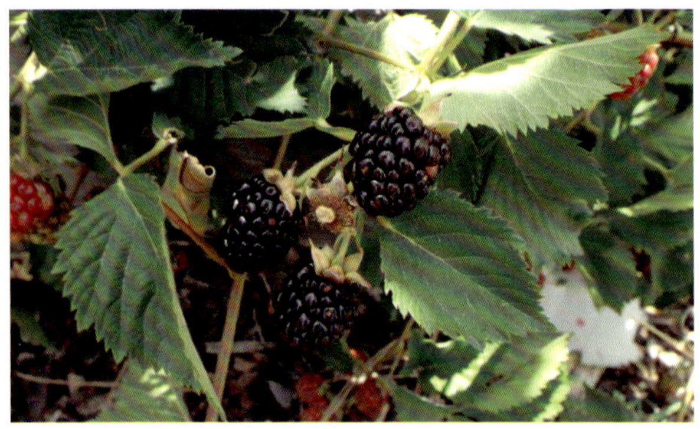

COLORS CREATED	blue, green, red, purple, pink, yellow
PARTS USED FOR PIGMENT	ripe berries
PLANT TYPE	perennial
HARDINESS ZONE	4

1. Mash the berries somewhat with a fork in water and simmer for at least 5 minutes. Blackberry color responds well to mordants.

Notes: Blackberry paint that is too thick will become sticky from the natural sugars. This paint is best used as a wash. Live plants shipped from SeedRenaissance.com in spring.

PLAIN BLACKBERRY

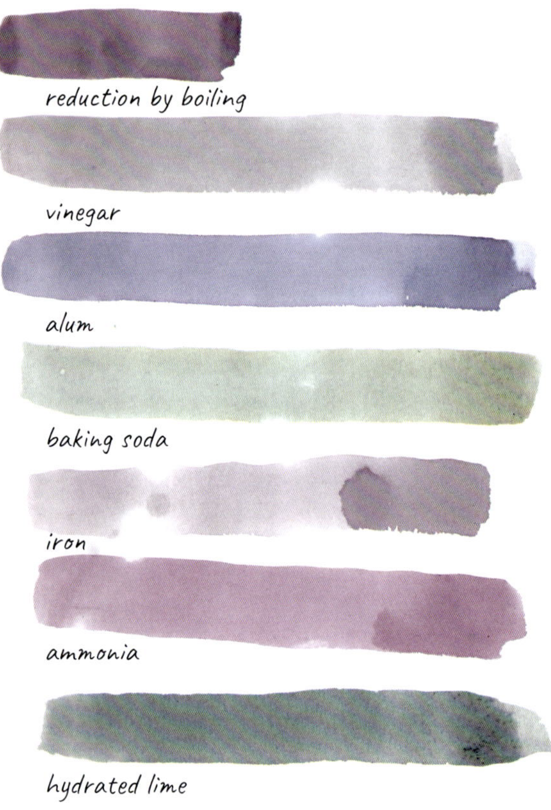

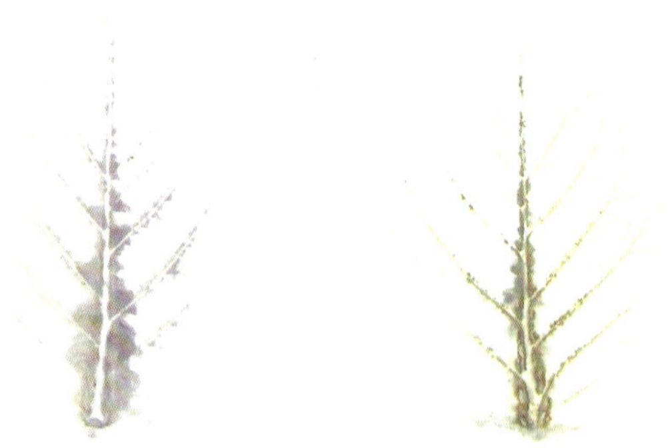

BLACKBERRY WITH GUM ARABIC

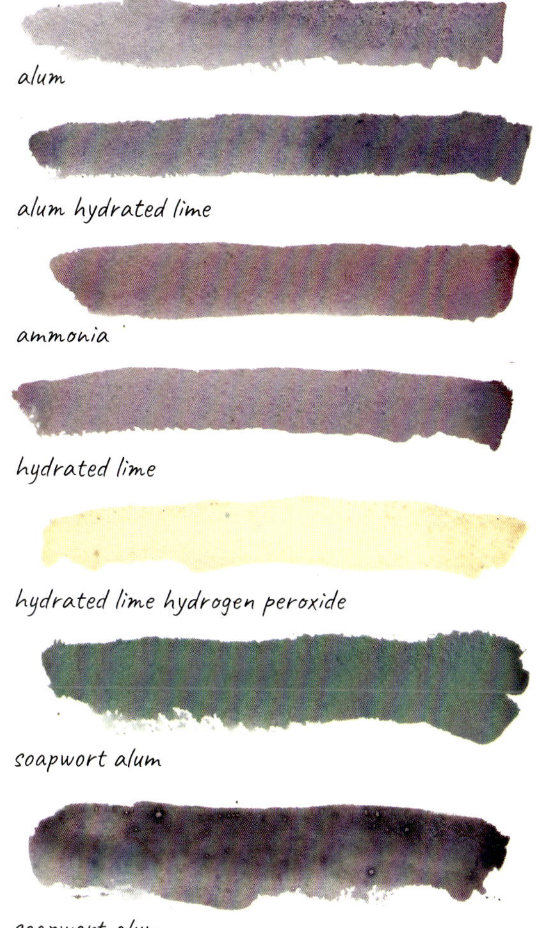

FRESH PRESSED BLACKBERRY JUICE

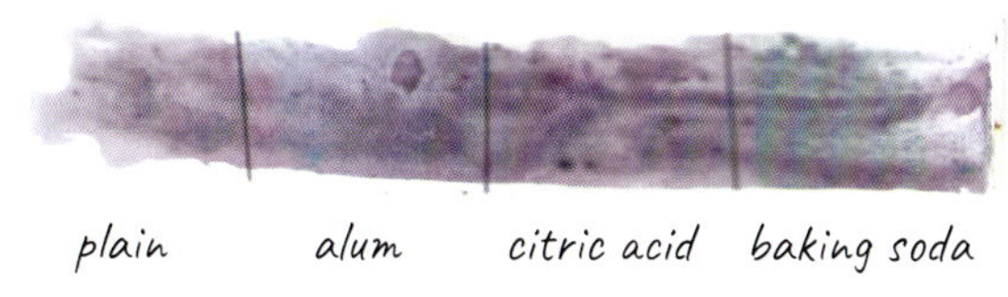

BLACKBERRY WITH EGG AND LINSEED OIL

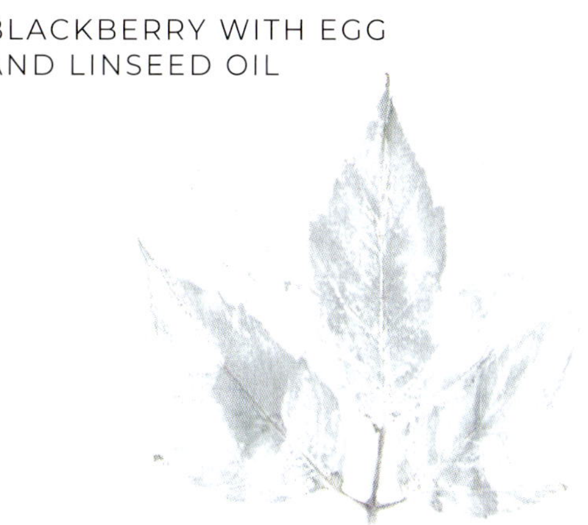

VACCINIUM SPECIES

Blueberries

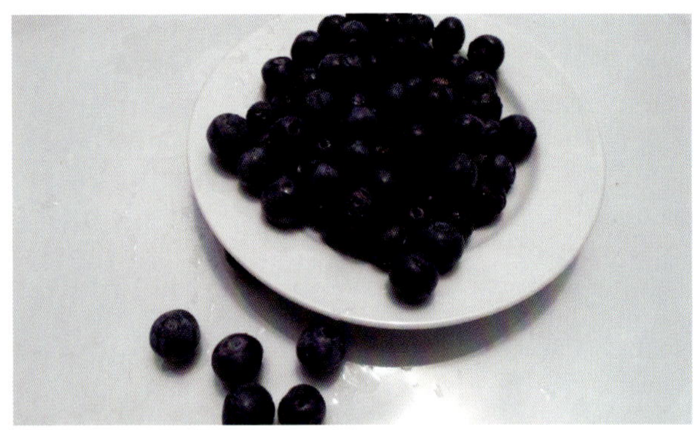

COLORS CREATED	blue
PARTS USED FOR PIGMENT	berries
PLANT TYPE	cultivated berry
HARDINESS ZONE	varies widely by cultivar

1. The skins of the fresh, uncooked berries made blue, and also when mordanted with alum, citric acid, and baking soda. Citric acid seemed to make a slightly darker shade. Berries, because of their natural sugar content, create a paint that is sticky even months or years after being dried, and thus do not make good art colors but are great for children's finger paints.

Notes: Requires acidic soil to produce berries.

BLUEBERRY SKIN

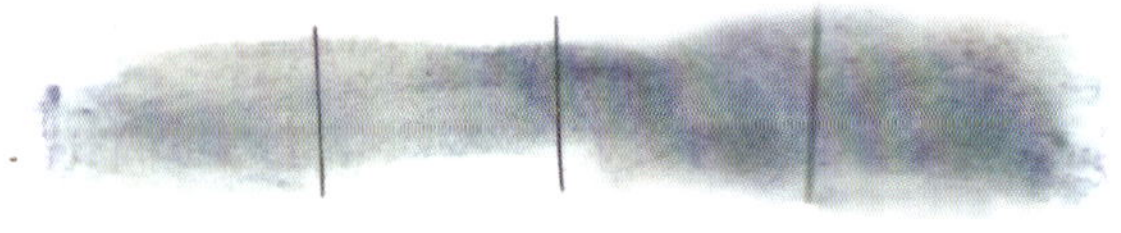

plain *alum* *citric acid* *baking soda*

FRESH MULLED UNCOOKED

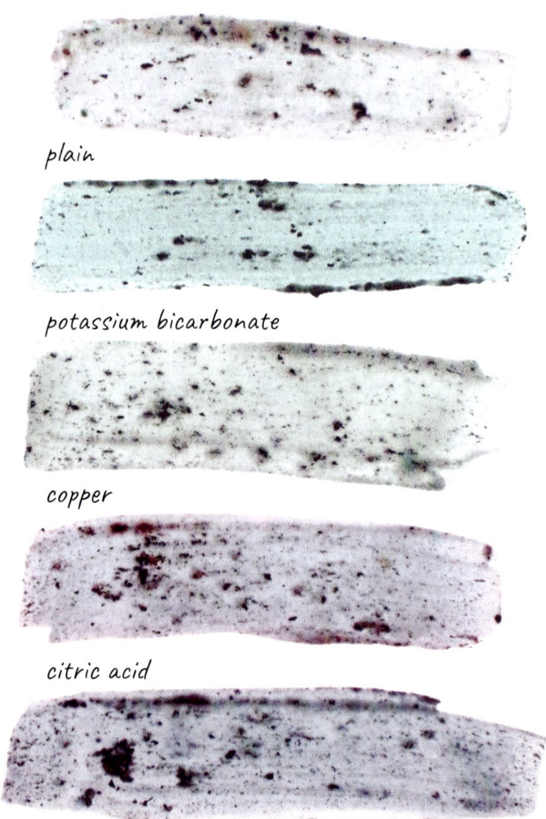

FORSYTHIA × INTERMEDIA

Border Forsythia

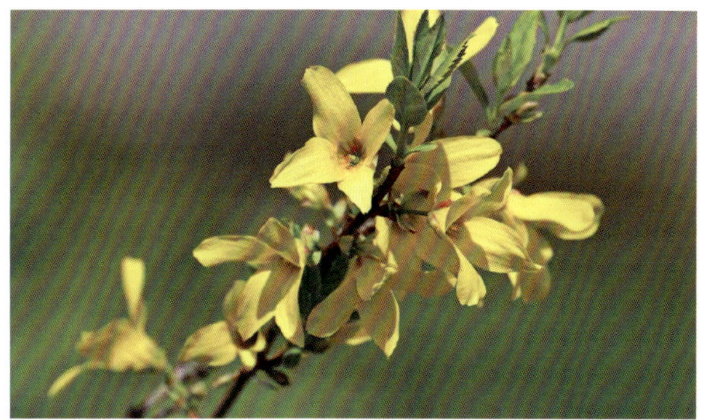

COLORS CREATED	yellow with most mordants
PARTS USED FOR PIGMENT	yellow flowers
PLANT TYPE	perennial tall bush
HARDINESS ZONE	4

1. Simmer for 10 minutes to make pigment or dye. Strain.
2. Simmer again to reduce liquid to desired color strength. Cooking too long will dull the colors.

Notes: A showy spring bloomer.

FRESH FLOWERS

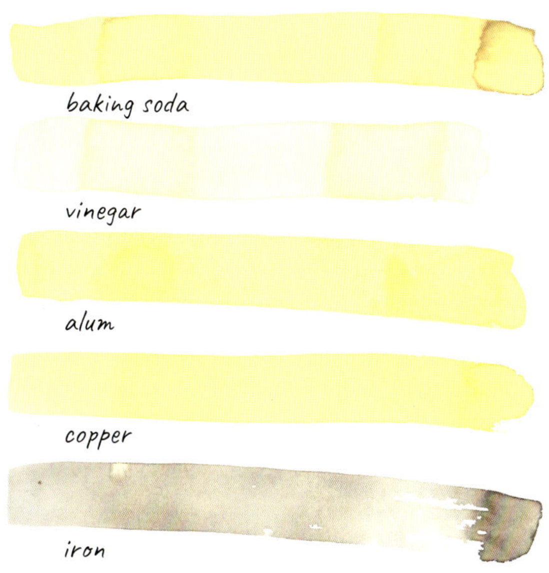

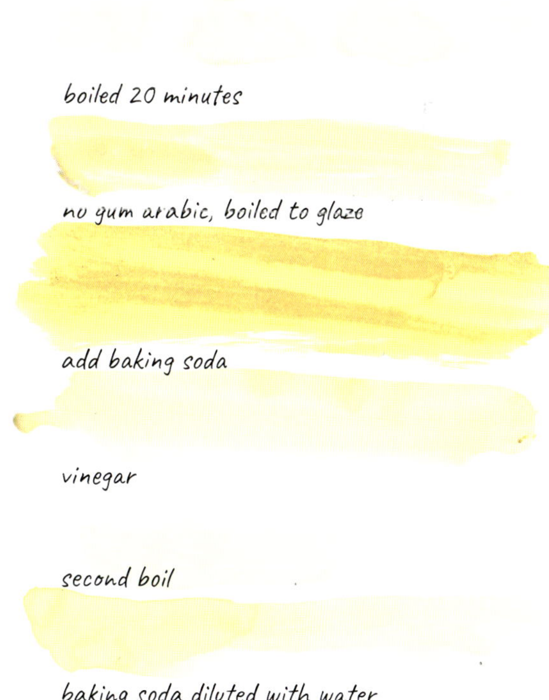

CALLISTEMON SPECIES

Bottlebrush

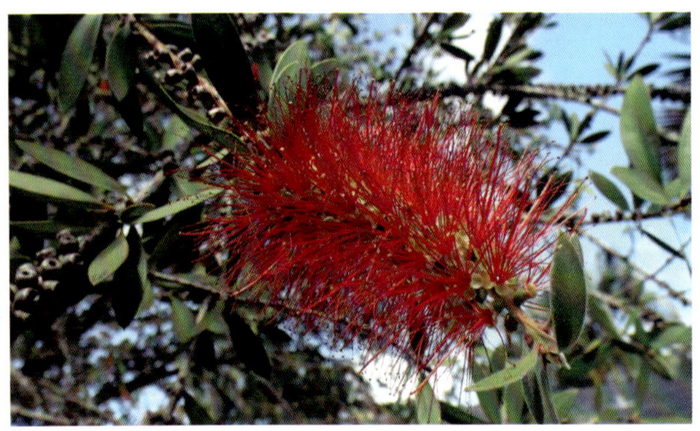

COLORS CREATED	purple, lavender, and blue with baking soda
PARTS USED FOR PIGMENT	red flowers
PLANT TYPE	tree
HARDINESS ZONE	tropical

1. Mull or press the fresh red flowers of some species. Boiling, more or less, destroys the colors.

Notes: On some species, the flowers are sticky.

FRESH MULLED RED PETALS

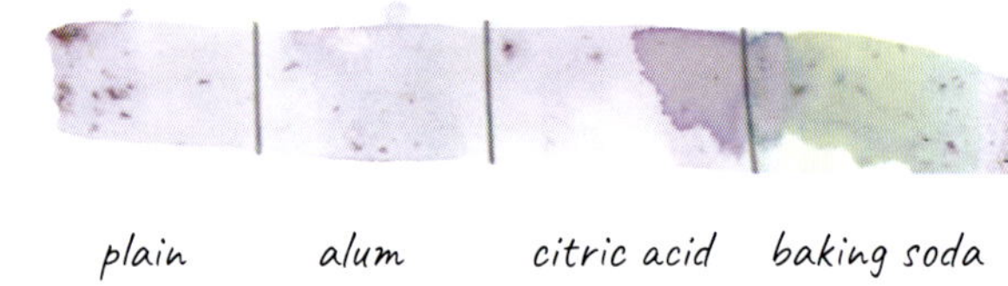

plain alum citric acid baking soda

BOILED RED PETALS

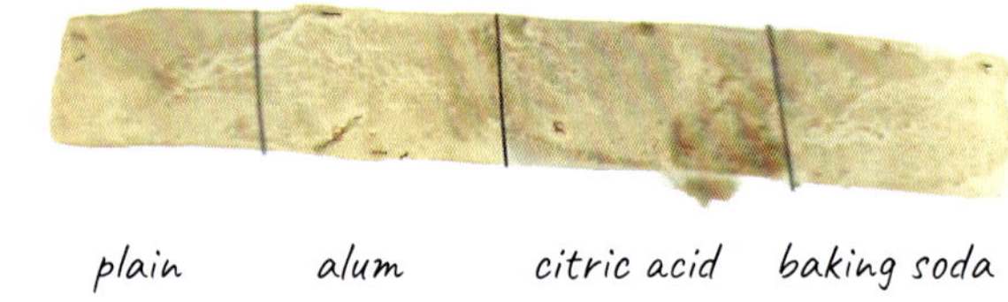

plain alum citric acid baking soda

SPOON-PRESSED FRESH RED PETALS

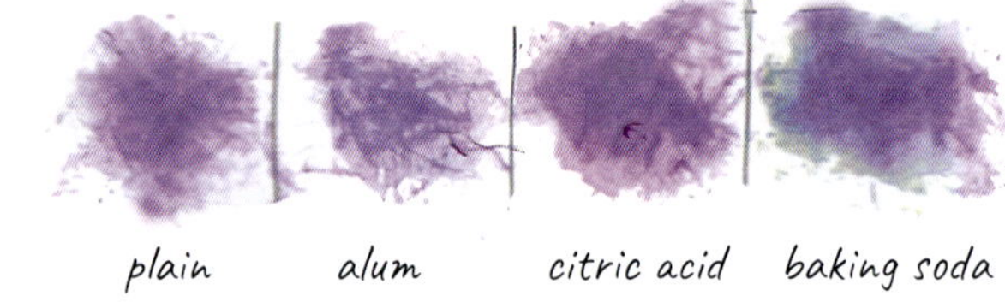

plain alum citric acid baking soda

RED PETALS OF STICKY FLOWER SPECIES

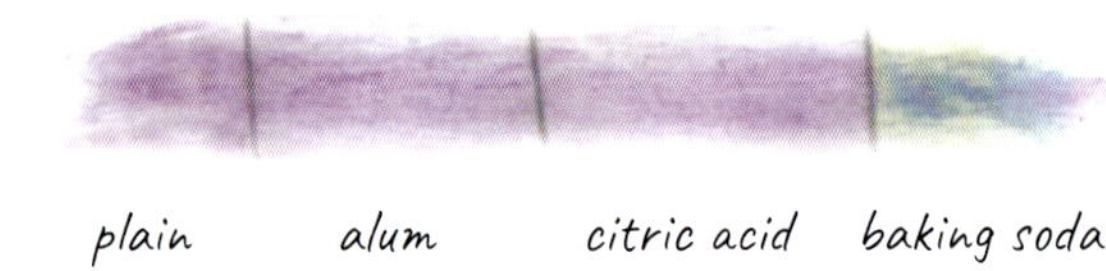

plain alum citric acid baking soda

Bougainvillea Species

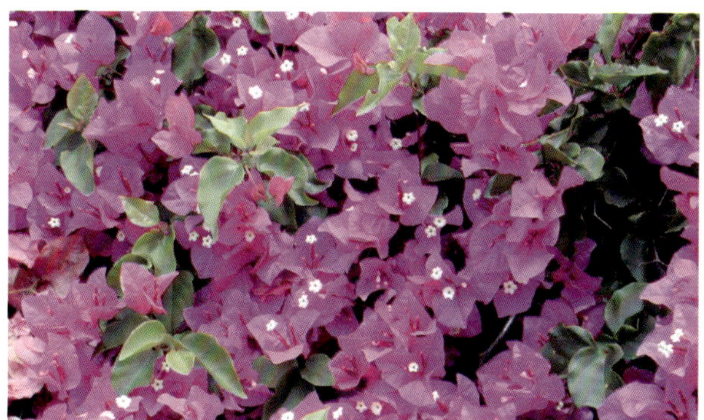

BOILED PUPRLE BOUGAINVILLEA

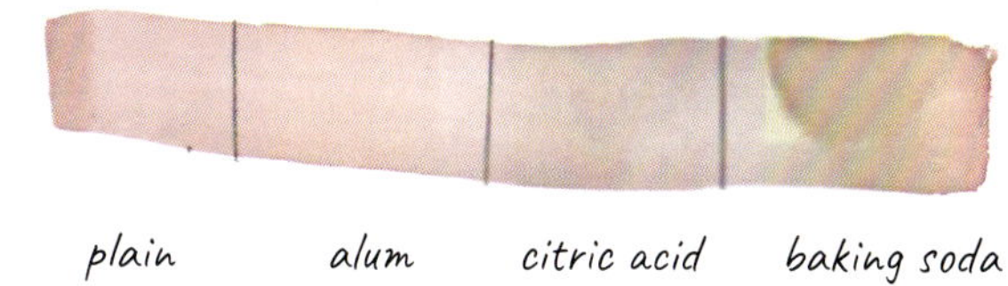

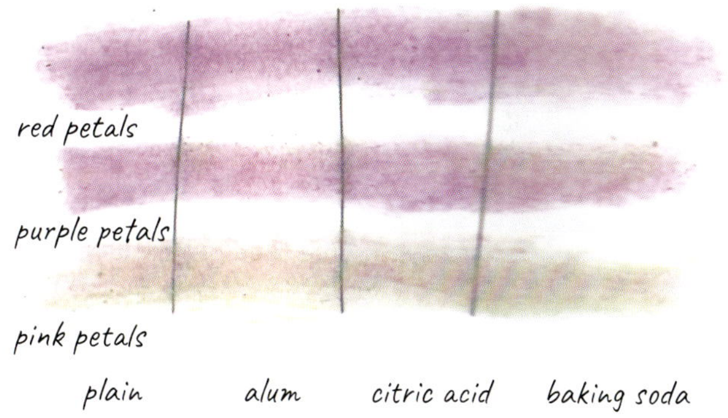

COLORS CREATED	red, violet
PARTS USED FOR PIGMENT	flowers
PLANT TYPE	perennial
HARDINESS ZONE	9

1. Purple flowers make red when cooked for 10 minutes. Red or purple petals make violet when used fresh for pigment.

RUBUS URSINUS OR RUBUS IDAEUS

Boysenberry

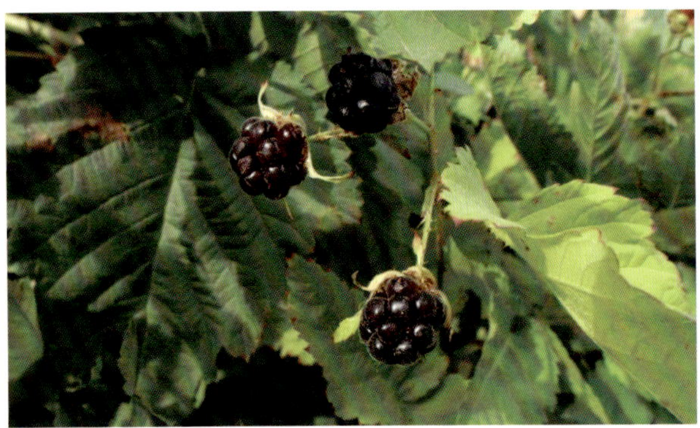

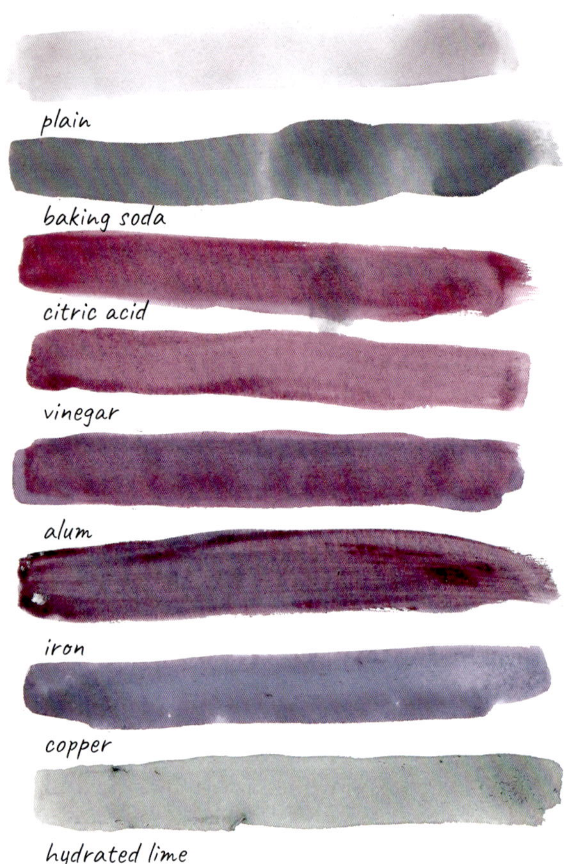

COLORS CREATED	red with citric acid, vinegar, alum, or iron; blue with vinegar of copper; beautiful grays with baking soda or lime; purple with fresh uncooked berries
PARTS USED FOR PIGMENT	ripe berries
PLANT TYPE	cultivated berry with very long vines
HARDINESS ZONE	5
GROWING	Live plants available at SeedRenaissance.com in spring.

1. Simmer for 10 minutes to make pigment or dye. Strain.
2. Simmer again to reduce liquid to desired color strength.

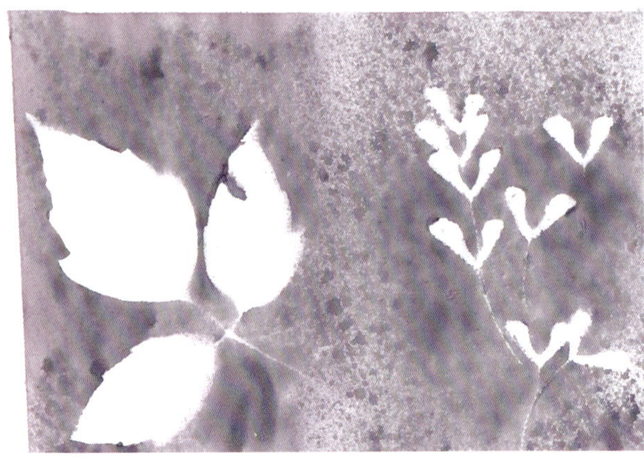

Boysenberry spray paint applied over leaves to form a negative image

PAUBRASILIA ECHINATA

Brazilwood

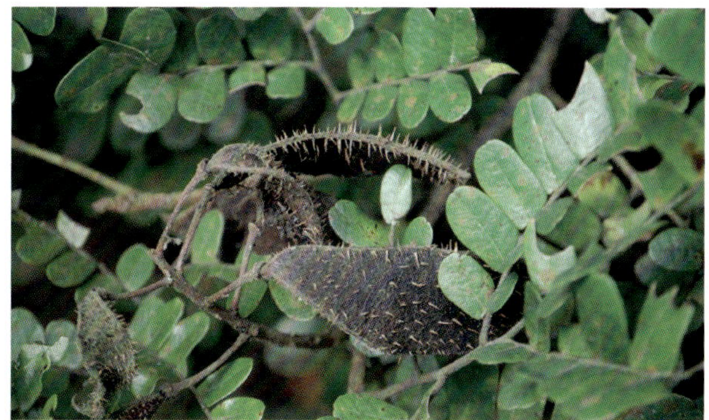

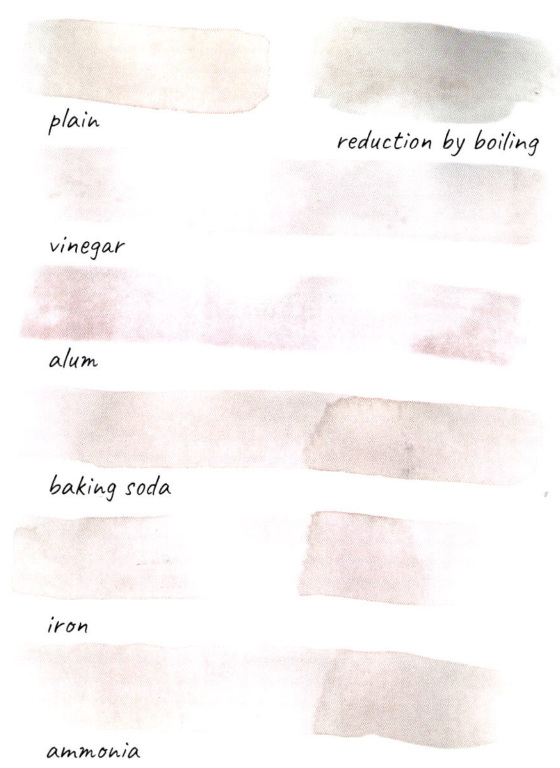

COLORS CREATED	pink when cooked, red when uncooked
PARTS USED FOR PIGMENT	powdered wood
PLANT TYPE	tree

1. Simmer for 10 minutes to make pigment or dye. Strain.
2. Simmer again to reduce liquid to desired color strength.

Notes: The more powder you use, the darker the color. Brazilwood is best mordanted with chalk or eggshell (calcium carbonate) to increase both the saturation and the lightfastness.

EPHEDRA NEVADENSIS

Brigham Tea

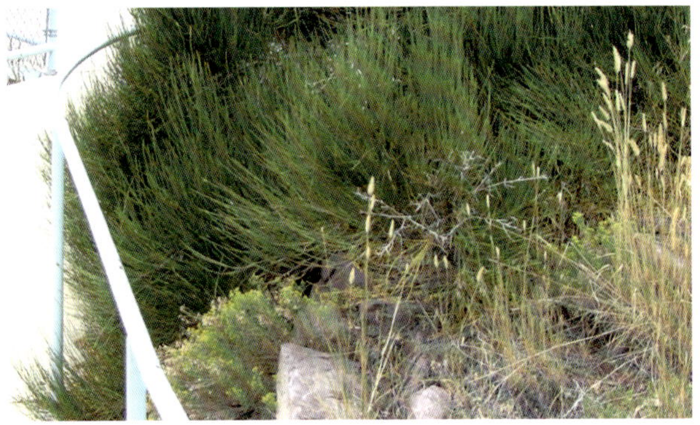

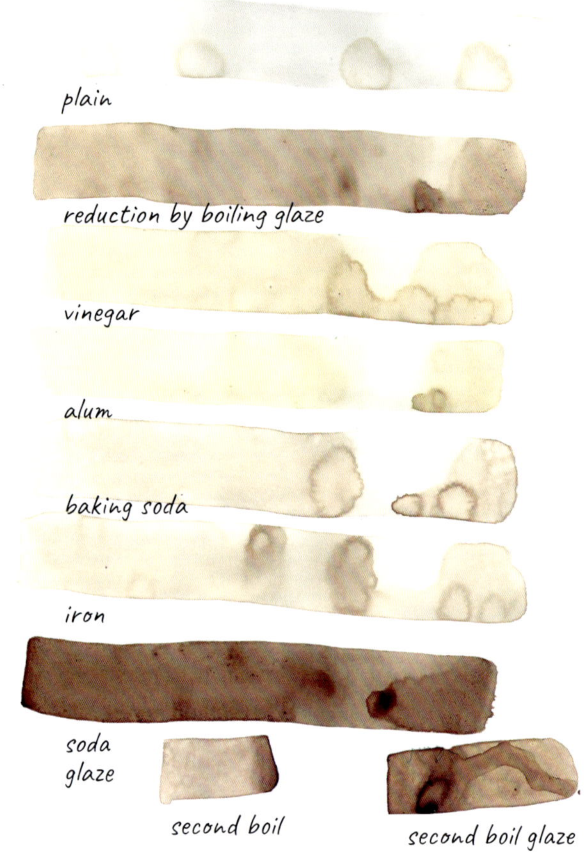

COLORS CREATED	brown with baking soda
PARTS USED FOR PIGMENT	stems, fresh or dried
PLANT TYPE	perennial
HARDINESS ZONE	6
SEEDING	Start indoors. Seeds available at SeedRenaissance.com.

1. Simmer for an hour to make pigment or dye. Strain.
2. Simmer again to reduce liquid to desired color strength.

Notes: Brigham tea is an important medical herb.

ERIOGONUM SPECIES

Buckwheat

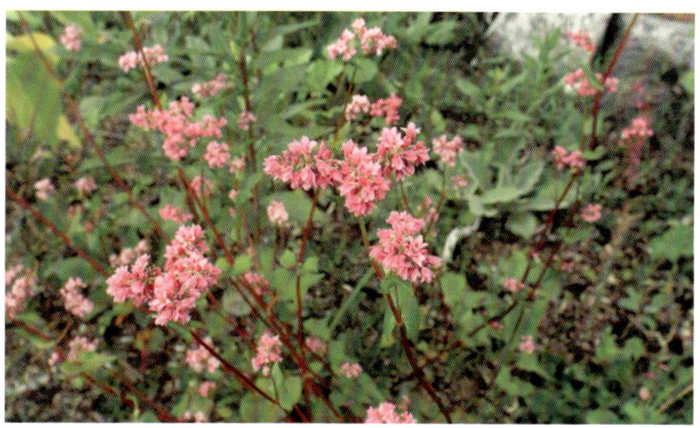

RED BUCKWEAT WILD FLOWERS

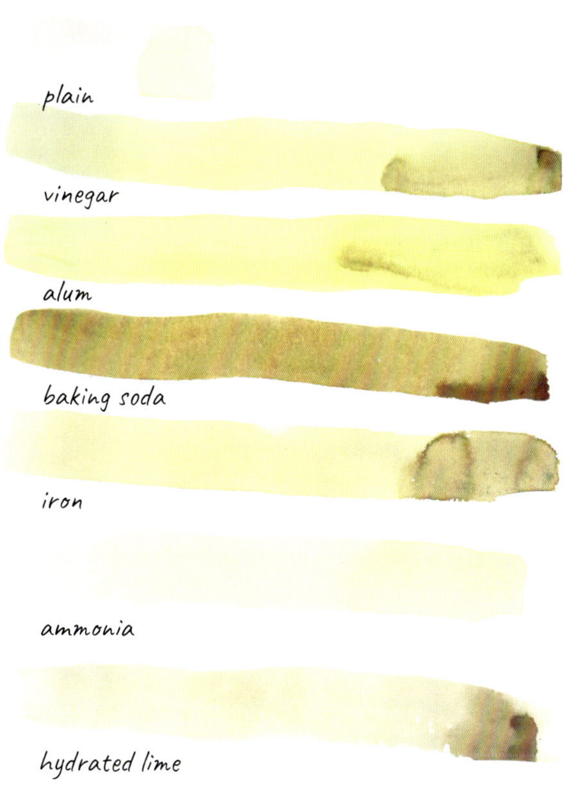

COLORS CREATED	yellow with alum, brown with baking soda
PARTS USED FOR PIGMENT	red flowers
PLANT TYPE	annual
GROWING	Seeds available at SeedRenaissance.com.

1. Simmer for 10 minutes to make pigment or dye. Strain.
2. Simmer again to reduce liquid to desired color strength.

RANUNCULUS SPECIES

Buttercups

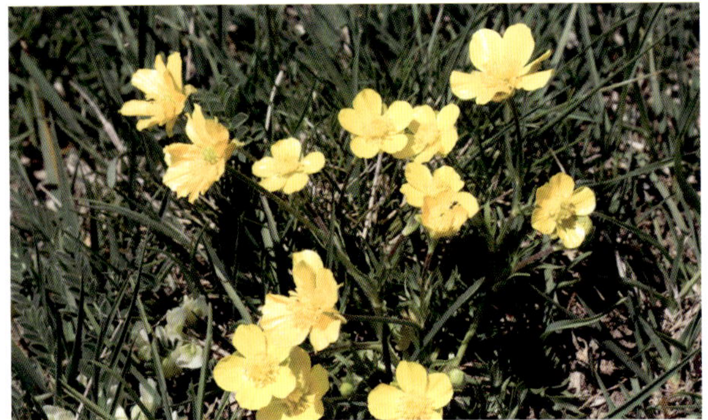

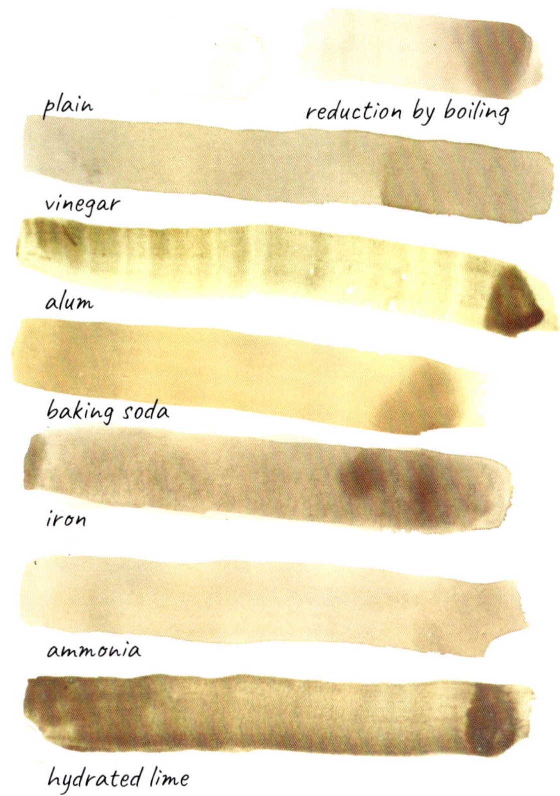

COLORS CREATED	brown
PARTS USED FOR PIGMENT	flowering stems
PLANT TYPE	bog-loving ground cover
HARDINESS ZONE	4
SEEDING	Plant directly outside in spring or autumn. Seeds available at SeedRenaissance.com.

1. Simmer for 15 minutes to make pigment or dye. Strain.
2. Simmer again to reduce liquid to desired color strength.

Notes: This plant spreads by rhizome and is invasive, but it does not spread where there is not a constant summer water supply.

BUDDLEIA DAVIDII

Butterfly Bush

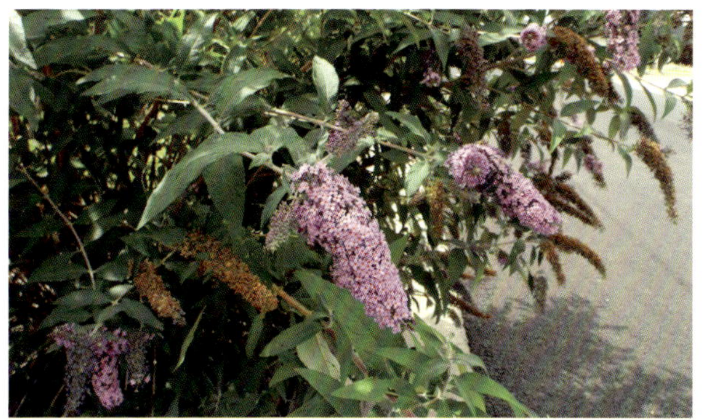

COLORS CREATED	yellow
PARTS USED FOR PIGMENT	purple flowering spikes
PLANT TYPE	perennial bush
HARDINESS ZONE	5

1. Simmer for 10 minutes to make pigment or dye. Strain.
2. Simmer again to reduce liquid to desired color strength.

BUTTERFLY BUSH FLOWERS

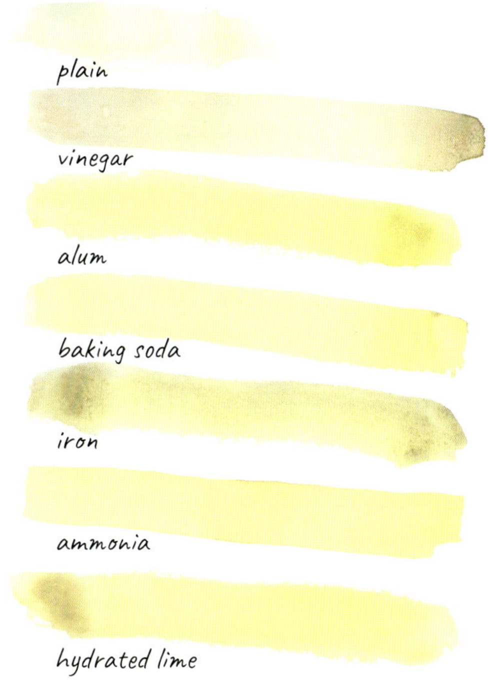

PURPLE BUTTERFLY BUSH NO LEAVES

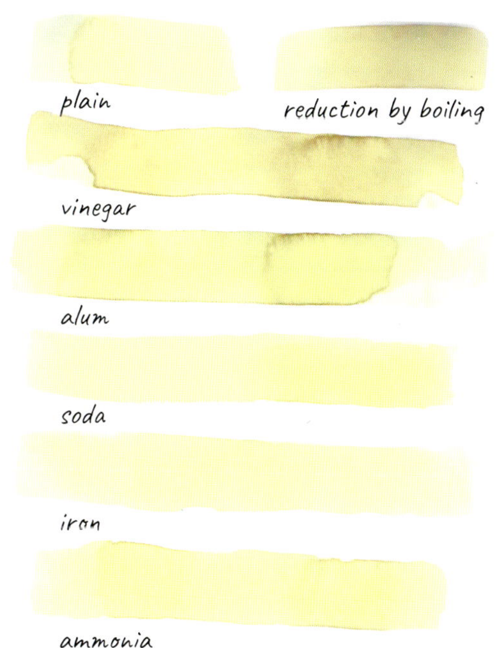

BRASSICA OLERACEA

Cabbage

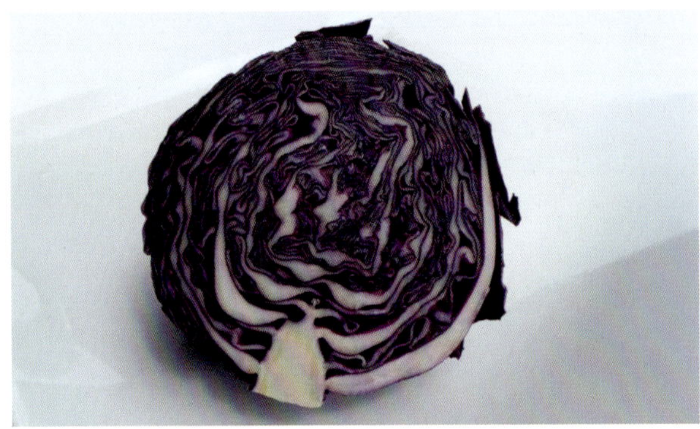

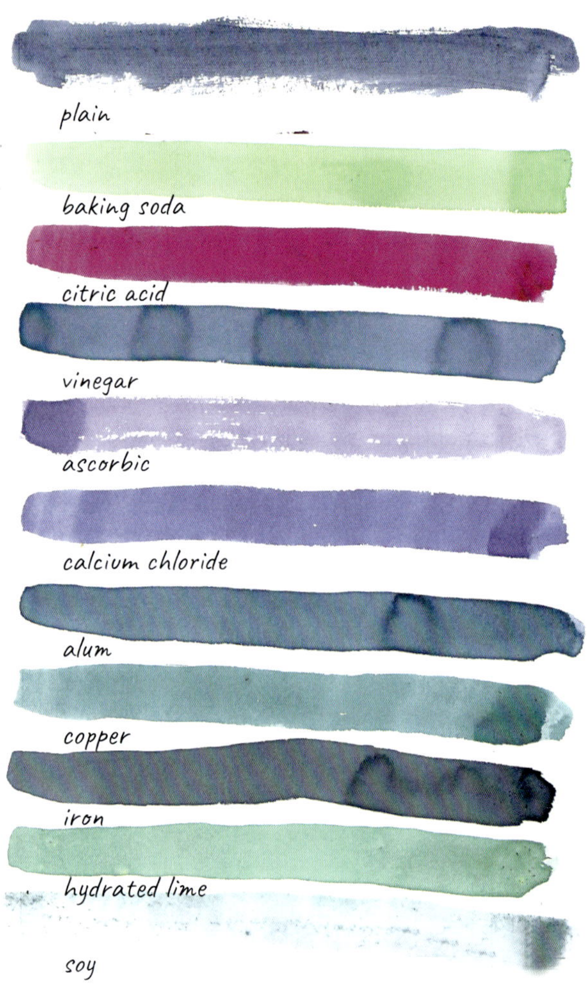

COLORS CREATED	blue, pink, red, green, purple, turquoise
PARTS USED FOR PIGMENT	leaves of purple cabbage
PLANT TYPE	biennial
HARDINESS ZONE	1
SEEDING	Plant directly outside in spring or start indoors. Seeds available at SeedRenaissance.com.

1. Simmer for 10 minutes to make pigment or dye. Strain.
2. Simmer again to reduce liquid to desired color strength. Purple cabbage responds well to mordants.

Notes: Paint will smell like cabbage, but the smell goes away totally when dried. Makes extraordinary colors that are fun to paint with.

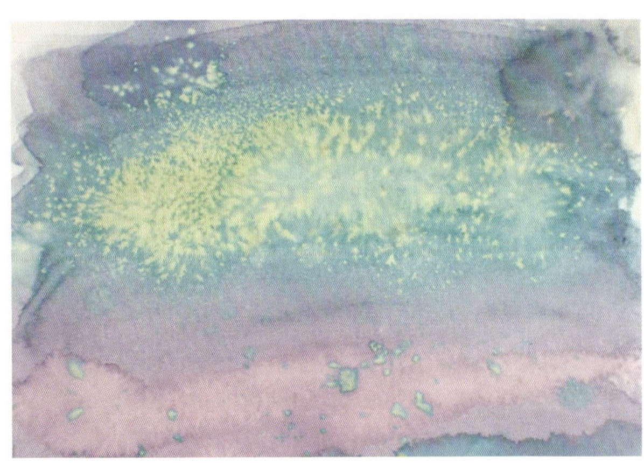

CACTACEAE SPECIES

Cactus

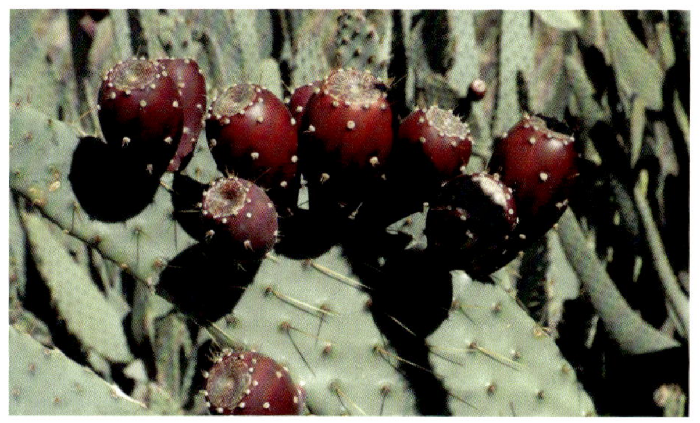

COLORS CREATED	red, brown
PARTS USED FOR PIGMENT	red fruit
PLANT TYPE	various cactus species
HARDINESS ZONE	varies by species

1. Simmer for 15 minutes to make pigment or dye. Strain.
2. Simmer again to reduce liquid to desired color strength.

Notes: Careful! I got cactus needles in my legs, arms, and fingers—which took days to pick out—when harvesting the fruit from wild cactus in the desert, but it was almost worth it because of the colors.

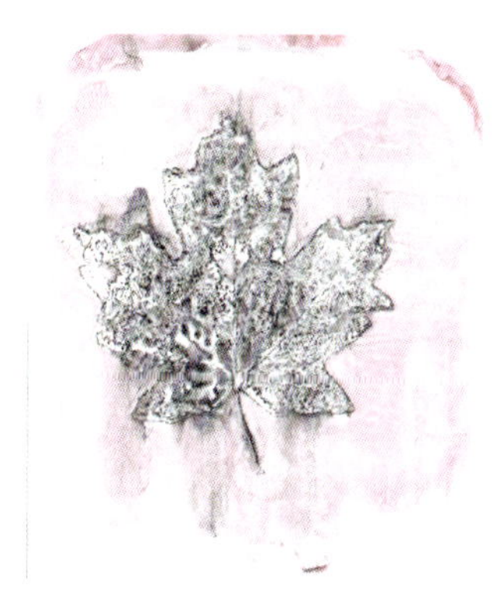

RED CACTUS FRUIT

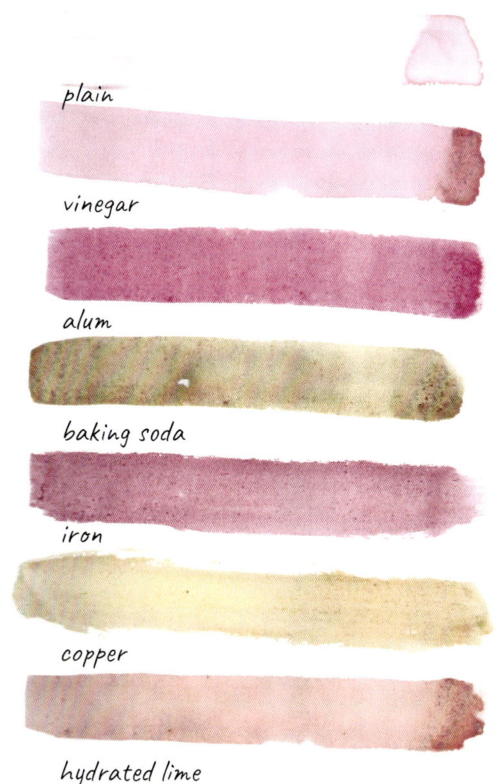

RED CACTUS FRUIT

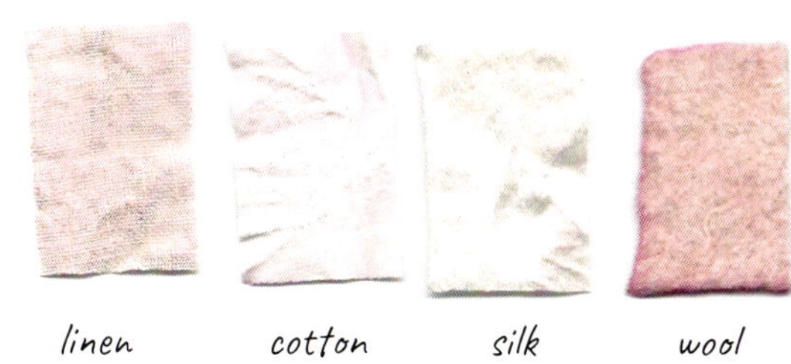

RED CACTUS ALUM ON ALUM ACETATE

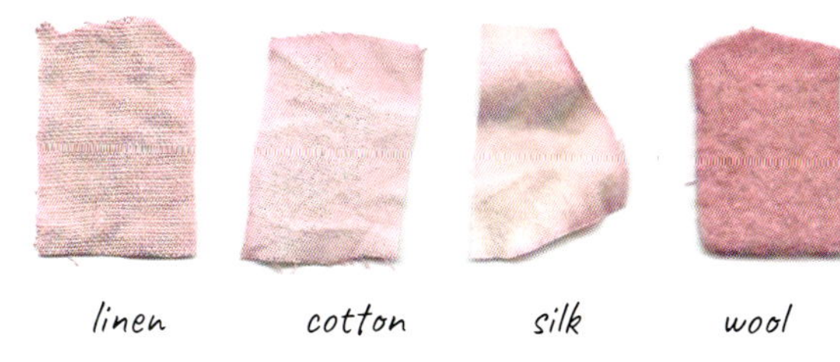

Calandrinia Species

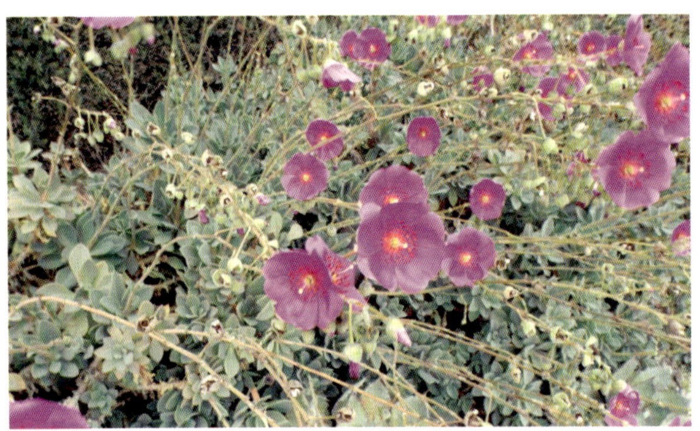

FRESH PRESSED GRANDIFLORA

COLORS CREATED	purple
PARTS USED FOR PIGMENT	fresh red petals
PLANT TYPE	landscape flower
HARDINESS ZONE	8

1. Using the fresh petals for pigment makes vibrant purples.

CALENDULA OFFICINALIS

Calendula

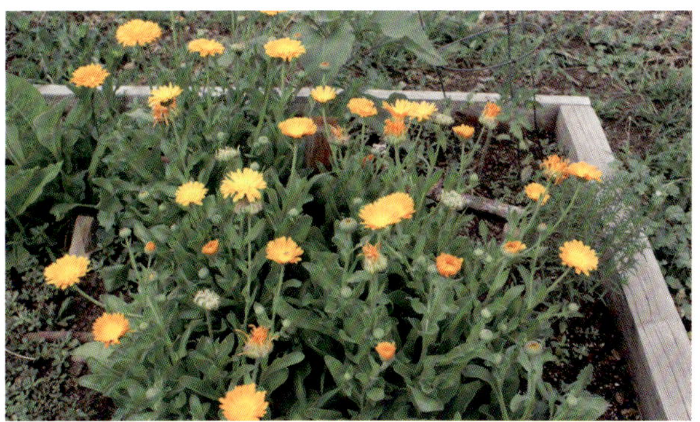

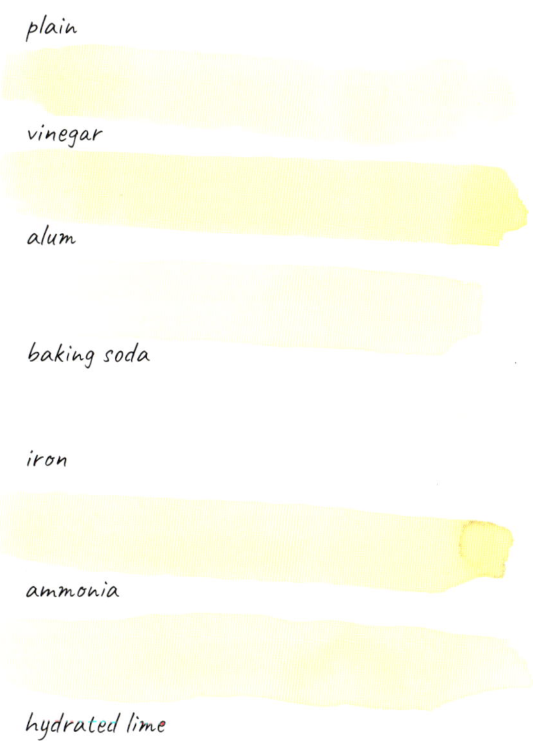

COLORS CREATED	yellow
PARTS USED FOR PIGMENT	petals only with no flower centers or sepals
PLANT TYPE	annual
SEEDING	Seeds available at SeedRenaissance.com.

1. Because calendula petals are high in resin, they must simmer for 30 minutes before they give off a good color. Alum creates the brightest yellow.

VERATRUM CALIFORNICUM

California False Hellebore

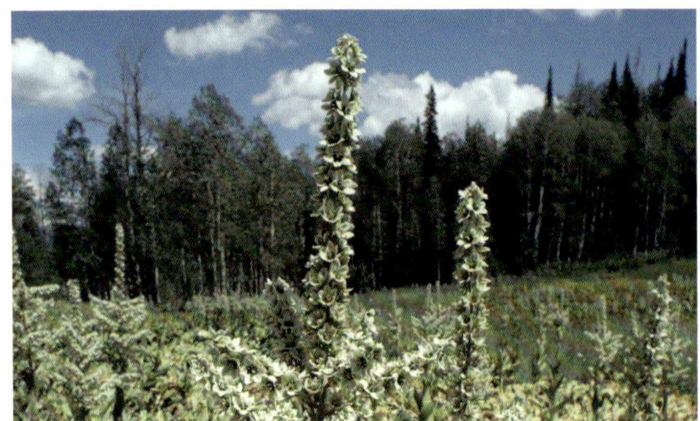

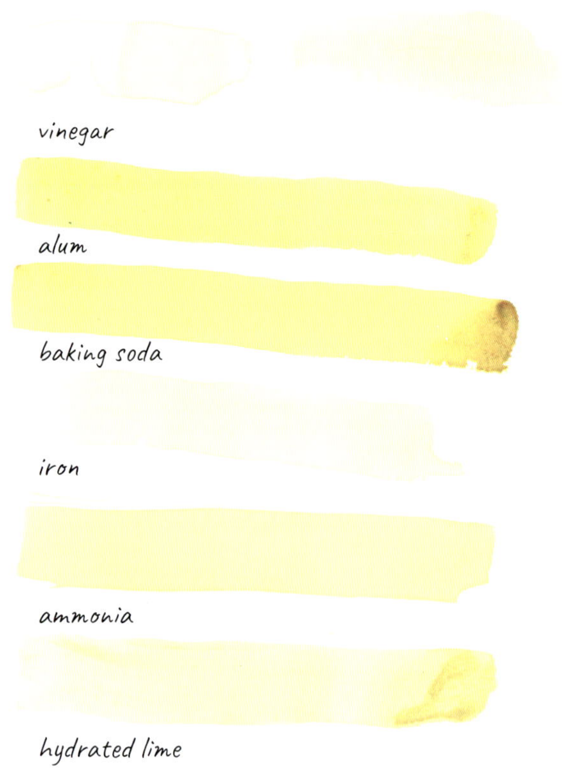

COLORS CREATED yellow

PARTS USED FOR PIGMENT flowering spikes

HARDINESS ZONE 4

1. Simmer for 15 minutes and reduce the liquid to create pale yellow. Alum or baking soda creates a strong neon yellow. Ammonia creates a strong matte yellow.

Notes: This plant is toxic and the roots are extremely poisonous. Don't eat it, of course. I've never had a problem handling it for dye purposes, but you should wear gloves.

CEANOTHUS SPECIES

California Lilacs

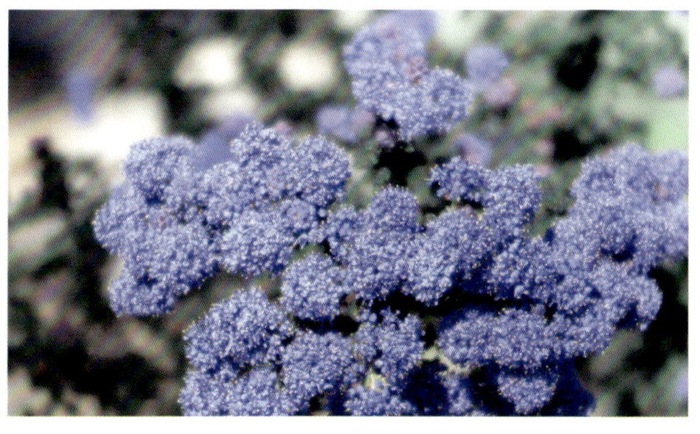

COLORS CREATED	blue when used fresh and uncooked
PARTS USED FOR PIGMENT	blue flowers
PLANT TYPE	small shrubs and trees
HARDINESS ZONE	7

1. Best used fresh for pigment and eco-prints. It is unlikely that the blue color survives being cooked.

Campanula Species

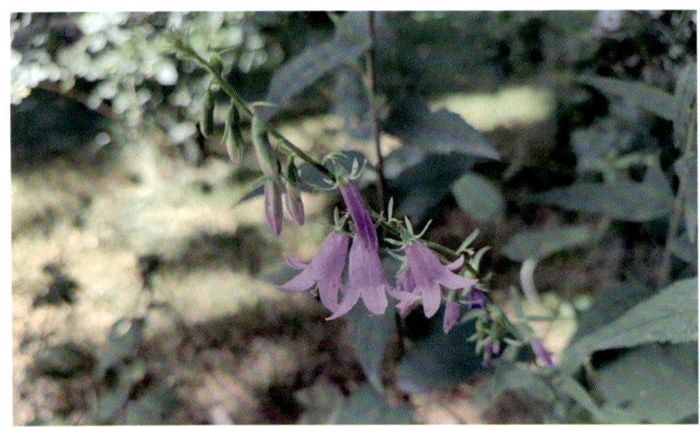

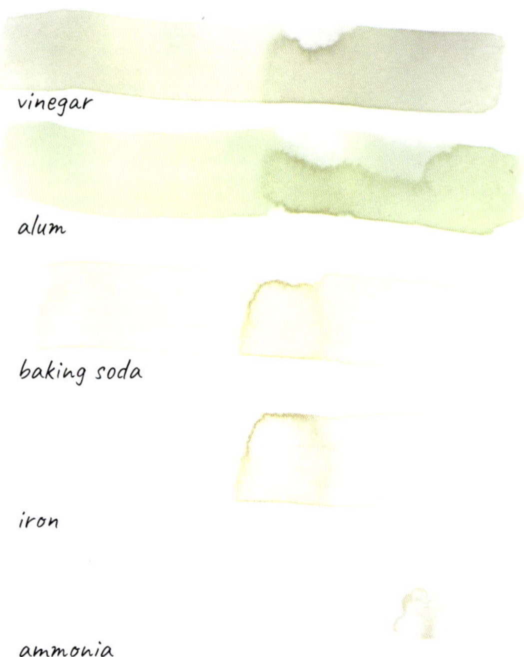

COLORS CREATED	green with alum
PARTS USED FOR PIGMENT	purple flower petals with no sepals
PLANT TYPE	perennial
HARDINESS ZONE	3

1. The plain color simmered for 10 minutes produces no usable color but then mordanting with alum creates green.

CANNA SPECIES

Canna Lily

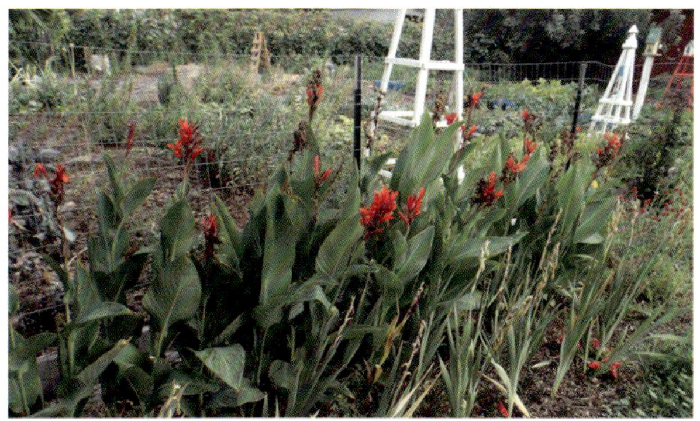

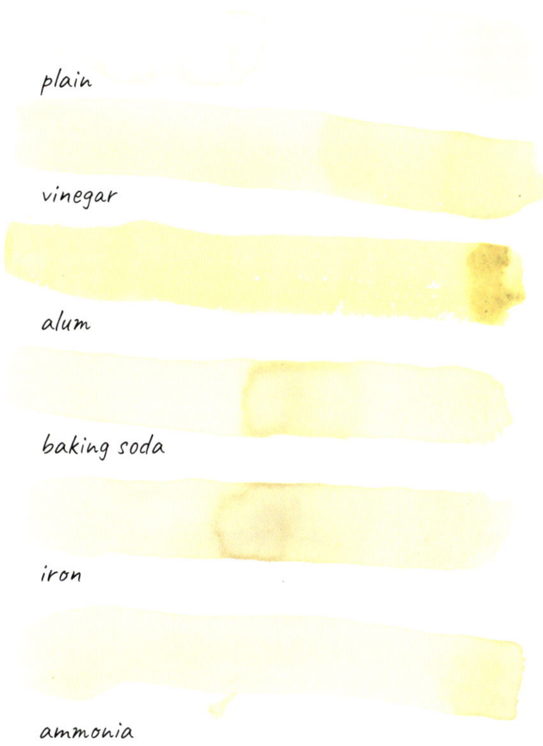

COLORS CREATED	bright yellow with alum
PARTS USED FOR PIGMENT	yellow petals
PLANT TYPE	perennial
HARDINESS ZONE	8

1. Simmer for 25 minutes to make pigment or dye. Strain.
2. Simmer again to reduce liquid to desired color strength.

DIANTHUS CARYOPHYLLUS

Carnation

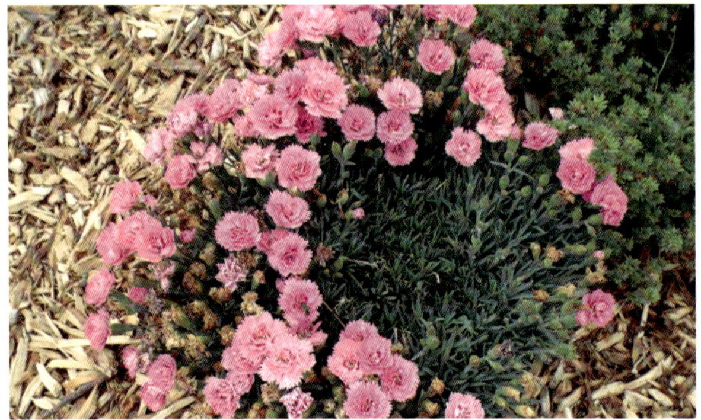

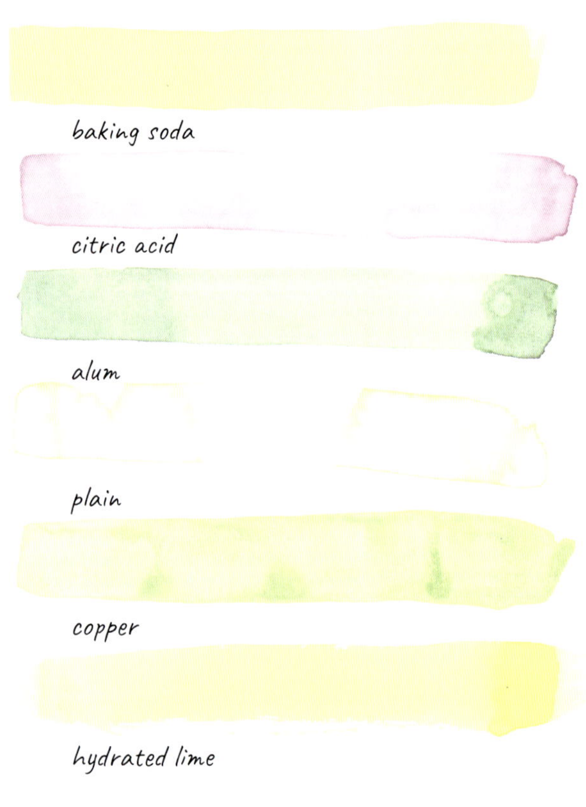

COLORS CREATED	pink with citric acid, green with alum or vinegar of copper, yellow with baking soda or hydrated lime
PARTS USED FOR PIGMENT	pink petals
PLANT TYPE	varies by species and cultivar
HARDINESS ZONE	varies by species and cultivar
SEEDING	Plant directly outside in spring or autumn. Seeds available at SeedRenaissance.com.

1. Simmer for 10 minutes to make pigment or dye. Strain.
2. Simmer again to reduce liquid to desired color strength.

Notes: When used fresh and uncooked, *Dianthus* also make strong colors, including purple, red, green, and gray. There are many cultivars and species of Dianthus, ranging from annuals to perennials to biennials and many hybrids too.

FRESH PRESSED PINK PETALS

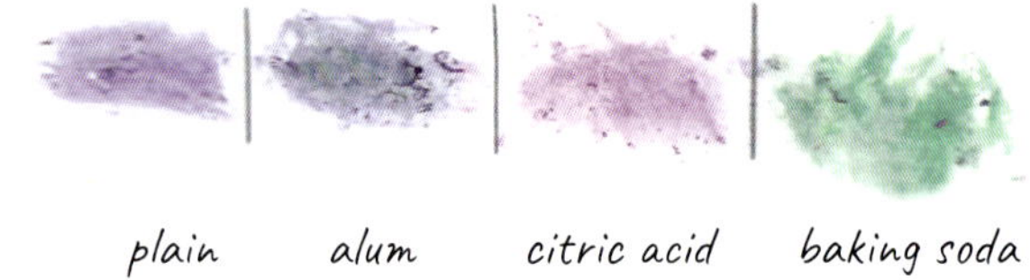

OCHNA SERRULATA

Carnival Bush

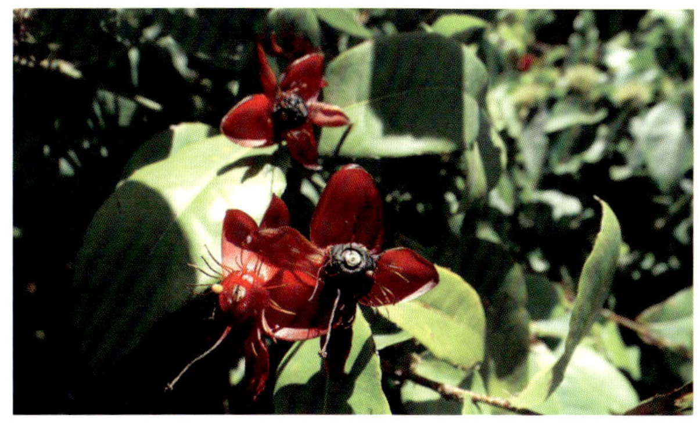

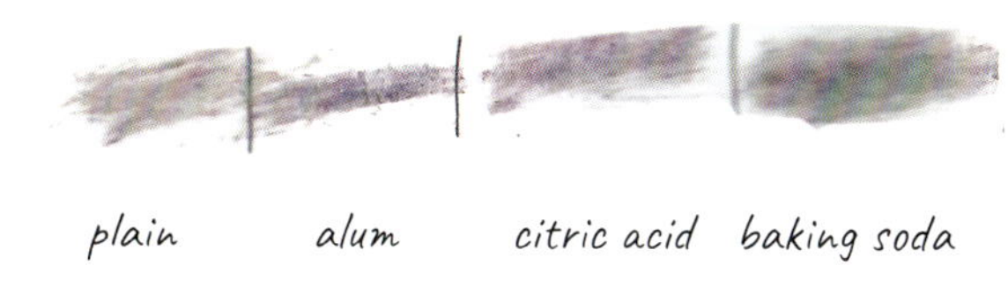

BOILED CARNIVAL BUSH

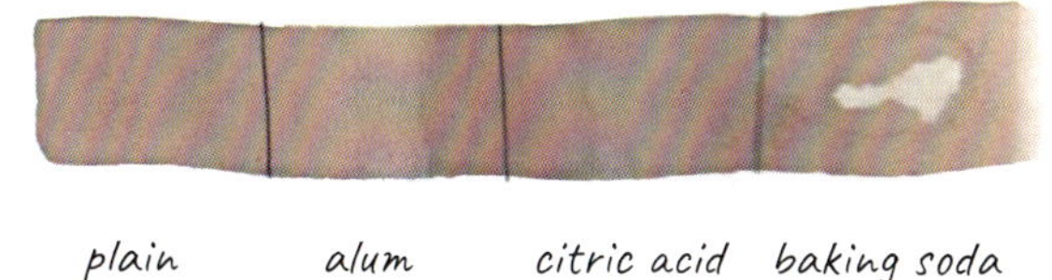

COLORS CREATED	red when cooked and purple when fresh, except with baking soda, which made green
PARTS USED FOR PIGMENT	red flowers
PLANT TYPE	flowering shrub
HARDINESS ZONE	9
SEEDING	Seeds available at SeedRenaissance.com.

1. Simmer for 10 minutes to make pigment or dye. Strain.
2. Simmer again to reduce liquid to desired color strength.

DAUCUS CAROTA

Carrot

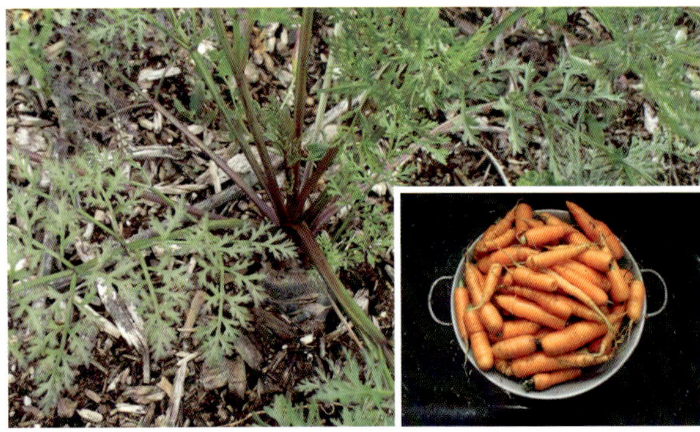

COLORS CREATED	orange from grated orange carrot; green, blue, purple from grated Black Nebula carrot; yellow from green carrot tops
PARTS USED FOR PIGMENT	root or green stems
PLANT TYPE	biennial
SEEDING	Seeds available at SeedRenaissance.com.

1. Simmer for 10 minutes to make pigment or dye. Strain.
2. Simmer again to reduce liquid to desired color strength. Works well with mordants.

Notes: Black Nebula carrots create blue dye even on cotton fabric.

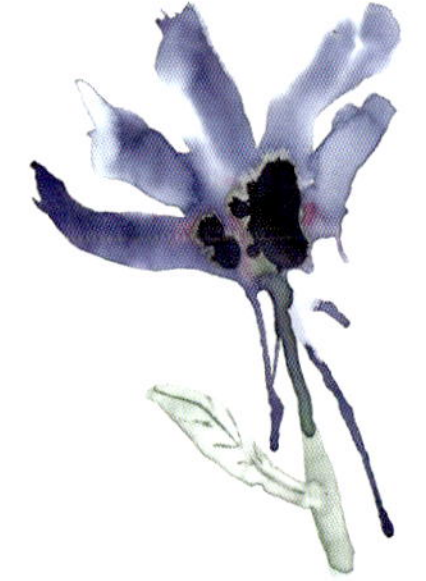

BLACK NEBULA GREEN TOPS

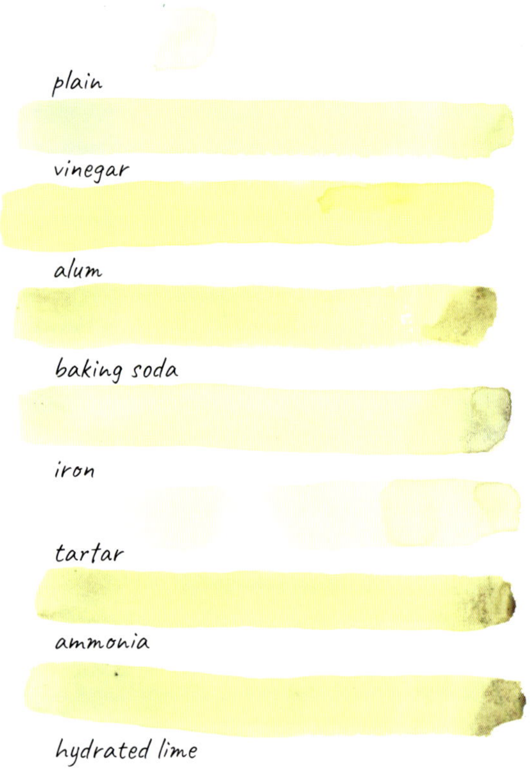

GRATED ORANGE CARROT

reduction by boiling

vinegar

alum

baking soda

hydrated lime

ammonia

BLACK NEBULA CARROT ROOT

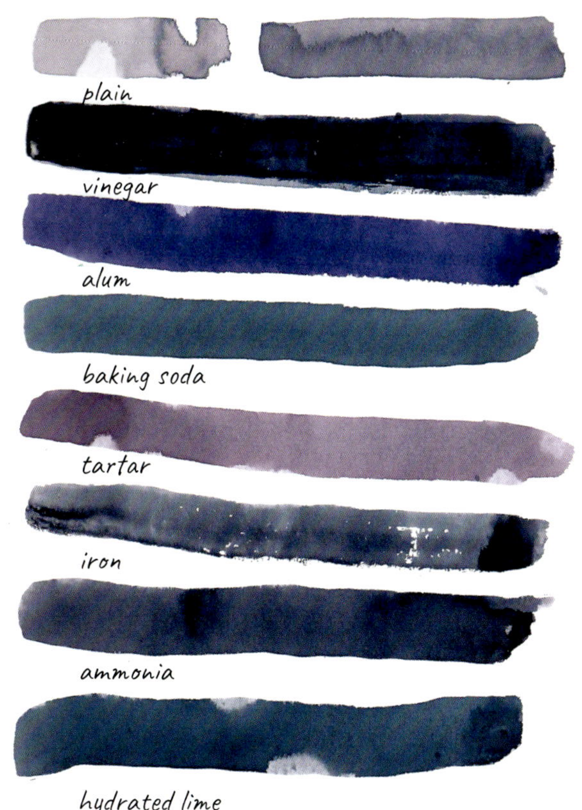

PLAIN BLACK NEBULA CARROT

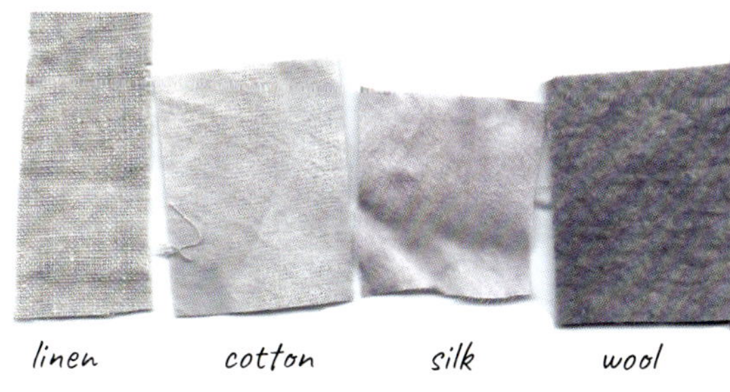

BLACK NEBULA CARROT WITH LIME

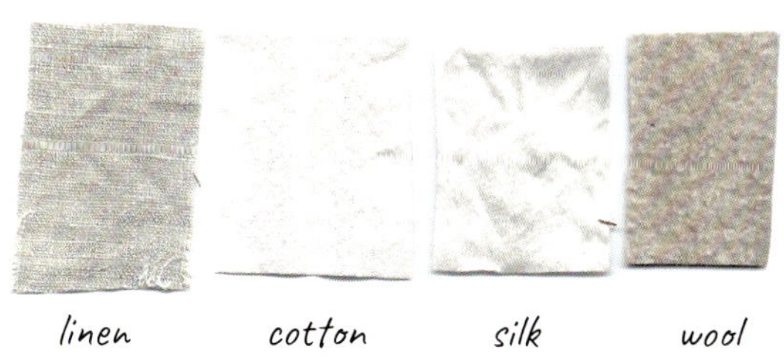

BLACK NEBULA ROOTS

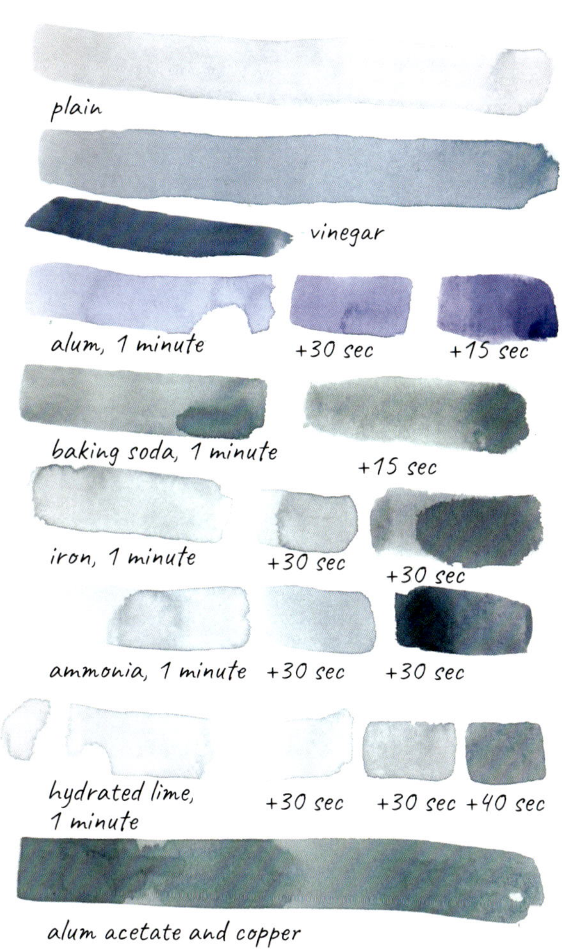

COPPER WITH ALUM ACETATE, THIRD PRESS

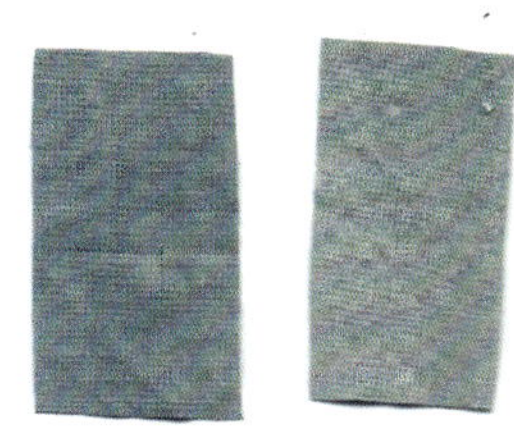

TYPHA SPECIES

Cattails

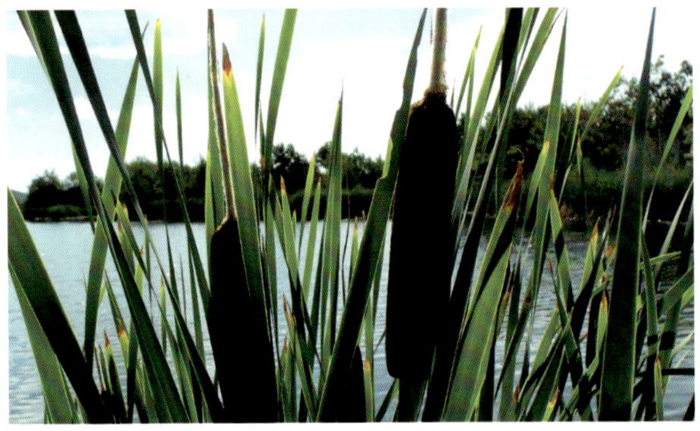

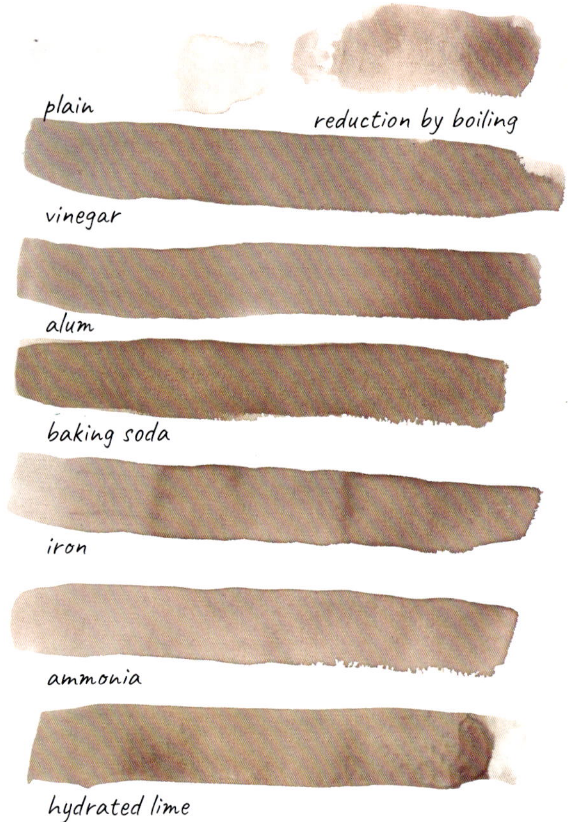

COLORS CREATED	brown (darkest with baking soda)
PARTS USED FOR PIGMENT	brown cigar-shaped flower heads
PLANT TYPE	perennial
HARDINESS ZONE	varies by species

1. Simmer for 30 minutes to make pigment or dye. Strain.
2. Simmer again to reduce liquid to desired color strength.

Notes: The color temporarily stained a stainless-steel pan and had to be removed with a copper scrubber.

CELOSIA PLUMOSA

Celosia

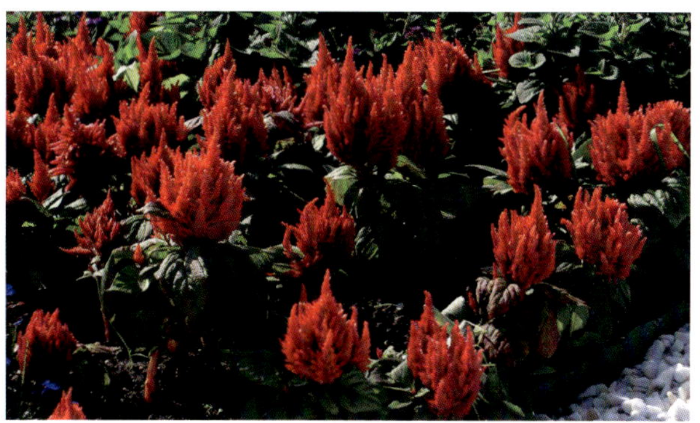

COLORS CREATED	vibrant red (from uncooked fresh flowers), brown with vinegar (when cooked), yellow with alum (when cooked)
PARTS USED FOR PIGMENT	feathery flower spikes, leaves
PLANT TYPE	annual

Notes: The cherry red celosia went through an interesting journey while cooking. About a minute after it started to simmer, it turned dark red, then as time went on, it went orange, back to cherry red, to yellow, and then to nearly white when the color was drained from it. It was fun to watch! Tangerine celosia flowers turned pale yellow when simmered, then green when reduced by steaming.

RED CELOSIA

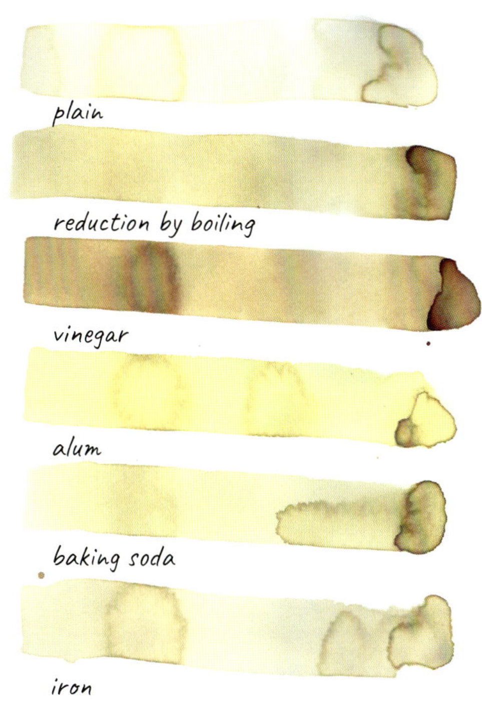

TANGERINE CELOSIA

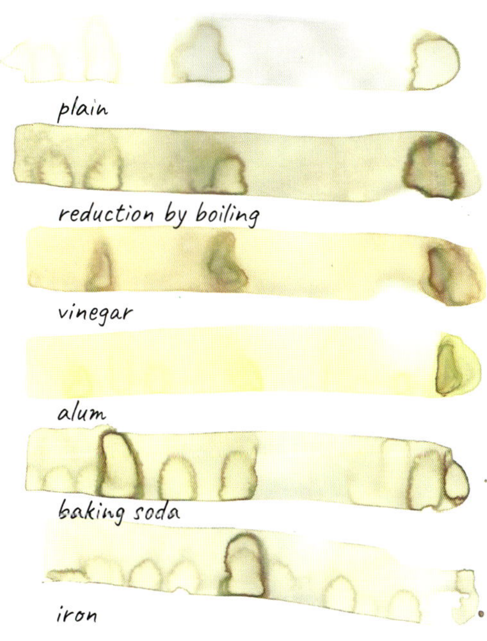

Charcoal and Soot

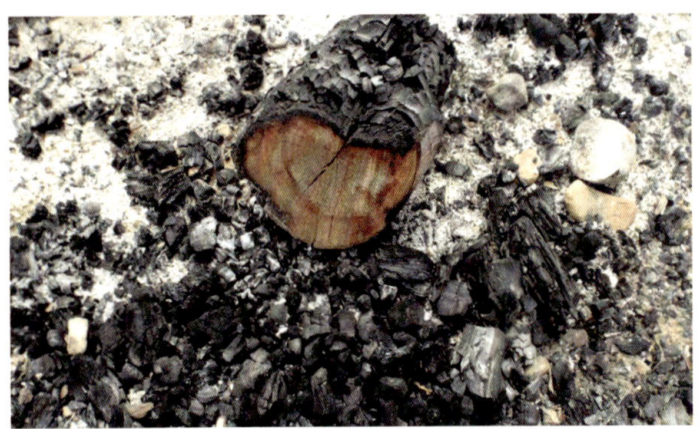

CASEIN MULLED CHARCOAL

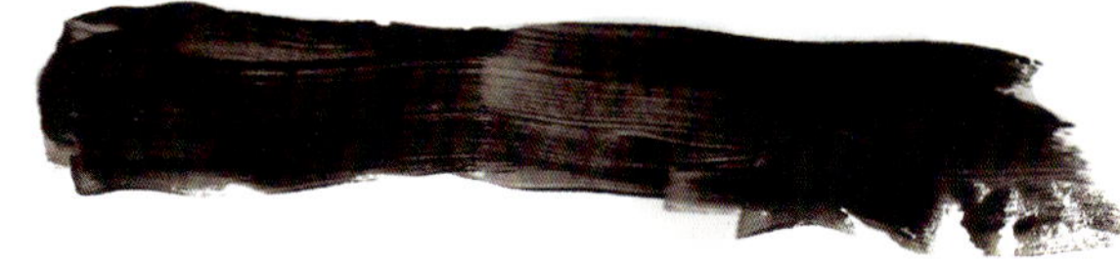

RECONSTITUTED CASEIN CHARCOAL

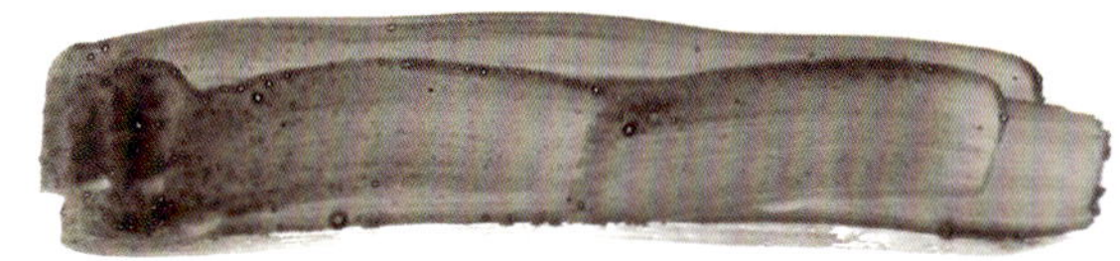

dried

COLORS CREATED	black, gray
PARTS USED FOR PIGMENT	charcoal, soot

1. In a bowl with water, gently crush small lumps of black charcoal without any ash with the back of a spoon to create a rough powder. Charcoal dust should not be inhaled, so this is why it is crushed underwater. Air dry and then store.

2. Use a glass or stone muller with a small amount of water to mull the charcoal into your choice of paint base. Soot can be collected by placing metal or other nonflammable surface above a candle.

Notes: Avoid using commercially produced charcoal because it often has additives to make it ignite easier.

ACALYPHA HISPIDA

Chenille

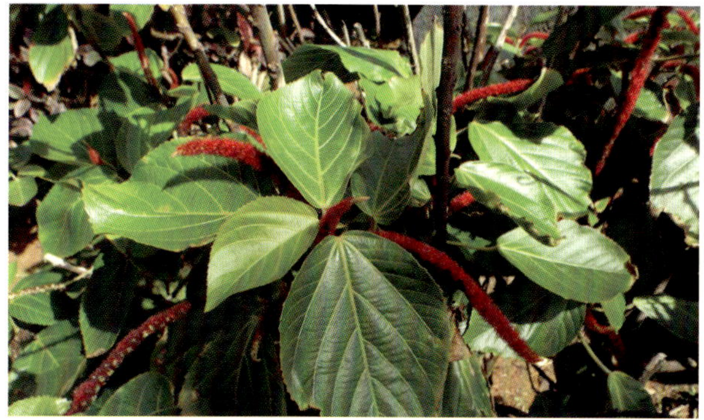

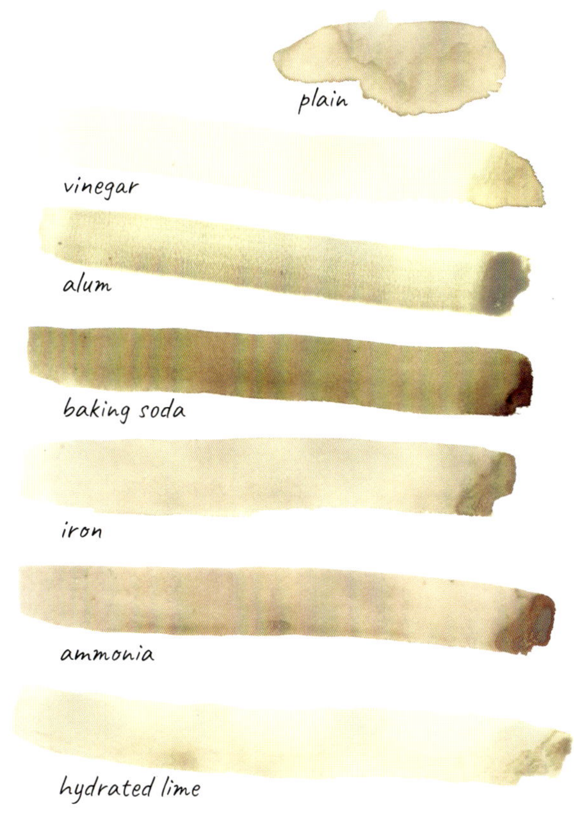

COLORS CREATED	purple with citric acid, brown with other mordants
PARTS USED FOR PIGMENT	fuzzy elongated flowers
PLANT TYPE	tropical

1. Simmer for 10 minutes to make pigment or dye. Strain.
2. Simmer again to reduce liquid to desired color strength.

Notes: Chenille makes a beautiful house plant but wants constant water.

BOILED WITH CITRIC ACID

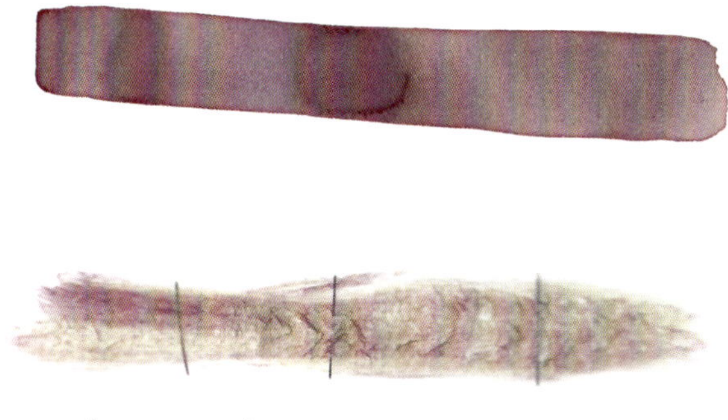

PRUNUS SPECIES

Cherries

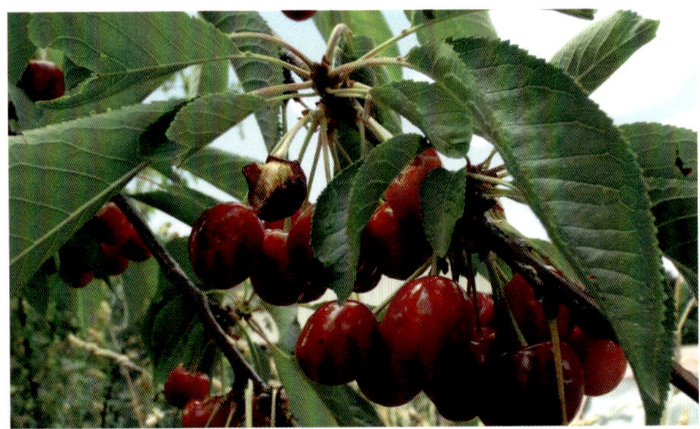

COLORS CREATED	purple with citric acid, blue with vinegar or alum, blue-gray with baking soda, purple when unmordanted or with iron or ammonia; rich reds with all mordants from bark and twigs
PARTS USED FOR PIGMENT	ripe berries, leaves, bark, twigs
PLANT TYPE	tree
HARDINESS ZONE	5

1. Mash berries and simmer for 10 minutes to create pigment or dye. Bark or pieces of branches or twigs are simmered for an hour. Cherry leaves simmered for 75 minutes create parchment and brown with baking soda. Leaves of the purple sand cherry bush, which is widely grown as a landscape bush for its beautiful foliage, are perhaps an unsung hero for their stunning colors of dye and pigment, used fresh or simmered for 10 minutes.

Notes: Alum and tartar mixed make a turquoise blue. Cherry leaves make excellent eco-prints. Purple sand cherry leaves make astonishing purple eco-prints unmordanted, or excellent green eco-prints when mordanted with vinegar of copper—the lines and veins are crisp.

RED CHERRIES

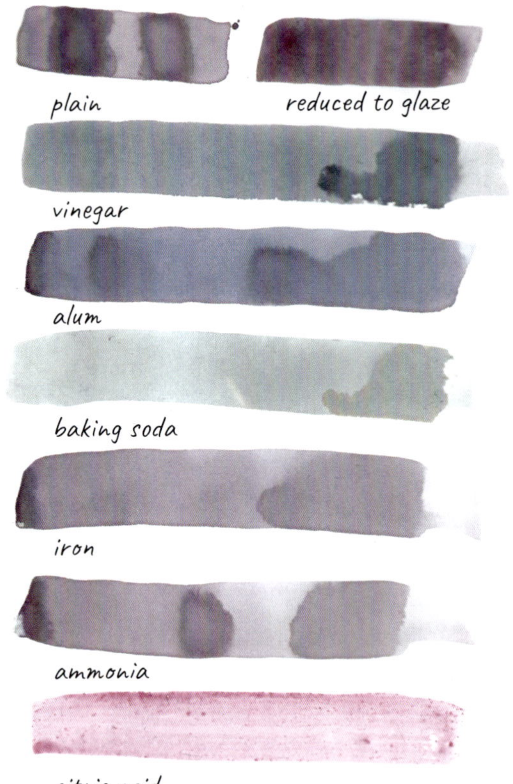

CHERRY BARK TWIGS

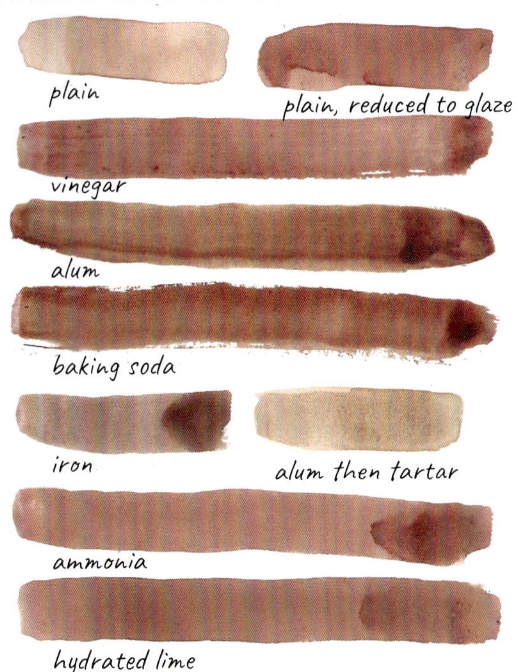

WILD CHOKEBERRIES

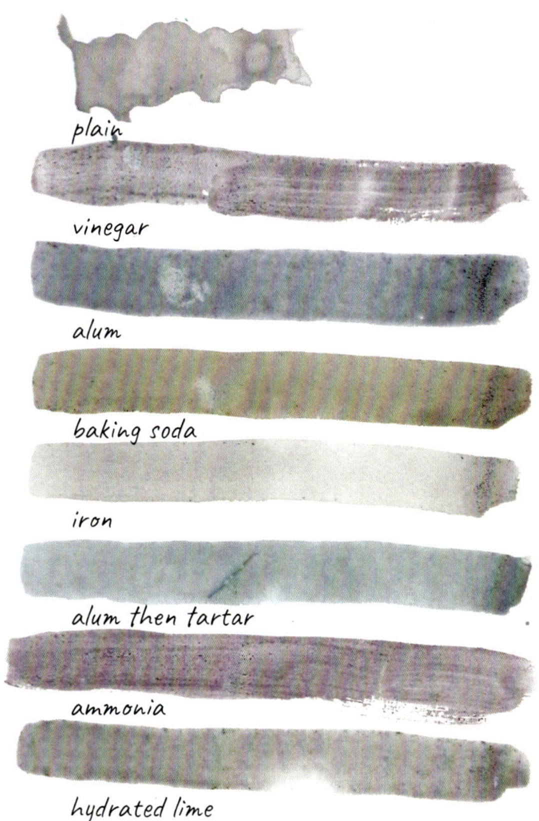

WILD CHERRY BARK WITH ALUM, TARTAR, AND GLAUBER'S SALT

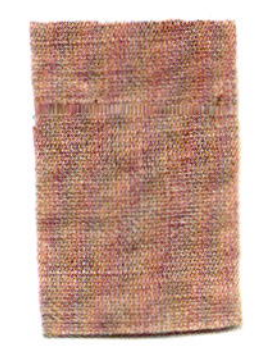

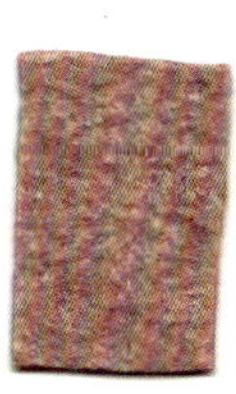

linen cotton silk wool

CHOKECHERRY TWIGS

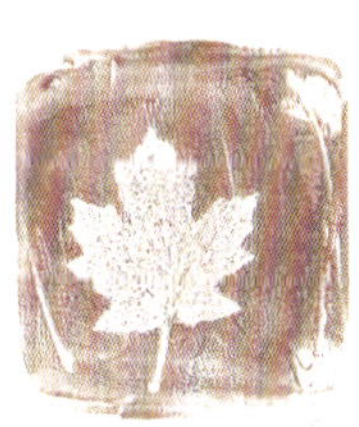

with egg, tartar, and linseed oil

FRESH PRESSED LEAF

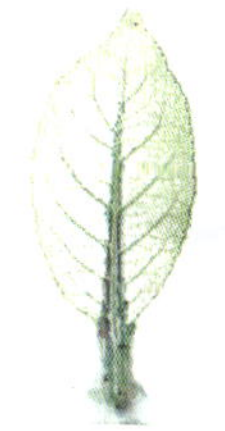

copper

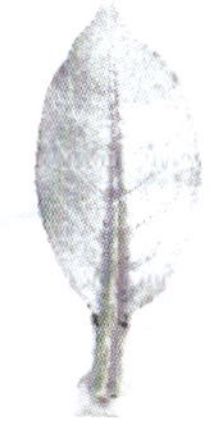

iron

CHERRY TREE LEAVES

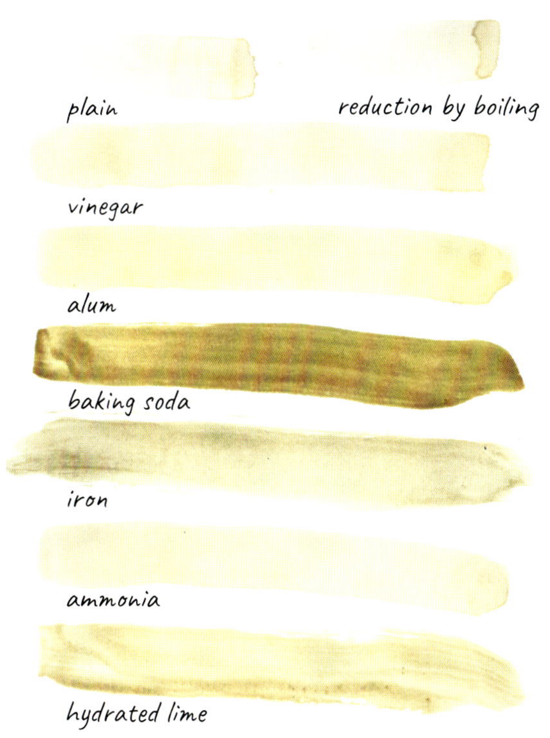

PURPLE SAND CHERRY LEAVES

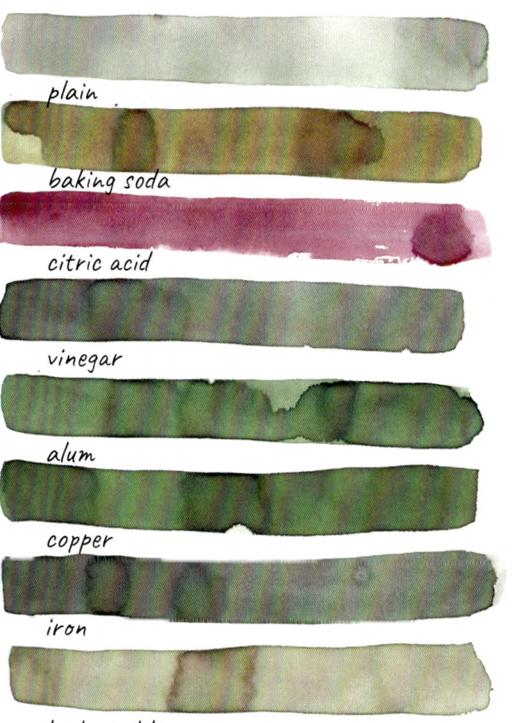

SALVIA HISPANICA

Chia

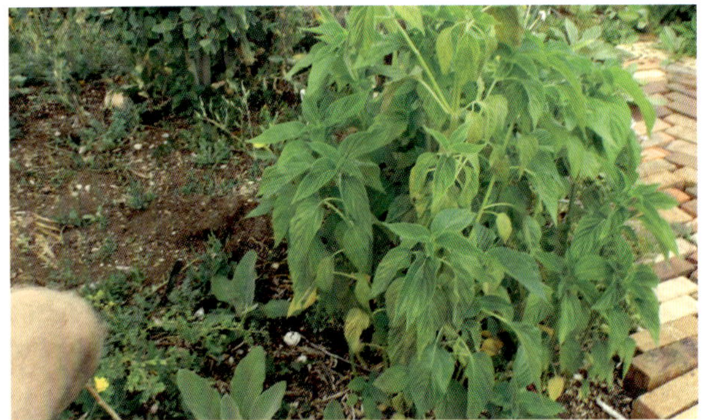

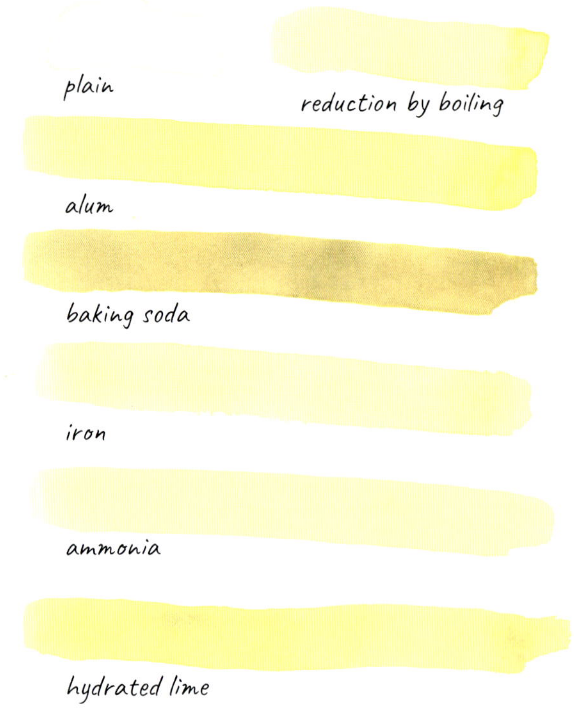

COLORS CREATED	yellow
PARTS USED FOR PIGMENT	leaves
PLANT TYPE	annual grain plant
SEEDING	Seeds available at SeedRenaissance.com.

1. Simmer for 10 minutes to make pigment or dye. Strain.
2. Simmer again to reduce liquid to desired color strength. Vinegar destroys the color and turns the dye liquid to clear.

Notes: This is the grain plant that makes the chia seeds that have become very popular for eating. Growing the grain requires roughly a 150-day frost-free season.

MORDANT MIX

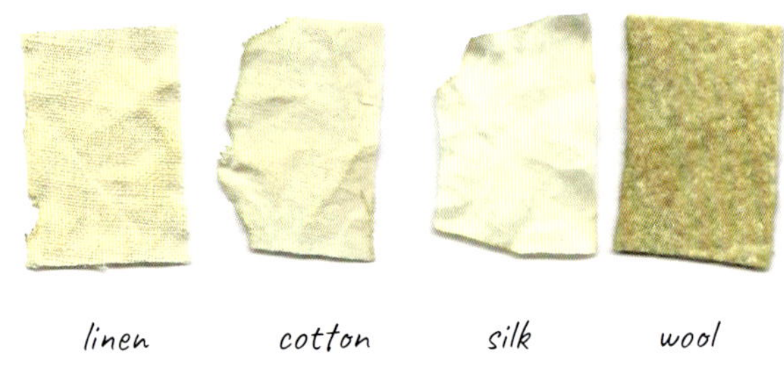

ASYSTASIA GANGETICA

Chinese Violets

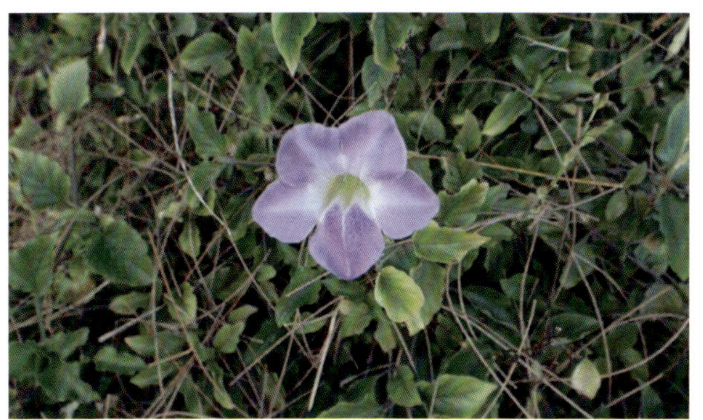

COLORS CREATED	green, yellow
PARTS USED FOR PIGMENT	Fresh uncooked leaves make green. Uncooked purple petals with baking soda make yellow.
PLANT TYPE	ground cover
HARDINESS ZONE	tropical

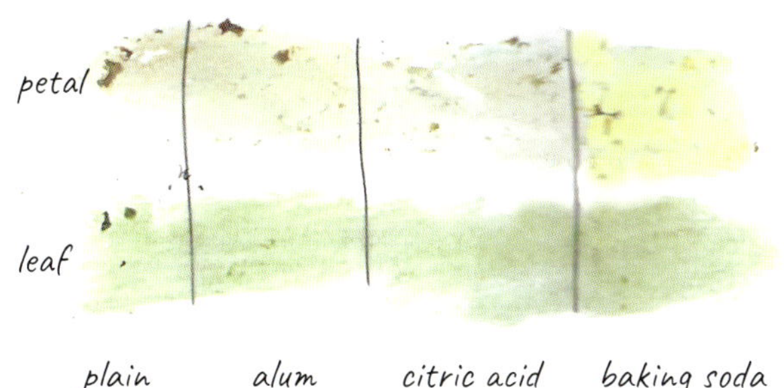

WEDELIA CHINENSIS

Chinese Wedelia

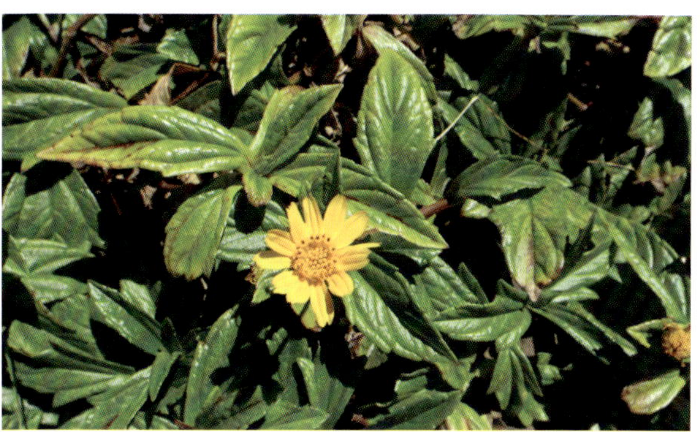

COLORS CREATED	yellow when used uncooked, brown when cooked
PARTS USED FOR PIGMENT	flowers
PLANT TYPE	ground cover
HARDINESS ZONE	8

1. Simmer for 10 minutes to make pigment or dye. Strain.
2. Simmer again to reduce liquid to desired color strength.

COOKED

baking soda

alum

plain

FRESH PRESSED FLOWERS

plain *alum* *citric acid* *baking soda*

Chrysanthemum Species

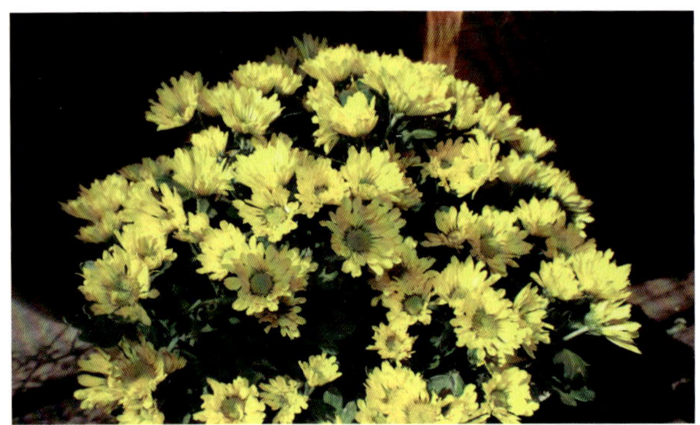

COLORS CREATED	purple, yellow (varies by petal color)
PARTS USED FOR PIGMENT	flower heads
PLANT TYPE	perennial
HARDINESS ZONE	5

1. Simmer for 10 minutes to make pigment or dye. Strain.
2. Simmer again to reduce liquid to desired color strength.

Notes: Purple flowers and citric acid make purple. Yellow flowers with alum make pale yellow.

YELLOW CHRYSANTHEMUMS

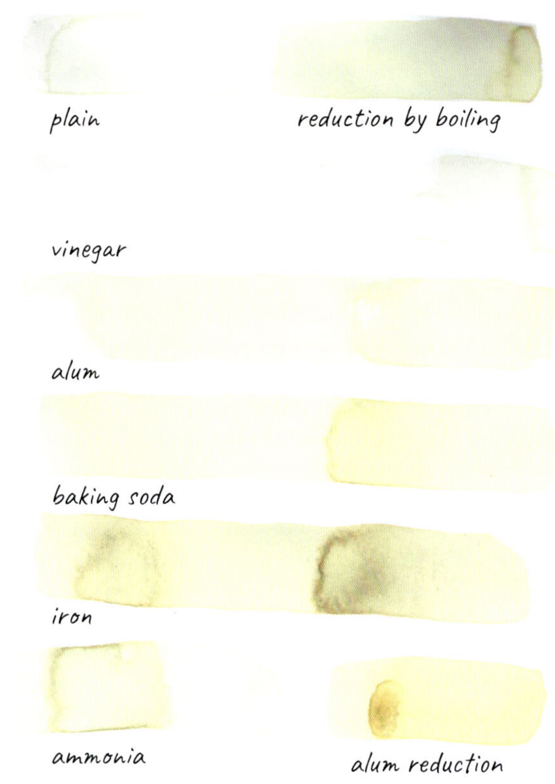

PURPLE CHRYSANTHEMUMS

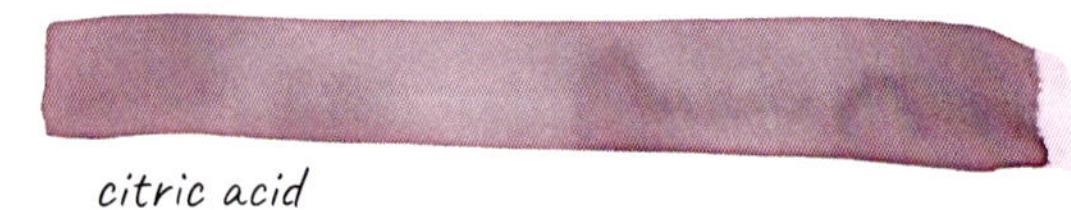

Citrus Trees and Fruit

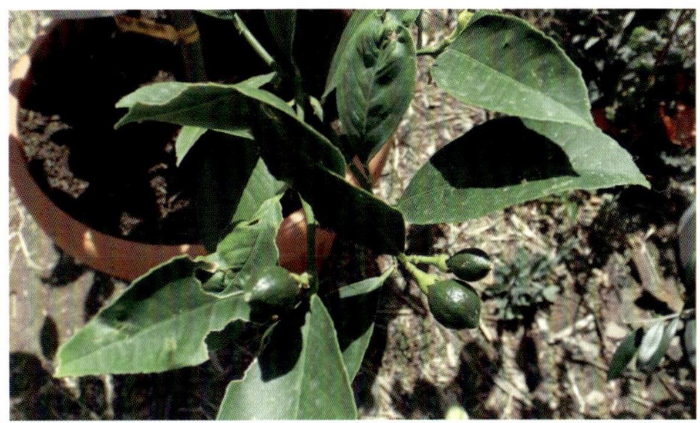

COLORS CREATED	leaves make green or yellow; fruit makes various colors
PARTS USED FOR PIGMENT	leaves of any citrus fruit
PLANT TYPE	perennial tree
HARDINESS ZONE	8

1. Simmer leaves for 30 minutes to make pigment or dye. Strain.
2. Simmer again to reduce liquid to desired color strength. Vinegar destroys the color and turns the liquid clear.

Notes: The pigment of both fruit and peels is sticky and does not dry well; they are best for children's finger paint.

LEMON LEAF

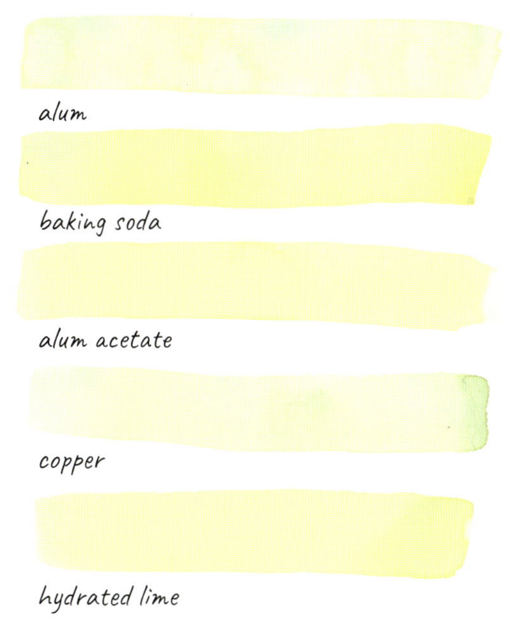

LEMON LEAF WITH COPPER

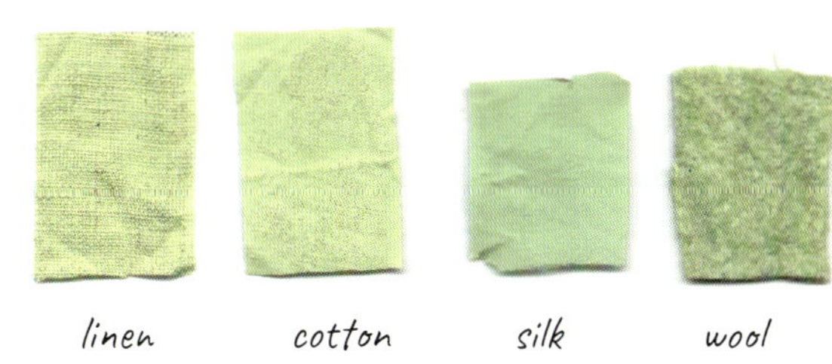

Clay

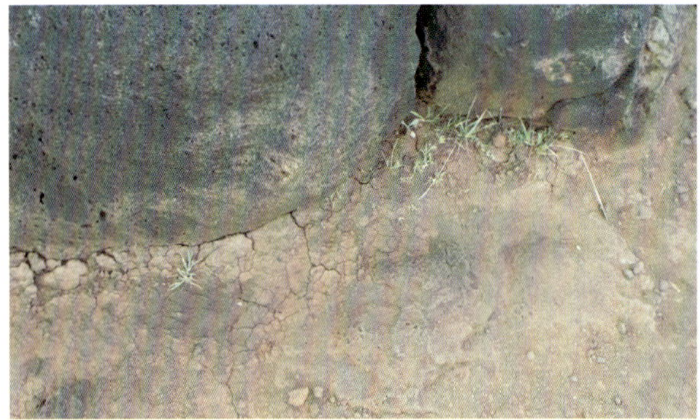

COLORS CREATED red, peach, green, purple

PARTS USED FOR PIGMENT clean clay

1. Clay from nature can be used as pigment whatever color it is. White clay is invaluable for dyeing for use as pigment or for making opaque paint when combined with other pigments. Clay pigments are some of the easiest to use for paint. Some boiled clays can make dye on fabric.

Notes: I always keep an eye out for good colors of natural clay when in nature. Naturally colored clays can also be purchased online.

VOLCANIC CLAY FROM LAHUE, HAWAII

VOLCANIC CLAY FROM LAHUE, HAWAII

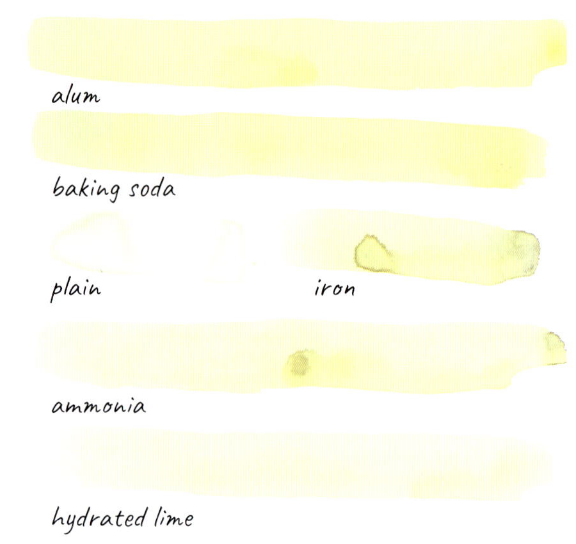

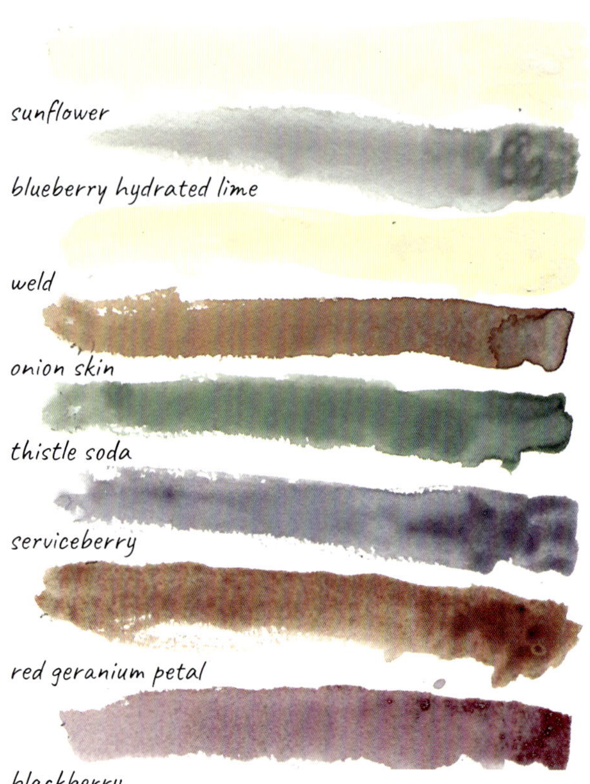

Clematis Species

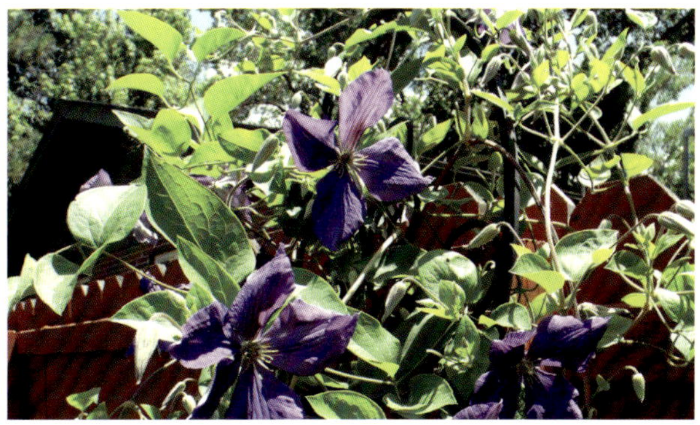

COLORS CREATED	red, green, brown, gray
PARTS USED FOR PIGMENT	petals of purple or red hybrids
PLANT TYPE	varies by species
HARDINESS ZONE	varies by species

1. Simmer for 10 minutes to make pigment or dye. Strain.
2. Simmer again to reduce liquid to desired color strength.

Notes: *Clematis* flowers only make pigment when at peak bloom. When I've tried to use dried flowers, there is no useful color.

WILD CLEMATIS

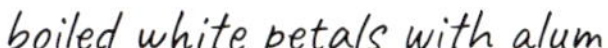

PURPLE FLOWERS

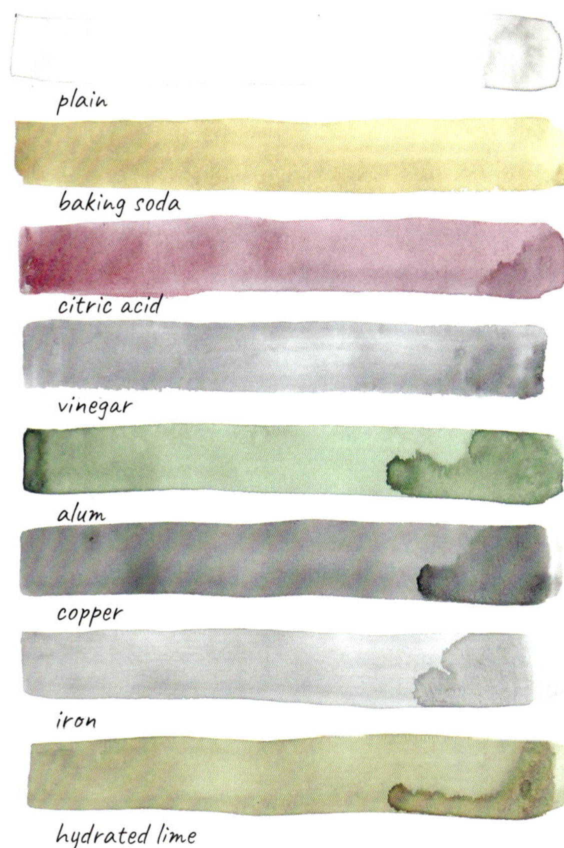

BOILED PURPLE CLEMATIS PETALS (NO MORDANTS)

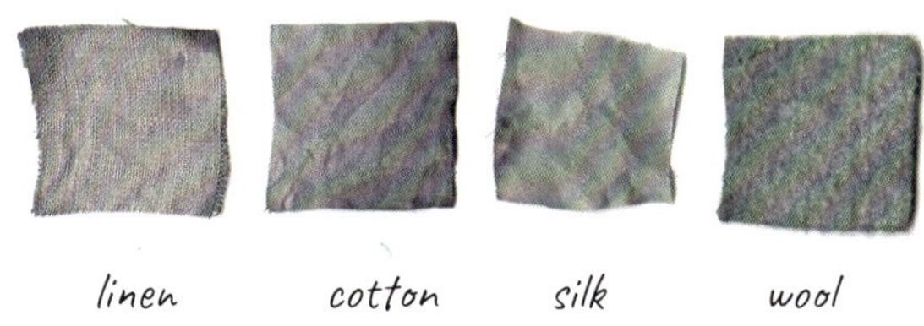

Cleome Species

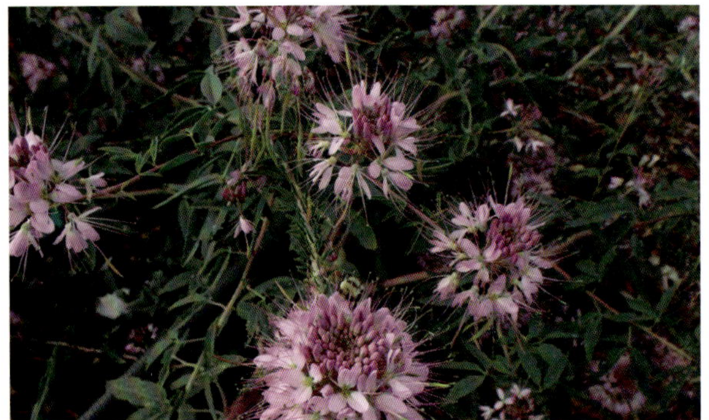

COLORS CREATED	pale green with alum, pale yellow with baking soda
PARTS USED FOR PIGMENT	leaves, stems, seed pods
PLANT TYPE	self-seeding annual
HARDINESS ZONE	4
SEEDING	Plant directly outside in autumn. Seeds available at SeedRenaissance.com

Special Use: Pottery paint. One of only a few herbs that can be used to create permanent pottery paint. Does not scrub off when used on greenware or bisque pottery, but it must be used in combination with other ingredients. To create an emulsion, cover clean aerial parts with water in a pan and simmer on the lowest temperature, lid off, for at least 1 hour. Strain out plant parts and reduce the liquid for brownish-yellow color, or reduce to a thick glaze and use in the Wild Botanical Pottery Paint recipe (see page 74).

Notes: Tolerant of drought and alkaline soils. Cleome seeds must freeze over winter or they will not germinate.

ROCKY MOUNTAIN BEEPLANT FLOWERS

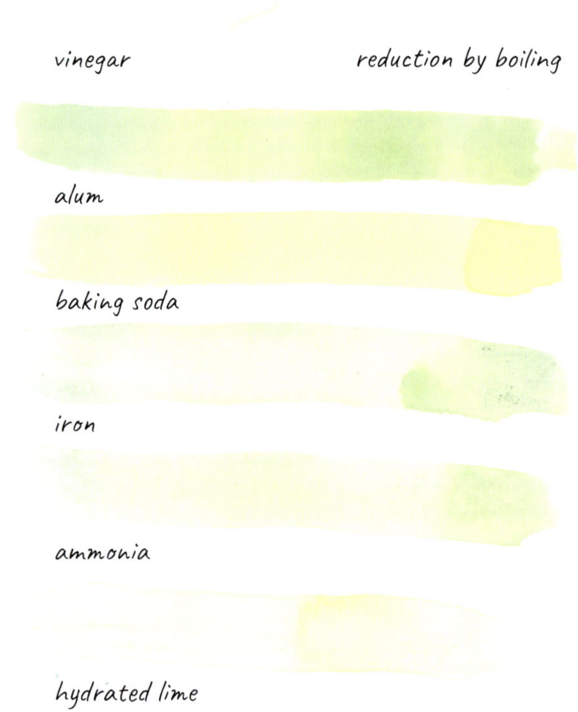

IMMATURE BEEPLANT NO FLOWERS

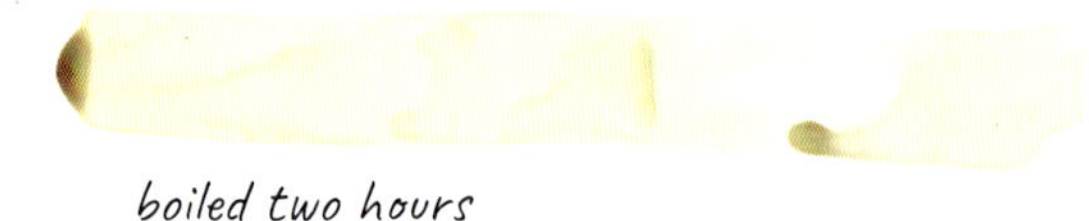

TRIFOLIUM SPECIES

Clover

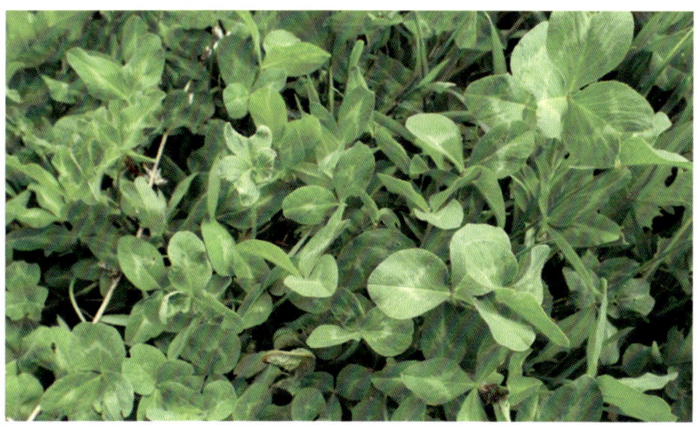

COLORS CREATED	yellow
PARTS USED FOR PIGMENT	flowers of various colors
PLANT TYPE	perennial
HARDINESS ZONE	5
SEEDING	Plant directly outside in autumn. Seeds available at SeedRenaissance.com.

1. Boil the flowers for 10 minutes with the lid on and reduce the liquid by steaming to produce a pale dirty yellow that does not change with a vinegar mordant. Alum creates a bright yellow. Baking soda creates an orangish yellow or orange, depending on saturation.

Notes: Red clover blooms in early summer. Some clovers, like white sweet clover and yellow sweet clover, have a strong smell when cooked.

RED CLOVER

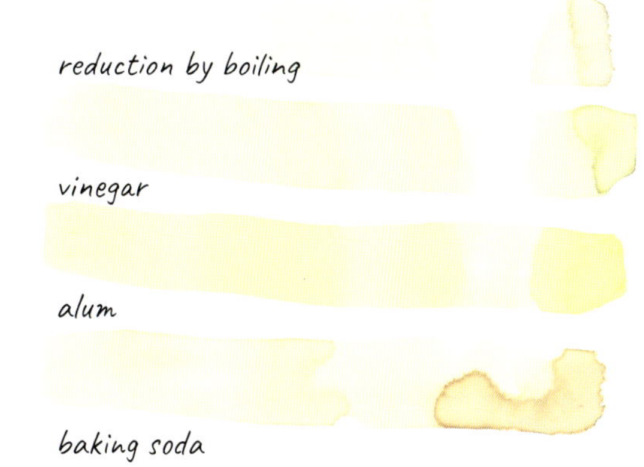

YELLOW CLOVER

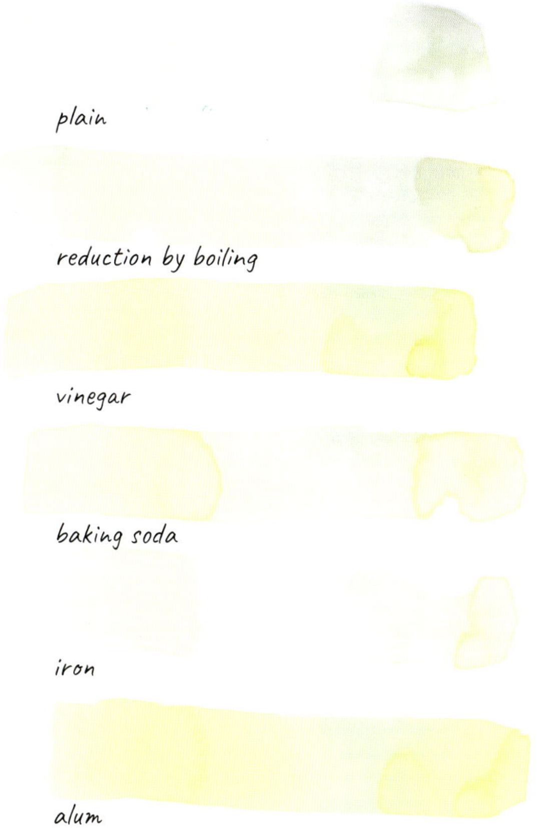

DACTYLOPIUS COCCUS

Cochineal

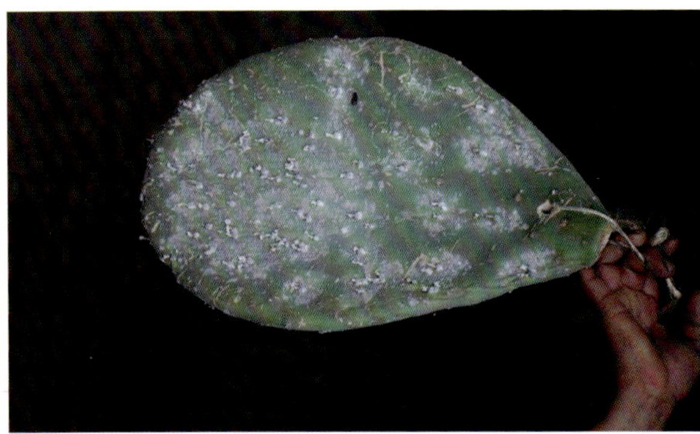

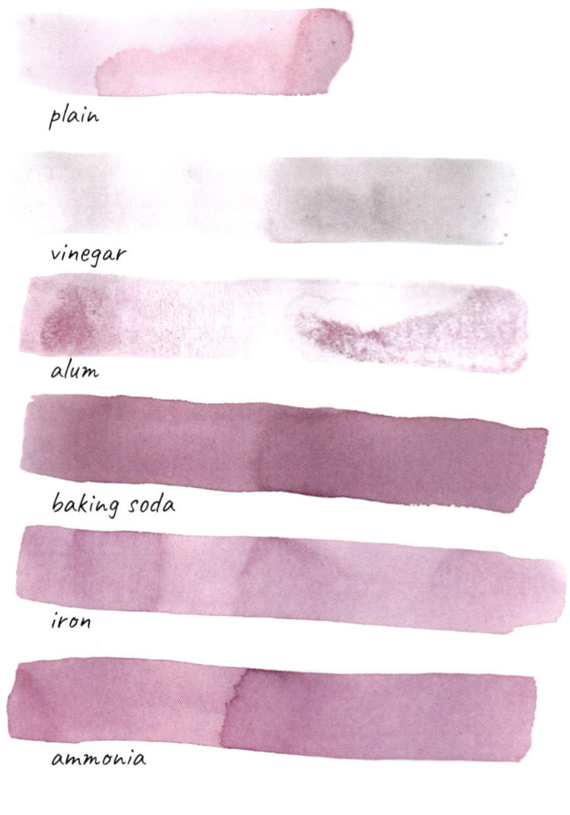

COLORS CREATED	red, pink, peachy oranges if carefully mixed with some botanical yellows
TYPE	tiny scale insect that lives on cactus pads

1. Crushed bugs can be simmered for 10 minutes on the stove or in a microwave to make pigment or dye, but they can also be mulled into paint without being cooked.

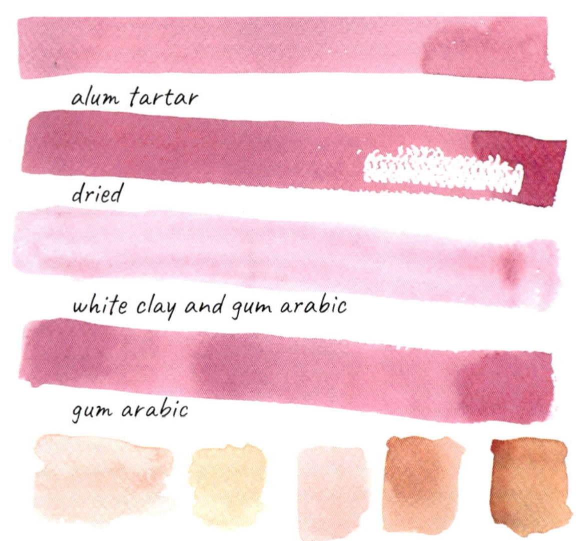

Notes: These tiny bugs are one of the most important sources of historic red dye, and are in demand again today because of concerns about synthetic red dyes, especially in food. Cochineal are approved as food grade dye in most countries, including the US. On ingredients lists they are often called carmine. Cochineal are farmed on cactus pads in Mexico. Fascinating documentaries about the endangered generational work to keep and harvest this crop are available online. Used to create red dye for thousands of years by the indigenous people of the Americas. Global trade of this dye began after the Spanish arrived.

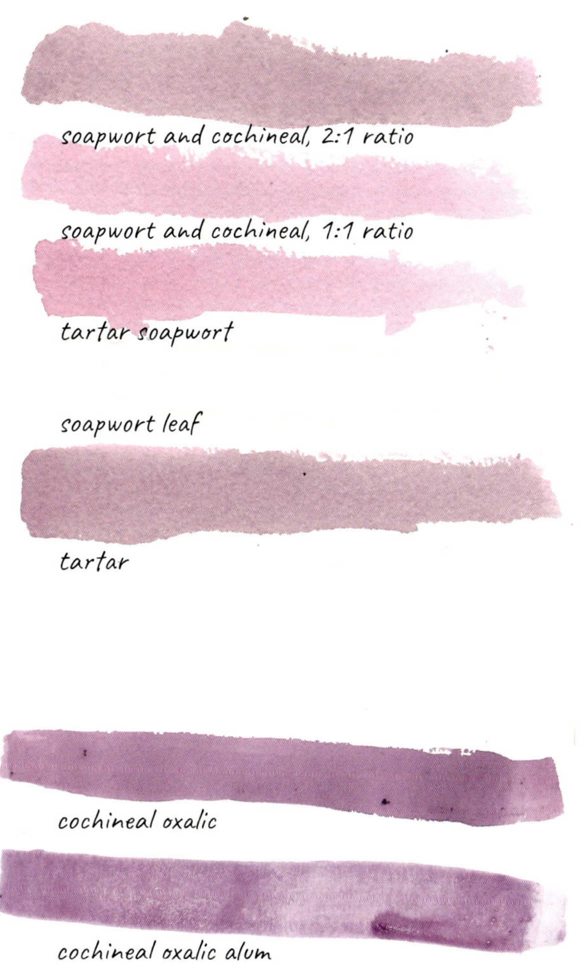

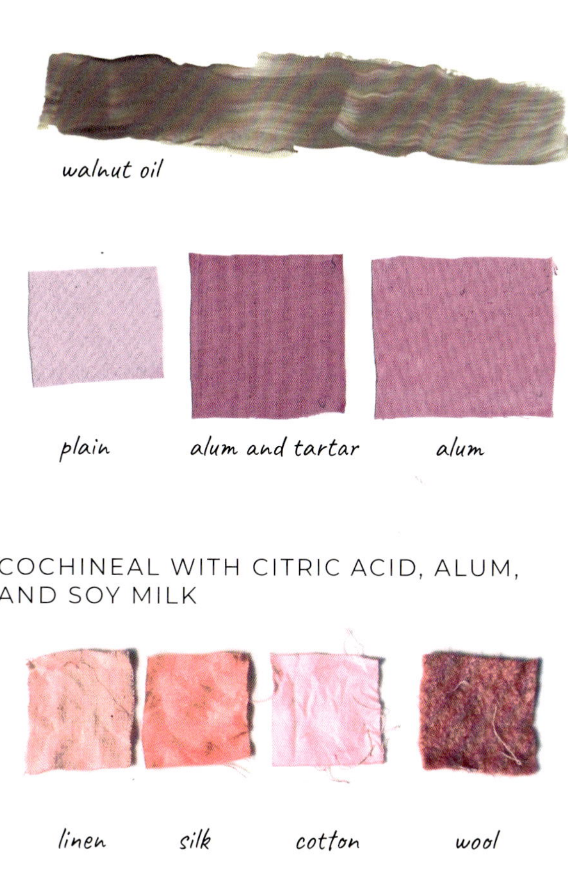

COCHINEAL WITH CITRIC ACID, ALUM, AND SOY MILK

linen silk cotton wool

XANTHIUM STRUMARIUM

Cocklebur

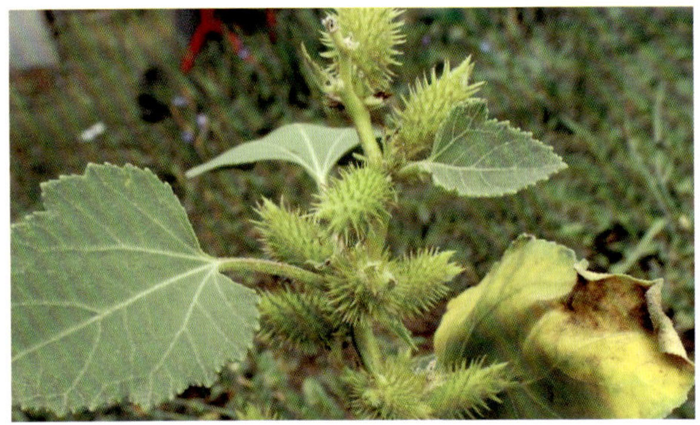

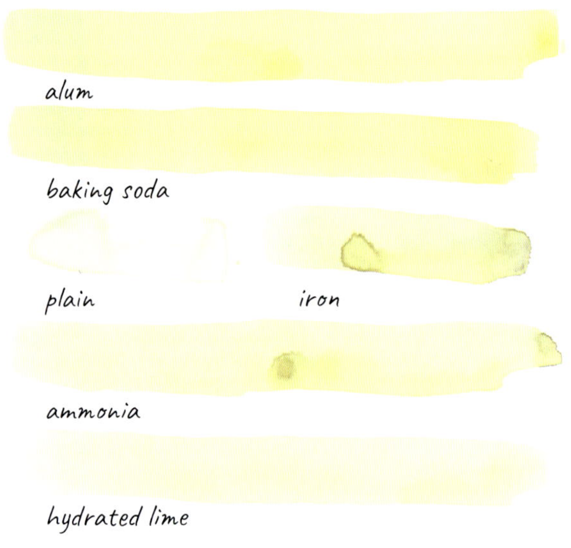

COLORS CREATED	yellow with alum
PARTS USED FOR PIGMENT	green burs, leaves, stems
PLANT TYPE	annual invasive weed

1. Simmer for 10 minutes to make pigment or dye. Strain.
2. Simmer again to reduce liquid to desired color strength.

Notes: Alum gives the best color. This is a great way to use up this unwanted weed.

PLECTRANTHUS SCUTELLARIOIDES

Coleus

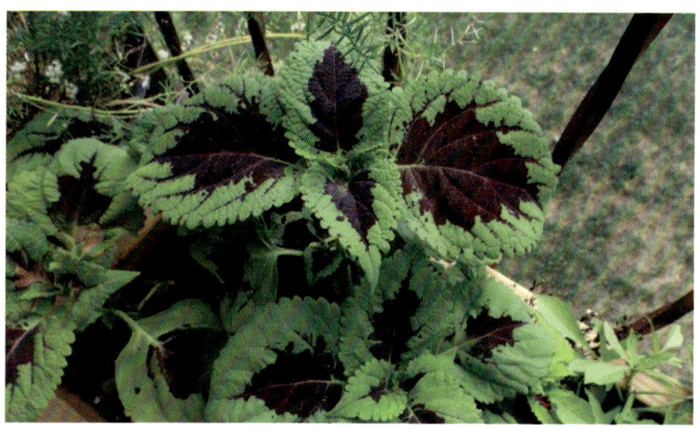

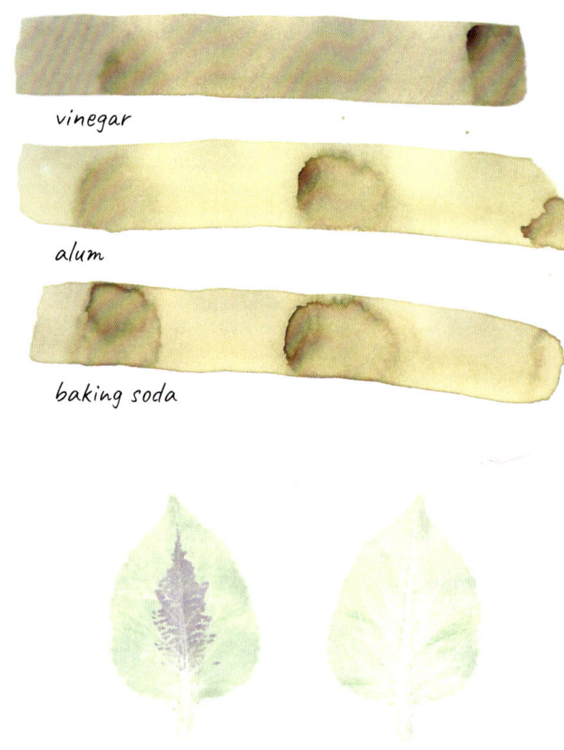

COLORS CREATED	golden brown
PARTS USED FOR PIGMENT	leaves
PLANT TYPE	annual

1. Simmer for 10 minutes to make pigment or dye. Strain.
2. Simmer again to reduce liquid to desired color strength.

Notes: While the color from the cooking is disappointing, coleus really shines as an eco-print on paper, where the leaves and colors print perfectly!

AQUILEGIA SPECIES

Columbines

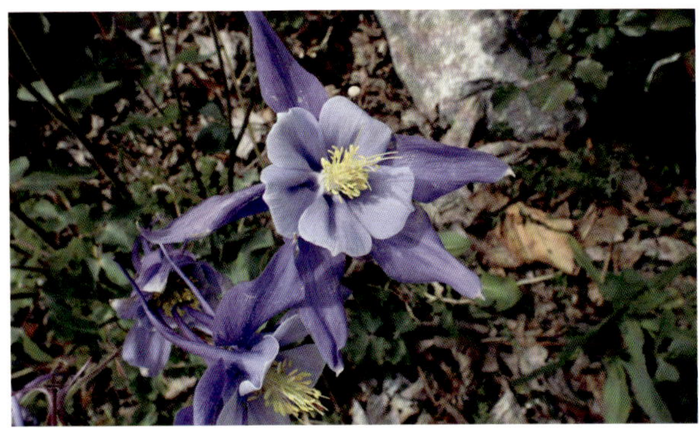

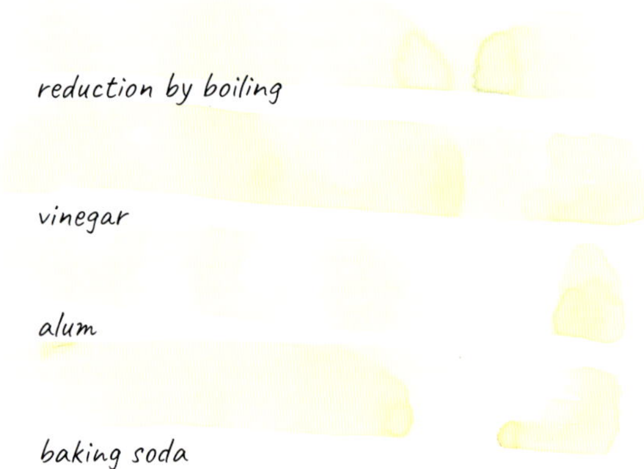

COLORS CREATED	yellow
PARTS USED FOR PIGMENT	blossoms
PLANT TYPE	perennial
HARDINESS ZONE	3

1. Simmer for 15 minutes to make pigment or dye. Strain.
2. Simmer again to reduce liquid to desired color strength.

Notes: Flowers bloom in early summer.

SYMPHYTUM OFFICINALE

Comfrey

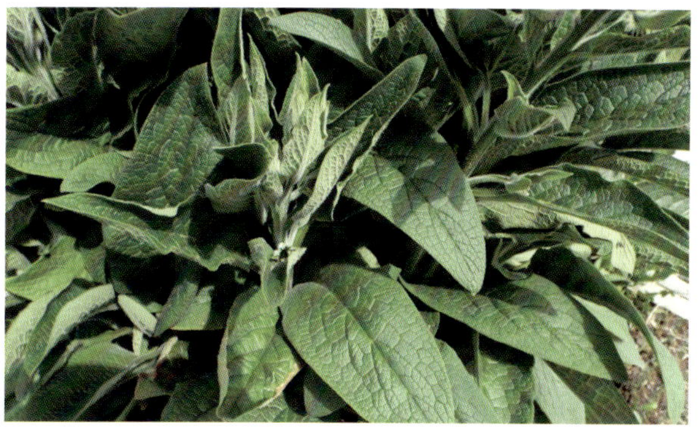

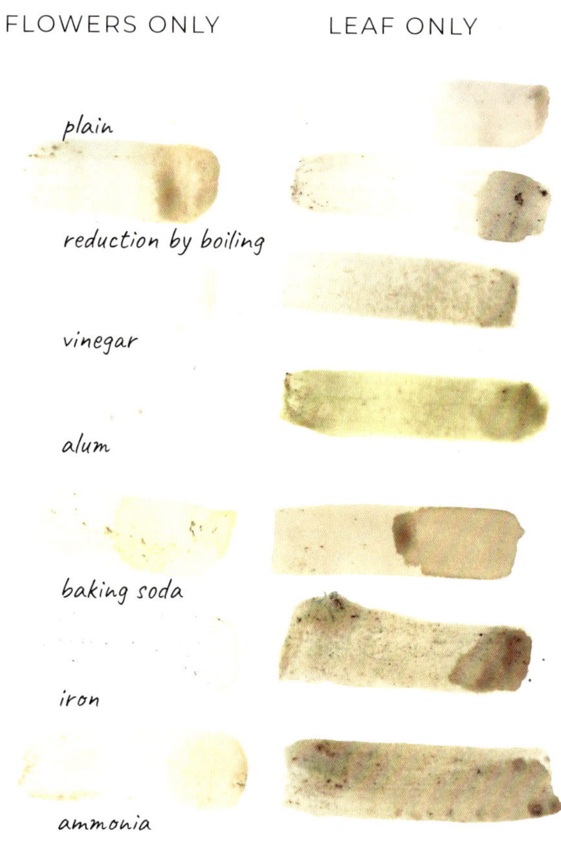

COLORS CREATED	brown
PARTS USED FOR PIGMENT	leaves
PLANT TYPE	perennial
HARDINESS ZONE	4

1. Simmer for 20 minutes to make pigment or dye. Strain.
2. Simmer again to reduce liquid to desired color strength.

RUDBECKIA AND *ECHINACEA* SPECIES

Coneflowers and Echinacea

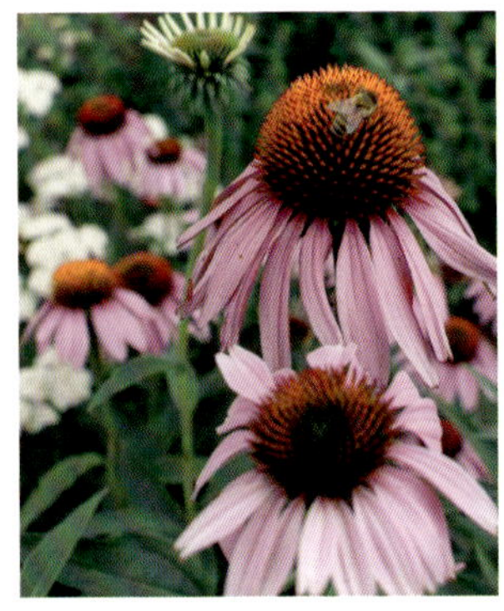

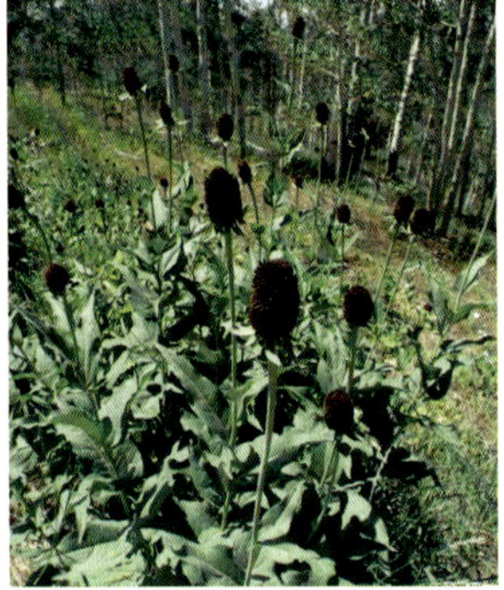

PETALS ONLY

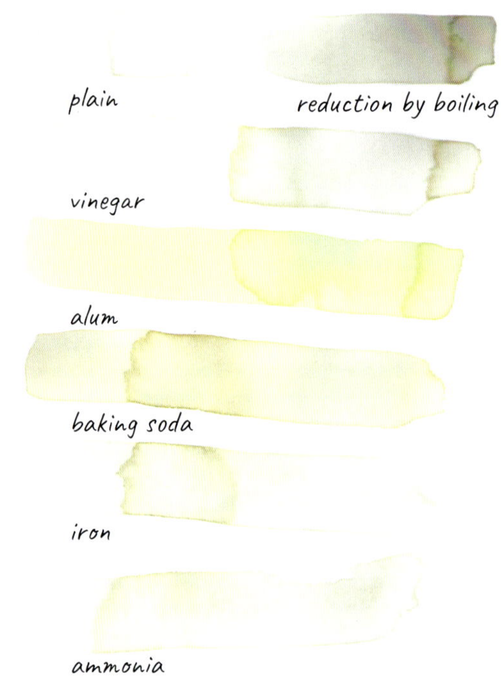

PURPUREA

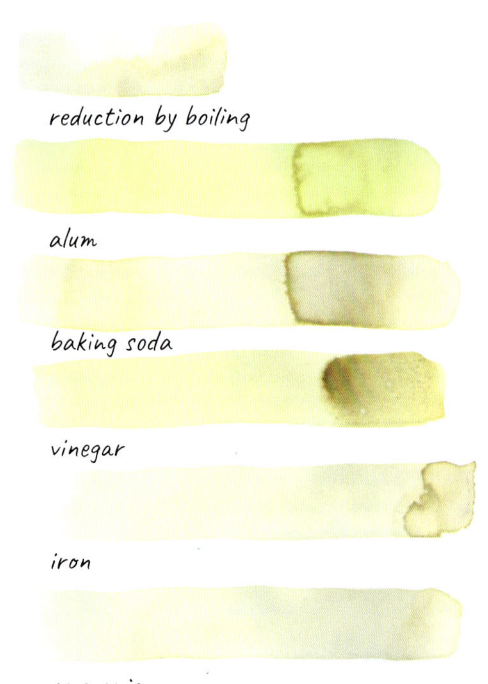

COLORS CREATED	*Echinacea purpurea* petals create yellow with alum and the whole flower head creates tans in addition to yellow with alum; Rocky Mountain and red prairie coneflowers create green with alum and yellow-brown with baking soda
PARTS USED FOR PIGMENT	petals or whole flower heads
PLANT TYPE	perennial
HARDINESS ZONE	3
SEEDING	Seeds available at SeedRenaissance.com

1. Simmer for 10 minutes to make pigment or dye. Strain.
2. Simmer again to reduce liquid to desired color strength.

PRAIRIE CORNFLOWER

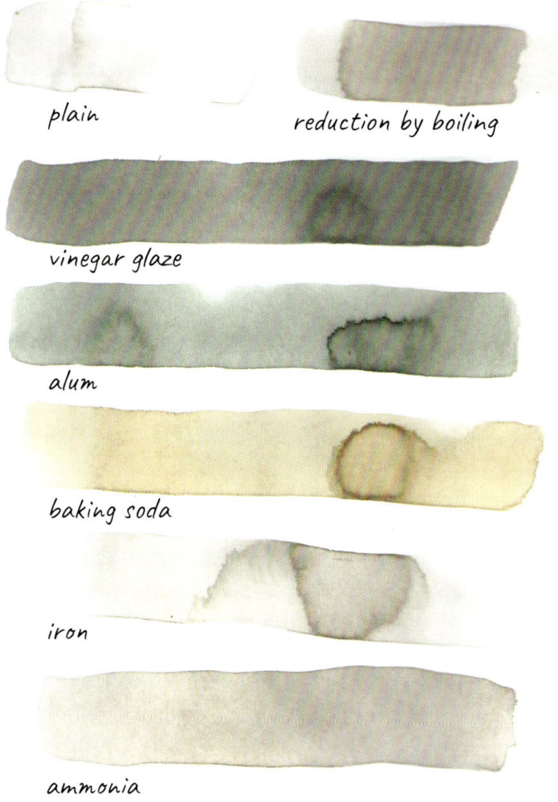

ROCKY MOUNTAIN

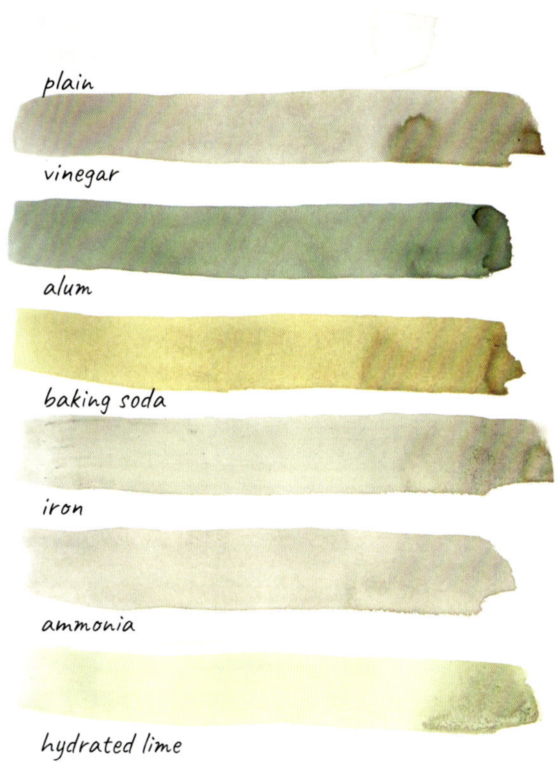

SYMPHORICARPOS ORBICULATUS

Coralberry

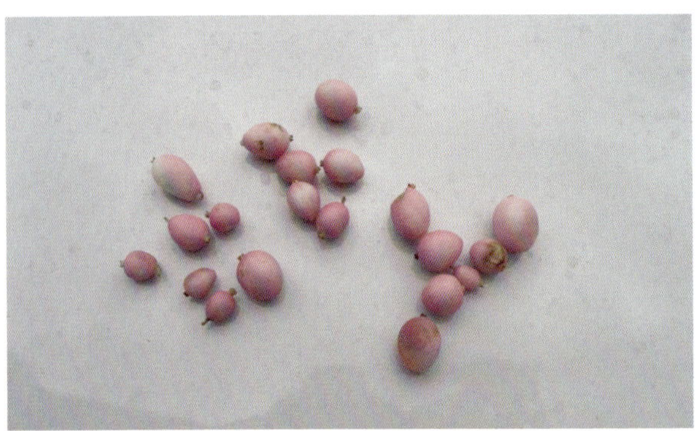

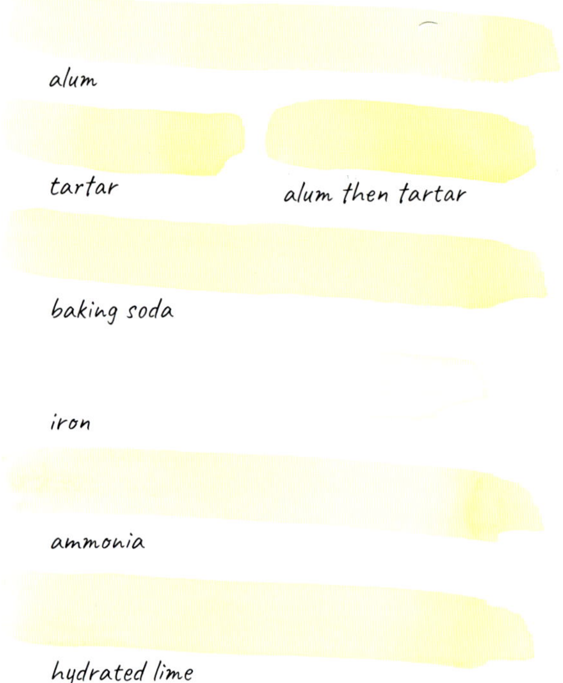

COLORS CREATED	yellow with alum and tartar
PARTS USED FOR PIGMENT	crushed ripe berries
PLANT TYPE	perennial
HARDINESS ZONE	2

1. Simmer for 20 minutes to make pigment or dye. Strain.
2. Simmer again to reduce liquid to desired color strength.

CORDYLINE FRUTICOSA

Cordyline

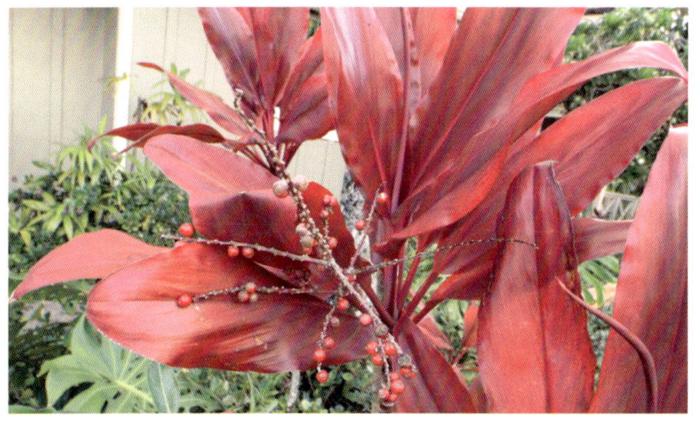

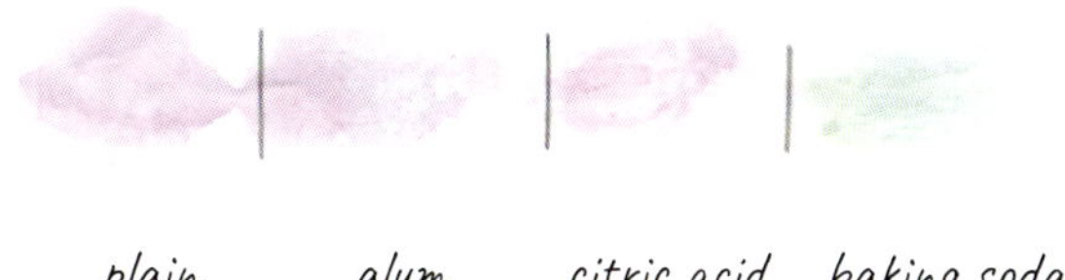

COLORS CREATED	pink and red with mordant, citric acid, or alum; green with baking soda
PARTS USED FOR PIGMENT	red berries from the purple-leaf variety
PLANT TYPE	tropical landscape plant
HARDINESS ZONE	10

1. I used the fresh juice of these berries as pigment. I have not yet tested a cooked version to see how the colors change. There is no end to the numbers of plants we can test for color, and that is half the fun!

ZEA MAYS

Corn

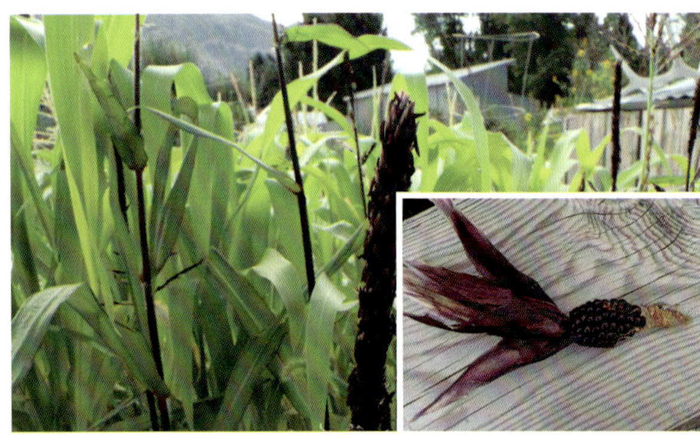

COLORS CREATED	purple, violet, green, gray, blue, brown
PARTS USED FOR PIGMENT	cob with corn and shuck or tassels of Double Red variety
PLANT TYPE	red kerneled garden sweet corn
HARDINESS ZONE	annual
SEEDING	Seeds available at SeedRenaissance.com.

1. Simmer for 10 minutes to make pigment or dye. Strain.
2. Simmer again to reduce liquid to desired color strength.

Notes: I'm still astonished that I was able to make blue dye from corn. The blue came from the liquid pigment of the cob and shuck, mordanted with alum. The blue hues became even more interesting when mulled into a glair and liquid gum arabic base, or a base of guar gum and liquid gum arabic. I have not been able to find any evidence of anyone else ever using corn to make blue dye.

DOUBLE RED SWEET CORN

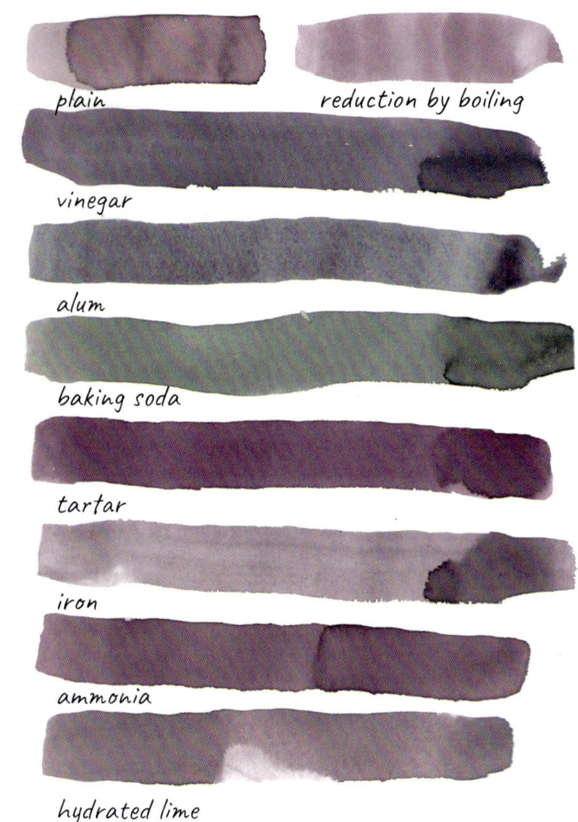

BOILED RED CORN LEAVES WITH TARTAR

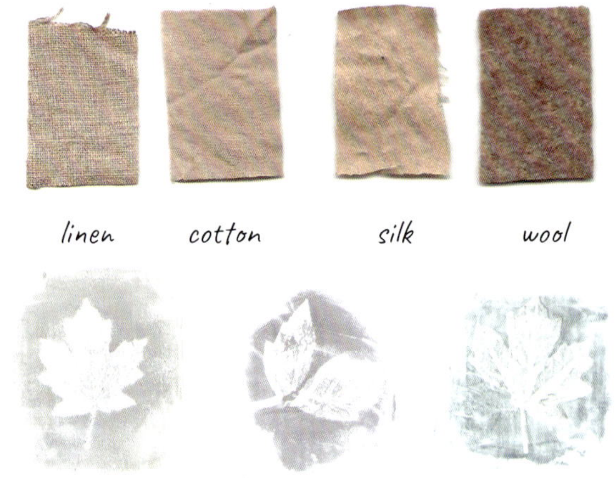

RED CORN TASSEL

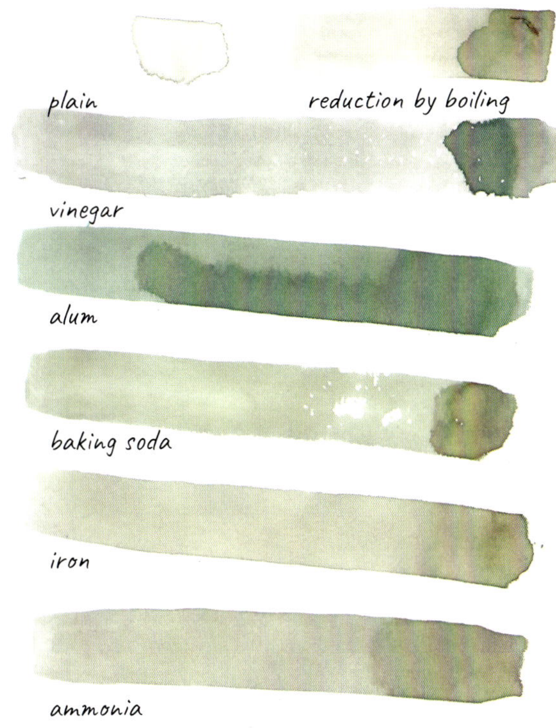

RED CORN COB BOILED WITH TARTAR, MULLED WITH GLAIR AND GUM ARABIC

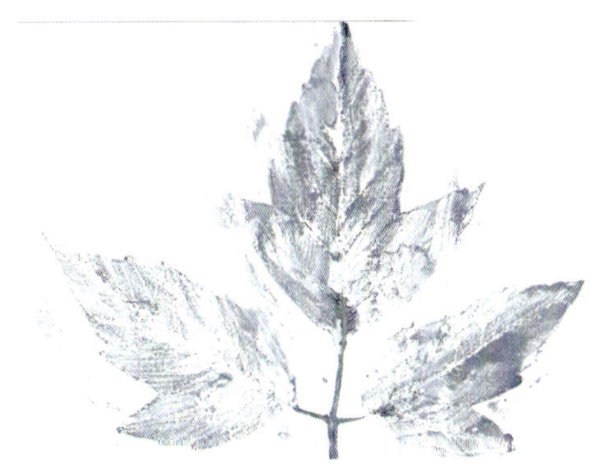

RED CORN TASSEL WITH VINEGAR

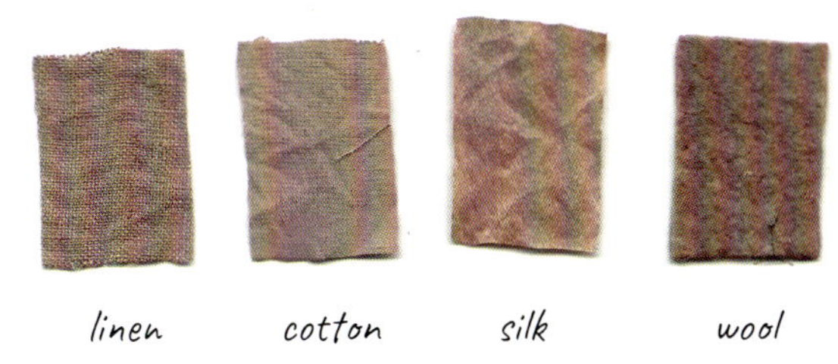

RED CORN TASSEL WITH TARTAR

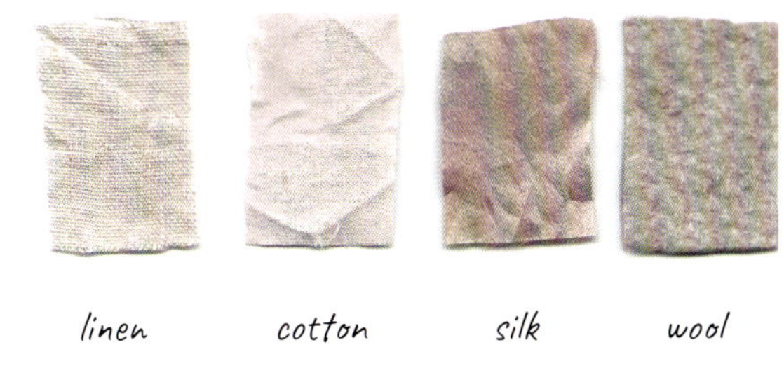

DOUBLE BOILED RED CORN TASSEL WITH TARTAR

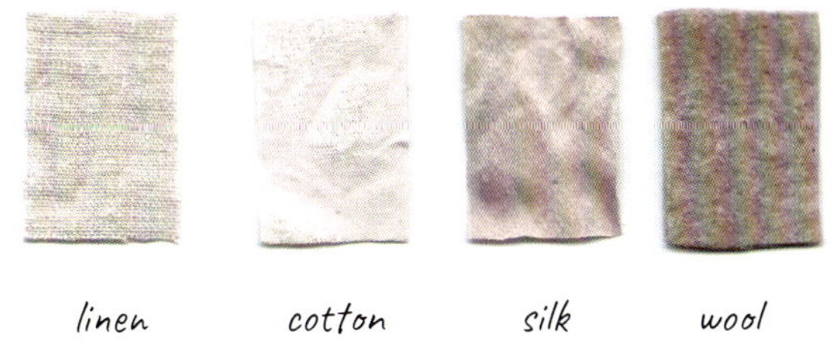

CENTAUREA CYANUS

Cornflower

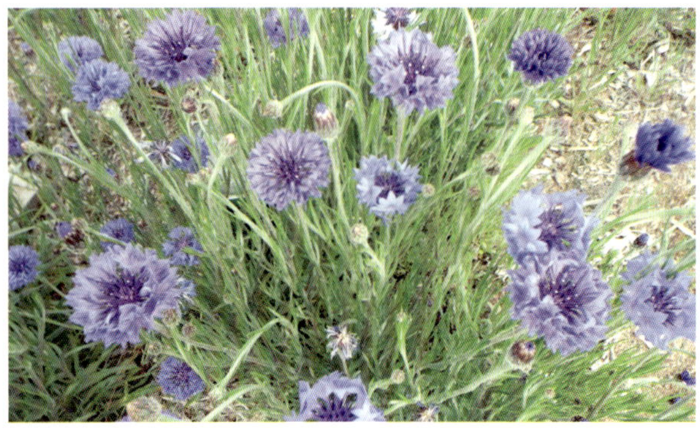

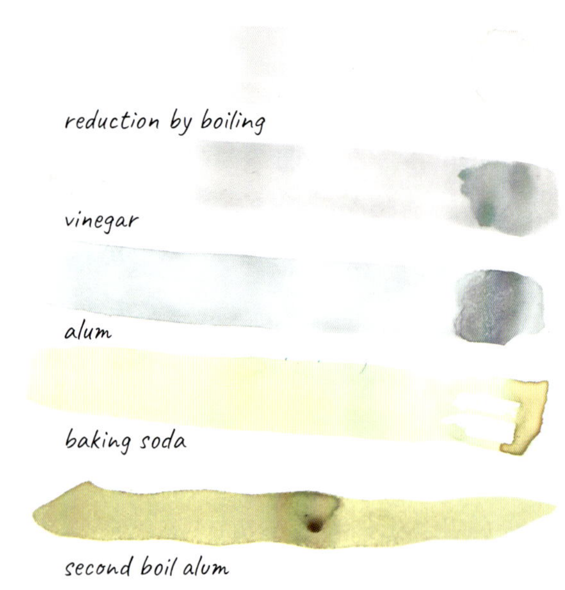

COLORS CREATED	blue, gray, brown, green
PARTS USED FOR PIGMENT	petals only
PLANT TYPE	self-seeding annual
SEEDING	Seeds available at SeedRenaissance.com.

1. The natural colors present and hidden in cornflower are both highly water soluble and VERY sensitive to mordants, which can make this plant somewhat tricky to work with. To begin, at peak bloom, separate the petals from any stems, sepals, and leaves and dry. Simmer petals for at least 10 minutes, then strain out the petals and discard or compost. This produces a pale gray.

2. Intensify the color by reducing the liquid at a steaming, not boiling, temperature. Boiling can over process and permanently darken the color. A red color that will age to become brown is created, but in my experiments, boiling the used petals a second time in fresh water produces a yellow color.

3. A slight amount of vinegar mordant produces a pink liquid that ages and dries to become purple. A little more vinegar creates a red liquid that ages and dries as pale green.

4. Alum creates a purple liquid that ages to be blue. A slight amount of baking soda mordant creates shades of green.

5. A little more baking soda creates yellows. Boiling the petals in fresh water with alum creates green shades that are brighter than the baking soda greens, but it never creates blues or purples again.

Notes: Adding any green part of the plant to the blue petals will ruin the color, which makes this plant fiddly to work with. I find that the petals pull nicely away from the green flower base (sepal) when they are fresh, but quite a few petals are needed to make even a small batch of color. The colors made from cornflowers disappear quickly if exposed to direct sunlight.

COSMOS BIPINNATUS

Cosmos

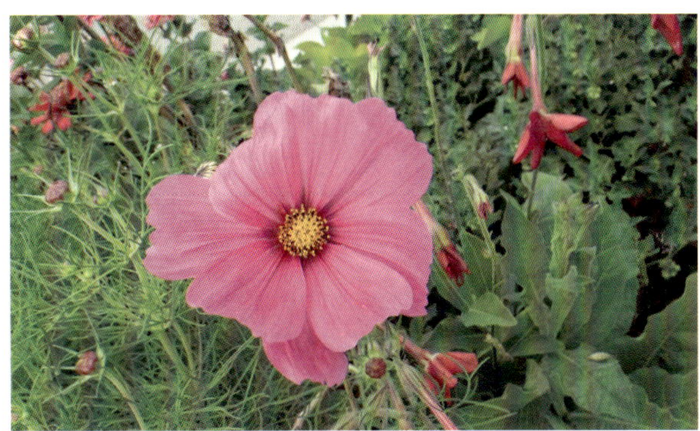

COLORS CREATED	white or red petals make yellow with alum and tartar; red petals make green with alum or yellow with baking soda; purple petals make no useful color
PARTS USED FOR PIGMENT	petals
PLANT TYPE	annual
SEEDING	Seeds available at SeedRenaissance.com.

1. Simmer for 10 minutes to make pigment or dye. Strain.
2. Simmer again to reduce liquid to desired color strength.

BOILED DARK PINK COSMOS PETALS WITH ALUM, TARTAR, AND GLAUBER'S SALT

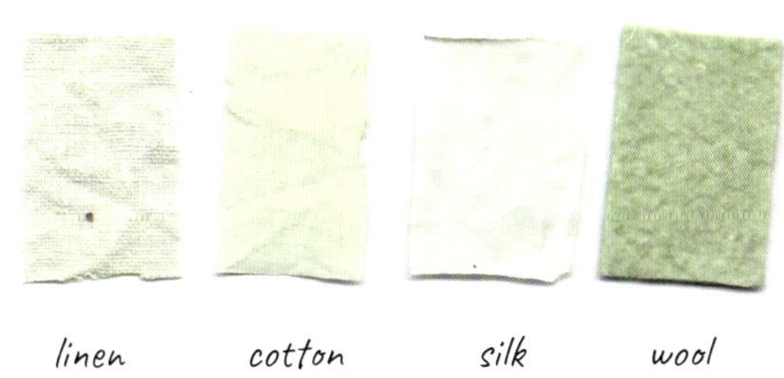

RED COSMOS PETALS

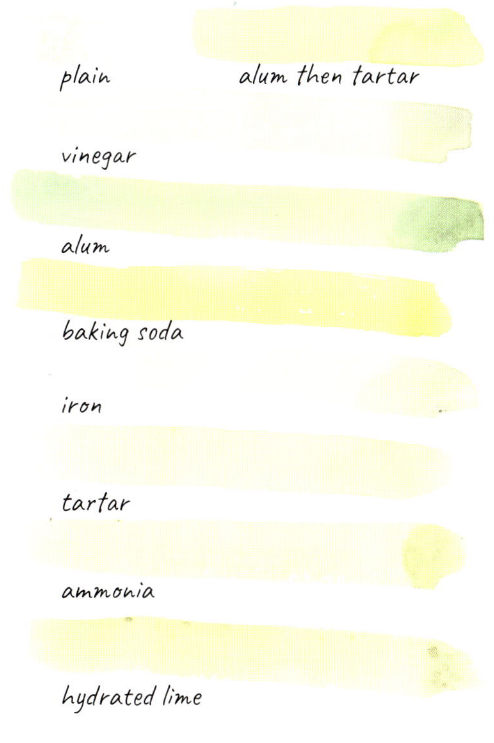

WHITE COSMOS PETALS

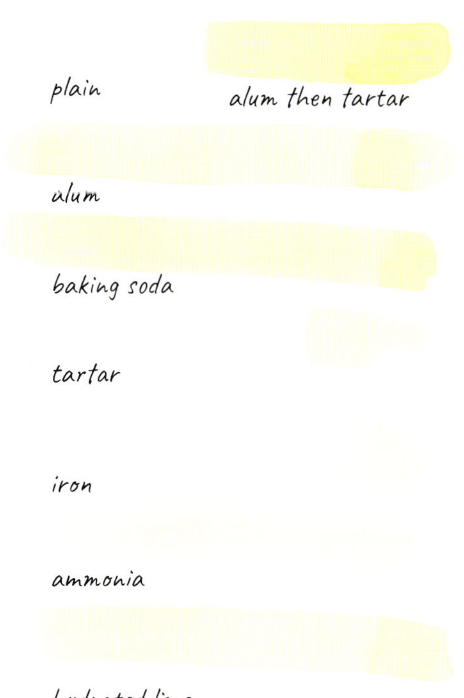

COSMOS SULPHUREUS

Cosmos Sulfur

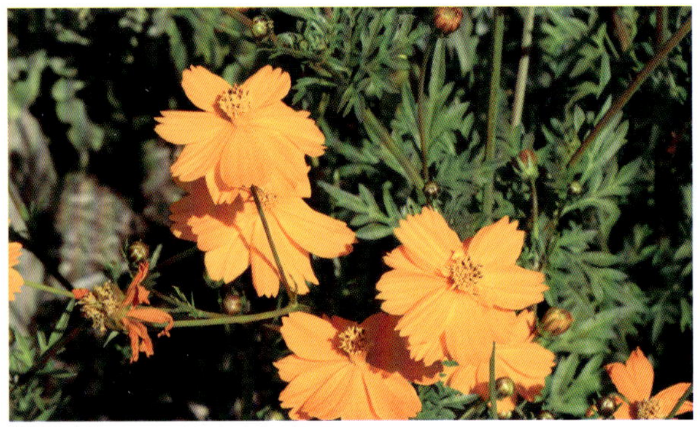

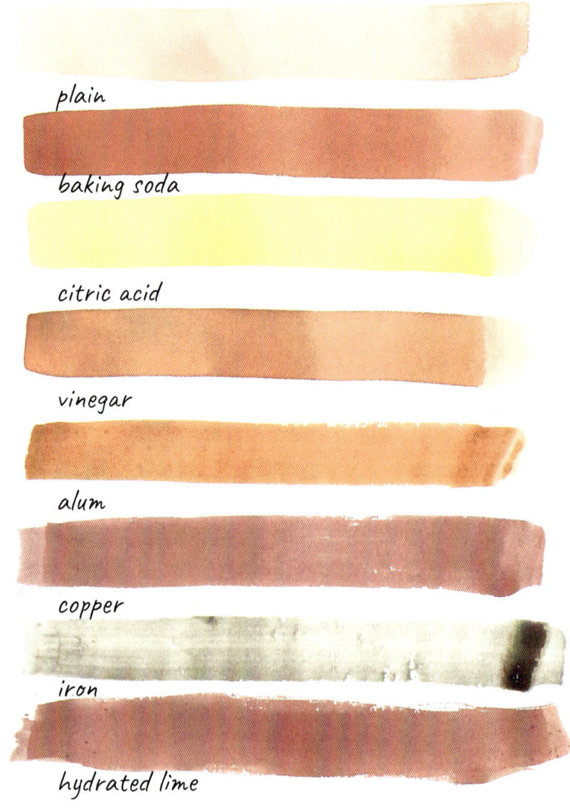

COLORS CREATED	red with baking soda, vinegar, vinegar of copper, or hydrated lime; orange with alum; yellow with citric acid
PARTS USED FOR PIGMENT	whole flower heads
PLANT TYPE	annual
SEEDING	Seeds available at SeedRenaissance.com.

1. Simmer for 10 minutes to make pigment or dye. Strain.
2. Simmer again to reduce liquid to desired color strength.

Notes: This plant also makes excellent eco-prints, creating a strong orange print with no mordant and a strong red print with vinegar of copper. This plant also makes an almost shiny gold on fabric.

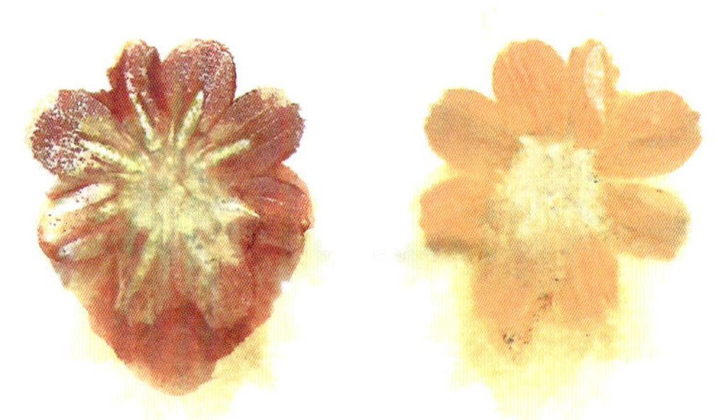

COTONEASTER LUCIDUS

Cotoneaster

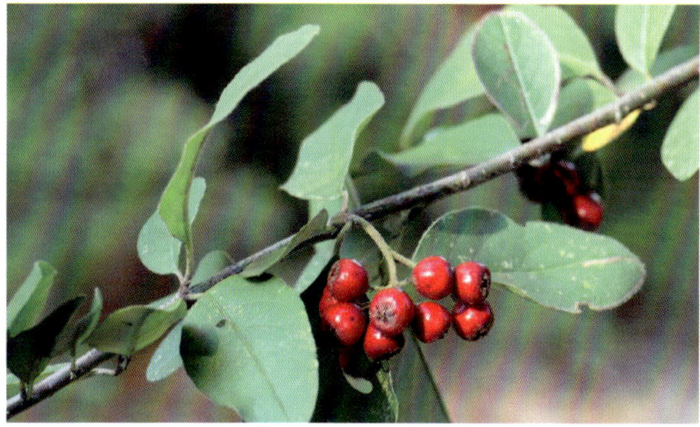

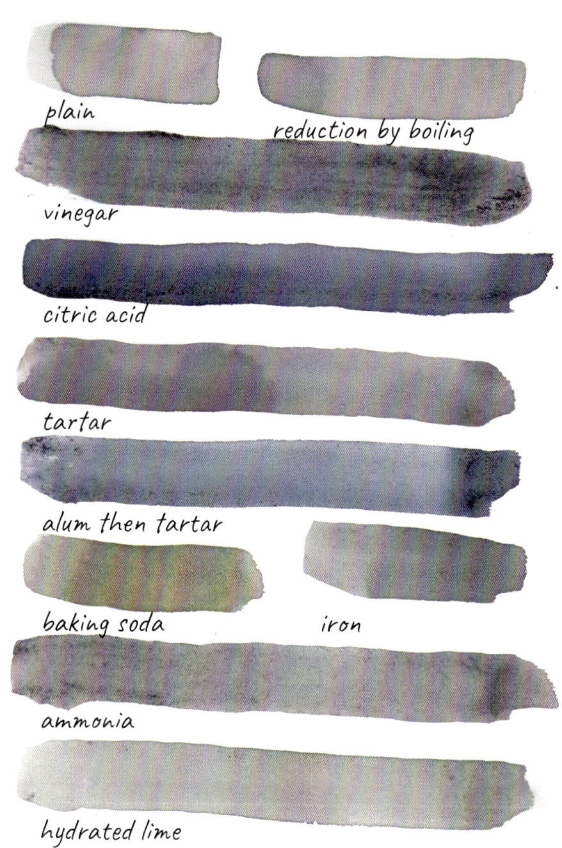

COLORS CREATED	dark blue with alum; medium blue with alum and tartar; purple without mordants or with most mordants
PARTS USED FOR PIGMENT	mashed ripe blue berries, fresh or dried
PLANT TYPE	perennial
HARDINESS ZONE	varies by species, but generally 5
SEEDING	Plant directly outside in spring or autumn. Seeds available at SeedRenaissance.com.

1. Simmer mashed berries for 10 minutes to make pigment or dye. Strain.
2. Simmer again to reduce liquid to desired color strength.

Notes: There are many species of cotoneaster, some with red or orange berries, and these are also good candidates for pigment and dye. This tall bush also turns fiery red in autumn. The blue dye must be washed with a pH-neutral soap or it will vanish.

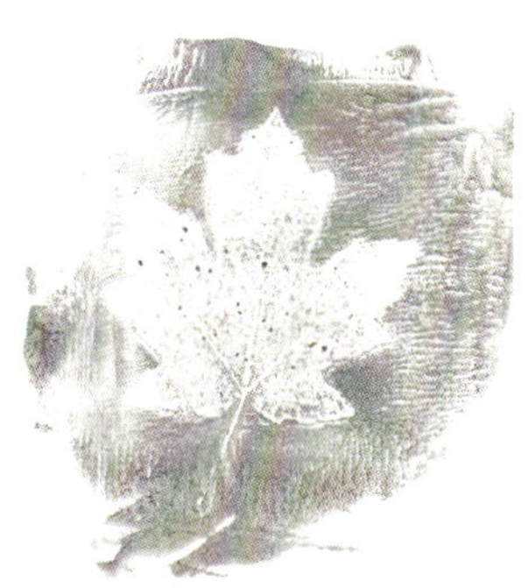

VACCINIUM SPECIES

Cranberry

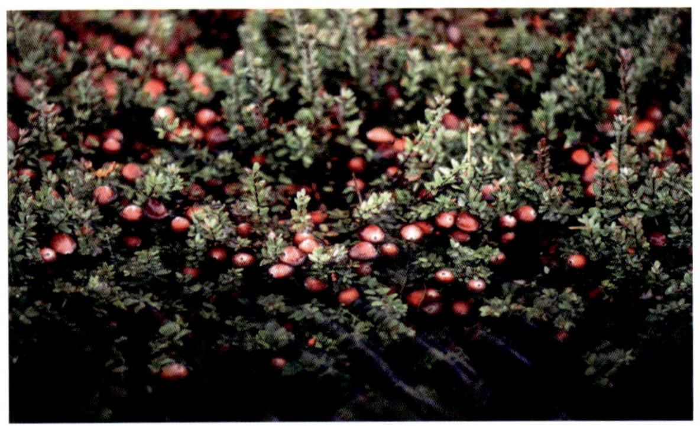

COLORS CREATED	red with vinegar, green with copper, gray or unstable colors with other mordants
PARTS USED FOR PIGMENT	ripe berries, fresh or unsweetened frozen
PLANT TYPE	perennial fruiting bush
HARDINESS ZONE	2

1. Simmer for 10 minutes to make pigment or dye. Strain.
2. Simmer again to reduce liquid to desired color strength.

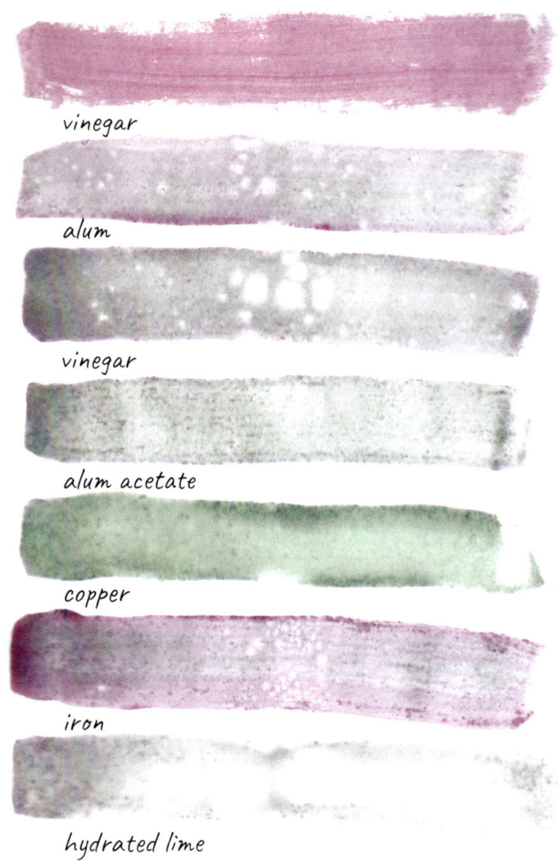

CRANBERRY WITH VINEGAR

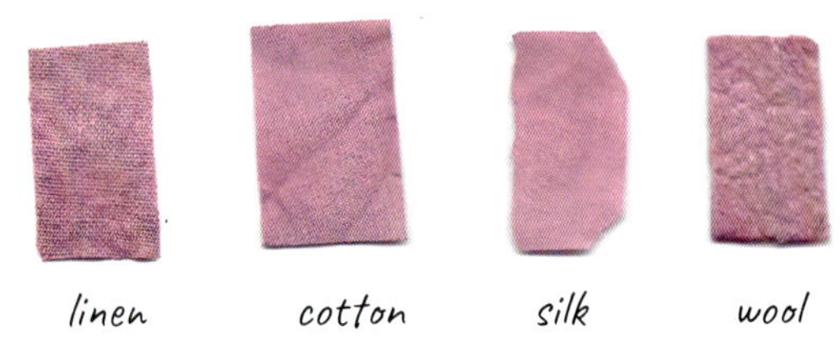

CRANBERRY WITH ALUM

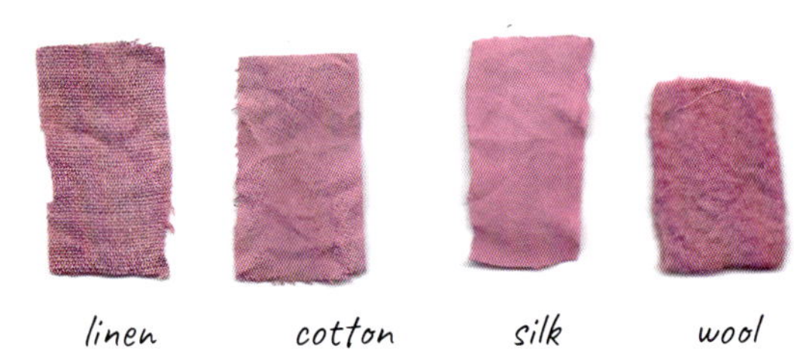

CRINUM ASIATICUM

Crinum Lily

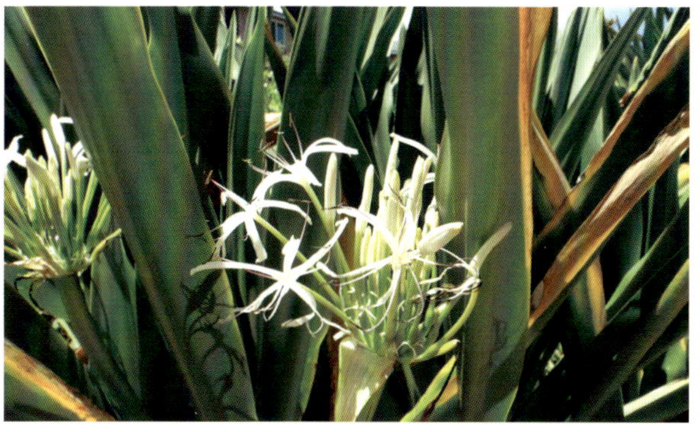

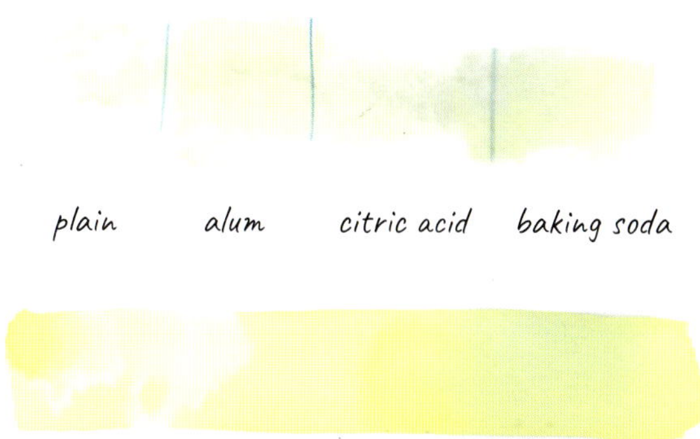

COLORS CREATED	strong yellow with baking soda, medium yellow with alum
PARTS USED FOR PIGMENT	white lily petals
PLANT TYPE	tropical

1. Simmer for 10 minutes to make pigment or dye. Strain.
2. Simmer again to reduce liquid to desired color strength.

RIBES SPECIES

Currants

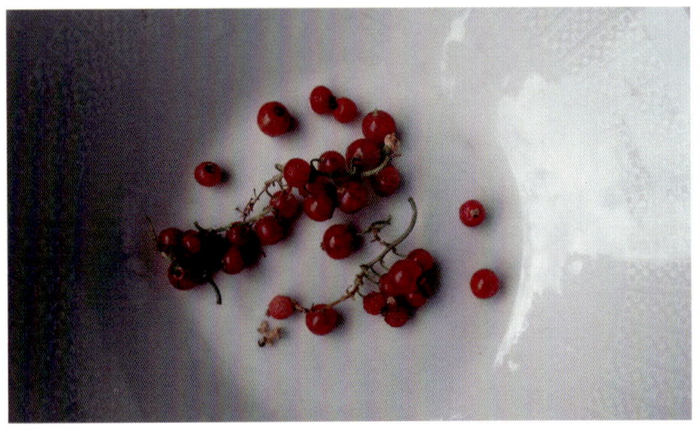

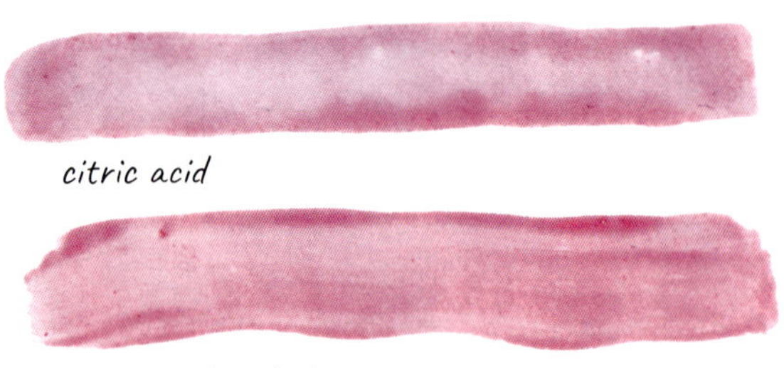

COLORS CREATED	red from red currants and citric acid
PARTS USED FOR PIGMENT	ripe red berries
PLANT TYPE	perennial
HARDINESS ZONE	3

1. Simmer for 10 minutes to make pigment or dye. Strain.
2. Simmer again to reduce liquid to desired color strength.

Notes: I have not been able to make a good color with any color of currant but red. You can add citric acid and alum to make the color more permanent.

NARCISSUS SPECIES

Daffodils

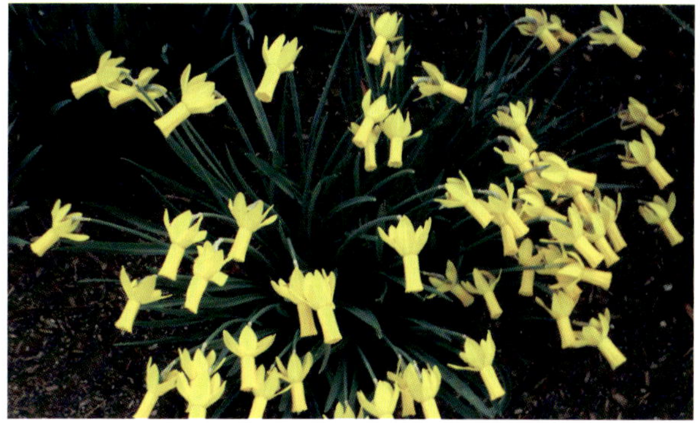

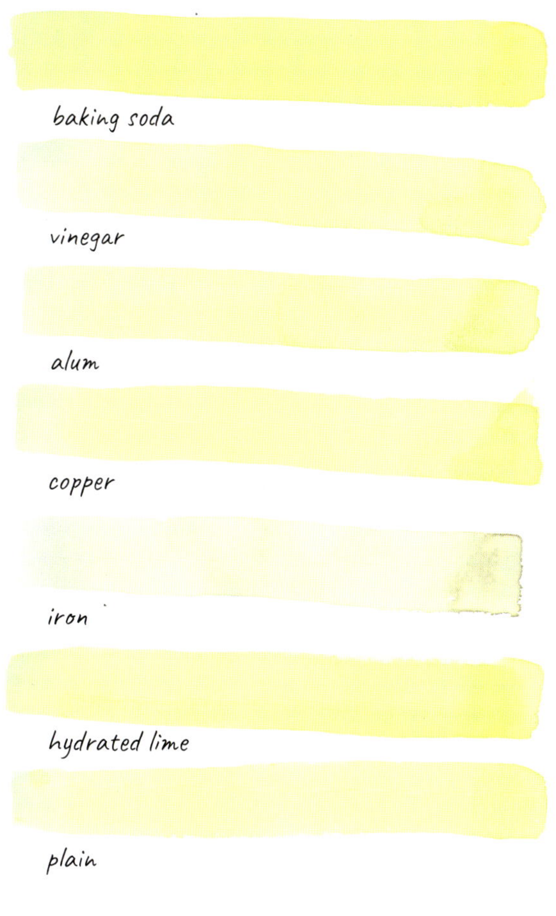

COLORS CREATED	yellow from baking soda, alum, or hydrated lime
PARTS USED FOR PIGMENT	yellow petal
PLANT TYPE	perennial bulbs
HARDINESS ZONE	3

1. Simmer for 10 minutes to make pigment or dye. Strain.
2. Simmer again to reduce liquid to desired color strength.

Notes: Makes a surprisingly great yellow dye on wool.

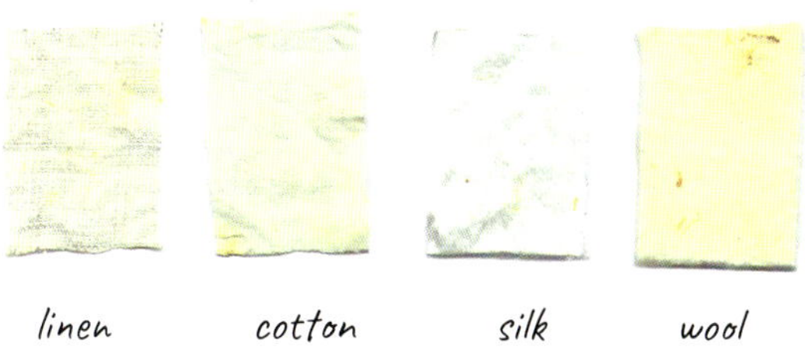

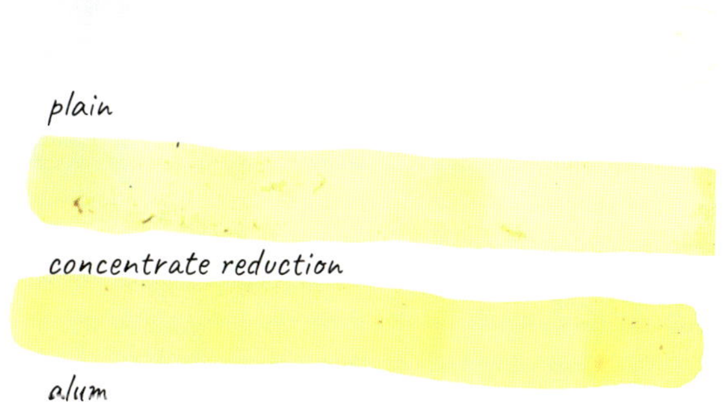

Dahlia Species

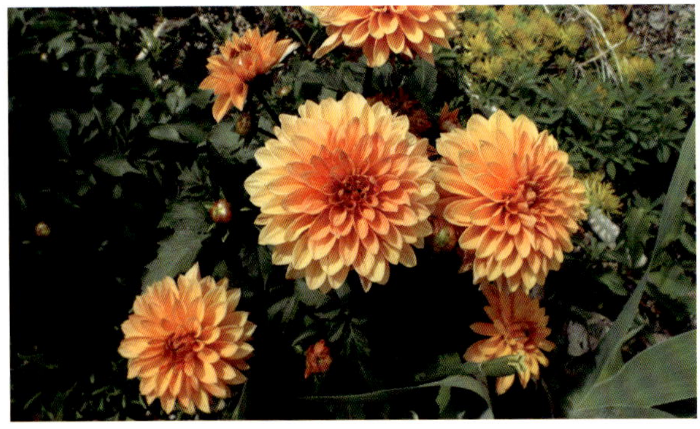

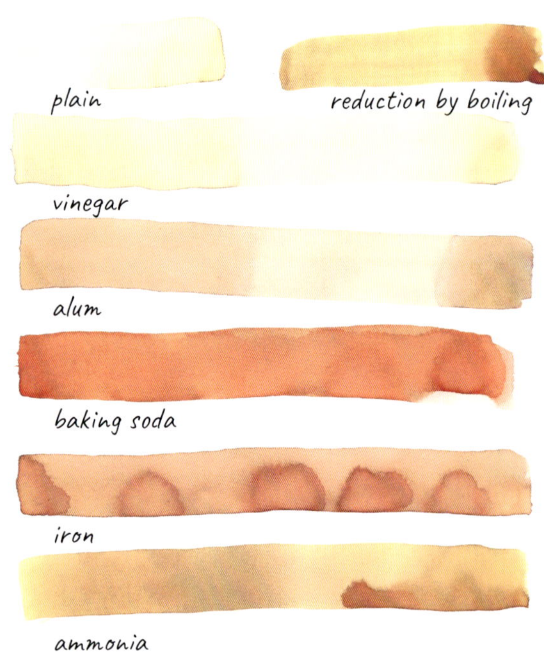

COLORS CREATED	red with baking soda or iron, terracotta without mordants or with ammonia, pale red with alum
PARTS USED FOR PIGMENT	red petals only (no sepals)
PLANT TYPE	landscape flower
HARDINESS ZONE	8

1. Simmer for 20 minutes to make pigment or dye. Strain.
2. Simmer again to reduce liquid to desired color strength.

Notes: Other colors of this flower may also make pigment and dye based on petal color.

FRESH MULLED ORANGE DAHLIA

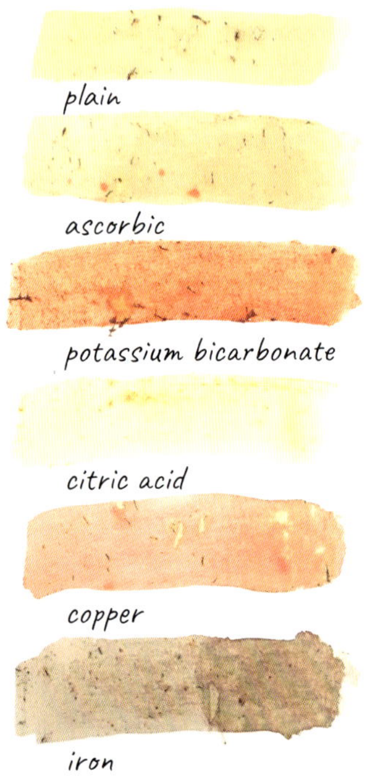

BELLIS PERENNIS

Daisies

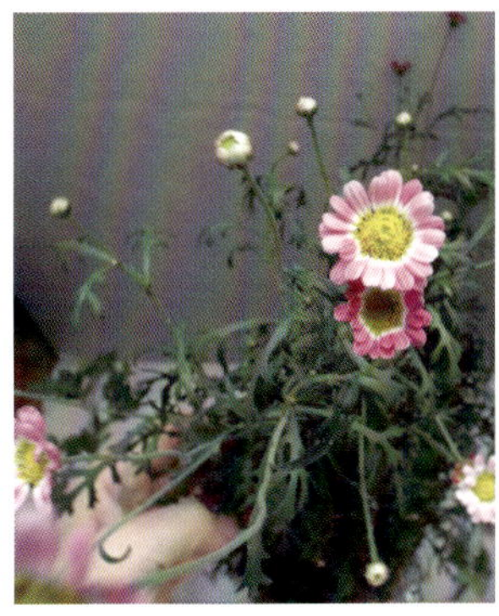

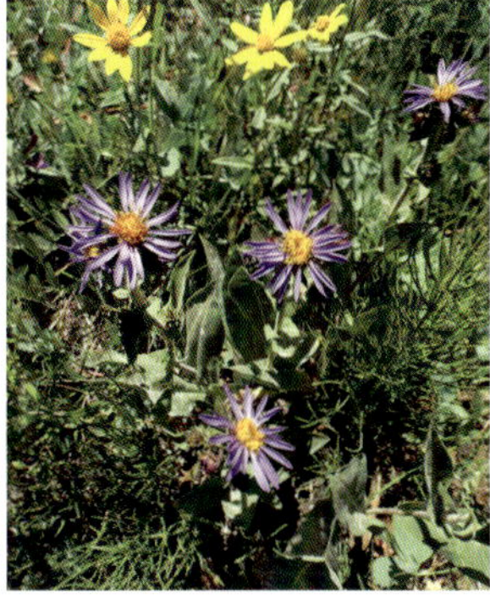

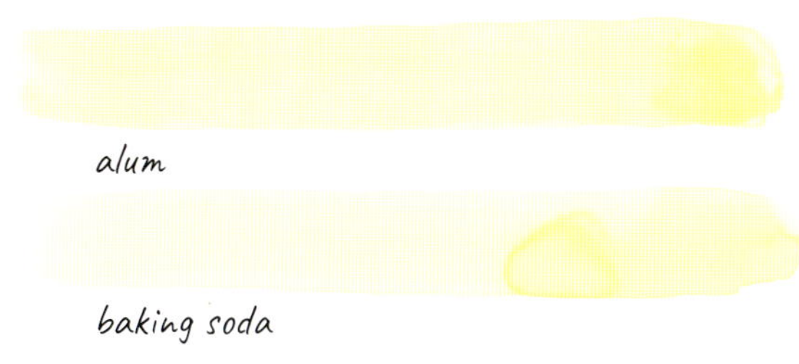

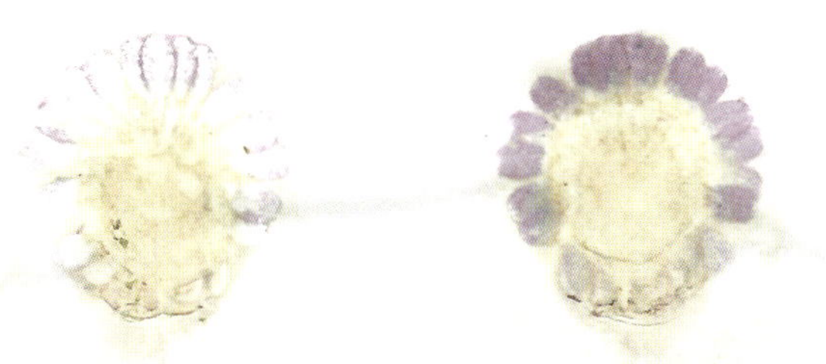

COLORS CREATED	yellows with alum and baking soda
PARTS USED FOR PIGMENT	petals only
PLANT TYPE	flower
HARDINESS ZONE	8

1. Simmer for 10 minutes to make pigment or dye. Strain.
2. Simmer again to reduce liquid to desired color strength.

Notes: Cherry red gerbera daisies created only tan. White petals alone of the Shasta daisy made nothing. So-called "painted daisy" made good eco-prints.

HESPERIS MATRONALIS

Dame's Rocket

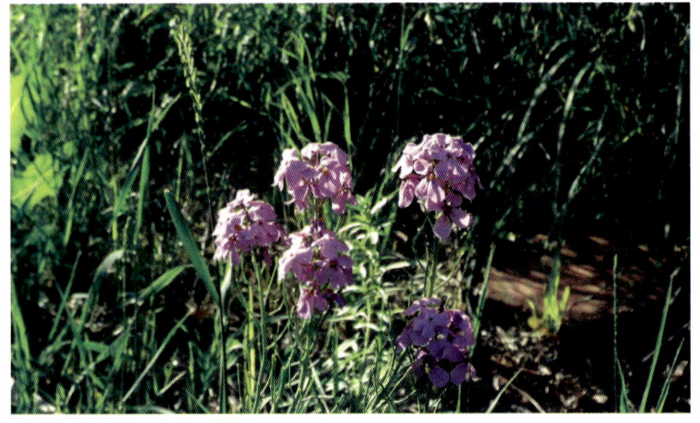

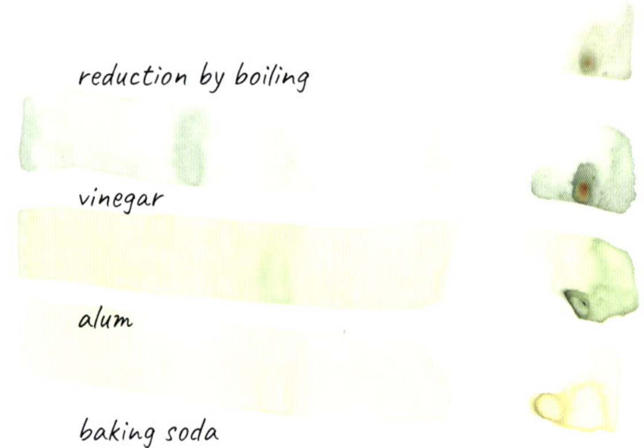

COLORS CREATED	pale yellow with alum
PARTS USED FOR PIGMENT	flower spikes with no leaves
PLANT TYPE	self-seeding annual

1. Simmer for 10 minutes to make pigment or dye. Strain.
2. Simmer again to reduce liquid to desired color strength.

Notes: Plants grow up to six feet tall and bloom in early summer. The color painted on green but changed to yellow.

FRESH MULLED

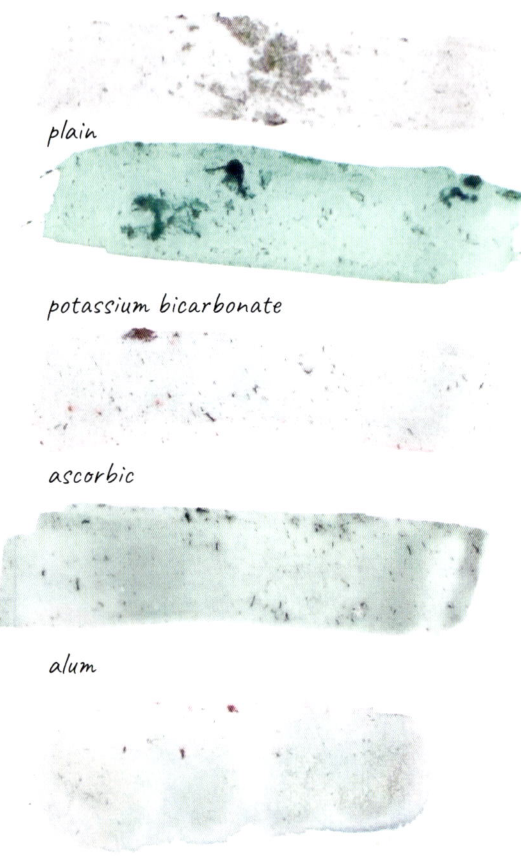

TARAXACUM OFFICINALE

Dandelion

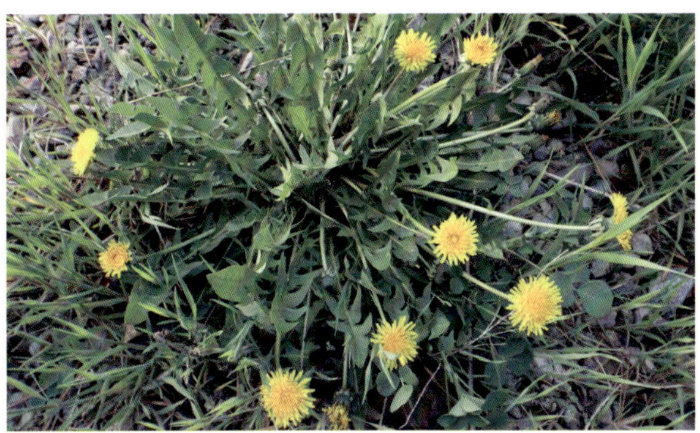

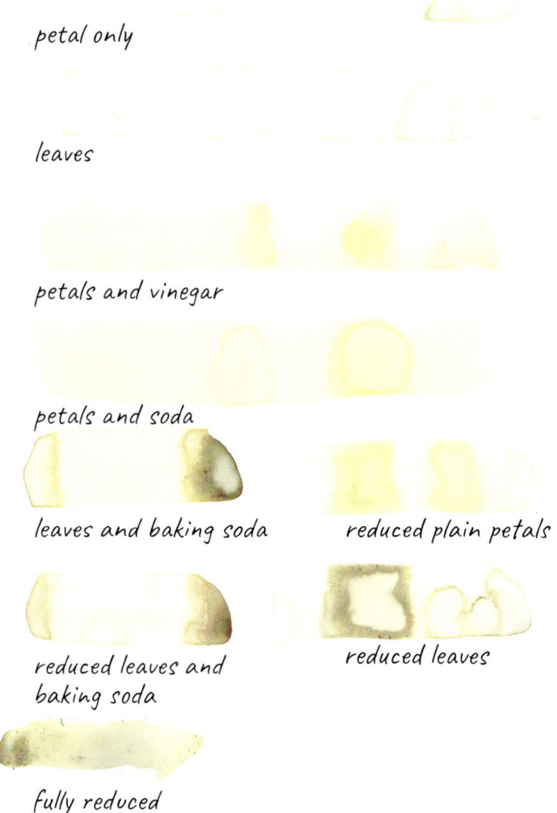

COLORS CREATED	pale yellow with vinegar or baking soda
PARTS USED FOR PIGMENT	petals
PLANT TYPE	perennial
HARDINESS ZONE	3

1. Simmer for 10 minutes to make pigment or dye. Strain.
2. Simmer again to reduce liquid to desired color strength.

Notes: The colors created with all other mordants, or without mordants, were unstable or nonexistent.

Datura Species

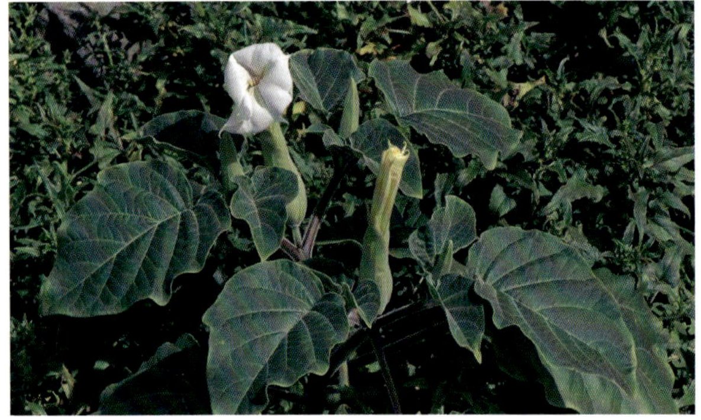

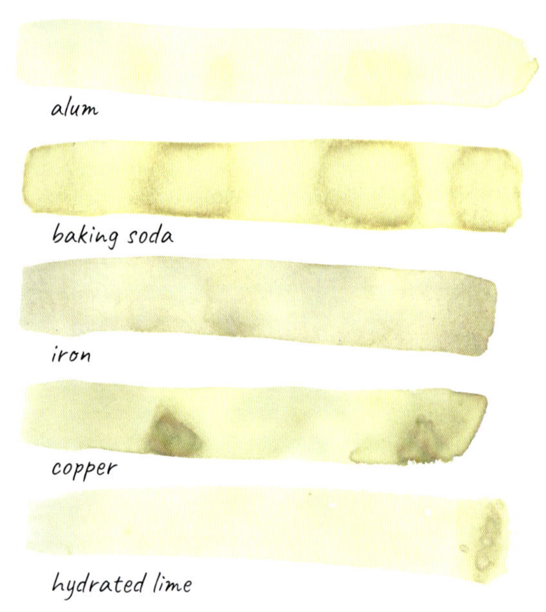

COLORS CREATED	pale yellow or pale brown from the leaves or white petals
PARTS USED FOR PIGMENT	leaves or petals
PLANT TYPE	root is perennial
HARDINESS ZONE	varies by species

1. Simmer for 20 minutes to make pigment or dye. Strain.
2. Simmer again to reduce liquid to desired color strength.

Notes: This plant is poisonous so don't eat it. I've never had a problem handling it for dye purposes.

HEMEROCALLIS SPECIES

Daylily

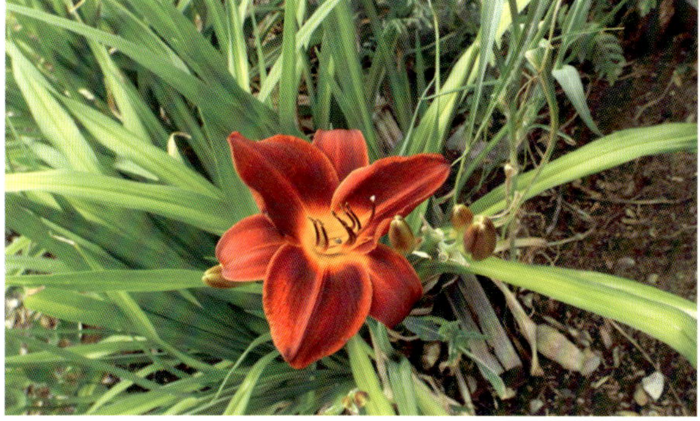

COLORS CREATED	red flowers create green with alum or vinegar, fresh orange petals create an orange-ish yellow with alum or baking soda, dried orange petals only create brown with baking soda
PARTS USED FOR PIGMENT	petals, fresh or dried
PLANT TYPE	perennial
HARDINESS ZONE	4

1. Simmer for 15 minutes to make pigment or dye. Strain.
2. Simmer again to reduce liquid to desired color strength.

RED DWARF DAYLILY

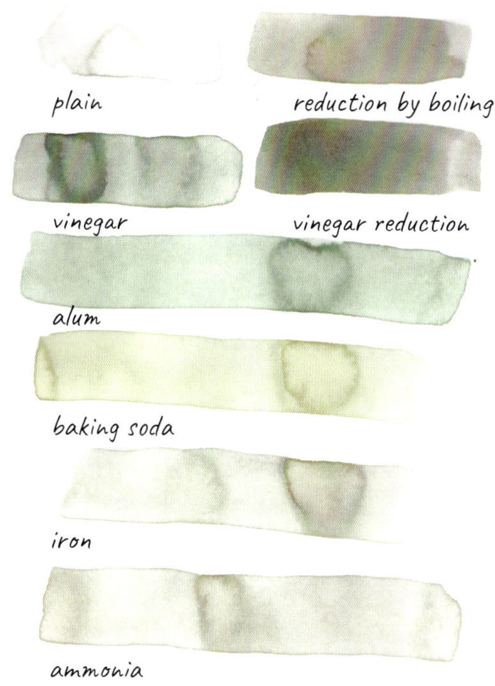

ORANGE NATURAL DAYLILY

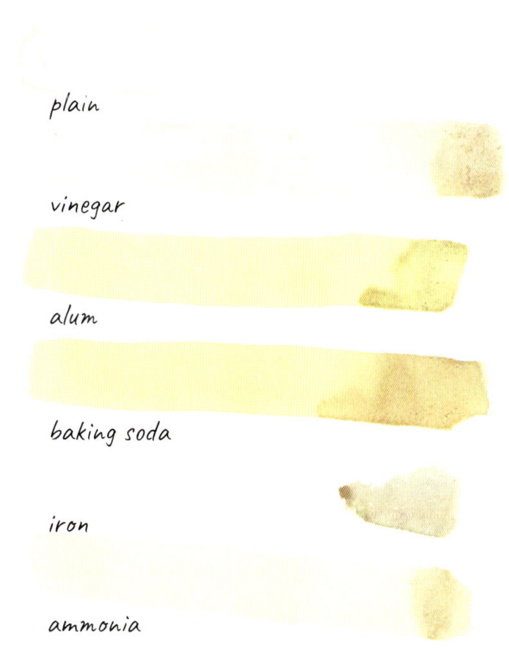

DELPHINIUM ELATUM

Delphinium

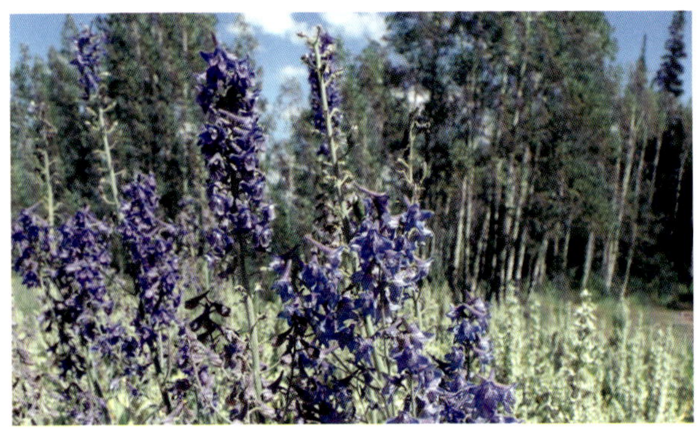

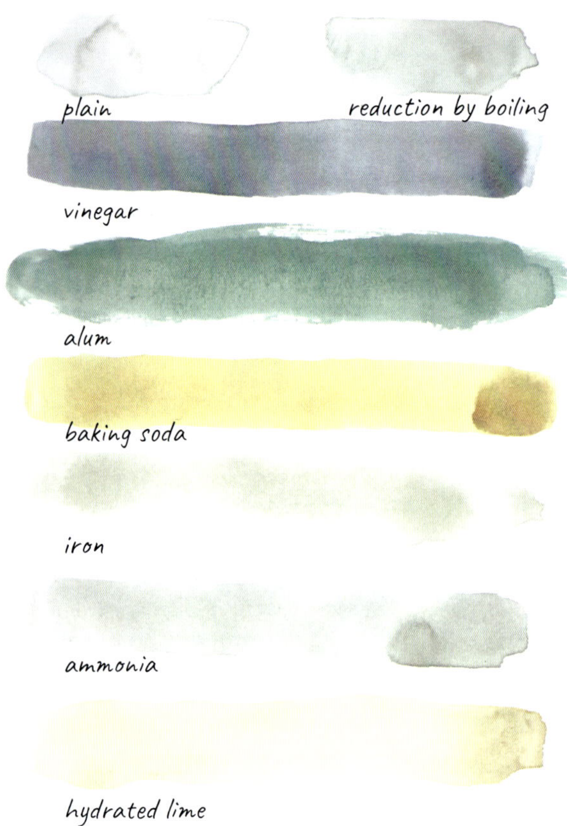

COLORS CREATED	blue with vinegar, green with alum, yellow with baking soda
PARTS USED FOR PIGMENT	blue petals
PLANT TYPE	varies widely by species and cultivar
SEEDING	Plant directly outside in spring or autumn. Seeds available at SeedRenaissance.com.

1. Simmer for 10 minutes to make pigment or dye. Strain.
2. Simmer again to reduce liquid to desired color strength.

Notes: Blue delphinium makes excellent blue eco-prints that turn green with vinegar of copper. If you live in a hot, arid climate like I do, you can grow delphiniums on the east side of your home where they get morning sun and full afternoon shade. They are perennial if watered.

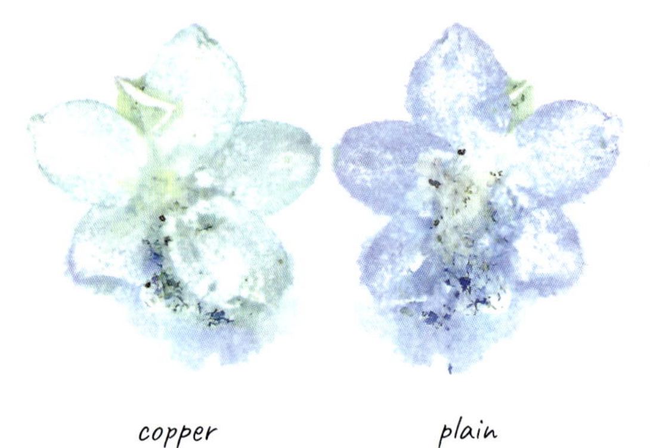

BAILEYA SPECIES

Desert Marigold

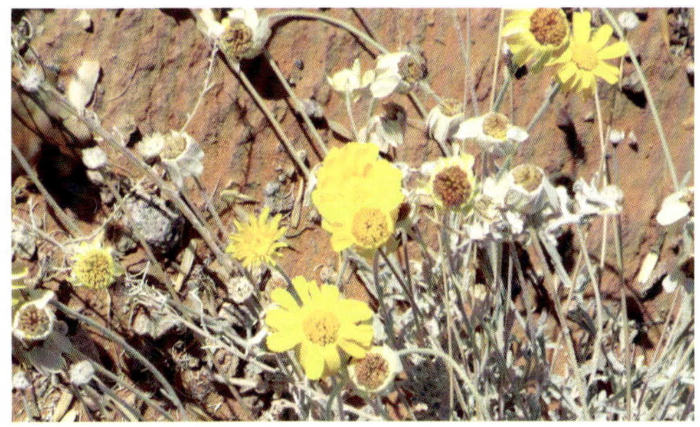

COLORS CREATED	yellow with various mordants
PARTS USED FOR PIGMENT	whole flower heads
PLANT TYPE	annual
HARDINESS ZONE	varies by species

1. Simmer for 10 minutes to make pigment or dye. Strain.
2. Simmer again to reduce liquid to desired color strength.

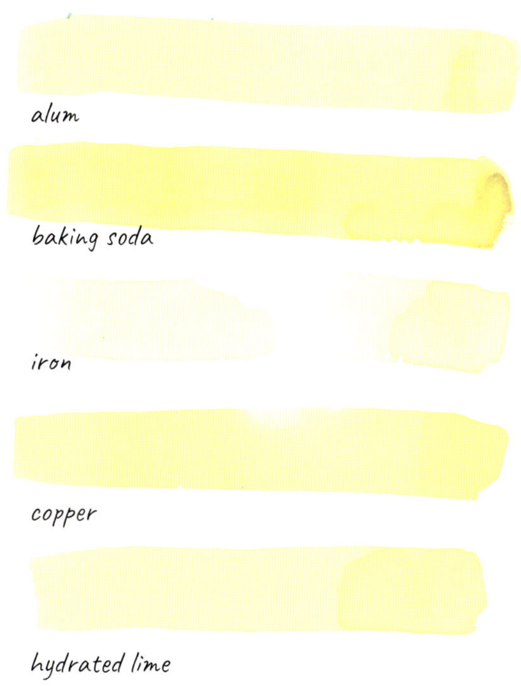

BOILED YELLOW FLOWERS (NO MORDANTS)

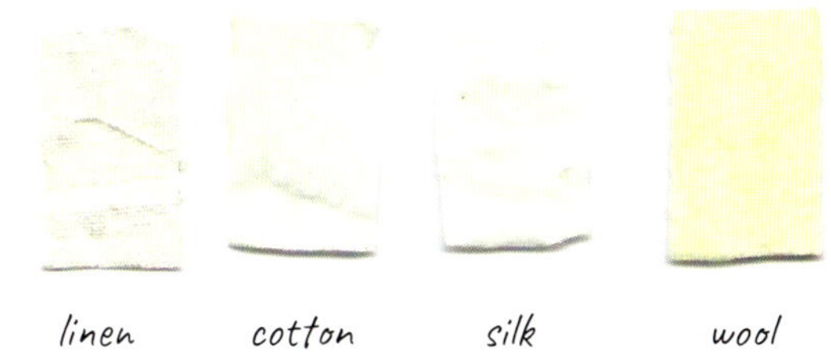

RUMEX SPECIES

Docks and Sorrels

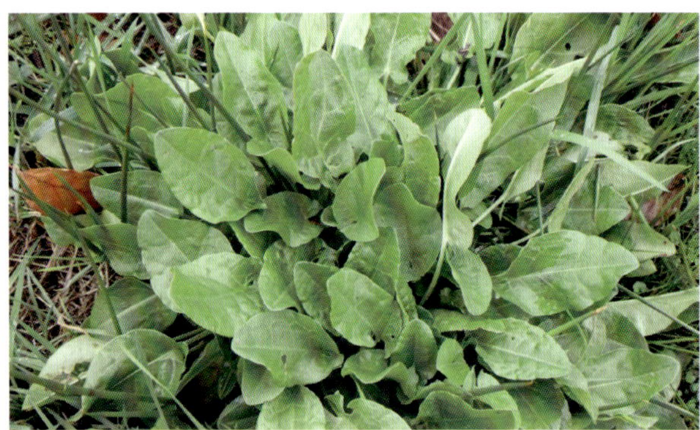

COLORS CREATED	red from roots of several species, yellowish brown from the flowering heads of burdock, yellowish red from green seeds
PARTS USED FOR PIGMENT	roots
PLANT TYPE	perennial
HARDINESS ZONE	4
SEEDING	Seeds available at SeedRenaissance.com.

1. Simmer roots for 20 minutes to make pigment or dye. Strain.
2. Simmer again to reduce liquid to desired color strength.

Notes: I believe the color is actually from the bark of the roots.

DOCK IMMATURE SEEDS

DOCK BURDOCK FLOWERS

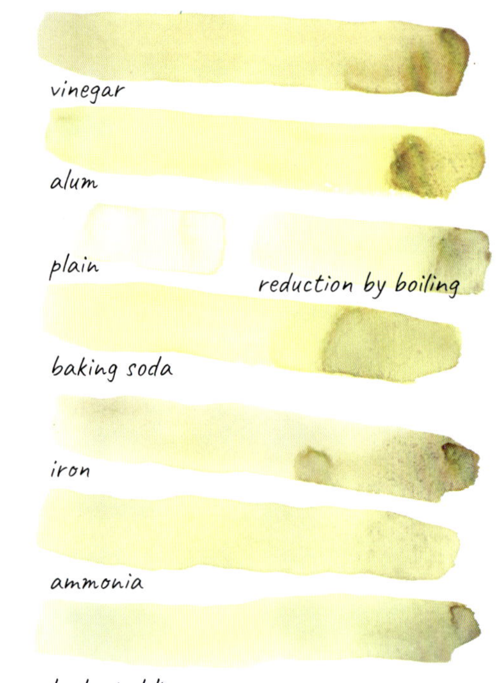

DOCK BURDOCK ROOT

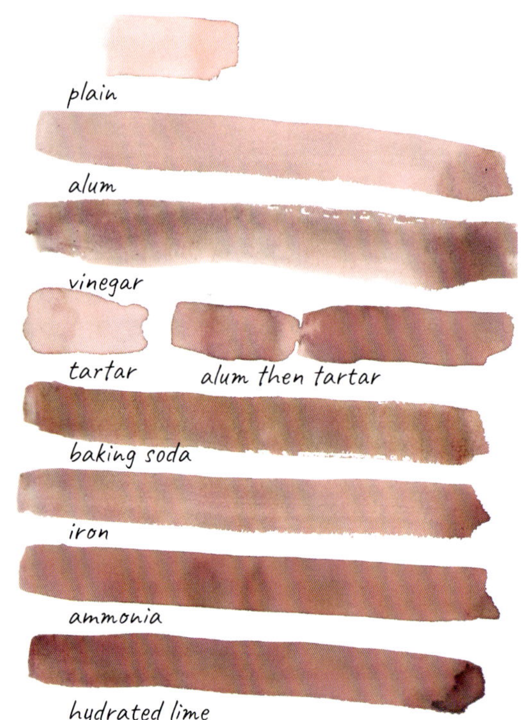

CORNUS SPECIES

Dogwood

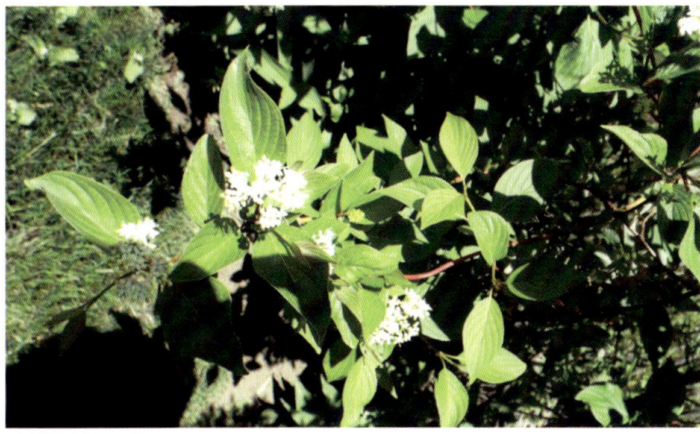

COLORS CREATED	brown or yellow, except when it makes red if you are lucky
PARTS USED FOR PIGMENT	twigs with bark
PLANT TYPE	perennial
HARDINESS ZONE	2

1. Simmer twigs with bark for 1 hour to make pigment or dye. Strain.
2. Simmer again to reduce liquid to desired color strength.

Notes: We have several species of dogwood that grow wild in our area, and I've taken samples from all of them repeatedly, but I have only gotten red from the dogwood growing in our backyard that my wife purchased at a nursery. I can't tell which dogwood ours is, except it is not red flowering dogwood or silky dogwood. I've included a photo of ours, in case one of you, my readers, can tell better than I can.

DOGWOOD LEAVES

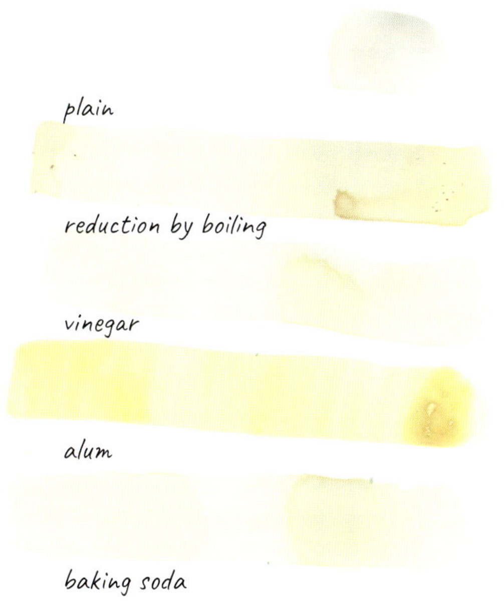

DOGWOOD MIG

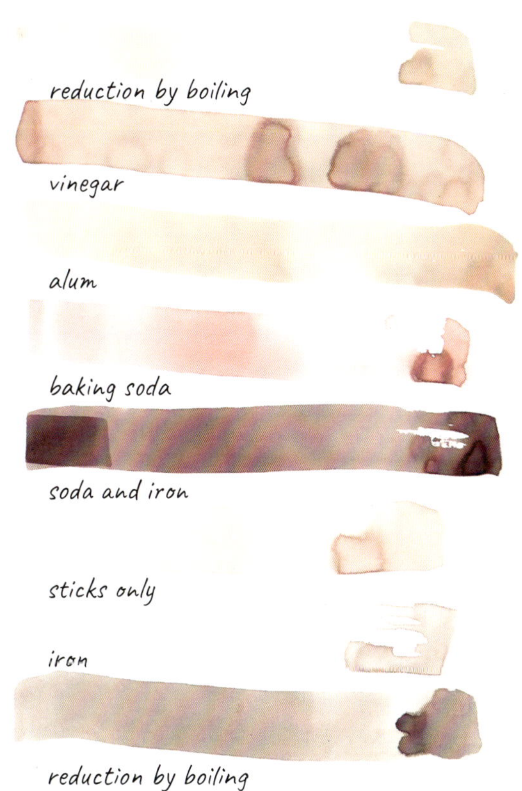

ANTHEMIS TINCTORIA

Dyer's Chamomile

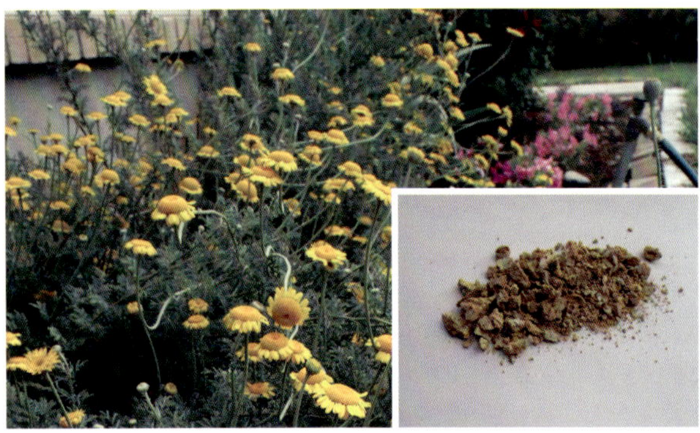

COLORS CREATED	yellow
PARTS USED FOR PIGMENT	flowers, fresh or dried at peak bloom
PLANT TYPE	perennial
HARDINESS ZONE	5
SEEDING	Seeds available at SeedRenaissance.com.

1. Simmer for 10 minutes or less to make pigment or dye. Overcooking the color will darken the yellow and make it muddy.

Notes: The cooked flowers can be boiled again with new water up to six times to produce more batches of good color. This is one of my favorite garden flowers. It is not the same as the chamomiles used for tea. The highly serrated leaves make excellent and visually interesting eco-prints.

FRESH PRESSED DYER'S CHAMOMILE LEAF

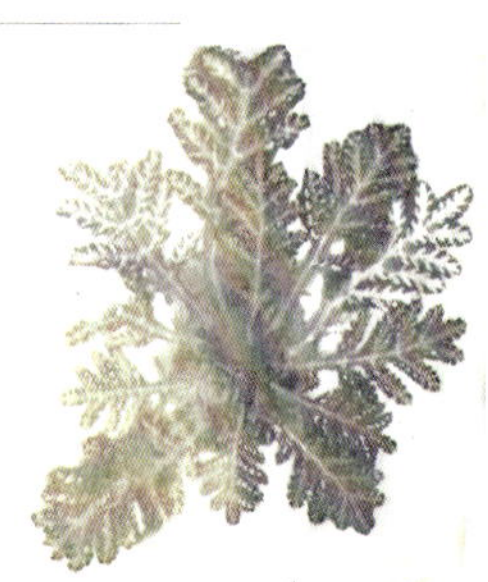

KELWAYS

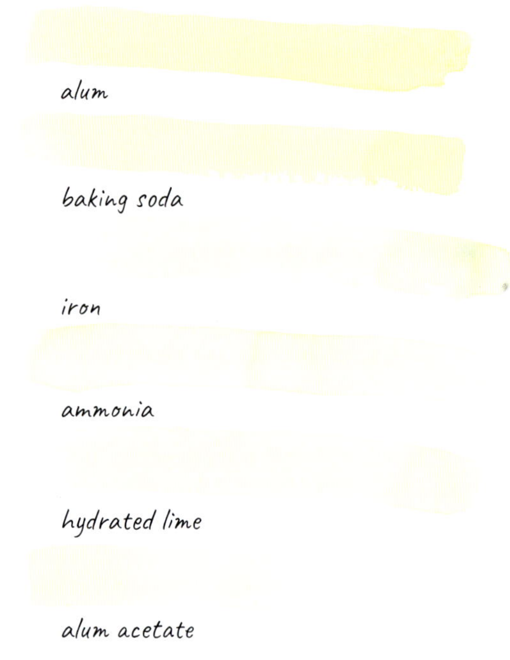

DRIED DYER'S CHAMOMILE

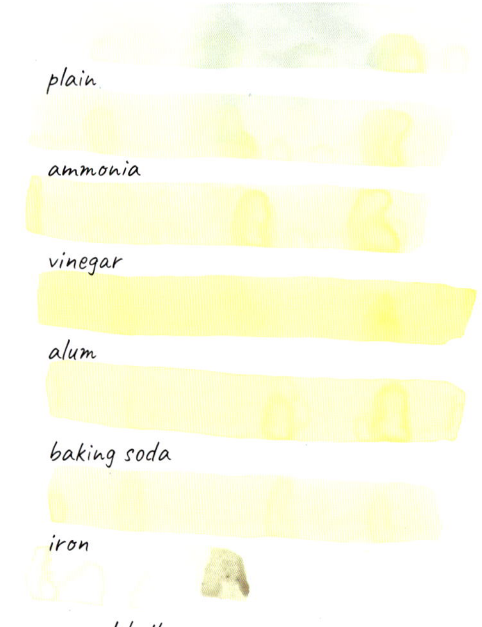

GENISTA TINCTORIA

Dyer's Greenweed

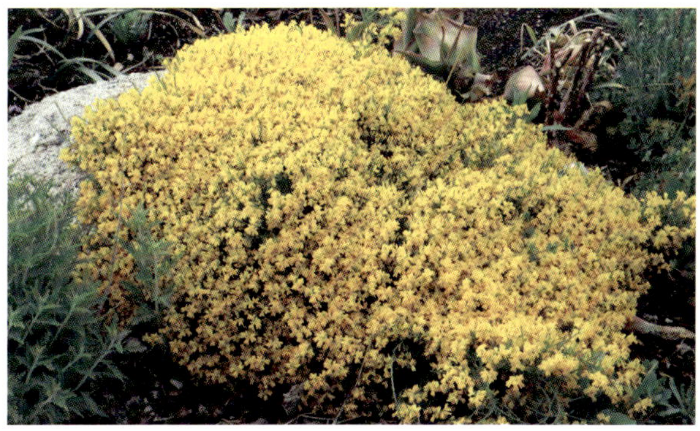

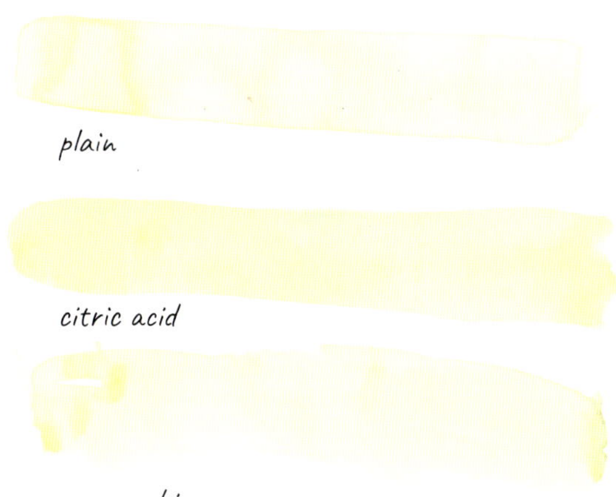

COLORS CREATED	yellow unmordanted and with most mordants
PARTS USED FOR PIGMENT	flowers, stems, leaves
PLANT TYPE	perennial low-growing shrub
HARDINESS ZONE	4

1. Simmer for 10 minutes to make pigment or dye. Strain.
2. Simmer again to reduce liquid to desired color strength.

Notes: This ground-hugging shrub makes a great spring flowering ground cover.

LILIUM LONGIFLORUM

Easter Lily

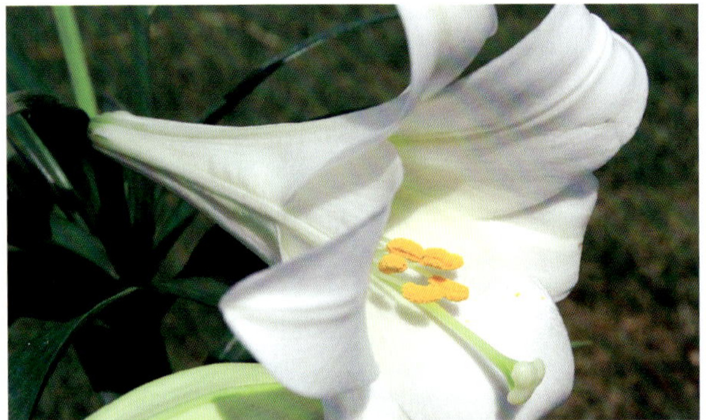

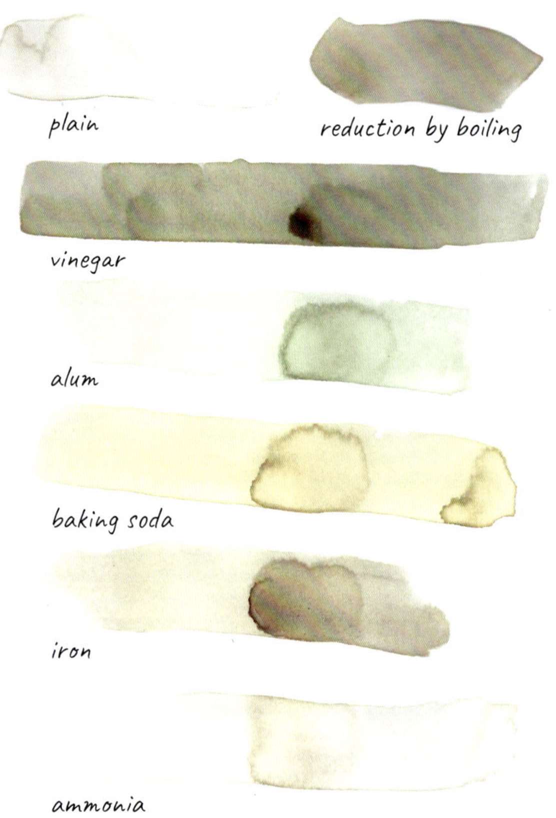

COLORS CREATED	red petals create army green with vinegar
PARTS USED FOR PIGMENT	flowers
PLANT TYPE	perennial
HARDINESS ZONE	4

1. Simmer for 10 minutes to make pigment or dye. Strain.
2. Simmer again to reduce liquid to desired color strength.

Eggshells and Seashells

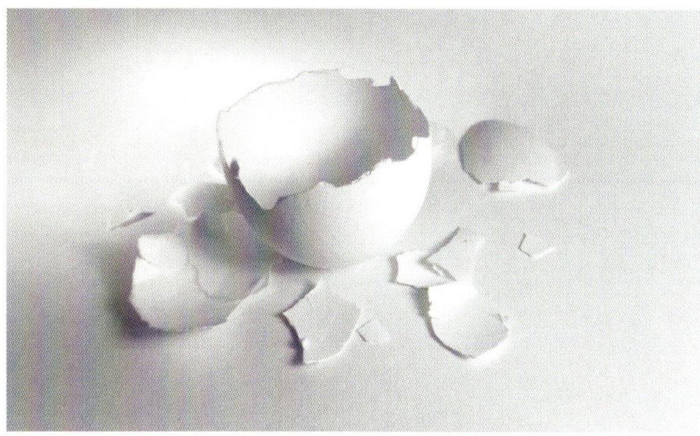

COLORS CREATED	white
PARTS USED FOR PIGMENT	clean shells, baked or boiled

1. See paint recipes in this book (see pages 68–77).

Notes: Natural calcium sources like these are a hugely important nontoxic source for white pigment, which cannot be created by flowers.

Coral background color: madder root with iron

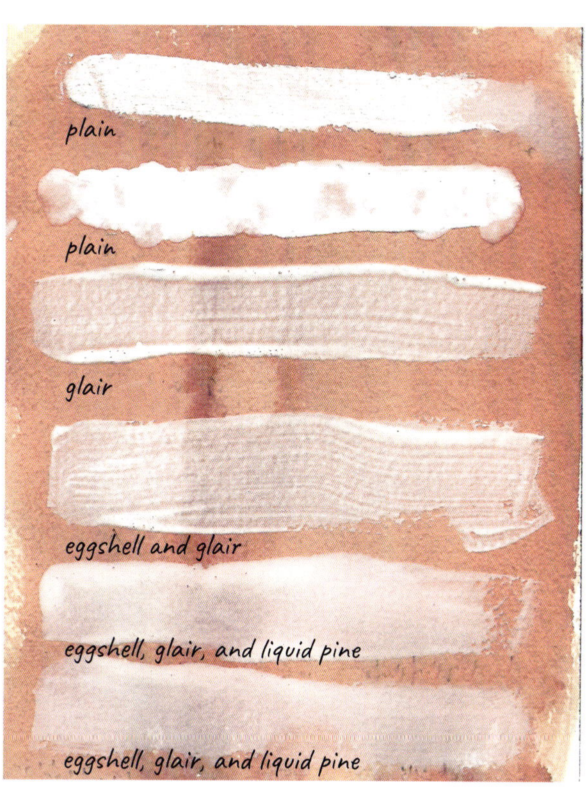

SAMBUCUS SPECIES

Elderberry

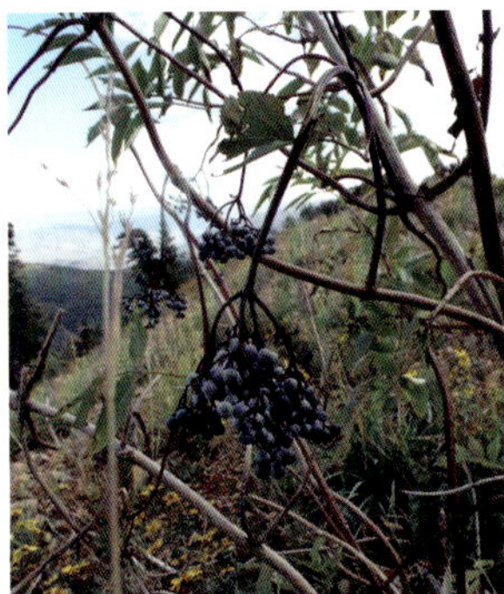

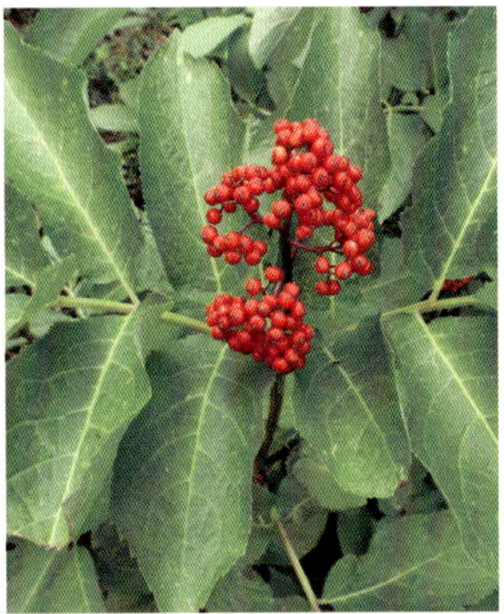

COLORS CREATED	fresh purple elderberries make blue with vinegar, green with baking soda, gray-blue with hydrated lime or iron, or purple unmordanted or with alum, tartar, or ammonia; fresh or dried blue elderberries make red or purple with most mordants; dried purple elderberries create green with vinegar and yellow with other mordants; red elderberries make yellow with alum, orange with baking soda, and brown with other mordants, except vinegar, which destroys the color to clear
PARTS USED FOR PIGMENT	berries
PLANT TYPE	perennial
HARDINESS ZONE	3

1. Simmer for 10 minutes to make pigment or dye. Strain.
2. Simmer again to reduce liquid to desired color strength.

BLUE ELDERBERRY

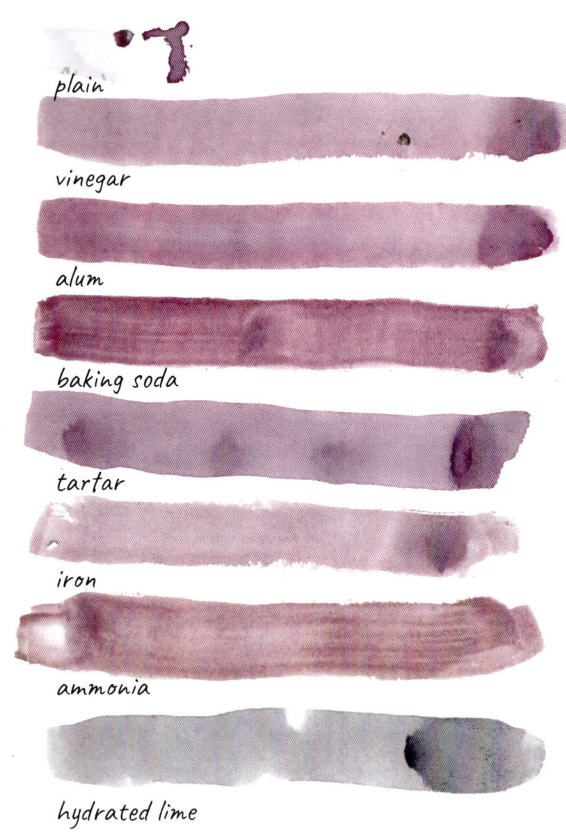

BOILED BLUE ELDERBERRIES (NO MORDANTS)

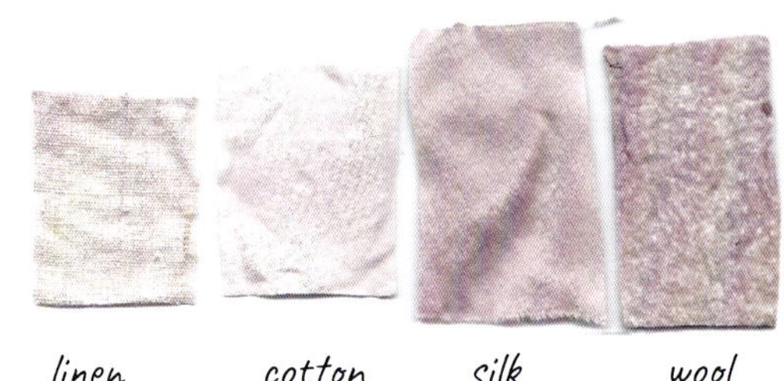

FRESH PURPLE ELDERBERRY

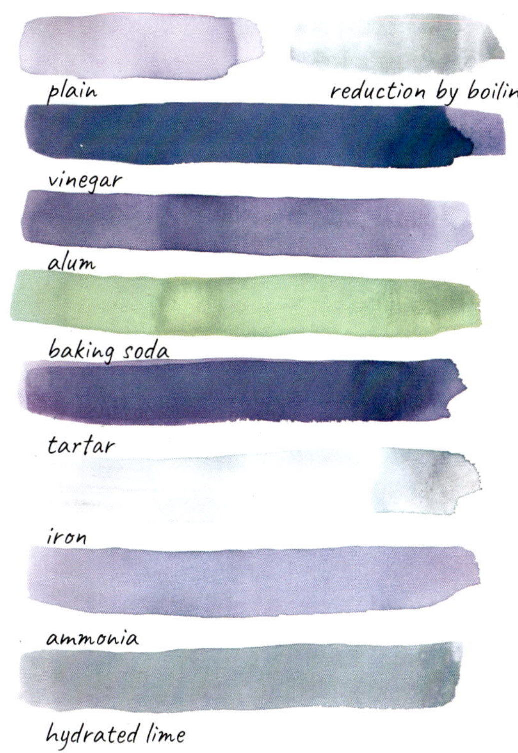

RED ELDERBERRY FLOWERS

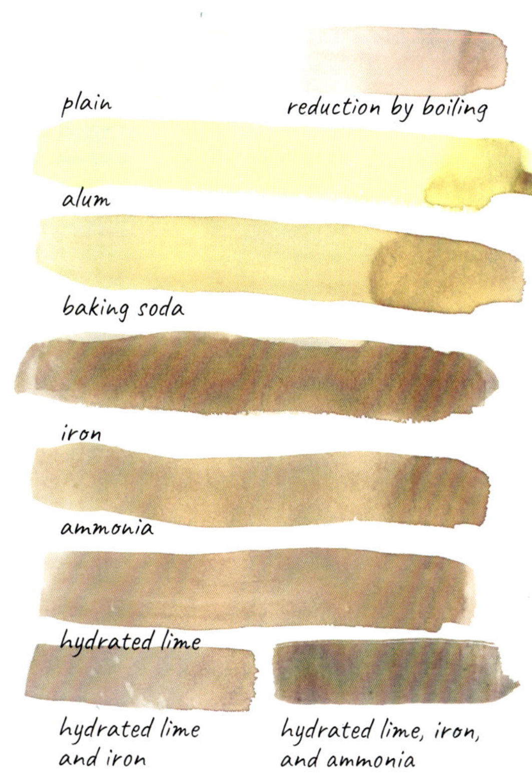

DRIED ELDERBERRY

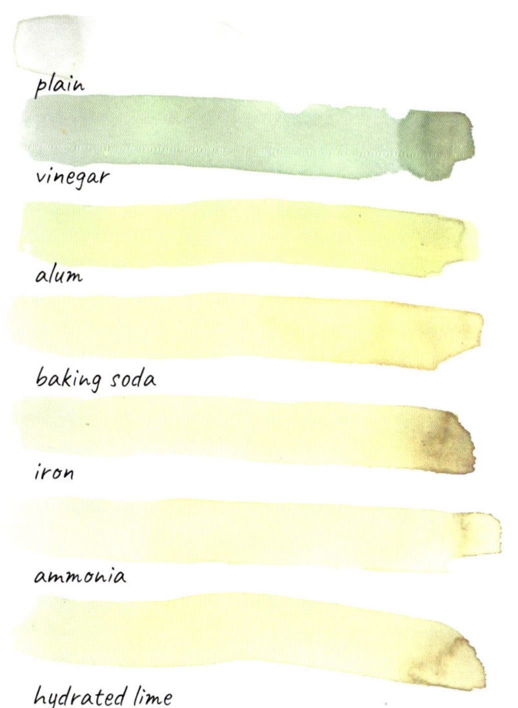

RED ELDERBERRY BERRIES

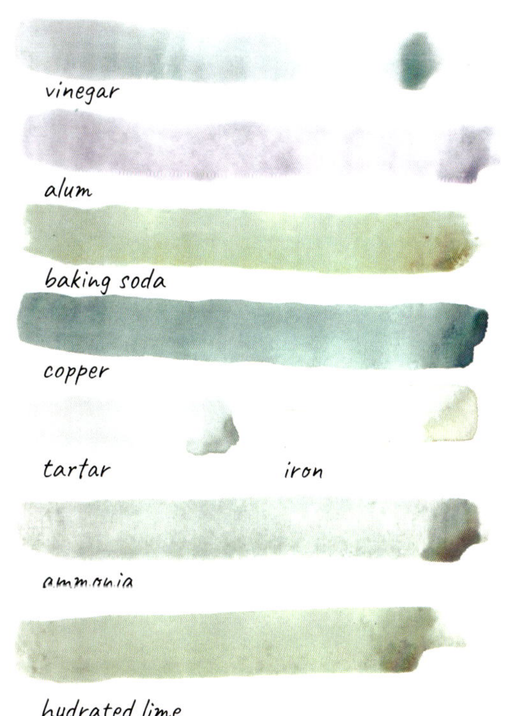

INULA HELENIUM

Elecampane

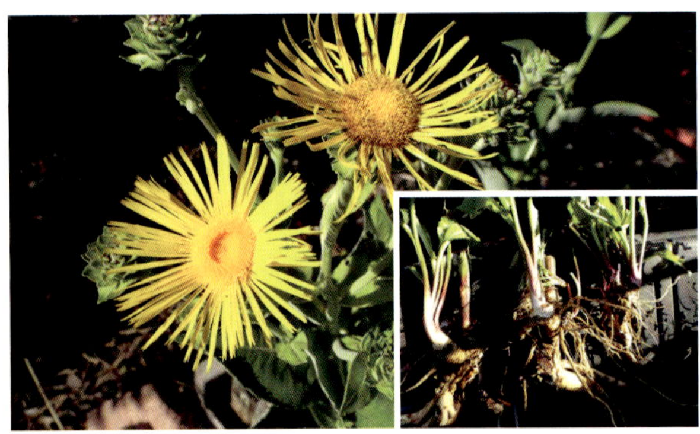

COLORS CREATED	yellow, and whatever color frustration is
PARTS USED FOR PIGMENT	flower heads
PLANT TYPE	perennial
HARDINESS ZONE	4
SEEDING	Seeds available at SeedRenaissance.com.

1. Simmer the whole flower heads for 10 minutes.

Notes: Alum or baking soda creates the strongest, brightest yellow. Roots boiled with bark made nothing, but a week of allowing the root to ferment in water made green; however, this green does not make dye or pigment. Many historical sources say the roots, when fermented with "stale urine" (urea) make blue. I've tried and tried and tried to make this blue with not even a hint of success. One more unusual note: The flowers smell so good while cooking that it makes you want to eat them. They smell like candy.

FERMENTED ELECAMPANE

vinegar

alum

baking soda

tartar

iron

ammonia

hydrated lime

WHOLE FLOWER PETALS ONLY

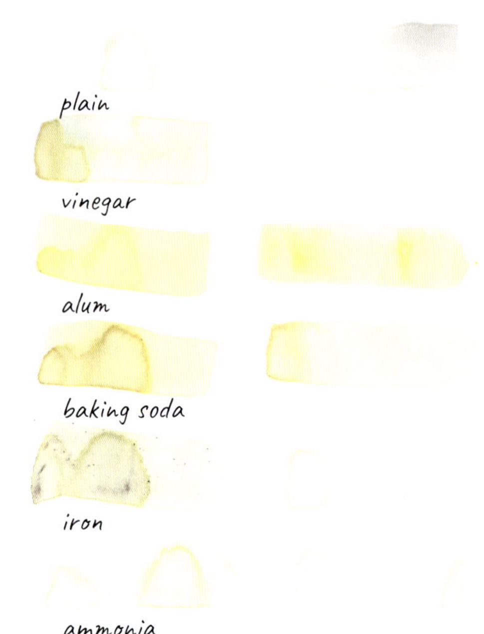

SCAEVOLA SPECIES

Fan Flower

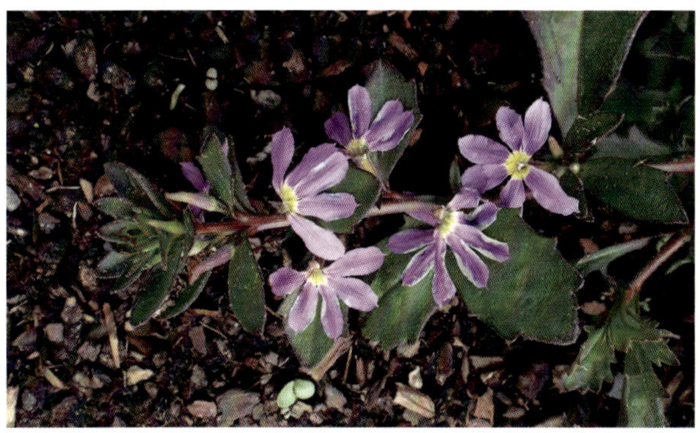

COLORS CREATED	blue
PARTS USED FOR PIGMENT	purple petals minus the yellow centers (which create yellow)
PLANT TYPE	low-growing landscape flower
HARDINESS ZONE	10 (commonly grown as an annual)

1. Best used fresh and uncooked as pigment.

Notes: I was at a restaurant in Los Angeles when I saw these flowers for the first time in my life, and since I had my travel-sized flower pressing book, I did a finger press and about fell on the floor when I saw the blue color. I now grow these in my yard in the Rocky Mountains as a summer annual. They are only happy on the east side of my house, which provides afternoon full shade, but they thrive there. I love printing and color blocking with these flowers, and so do my students. These flowers also make excellent blue eco-prints.

FRESH MULLED

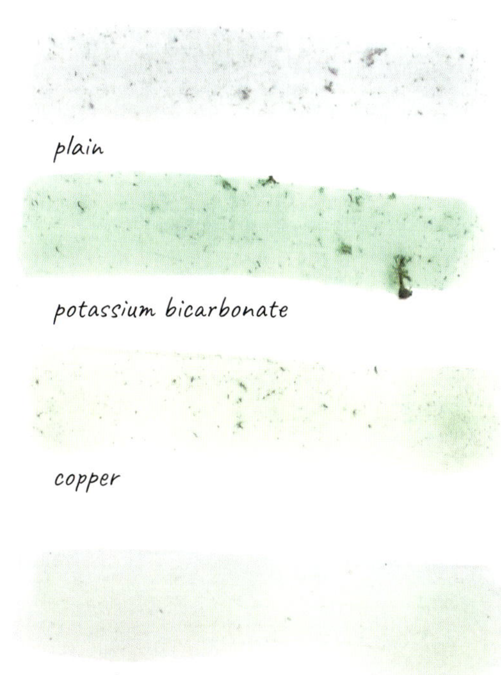

FRESH PRESSED FAN FLOWERS ON PAPER

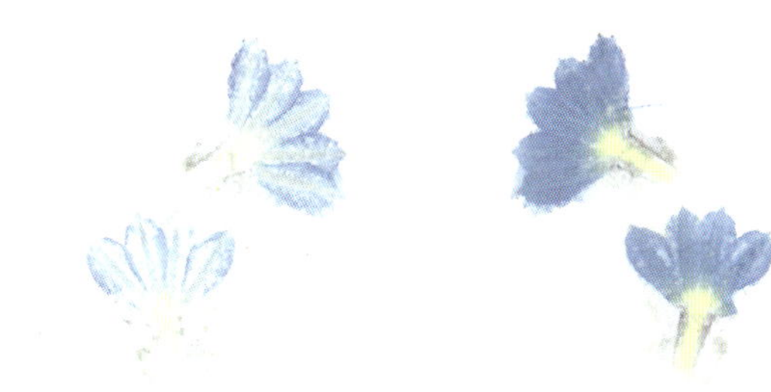

Fennel Leaves

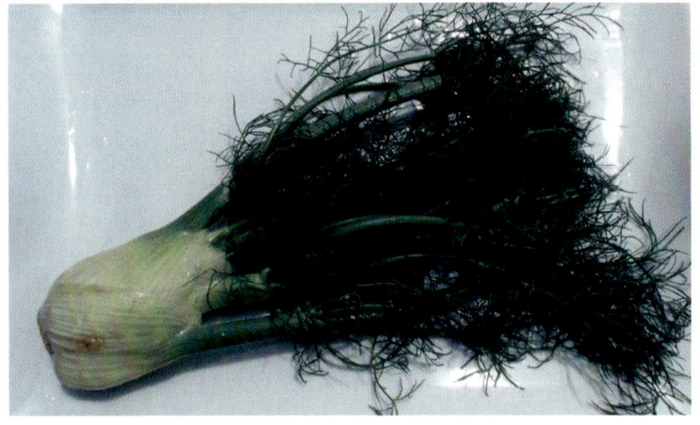

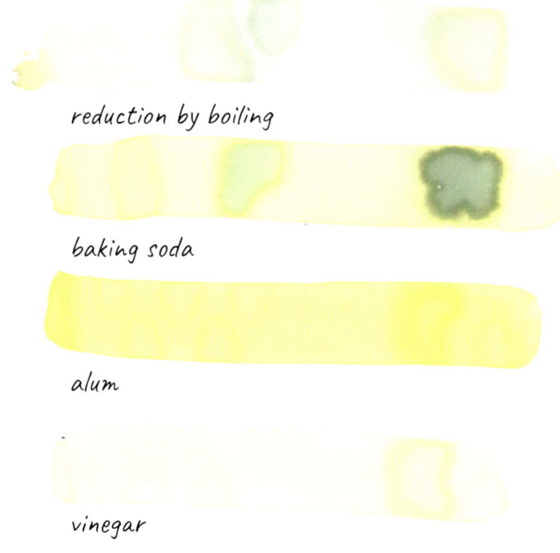

COLORS CREATED	yellow with alum
PARTS USED FOR PIGMENT	leaves, stems, tendrils
PLANT TYPE	self-seeding annual
SEEDING	Seeds available at SeedRenaissance.com.

1. Simmer for 15 minutes to make pigment or dye. Strain.
2. Simmer again to reduce liquid to desired color strength.

Notes: Processing this color fills your house with the sweet odor of anise tea.

TANACETUM PARTHENIUM

Feverfew

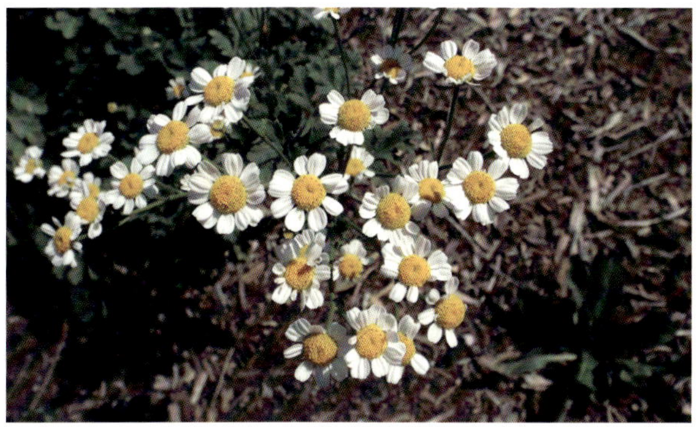

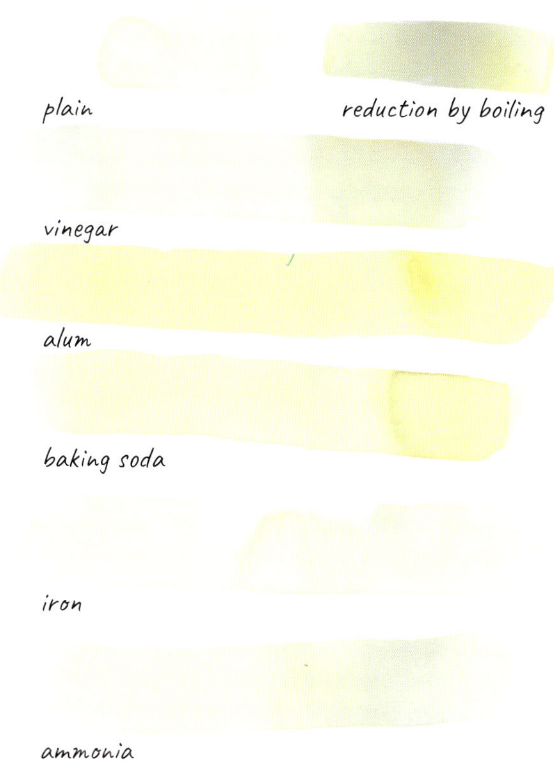

COLORS CREATED	yellow with alum
PARTS USED FOR PIGMENT	flowers
PLANT TYPE	perennial
HARDINESS ZONE	5
SEEDING	Seeds available at SeedRenaissance.com.

1. Simmer for 10 minutes to make pigment or dye. Strain.
2. Simmer again to reduce liquid to desired color strength.

Ficus Species

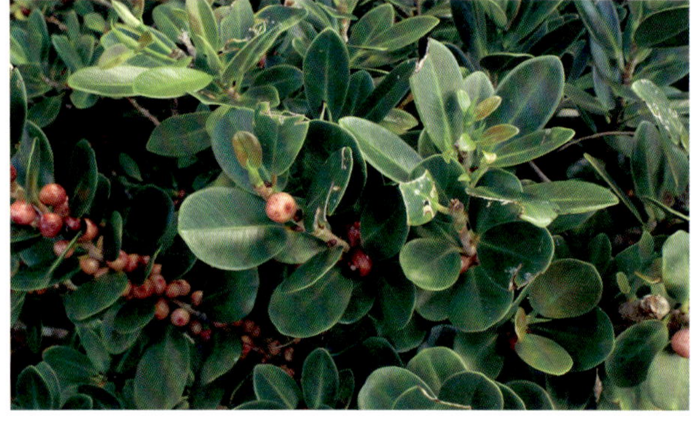

COLORS CREATED	blue with alum
PARTS USED FOR PIGMENT	red berries of certain tropical *Ficus* species
PLANT TYPE	shrub
HARDINESS ZONE	tropical

1. Likely best used fresh.

CHAMERION ANGUSTIFOLIUM

Fireweed

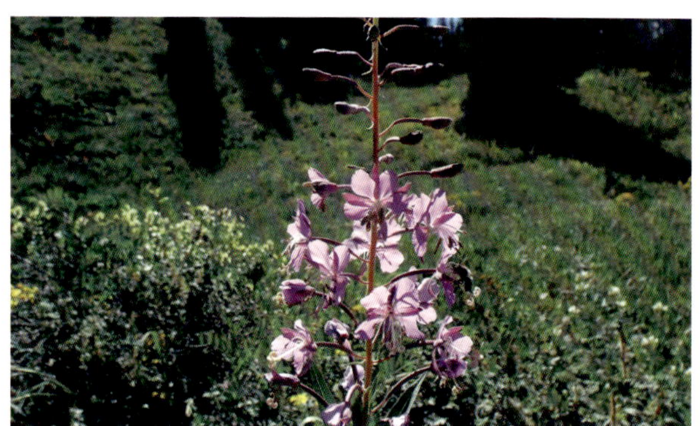

COLORS CREATED	yellow with alum
PARTS USED FOR PIGMENT	red flowers
SEEDING	Plant directly outside in spring or autumn. Seeds available at SeedRenaissance.com.

1. Simmer for 20 minutes to make pigment or dye. Strain.
2. Simmer again to reduce liquid to desired color strength.

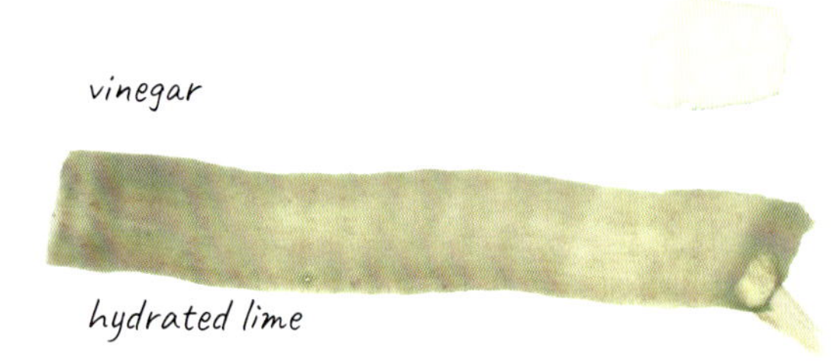

ERIGERON SPECIES

Fleabane

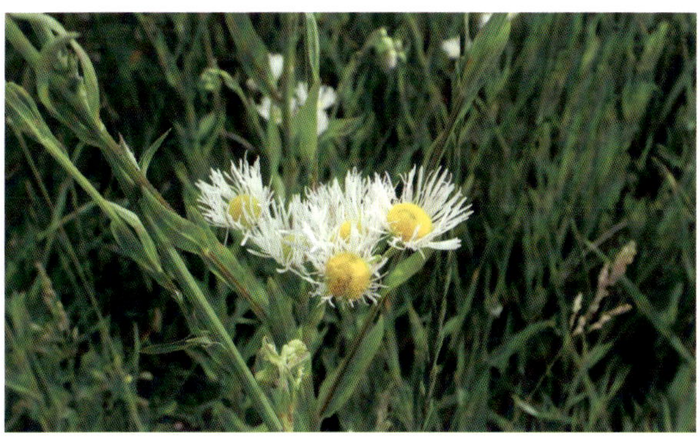

COLORS CREATED	yellow with alum, vinegar, or baking soda
PARTS USED FOR PIGMENT	flowers, leaves, stem

1. Simmer for 20 minutes to make pigment or dye. Strain.
2. Simmer again to reduce liquid to desired color strength.

Notes: The flowers can be boiled a second time to create the same colors. Fleabane can be all but impossible to discern from some wild daisy species. This plant was historically used to repel fleas.

LEAVES AND STEMS

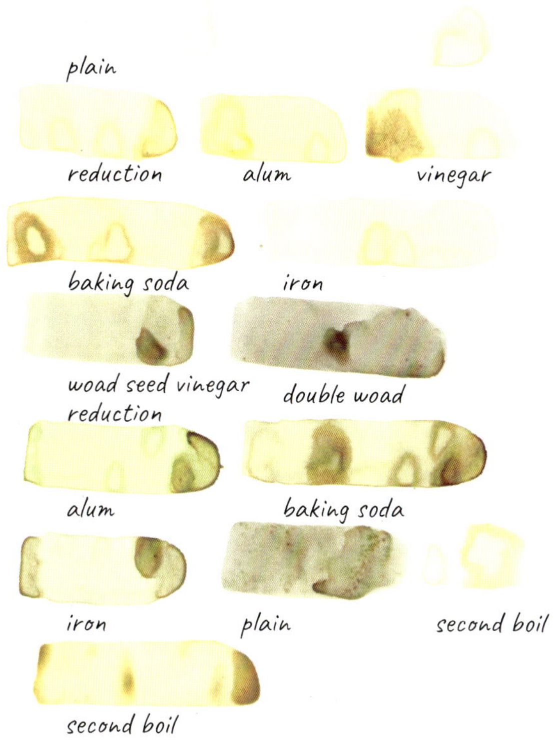

BOILED FLOWERS

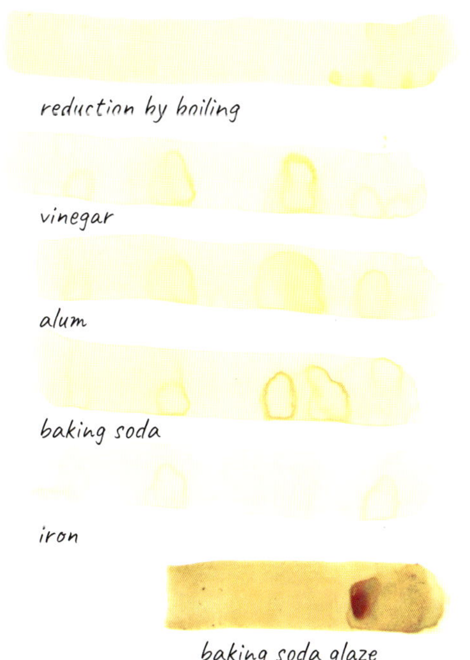

Fritillaria Species

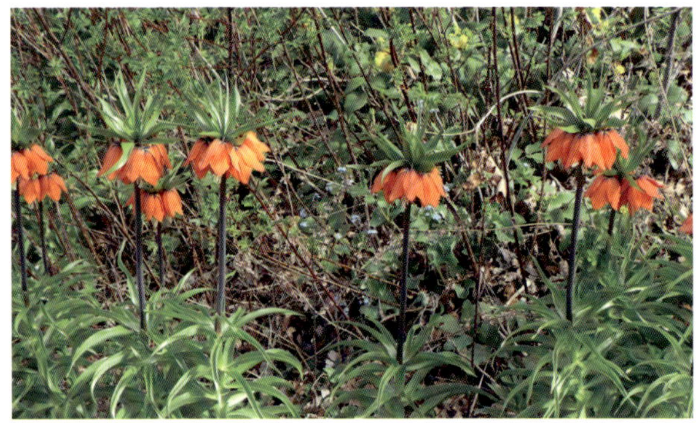

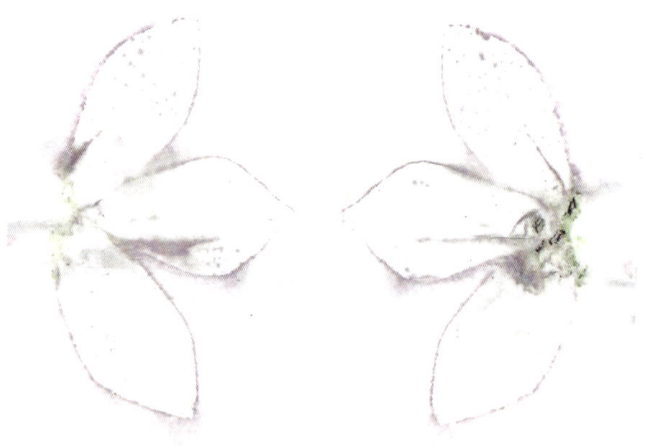

COLORS CREATED	green
PARTS USED FOR PIGMENT	leaves
PLANT TYPE	hardy bulb
HARDINESS ZONE	4

1. Because the petals are so showy and the flowers are so expensive, it is best to use this fresh when the petals begin to wilt. That way, you can have your flowers and eco-print them too.

Notes: Leaves and flowers make remarkable eco-prints.

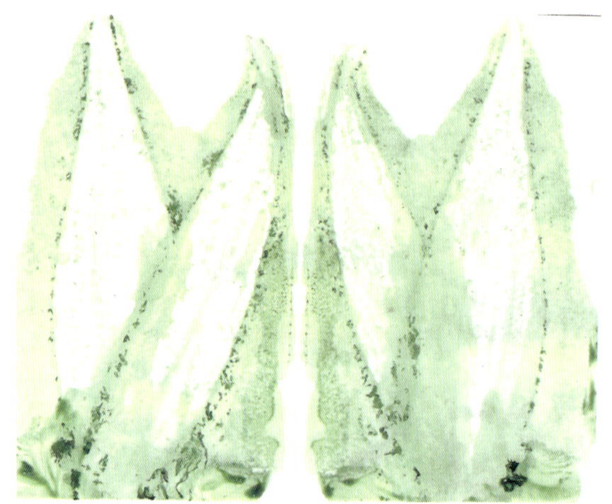

FUCHSIA SPECIES

Fuchsia Bells

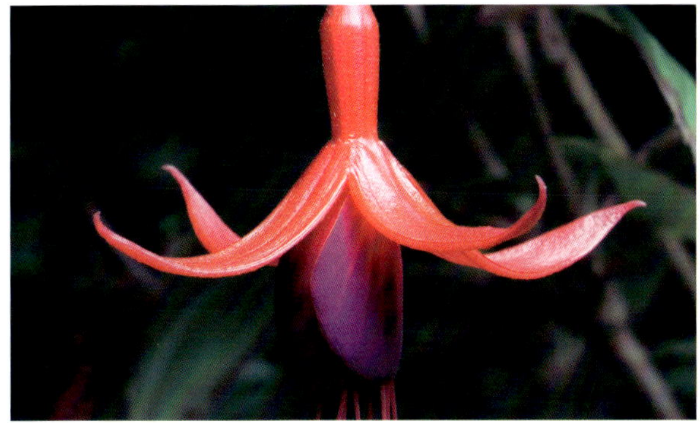

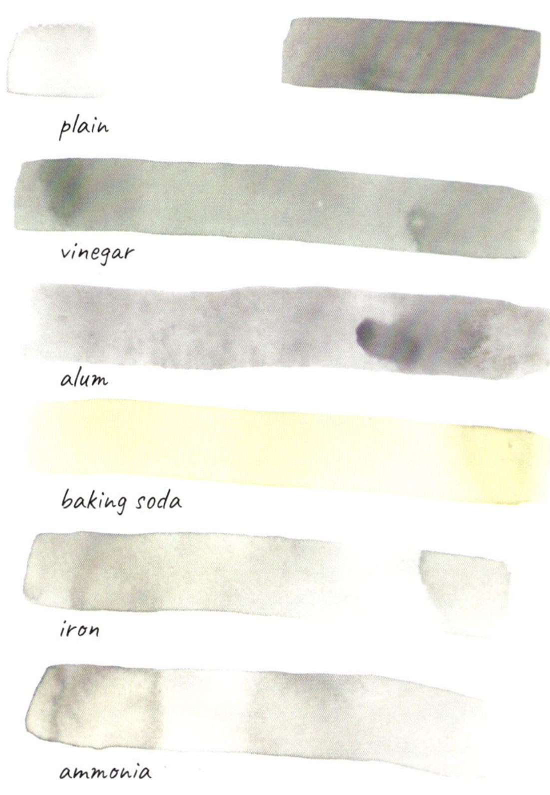

COLORS CREATED	gray, green, purple
PARTS USED FOR PIGMENT	flower petals only (no sepals)
PLANT TYPE	varies by species
HARDINESS ZONE	varies by species

1. Simmer for 15 minutes to make pigment or dye. Strain.
2. Simmer again to reduce liquid to desired color strength.

CHLOROPHORA TINCTORIA

Fustic

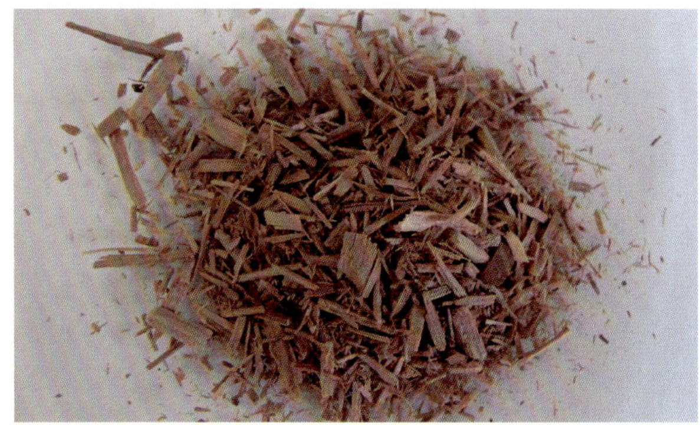

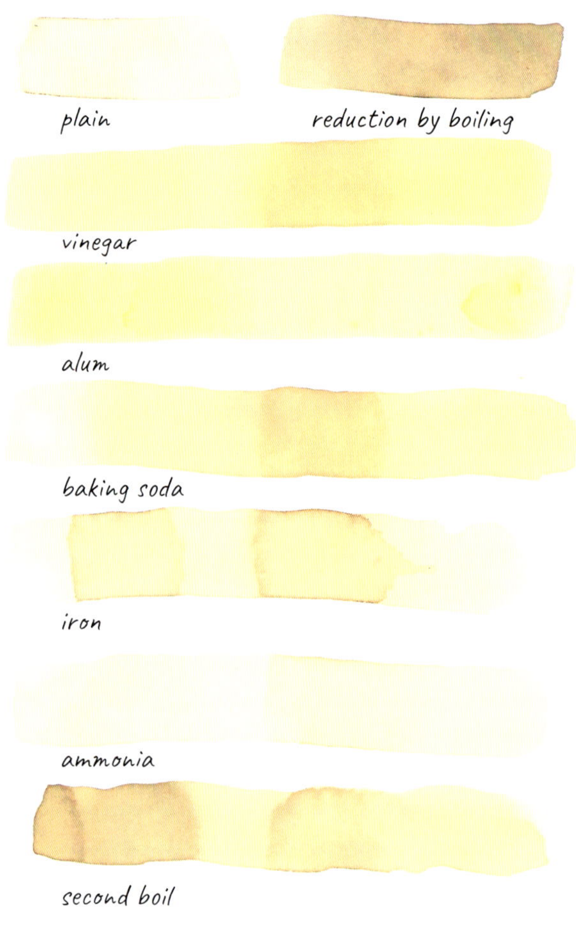

COLORS CREATED	yellow with alum, brown with other mordants
PARTS USED FOR PIGMENT	heartwood shavings
PLANT TYPE	tree

1. Simmer for 10 minutes to make pigment or dye. Strain.
2. Simmer again to reduce liquid to desired color strength.

Notes: A second boil of the shavings in fresh water makes the same colors.

GARDENIA JASMINOIDES

Gardenia

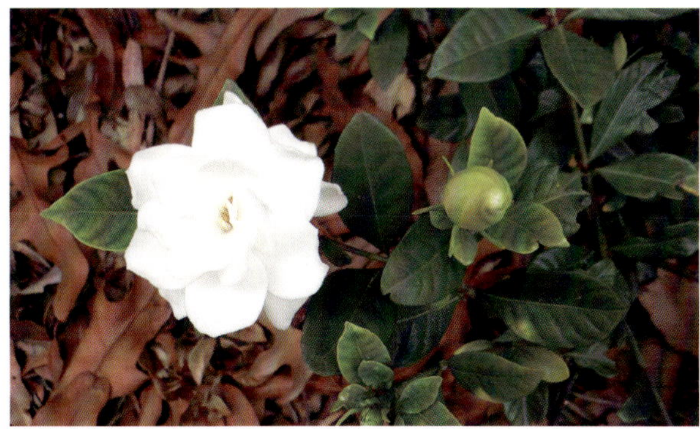

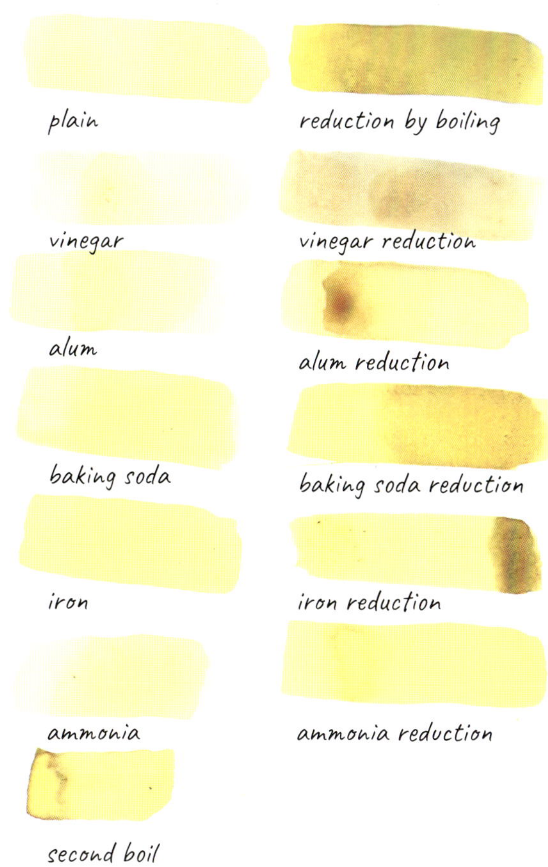

COLORS CREATED	bright yellow with most mordants
PARTS USED FOR PIGMENT	dried seed pod, crushed enough to open the pod
PLANT TYPE	perennial vining shrub
HARDINESS ZONE	8

1. Simmer for 10 minutes to make pigment or dye. Strain.
2. Simmer again to reduce liquid to desired color strength.

Notes: Boiling the pods a second time with fresh water creates a new batch of the same colors. The pods can be used up to four times.

CORDIA SPECIES

Geiger Tree

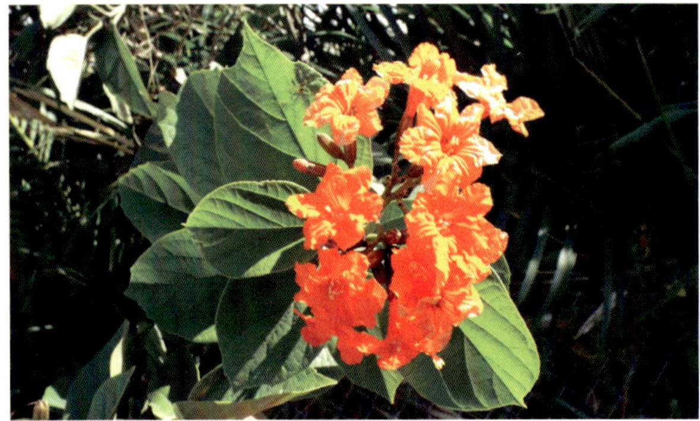

FRESH PRESSED RED PETALS

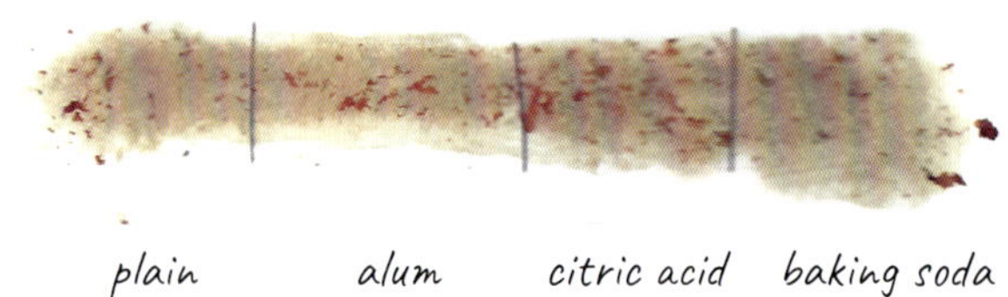

COLORS CREATED	brown with most mordants
PARTS USED FOR PIGMENT	red flowers
PLANT TYPE	tropical tree

1. While I tested fresh petals, it is likely the color does not change when cooked. I suspect the orange flowered species makes the same brown.

Geranium and *Pelargonium* Species

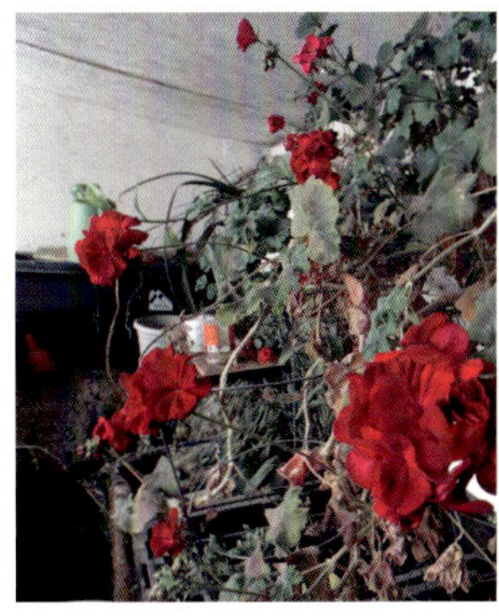
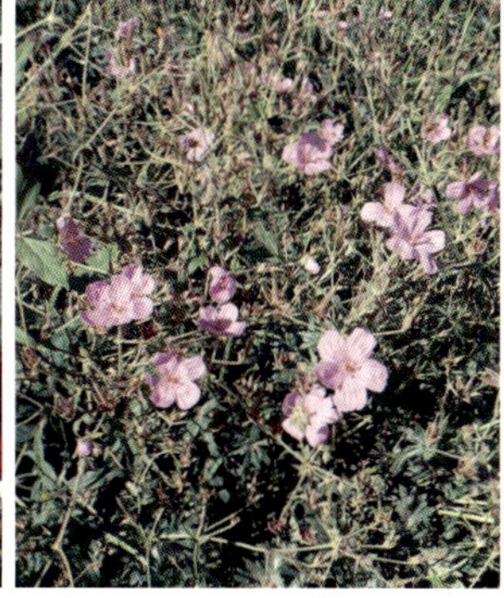

COLORS CREATED	blue, purple, violet, red
PARTS USED FOR PIGMENT	petals
HARDINESS ZONE	varies by species
SEEDING	Plant directly outside in spring or autumn. Seeds available at SeedRenaissance.com.

1. Simmer for 10 minutes to make pigment or dye. Strain.
2. Simmer again to reduce liquid to desired color strength.

Notes: Fresh petals of *Pelargonium* "Aldebaran"—a historic variety—made blue when mulled into milk paint base.

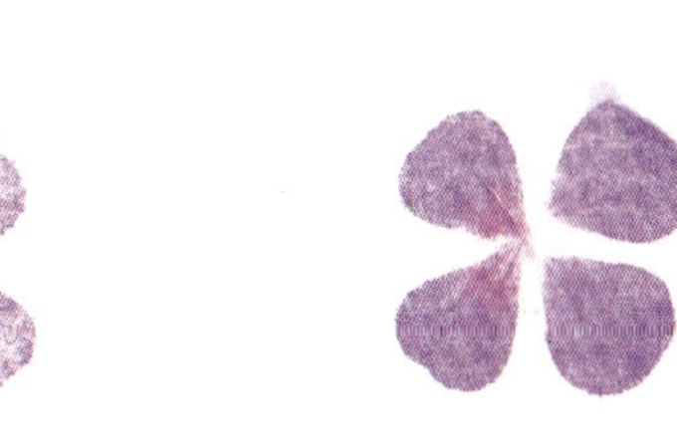

GERANIUM ALDEBARAN

fresh, milk

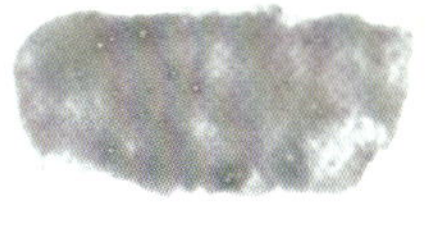
extra petals

milk completely ground

RED GERANIUM PETALS WITH GUM ARABIC

FRESH MULLED RED

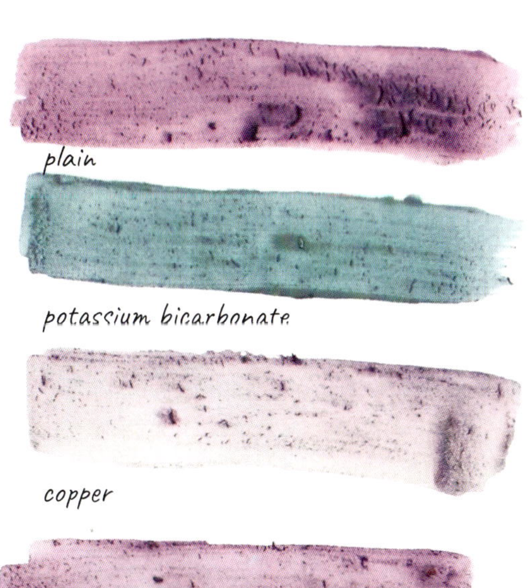
plain

potassium bicarbonate

copper

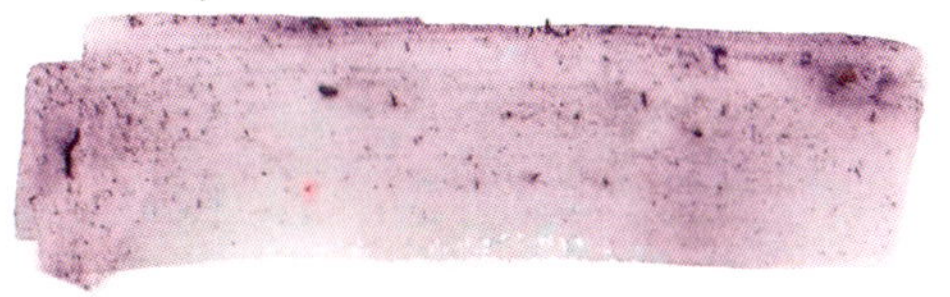
ascorbic

alum

ALPINIA PURPURATA

Ginger Red

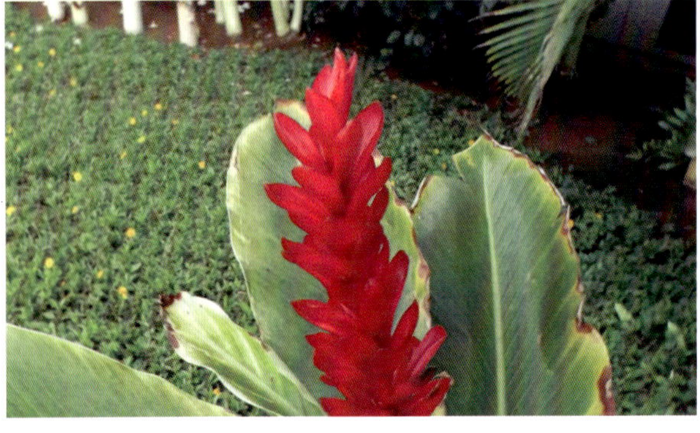

RED PLUME

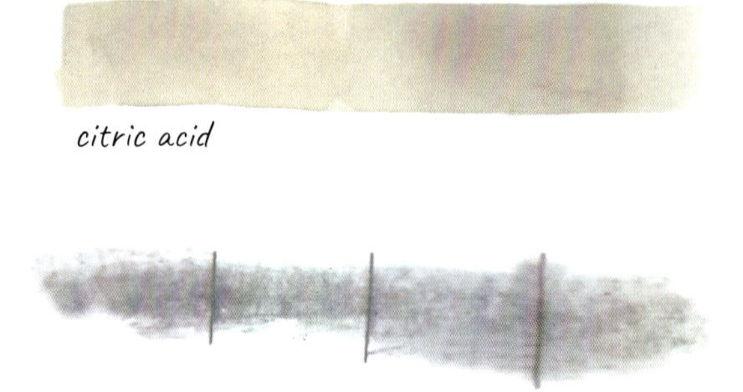

COLORS CREATED	gray when used fresh, brown when cooked
PARTS USED FOR PIGMENT	red plume flowers
PLANT TYPE	large tropical flower

1. Best used fresh.

Notes: This is not the same species of ginger sold in grocery stores.

Gladiolus Species

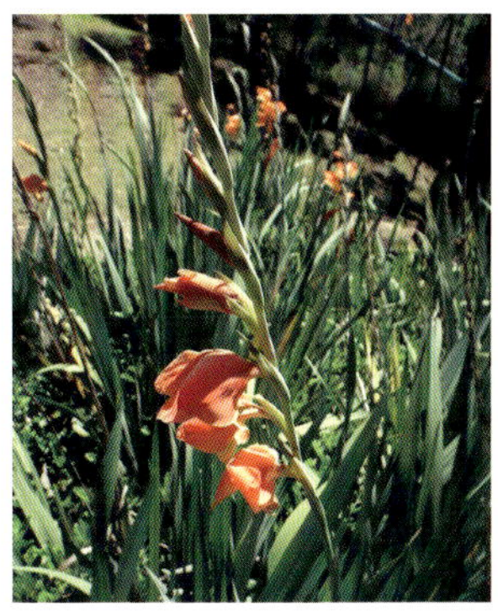

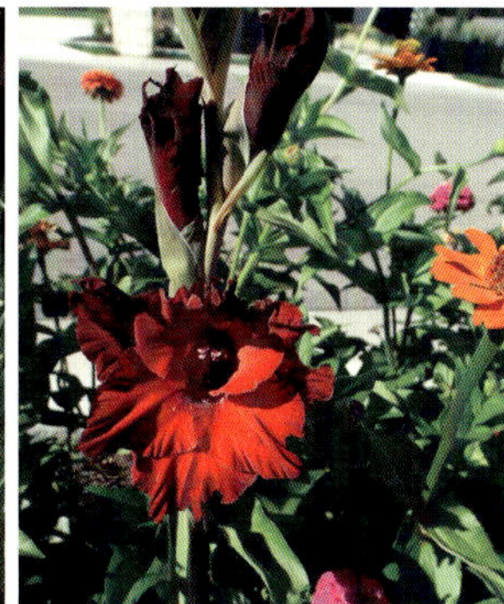

COLORS CREATED	pink with citric acid, various grayish tones with other mordants
PARTS USED FOR PIGMENT	deep red flowers
PLANT TYPE	summer bulb, grown as an annual in winter climates
HARDINESS ZONE	8

1. Simmer for 10 minutes to make pigment or dye. Strain.
2. Simmer again to reduce liquid to desired color strength.

Notes: The flowers also make excellent pigment when used fresh and uncooked. The flowers contain a lot of dye.

FRESH MULLED

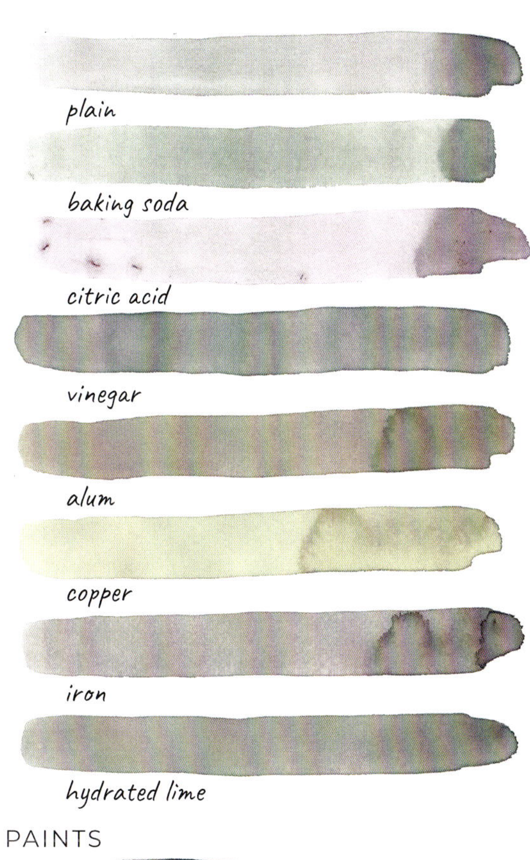

PAINTS

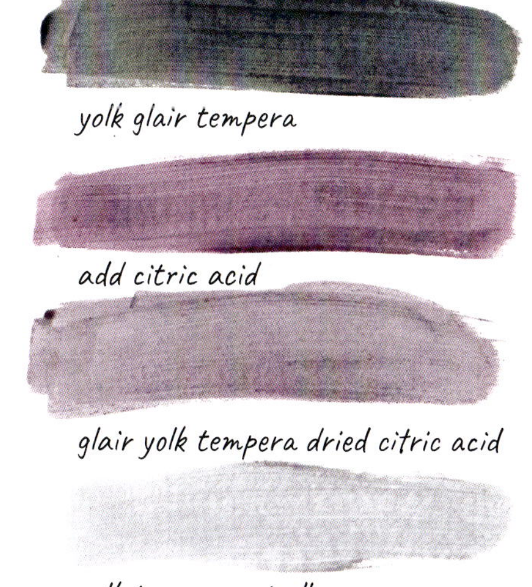

CASSIA AND *SENNA* SPECIES

Golden Showers Tree

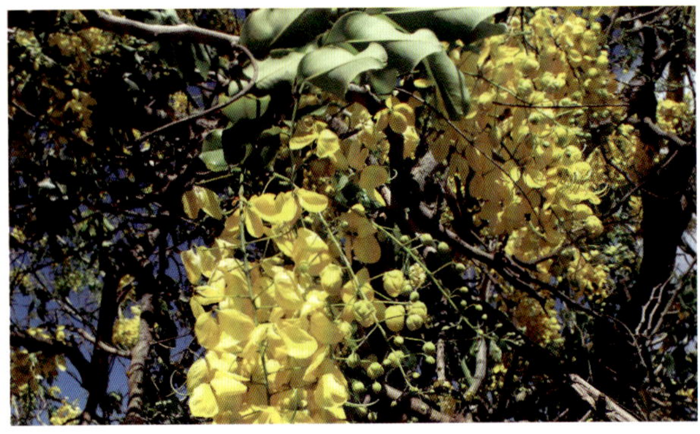

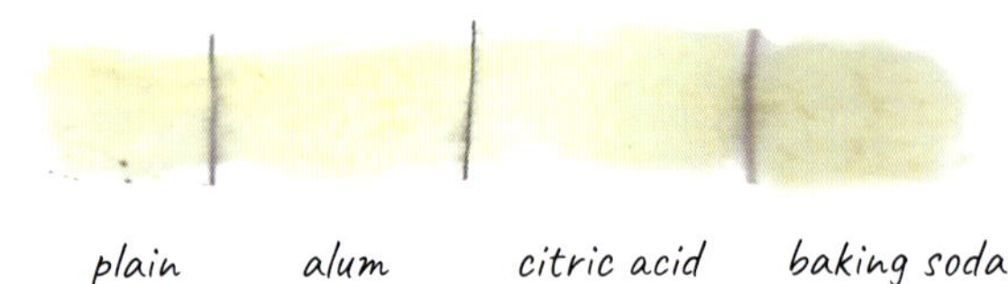

COLORS CREATED	yellow with alum, pale yellow with other mordants
PARTS USED FOR PIGMENT	yellow flowers
PLANT TYPE	tree
HARDINESS ZONE	varies by species
SEEDING	Plant directly outside in spring or autumn. Seeds available at SeedRenaissance.com.

1. Simmer for 10 minutes to make pigment or dye. Strain.
2. Simmer again to reduce liquid to desired color strength.

Notes: Species with red and orange flowers likely make dye also.

SOLIDAGO SPECIES

Goldenrod

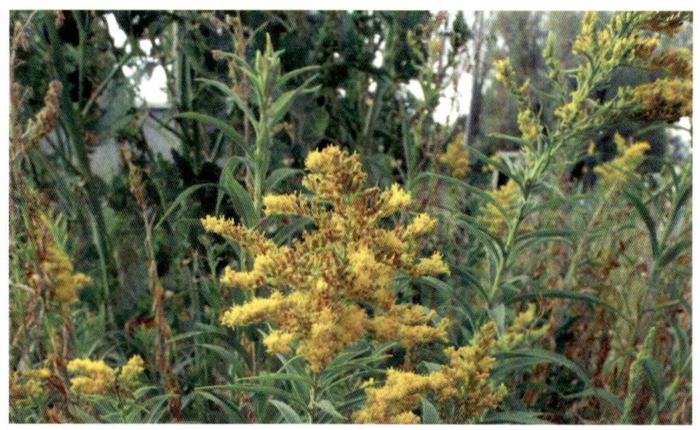

COLORS CREATED	yellow with most mordants
PARTS USED FOR PIGMENT	yellow flowering stems (no leaves)
PLANT TYPE	perennial
HARDINESS ZONE	4
SEEDING	Plant directly outside in spring or autumn. Seeds available at SeedRenaissance.com.

1. Simmer for 10 minutes to make pigment or dye. Strain.
2. Simmer again to reduce liquid to desired color strength.

PAINTS

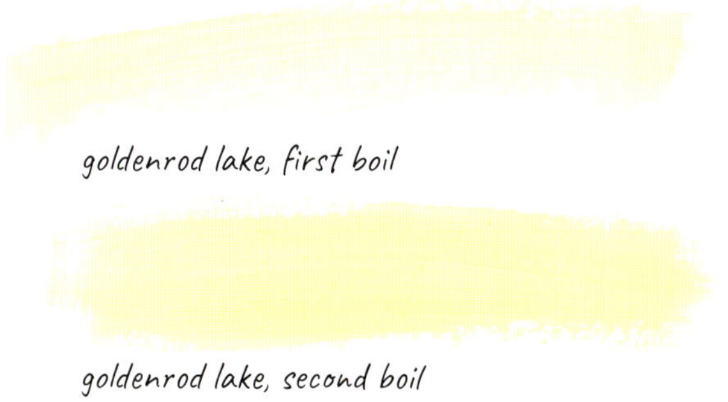

PLAIN BOILED

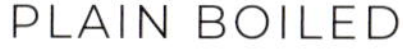

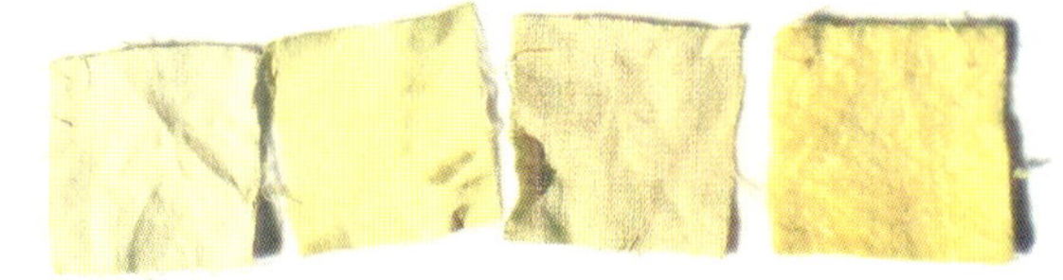

BOILED WITH SOY

COLD DYE WITH SOY

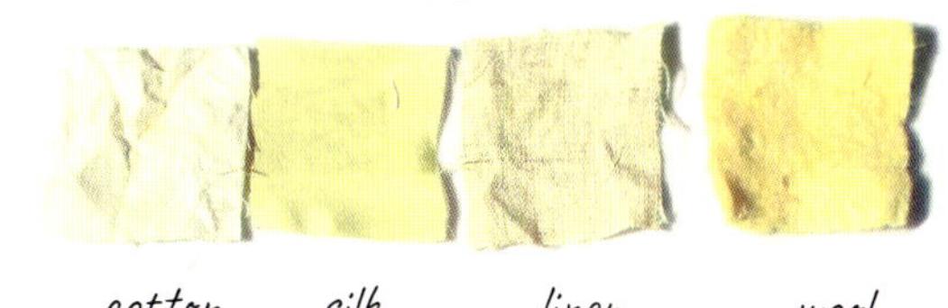

cotton silk linen wool

FLOWERS ONLY

RIBES SPECIES

Gooseberries

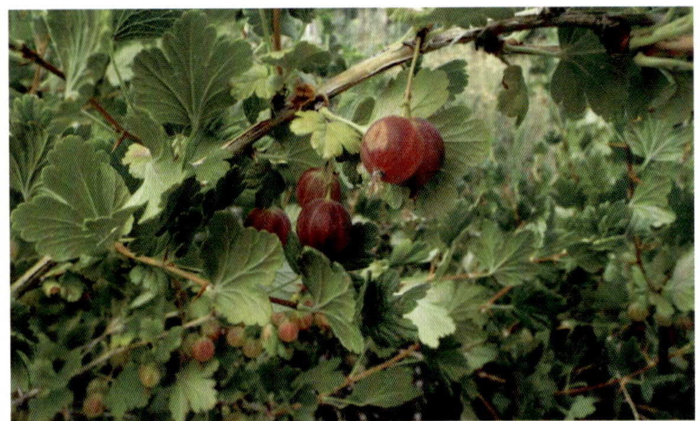

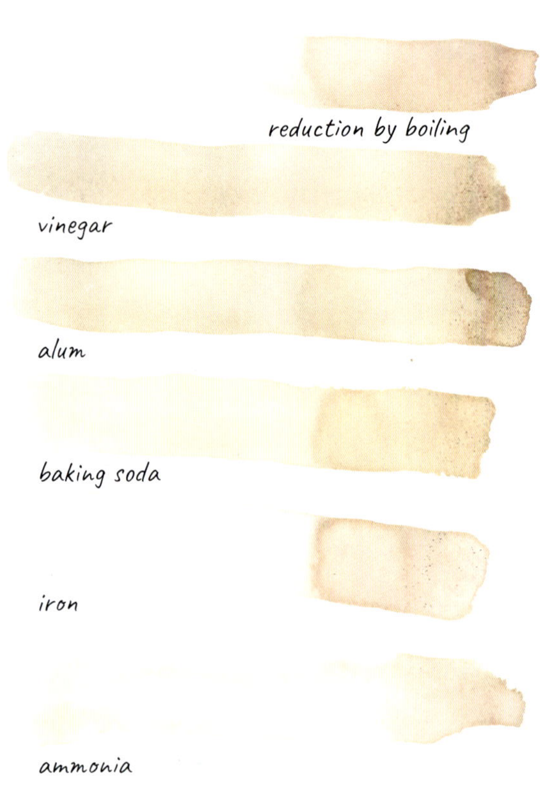

COLORS CREATED	brown
PARTS USED FOR PIGMENT	ripe red berries
PLANT TYPE	perennial
HARDINESS ZONE	3

1. Simmer for 40 minutes to make pigment or dye. Strain.
2. Simmer again to reduce liquid to desired color strength.

VITUS SPECIES

Grapes

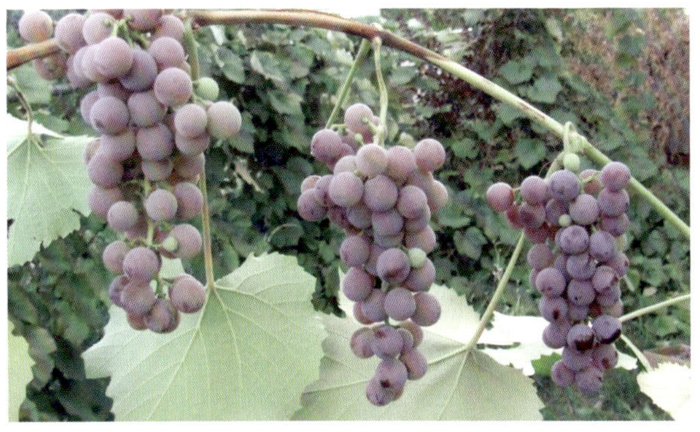

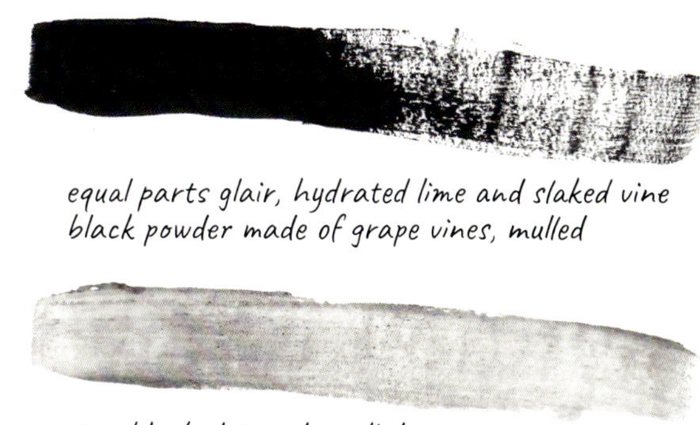

equal parts glair, hydrated lime and slaked vine black powder made of grape vines, mulled

vine black glair only mulled

COLORS CREATED	purple, black, red
PARTS USED FOR PIGMENT	purple fruit
PLANT TYPE	perennial
HARDINESS ZONE	varies by species and cultivar
SEEDING	Live plants available for shipping in spring at SeedRenaissance.com.

1. Simmer for 10 minutes to make pigment or dye. Strain.
2. Simmer again to reduce liquid to desired color strength.

Notes: Vine black powder is made from grape vines (see page 76). Pigments and dyes made from the fruit are so sugary and sticky and impossible to dry that they are best used as children's finger paints.

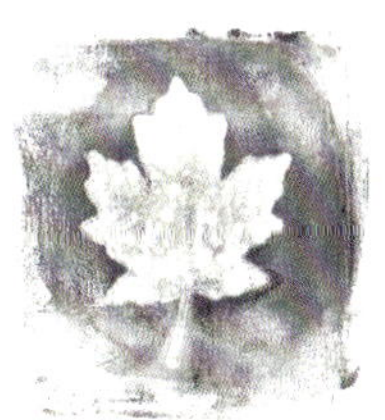

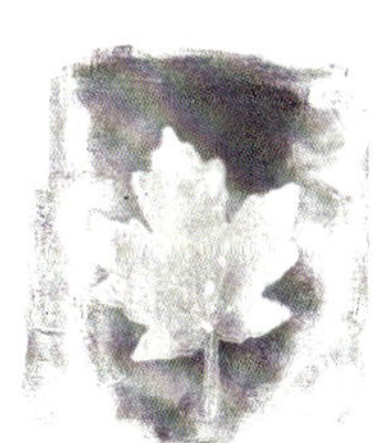

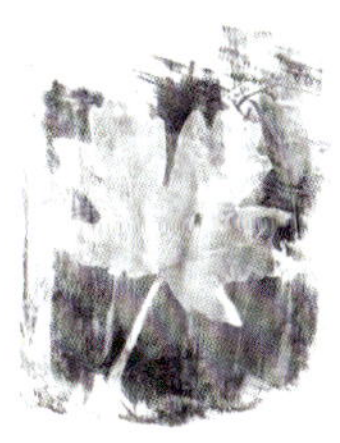

BOILED CONCORD GRAPE WITH COPPER, HYDRATED LIME, AND LIQUID PINE

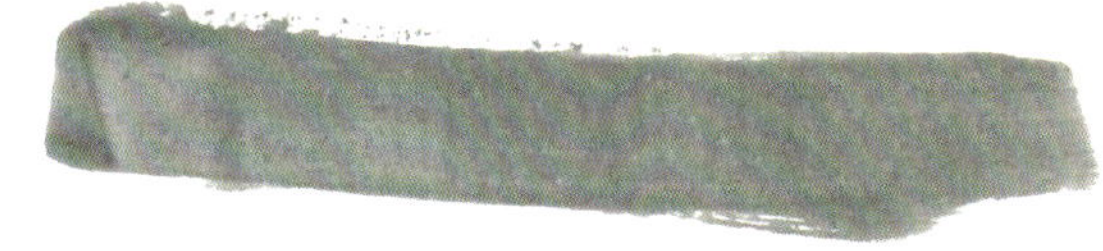

CONCORD GRAPE WITH COPPER

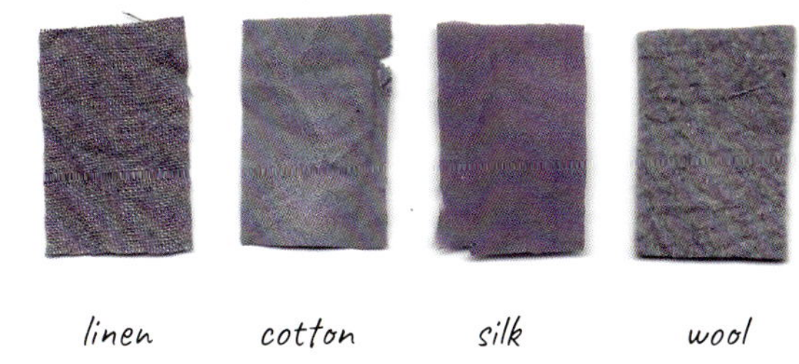

linen *cotton* *silk* *wool*

CHELIDONIUM MAJUS

Greater Celandine

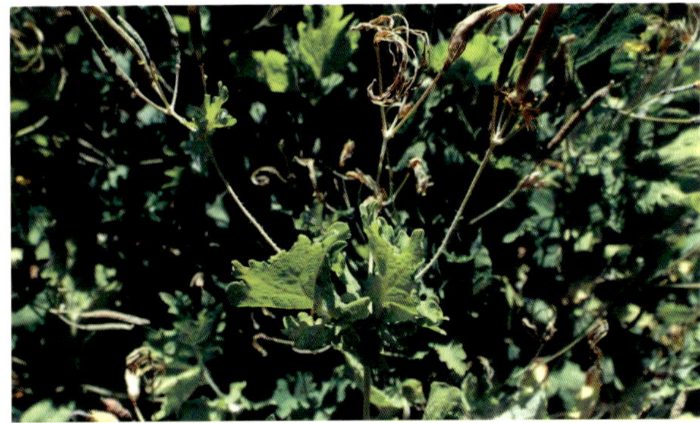

COLORS CREATED	yellow with alum, brown with most mordants
PARTS USED FOR PIGMENT	leaves, stems
PLANT TYPE	perennial
HARDINESS ZONE	4

1. Simmer for 10 minutes to make pigment or dye. Strain.
2. Simmer again to reduce liquid to desired color strength.

Notes: If you break a stem of the plant, an orange ooze will come out that is toxic if ingested. I have not had any problem handling the plant for dye purposes and it has a long history of use for dye.

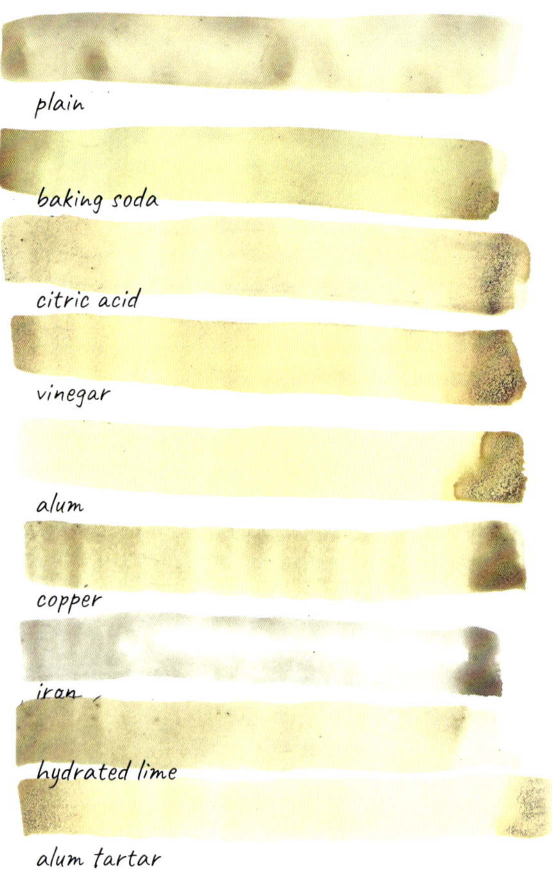

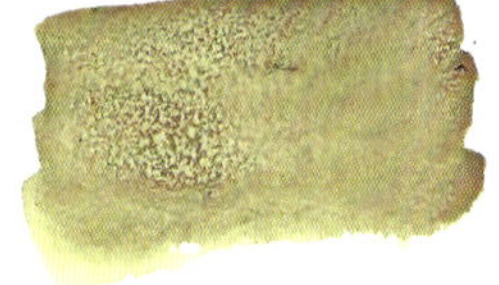

GREATER CELANDINE WITH ALUM

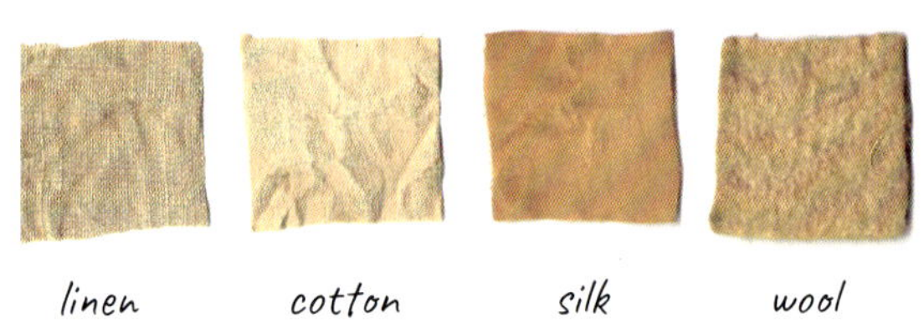

GUAIACUM OFFICINALE

Guaiac Wood

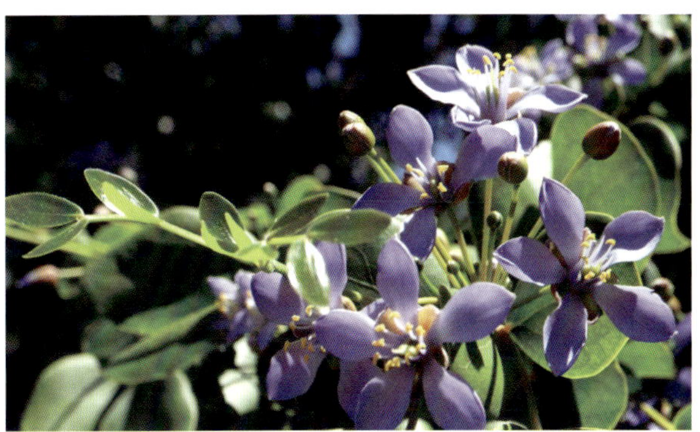

COLORS CREATED	blue when unmordanted or with alum or citric acid; green with baking soda
PARTS USED FOR PIGMENT	blue flowers
PLANT TYPE	tropical

1. Best used fresh; color is obliterated when cooked.

FRESH PRESSED PETALS

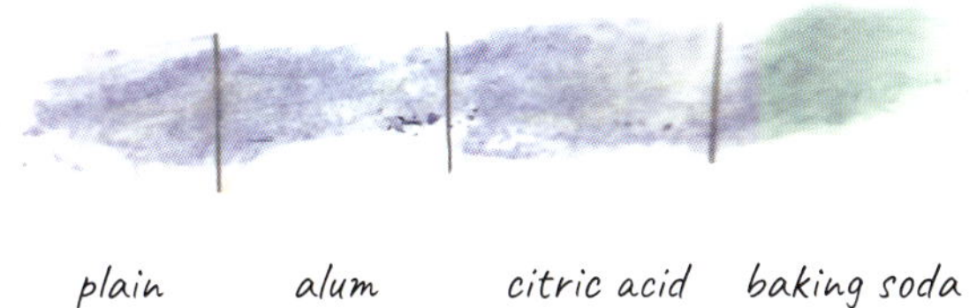

VARIOUS SPECIES

Hawkweed

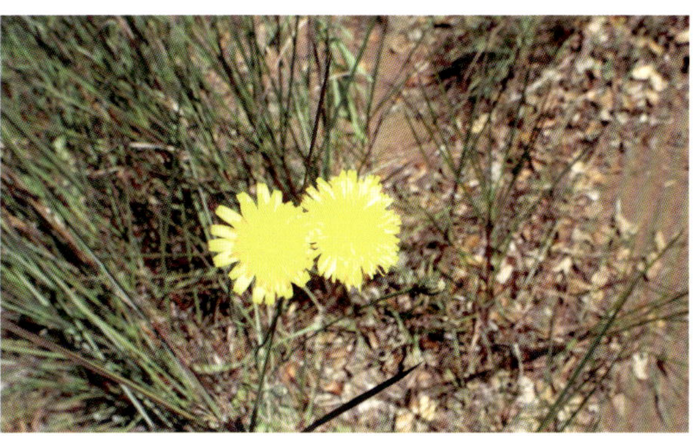

COLORS CREATED	yellow with most mordants
PARTS USED FOR PIGMENT	flowers
HARDINESS ZONE	varies by species

1. Best used fresh.

Notes: Because there are so many species, it is possible that some create brown when cooked.

FRESH PRESSED PETALS

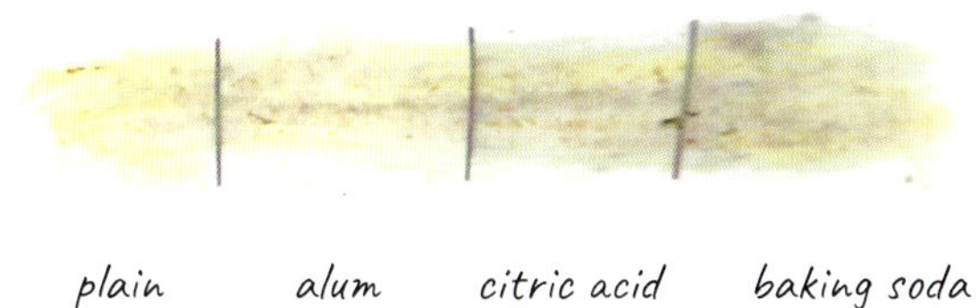

CRATAEGUS SPECIES

Hawthorn

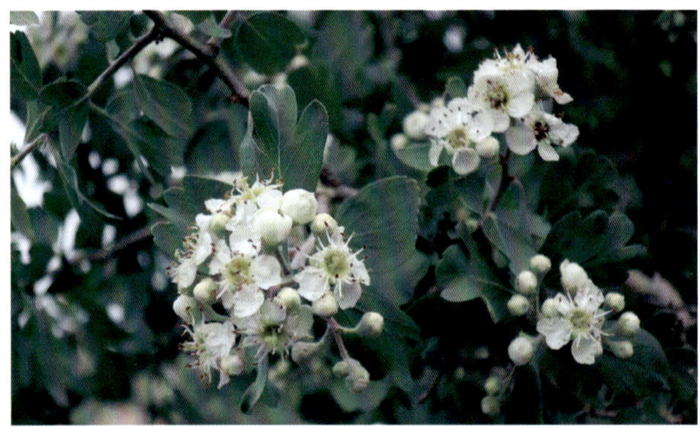

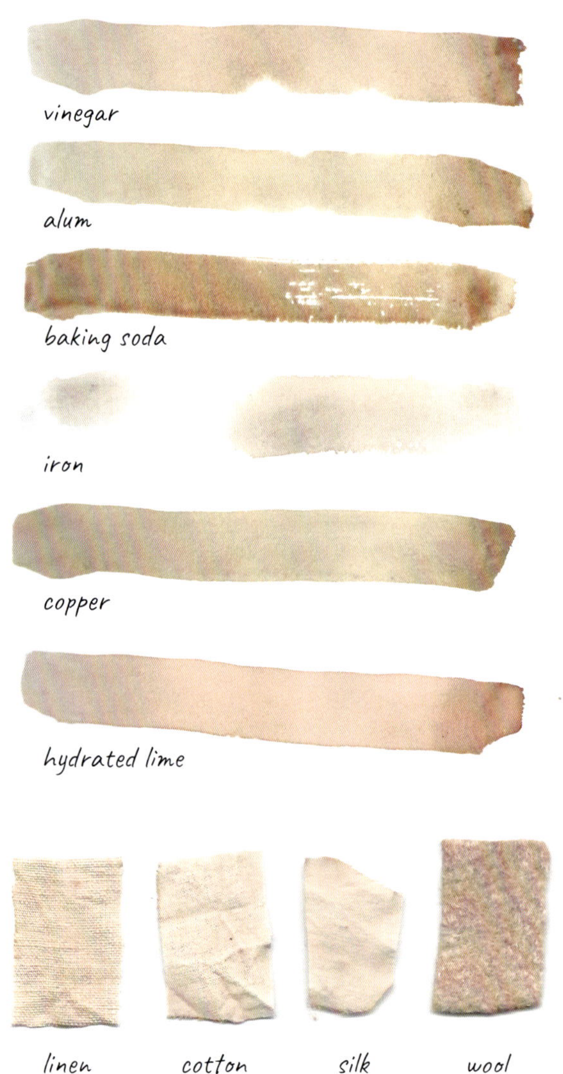

COLORS CREATED	red with hydrated lime, brown with most mordants
PARTS USED FOR PIGMENT	ripe red berries
PLANT TYPE	tree
HARDINESS ZONE	varies by species

1. Simmer for 30 minutes to make pigment or dye. Strain.
2. Simmer again to reduce liquid to desired color strength.

CORYLUS SPECIES

Hazelnut

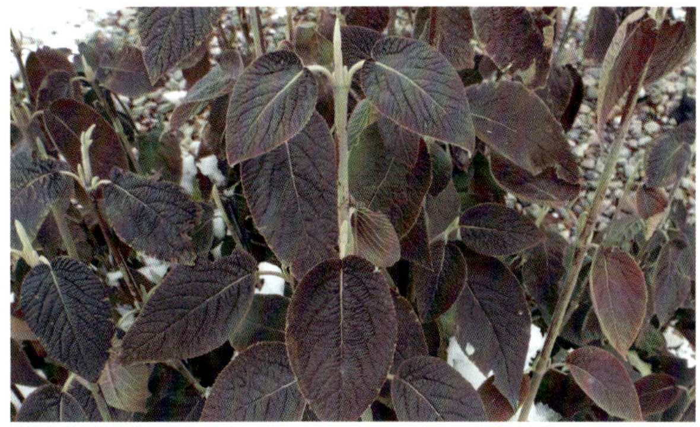

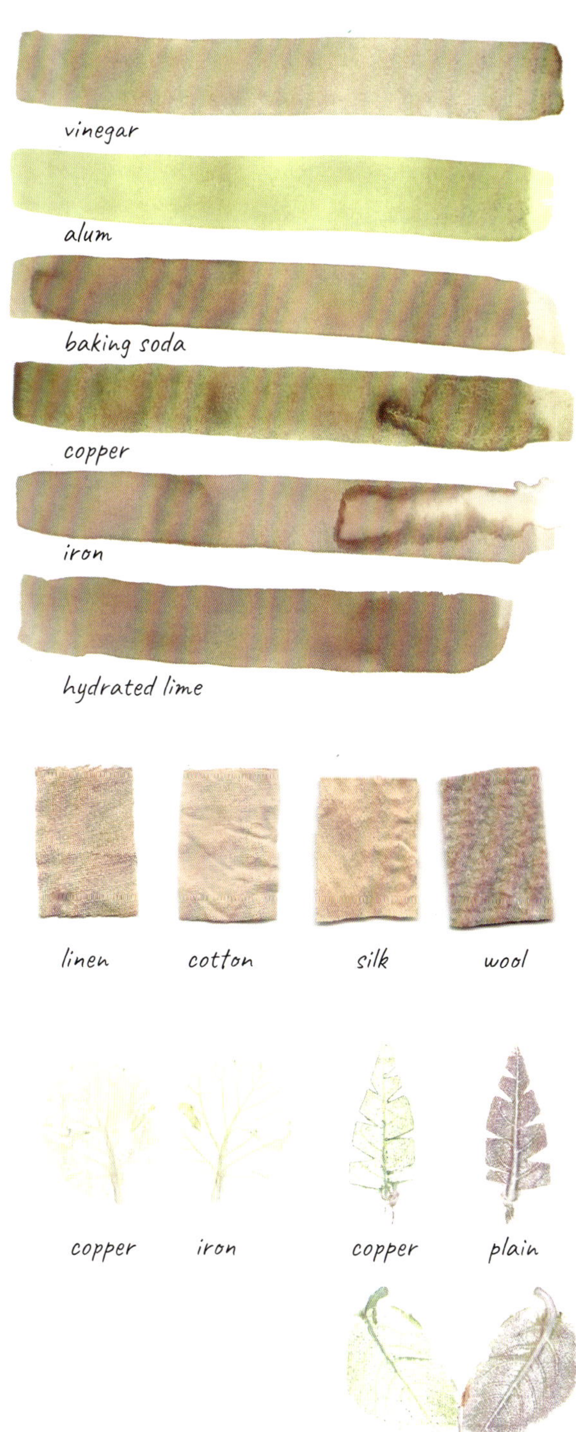

COLORS CREATED	green with alum, brown with most mordants
PARTS USED FOR PIGMENT	leaves
PLANT TYPE	bush
HARDINESS ZONE	generally hardy but varies by species
SEEDING	Plant directly outside in spring or autumn. Seeds available at SeedRenaissance.com.

1. Hazelnut leaves give the best color when used fresh and uncooked.

Notes: Purple hazelnut leaves make amazingly detailed eco-prints and print purple with no mordant and green with vinegar of copper. The best colors come from the nutless commercial landscape bushes with purple leaves. Hazelnut hulls likely make brown dye (mine are not ripe yet or I could test them!).

FRESH PRESSED WITH IRON

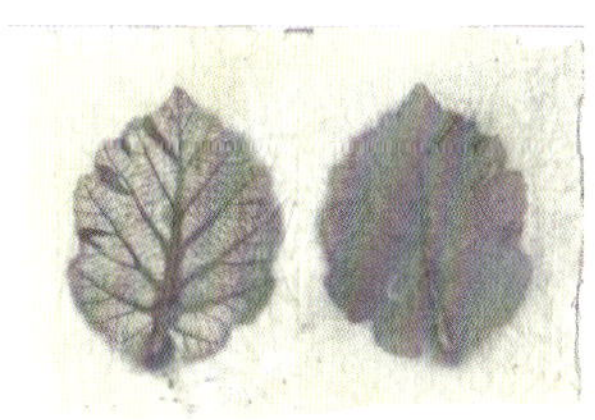

HELLEBORUS ORIENTALIS

Hellebore

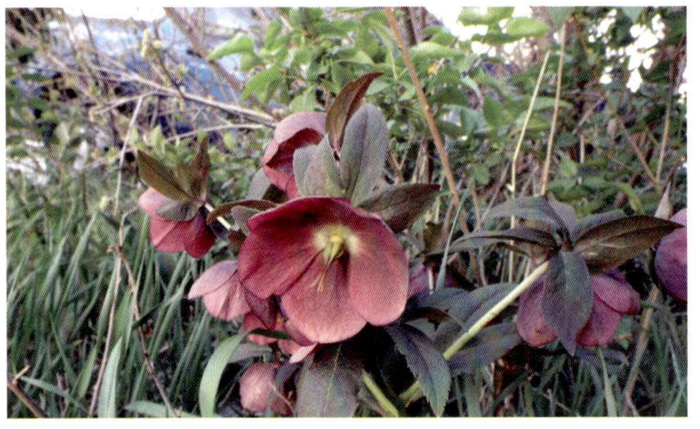

COLORS CREATED	pink
PARTS USED FOR PIGMENT	red flowers
PLANT TYPE	perennial spring flower
HARDINESS ZONE	3
SEEDING	Plant directly outside in spring or autumn. Seeds available at SeedRenaissance.com.

Notes: These flowers are best used fresh to make astonishing eco-prints.

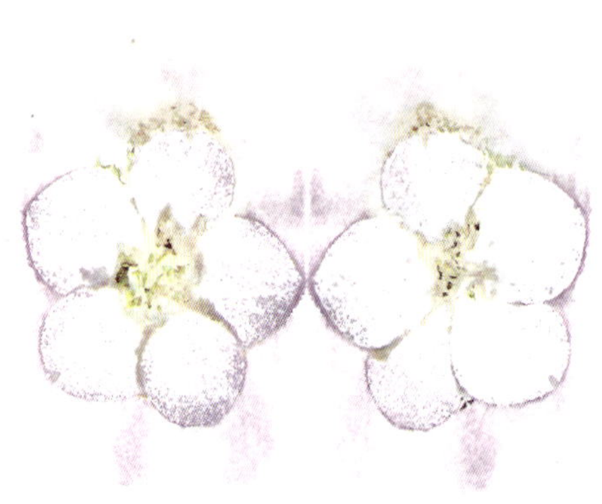

Heuchera Species

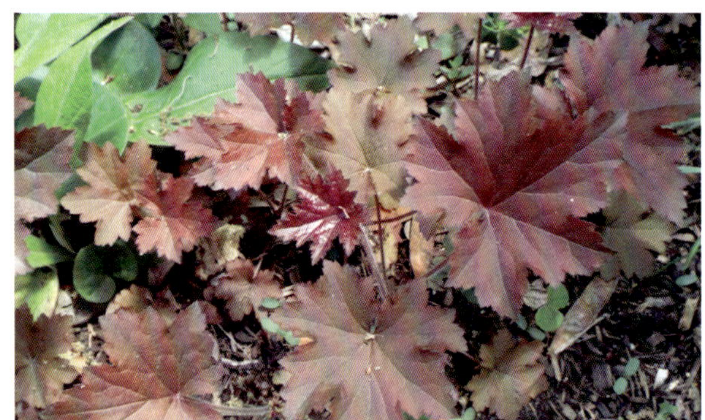

COLORS CREATED	blueish purple when fresh leaves are pressed, cooked colors make hues of brown
PARTS USED FOR PIGMENT	purple leaves
PLANT TYPE	ground cover
HARDINESS ZONE	varies by species

Notes: Best used fresh for pigment.

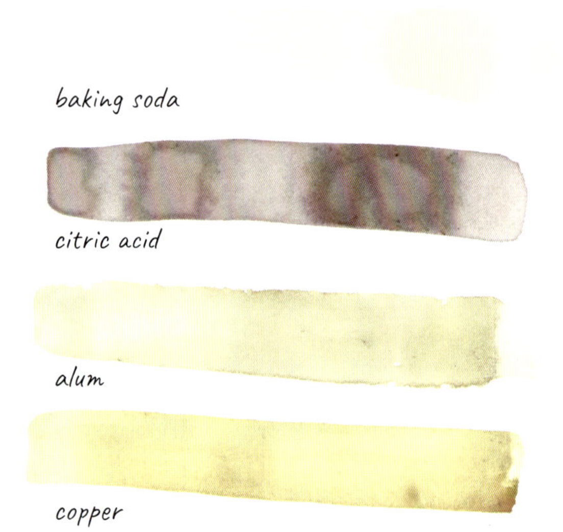

Hibiscus Species

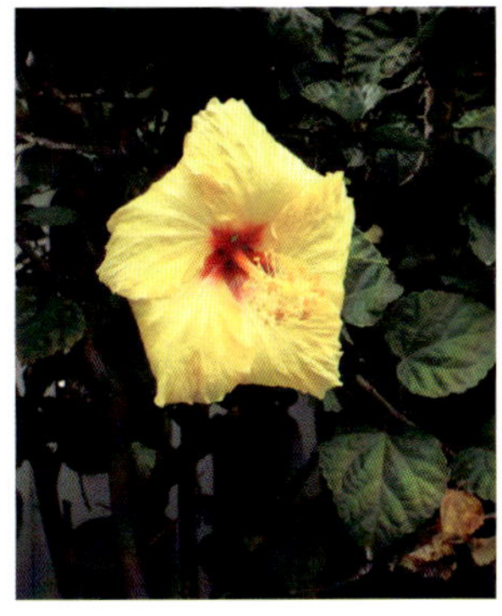
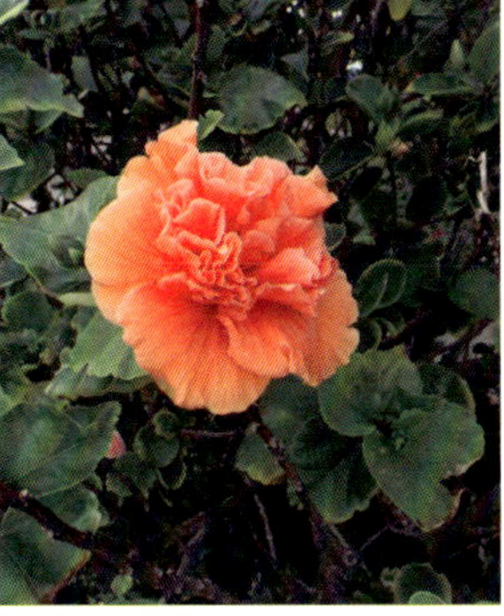

COLORS CREATED: some fresh red leaves make blue with alum, violet with citric acid, green with baking soda, and reddish black unmordanted; other species of red leaves make blue with baking soda and gray-green with other mordants; yellow petals make yellow and orange with various mordants

PARTS USED FOR PIGMENT: flowers or leaves

HARDINESS ZONE: varies widely but most non-hybrids are tropical

1. Try fresh petals first to see what colors they make and then try simmering the petals for 10 minutes to see how the colors change.

FRESH PRESSED RED PETALS

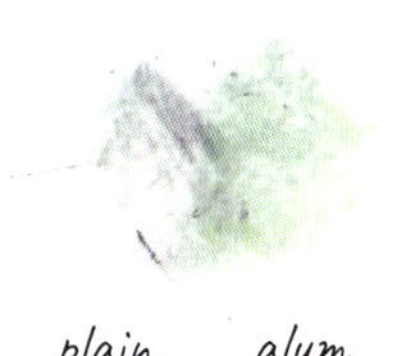

plain alum

FRESH PRESSED YELLOW PETALS

plain alum

YELLOW PETALS

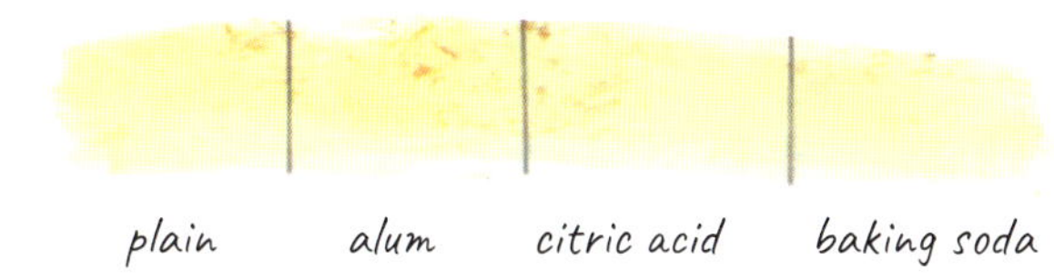

plain alum citric acid baking soda

FRESH PRESSED PINK PETALS

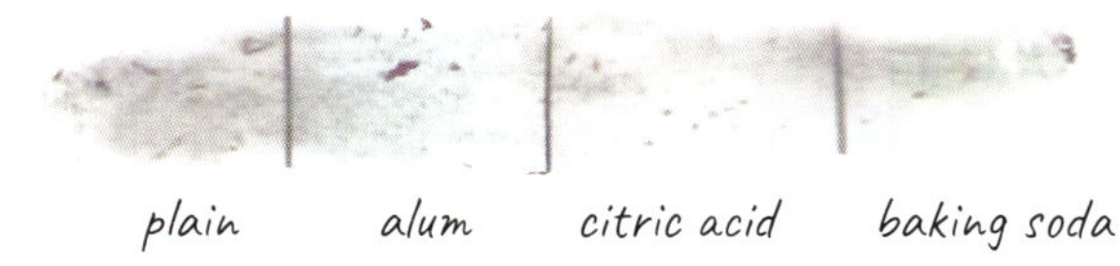

plain alum citric acid baking soda

FRESH PRESSED RED PETALS

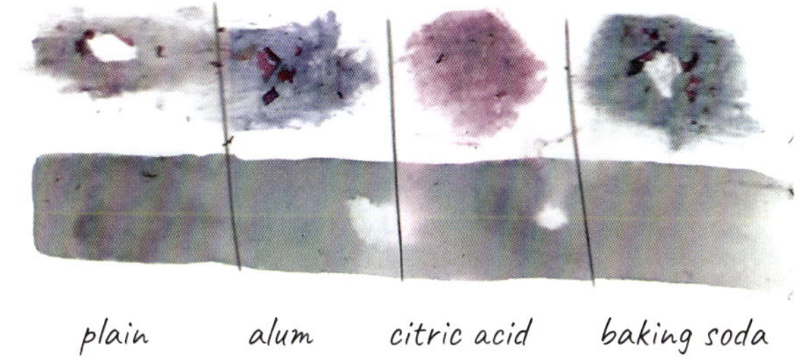

plain alum citric acid baking soda

HIBISCUS SHOEBLACK

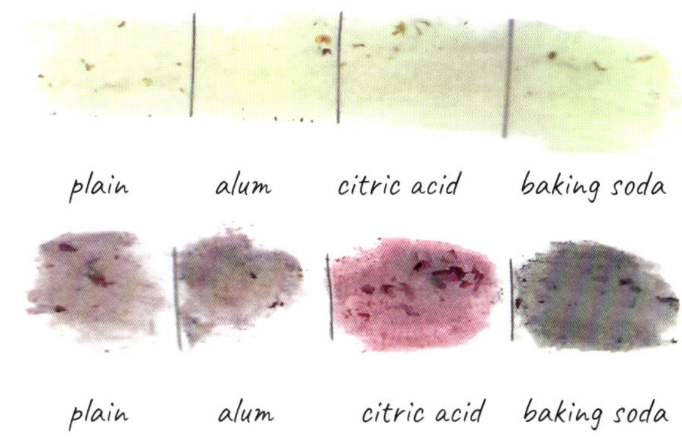

plain alum citric acid baking soda

plain alum citric acid baking soda

CARYA SPECIES

Hickory

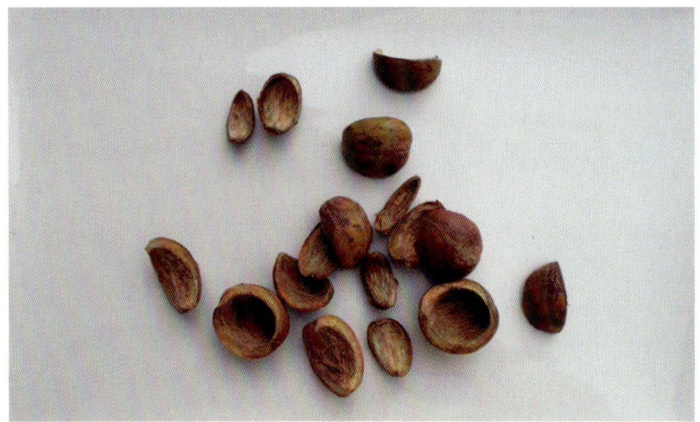

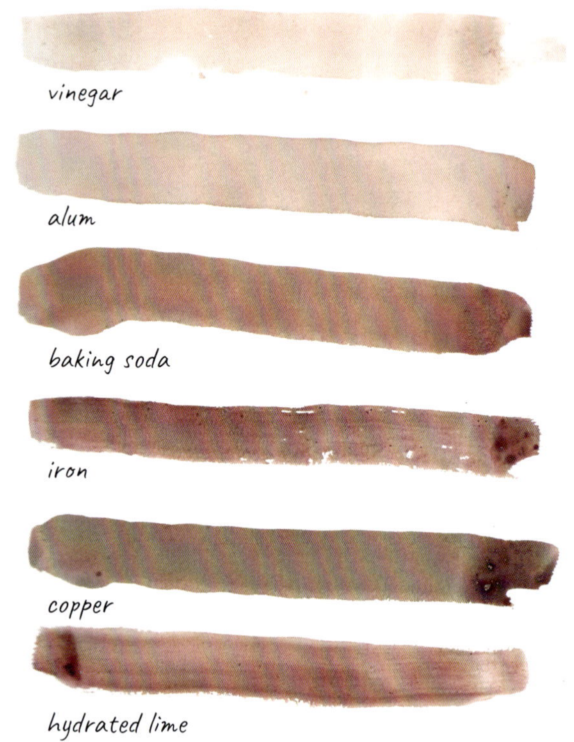

COLORS CREATED	brown with most mordants, yellow with hydrated lime
PARTS USED FOR PIGMENT	hulls
PLANT TYPE	tree
HARDINESS ZONE	varies by species

1. Simmer for 75 minutes to make pigment or dye. Strain.
2. Simmer again to reduce liquid to desired color strength.

Notes: Shagbark hulls make reddish brown on fabric with most mordants.

BOILED HICKORY NUT HULLS WITH HYDRATED LIME

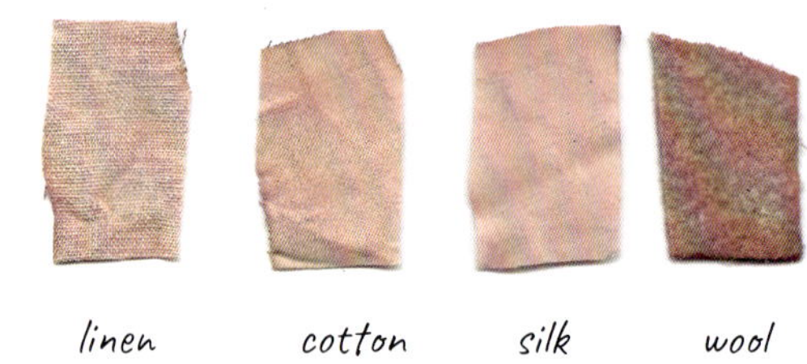

PLAIN BOILED SHAGBARK HICKORY HULLS

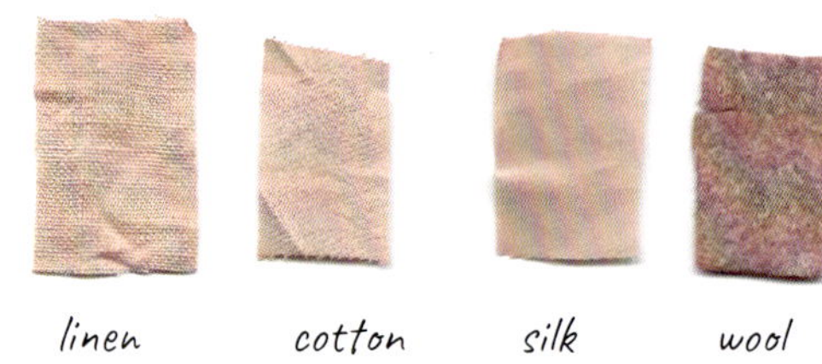

ALCEA ROSEA

Hollyhock

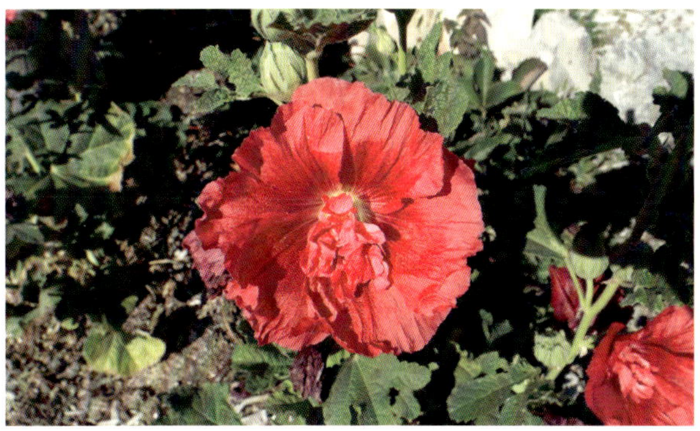

COLORS CREATED	black petals create green with alum and grayish hues with other mordants, red petals create purple with citric acid and yellow with baking soda and alum
PARTS USED FOR PIGMENT	petals only (no sepals)
PLANT TYPE	biennial
HARDINESS ZONE	3
SEEDING	Seeds available at SeedRenaissance.com.

1. Simmer for 75 minutes to make pigment or dye. Strain.
2. Simmer again to reduce liquid to desired color strength.

Notes: The flowers make a thick liquid regardless of mordants, making it ideal for children's finger paints. The liquid, when used as paint or ink, is granular and bumpy, creating an interesting effect on paper.

BLACK HOLLYHOCK

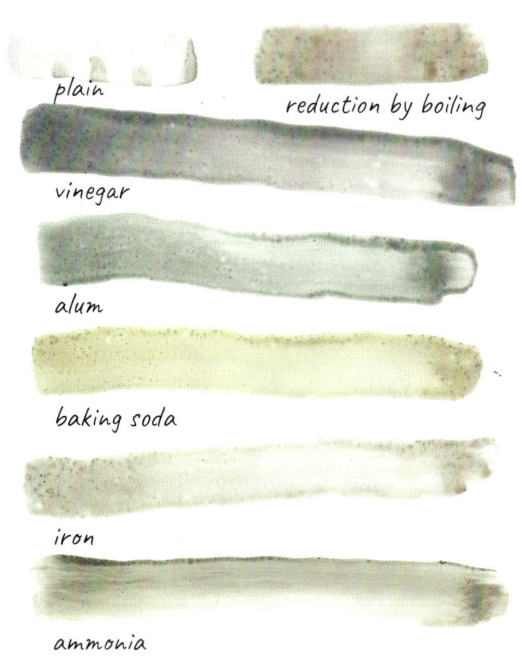

RED HOLLYHOCK PETALS

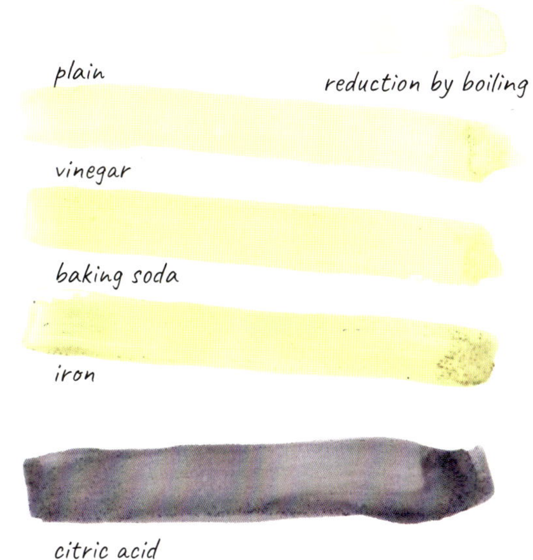

LONICERA SPECIES

Honeysuckle

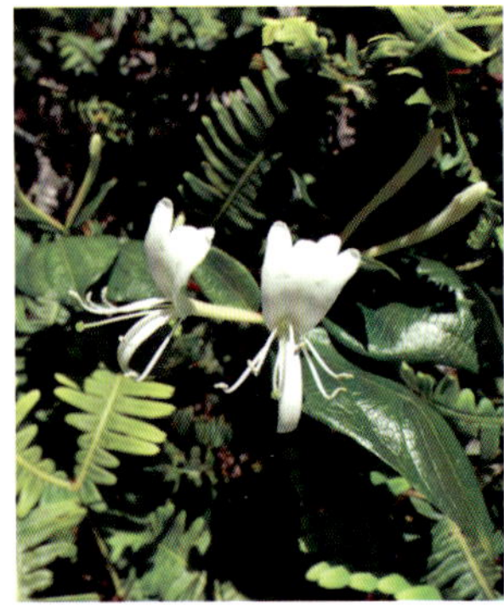
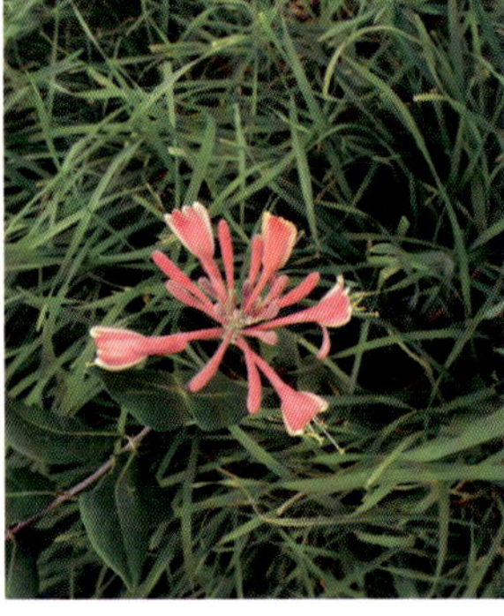

JAPANESE HONEYSUCKLE WHITE PETALS

TWINBERRY HONEYSUCKLE

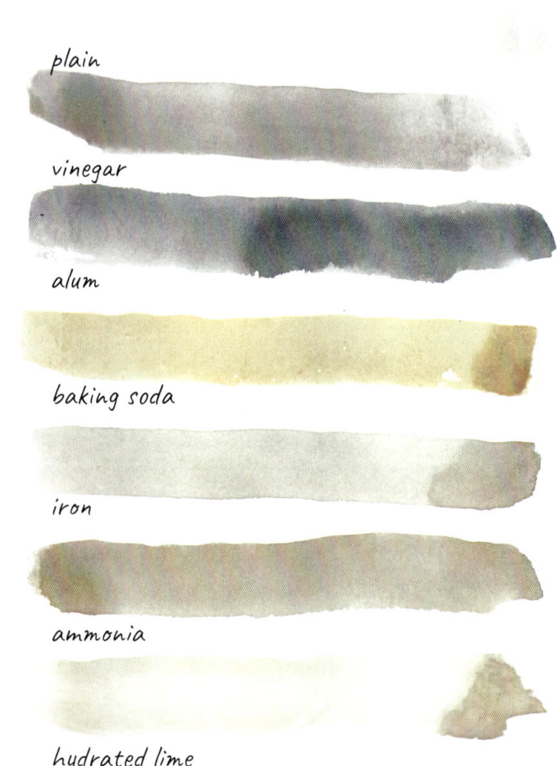

RED HONEYSUCKLE

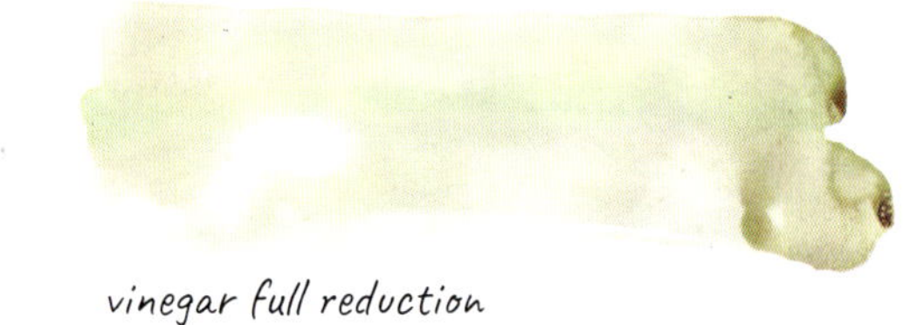

COLORS CREATED	hybrid red petals make yellow with baking soda and brown hues with other mordants, white Japanese honeysuckle creates yellow with alum, twinberry honeysuckle creates a beautiful gray with alum or orange with baking soda
PARTS USED FOR PIGMENT	flower petals
PLANT TYPE	perennial
HARDINESS ZONE	4

1. Simmer for 10 minutes to make pigment or dye. Strain.
2. Simmer again to reduce liquid to desired color strength.

Notes: A second boil of the same petals created the same colors. The yellow created with baking soda mordant initially appears as green but decomposes to yellow as the liquid cools and ages. Honeysuckle flowers are renowned for their natural edible "honey" and any honeysuckle paint that is too layered or too thick will become sticky, although the sugar does not appear in simple washes of color.

EQUISETUM SPECIES

Horsetail Grass

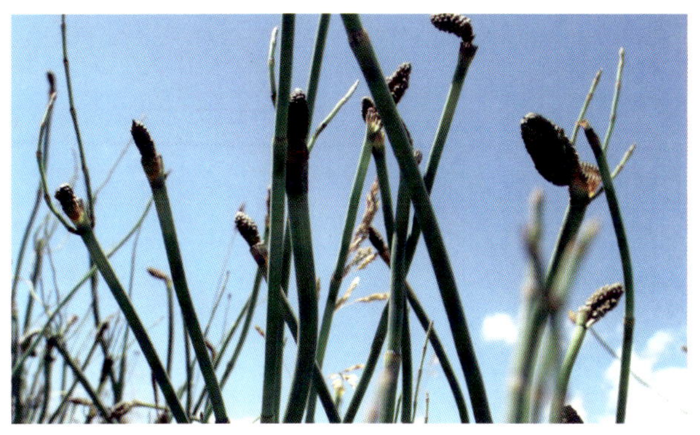

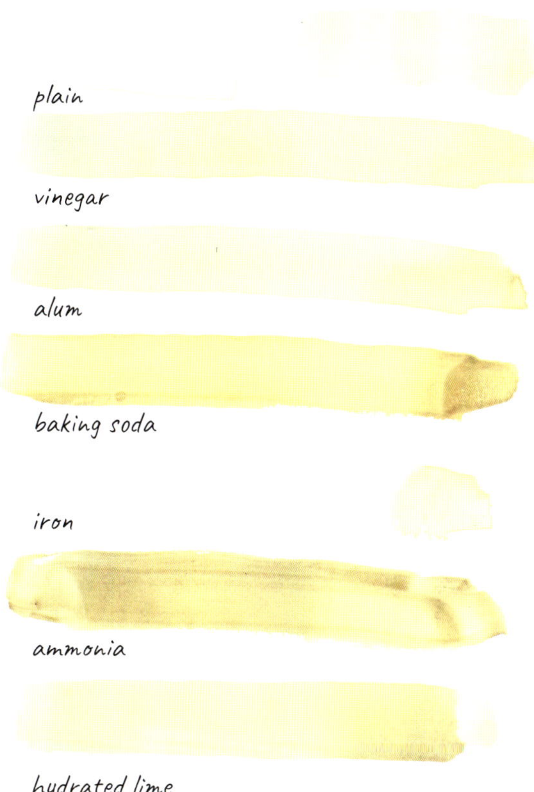

COLORS CREATED	yellow with most mordants
PARTS USED FOR PIGMENT	reeds
PLANT TYPE	perennial
HARDINESS ZONE	4

1. Simmer for 10 minutes to make pigment or dye. Strain.
2. Simmer again to reduce liquid to desired color strength.

CYNOGLOSSUM OFFICINALE

Houndstongue

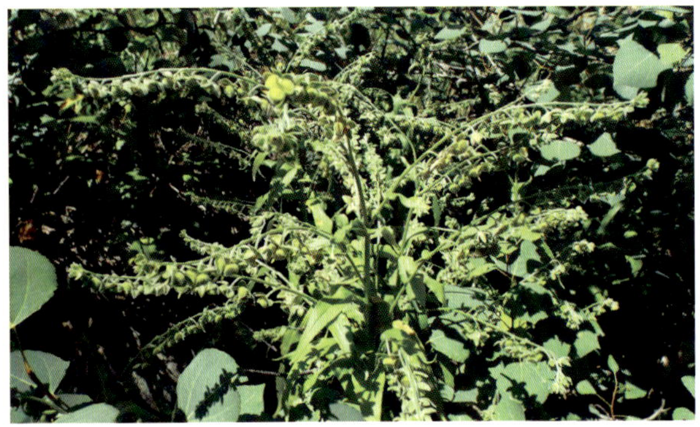

COLORS CREATED	yellow with alum, orange with baking soda
PARTS USED FOR PIGMENT	flowering tops
PLANT TYPE	perennial
HARDINESS ZONE	5

1. Simmer for 10 minutes to make pigment or dye. Strain.
2. Simmer again to reduce liquid to desired color strength.

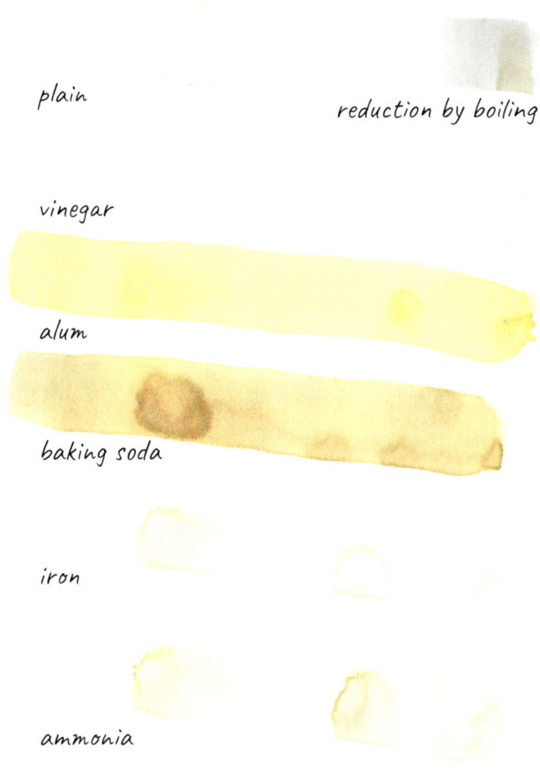

HYACINTHUS SPECIES

Hyacinths

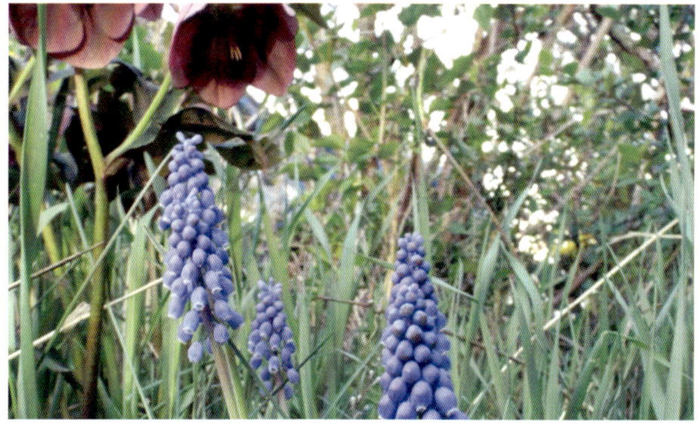

COLORS CREATED	turquoise with vinegar and alum, green with copper, purple when unmordanted
PARTS USED FOR PIGMENT	blue flowers
PLANT TYPE	perennial bulb flowers
HARDINESS ZONE	3

1. Simmer for 10 minutes to make pigment or dye. Strain.
2. Simmer again to reduce liquid to desired color strength.

Notes: Adding hydrated lime created the most interesting and unexpected starry night paint. Grape hyacinths (*Muscari armeniacum*) make a more muted palette of colors when cooked but result a great blue when used fresh for pigment.

DRIED THEN BOILED BLUE HYACINTH PETALS (NO MORDANTS)

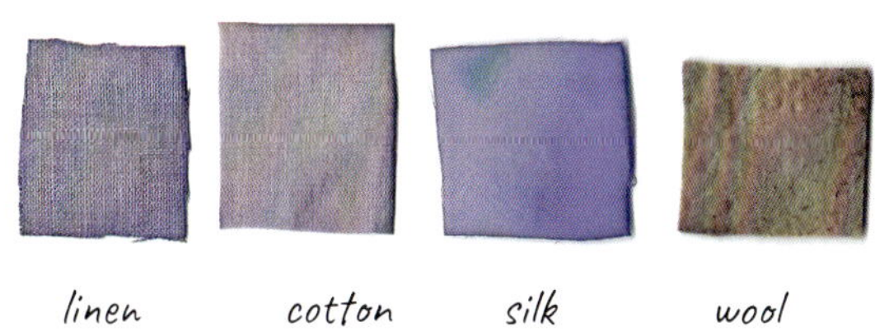

BLUE HYACINTH

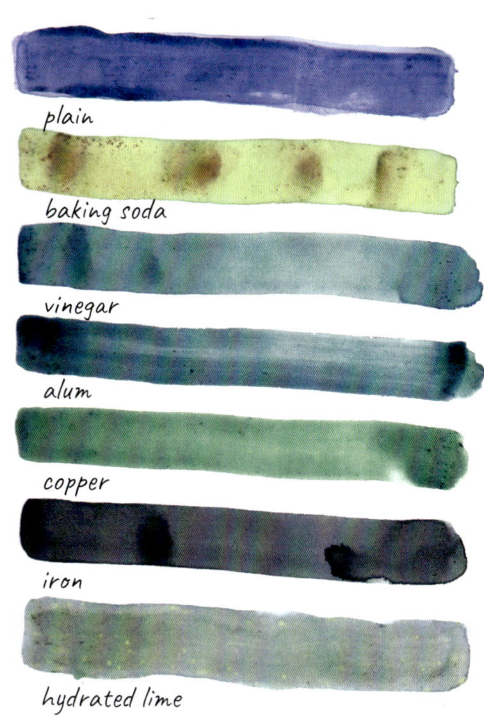

HYACINTH BULB FLOWERS

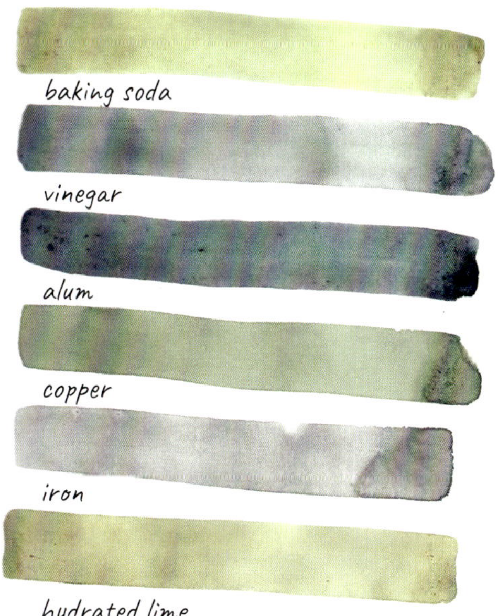

HYDRANGEA MACROPHYLLA

Hydrangea

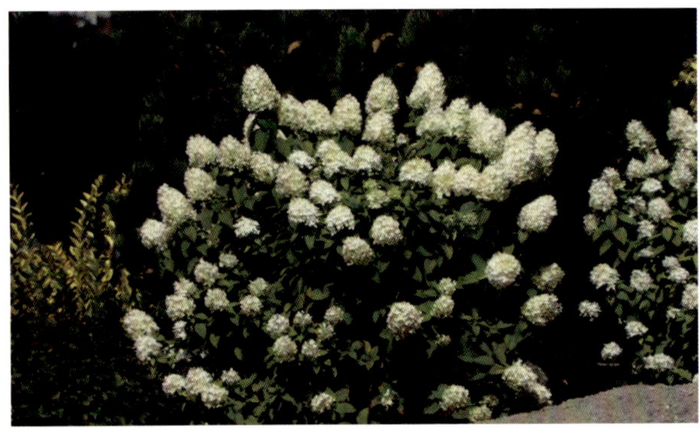

COLORS CREATED	yellows
PARTS USED FOR PIGMENT	flower heads (no leaves)
PLANT TYPE	perennial
HARDINESS ZONE	6

1. Simmer for 10 minutes to make pigment or dye. Strain.
2. Simmer again to reduce liquid to desired color strength.

Notes: Blue hydrangea flowers created yellows and greenish yellows when used fresh and uncooked. Lime green flowers created neon yellow with alum and baking soda.

YELLOW HYDRANGEA

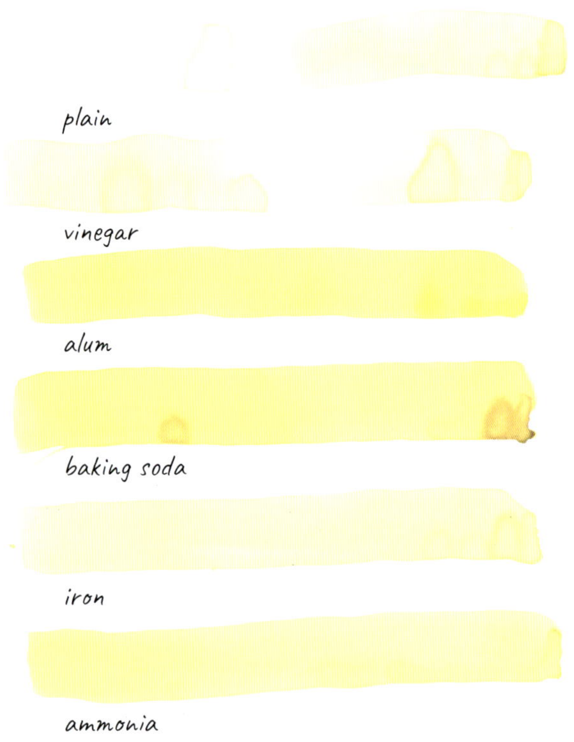

BOILED BLUE HYDRANGEA PETALS

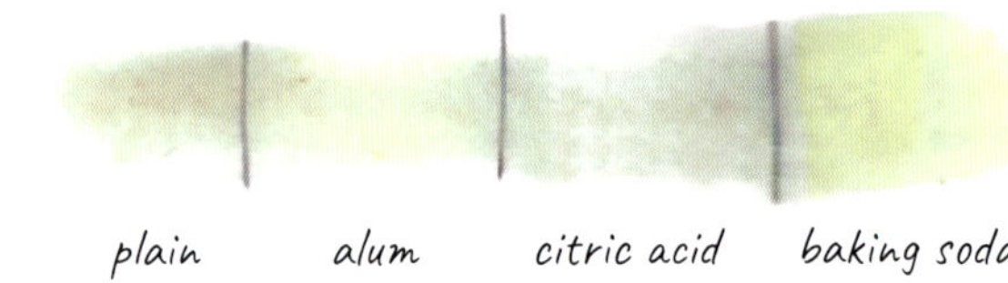

TERMINALIA CATAPPA

Indian Almond

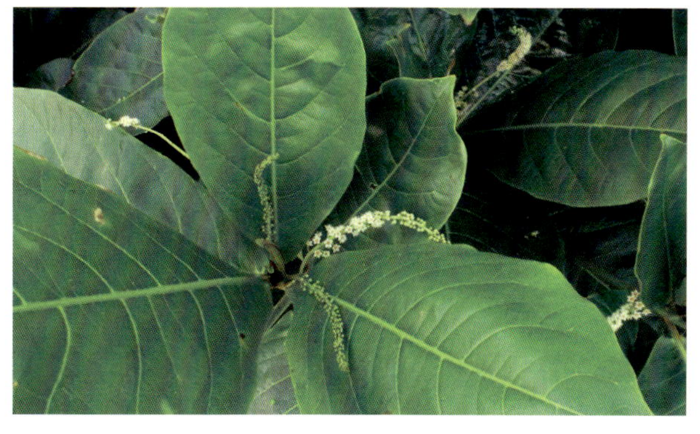

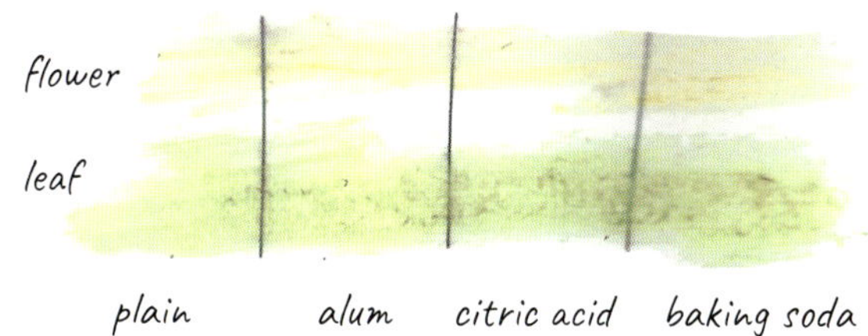

COLORS CREATED	green
PARTS USED FOR PIGMENT	fresh leaves
PLANT TYPE	tree
HARDINESS ZONE	10

1. Best used fresh as pigment.

CASTILLEJA SPECIES

Indian Paintbrush

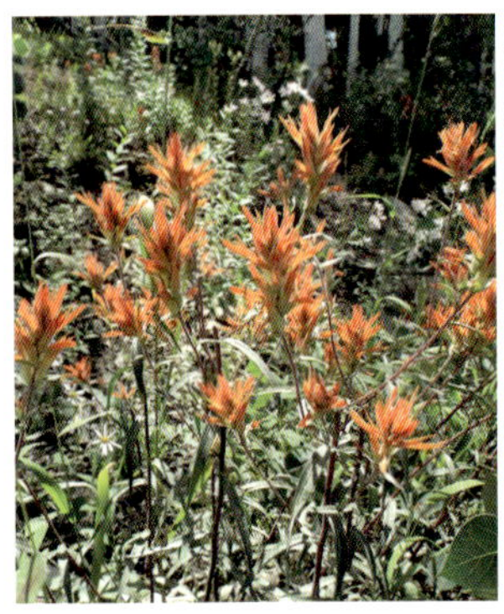
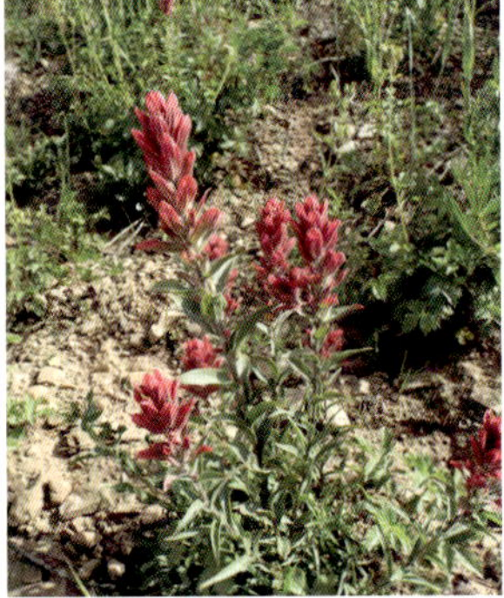

COLORS CREATED	yellow with most mordants (from yellow or orange flowers), green with alum and hues of brown with most mordants (from red flowers)
PARTS USED FOR PIGMENT	flowering spikes
PLANT TYPE	varies by species
HARDINESS ZONE	varies by species

1. Simmer for 10 minutes to make pigment or dye. Strain.
2. Simmer again to reduce liquid to desired color strength.

Notes: The color temporarily stained a stainless-steel pan and had to be scrubbed out with a copper scrubber, which often indicates lightfastness.

LIME GREEN INDIAN PAINTBRUSH

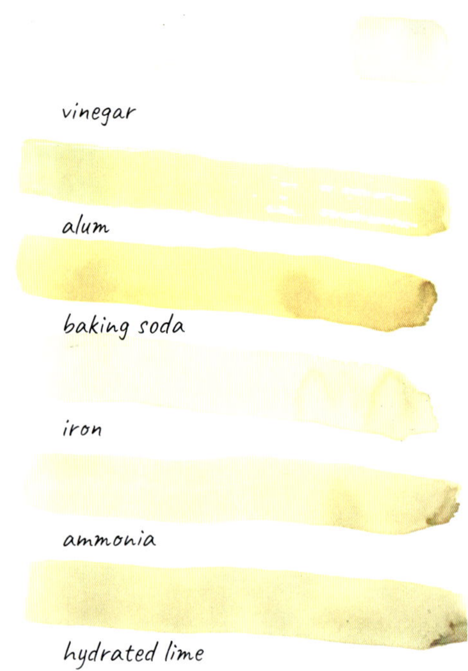

DARK RED INDIAN PAINTBRUSH

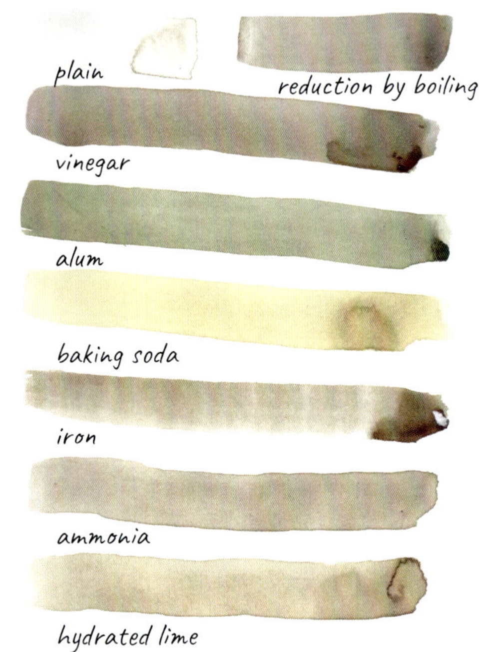

INDIGOFERA SPECIES

Indigo and False Indigo

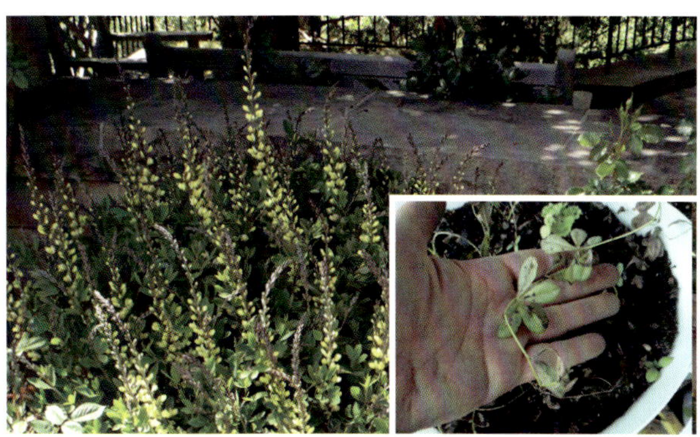

COLORS CREATED	blue
PARTS USED FOR PIGMENT	leaves, powdered extract of leaves
HARDINESS ZONE	true indigo is zone 11; false indigos are hardier

Notes: Leaves are processed in the same way as woad, as described in this book (see page 352). Indigo and false indigos are much harder to grow than woad in winter climates, even if you have eight geothermal greenhouses. Both indigo and woad have a strong smell when fermenting, which might offend your neighbors. This is why people buy indigo extract. False Indigos do not produce as much blue extract as the true tropical plant but are sure easier to grow.

INDIGO POWDER MULLED WITH WHOLE EGG AND LINSEED OIL

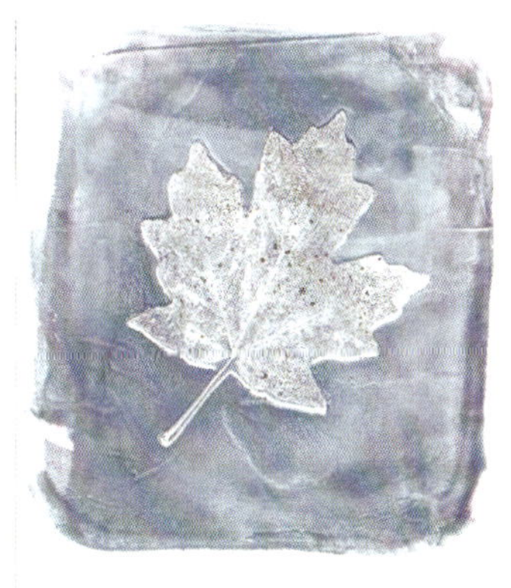

FRESH LEAVES OF INDIGO TINCTORIA BOILED WITH SALT

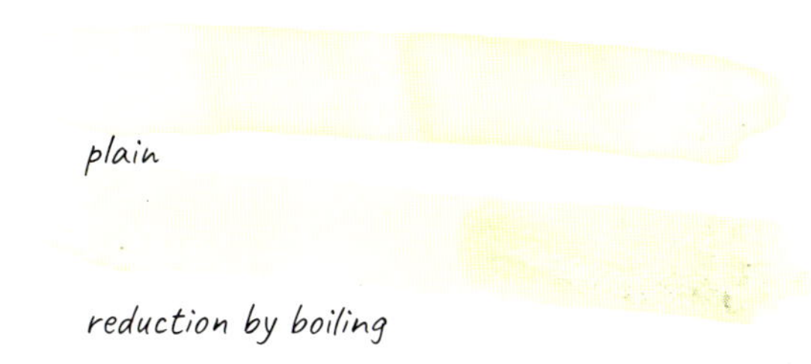

plain

reduction by boiling

GLAIR PAINTS

plus liquid pine

plus quark

INDIGO POWDER MULLED WITH LIQUID PINE, GLAIR, AND HYDRATED LIME

IRIDACEAE SPECIES

Iris

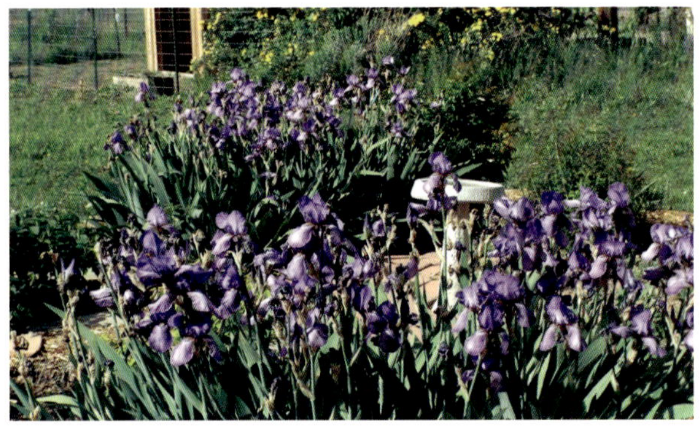

COLORS CREATED	green and orange (from purple blossoms), yellow and orange (from gold and violet blossoms)
PARTS USED FOR PIGMENT	blossoms, fresh or dried
PLANT TYPE	perennial
HARDINESS ZONE	3

1. Simmer for 10 minutes to make pigment or dye. Strain.
2. Simmer again to reduce liquid to desired color strength.

Notes: Gold and violet iris petals, dried, made pale orange when boiled and orange when reduced. The strongest orange came with a mordant of vinegar. Iron produced a pale orange, alum made a yellow-orange, and baking soda made a pale orange.

THREE COLOR IRIS

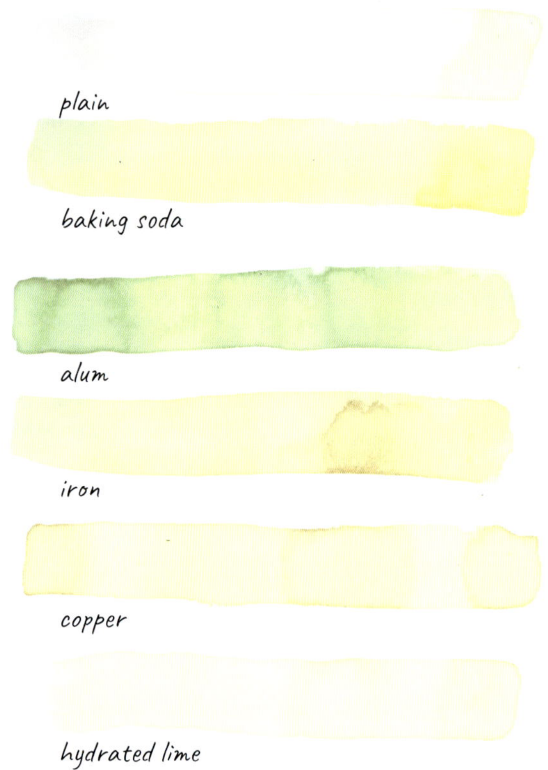

BOILED PURPLE IRIS PETALS WITH ALUM

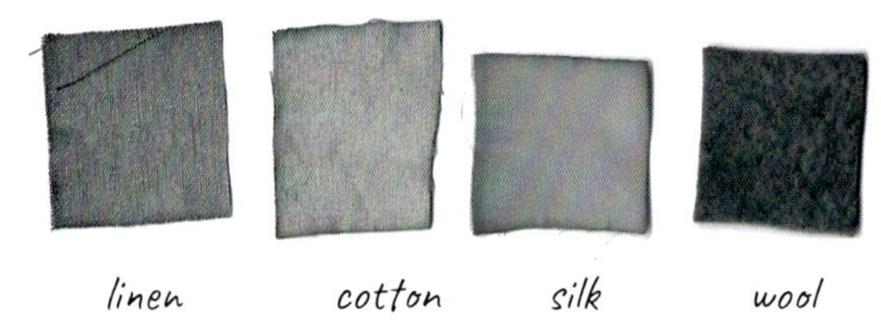

FRESH PRESSED PURPLE IRIS PETAL

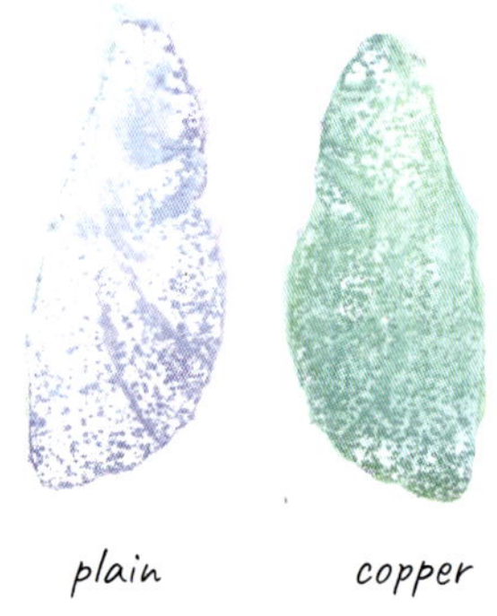

PURPLE IRIS

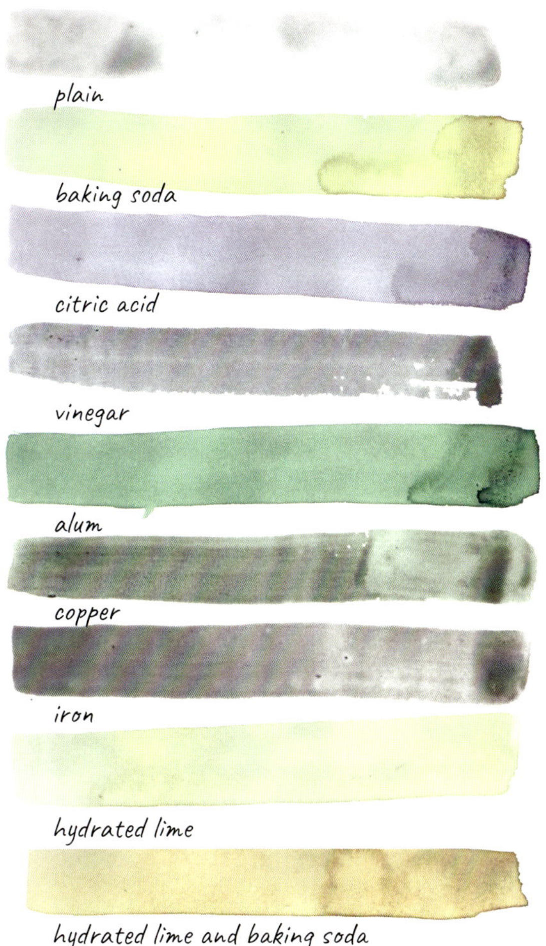

BOILED PURPLE IRIS PETALS WITH ALUM

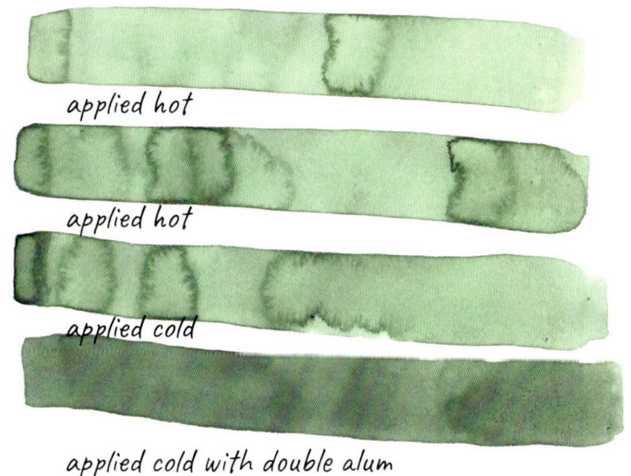

DRIED YELLOW IRIS

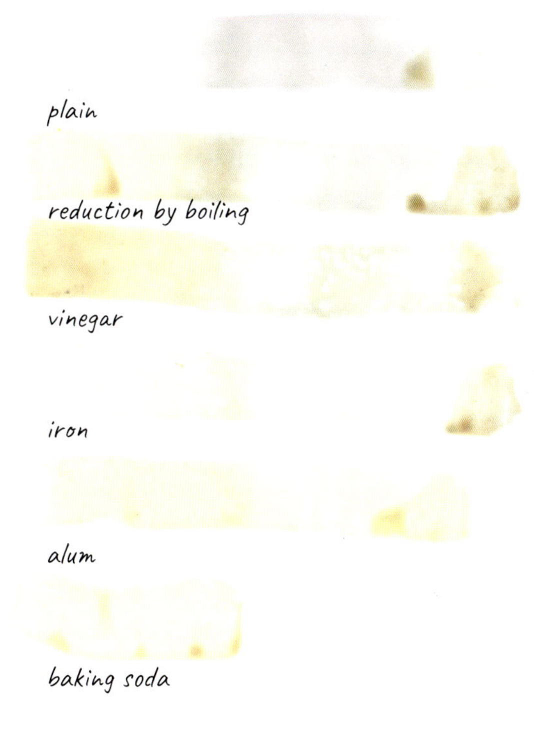

YELLOW IRIS

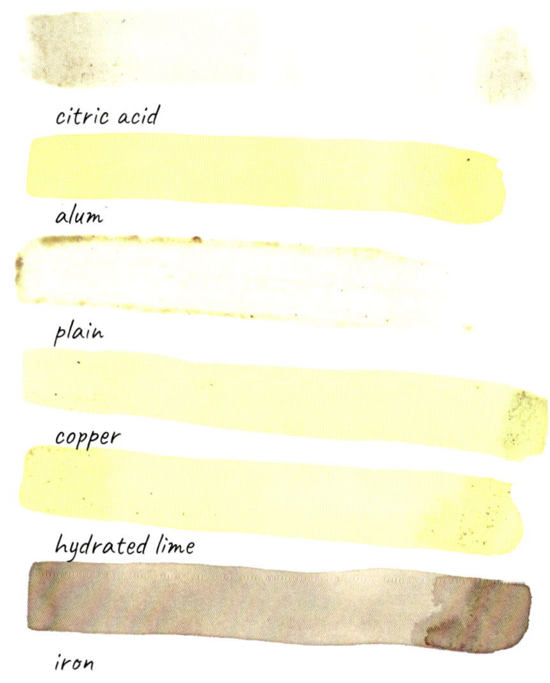

JUNIPERUS SPECIES

Juniper

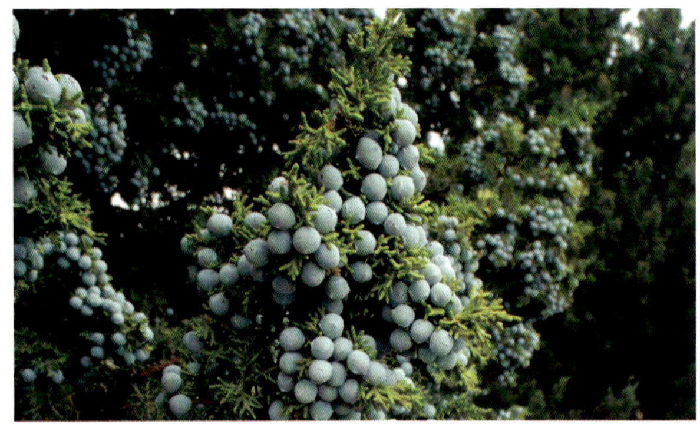

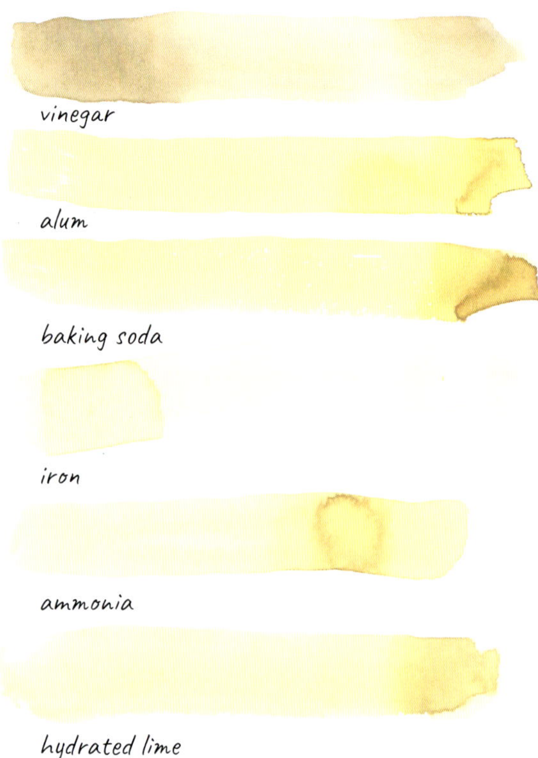

COLORS CREATED	yellow with most mordants
PARTS USED FOR PIGMENT	berries
PLANT TYPE	tree
HARDINESS ZONE	3

1. Simmer for 10 minutes to make pigment or dye. Strain.
2. Simmer again to reduce liquid to desired color strength.

KERRIA LACCA

Lac

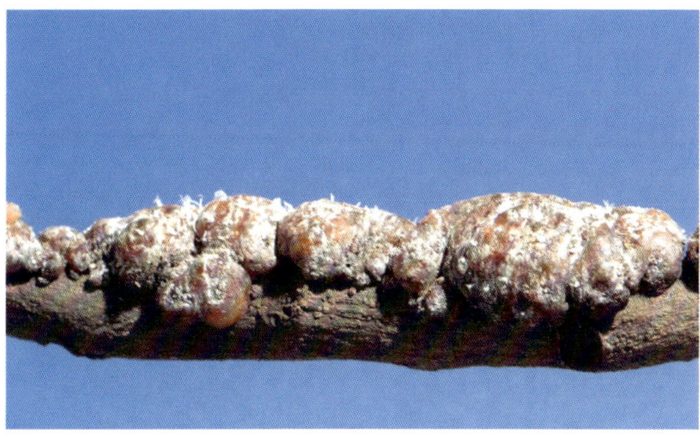

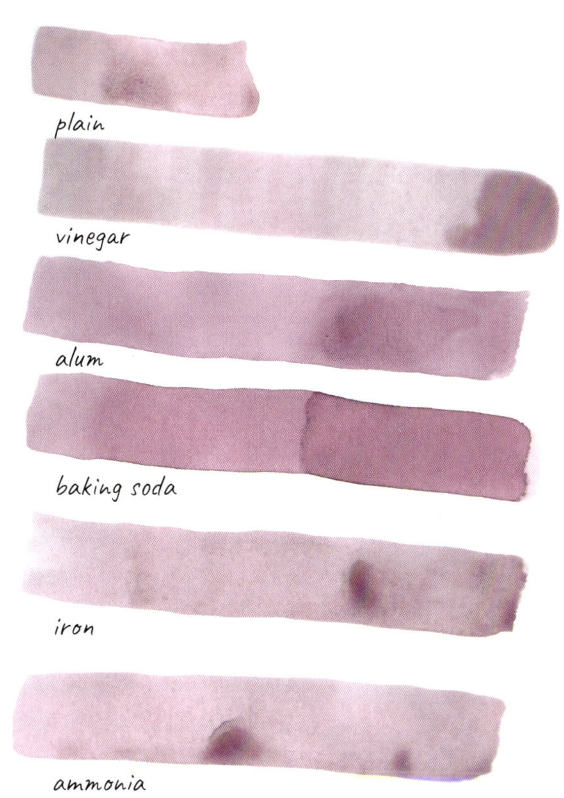

COLORS CREATED	purple
PARTS USED FOR PIGMENT	resin extract

1. Simmer for 10 minutes to make pigment or dye. Strain.
2. Simmer again to reduce liquid to desired color strength.

Notes: Historically, lac has been a hugely important source of purple dye and pigment. Lac is fig tree resin metabolized by specific insects. With lac there is no lack—meaning a little bit of lac powder goes a long way. Only the tiniest pinch is needed to make watercolor, for example—but use a spoon because it stains. Far smaller amounts are used than most of the color sources listed in this book.

PAINTS

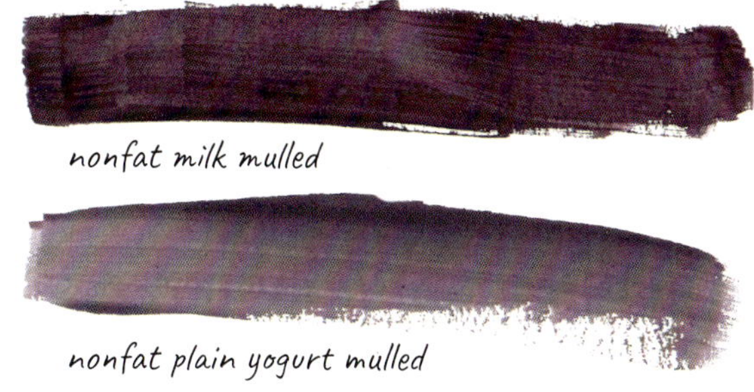

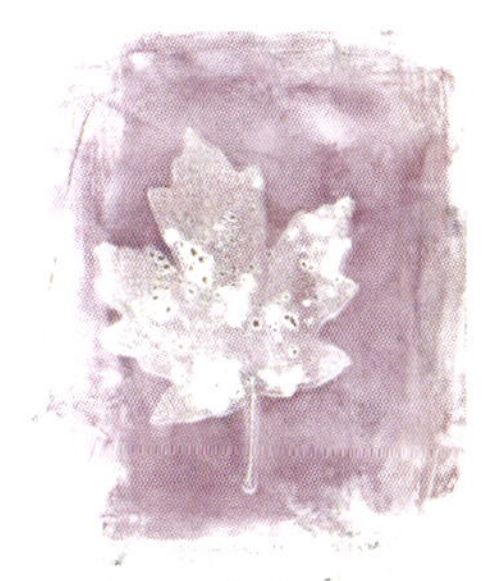

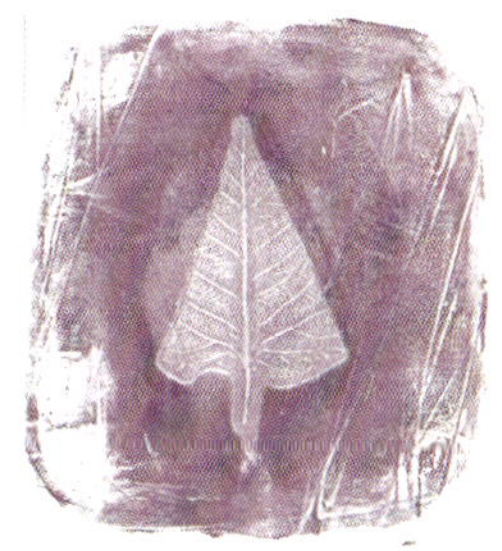

LANTANA CAMARA

Lantana

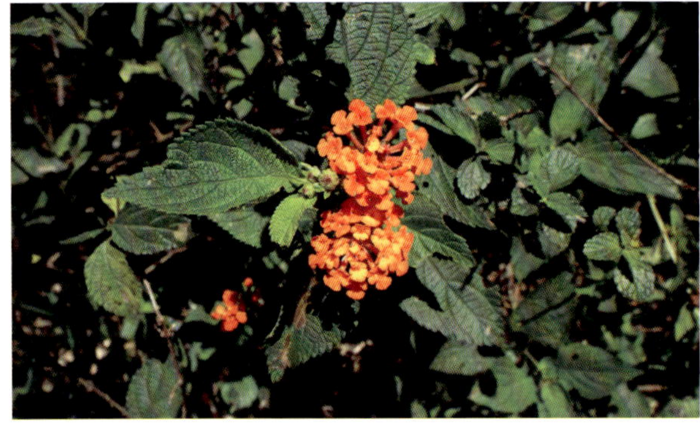

RED LANTANA

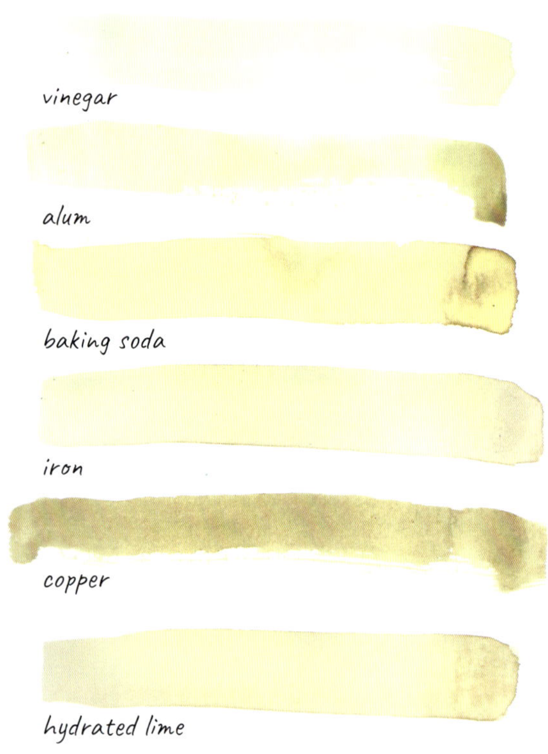

COLORS CREATED	yellow with baking soda
PARTS USED FOR PIGMENT	flowers
PLANT TYPE	tropical

1. Simmer for 10 minutes to make pigment or dye. Strain.
2. Simmer again to reduce liquid to desired color strength.

CONSOLIDA SPECIES

Larkspur

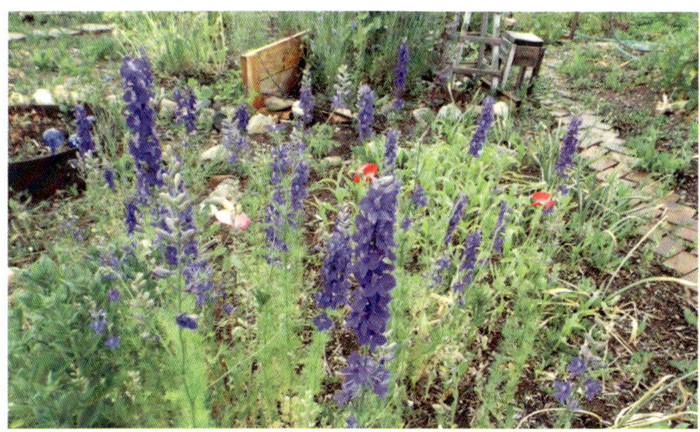

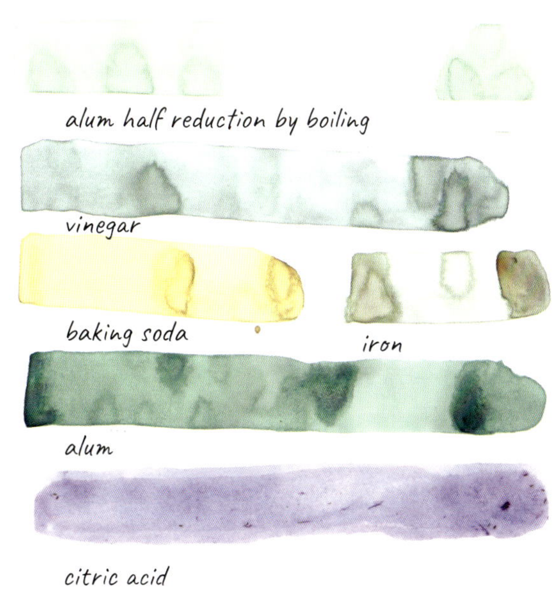

COLORS CREATED	purples, blues, and greens when used fresh; yellow with baking soda and green with most mordants when cooked
PARTS USED FOR PIGMENT	flowering spikes
PLANT TYPE	perennial
HARDINESS ZONE	2
SEEDING	Seeds available at SeedRenaissance.com.

FRESH PRESSED BLUE PETALS

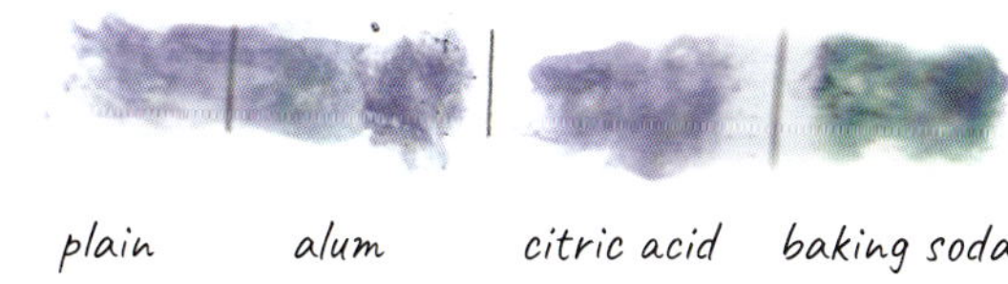

1. Simmer for 10 minutes to make pigment or dye. Strain.
2. Simmer again to reduce liquid to desired color strength.

Notes: Larkspur makes excellent blue eco-prints.

METROSIDEROS POLYMORPHA

Lehua Tree

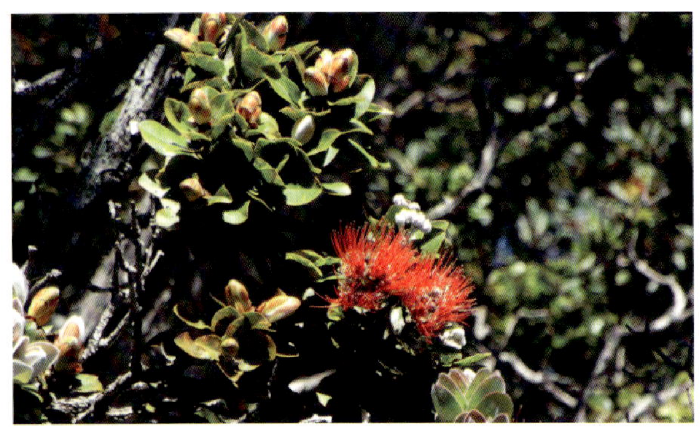

FRESH PRESSED PETALS

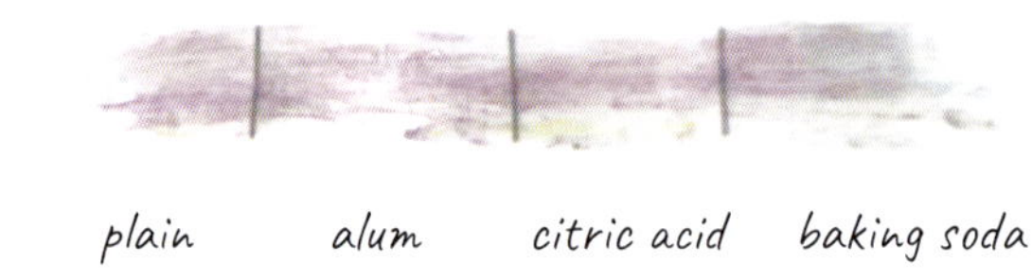

FRESH PRESSED RED FLOWERS

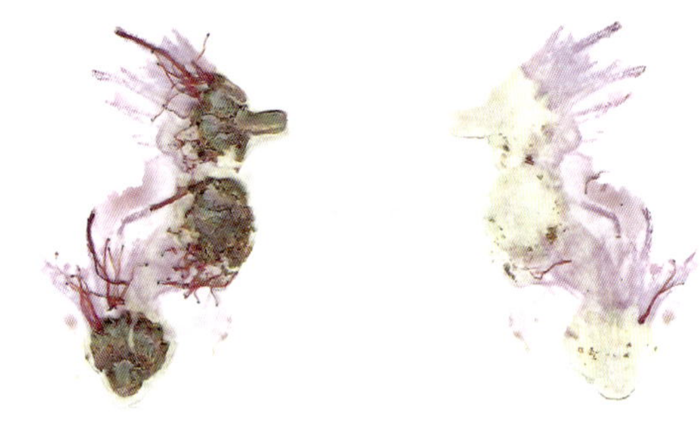

COLORS CREATED	purple
PARTS USED FOR PIGMENT	fresh red thread-like flowers
PLANT TYPE	tropical tree
HARDINESS ZONE	10

1. I have only been able to test this while fresh, but I suspect the color does not withstand cooking, except possibly with a citric acid mordant.

LACTUCA SPECIES

Lettuce

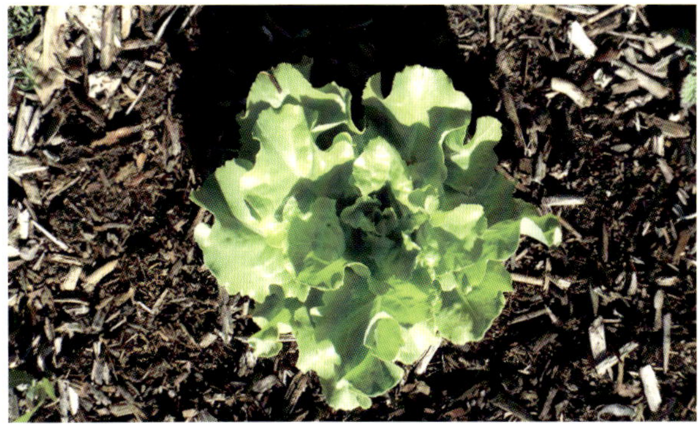

COLORS CREATED	yellow with most mordants
PARTS USED FOR PIGMENT	fresh or dried leaves, stems, flowers
PLANT TYPE	annual
SEEDING	Seeds available at SeedRenaissance.com.

1. Simmer for 10 minutes to make pigment or dye. Strain.
2. Simmer again to reduce liquid to desired color strength.

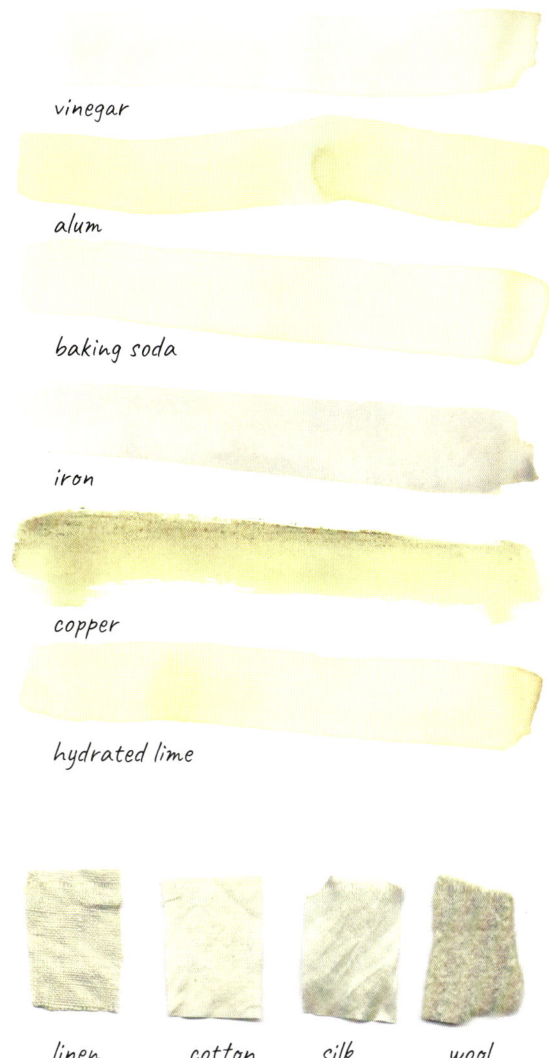

Lilies (Various Species)

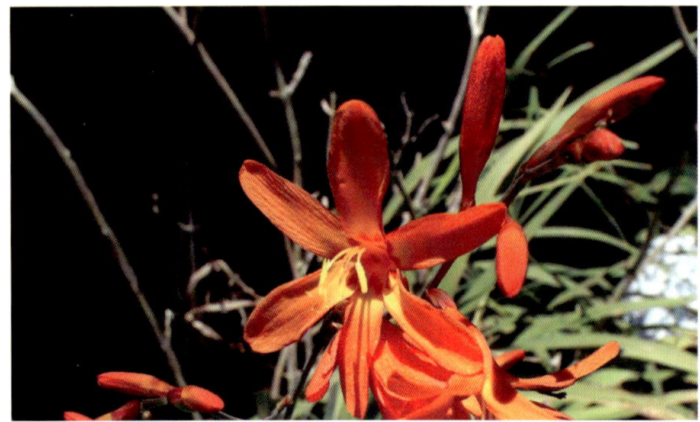

RED LILIES

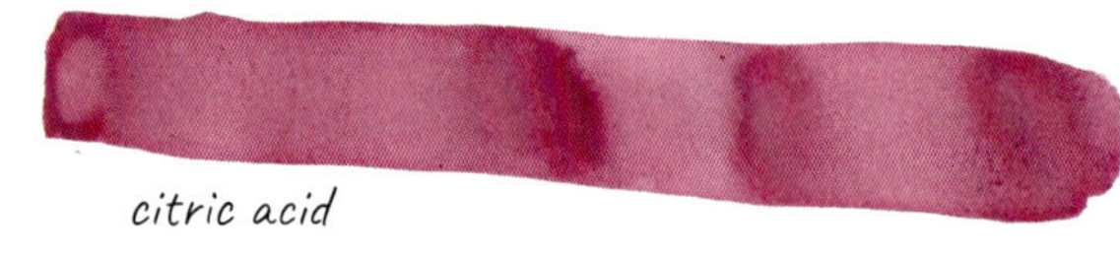

YELLOW LILIES

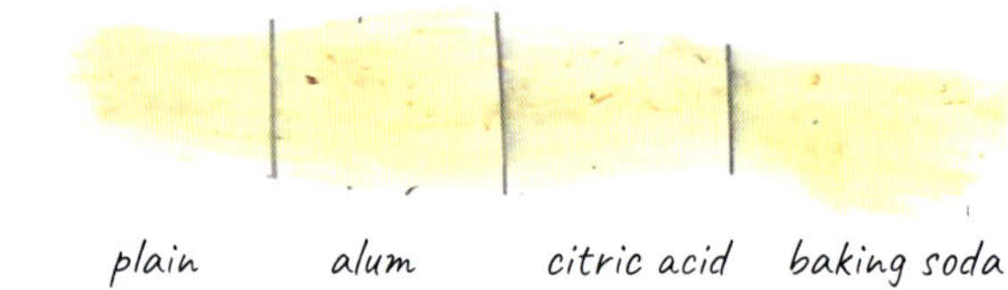

CROCOSMIA

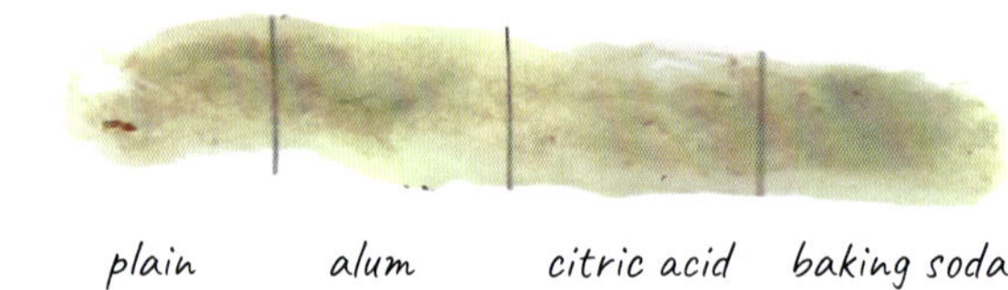

COLORS CREATED	yellow or brown from fresh yellow petals, green from fresh red petals, red from cooked red petals with citric acid
PARTS USED FOR PIGMENT	petals
HARDINESS ZONE	perennial

1. Simmer for 10 minutes to make pigment or dye. Strain.
2. Simmer again to reduce liquid to desired color strength.

Lobelia Species

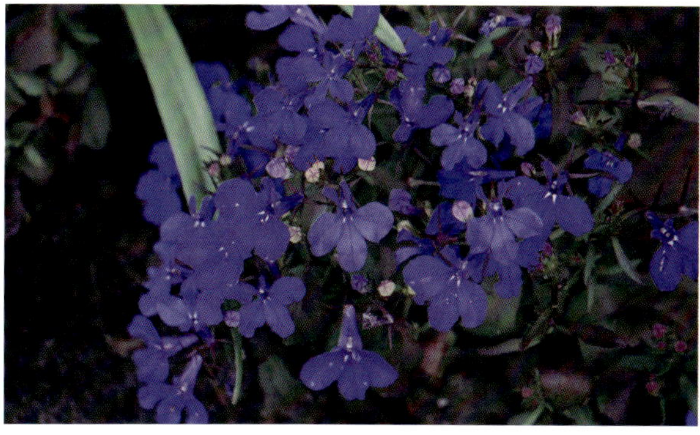

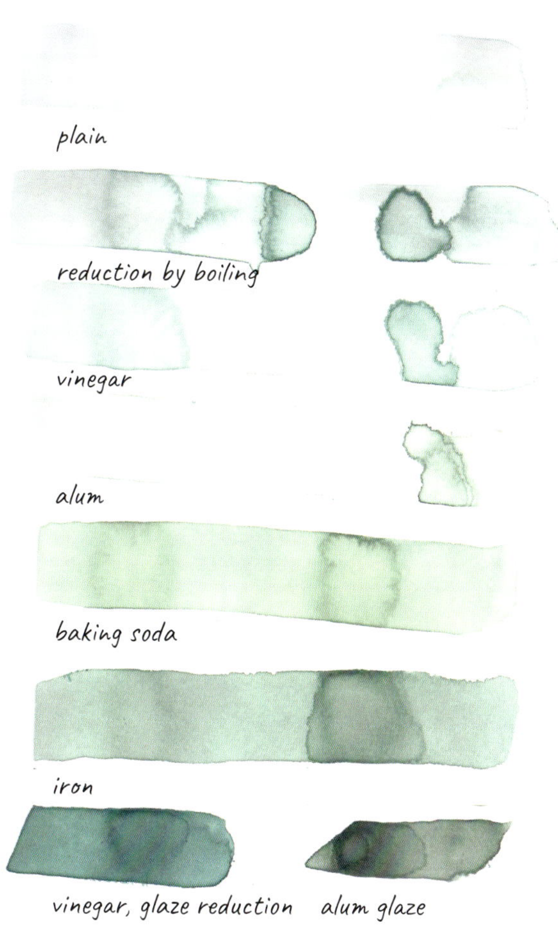

COLORS CREATED	blue from fresh pressed blue petals, green when cooked with most mordants
PARTS USED FOR PIGMENT	blooming flower stems
PLANT TYPE	flowering ground cover
HARDINESS ZONE	9

HAEMATOXYLUM CAMPECHIANUM

Logwood Tree

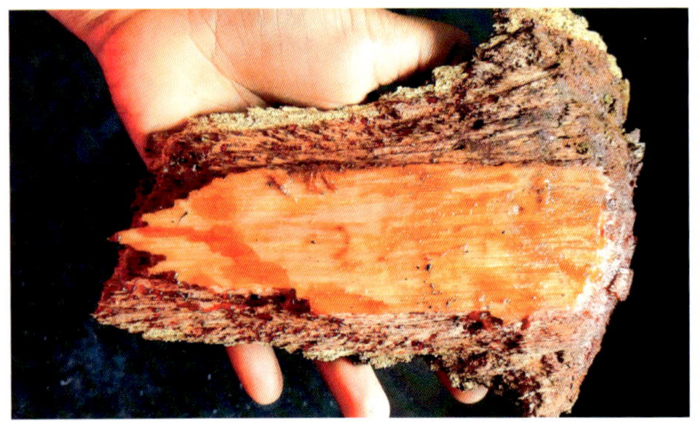

COLORS CREATED	purple with logwood, browns with other mordants
PARTS USED FOR PIGMENT	heartwood shavings
PLANT TYPE	tree
HARDINESS ZONE	10

1. Simmer for 10 minutes to make pigment or dye. Strain.
2. Simmer again to reduce liquid to desired color strength.

Notes: A little bit of shavings goes a long way. A second boil of the shavings, in fresh water, creates the same colors and can be used three or four times.

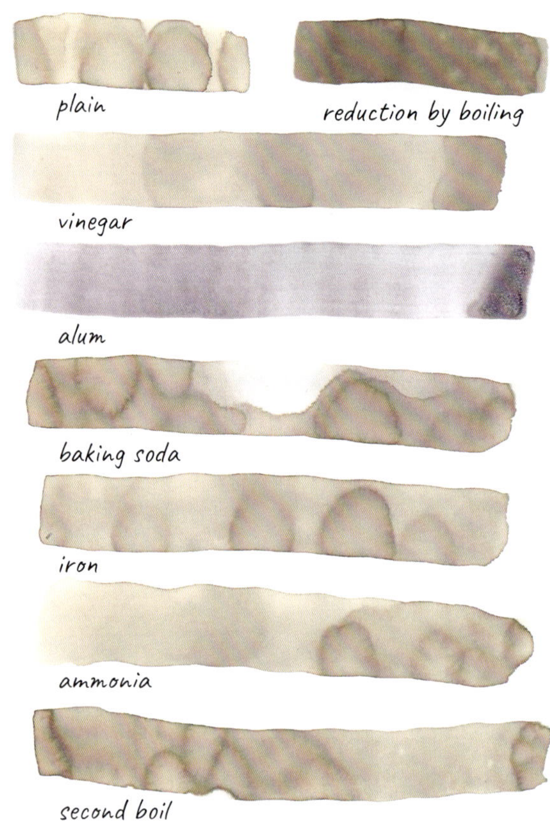

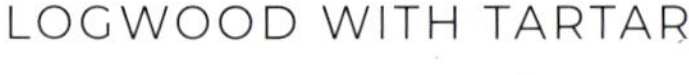

LOGWOOD WITH TARTAR

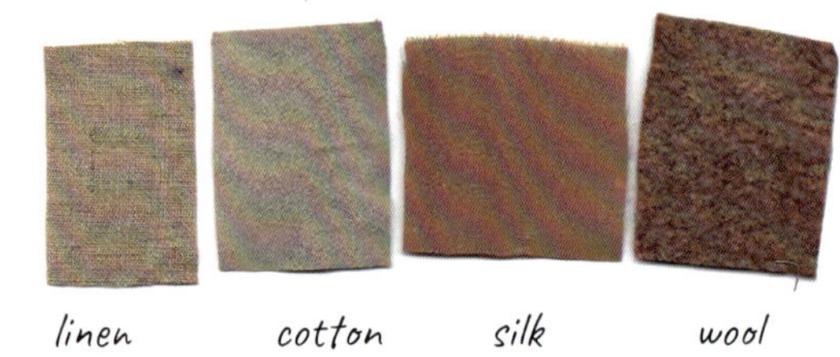

LOGWOOD WITH ALUM

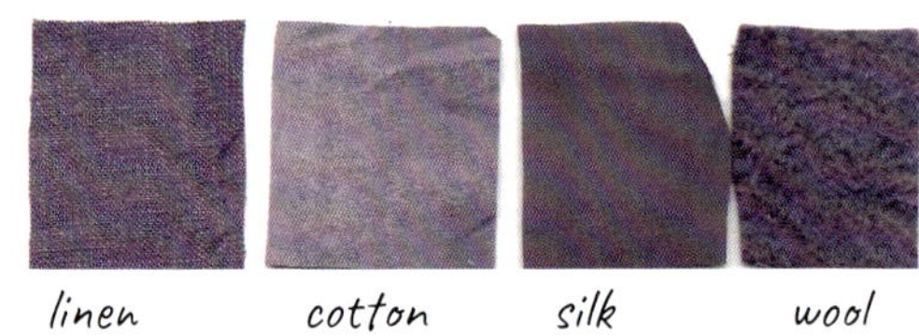

LITCHI CHINENSIS

Lychee

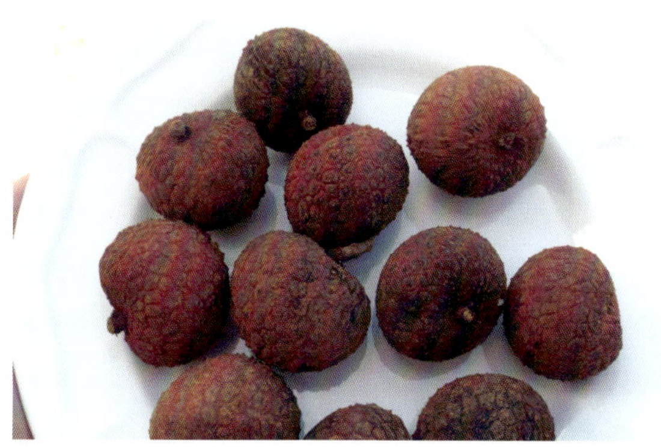

COLORS CREATED	gray with most mordants or unmordanted, brown with baking soda
PARTS USED FOR PIGMENT	skin of the lychee fruit
PLANT TYPE	fruiting tree
HARDINESS ZONE	9

1. Simmer for 10 minutes to make pigment or dye. Strain.
2. Simmer again to reduce liquid to desired color strength.

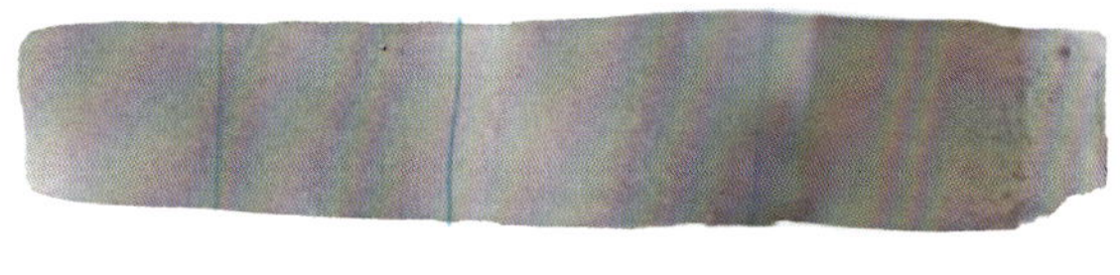

plain alum citric acid baking soda

CATHARANTHUS ROSEUS

Madagascar Periwinkle

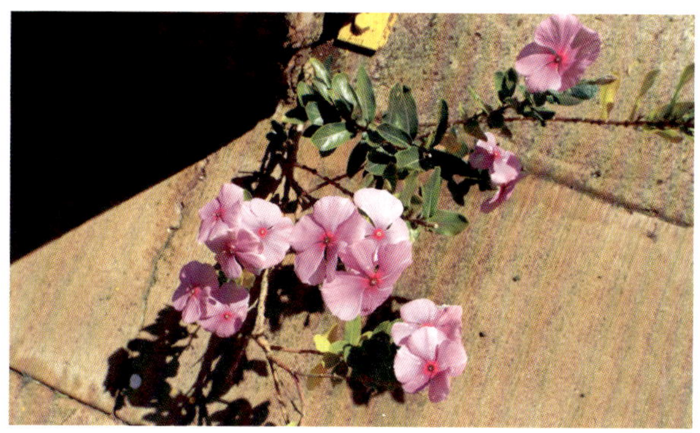

COLORS CREATED	blue unmordanted, green with baking soda
PARTS USED FOR PIGMENT	red flowers
PLANT TYPE	tropical landscape flower
HARDINESS ZONE	10

1. I tested the flowers fresh; the colors are likely not the same when cooked.

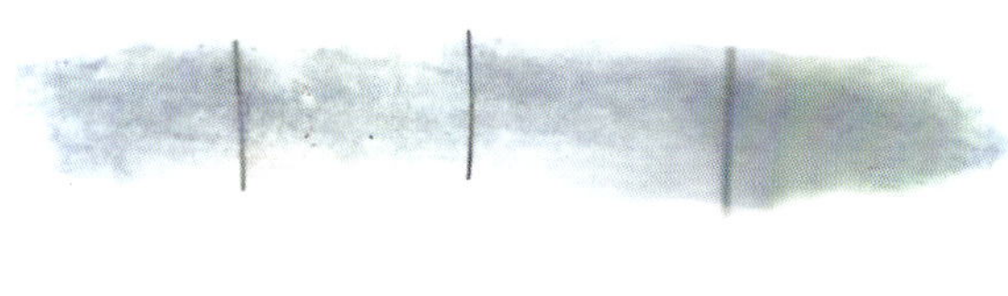

plain alum citric acid baking soda

RUBIA TINCTORUM

Madder Root

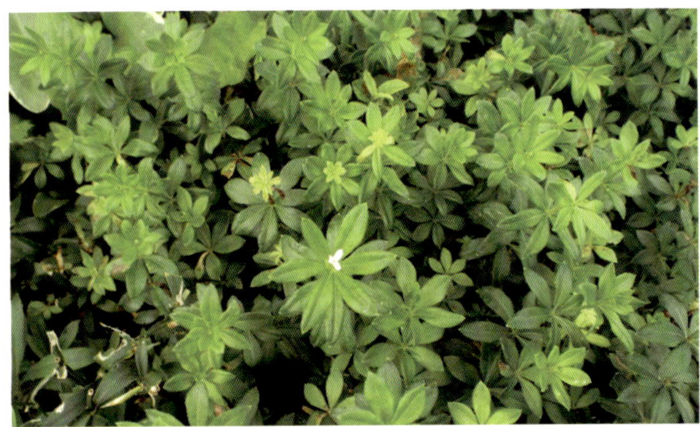

MADDER WHOLE ROOT

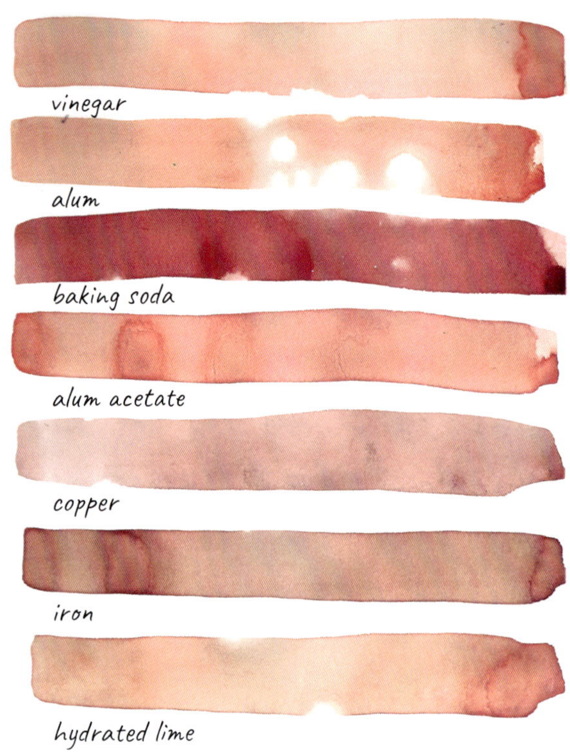

COLORS CREATED	red, pink, orange with citric acid, brown with cream of tartar
PARTS USED FOR PIGMENT	roots, berries
PLANT TYPE	perennial
HARDINESS ZONE	4
SEEDING	Seeds available at SeedRenaissance.com.

1. The raw fresh root simply blended with water will produce orange, peach, and coral colors depending on saturation. Heating to just begin steaming will produce peach tones. Simmering for 10 minutes produces coral tones. Simmering 20 minutes produces red tones. Steaming until the color is thickened produces orange and red tones depending on saturation. Both vinegar and baking soda mordants produce brick red tones, while baking soda produces the darkest hues. A second boil of the same roots in new water produces pink or peach. Cream of tartar mordant makes brown. Iron mordant makes brown. Iron mordant boiled to paste makes a true dark brown, which is not always an easy color to achieve. Even a third boil of the same roots in fresh water each time with an iron mordant makes the same true brown. Madder roots have so much color in them they can be reprocessed many times.
2. A fourth boil of the same roots with no reduction and no mordant makes pink, and a full reduction of the same makes a true red. A fifth boil and reduction made brick red. All shades can be made lighter with more water or darker by simmering to reduce.

Notes: The root produces the best-quality colors when chopped and dried before use, but I have also used fresh roots many times with happy results. I rinse and chop the fresh roots from my garden, press the pieces with the back of a spoon to braid them, and then let them dry completely before storing for later use. Roots taken in summer instead of spring or autumn may result in somewhat paler colors. Madder root is renowned not only for the range of tones it creates but also for the lightfast quality of the colors. Like iron rust, madder root is resistant to fading in ultraviolet light, which makes it ideal for exterior lightfast colors.

CRUSHED MADDER BERRIES

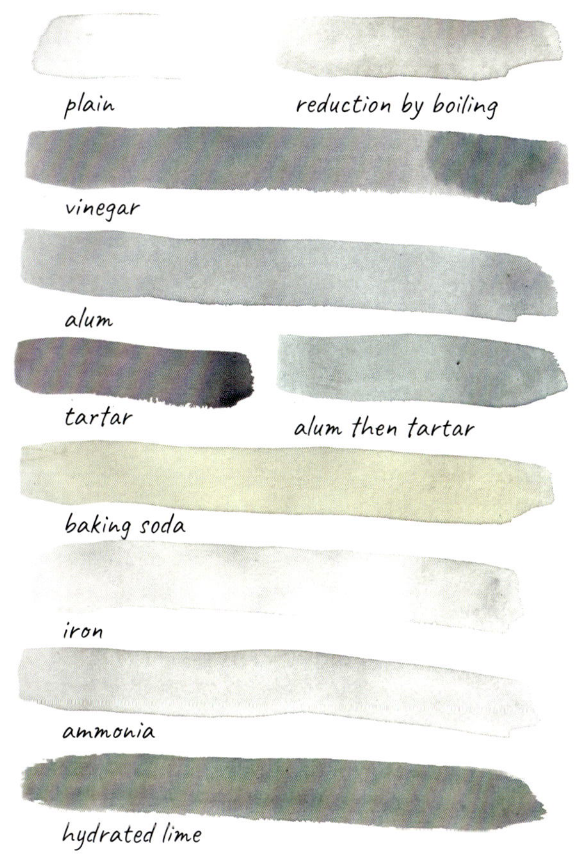

MADDER WITH SODA

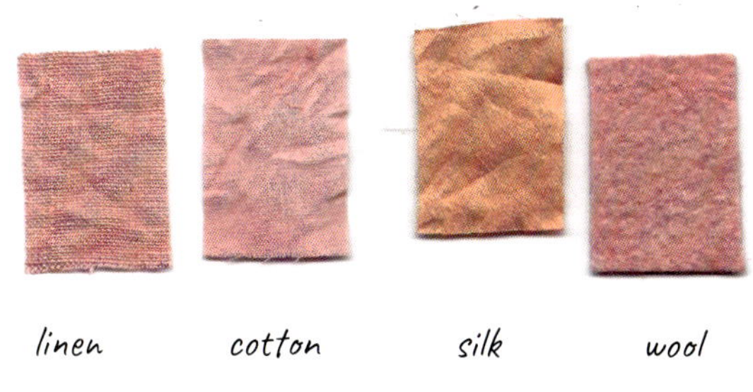

MADDER INNER ROOT

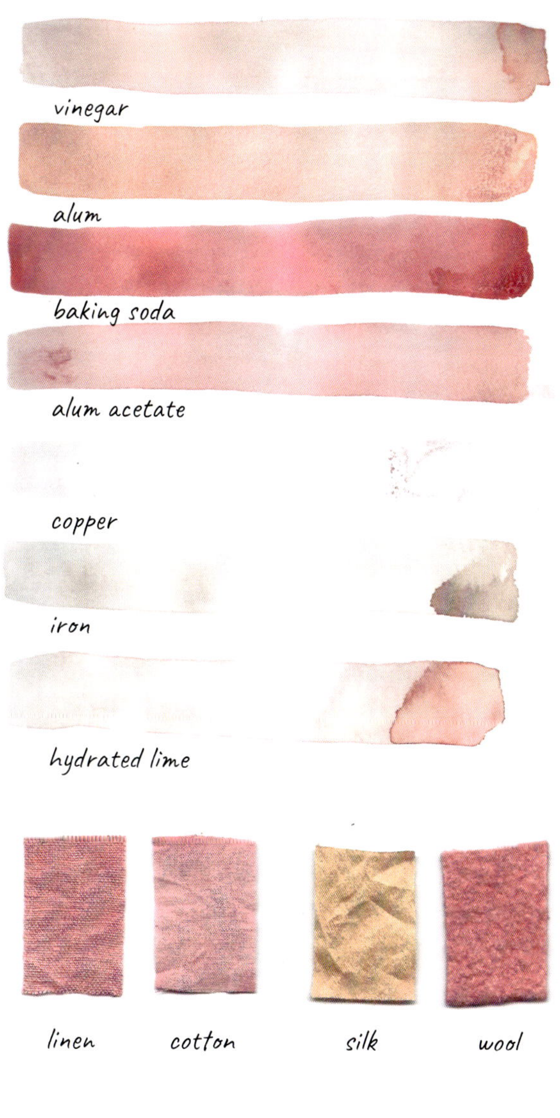

MADDER OUTER BARK

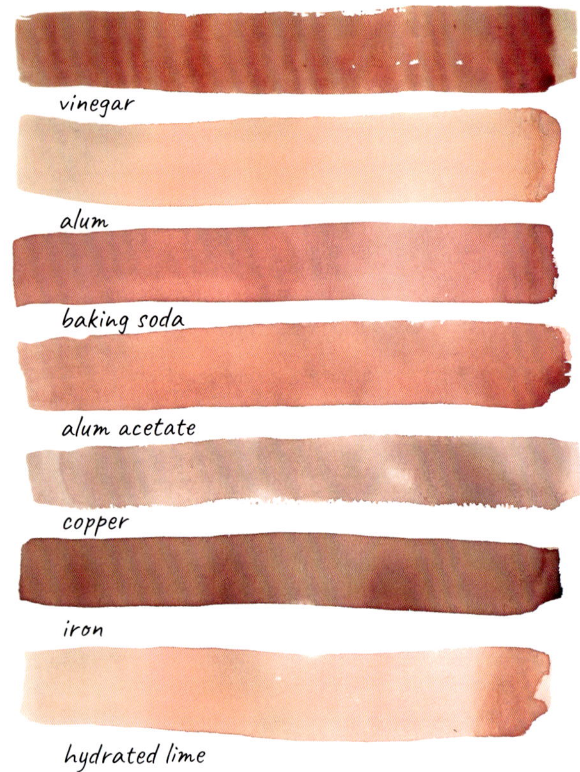

CASEIN GLAIR PAINT

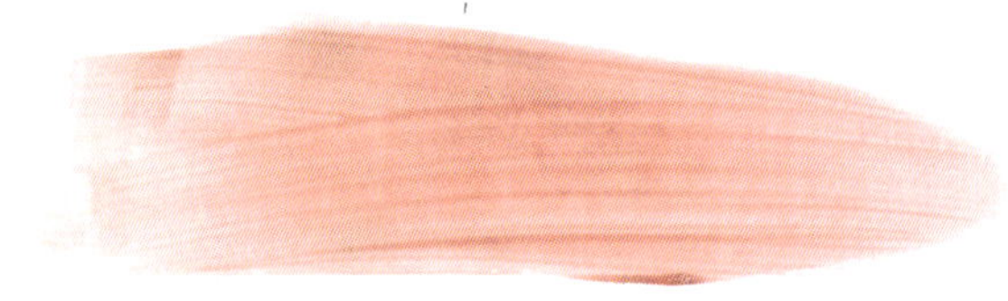

GLAIR ACRYLIC PAINT

GOUACHE PAINT

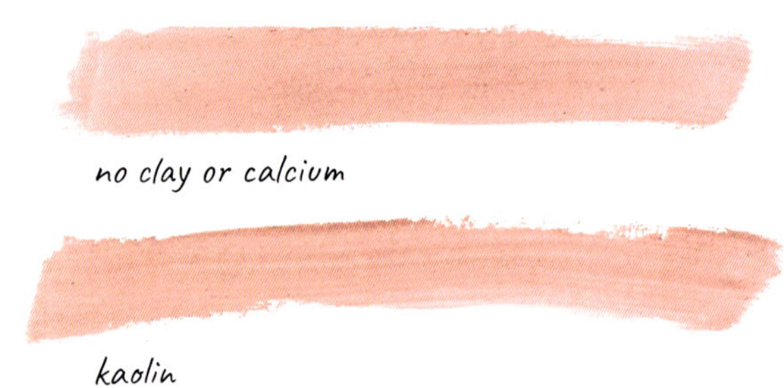

PLAIN MADDER OUTER BARK

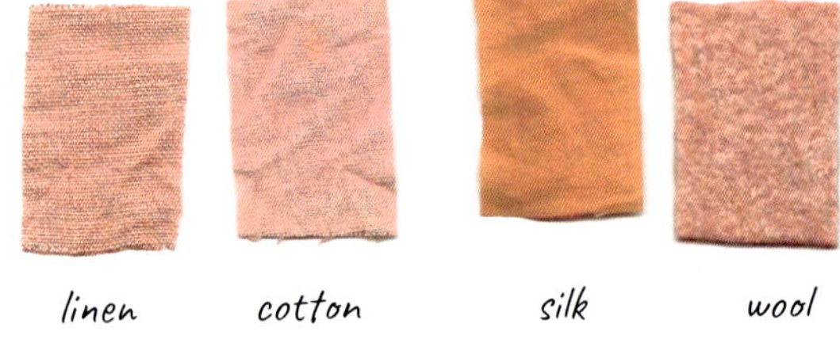

BOILED MADDER ROOT DYE

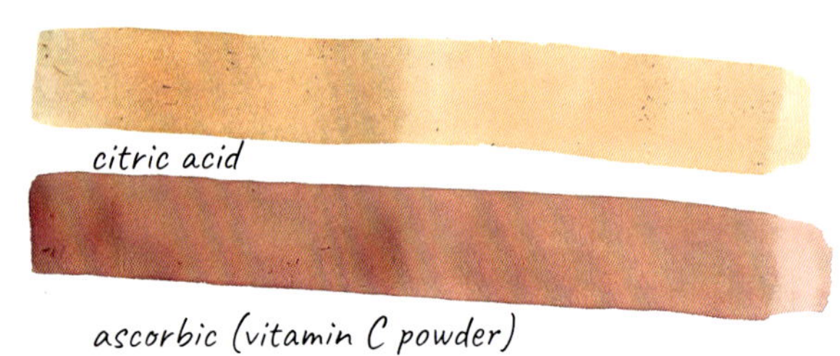

MADDER OUTER BARK WITH ALUM, VINEGAR, AND ALUM ACETATE

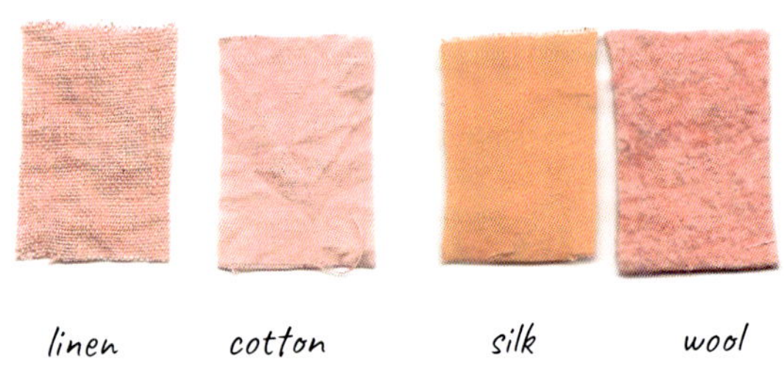

MADDER WITH YELLOW ONION

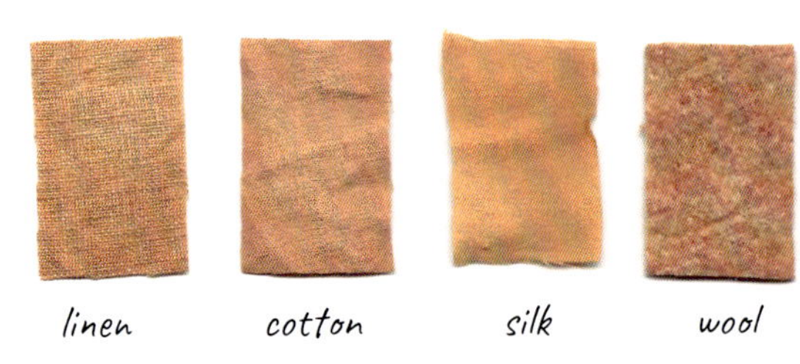

FRESH MADDER

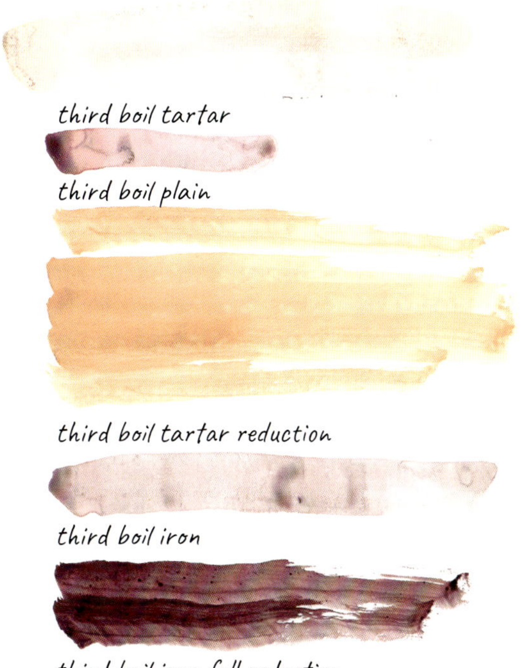

RAW MADDER

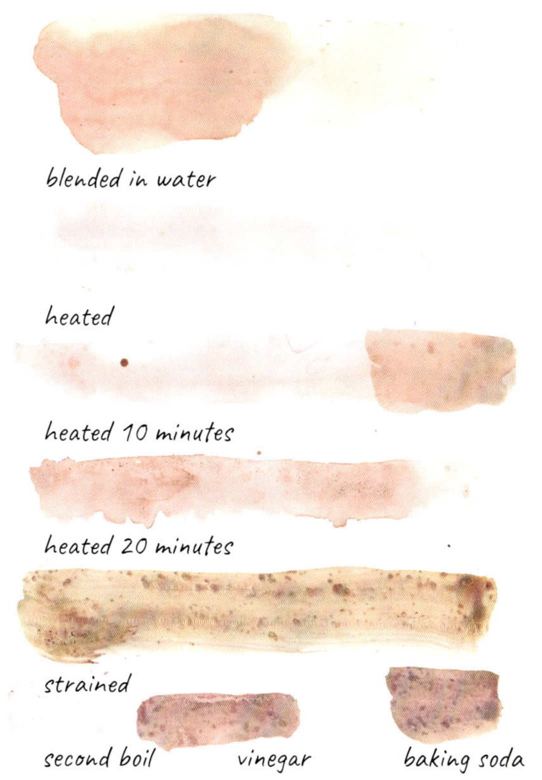

STEAMED MADDER ROOT (NOT BOILED)

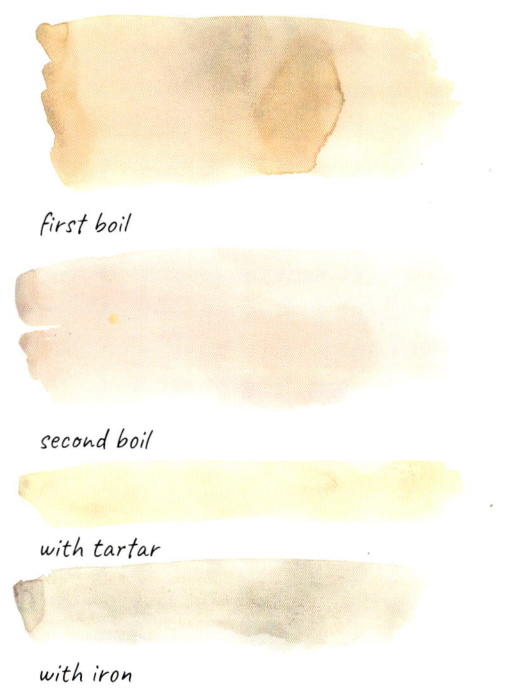

BOILED MADDER ROOT

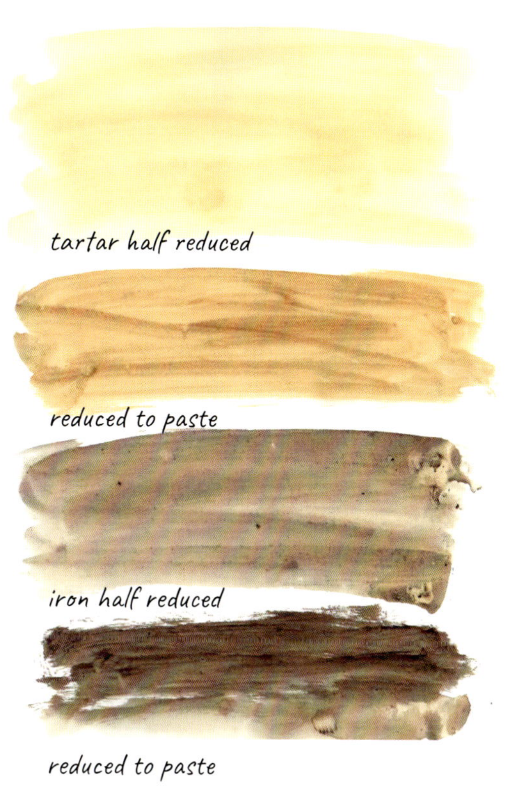

PERISTROPHE ROXBURGHIANA

Magenta Plant

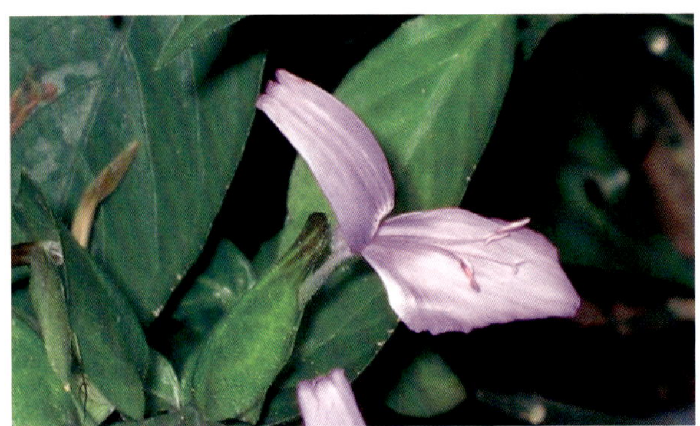

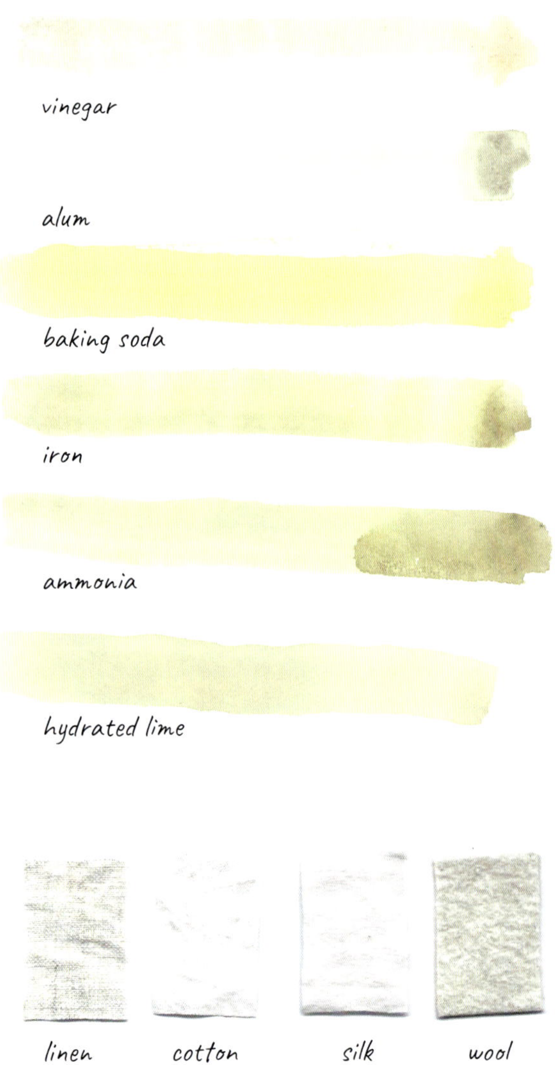

COLORS CREATED	yellow with baking soda, magenta (if you are lucky)
PARTS USED FOR PIGMENT	leaves
PLANT TYPE	tropical
HARDINESS ZONE	10

1. In tropical areas of the world, this plant is widely used to make a tea that is used as a magenta food dye. I managed to get a plant shipped to me, but I could never make it turn to red, but this was before I had discovered the use of citric acid, which would probably have helped. The plant lived most of the winter in my greenhouse but gave up the ghost in February, darn it.

BASELLA ALBA

Malabar Spinach

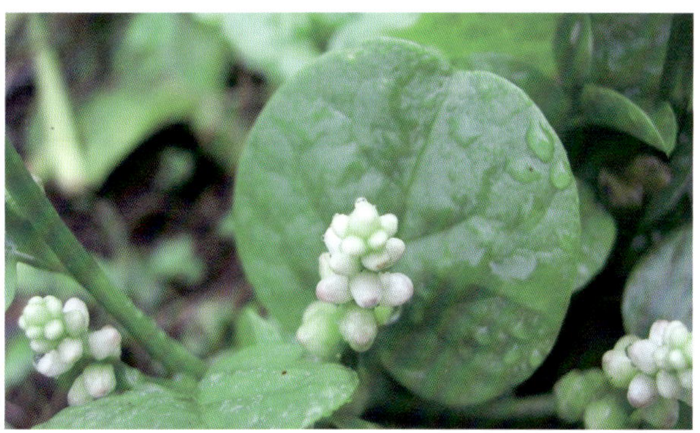

COLORS CREATED	purple
PARTS USED FOR PIGMENT	berries
PLANT TYPE	heat-loving leafy vegetable
HARDINESS ZONE	7
SEEDING	Seeds available at SeedRenaissance.com.

1. Use fresh or simmer for 10 minutes to make pigment or dye. Strain.
2. Simmer again to reduce liquid to desired color strength.

Notes: Not the same species as common garden spinach. This vining plant grows 10–12 feet long and is a favorite of green smoothie lovers, although it turns the smoothie purple with the berries or perhaps with enough of the vine. I've not had luck getting purple from the purple stems.

FRESH MALABAR BERRY JUICE

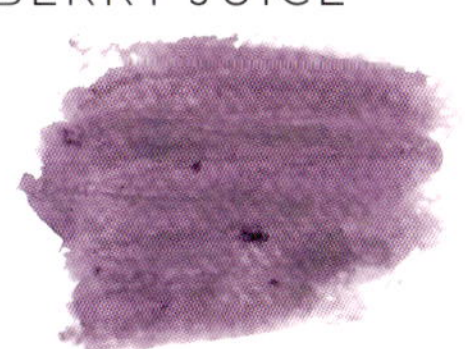

FRESH MALABAR BERRY MILK

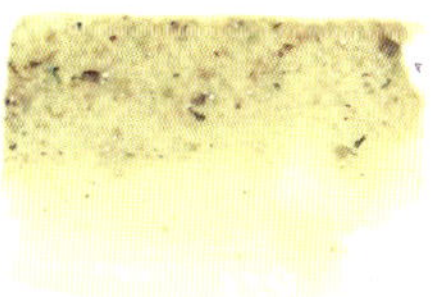

SYZYGIUM MALACCENSE

Malay Apple

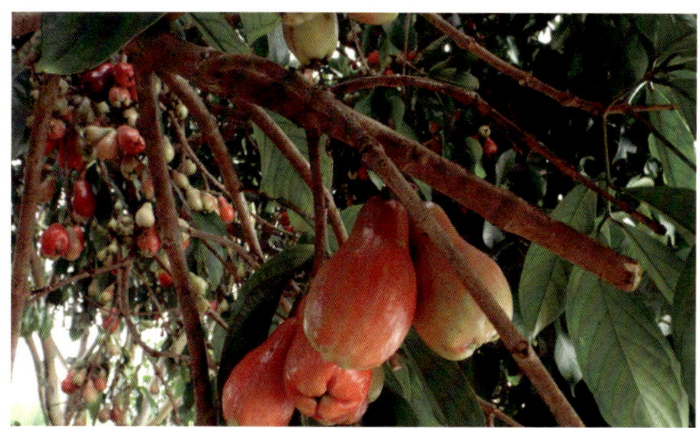

COLORS CREATED	purple when unmordanted, blue with alum, red with citric acid, green with baking soda
PARTS USED FOR PIGMENT	white flesh
PLANT TYPE	tropical fruit tree
HARDINESS ZONE	9

1. I tested the fresh fruit on the side of the road in Hawaii and did not have a chance to try cooking it, unfortunately. It would be interesting to see what happens when it's cooked.

Notes: I have read that the bark makes a brown dye, which is not surprising. I have also read that the ancient Polynesian people used this fruit for dyeing, but I cannot find any modern evidence of people using it for that purpose today, which is odd considering how rare botanical blue dye is.

FRESH PRESSED

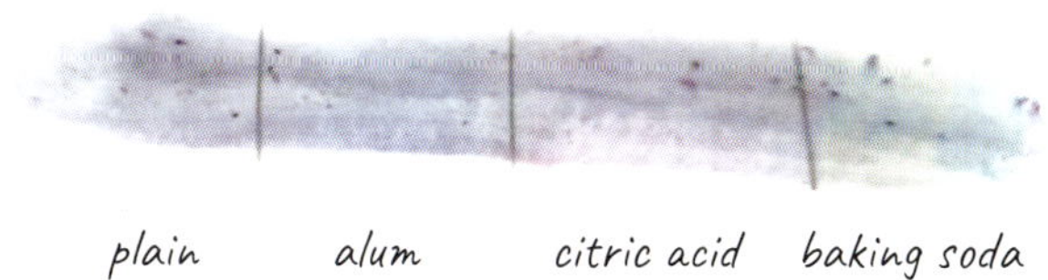

plain alum citric acid baking soda

MALVA AND *SPHAERALCEA* SPECIES

Mallows and Globe Mallows

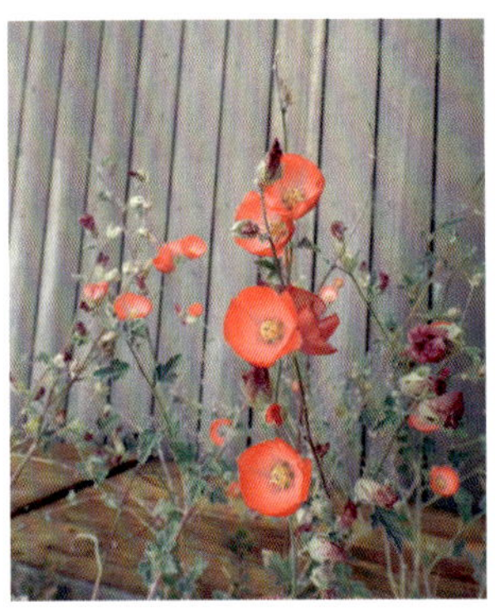

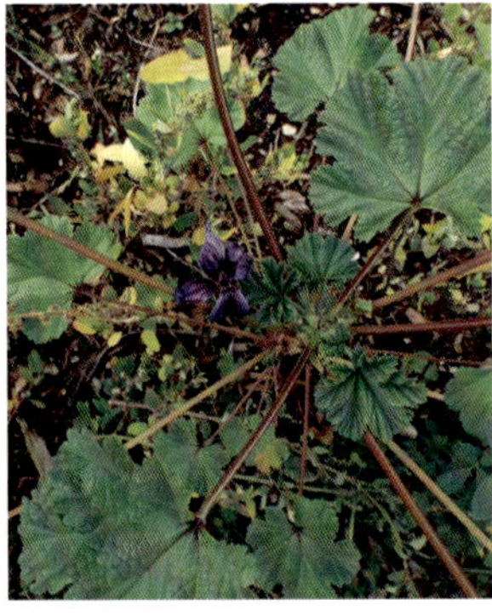

FRESH PRESSED DESERT MALLOW

plain *citric acid*

COMMON MALLOW

vinegar

COLORS CREATED	red petals make red; yellow petals make yellow
PARTS USED FOR PIGMENT	leaves, stems, flowers, fresh or dried
PLANT TYPE	perennial
HARDINESS ZONE	varies by species

1. When yellow flowers are boiled for at least 15 minutes, the plant produces a medium natural yellow that does not change with a mordant of vinegar but becomes a bright lemon yellow with a mordant of baking soda. Red flowers made red when fresh pressed without mordant and bright red with citric acid.

Special Use: Pottery paint. One of only a few herbs that can be used to create permanent pottery paint when heated in a kiln to 1,800 degrees. Does not scrub off when used on greenware or bisque pottery, but it must be used in combination with other ingredients. To create an emulsion, cover clean aerial parts with water in a pan and simmer on the lowest temperature, lid off, for at least 1 hour. Strain and discard plant matter. Continue to simmer the strained liquid until nothing is left in the pan but a thick liquid. Use the Wild Botanical Pottery Paint recipe (see page 74).

Notes: Tolerant of drought and alkaline soils.

MANDEVILLA SPECIES

Mandevilla Vine

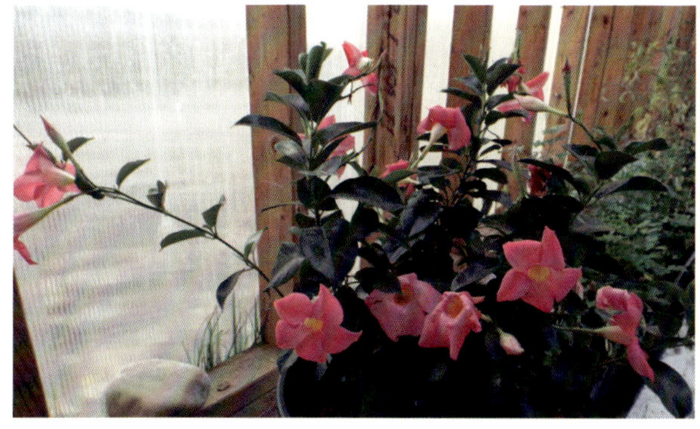

COLORS CREATED	purple when fresh and unmordanted; blue when mordanted with vinegar of copper; green in milk paint; purple, violet, and blue-gray with alum when cooked
PARTS USED FOR PIGMENT	blossoms, fresh or dried at peak bloom
PLANT TYPE	tropical vining flower
HARDINESS ZONE	10

1. Simmer for 10 minutes to make pigment or dye. Strain.
2. Simmer again to reduce liquid to desired color strength.

MILK PAINT OF DRIED RED PETALS

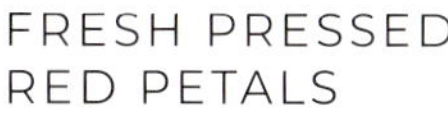

FRESH PRESSED RED PETALS

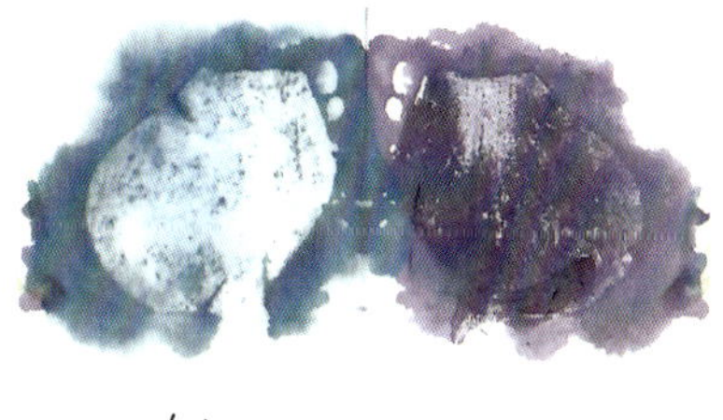

DRIED RED MANDEVILLA FLOWERS

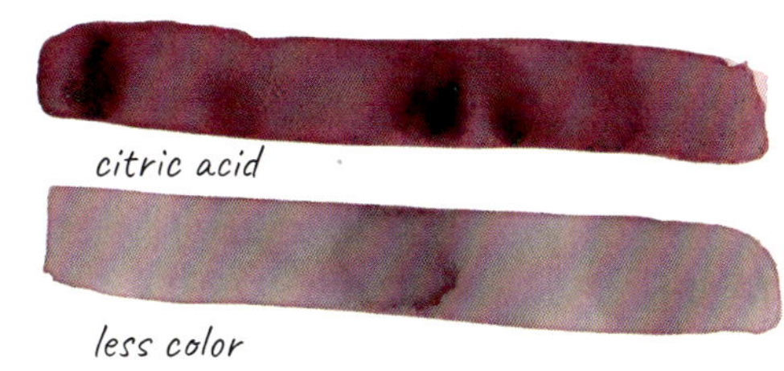

FRESH DARK RED MANDEVILLA FLOWERS

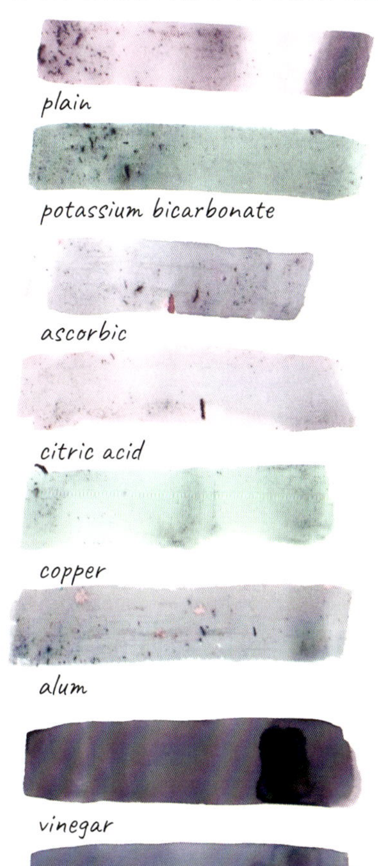

ACER SPECIES

Maples

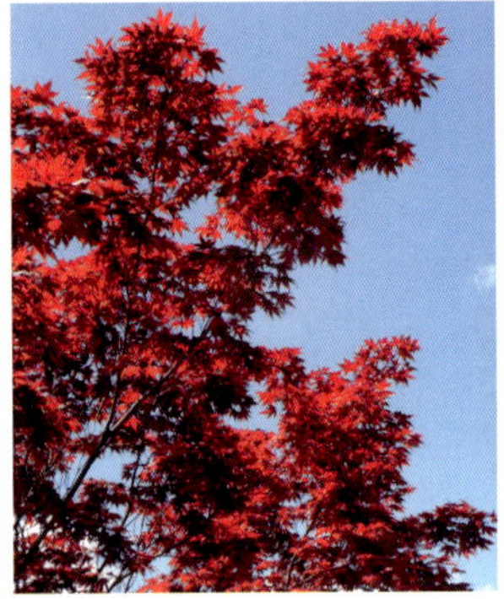

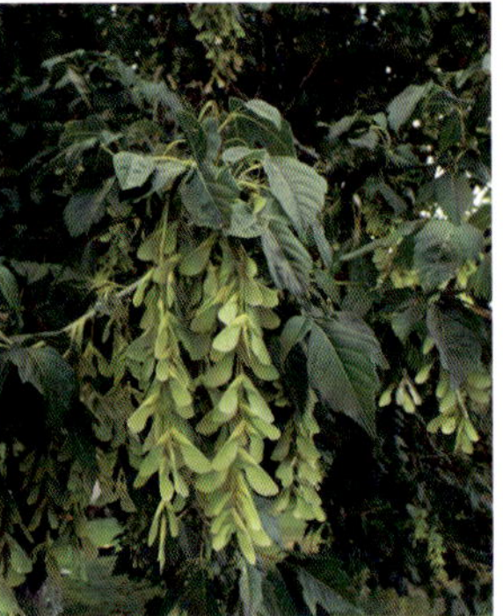

COLORS CREATED	brown, red with citric acid, green with alum and vinegar of copper, orange with baking soda
PARTS USED FOR PIGMENT	leaves
PLANT TYPE	tree
HARDINESS ZONE	varies by species

Notes: Maple leaves of all kinds make great eco-prints when painted or inked and then pressed. Japanese maples make excellent eco-prints; the purple leaves print purple with no mordant and turn green with vinegar of copper. Maple "heli-copter" seeds make no useful color.

RED JAPANESE MAPLE

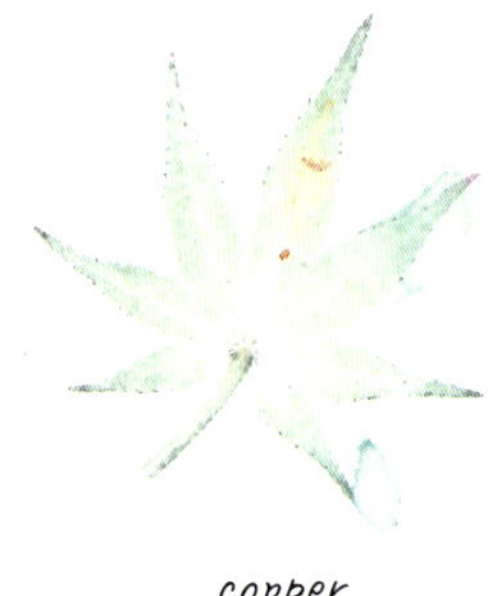

copper

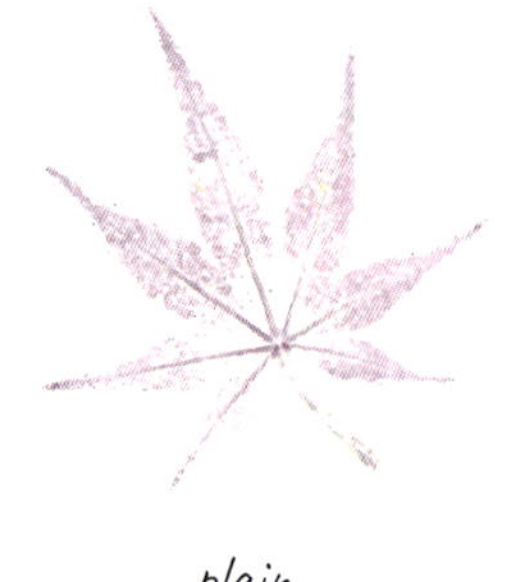

plain

RED JAPANESE MAPLE

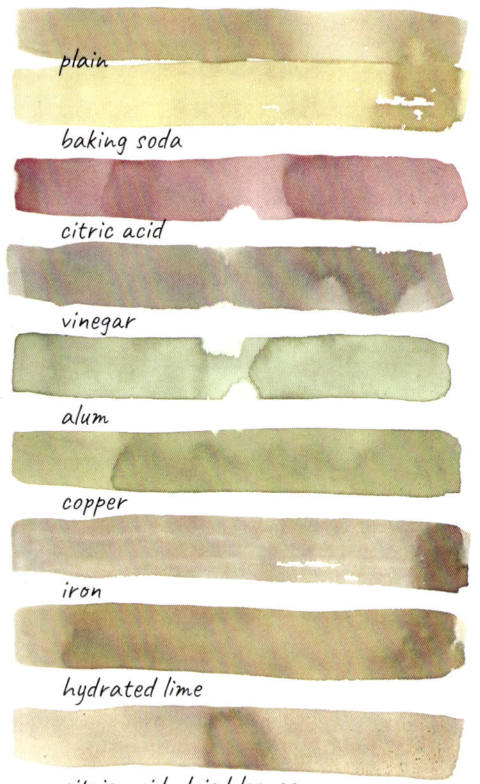

RED MAPLE

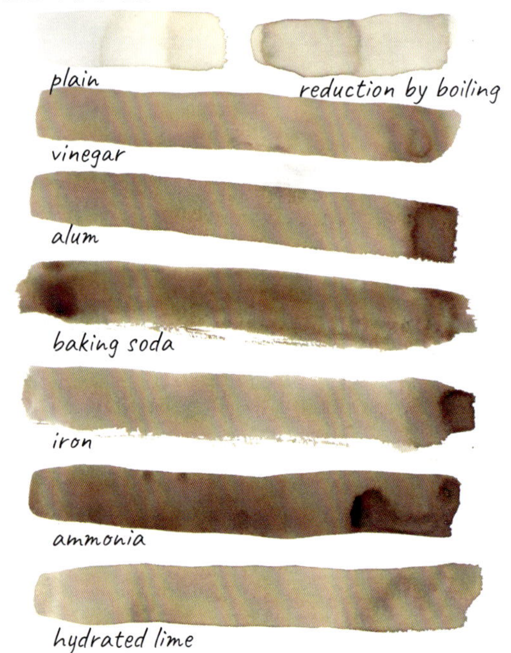

TAGETES SPECIES

Marigold

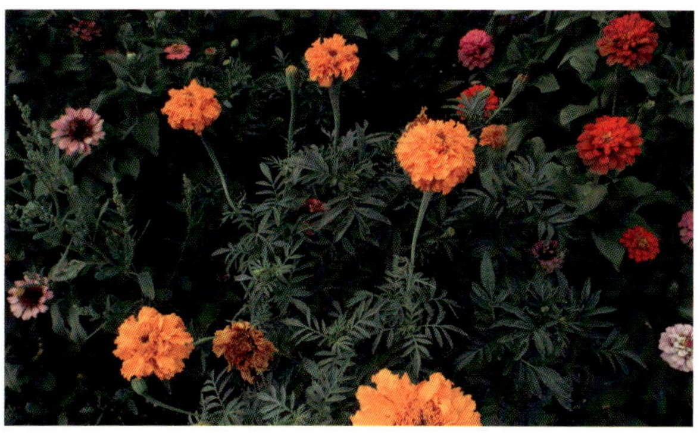

COLORS CREATED	oranges
PARTS USED FOR PIGMENT	petals only (no sepals)
PLANT TYPE	annual
SEEDING	Plant directly outside in spring or autumn. Seeds available at SeedRenaissance.com.

1. The petals are slow to give up their color. Simmer orange petals for 40 minutes to create a pale dirty orange that becomes a medium dirty orange when the liquid is reduced.
2. Vinegar or ammonia creates pumpkin orange. Alum creates a bright, clear citrus orange. Baking soda creates burnt orange. Iron creates dirty orange.

Notes: "Orange Hawaii" cultivars make especially brilliant orange colors. Flowers smell wonderful when working with them. I air dry my garden marigolds and use them year-round for orange pigment and dye, especially with ascorbic acid.

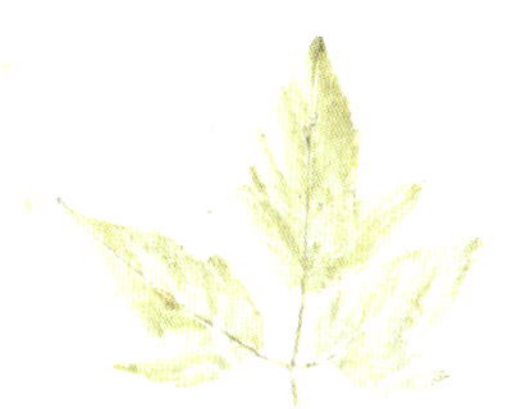

ORANGE HAWAII MARIGOLD

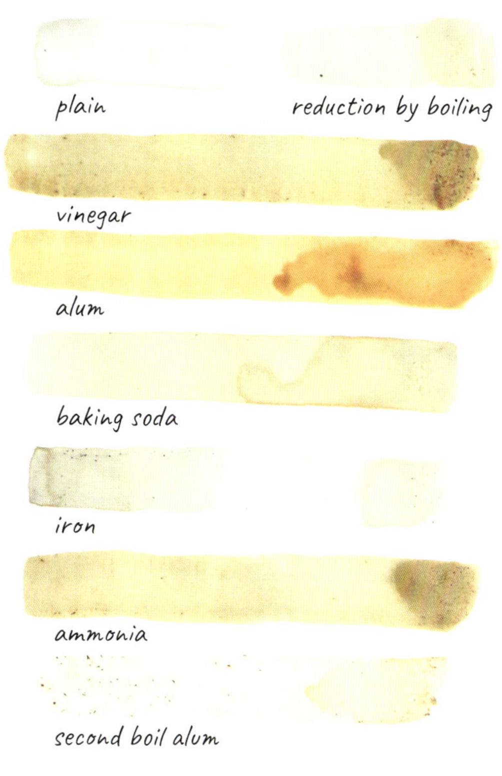

STEAMED MARIGOLD

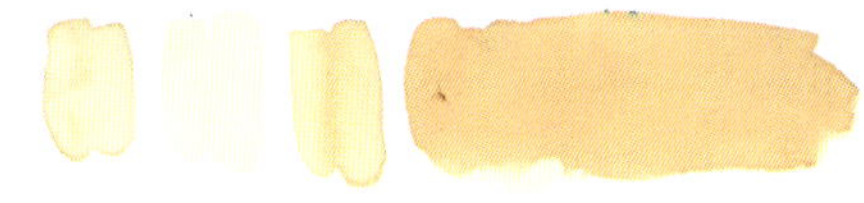

MARIGOLD PAINTS

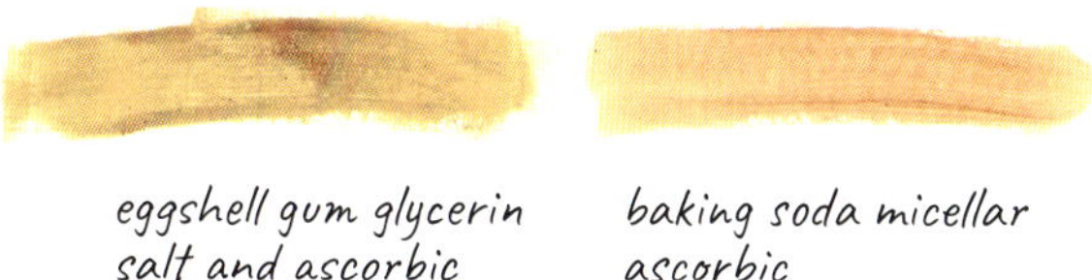

eggshell gum glycerin salt and ascorbic

baking soda micellar ascorbic

MARIGOLD WITH ALUM TARTAR

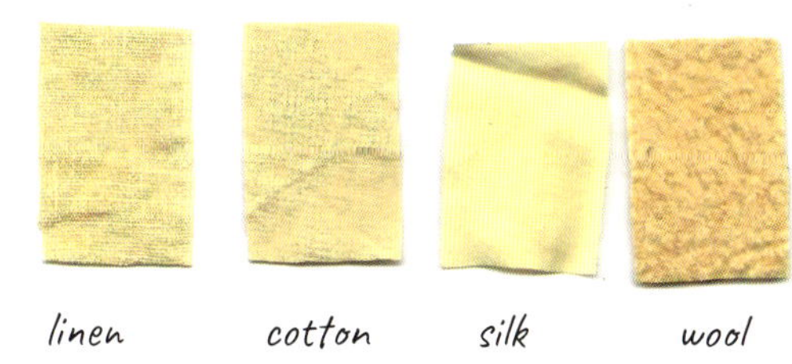

linen *cotton* *silk* *wool*

PROSOPIS SPECIES

Mesquite

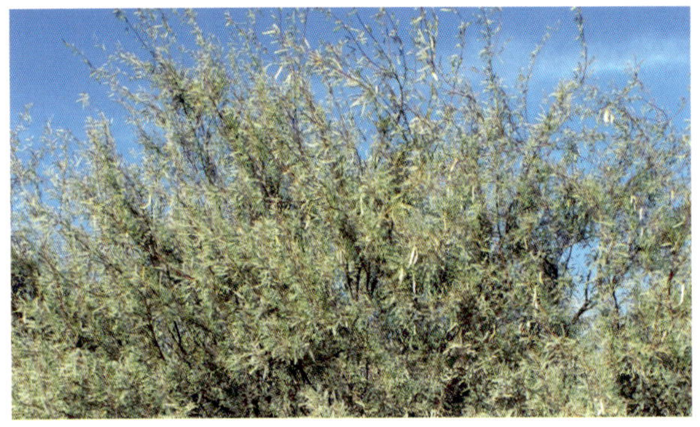

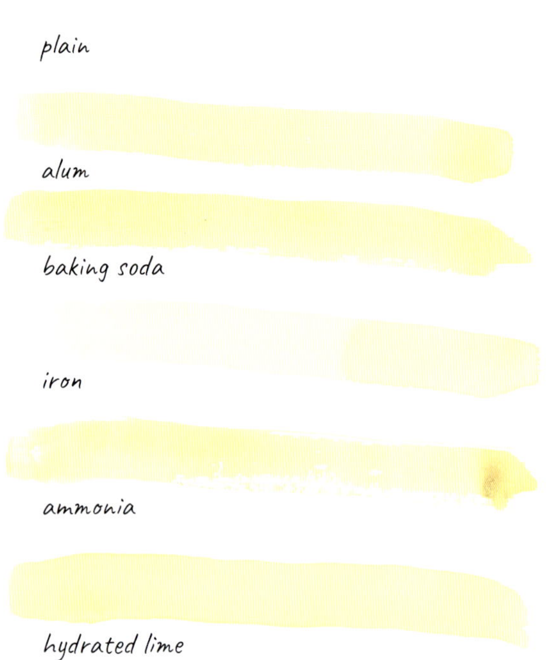

COLORS CREATED	yellow with most mordants
PARTS USED FOR PIGMENT	leaves, twigs
PLANT TYPE	short tree
HARDINESS ZONE	7

1. Simmer for 10 minutes to make pigment or dye. Strain.
2. Simmer again to reduce liquid to desired color strength.

Special Use: The beans and sap-covered sections of bark have long been used to make permanent pottery paint that can withstand the 1,800 degree temperatures of the wood-fired kiln. Both are boiled in water, strained, and then boiled again to reduce to an almost oily substance. The bean paint is thicker than the resin paint, but the resin paint is famed for being shiny black if fired correctly, which is usually for a short time directly on hot coals. The resin paint is one of only a very few botanical pottery paints that can be used without adding any other ingredients. Both paints can be stored long-term. I have a jar of mesquite leaf paint sitting in my cupboard right now.

RATIBIDA SPECIES

Mexican Hat

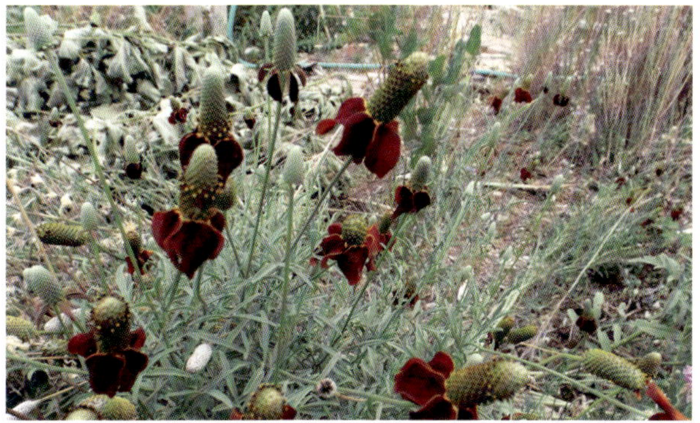

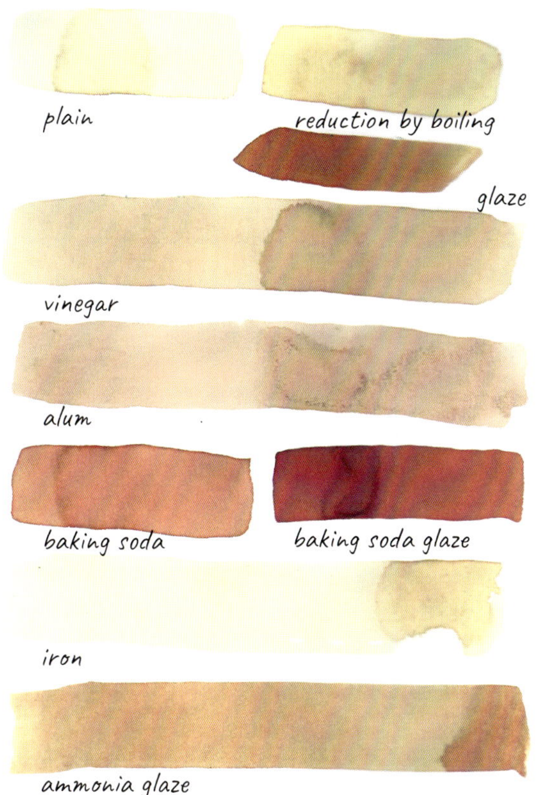

COLORS CREATED	reds
PARTS USED FOR PIGMENT	petals
PLANT TYPE	annual
HARDINESS ZONE	4
SEEDING	Seeds available at SeedRenaissance.com.

1. Simmer for 10 minutes to make pigment or dye. Strain.
2. Simmer again to reduce liquid to desired color strength.

JUSTICIA SPICIGERA

Mexican Honeysuckle

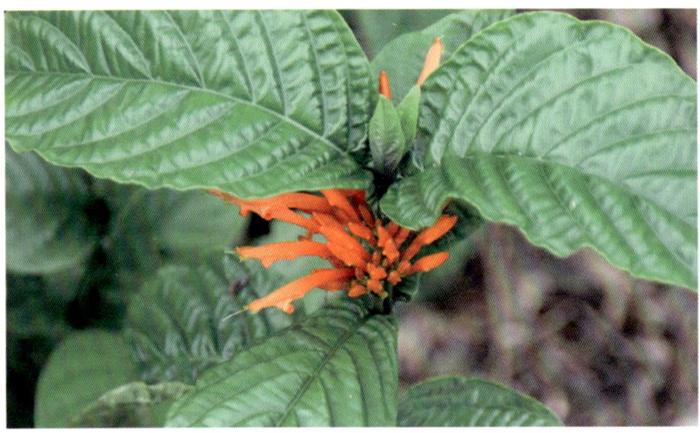

DRY TEA STEM LEAVES

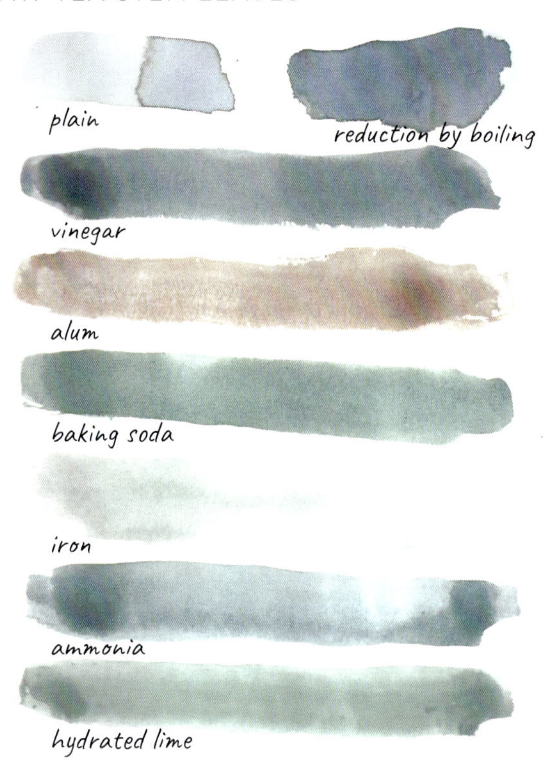

COLORS CREATED	blue, green
PARTS USED FOR PIGMENT	stems, leaves
PLANT TYPE	tropical tender annual
HARDINESS ZONE	8

1. Mexican honeysuckle, or muicle, has long been used as tea and botanical food coloring, and dried loose tea of the leaves and stems is sold online. The color changes easily. If you soak the leaves and stems in water, the water slowly turns pink and then red. When simmered, the water can also be slow to change color, but after a few minutes turns pink and then red and then purple after boiling for a while. Boiling the water for 15 minutes produced a pale pink that dried violet.

2. The same liquid, reduced, created blue with black edges. Vinegar created a turquoise blue-green. Alum made a mauve-pink. Baking soda or ammonia made a smoky green. Iron seemed to destroy the color. Hydrated lime made a beautiful old-fashioned green with gray undertones. A second boil for 5 minutes created a pale blue. I experimented a lot with this plant. Boiling the leaves and stems for 1 hour created a red liquid that dried blue, but vinegar, alum, baking soda, ammonia, or hydrated lime made true black. If the black was not applied thinly, it was sticky and tar-like for several days. There is a hint of green undertones to the black, especially with ammonia. Using about 2 teaspoons of dried loose leaves and stems per cup of water made pale blue when simmered for 10 minutes. The color was red when applied but dried blue. I reduced this liquid in the microwave for 30 to 90 seconds at a time and gradually, as the liquid thickened, the color when dry turned from blue to blue-green to green. A third boil created lavender. Another boil, following the same pattern, made a gray-green that gradually darkened to forest green without the hints of blue. The color seems to be fickle, depending on how much color is in the leaves and stems, and is highly changeable spending on volume, temperature, and mordants. This is a fun plant to play with.

REDUCTION GLAZE

second boil

vinegar

alum

baking soda

ammonia

hydrated lime

15 minute reduction by boiling

BOILED LEAVES (NO MORDANTS)

linen cotton silk wool

FIRST BOIL

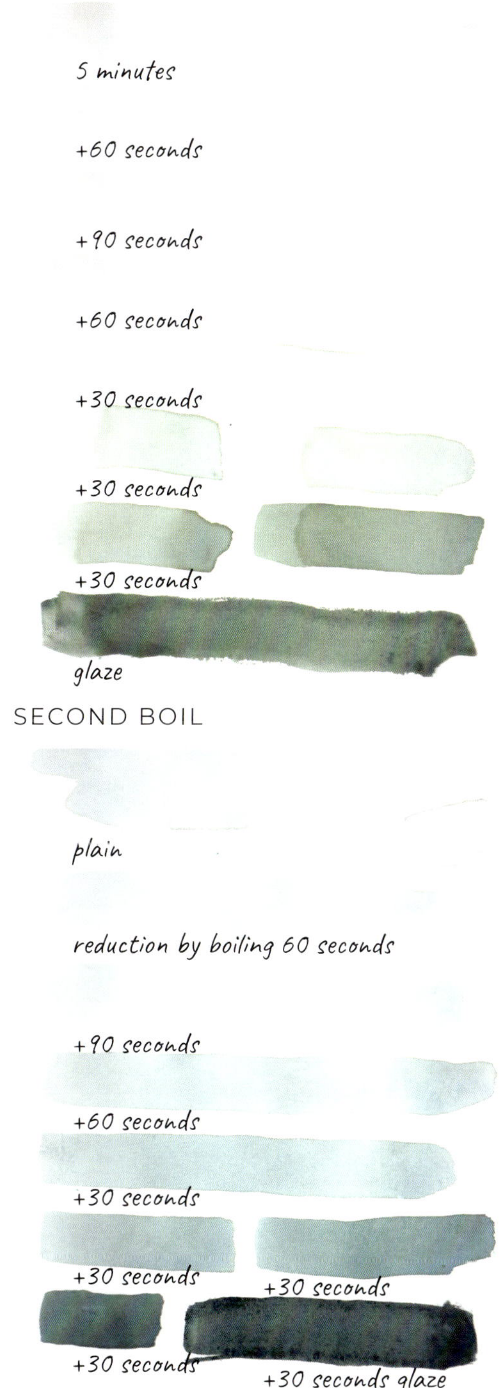

TITHONIA DIVERSIFOLIA

Mexican Sunflower

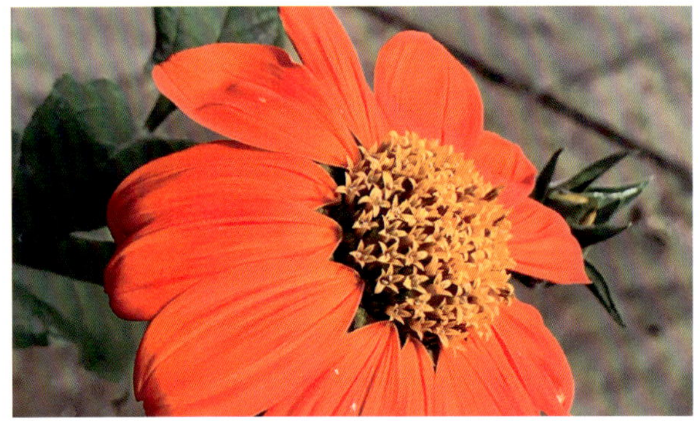

WHOLE FLOWER	PETALS ONLY

reduction by boiling

vinegar

alum

baking soda

iron

ammonia

COLORS CREATED	yellow with alum
PARTS USED FOR PIGMENT	flower centers (no petals)
PLANT TYPE	annual
HARDINESS ZONE	10

1. Simmer for 10 minutes to make pigment or dye. Strain.
2. Simmer again to reduce liquid to desired color strength.

Notes: When composted, this plant is said to make a rich "vegan manure." The color stained a stainless-steel pan, which may indicate lightfastness.

ASCLEPIAS SPECIES

Milkweed

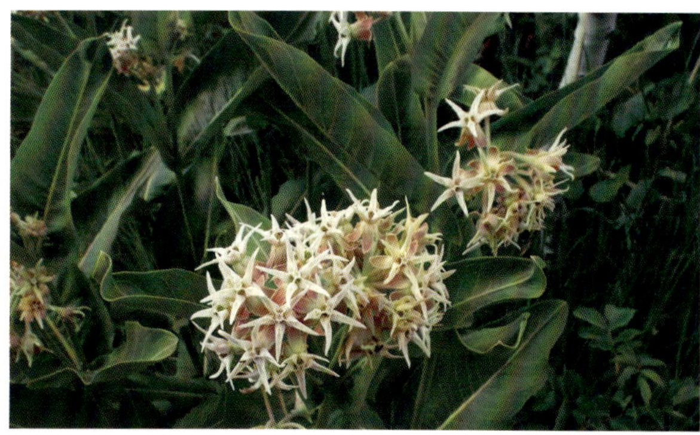

COLORS CREATED	pink with citric acid, vibrant yellow with alum, yellow with most mordants
PARTS USED FOR PIGMENT	flowering stems
PLANT TYPE	perennial from the roots
HARDINESS ZONE	3
SEEDING	Plant directly outside in spring or autumn. Seeds available at SeedRenaissance.com.

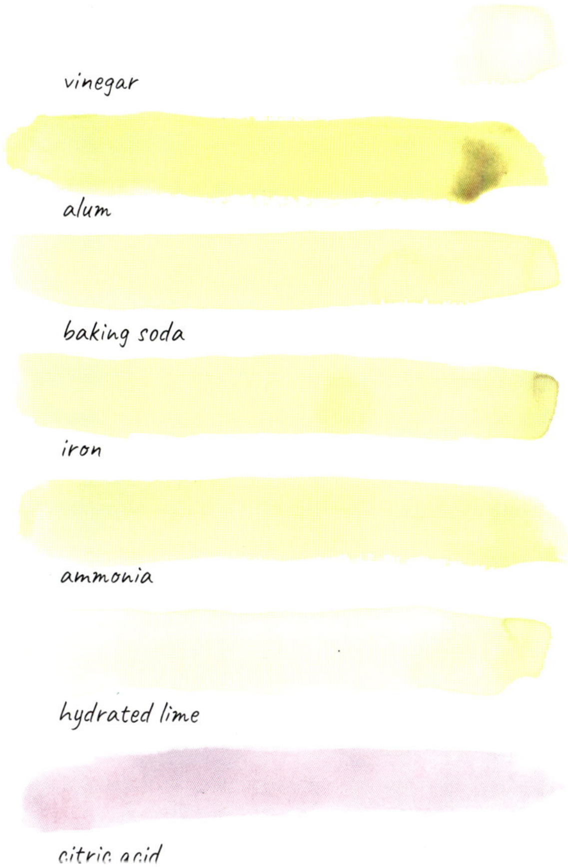

1. Simmer for 10 minutes to make pigment or dye. Strain.
2. Simmer again to reduce liquid to desired color strength.

Notes: Milkweed flowers are a delicious sweet wild edible. For more information, see my books on wild edible plants. They are also important plants to butterflies, so take one or two flowers only where there are large populations of the plant.

ALBIZIA AND *CALLIANDRA* SPECIES

Mimosa Silk Trees

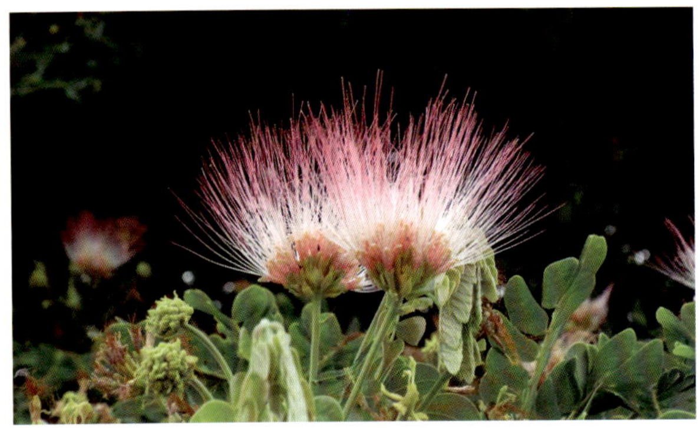

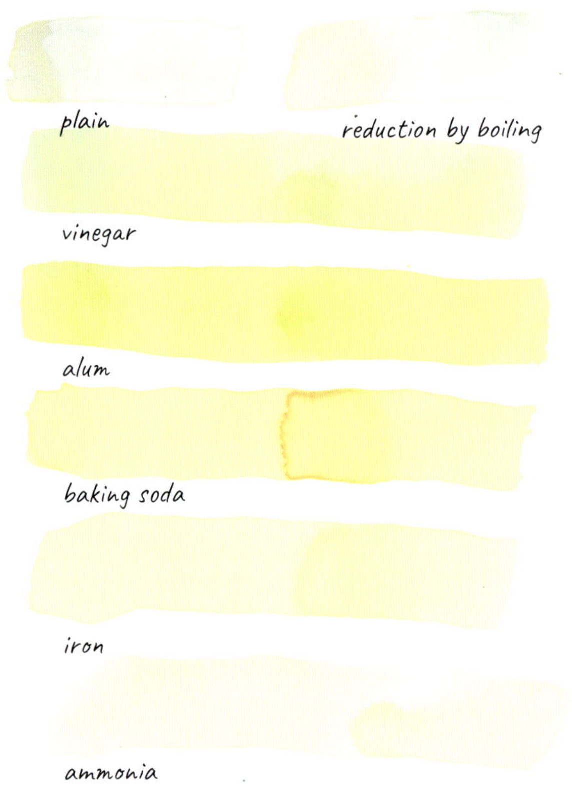

COLORS CREATED	yellow with alum from the *Albizia* species when cooked; purple, green, and gray from *Calliandra* species when used fresh
PARTS USED FOR PIGMENT	pink silk of the blossoms
PLANT TYPE	tree
HARDINESS ZONE	*Albizia* is zone 6; *Calliandra* is zone 10

1. Simmer for 10 minutes to make pigment or dye. Strain.
2. Simmer again to reduce liquid to desired color strength.

FRESH PRESSED RED FLOWERS

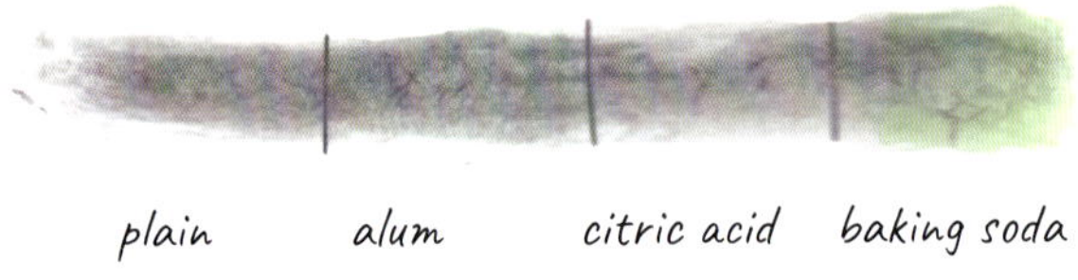

FRESH PRESSED RED FLOWERS

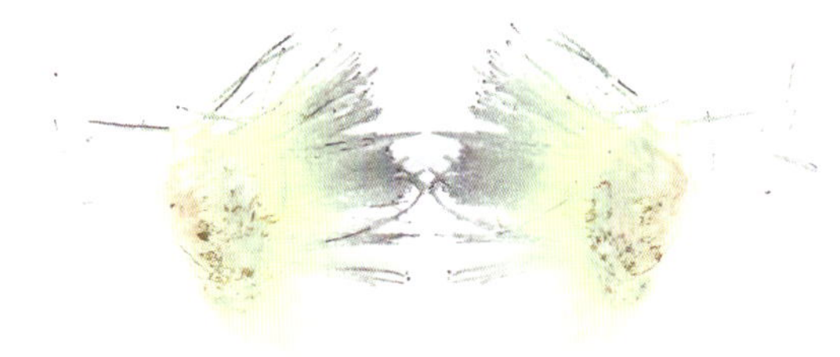

VARIOUS SPECIES

Mints

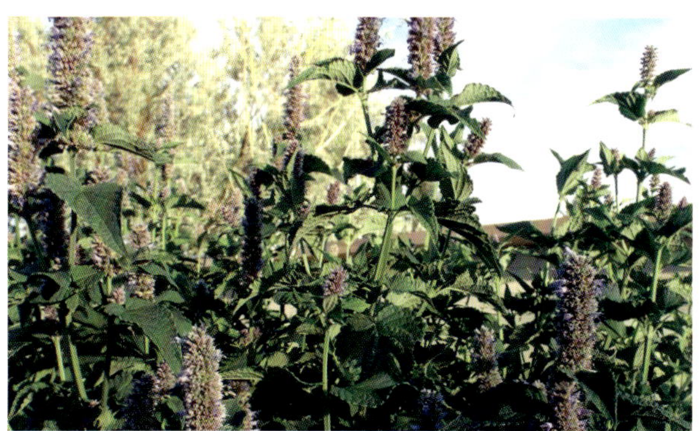

COLORS CREATED	green when used fresh, green and brown when cooked
PARTS USED FOR PIGMENT	leaves, stems
PLANT TYPE	varies by species
HARDINESS ZONE	generally hardy
SEEDING	Seeds available at SeedRenaissance.com.

1. Simmer for 10 minutes to make pigment or dye. Strain.
2. Simmer again to reduce liquid to desired color strength.

Notes: Mint leaves make a good green lake pigment; see the lake pigment recipes in this book (see pages 54–55).

MINT ANISE HYSSOP

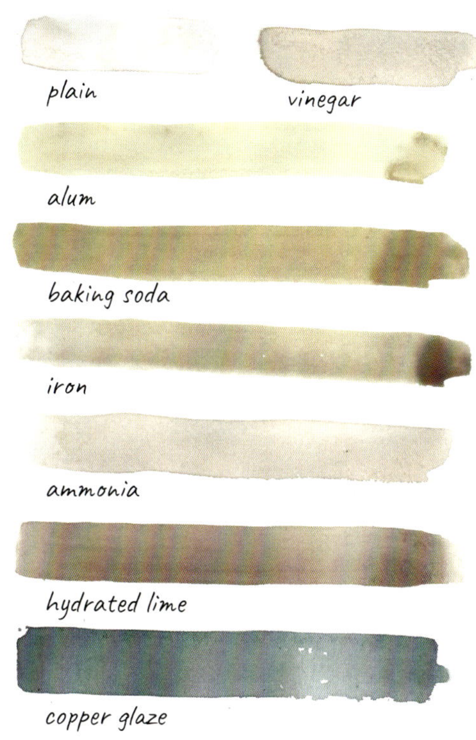

HORSEMINT

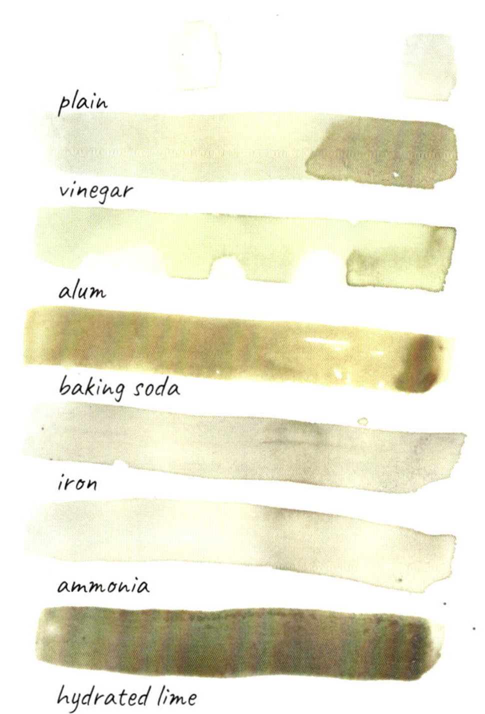

Monarda Species

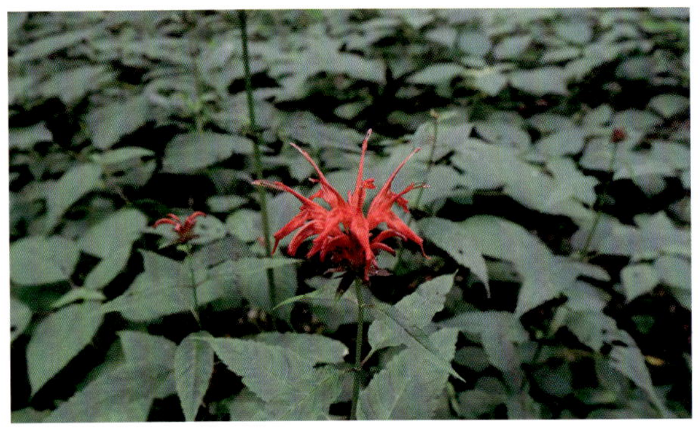

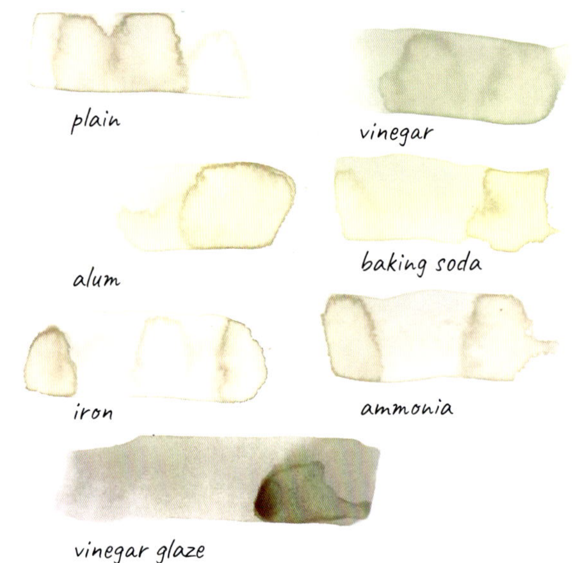

COLORS CREATED	strong reds and greens when used fresh
PARTS USED FOR PIGMENT	flowers
PLANT TYPE	perennial
HARDINESS ZONE	4

1. Best when used fresh and uncooked.

FRESH PRESSED RED FLOWERS

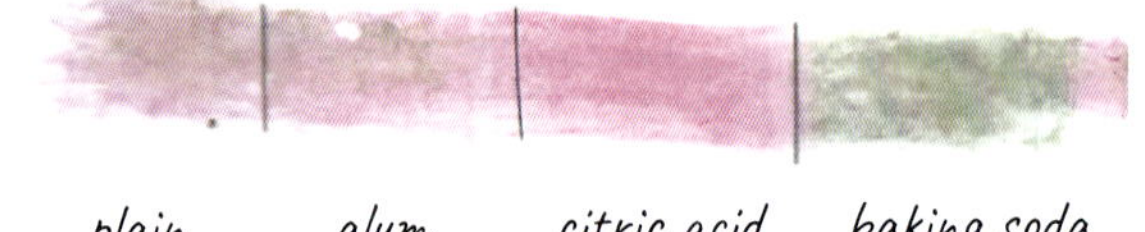

FRASERA SPECIOSA

Monument Plant

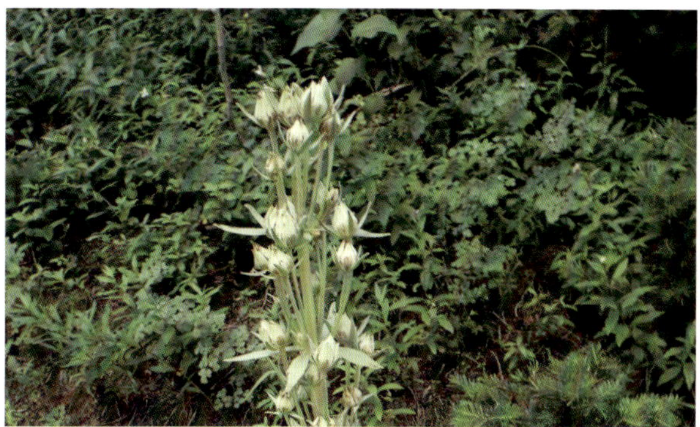

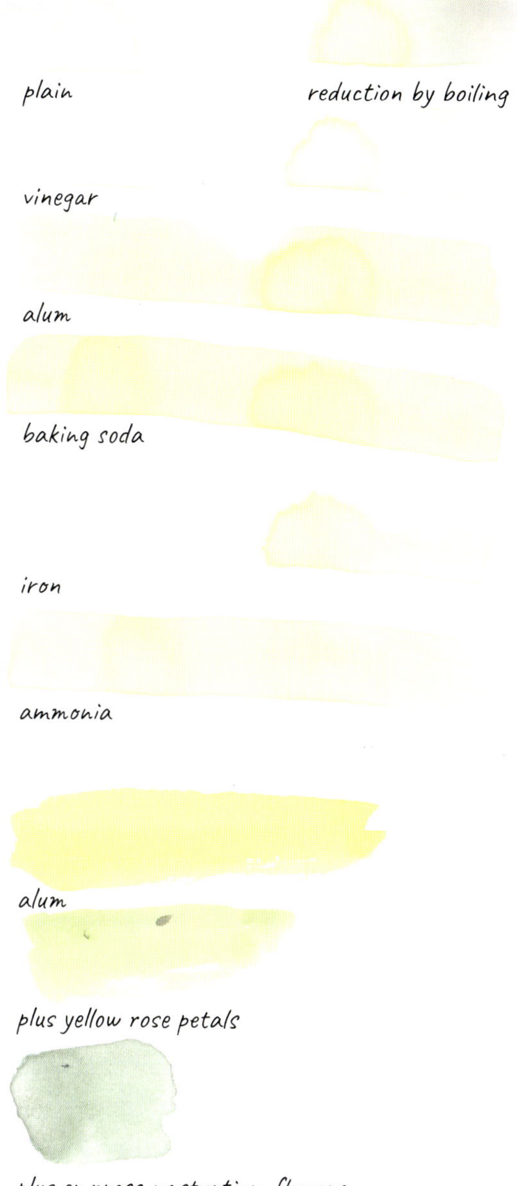

COLORS CREATED	yellow with alum
PARTS USED FOR PIGMENT	flower spike
PLANT TYPE	perennial
HARDINESS ZONE	3

1. Simmer for 10 minutes to make pigment or dye. Strain.
2. Simmer again to reduce liquid to desired color strength.

Notes: Although this plant is perennial, it only flowers once.

PORTULACA GRANDIFLORA

Moss Rose

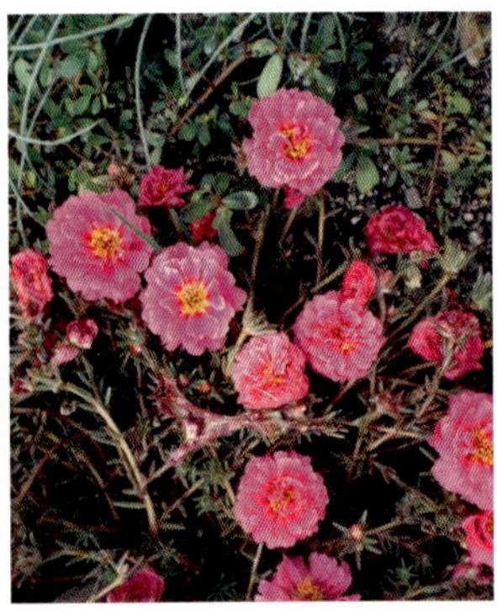

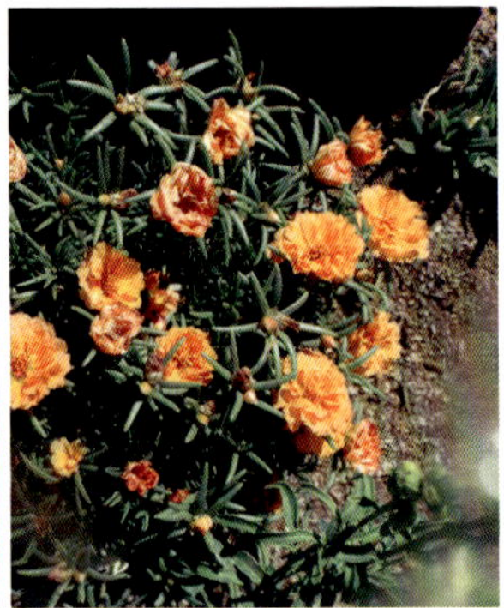

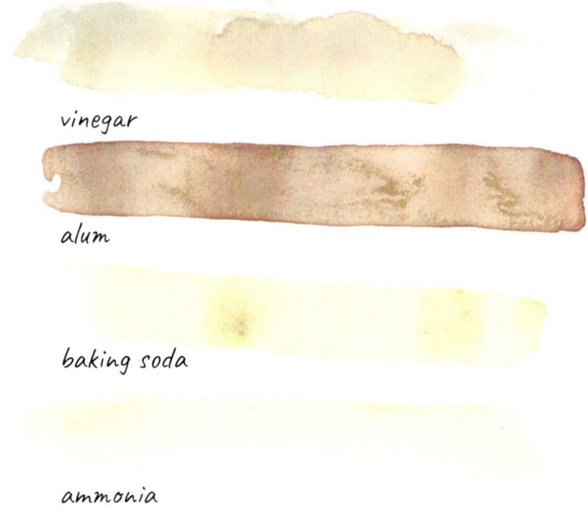

COLORS CREATED	pink with alum and probably also citric acid and ascorbic acid (vitamin C)
PARTS USED FOR PIGMENT	flowers
PLANT TYPE	annual self-seeding succulent
SEEDING	Seeds available at SeedRenaissance.com.

1. Simmer for 10 minutes to make pigment or dye. Strain.
2. Simmer again to reduce liquid to desired color strength.

MORUS SPECIES

Mulberry

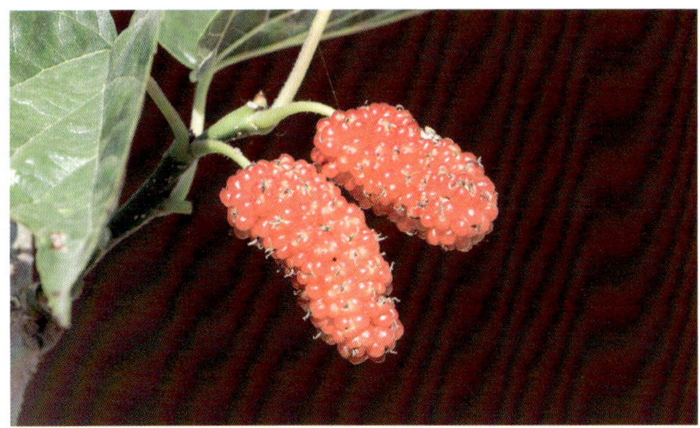

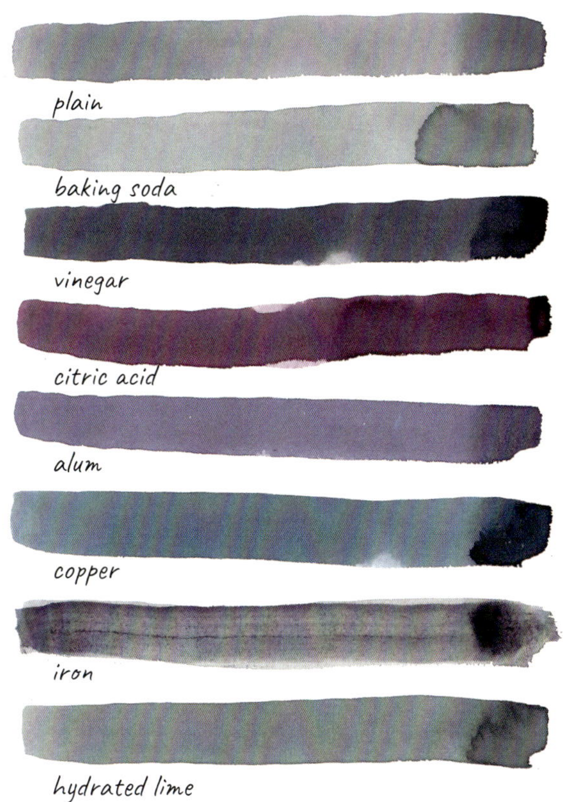

COLORS CREATED	blue with copper and vinegar, purple with alum, violet with citric acid, gray with other mordants
PARTS USED FOR PIGMENT	ripe red or black berries
PLANT TYPE	trees and bushes
HARDINESS ZONE	varies by species

1. Simmer for 10 minutes to make pigment or dye. Strain.
2. Simmer again to reduce liquid to desired color strength.

BOILED BLACK MULBERRIES

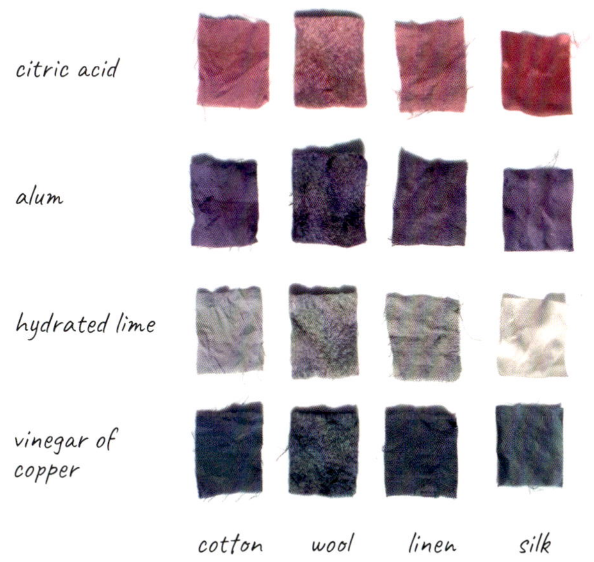

VERBASCUM THAPSUS

Mullein

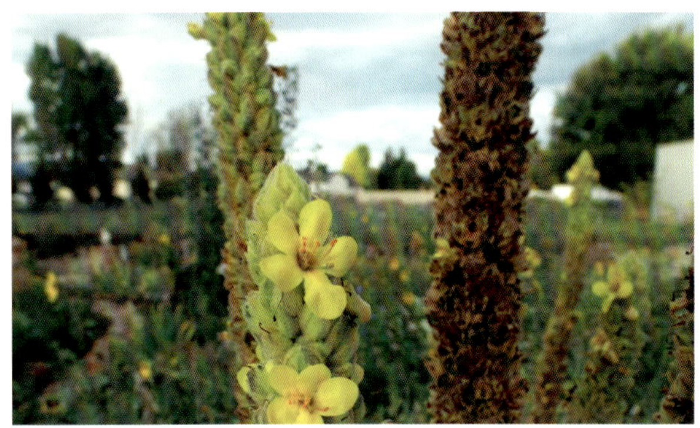

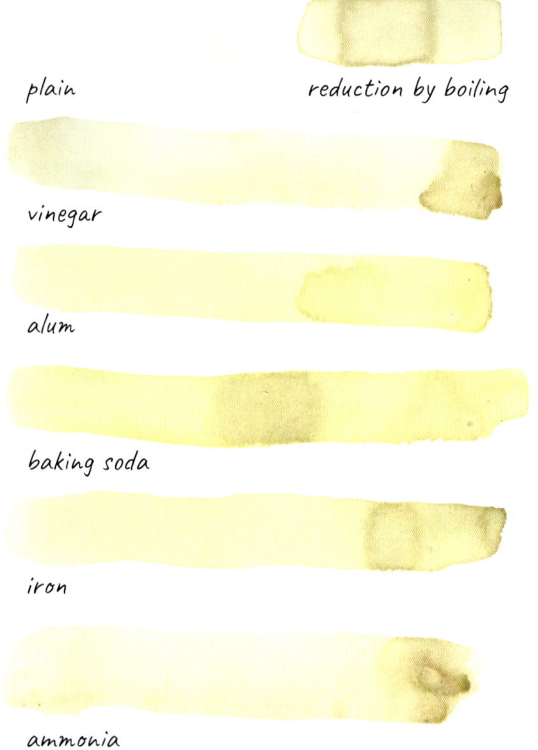

COLORS CREATED	yellow with most mordants
PARTS USED FOR PIGMENT	yellow flower spikes
PLANT TYPE	biennial
HARDINESS ZONE	3
SEEDING	Seeds available at SeedRenaissance.com.

1. Simmer for 10 minutes to make pigment or dye. Strain.
2. Simmer again to reduce liquid to desired color strength.

Notes: These towering flowers are also an important source of autumn and winter food for some bird species.

Mushrooms (Various Species)

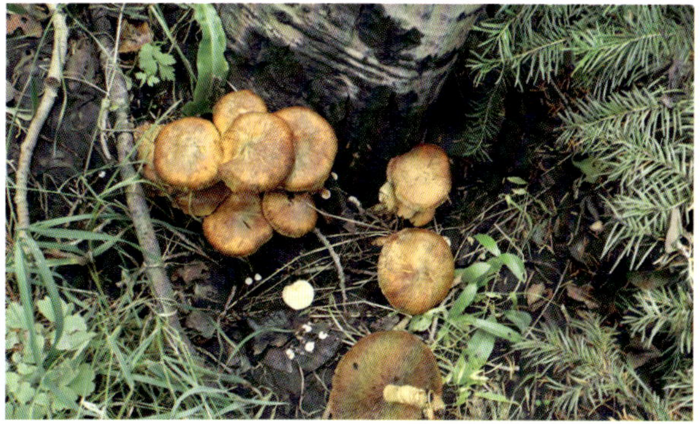

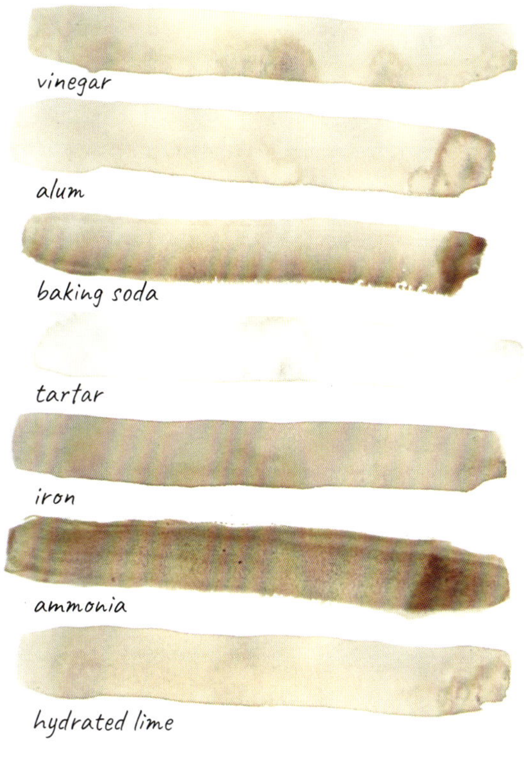

COLORS CREATED	browns (and sometimes other colors)
PARTS USED FOR PIGMENT	mushrooms

1. Simmer for 10 minutes to make pigment or dye. Strain.
2. Simmer again to reduce liquid to desired color strength.

Notes: No one knows how many species of mushrooms there are worldwide; experts disagree considerably, with estimates ranging from tens of thousands to millions. Most mushrooms are fairly localized. I tested every mushroom I could find in my area and only ever got brown colors, but I live in an arid cold climate. Other people have been able to make interesting dyes from mushrooms in their local area.

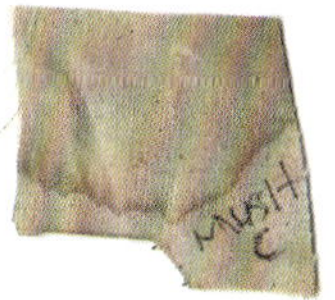

cotton

TROPAEOLUM MAJUS

Nasturtiums

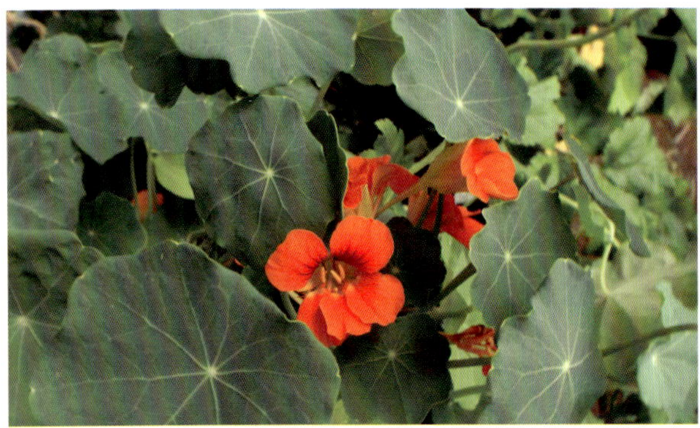

NASTURTIUM BLOSSOMS

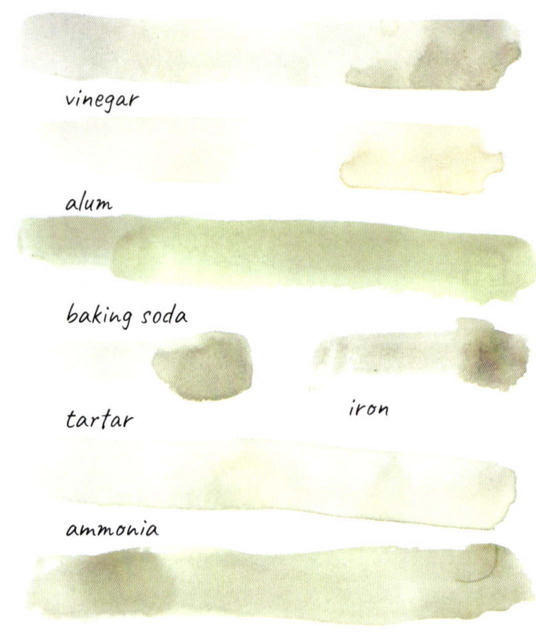

COLORS CREATED	violet from dark red Empress of India nasturtium flowers cooked with citric acid, pale greens from lighter red flowers with most mordants; flowers used fresh and uncooked also make good colors

1. Simmer for 10 minutes to make pigment or dye. Strain.
2. Simmer again to reduce liquid to desired color strength.

Notes: With alum, tartar, and Glauber's salt, the flower made an almost silver dye on fabrics that was unexpected.

EMPRESS OF INDIA NASTURTIUM

FRESH MULLED ORANGE PETALS

FRESH MULLED RED

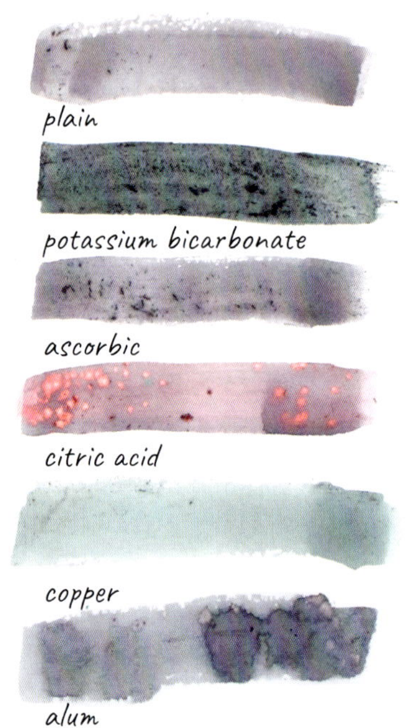

PHYSOCARPUS OPULIFOLIUS

Ninebark Purple

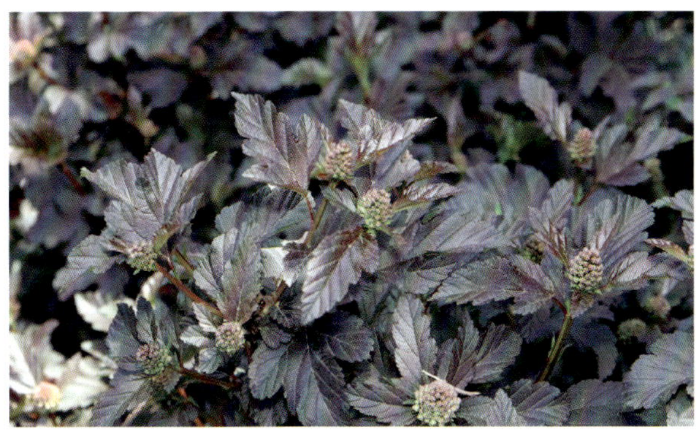

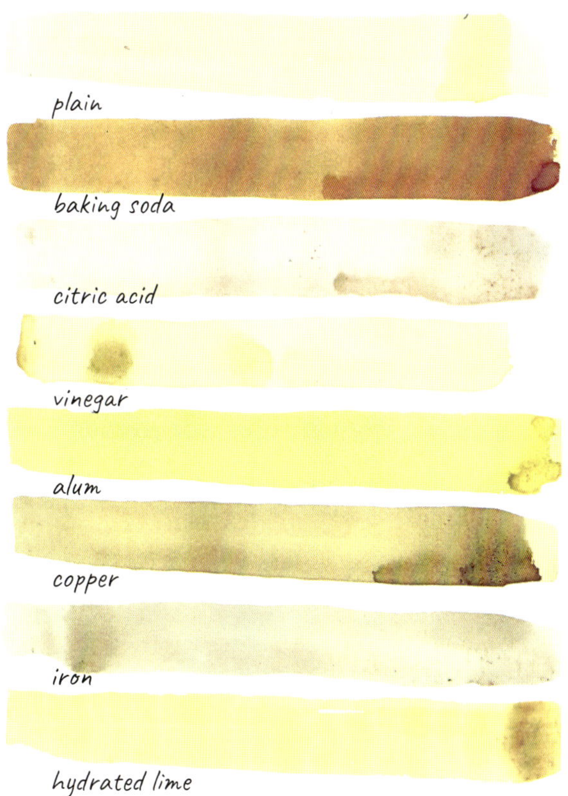

COLORS CREATED	yellow with alum
PARTS USED FOR PIGMENT	purple leaves
PLANT TYPE	landscape shrub
HARDINESS ZONE	2
SEEDING	Seeds available at SeedRenaissance.com.

1. Simmer for 10 minutes to make pigment or dye. Strain.
2. Simmer again to reduce liquid to desired color strength.

THEVETIA PERUVIANA AND *OLEANDER* SPECIES

Oleander

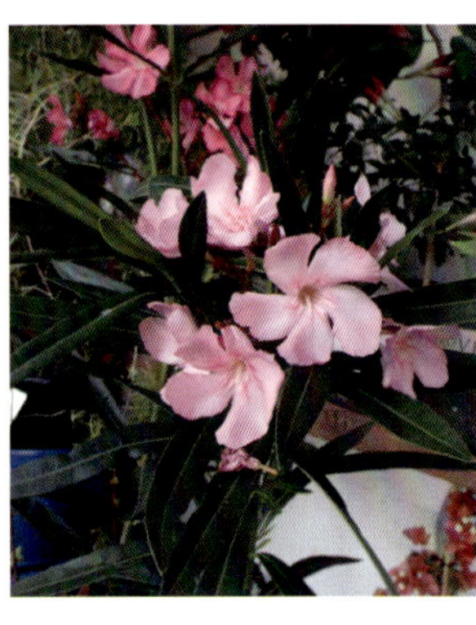

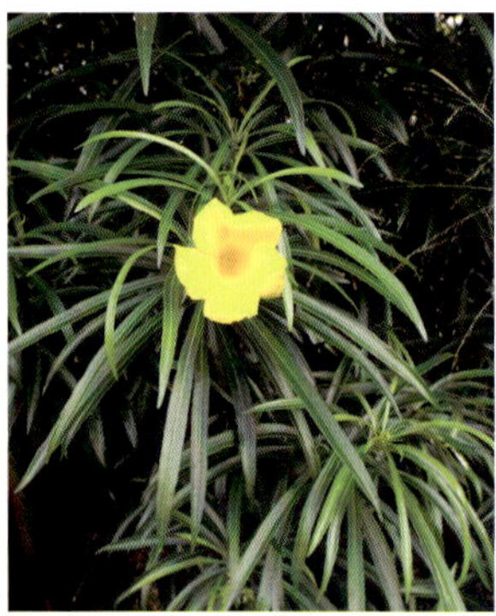

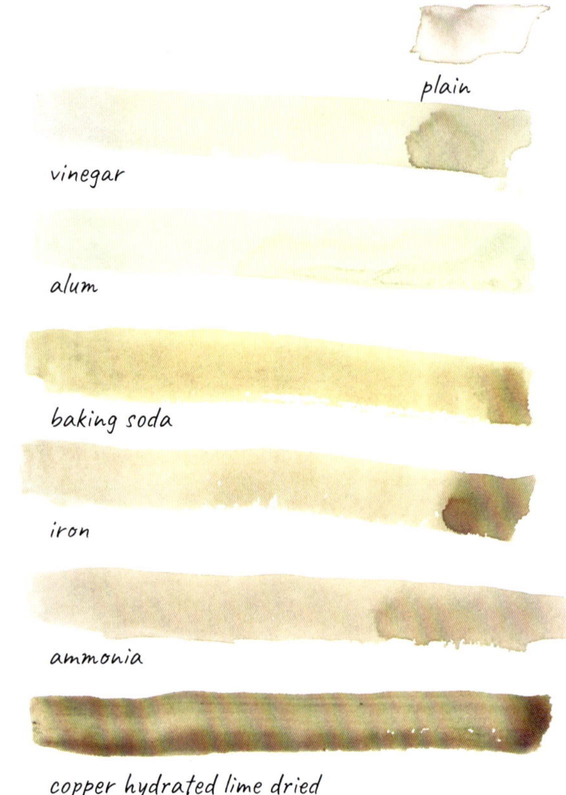

COLORS CREATED	strong yellow from *Thevetia*, brown from pink *Oleander* flowers
PARTS USED FOR PIGMENT	flowers
PLANT TYPE	flowering landscape bush
HARDINESS ZONE	*Thevetia* is zone 9; *Oleander* is zone 8

1. Simmer for 10 minutes to make pigment or dye. Strain.
2. Simmer again to reduce liquid to desired color strength.

PINK OLEANDER MILK

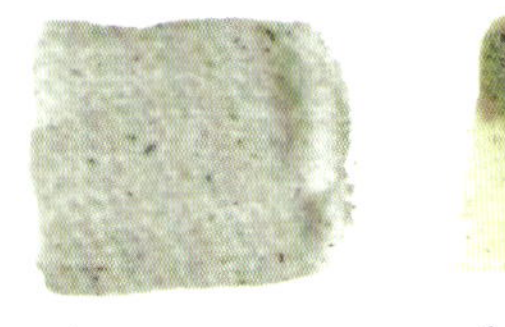

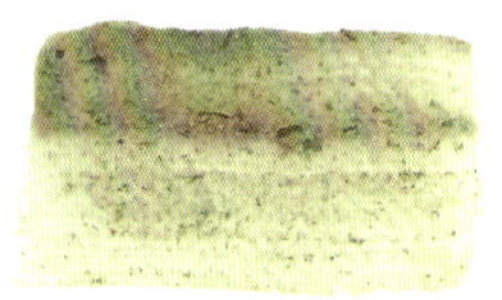

ALLIUM CEPA

Onion

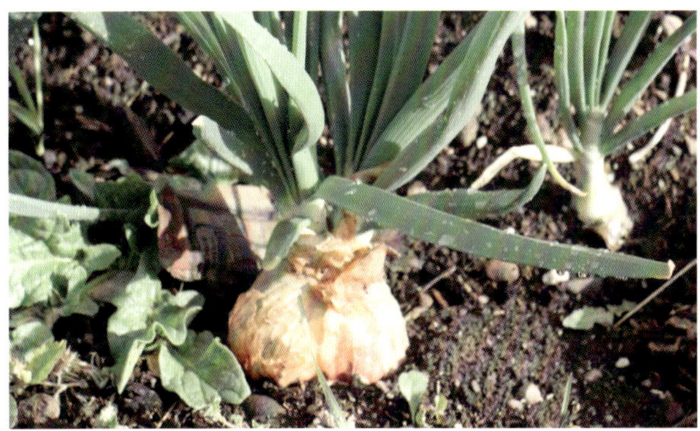

COLORS CREATED	red, brown, orange
PARTS USED FOR PIGMENT	skins or whole small onions
PLANT TYPE	perennial
HARDINESS ZONE	4
SEEDING	Seeds available at SeedRenaissance.com.

1. Simmering for a few minutes produces pale orange. Steam reducing produces true orange. Browns are created by increasing the amount of onion skin cooked. Even boiled three and four times, with new water each time, the onion skins continue to produce a strong orange color.

Notes: The colors have no scent once dried. Dried red onion peels made brown and darker brown when reduced. Vinegar made the color lighter when half reduced and a deep brown when reduced to a glaze. Alum made a yellow-brown when half reduced and a dark brown when reduced to a glaze that stained my glass bowl. Baking soda made an orange-brown and a rich walnut color when reduced. Iron made a medium brown when half reduced and a gorgeous mahogany brown when reduced to a glaze.

EGYPTIAN WALKING ONION

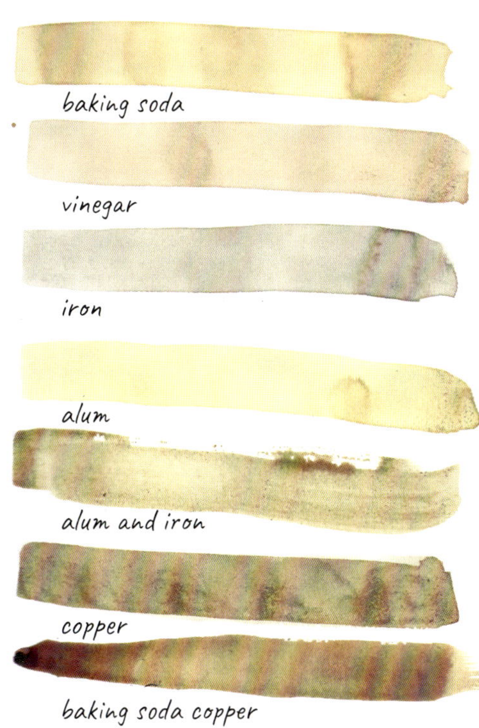

DRIED ONION AND GARBANZO

EGYPT ONION

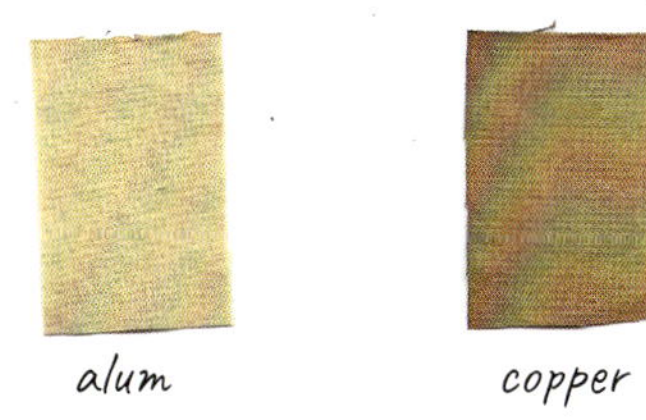

ATRIPLEX HORTENSIS

Orach Spinach

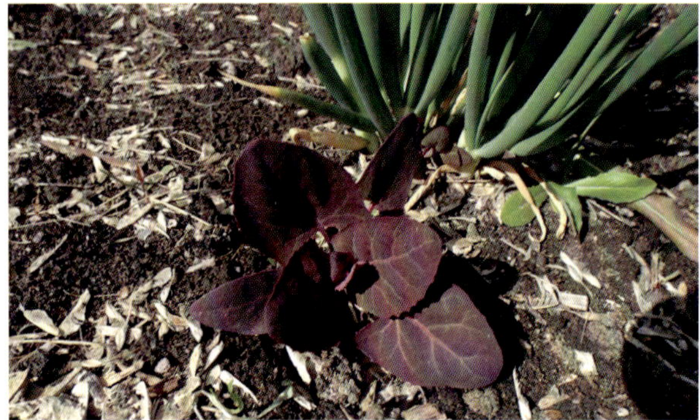

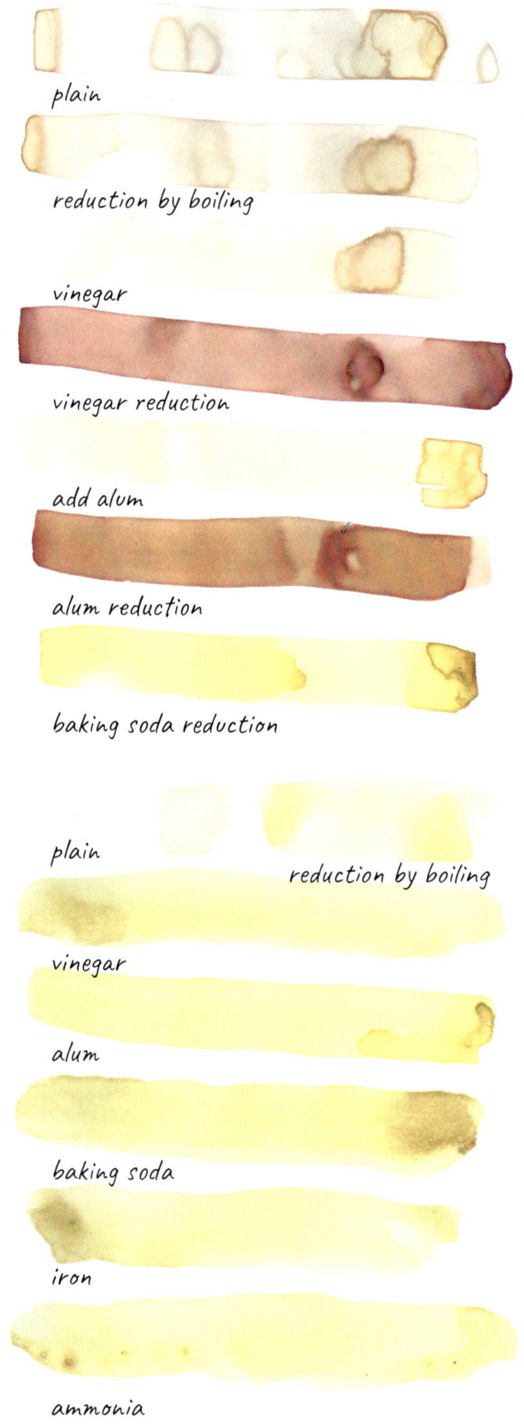

COLORS CREATED	red with vinegar, orange with alum, yellow with baking soda, brown and peach with other mordants
PARTS USED FOR PIGMENT	leaves and stems of young purple plants
PLANT TYPE	self-seeding annual
SEEDING	Seeds available at SeedRenaissance.com.

1. Simmer for 10 minutes to make pigment or dye. Strain.
2. Simmer again to reduce liquid to desired color strength.

ORIGANUM VULGARE

Oregano

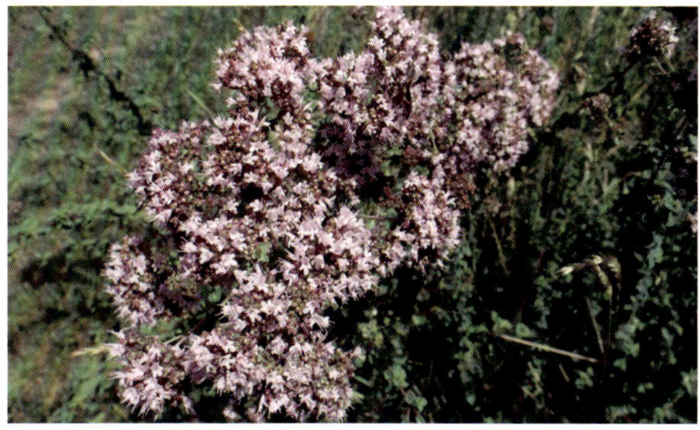

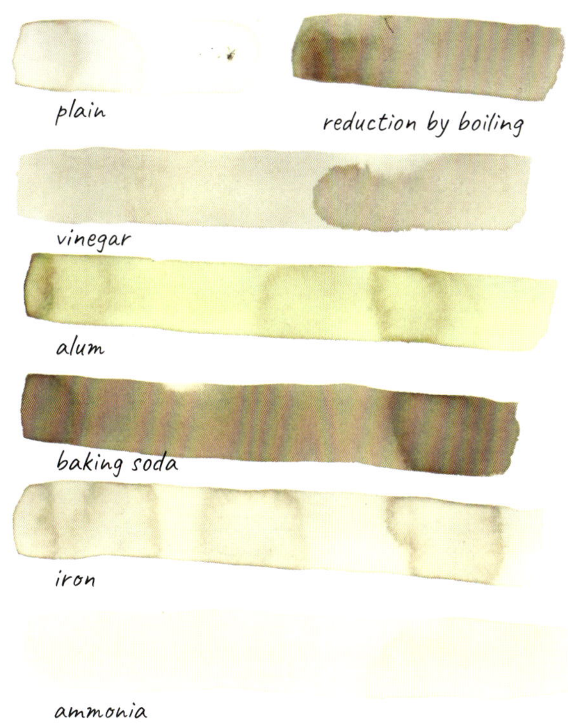

COLORS CREATED	browns
PARTS USED FOR PIGMENT	purple flowering tops
PLANT TYPE	perennial
HARDINESS ZONE	4
SEEDING	Seeds available at SeedRenaissance.com.

1. Simmer for 10 minutes to make pigment or dye. Strain.
2. Simmer again to reduce liquid to desired color strength.

Notes: Smells great while you are working with it but dries with no smell.

MAHONIA AQUIFOLIUM

Oregon Grape

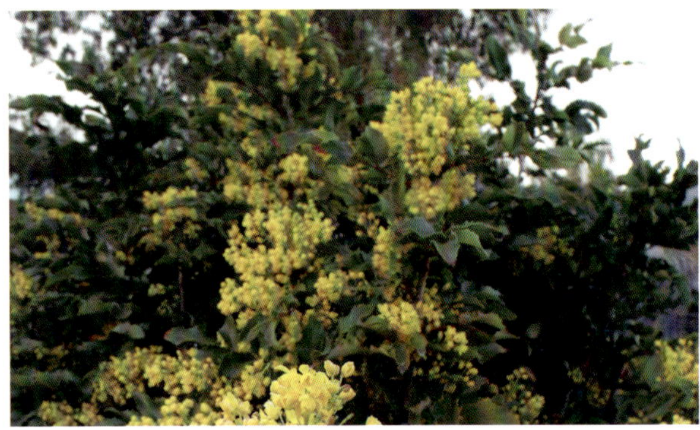

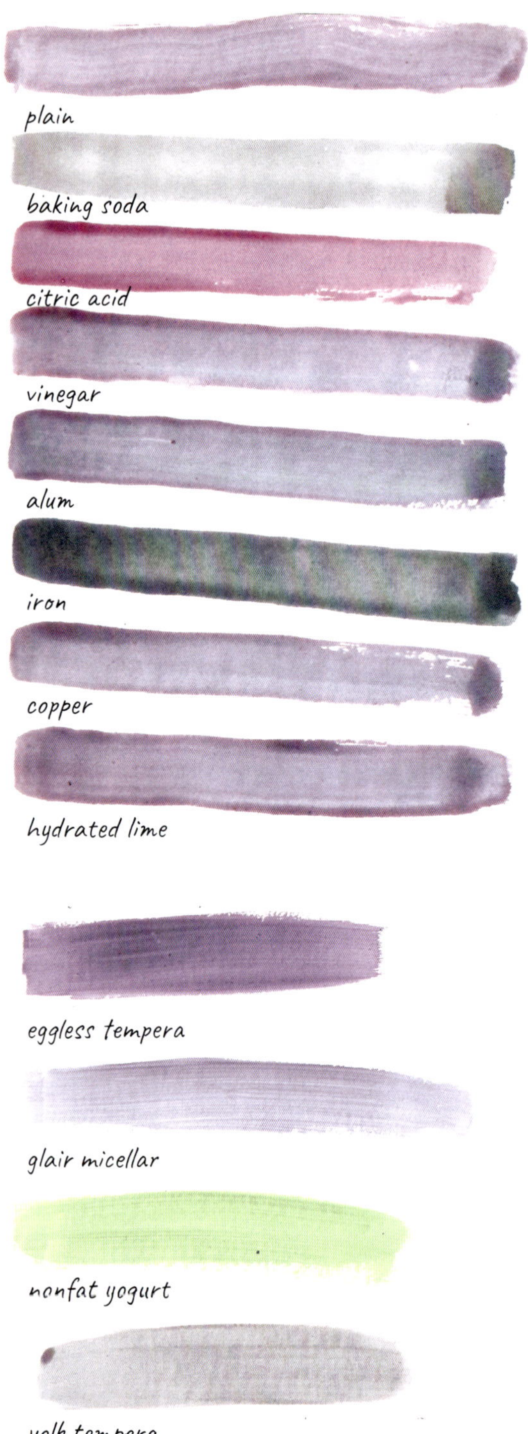

COLORS CREATED	violet, purple, gray, and strong greens in milk paint
PARTS USED FOR PIGMENT	ripe blue berries
PLANT TYPE	perennial shrub
HARDINESS ZONE	5

1. Simmer for 10 minutes to make pigment or dye. Strain.
2. Simmer again to reduce liquid to desired color strength.

MACLURA POMIFERA

Osage Orange

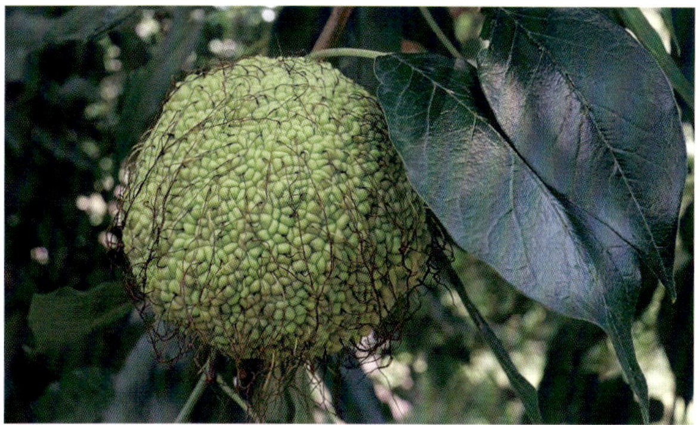

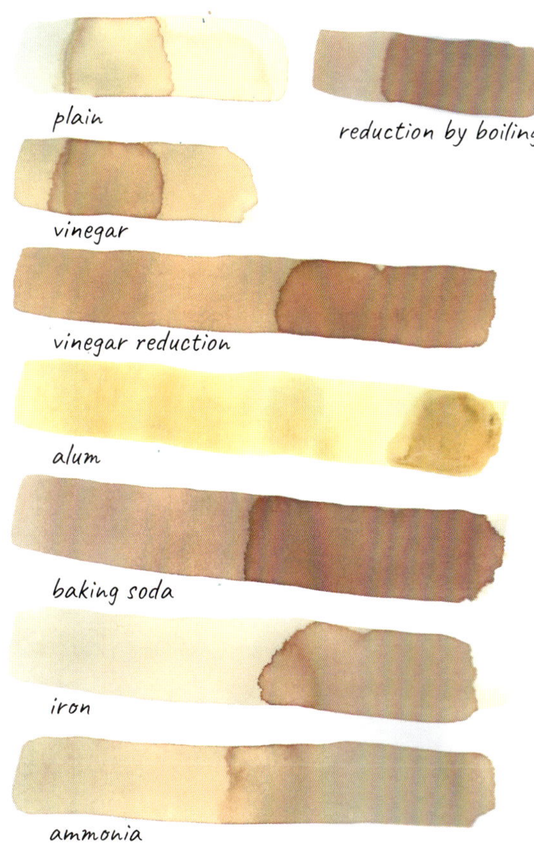

COLORS CREATED	orange with alum, reds and browns with most mordants
PARTS USED FOR PIGMENT	heartwood shavings
PLANT TYPE	tree
HARDINESS ZONE	5

1. Boil (not simmer) the shavings for 15 minutes to make pigment or dye. Strain.
2. Simmer again to reduce liquid to desired color strength.

Notes: A second boil in fresh water creates the same colors and the shavings can be used three or more times. The color temporarily stains a stainless-steel pan and has to be scrubbed out with a copper scrubber, which is often an indication of lightfastness.

PARKINSONIA SPECIES

Palo Verde

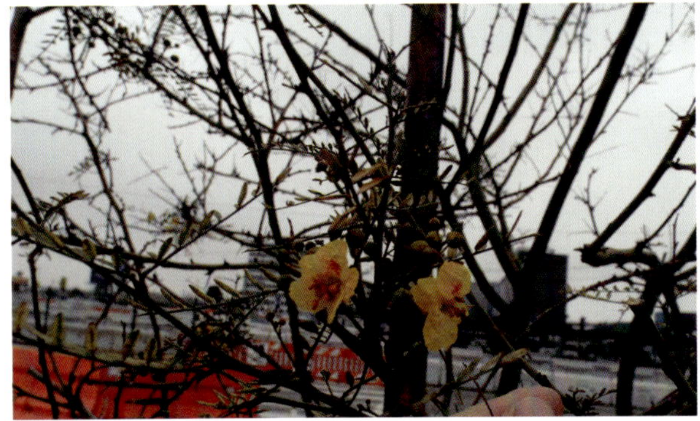

COLORS CREATED	red, green, yellow, brown
PARTS USED FOR PIGMENT	red base of yellow flowers, bark
PLANT TYPE	shrub
HARDINESS ZONE	8

1. Simmer for 10 minutes to make pigment or dye. Strain.
2. Simmer again to reduce liquid to desired color strength.

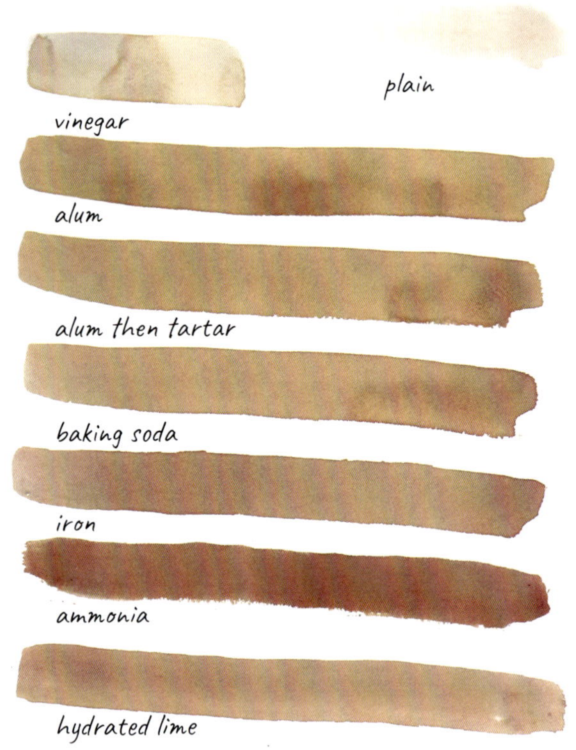

PRESSED FLOWERS

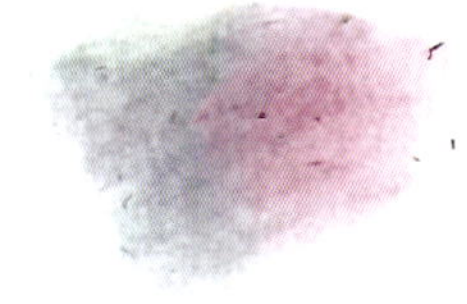

plain citric acid

PALO VERDE YELLOW PETALS

VIOLA X WITTROCKIANA

Pansy

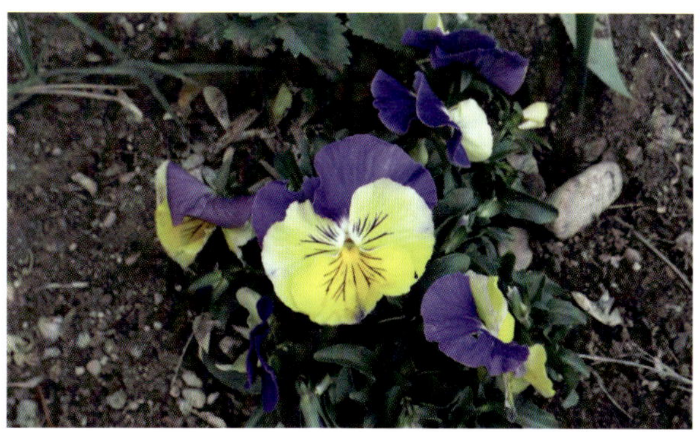

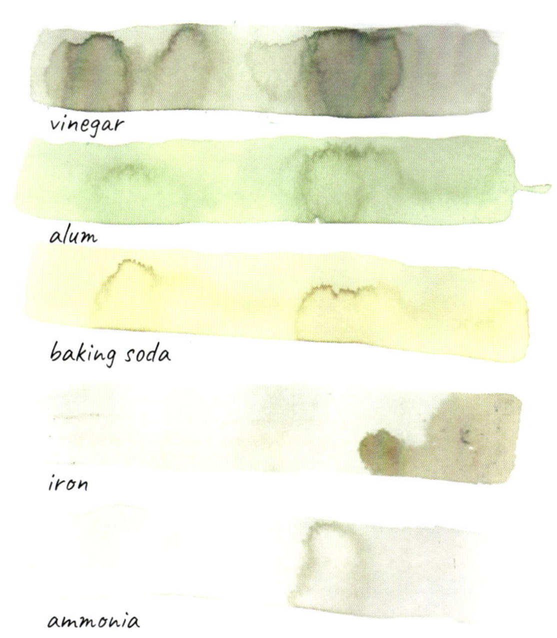

COLORS CREATED	orange and yellow from fresh orange petals, green and yellow from cooked purple petals
PARTS USED FOR PIGMENT	flower petals (no sepals)
PLANT TYPE	annual
HARDINESS ZONE	6
SEEDING	Seeds available at SeedRenaissance.com.

1. Simmer for 10 minutes to make pigment or dye. Strain.
2. Simmer again to reduce liquid to desired color strength.

Notes: Pansies, especially those with thin black patterns, make remarkable eco-prints when used fresh.

FRESH PRESSED YELLOW PETALS

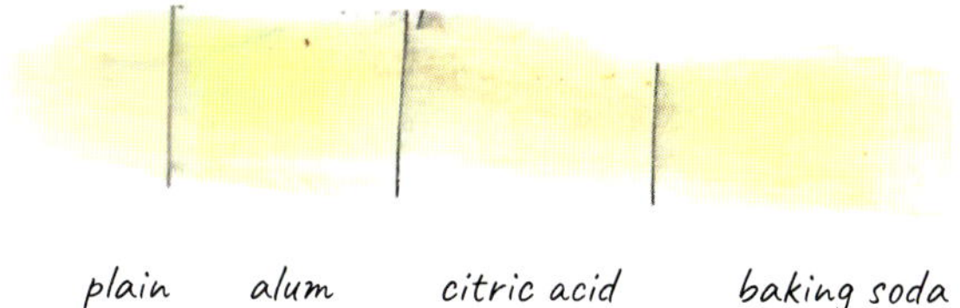

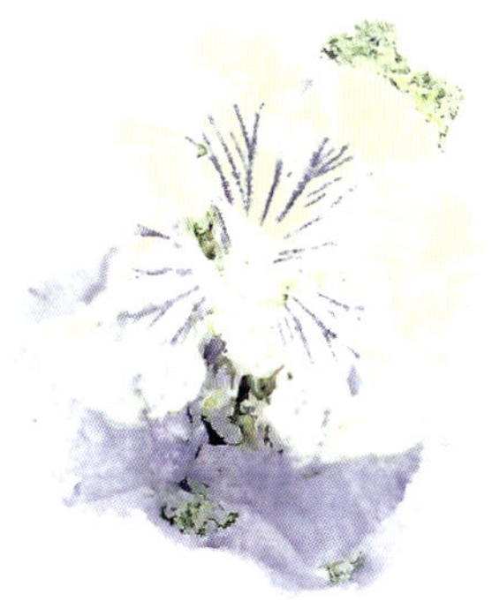

PRUNUS PERSICA

Peach Tree

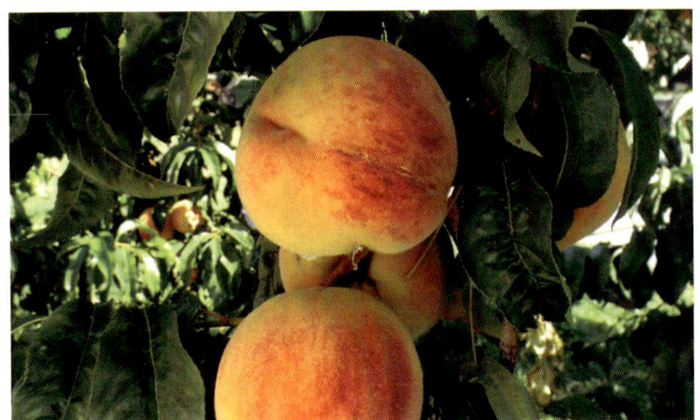

COLORS CREATED	yellow with most mordants
PARTS USED FOR PIGMENT	fresh green leaves
PLANT TYPE	fruit tree
HARDINESS ZONE	4

1. Simmer for 10 minutes to make pigment or dye. Strain.
2. Simmer again to reduce liquid to desired color strength.

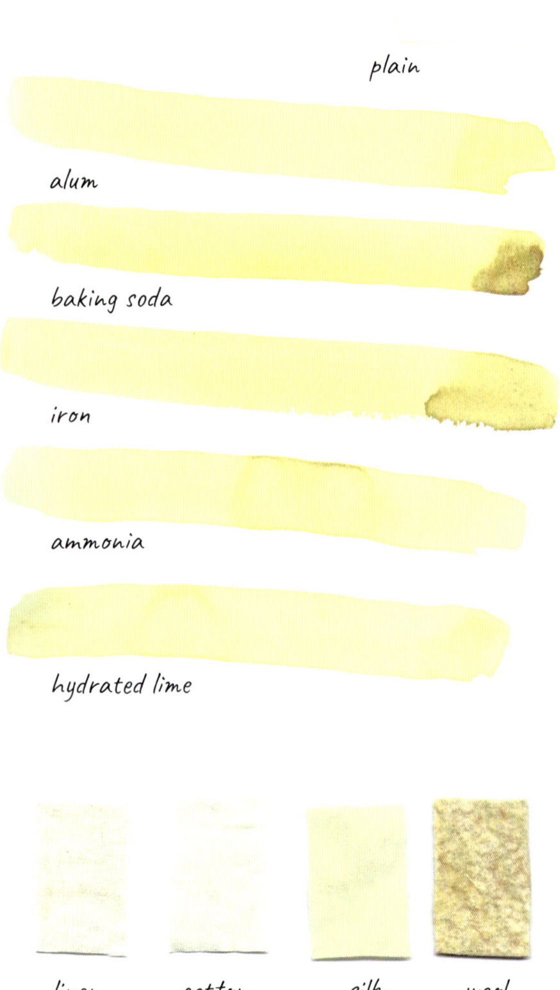

ANAPHALIS MARGARITACEA

Pearly Everlasting

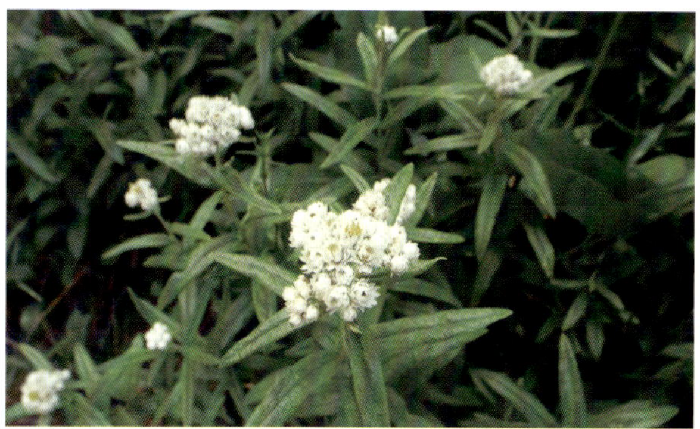

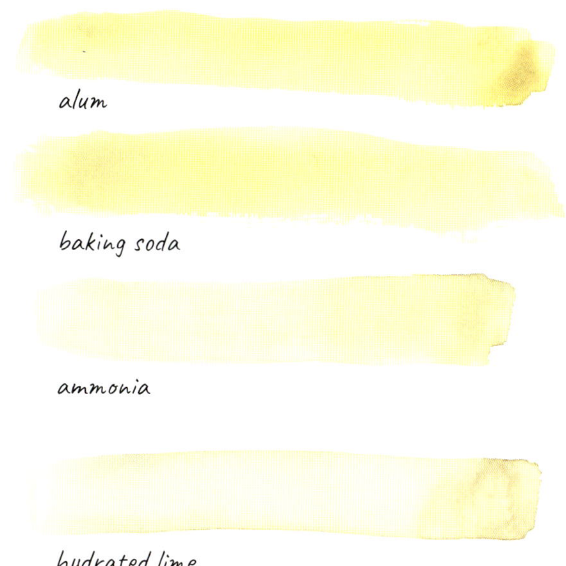

COLORS CREATED	yellow with alum and baking soda
PARTS USED FOR PIGMENT	white flowers
PLANT TYPE	perennial
HARDINESS ZONE	2
SEEDING	Plant directly outside in spring or autumn.

1. Simmer for 10 minutes to make pigment or dye. Strain.
2. Simmer again to reduce liquid to desired color strength.

CARYA SPECIES

Pecans

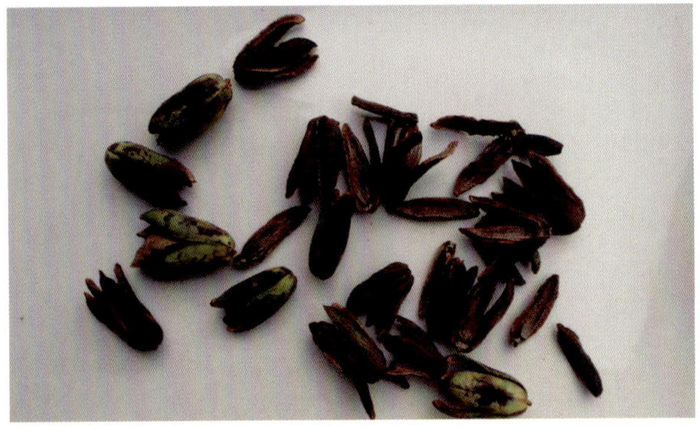

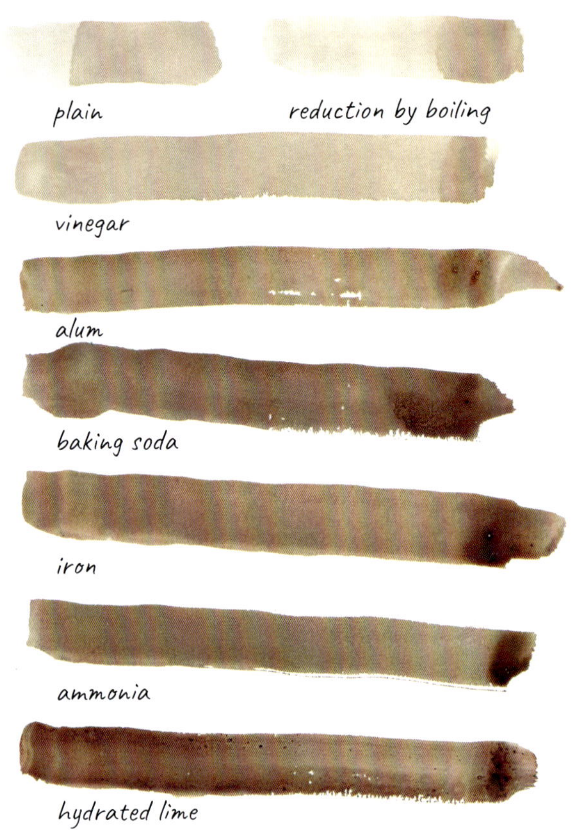

COLORS CREATED	brown
PARTS USED FOR PIGMENT	hulls
PLANT TYPE	nut tree
HARDINESS ZONE	5
SEEDING	Seeds available at SeedRenaissance.com.

1. Simmer for 75 minutes to make pigment or dye. Strain.
2. Simmer again to reduce liquid to desired color strength.

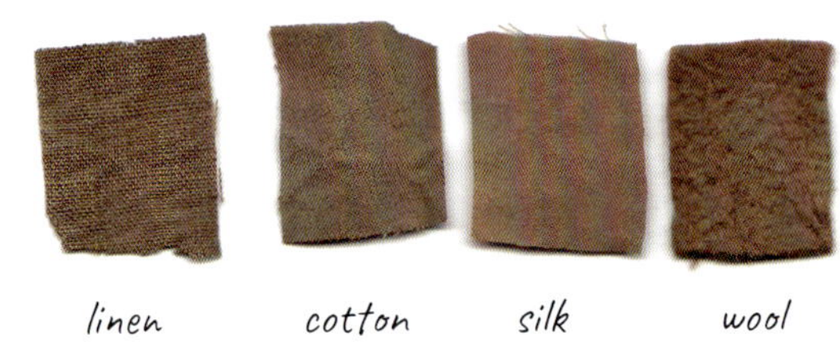

WITH EGG AND LINSEED OIL

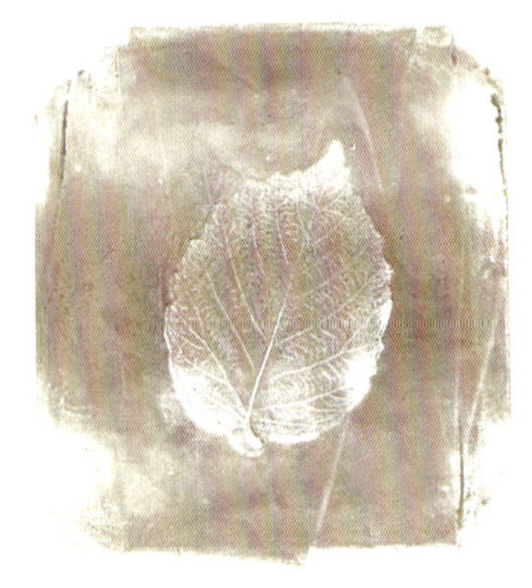

Penstemon Species

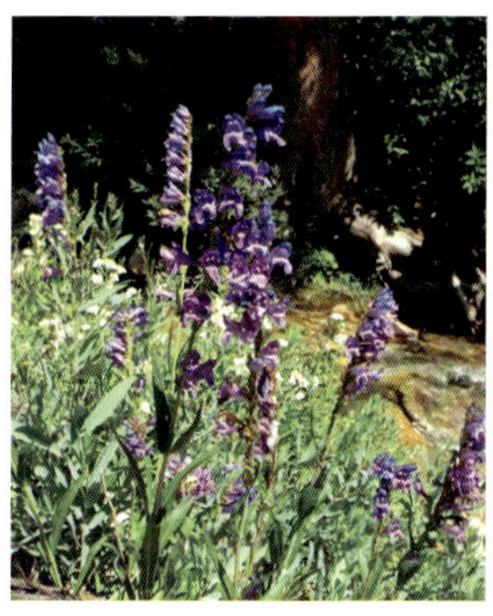
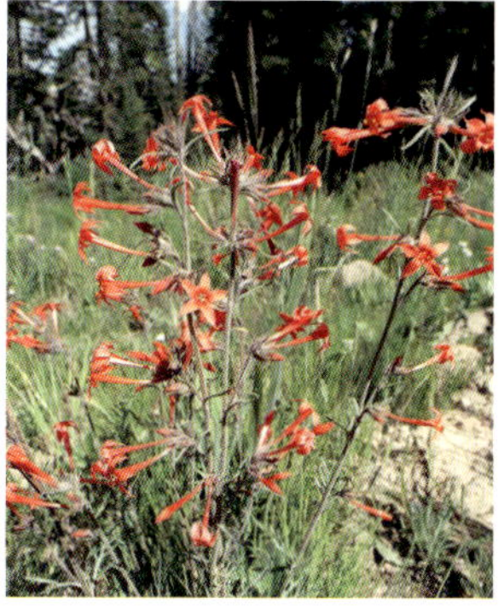

BLUE PENSTEMON FLOWERS

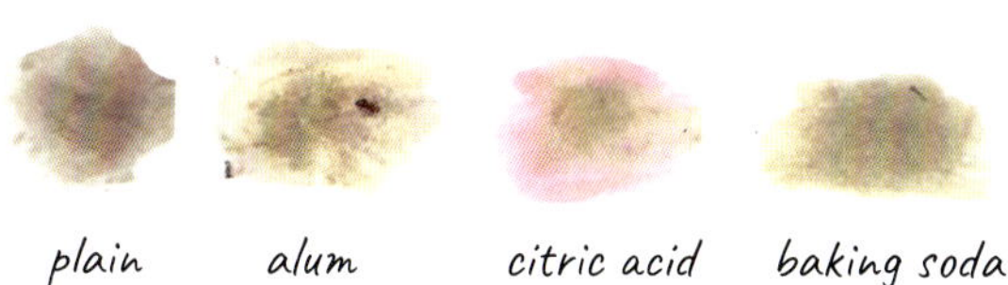

COLORS CREATED	red, yellow, brown
PARTS USED FOR PIGMENT	blossoms
PLANT TYPE	annual
HARDINESS ZONE	3

1. Simmer for 20 minutes to make pigment or dye. Strain.
2. Simmer again to reduce liquid to desired color strength.

Notes: The blooms likely also make good eco-prints.

PAEONIA SPECIES

Peony

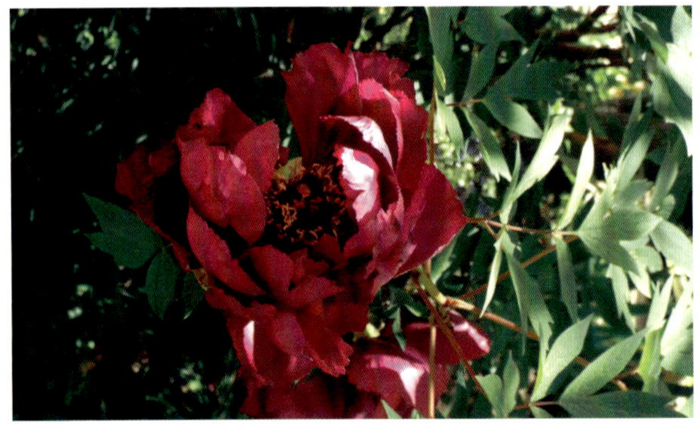

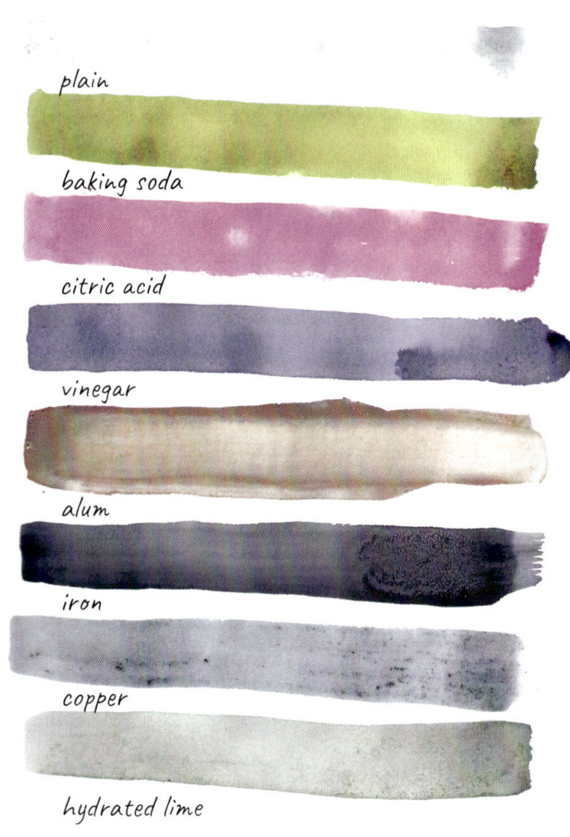

COLORS CREATED	green with baking soda, red with citric acid, purple with vinegar, brown with alum, black with iron, blueish gray with vinegar of copper
PARTS USED FOR PIGMENT	red petals
PLANT TYPE	perennial
SEEDING	Plant directly outside in spring or autumn. Seeds available at SeedRenaissance.com.

1. Simmer for 10 minutes to make pigment or dye. Strain.
2. Simmer again to reduce liquid to desired color strength.

RED PEONY PETALS WITH CITRIC ACID

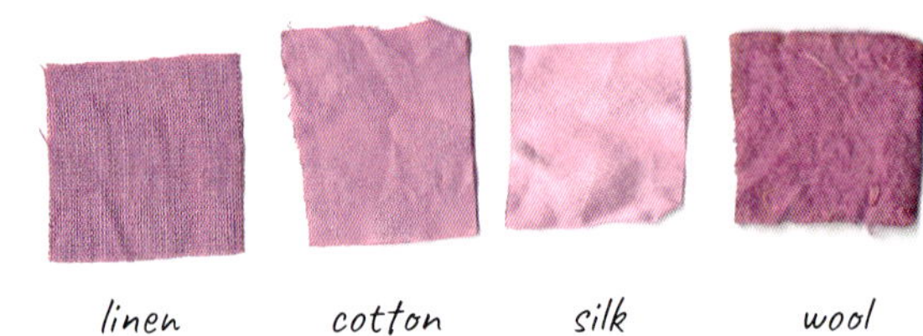

JATROPHA INTEGERRIMA

Peregrina

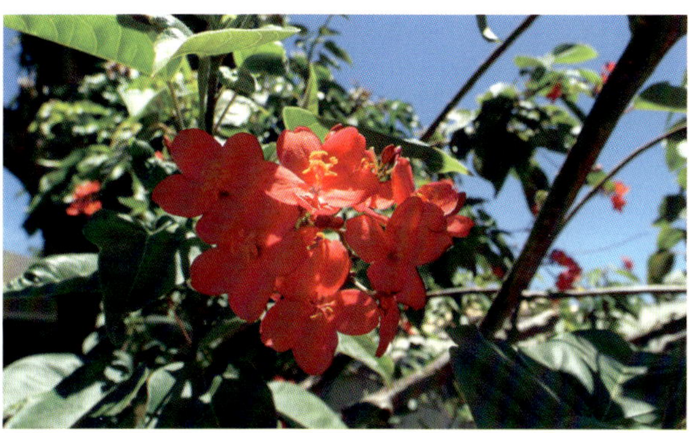

COLORS CREATED	purple and green when used fresh, reddish brown when cooked
PARTS USED FOR PIGMENT	petals
PLANT TYPE	shrub or small tree
HARDINESS ZONE	9

1. Simmer for 10 minutes to make pigment or dye. Strain.
2. Simmer again to reduce liquid to desired color strength.

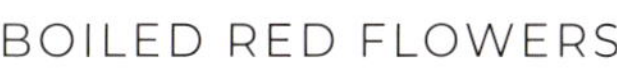

BOILED RED FLOWERS

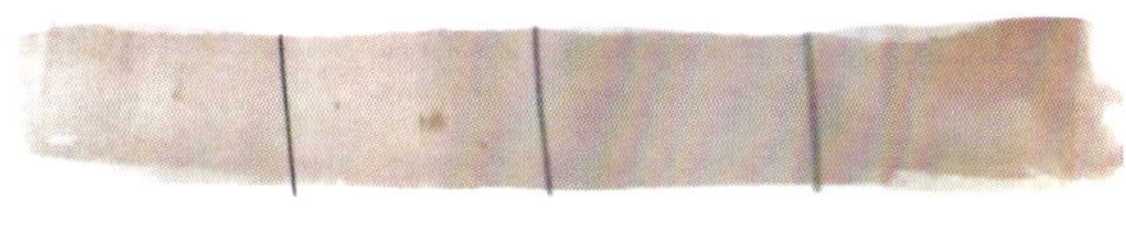

FRESH PRESSED RED FLOWERS

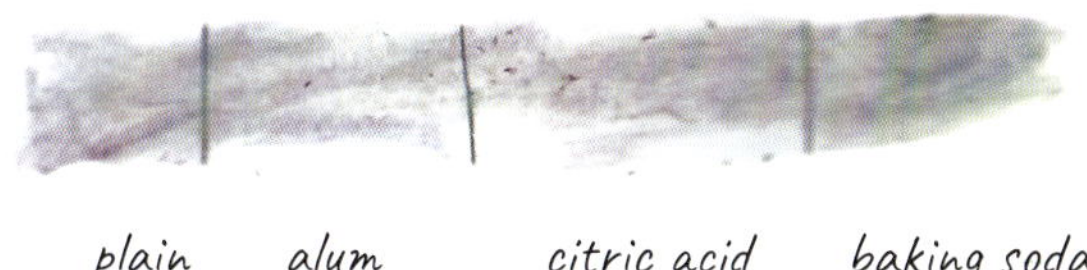

LATHYRUS LATIFOLIUS

Perennial Peavine

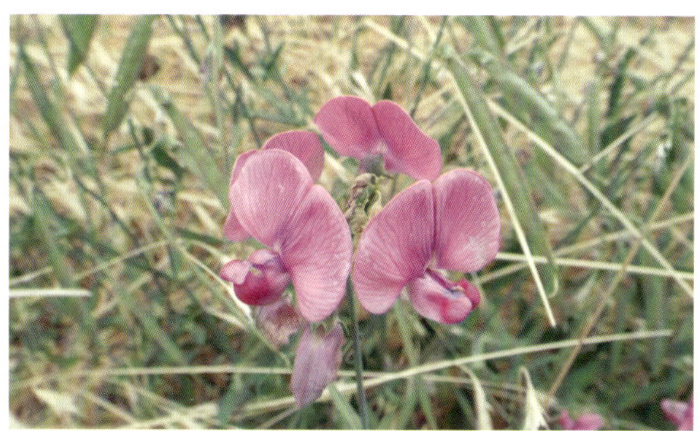

COLORS CREATED	green with alum, yellow with baking soda
PARTS USED FOR PIGMENT	petals only (no sepals)
PLANT TYPE	perennial
HARDINESS ZONE	3

1. Simmer for 10 minutes to make pigment or dye. Strain.
2. Simmer again to reduce liquid to desired color strength.

PETUNIA HYBRIDA

Petunia

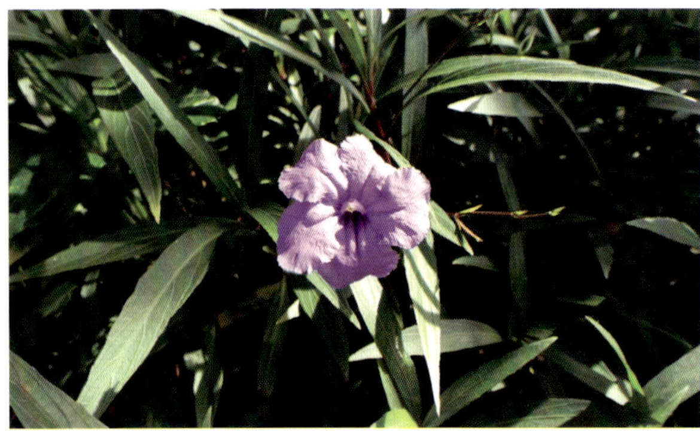

COLORS CREATED	blue with alum, green with vinegar or vinegar of copper, gray with iron, greenish brown with baking soda
PARTS USED FOR PIGMENT	petals
PLANT TYPE	annual

1. Simmer for 20 minutes to make pigment or dye. Strain.
2. Simmer again to reduce liquid to desired color strength.

Notes: When pressed fresh, petunias make excellent but sticky colors. Velvet petunias make rich colors. Some hybrids make pastels.

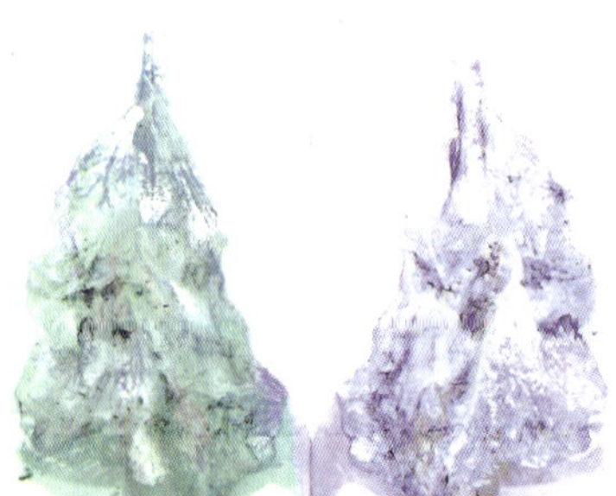

CHANTER ALTO RED PETUNIA

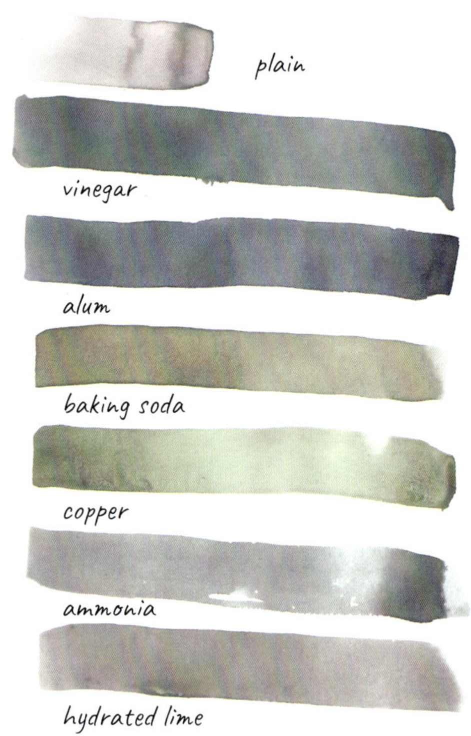

PETUNIA STEEPED

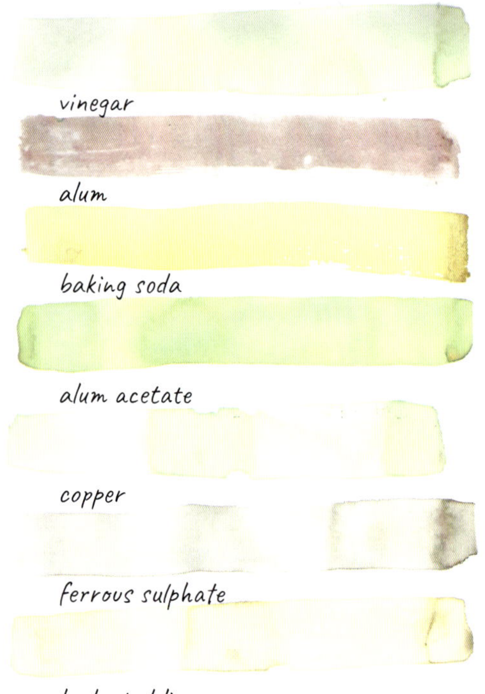

Phlox Species and Hybrids

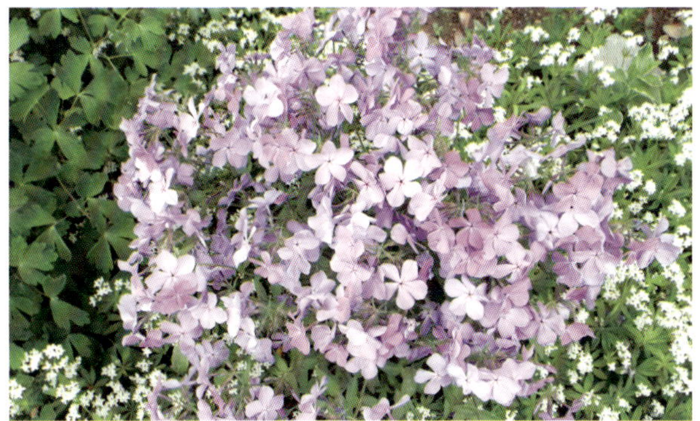

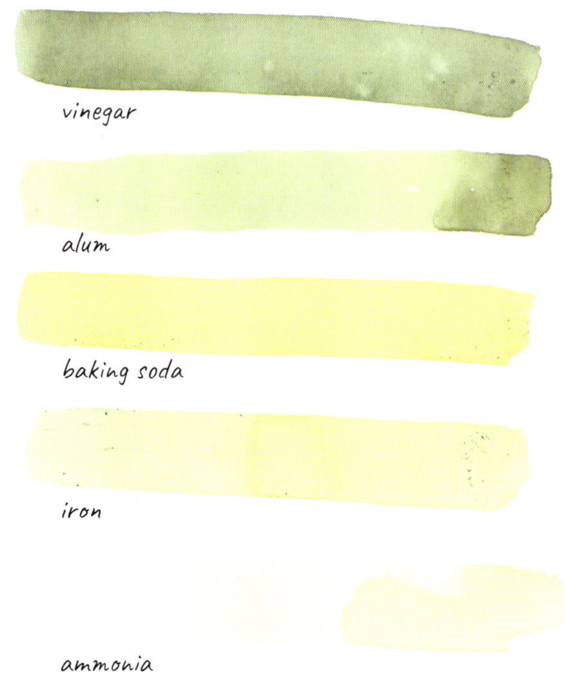

COLORS CREATED	green with vinegar, yellow with baking soda
PARTS USED FOR PIGMENT	red petals only (no sepals)
PLANT TYPE	varies by species
HARDINESS ZONE	varies by species

1. Simmer for 10 minutes to make pigment or dye. Strain.
2. Simmer again to reduce liquid to desired color strength.

Notes: Fresh pressed petals make excellent eco-prints.

PRUNUS DOMESTICA

Plum

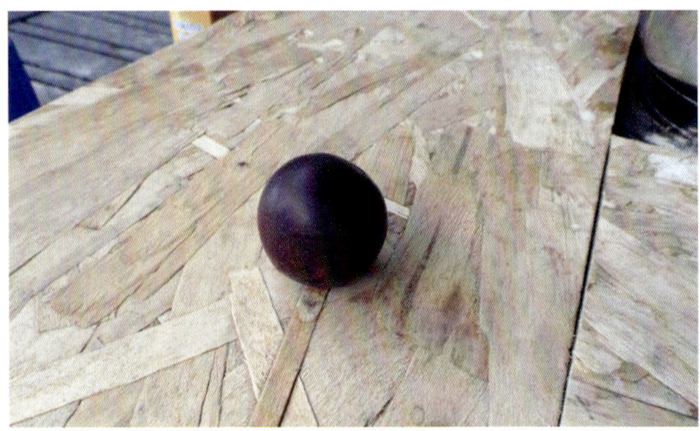

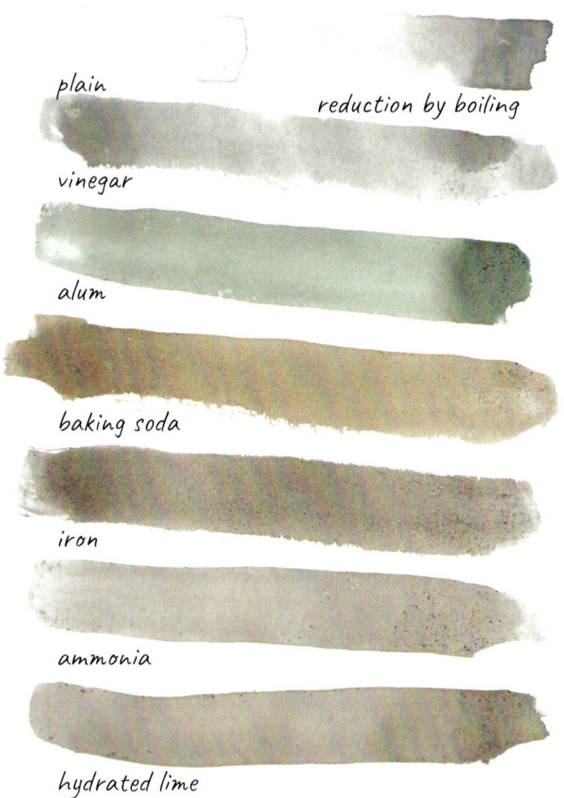

COLORS CREATED	green with alum, brown or gray with most mordants
PARTS USED FOR PIGMENT	skin of a ripe or overripe plum fruit
PLANT TYPE	perennial
HARDINESS ZONE	4

1. Simmer for 30 minutes to make pigment or dye. Strain.
2. Simmer again to reduce liquid to desired color strength.

Notes: Using the fruit with the skin makes the pigment sticky. To avoid this, use only the skin. I found it easiest to separate the skin from the fruit by allowing the fruit to become overripe, then squeezing the fruit out of the skin.

Plumeria Species

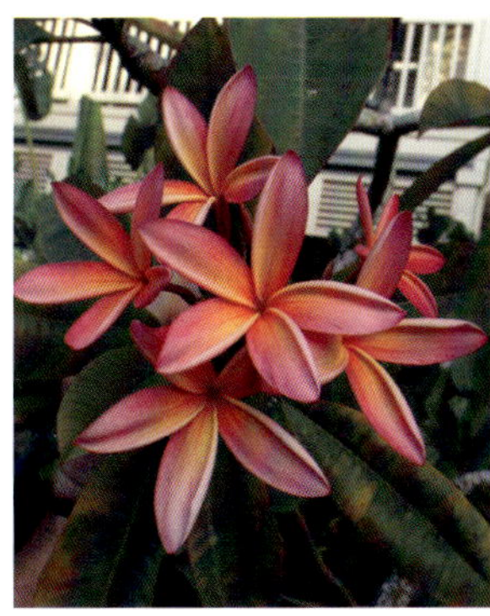

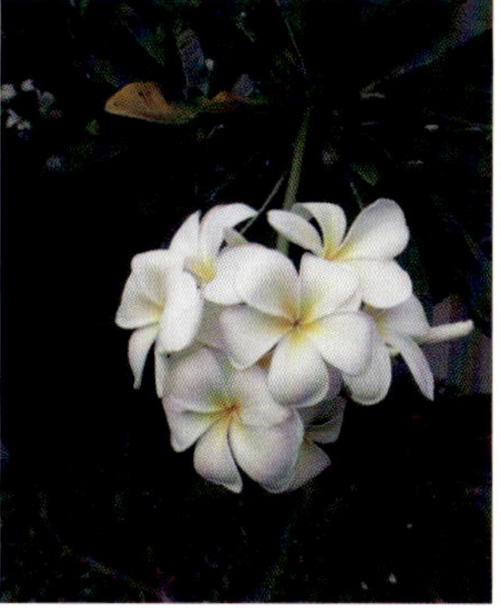

FRESH PRESSED WHITE PETALS

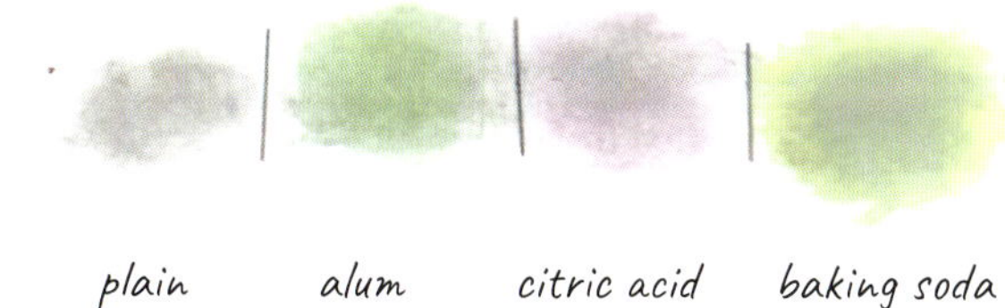

COLORS CREATED	green with alum or baking soda, pink with citric acid, gray unmordanted
PARTS USED FOR PIGMENT	red or pink flowers
PLANT TYPE	tropical
HARDINESS ZONE	10

1. Best when pressed fresh and uncooked.

EUPHORBIA PULCHERRIMA

Poinsettia

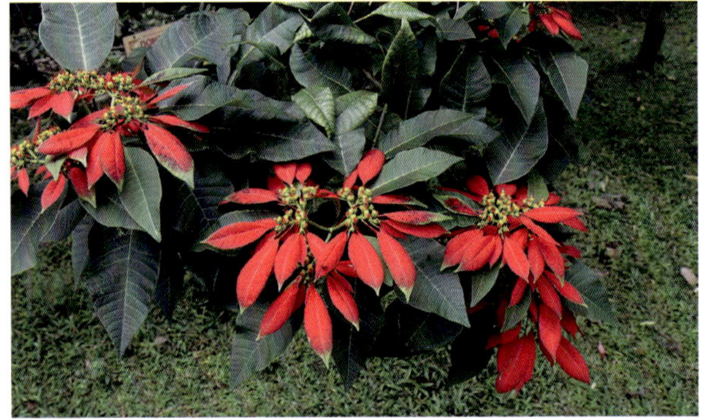

COLORS CREATED	green with most mordants
PARTS USED FOR PIGMENT	red leaves, fresh or dried
PLANT TYPE	houseplant
HARDINESS ZONE	9

1. Simmer for 10 minutes to make pigment or dye. Strain.
2. Simmer again to reduce liquid to desired color strength.

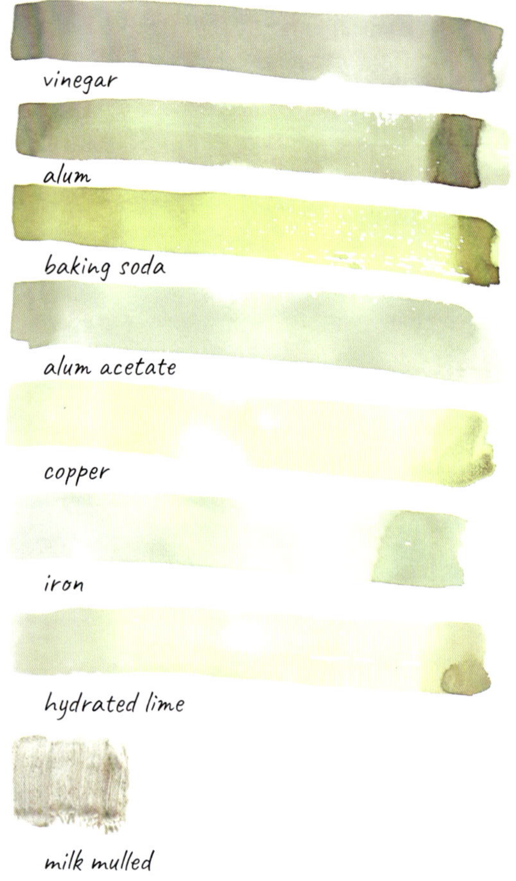

PLAIN POINSETTIA

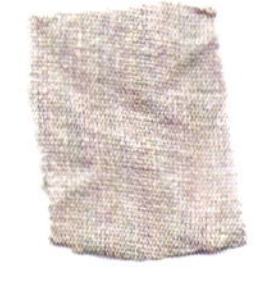
linen

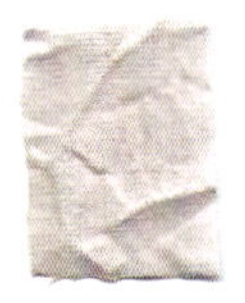
cotton

silk

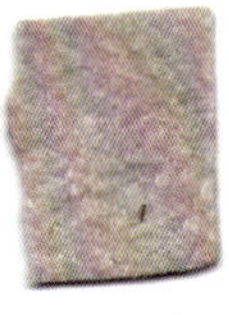
wool

POINSETTIA WITH VINEGAR

linen

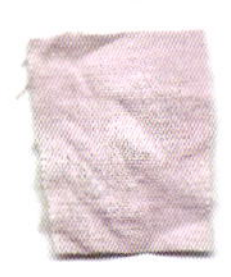
cotton

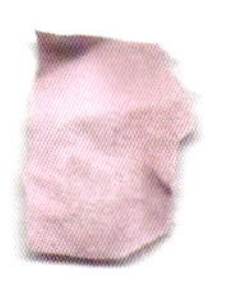
silk

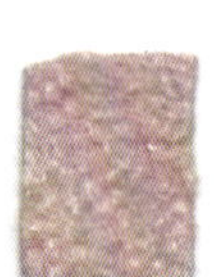
wool

POINSETTIA ALUM

linen

cotton

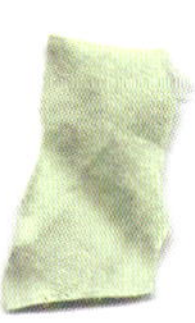
silk

wool

PHYTOLACCA AMERICANA

Poke

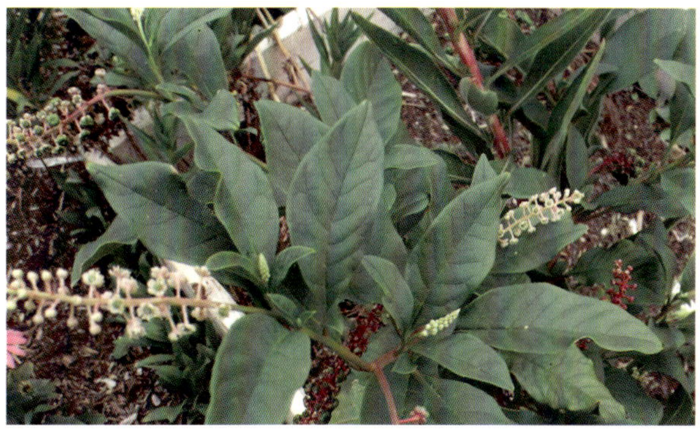

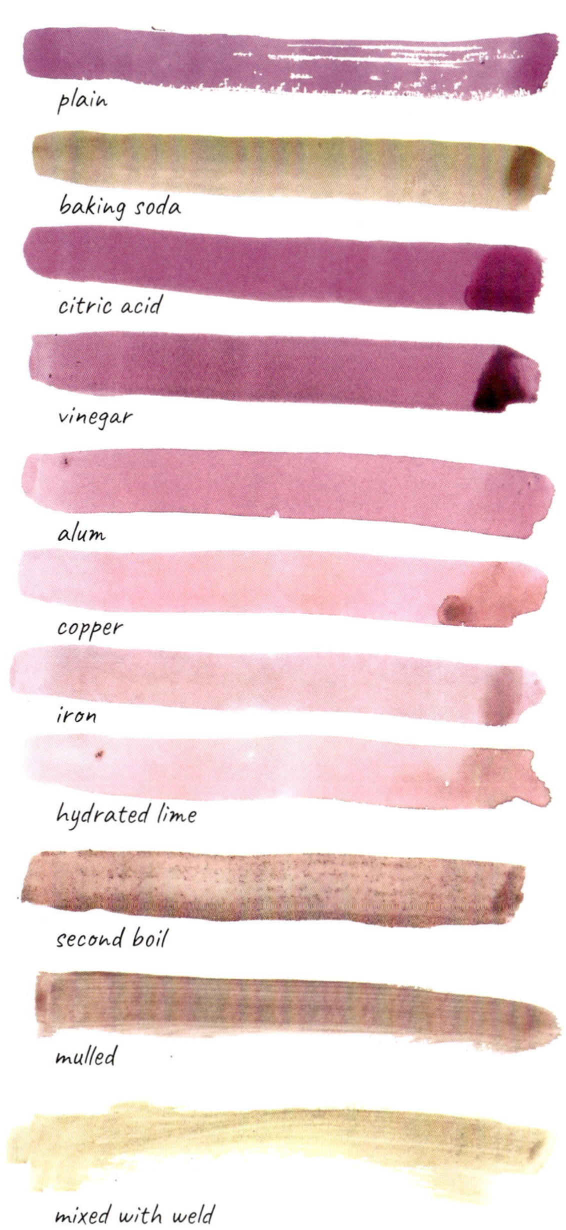

COLORS CREATED	reds, oranges
PARTS USED FOR PIGMENT	ripe berries
PLANT TYPE	berry bush
HARDINESS ZONE	4
SEEDING	Seeds available at SeedRenaissance.com.

1. Simmer for 10 minutes to make pigment or dye. Strain.
2. Simmer again to reduce liquid to desired color strength.

Notes: This plant requires acidic soil and a long growing season. The plant is poisonous and the berries are not to be eaten, but they have a long history of use for dyeing. I've had no problems using the berries for dye.

FRESH PRESSED LEAF WITH IRON

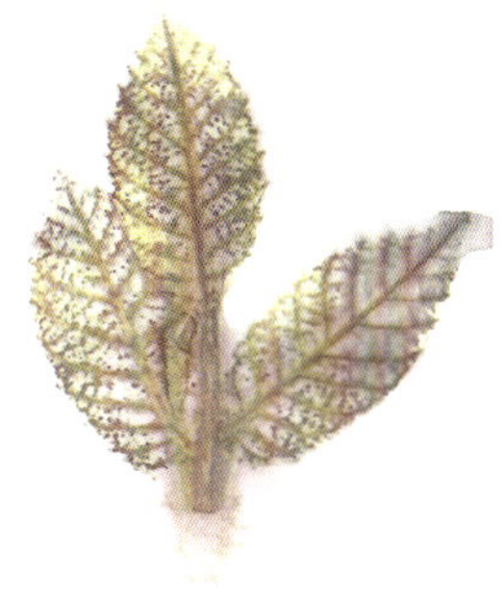

PUNICA GRANATUM

Pomegranate

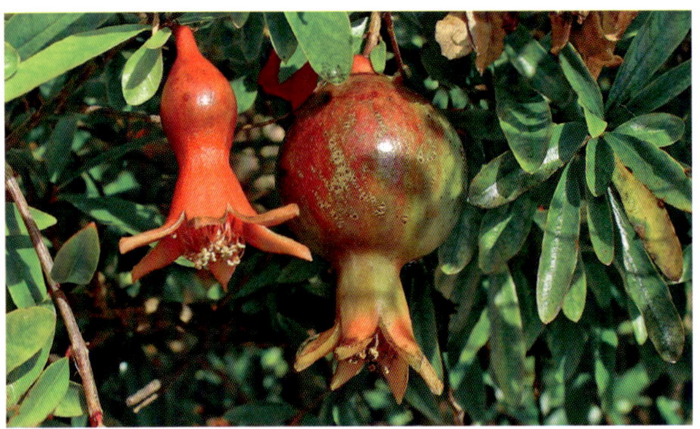

COLORS CREATED	purple and perhaps red with citric acid or ascorbic acid from seeds, yellow and brown from skin
PARTS USED FOR PIGMENT	fleshy seeds, skin
PLANT TYPE	tree
HARDINESS ZONE	8

1. Simmer for 10 minutes to make pigment or dye. Strain.
2. Simmer again to reduce liquid to desired color strength.

Notes: Extremely sticky paint when cooked, so it is best used as children's finger paint. When used on fabric as dye, the sticky sugars wash away.

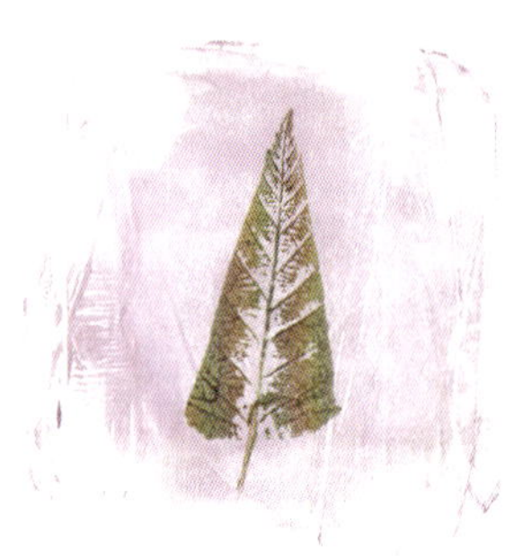

POMEGRANATE SKIN

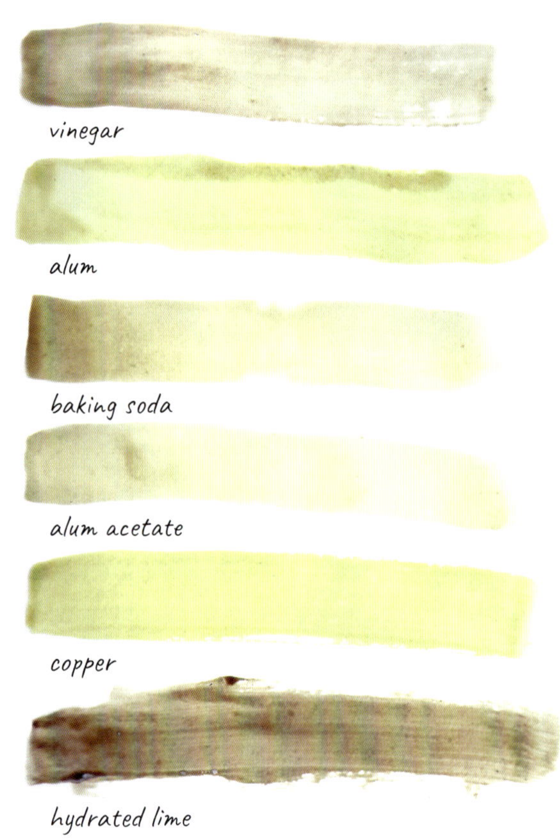

POMEGRANATE SEED WITH ALUM AND ALUM ACETATE

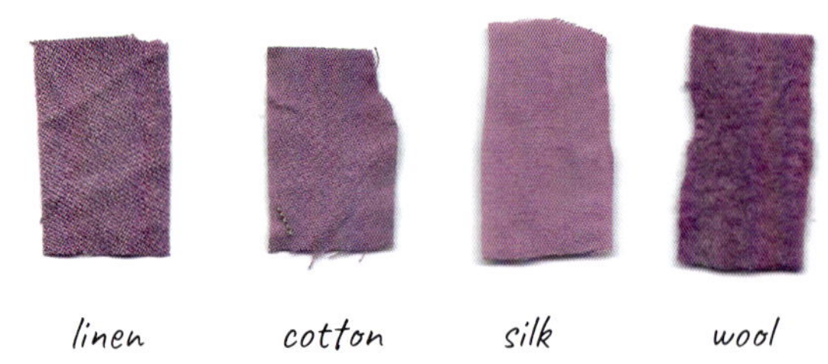

PAPAVER RHOEAS

Poppies

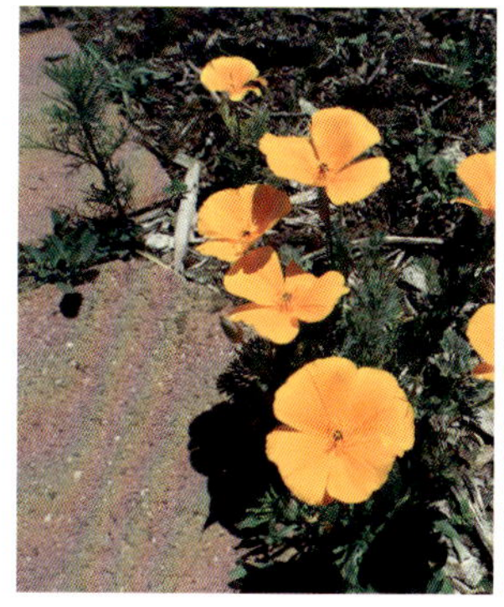

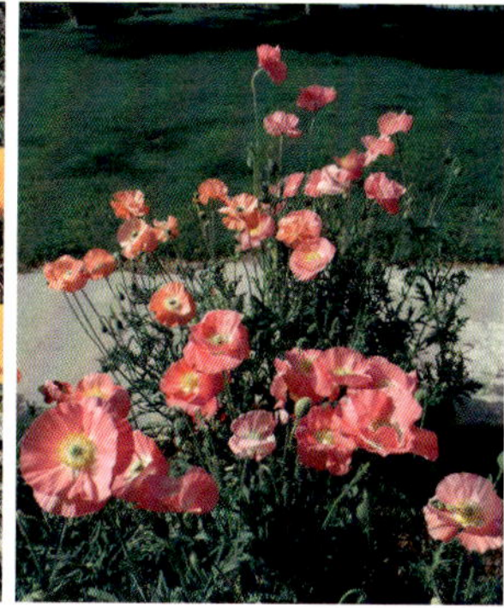

COLORS CREATED	red and green when cooked, purple and greens with citric acid when used fresh and uncooked
PARTS USED FOR PIGMENT	red petals, used fresh or dried at peak bloom
PLANT TYPE	self-seeding annual or perennial
HARDINESS ZONE	1
SEEDING	Seeds available at SeedRenaissance.com.

1. Simmer for 10 minutes to make pigment or dye. Strain.
2. Simmer again to reduce liquid to desired color strength.

DRIED PINK SHIRLEY PETALS

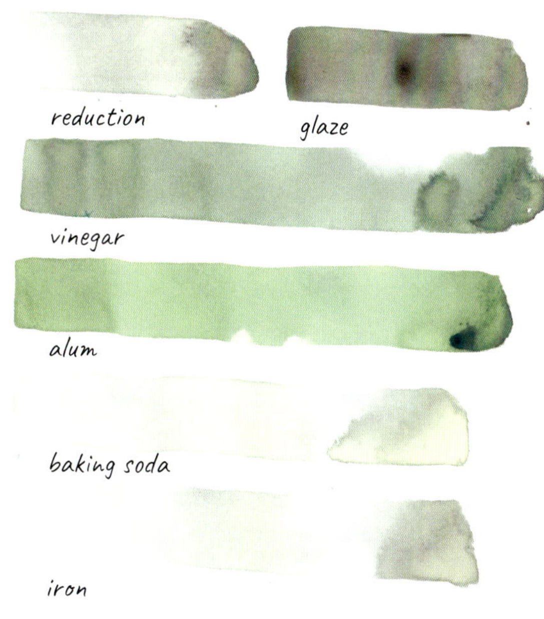

RED POPPY

PURPLE GRAPE POPPY

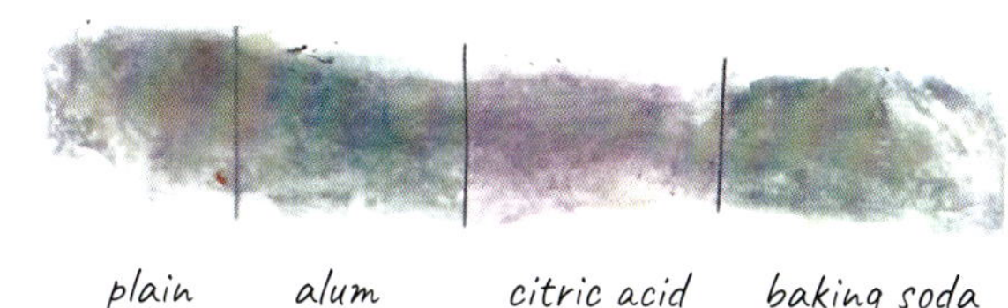

SCHINOPSIS LORENTZII

Quebracho Tree

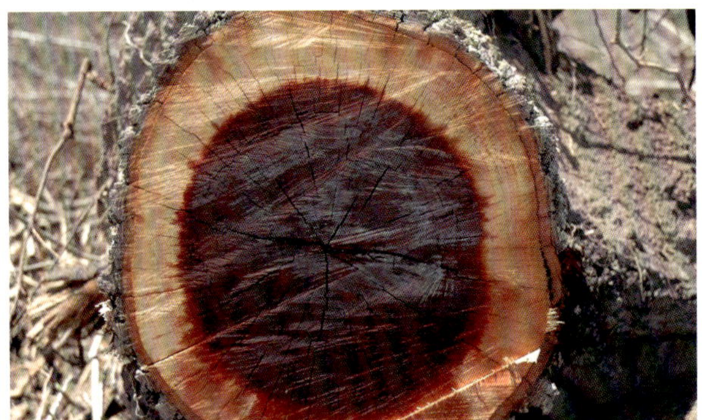

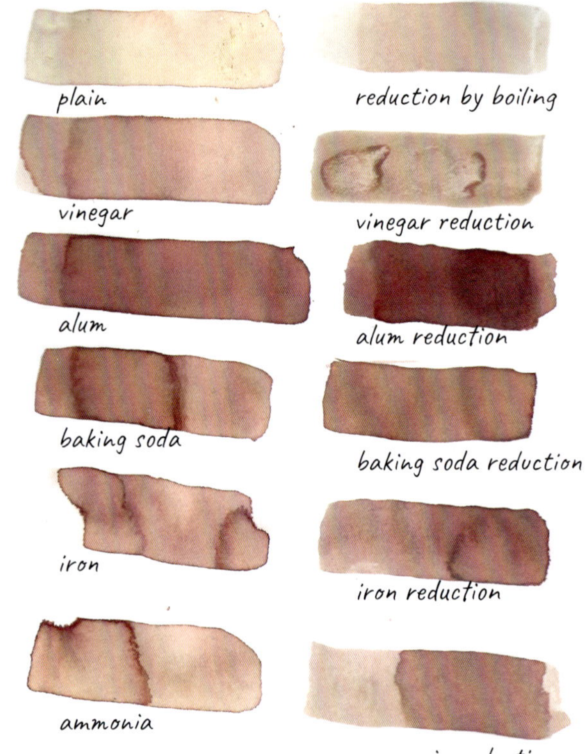

COLORS CREATED	pink and red with most mordants
PARTS USED FOR PIGMENT	heartwood
PLANT TYPE	tree

1. Simmer for 10 minutes to make pigment or dye. Strain.
2. Simmer again to reduce liquid to desired color strength.

Rabbitbrush (Various Species)

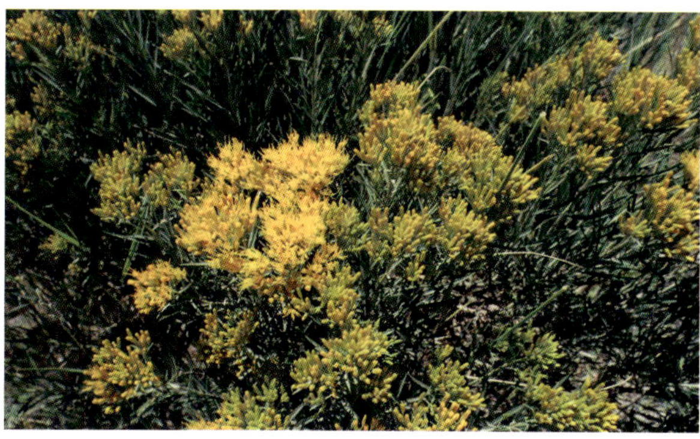

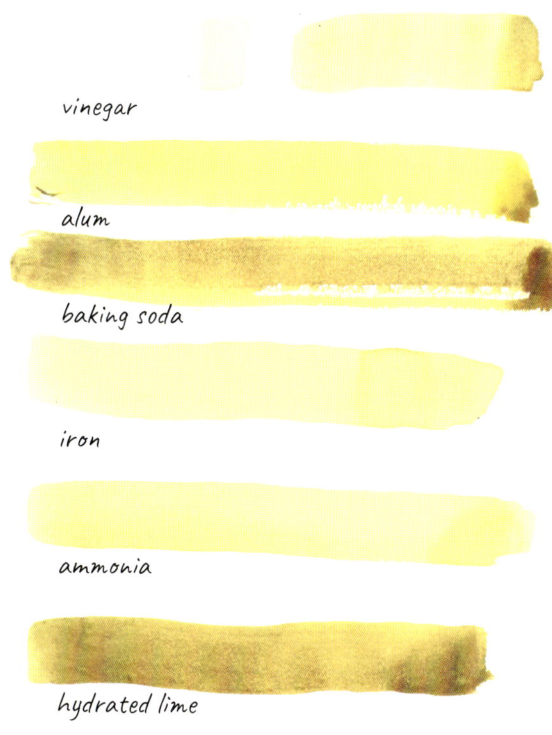

COLORS CREATED	yellow with alum
PARTS USED FOR PIGMENT	flowers
PLANT TYPE	perennial shrub
HARDINESS ZONE	varies by species

1. Simmer for 15 minutes to make pigment or dye. Strain.
2. Simmer again to reduce liquid to desired color strength.

RAPHANUS RAPHANISTRUM

Radish

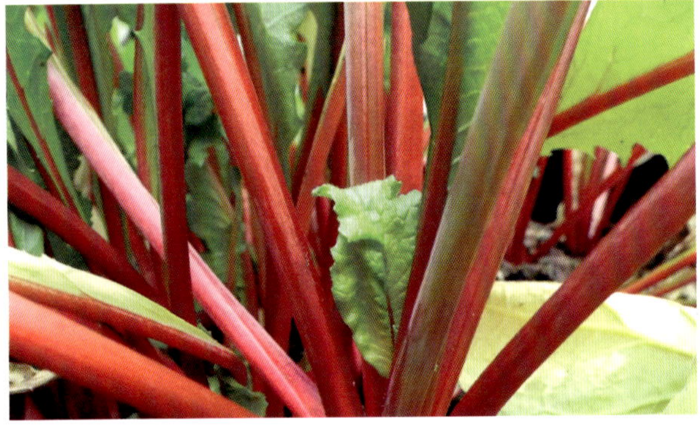

COLORS CREATED	blue, pink, red, yellow, green
PARTS USED FOR PIGMENT	leaves, stems

1. Simmer for 10 minutes to make pigment or dye. Strain.
2. Simmer again to reduce liquid to desired color strength.

Notes: If you are astonished at the colors that can come from a radish—especially blue—so was I. This particular radish is red throughout and stays red when cooked, which is the key to how it gives such great colors. Even stems of the leaves make pastels.

BOILED RED RADISH ROOT WITH ALUM

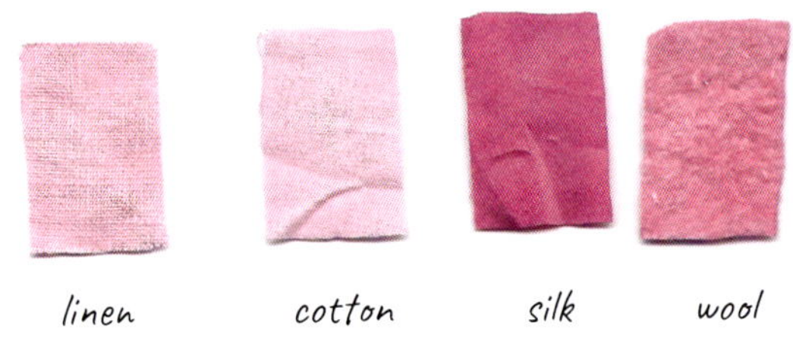

RED BEAUTY RADISH LEAF STEMS

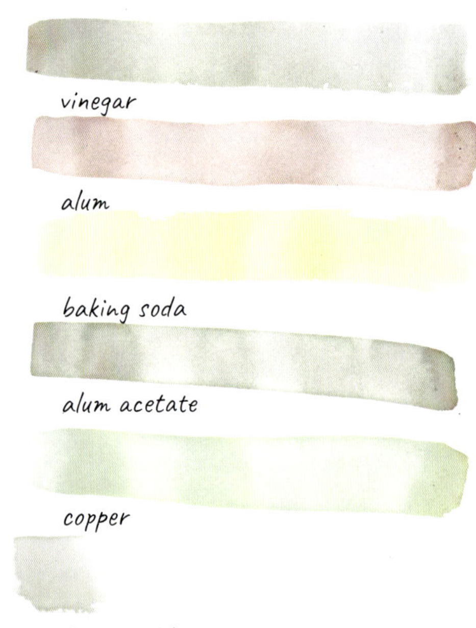

GRATED RED BEAUTY RADISH

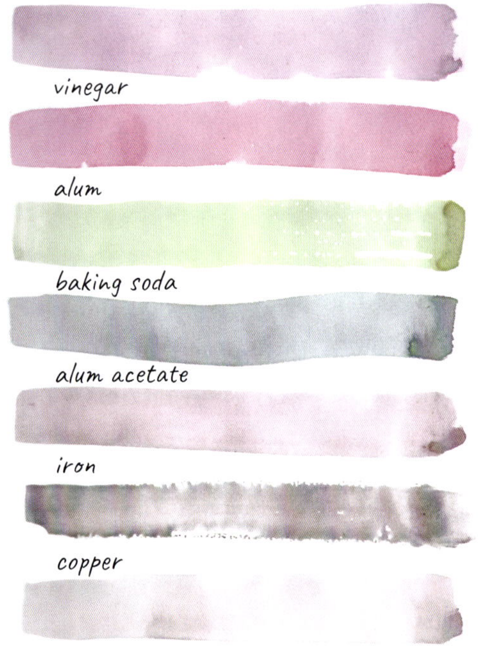

RUBUS IDAEUS

Raspberries

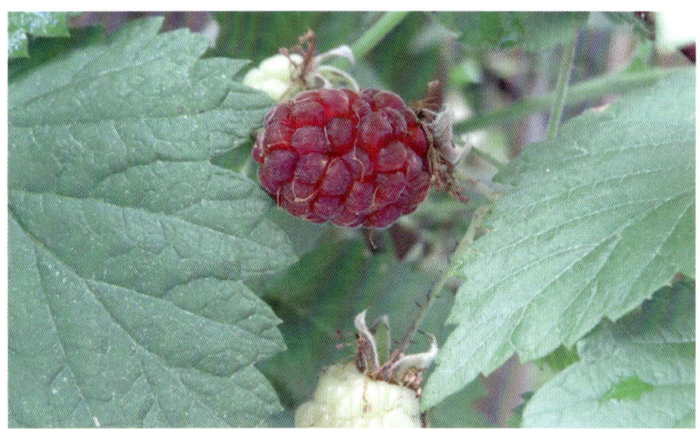

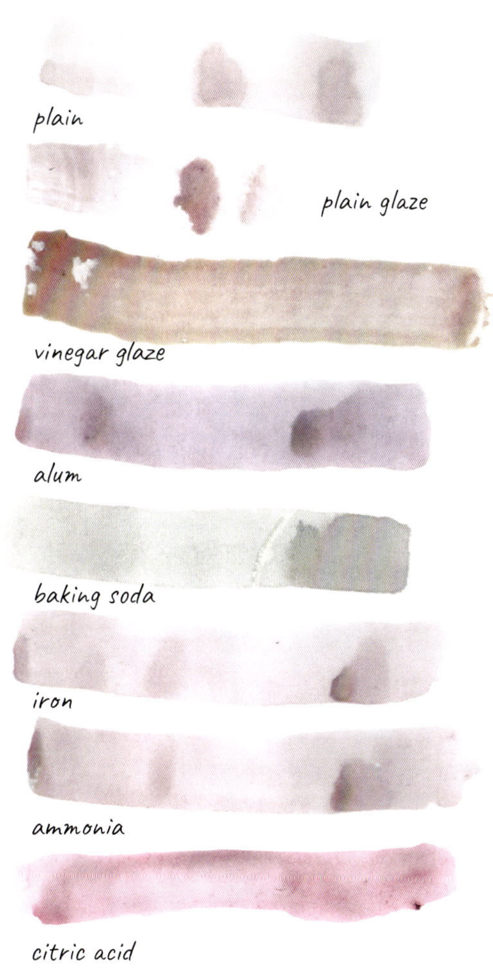

COLORS CREATED	red or purple with most mordants, gray with baking soda
PARTS USED FOR PIGMENT	ripe berries
PLANT TYPE	perennial
HARDINESS ZONE	4

1. Simmer for 10 minutes to make pigment or dye. Strain.
2. Simmer again to reduce liquid to desired color strength.

Note: Raspberry leaves make great eco-prints. The best red is created with citric acid.

ALNUS RUBRA

Red Alder

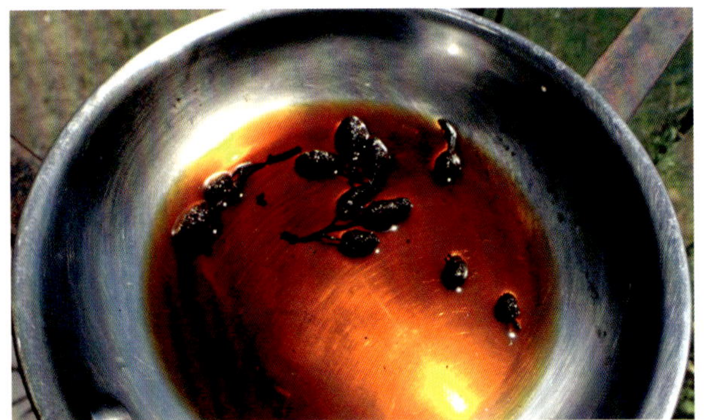

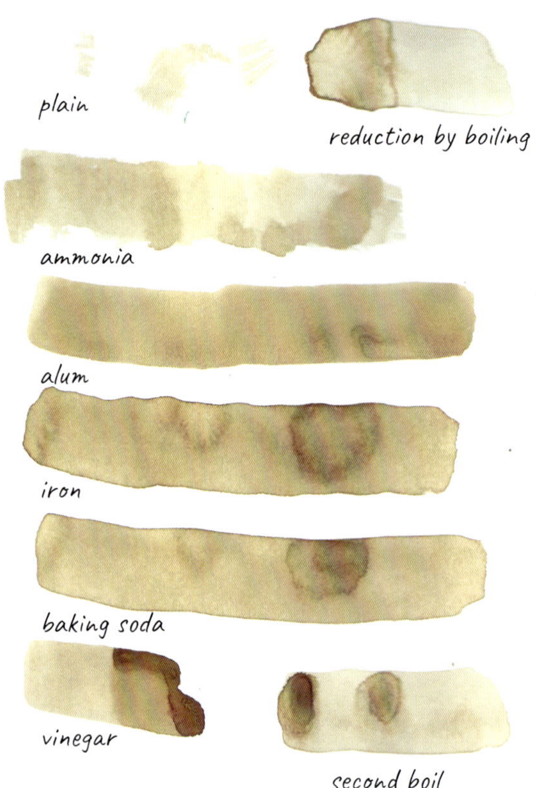

COLORS CREATED	tan, brown
PARTS USED FOR PIGMENT	fresh brown cones picked in summer
PLANT TYPE	tree
HARDINESS ZONE	6

1. Cook at a full boil (not a simmer) for 30 minutes to produce pigment or dye.

Notes: Alder makes such a good stain that it naturally stains other wood in nature.

AMARANTHUS CRUENTUS

Red Amaranth

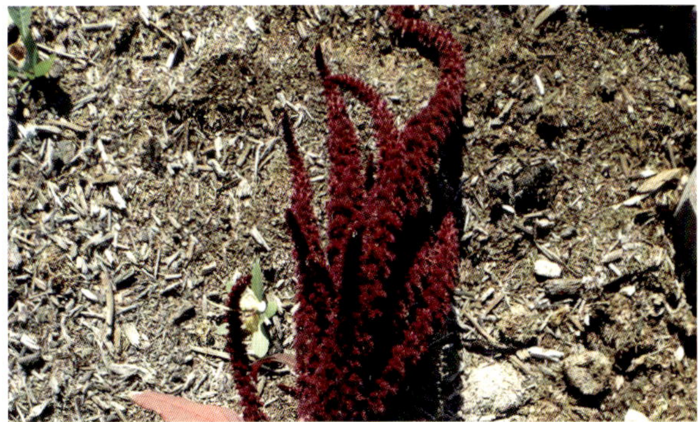

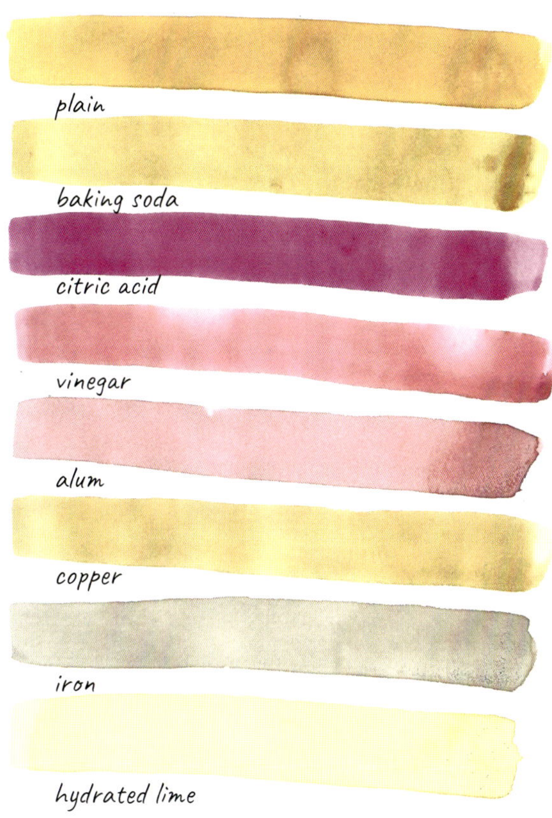

COLORS CREATED	orange; brown with baking soda or copper; red with citric acid, vinegar, or alum; gray with iron; yellow with hydrated lime
PARTS USED FOR PIGMENT	seed stalks, leaves, stems
PLANT TYPE	annual
SEEDING	Plant directly outside in spring or autumn. Seeds available at SeedRenaissance.com.

1. Simmer for 10 minutes to make pigment or dye. Strain.
2. Simmer again to reduce liquid to desired color strength.

Notes: This variety of amaranth, which is purple, is said to have been cultivated by the Hopi tribe for dye for thousands of years, beginning long before the tribe emigrated to present day Arizona. Apparently, they soaked the grain overnight to use in piki wafer bread, which turned the bread pink. Of course, they also used it for dye and paint. The pigment in the plant seems to sit over the chlorophyll because when the plant is cooked to release its dye, it turns green. This plant also makes an excellent and easy red lake pigment of alum; see the lake pigment recipes in this book (see page 54–55).

RHEUM SPECIES

Rhubarb

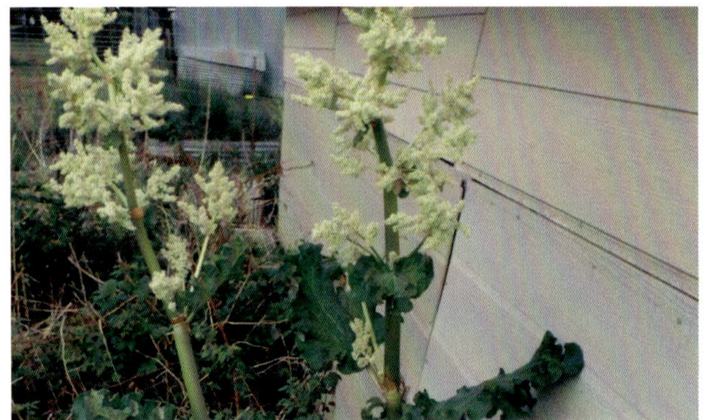

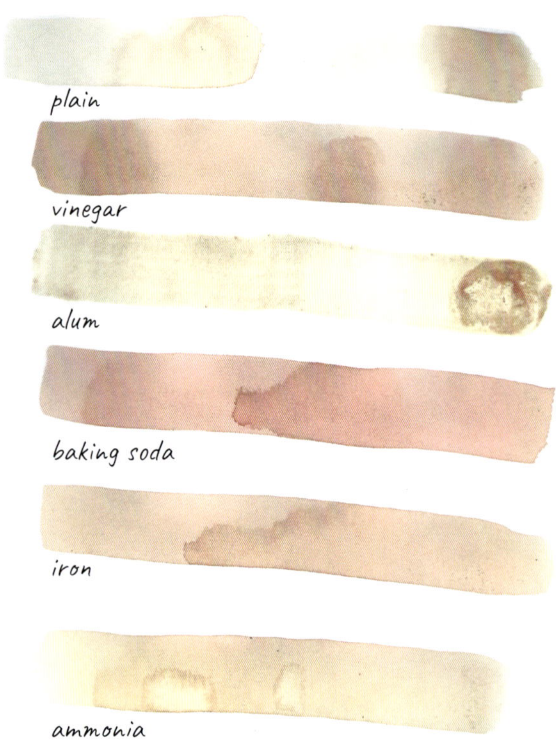

COLORS CREATED	pink with baking soda
PARTS USED FOR PIGMENT	root powder
PLANT TYPE	perennial
HARDINESS ZONE	6

1. Simmer for 10 minutes to make pigment or dye. Strain.
2. Simmer again to reduce liquid to desired color strength.

ASPALATHUS LINEARIS

Rooibos

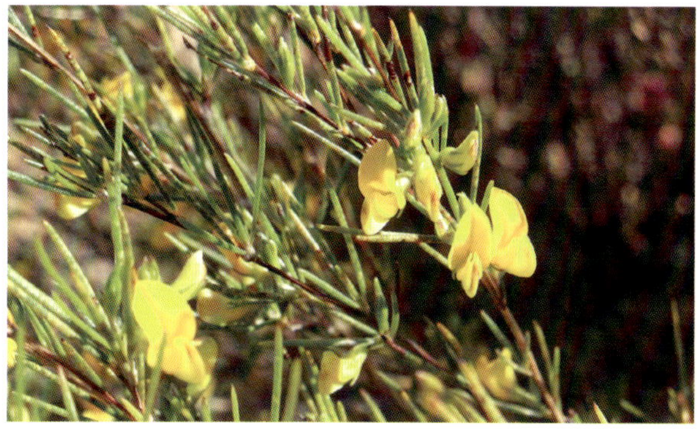

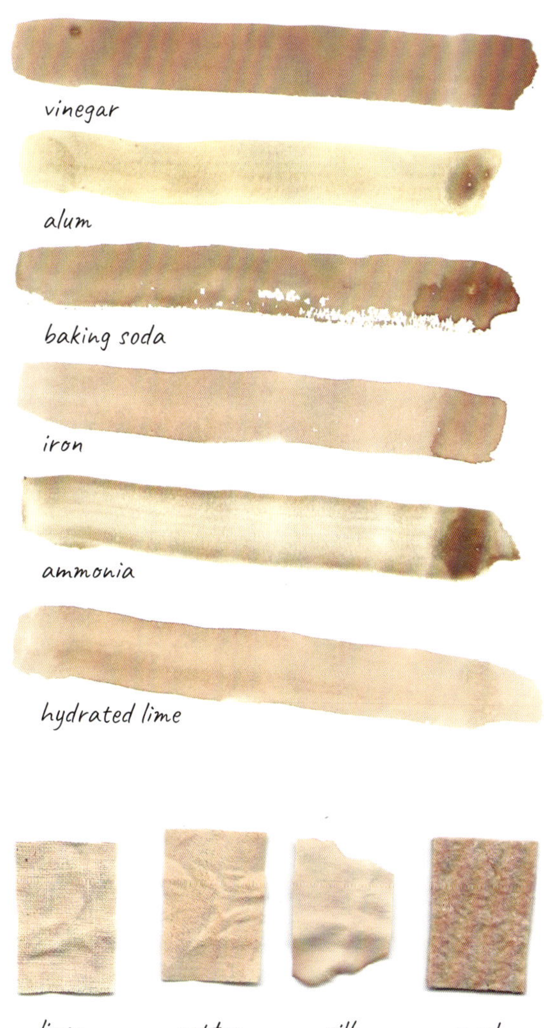

COLORS CREATED	brown
PARTS USED FOR PIGMENT	rooibos tea bags (leaves)
PLANT TYPE	shrub native to South Africa
HARDINESS ZONE	8

1. Make tea. Strain if necessary.
2. Simmer again to reduce liquid to desired color strength.

Notes: Rooibos has long been sold as a caffeine-free alternative to traditional tea and touted for its health benefits.

ROSA SPECIES

Roses

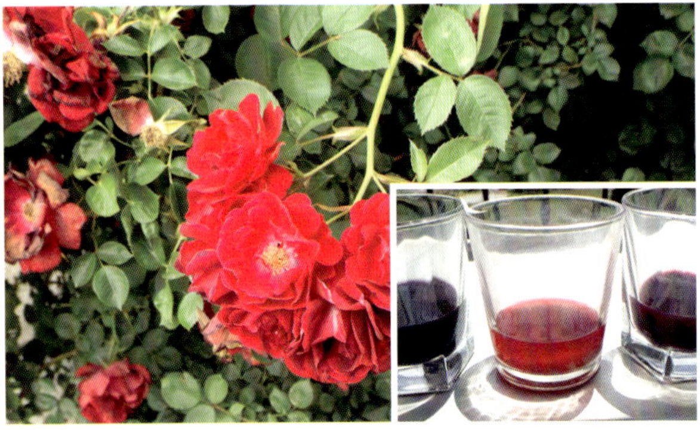

COLORS CREATED	red, pink, peach, yellow, green, brown, black (varies by petal color)
PARTS USED FOR PIGMENT	petals
PLANT TYPE	perennial
HARDINESS ZONE	varies

1. Simmer for 10 minutes to make pigment or dye. Strain.
2. Simmer again to reduce liquid to desired color strength.

Notes: Most plant material does not have to be stirred while it is boiling, but roses do. Roses lose their color by blanching wherever they are in direct contact with the boiling water, and the petals float, so stirring every couple of minutes makes sure you get all the color out of the petals. Combine with citric acid to get the best red colors. Rose leaves make excellent eco-prints.

RED ROSE

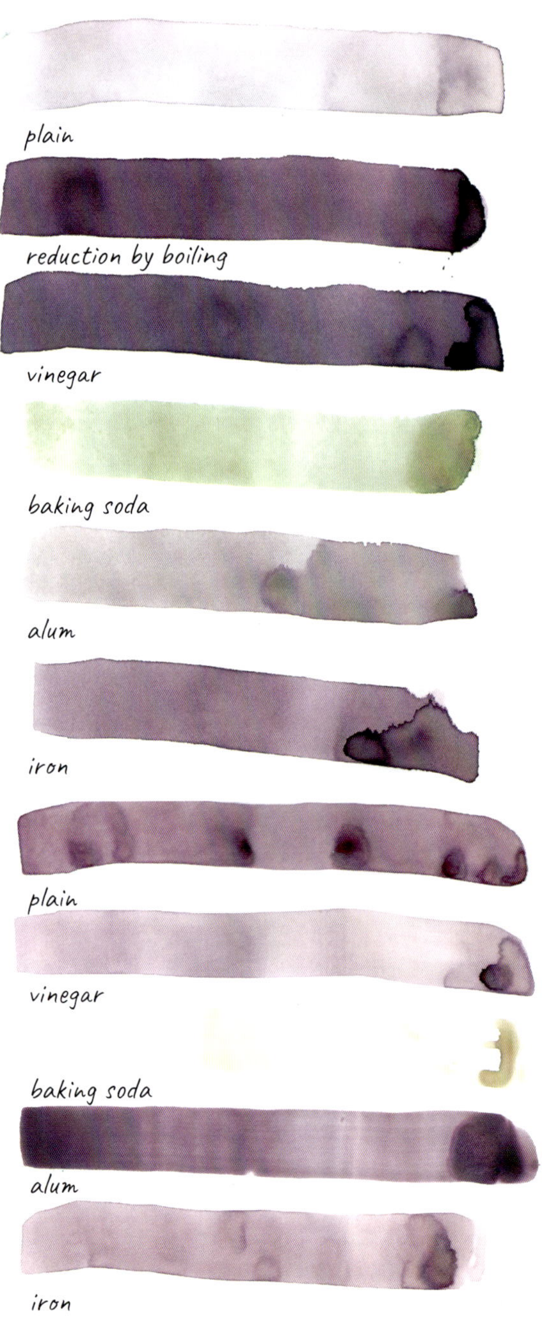

COPPER ROSE

COLD BLEND WITH CITRIC ACID

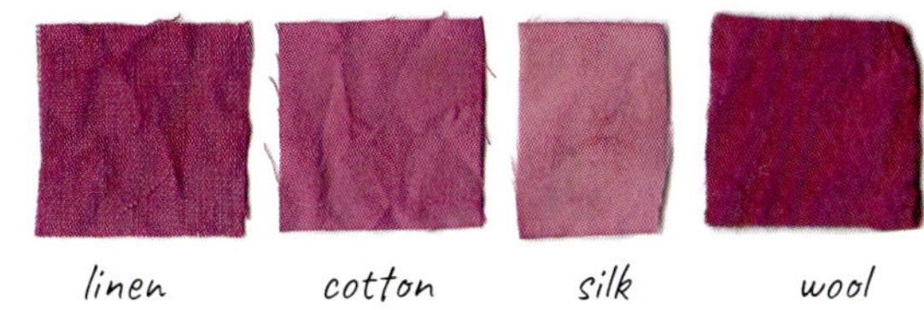

BOILED WITH CITRIC ACID

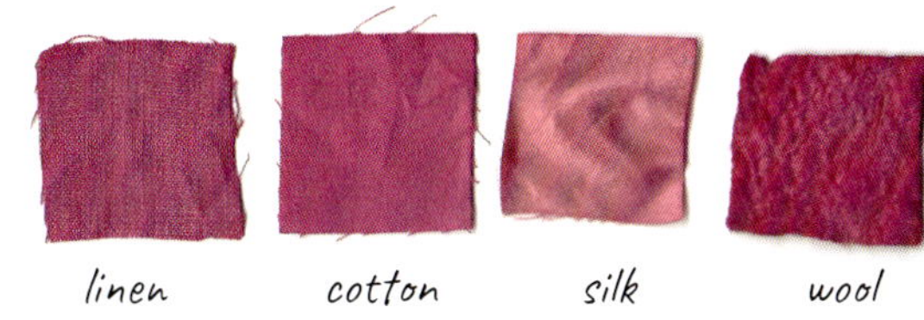

COLD BLEND WITH BAKING SODA

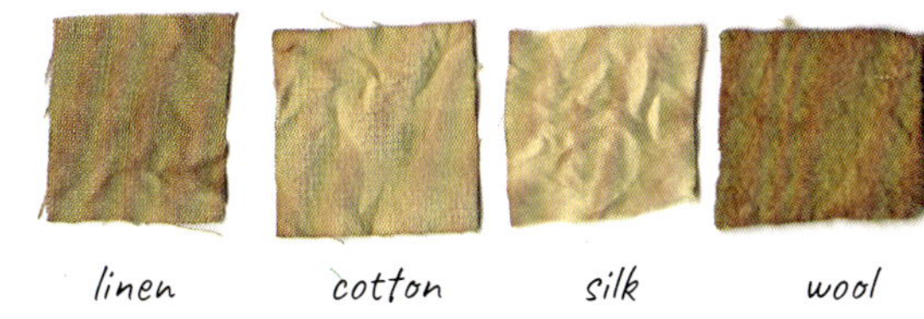

PLAIN COLD BLEND

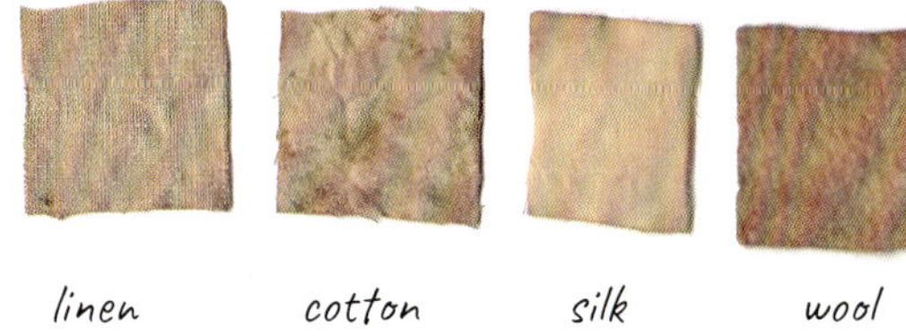

FRESH PRESSED RED PETALS

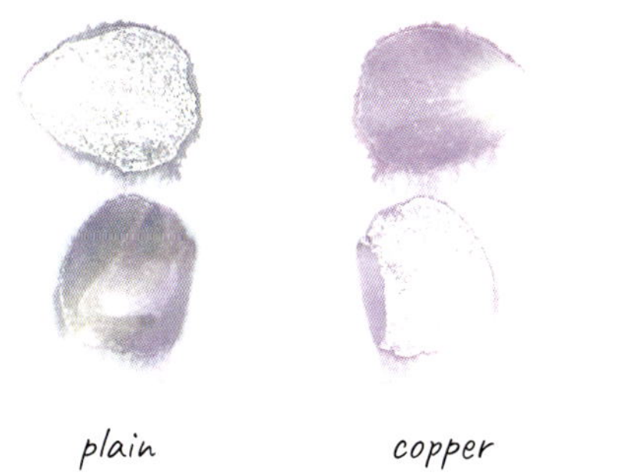

ROSE OF SHARON PETALS ONLY

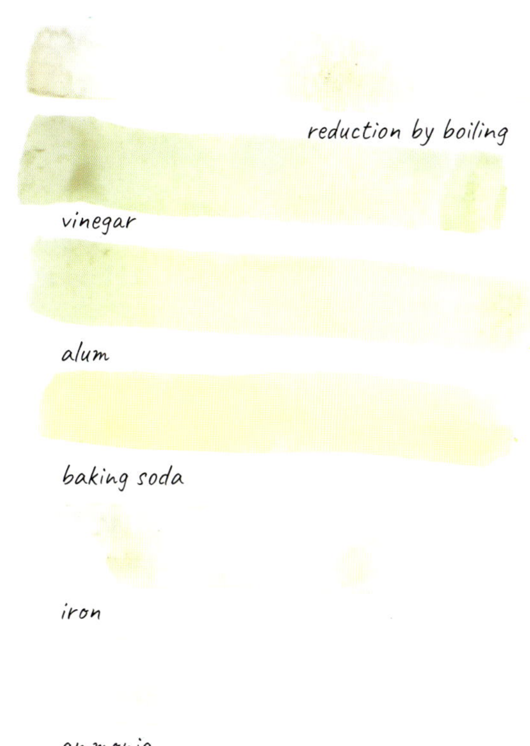

ROSE HIPS

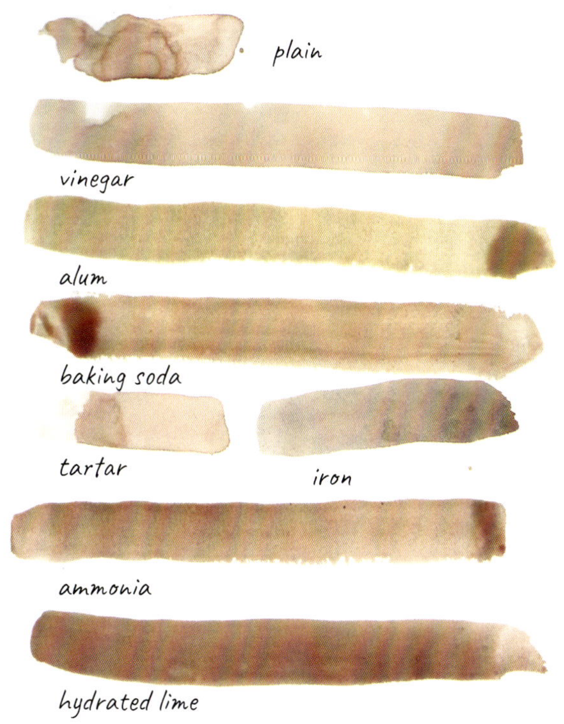

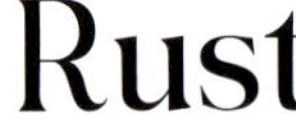

Rust

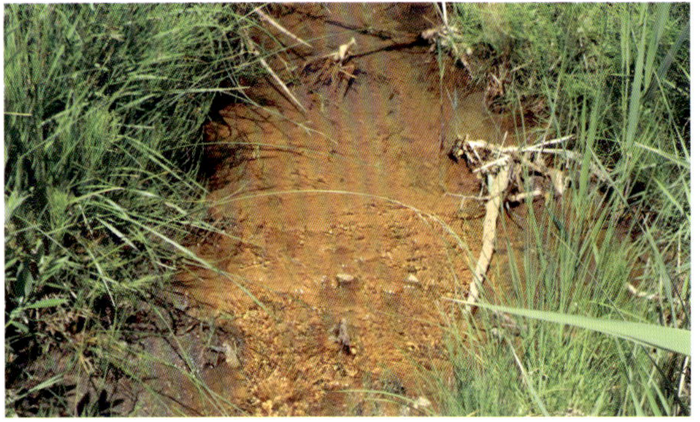

COLORS CREATED	red
PARTS USED FOR PIGMENT	any iron source, such as rusty nails

1. Put nails in a jar, without a lid, cover with water, and add a splash of vinegar and wait a few days.
2. If you want to create rust quickly, add a splash of hydrogen peroxide and wait a few hours. Mull the rust in a little water using a stone or glass muller.

Notes: Although it is not strictly botanical, rust is one of the most important historic sources of dye and pigment and is still widely used today. Like madder root, iron oxides (rust) are resistant to fading in ultraviolet light, which makes it ideal for exterior lightfast colors. Many Native American rock art paintings made with iron oxide paint still have not faded centuries later! Natural rust deposits exist widely in nature and were collected and used by the Native Americans for color. Look for natural rust deposits on roadsides. Iron rust is also an essential ingredient in red pottery paint. See pottery paint recipes in this book (see page 74).

RUBUS SPECTABILIS

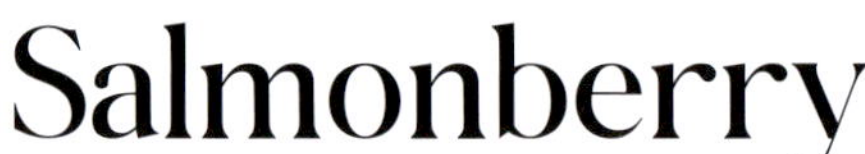

Salmonberry

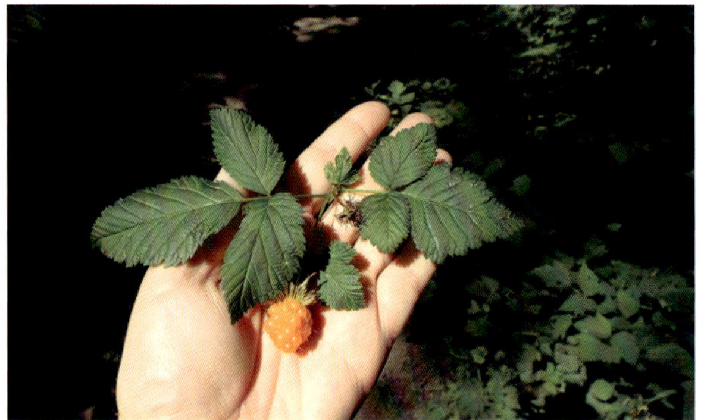

COLORS CREATED	salmon
PARTS USED FOR PIGMENT	ripe berries
PLANT TYPE	perennial
HARDINESS ZONE	5

1. Simmer for 10 minutes to make pigment or dye. Strain.
2. Simmer again to reduce liquid to desired color strength.

Notes: Paint and pigment of this berry are thick and unwieldy, so are best used as children's finger paints.

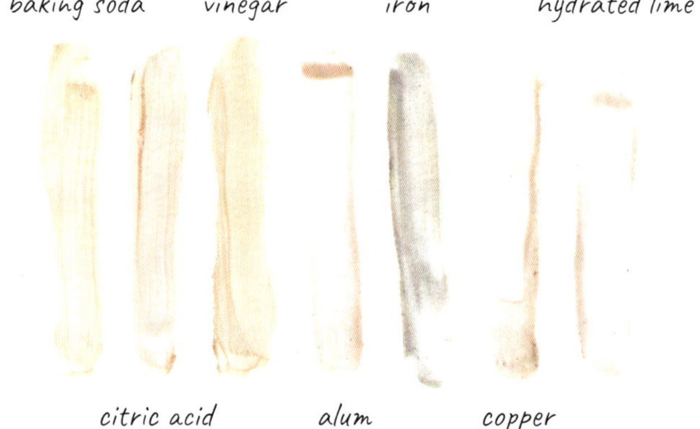

TRAGOPOGON SPECIES

Salsify

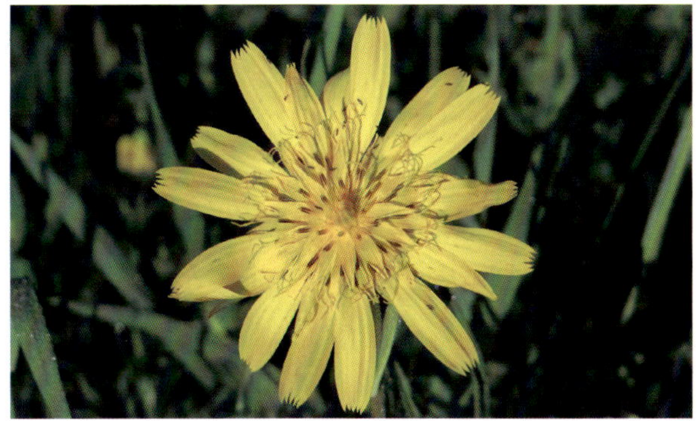

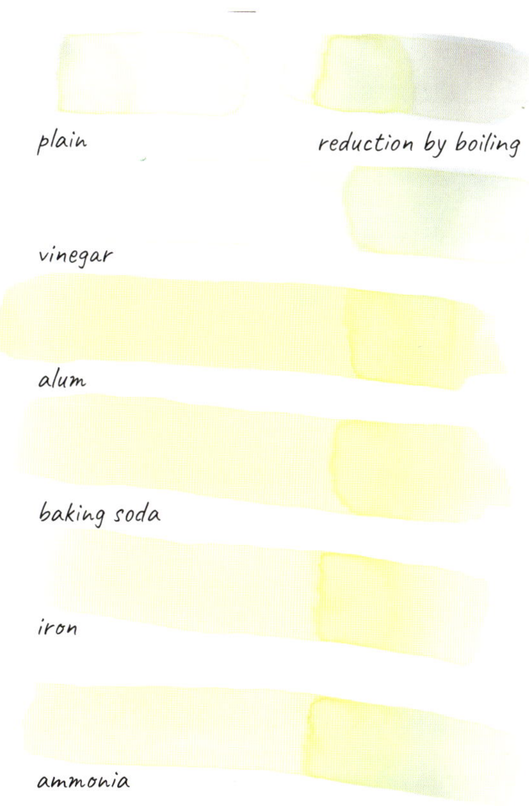

COLORS CREATED	yellow with most mordants
PARTS USED FOR PIGMENT	flowers
PLANT TYPE	perennial
HARDINESS ZONE	5

1. Simmer for 15 minutes to make pigment or dye. Strain.
2. Simmer again to reduce liquid to desired color strength.

SALVIA SPECIES

Salvias and Sages

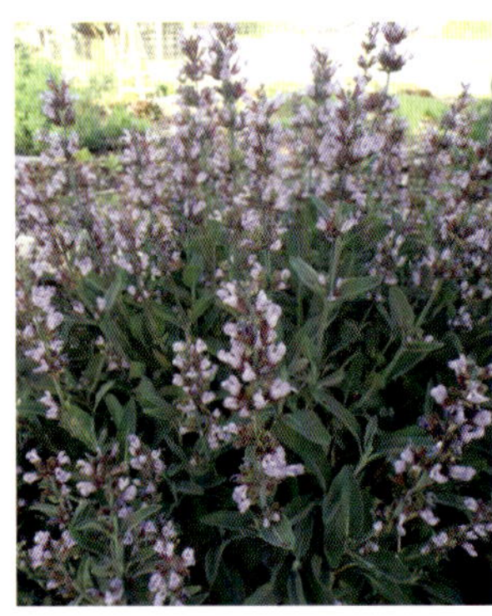

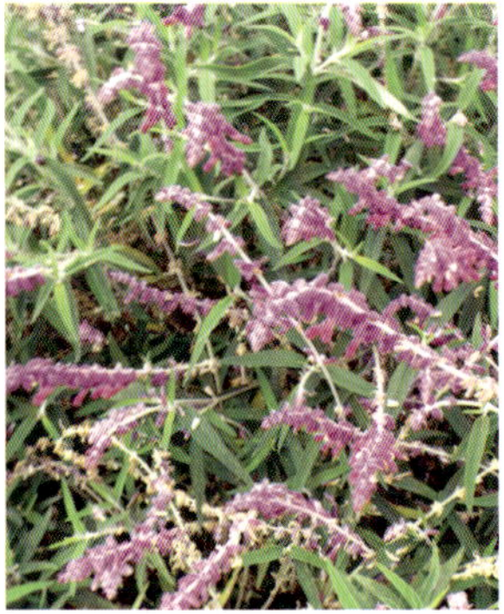

COLORS CREATED	yellow with most mordants, brown with baking soda, blue from uncooked *Salvia leucantha*
PARTS USED FOR PIGMENT	purple flower stems
PLANT TYPE	perennial
SEEDING	Plant directly outside in spring or autumn. Seeds available at SeedRenaissance.com.

1. Simmer for 15 minutes to make pigment or dye. Strain.
2. Simmer again to reduce liquid to desired color strength.

CLARY SAGE

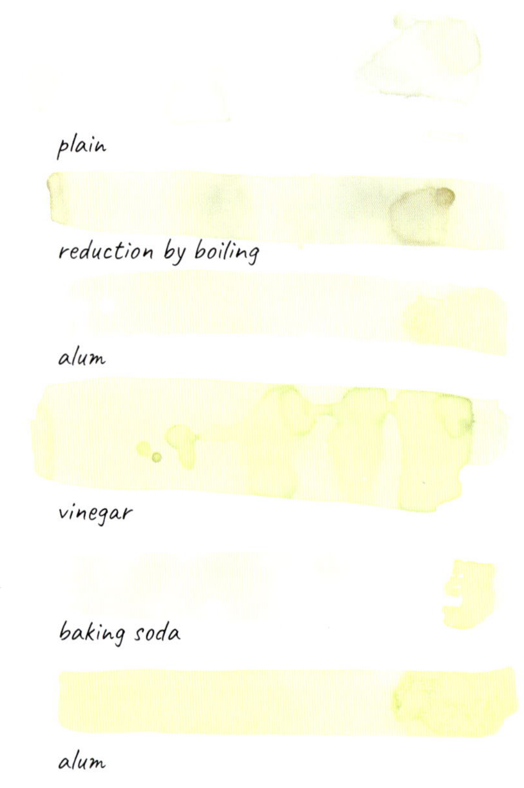

FRESH PRESSED

PTEROCARPUS SPECIES

Sandalwood

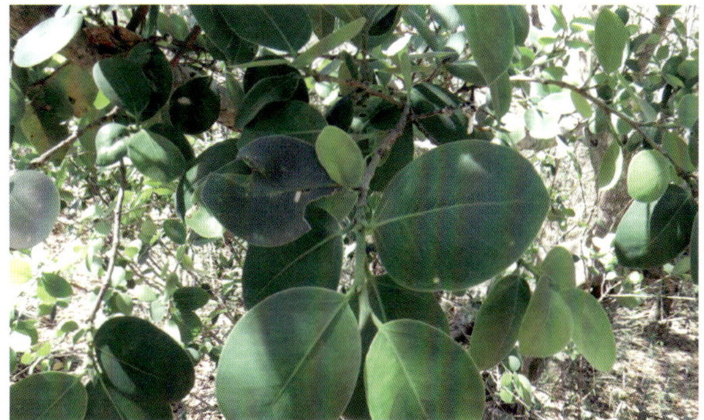

COLORS CREATED	red with most mordants, brown with alum
PARTS USED FOR PIGMENT	wood shavings extracted in alcohol
PLANT TYPE	tree

1. Simmer for 20 minutes to make pigment or dye. Strain.
2. Simmer again to reduce liquid to desired color strength.

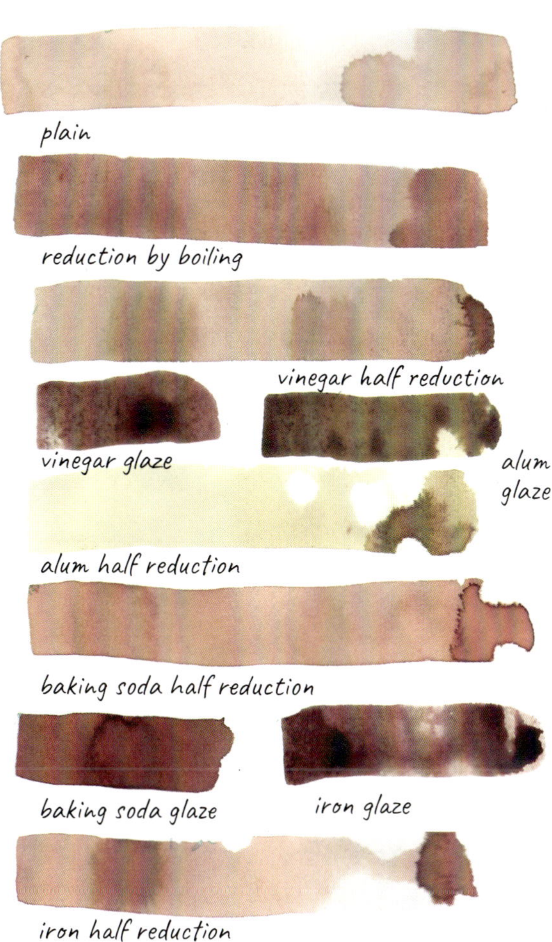

SCUTELLARIA BAICALENSIS

Skullcap Baikal

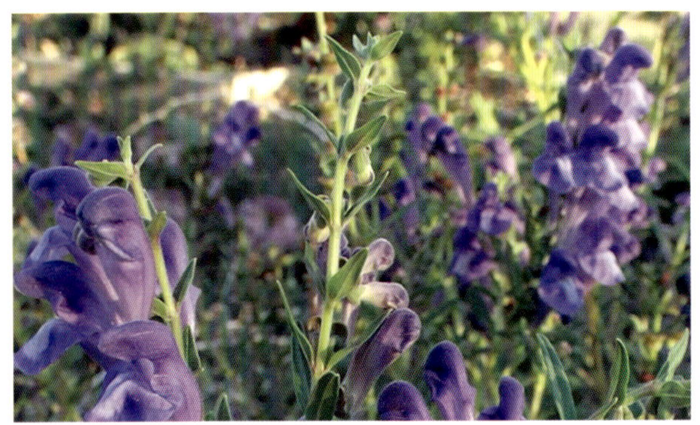

COLORS CREATED	blue and green when uncooked, yellow when cooked
PARTS USED FOR PIGMENT	purple petals only (no sepals)
PLANT TYPE	perennial
HARDINESS ZONE	4
SEEDING	Plant directly outside in spring or autumn. Seeds available at SeedRenaissance.com.

1. Best used fresh and uncooked as pigment. For yellow, simmer for 15 minutes to make pigment or dye. Strain.
2. Simmer again to reduce liquid to desired color strength.

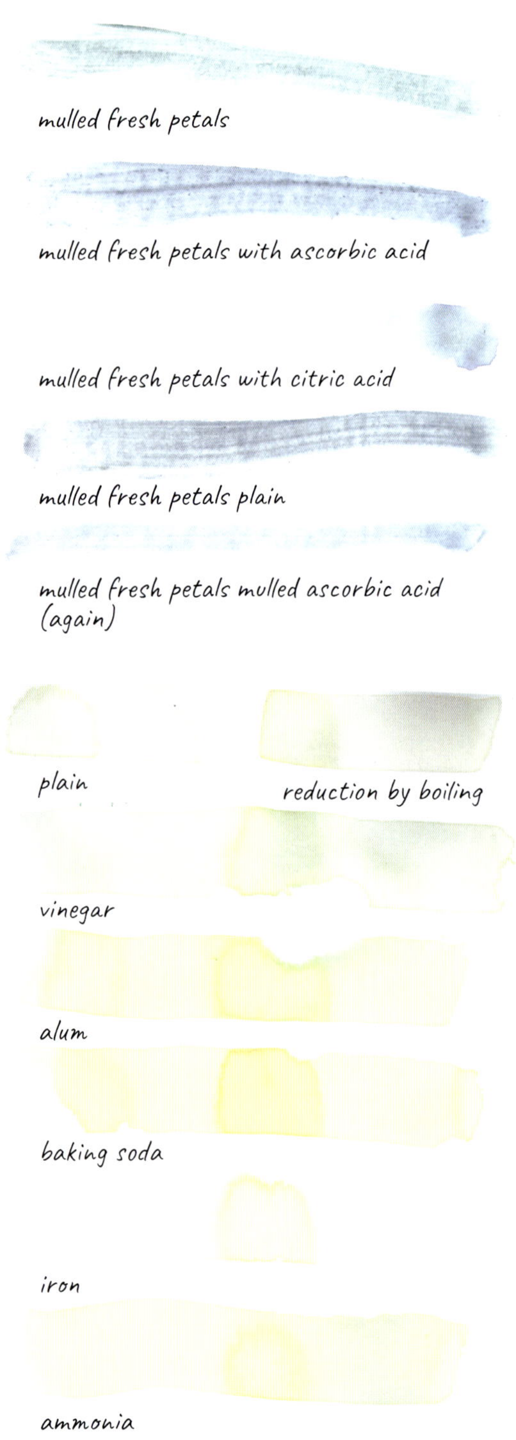

AMELANCHIER SPECIES

Serviceberry

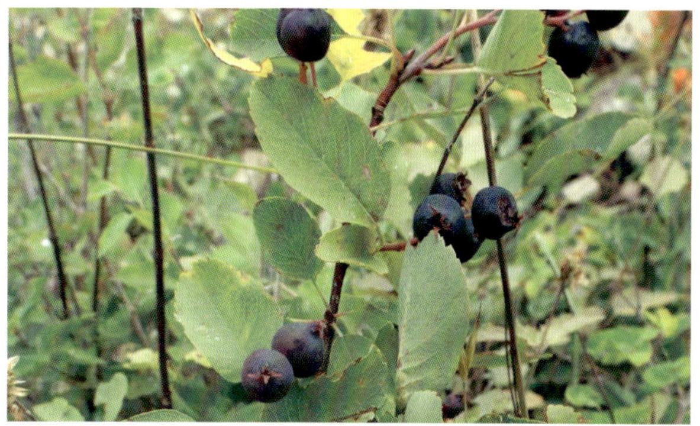

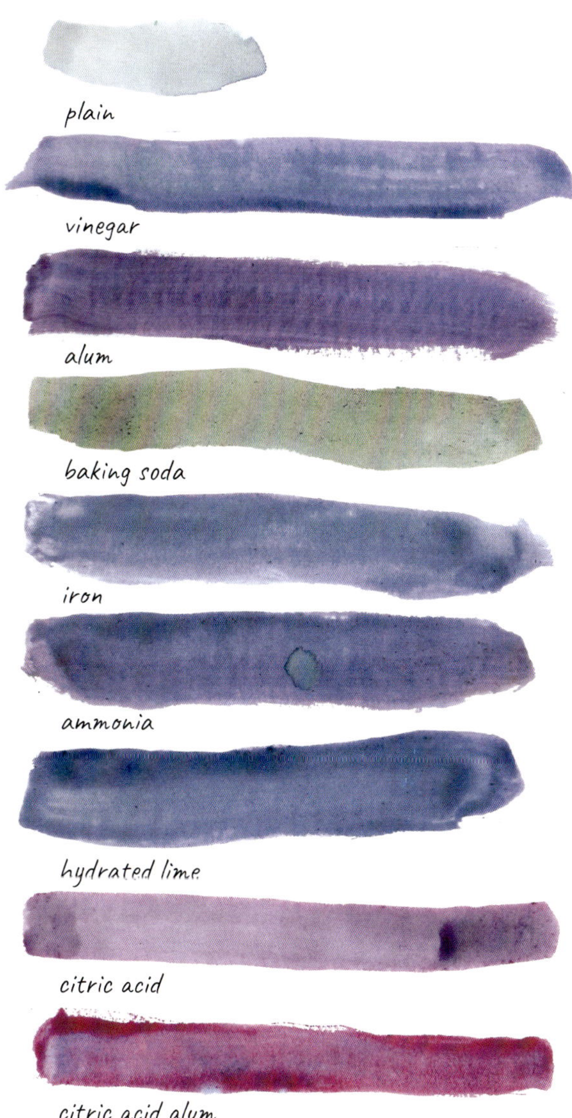

COLORS CREATED	blue with alum or hydrated lime, purple with citric acid, red with citric acid and alum, green with baking soda
PARTS USED FOR PIGMENT	mashed berries
PLANT TYPE	perennial
HARDINESS ZONE	4
SEEDING	Plant directly outside in spring or autumn. Seeds available at SeedRenaissance.com.

1. Simmer for 20 minutes to make pigment or dye. Strain.
2. Simmer again to reduce liquid to desired color strength.

Notes: To get the colors you see here, you need to pick serviceberries at peak ripeness. Old berries create blue with alum and brown with most other mordants. These are my favorite wild berries for eating and I grow them in my yard. The flavor is not to be missed. I love to eat these while hiking in autumn.

SPINACIA OLERACEA

Spinach

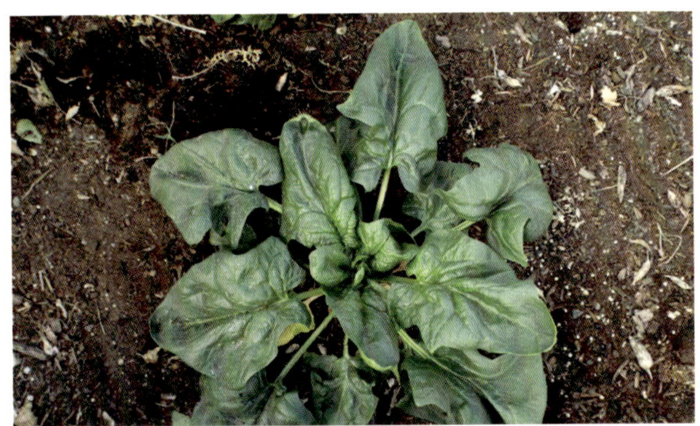

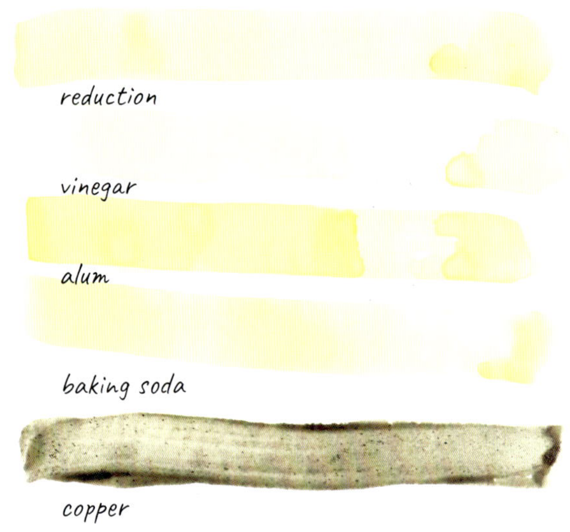

COLORS CREATED	green when uncooked, yellow when cooked
PARTS USED FOR PIGMENT	leaves
PLANT TYPE	annual
HARDINESS ZONE	Seeds available at SeedRenaissance.com.

1. Simmer for 15 minutes to make pigment or dye. Strain.
2. Simmer again to reduce liquid to desired color strength.

FRESH PRESSED LEAVES

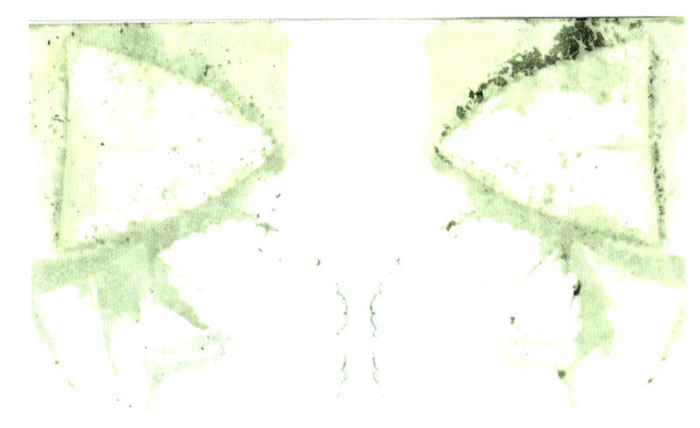

SPIRAEA JAPONICA

Spirea

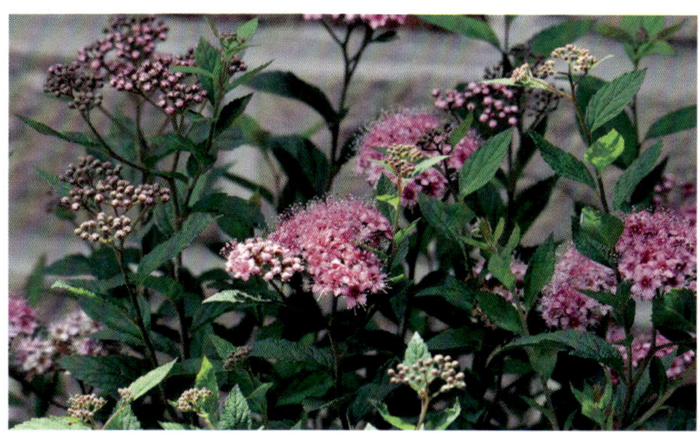

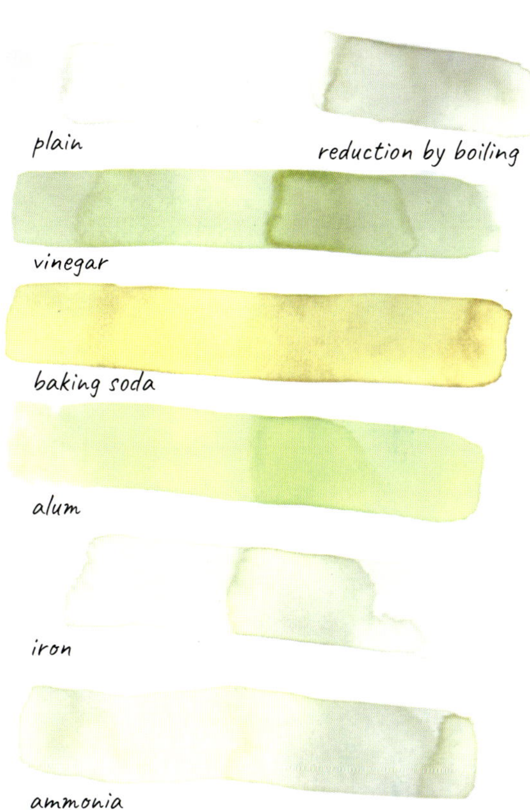

COLORS CREATED	green with vinegar or alum, yellow with baking soda
PARTS USED FOR PIGMENT	flower heads with no leaves
PLANT TYPE	perennial
HARDINESS ZONE	3

1. Simmer for 15 minutes to make pigment or dye. Strain.
2. Simmer again to reduce liquid to desired color strength.

CUCURBITA SPECIES

Squash

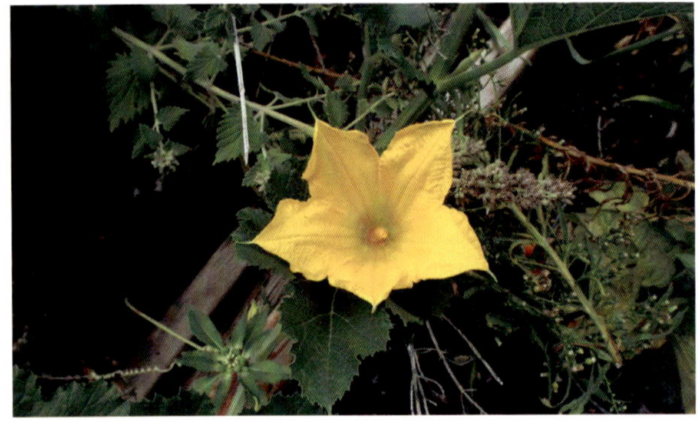

COLORS CREATED	yellow
PARTS USED FOR PIGMENT	flower heads with no leaves
PLANT TYPE	perennial
HARDINESS ZONE	3

1. The brightest yellow comes when used uncooked. To cook, simmer for 10 minutes to make pigment or dye. Strain.
2. Simmer again to reduce liquid to desired color strength.

St. John's Wort (Various Species)

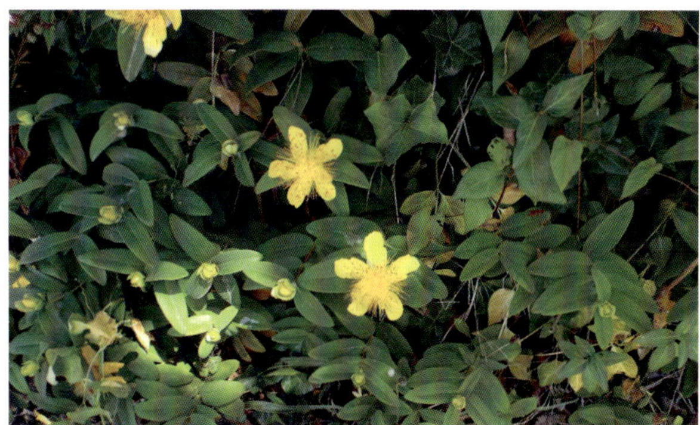

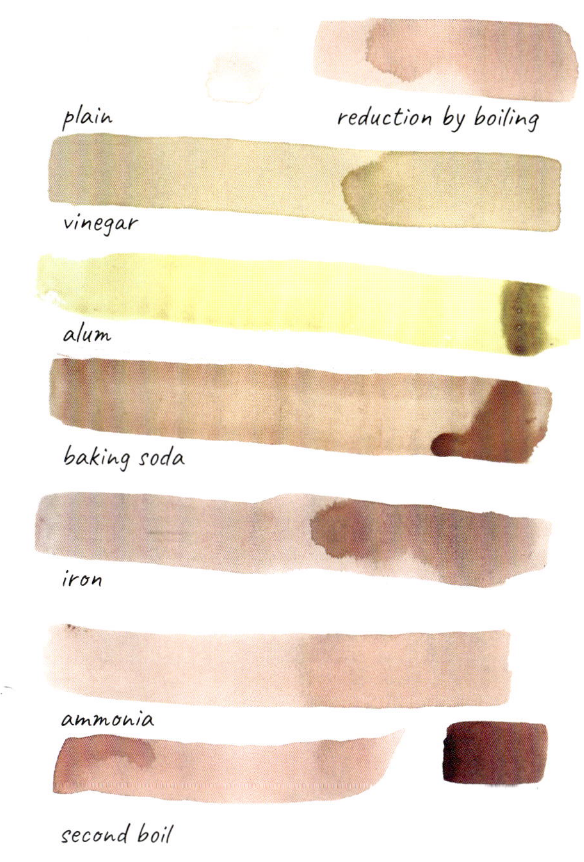

COLORS CREATED	red with most mordants, yellow with alum, brown with vinegar
PARTS USED FOR PIGMENT	flowering tops, fresh or dried
PLANT TYPE	perennial
HARDINESS ZONE	4

1. Simmer for 20 minutes to make pigment or dye. Strain.
2. Simmer again to reduce liquid to desired color strength.

Notes: When used fresh, the flowers of Greater St. John's wort make an orange-yellow.

FRESH PRESSED YELLOW FLOWERS

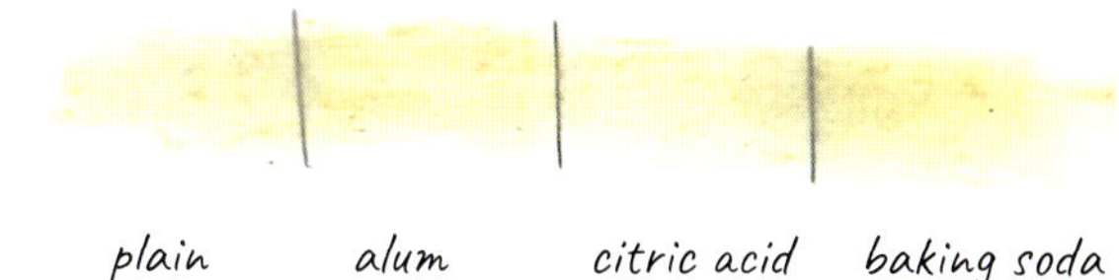

MATTHIOLA INCANA

Stock

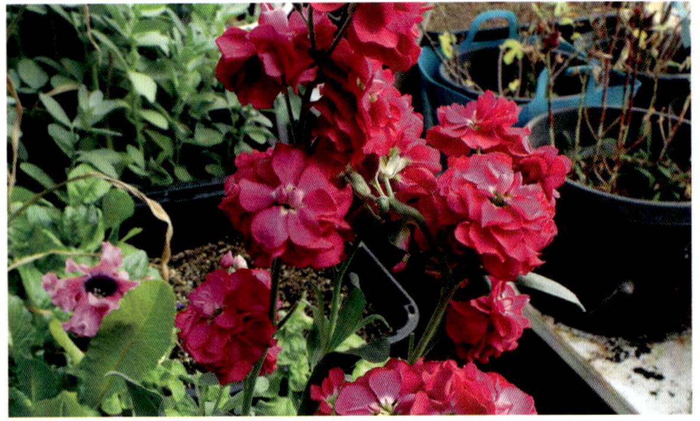

COLORS CREATED	red, green, purple
PARTS USED FOR PIGMENT	red or purple flowers
PLANT TYPE	annual

1. Unlike perhaps every other flower in the book, stock makes its color only when steeped or used fresh. To steep, pour boiling water over the flowers, just enough to cover them.

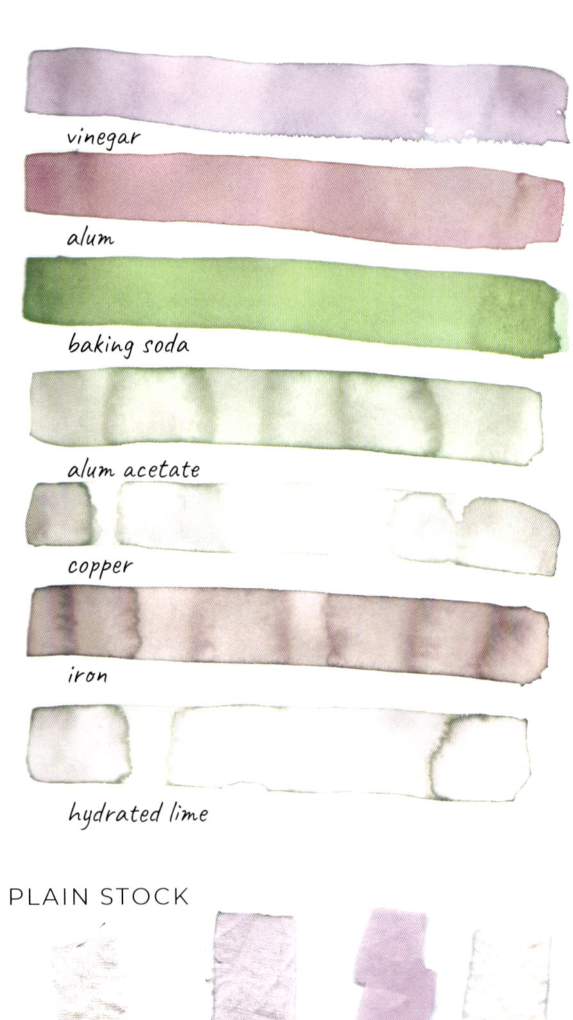

PLAIN STOCK

linen cotton silk wool

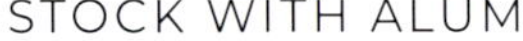

STOCK WITH ALUM

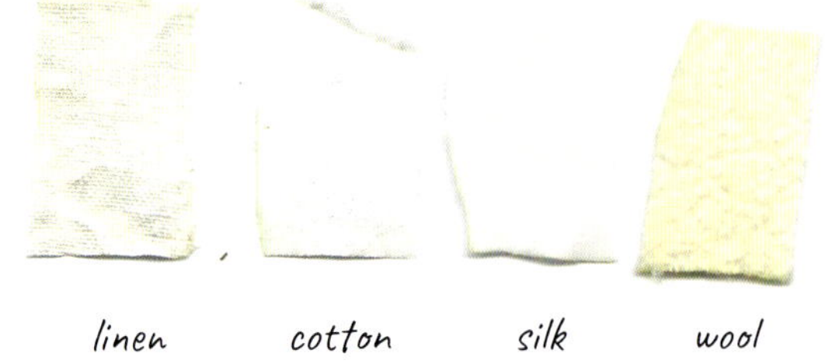

linen cotton silk wool

SEDUM SPECIES

Stonecrops

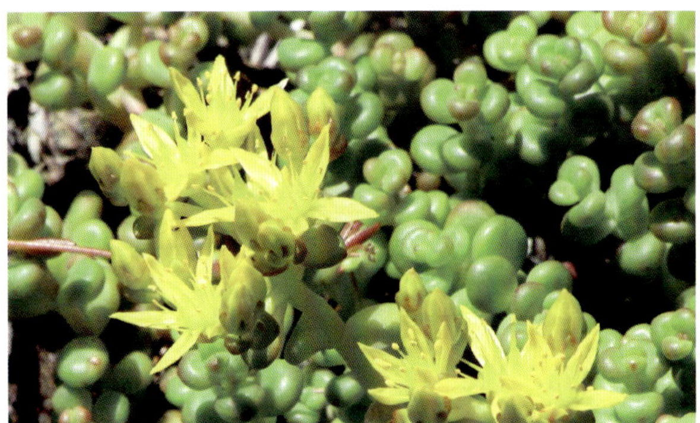

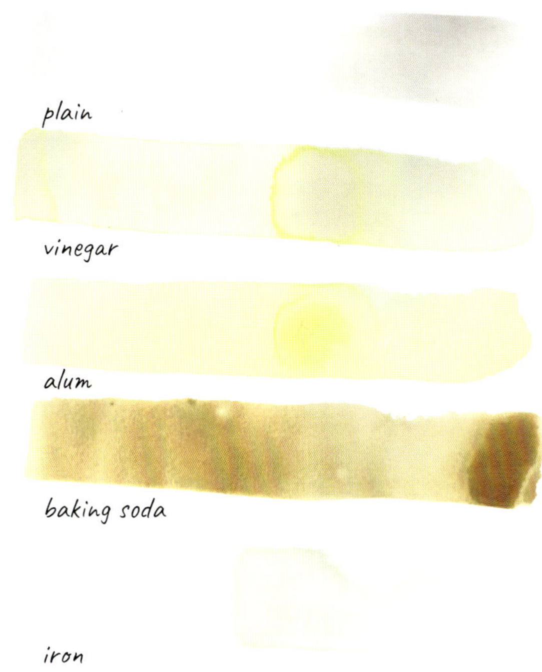

COLORS CREATED	yellow with alum, brown with baking soda
PARTS USED FOR PIGMENT	flowering stems
PLANT TYPE	perennial
HARDINESS ZONE	3

1. Simmer for 60 minutes to make pigment or dye. Strain.
2. Simmer again to reduce liquid to desired color strength.

Notes: There are easier ways to get these colors than to cook this for an hour.

FRAGARIA SPECIES

Strawberries

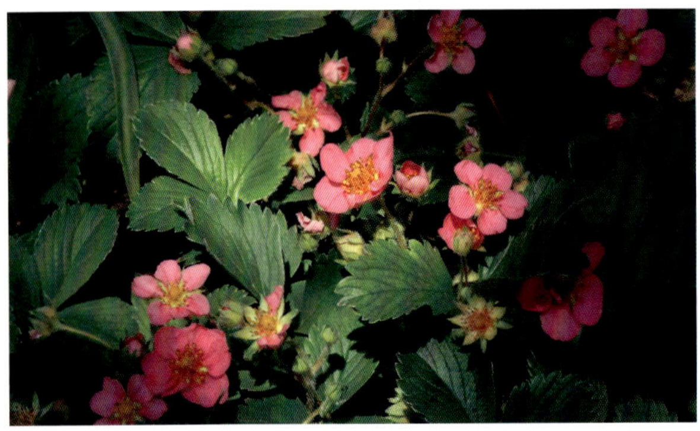

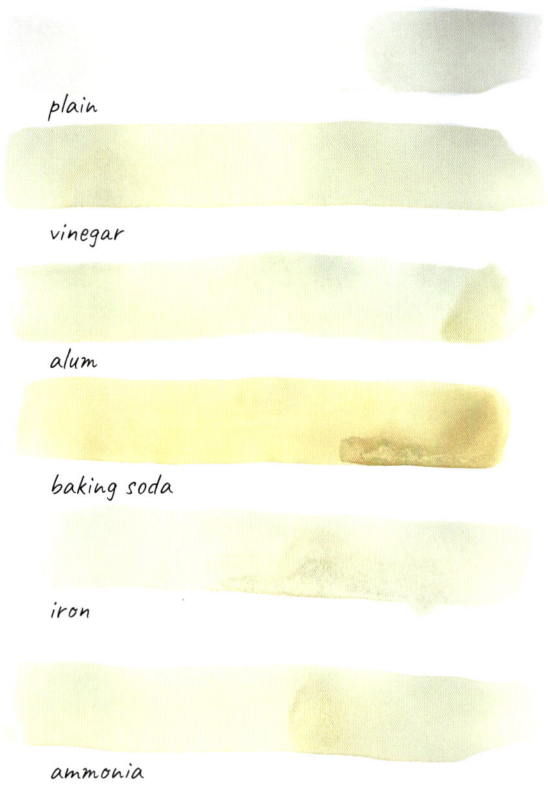

COLORS CREATED	pink, yellow
PARTS USED FOR PIGMENT	leaves, flowers
PLANT TYPE	garden berry and others

1. Fresh pressed leaves mordanted with iron make stunning eco-prints. Pink flowering strawberries like Gasana can be used fresh to make pink eco-prints.

Notes: The yellow flowers of False Wild Strawberries (*Potentilla indica*) make orange with baking soda. These flowers are often grown as perennial ground covers.

FRESH PRESSED LEAF WITH IRON

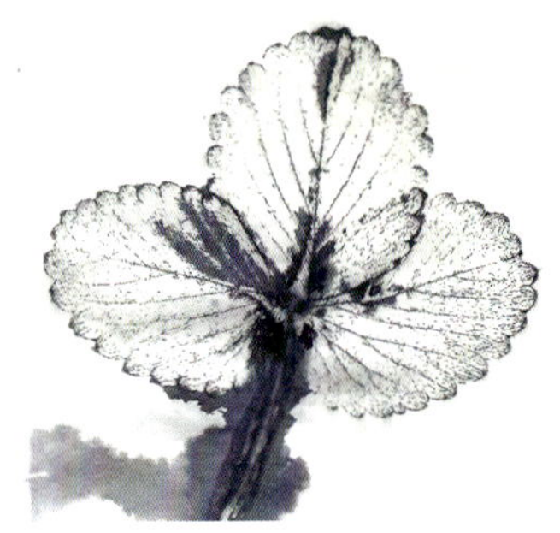

XEROCHRYSUM BRACTEATUM

Strawflowers

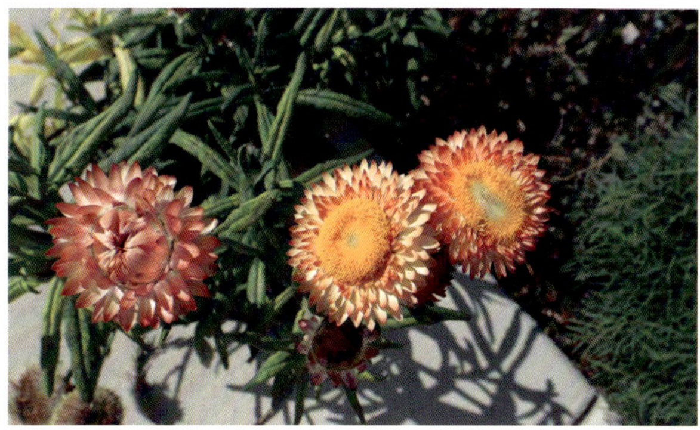

COLORS CREATED	yellow with most mordants
PARTS USED FOR PIGMENT	flowers
PLANT TYPE	landscape flower
HARDINESS ZONE	annual

1. Simmer for 10 minutes to make pigment or dye. Strain.
2. Simmer again to reduce liquid to desired color strength.

RHUS SPECIES

Sumac

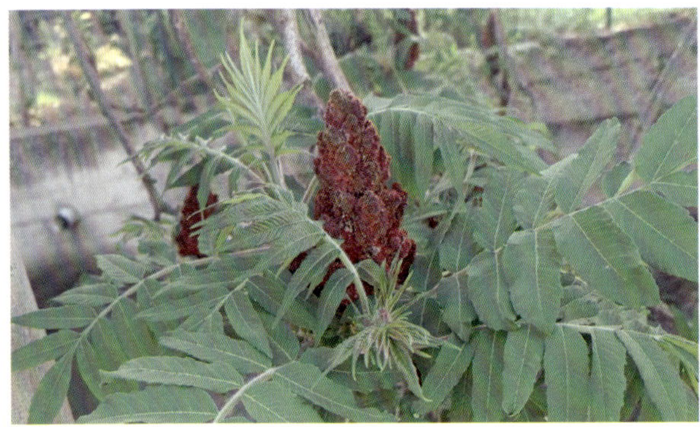

COLORS CREATED	red and brown from the fruit; green, yellow, and brown from the leaves
PARTS USED FOR PIGMENT	leaves, berries
PLANT TYPE	perennial
HARDINESS ZONE	hardy but varies by species

1. Simmer for 10 minutes to make pigment or dye. Strain.
2. Simmer again to reduce liquid to desired color strength.

SUMAC FRUIT

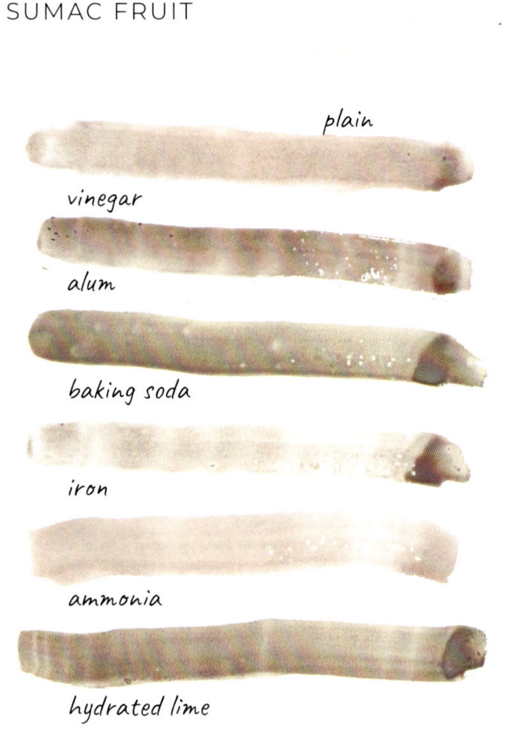

SUMAC LEAVES

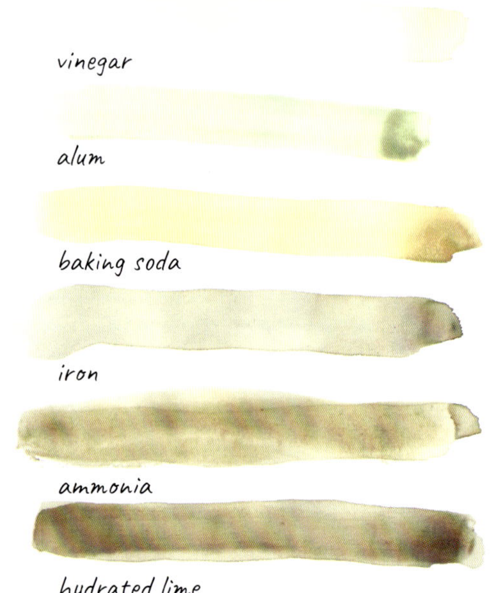

HELIANTHUS ANNUUS

Sunflower

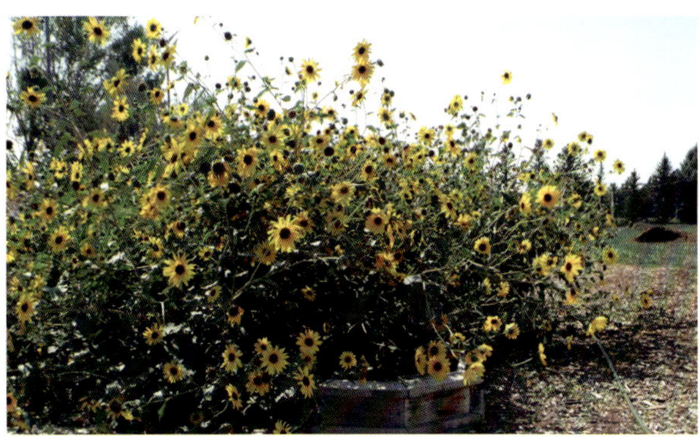

COLORS CREATED	yellow, brown, black
PARTS USED FOR PIGMENT	petals, leaves, stems, fresh or dried
PLANT TYPE	self-seeding annual
HARDINESS ZONE	4

1. Simmer petals for 10 minutes to make pigment or dye. Strain.
2. Simmer again to reduce liquid to desired color strength.

Special Use: Pottery paint. One of only a few herbs that can be used to create permanent pottery paint that withstands 1,800-degree kiln temperatures. Does not scrub off when used on greenware or bisque pottery but must be used in combination with other ingredients. To create an emulsion, cover clean aerial parts with water in a pan and simmer on the lowest temperature, lid off, for at least 1 hour. Strain and discard plant matter. Continue to simmer the strained liquid until nothing is left in the pan but a thick liquid.

Notes: Tolerant of drought and alkaline soils. Alum, baking soda, and ammonia make a strong bright yellow. Iron makes a dirty yellow. After the yellow petals were processed, they appeared to still be rich in color and ready for a second boil in fresh water, but a second boil produced no color and the petals began to disintegrate.

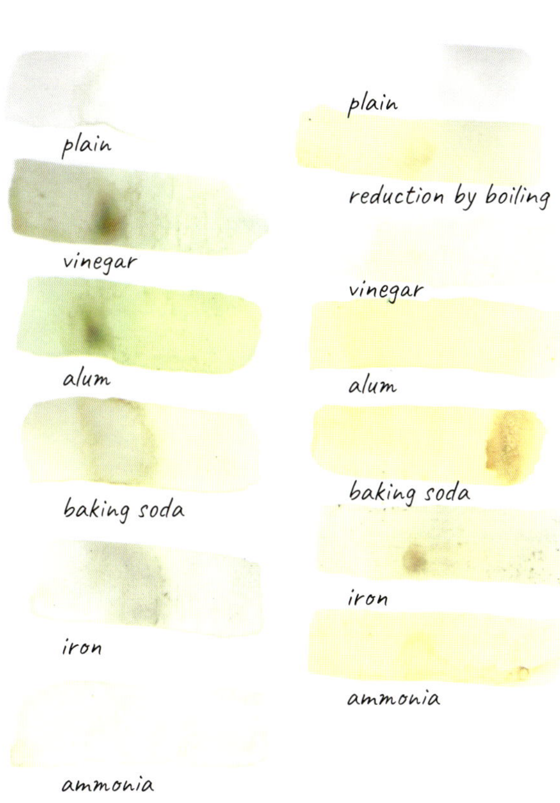

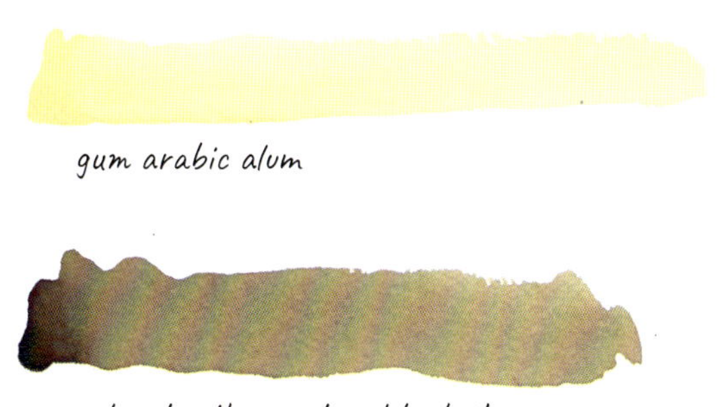

TANACETUM VULGARE

Tansy

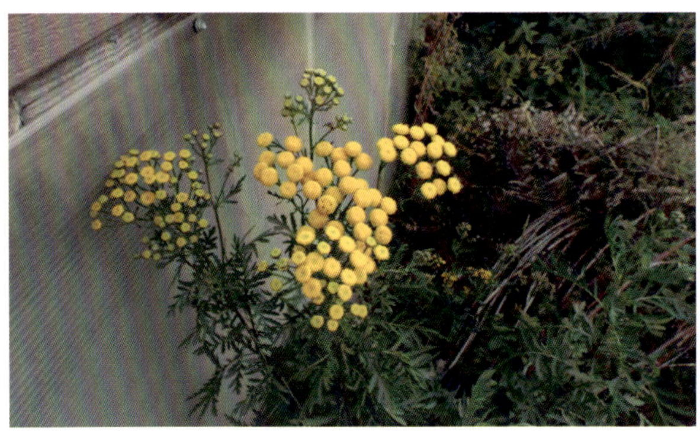

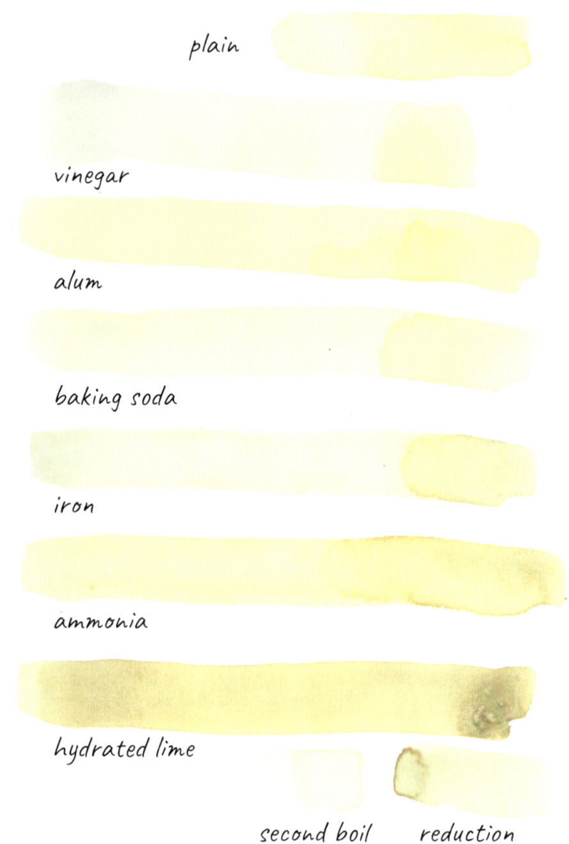

COLORS CREATED	green when pressed fresh and uncooked, yellow when cooked
PARTS USED FOR PIGMENT	flowers, leaves
PLANT TYPE	perennial
HARDINESS ZONE	4
SEEDING	Seeds available at SeedRenaissance.com.

1. Simmer for 10 minutes to make pigment or dye. Strain.
2. Simmer again to reduce liquid to desired color strength.

Notes: Tansy leaves make excellent eco-prints.

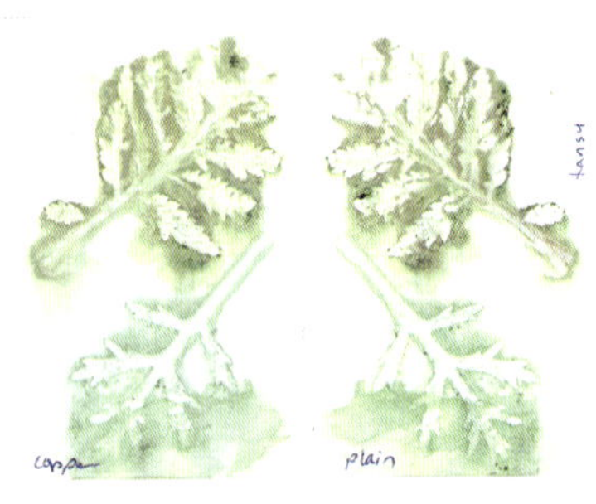

DRIED TANSY

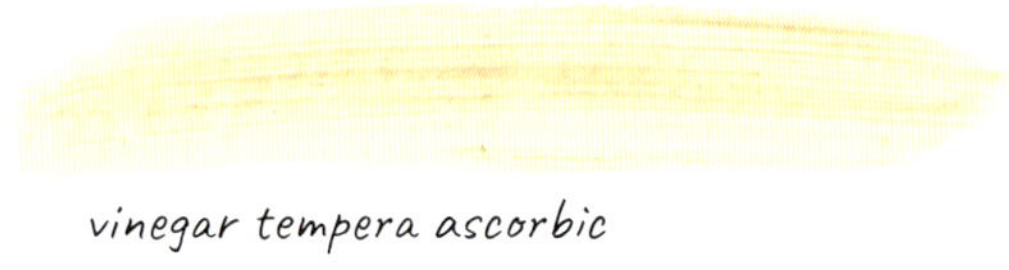

DIPSACUS FULLONUM

Teasel

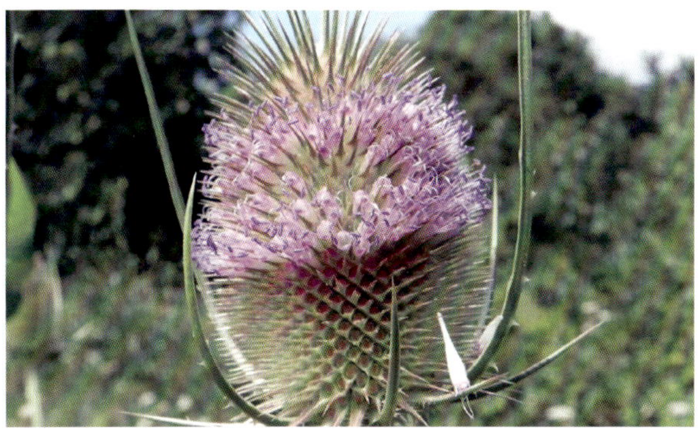

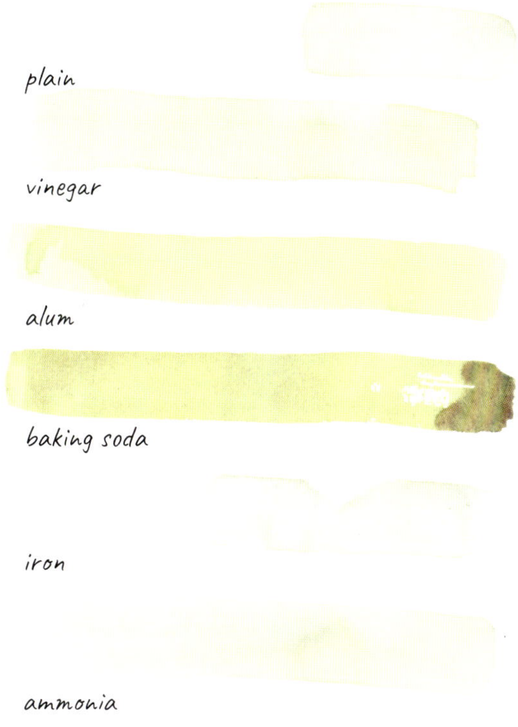

COLORS CREATED	yellow with alum
PARTS USED FOR PIGMENT	flowering coneheads
PLANT TYPE	biennial
HARDINESS ZONE	4

1. Simmer for 10 minutes to make pigment or dye. Strain.
2. Simmer again to reduce liquid to desired color strength.

Notes: Flowering coneheads are spiky and large. To boil them, I had to turn them in the pan so all the flowers could be cooked without using excess water. Flowers are tiny and lavender.

RUBUS PARVIFLORUS

Thimbleberry

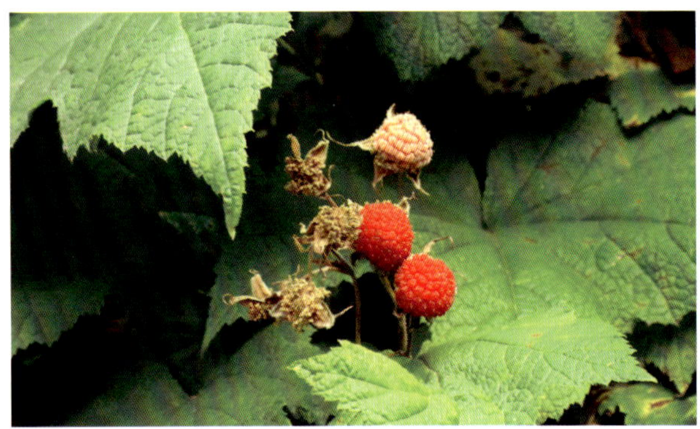

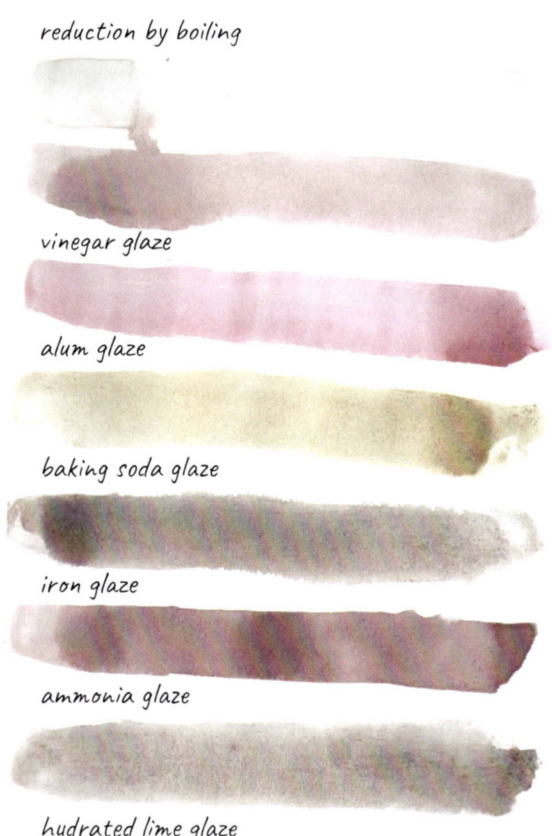

COLORS CREATED	red, brown
PARTS USED FOR PIGMENT	ripe berries
PLANT TYPE	perennial
HARDINESS ZONE	3
SEEDING	Plant directly outside in spring or autumn. Seeds available at SeedRenaissance.com.

1. Simmer for 20 minutes to make pigment or dye. Strain.
2. Simmer again to reduce liquid to desired color strength.

Notes: The only reason these berries are not sold in stores is because they fall apart so easily that they cannot be shipped. A cousin of raspberries and blackberries, they are a favorite treat for forest hikers.

CARDUUS SPECIES

Thistle

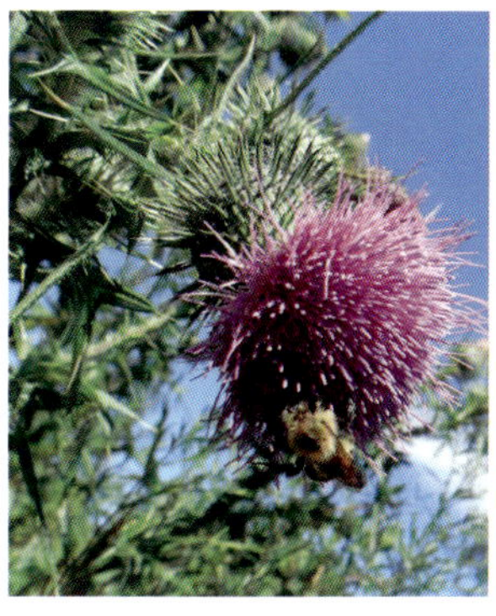

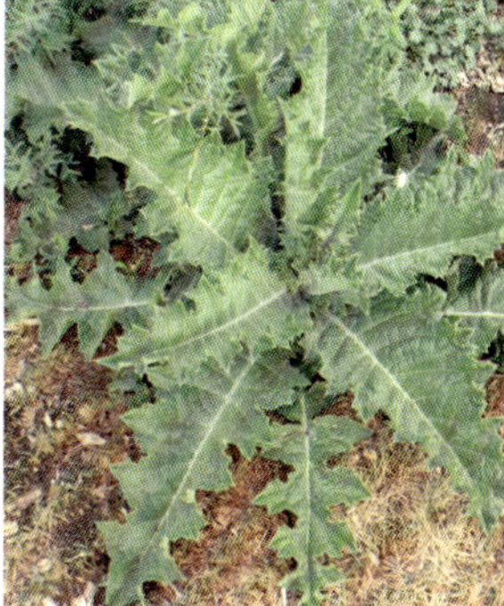

COLORS CREATED	green with baking soda and time, yellow with alum, brown with other mordants
PARTS USED FOR PIGMENT	leaves, stems, flowers

1. Simmer whole purple flower heads for 20 minutes to create yellow with alum.
2. For leaves, boil at least 15 minutes, strain, and then reduce by simmering to produce a dirty yellow that turns to a strong, bright yellow with a mordant of baking soda. Interestingly, this yellow decomposes in about 12 hours to become a beautiful strong and bright leaf green that makes wonderful paint after cooling and sitting.

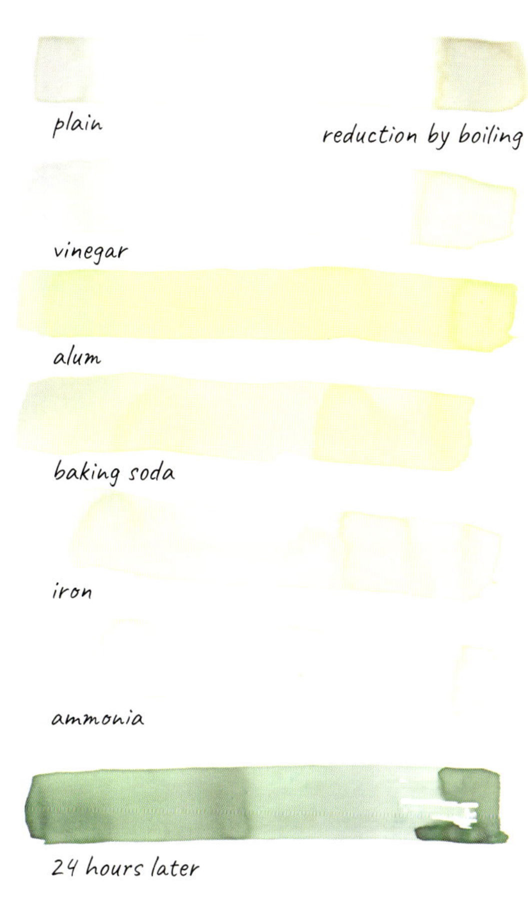

DRIED THISTLE

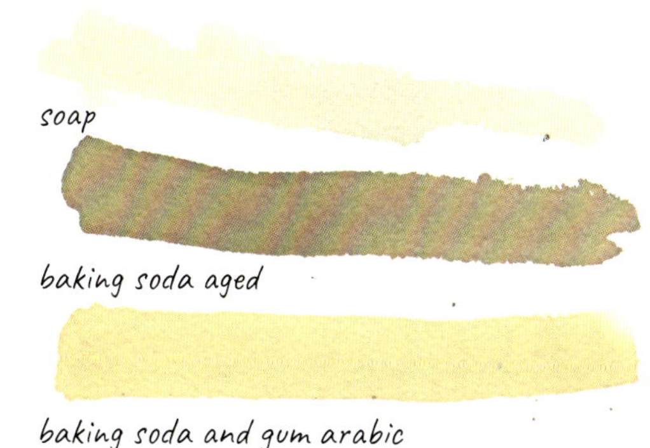

Tibouchina Species

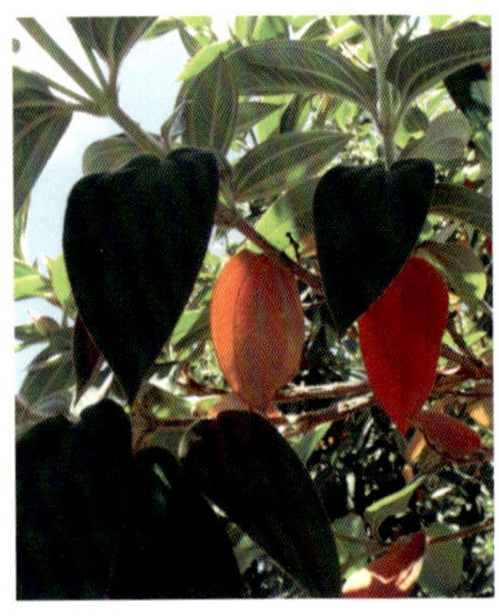

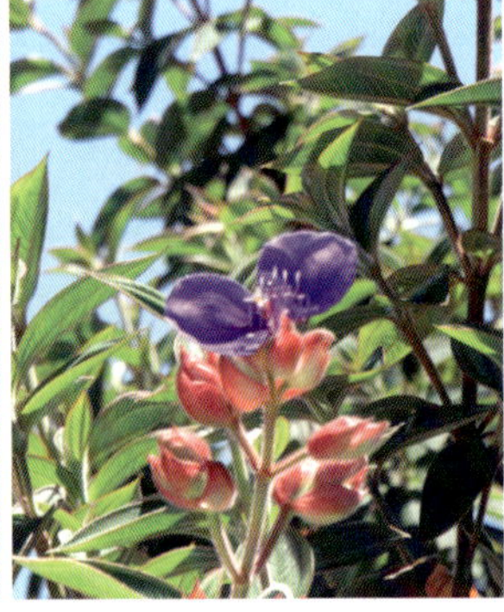

FRESH PRESSED PURPLE TREE FLOWERS

plain alum citric acid baking soda

FRESH PRESSED RED LEAF

plain alum citric acid baking soda

COLORS CREATED	blue without mordant or with alum or citric acid, green with baking soda
PARTS USED FOR PIGMENT	flowers
PLANT TYPE	tropical
HARDINESS ZONE	10

1. Best used uncooked.

SOLANUM LYCOPERSICUM

Tomato

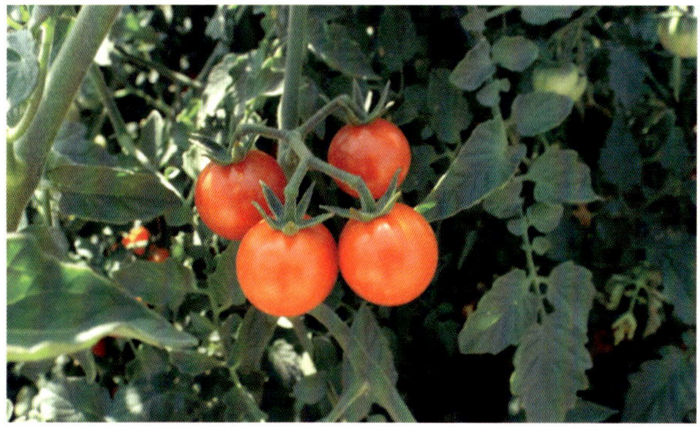

COLORS CREATED	yellow, brown
PARTS USED FOR PIGMENT	vine, leaves
PLANT TYPE	garden vegetable
HARDINESS ZONE	annual
SEEDING	Seeds available at SeedRenaissance.com.

1. Simmer for 30 minutes to make pigment or dye. Strain.
2. Simmer again to reduce liquid to desired color strength.

TOMATO VINE AND LEAVES

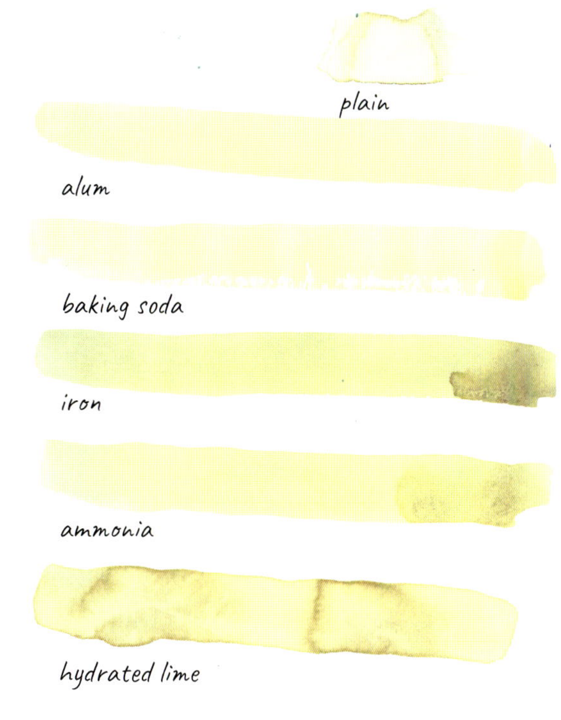

SUNSHINE TOMATO

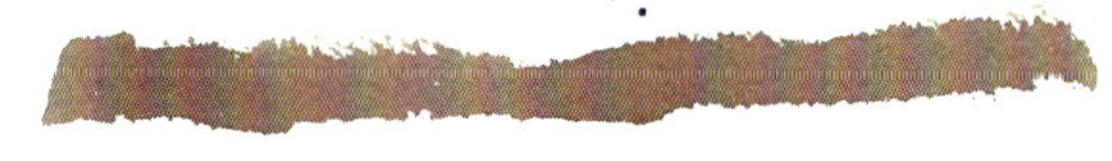

TOMATO VINE WITH COPPER ACETATE

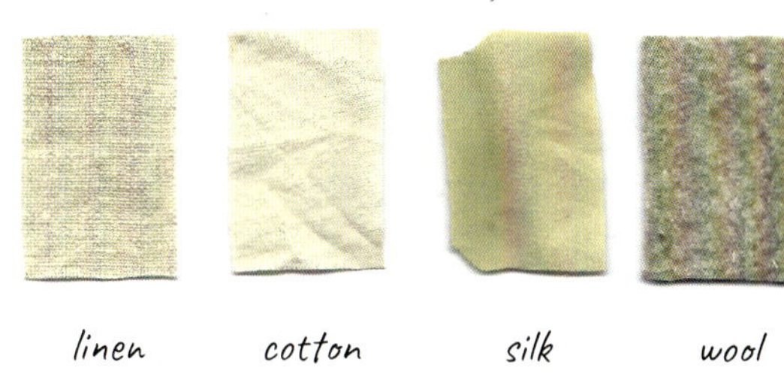

CAMPSIS RADICANS

Trumpet Vine

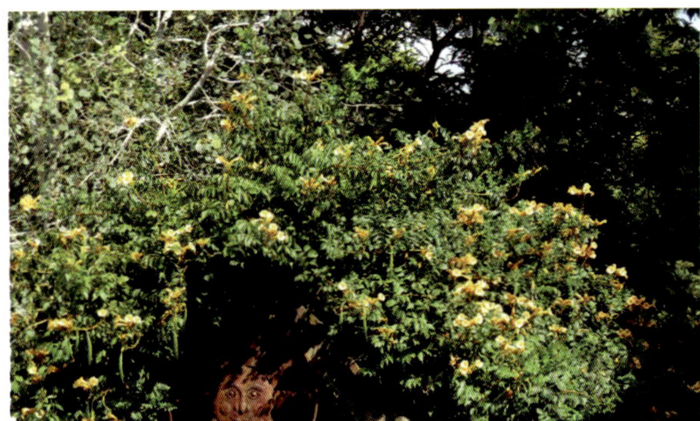

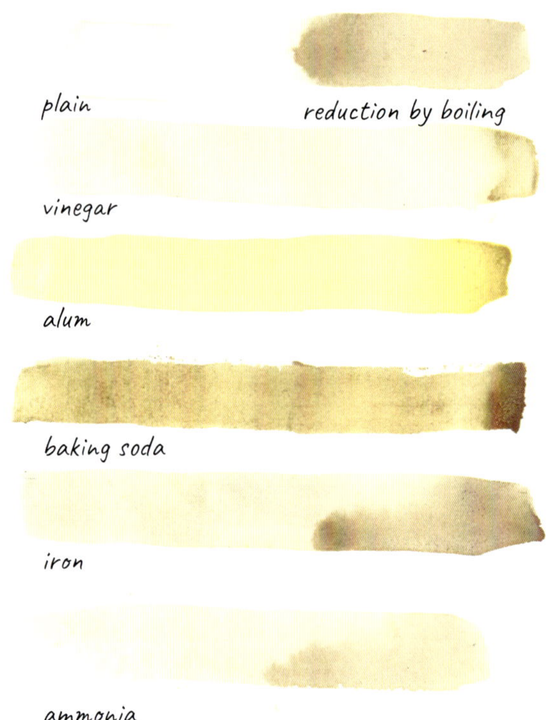

COLORS CREATED	yellow with alum
PARTS USED FOR PIGMENT	flowers only (no sepals or leaves)
PLANT TYPE	perennial vine
HARDINESS ZONE	5

1. Simmer for 30 minutes to make pigment or dye. Strain.
2. Simmer again to reduce liquid to desired color strength.

TULIPA SPECIES

Tulips

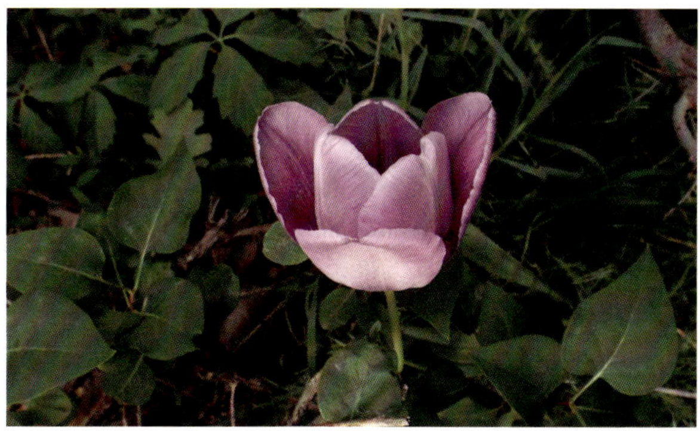

FRESH MULLED PURPLE TULIPS

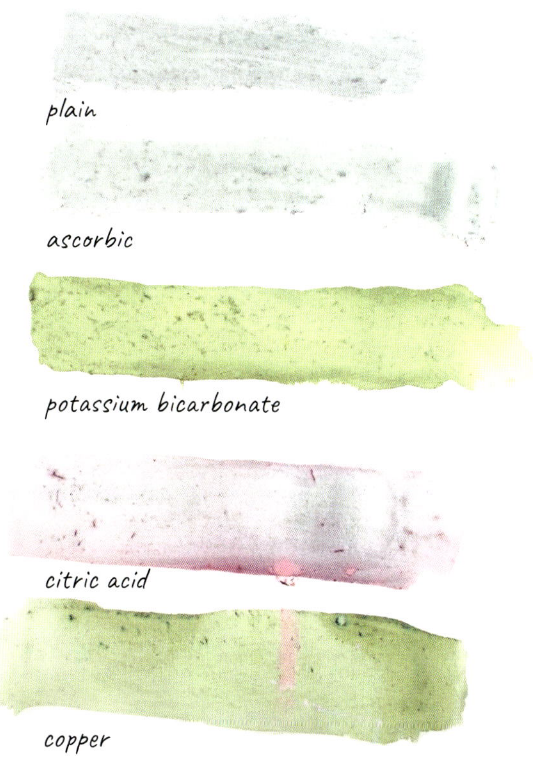

COLORS CREATED	red, brown, and gray from red tulips; yellow from yellow petals
PARTS USED FOR PIGMENT	petals, fresh or dried
PLANT TYPE	perennial
HARDINESS ZONE	3
GROWING	Plant bulbs directly outside in autumn.

1. Do not boil petals. Instead, soak the petals in water overnight. Bring this liquid to a steaming but not boiling temperature to reduce to desired color.
2. Add mordant to hot liquid as desired.

CURCUMA LONGA

Turmeric

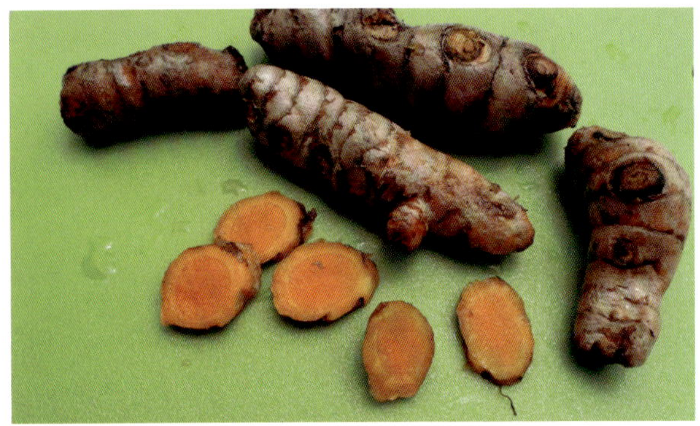

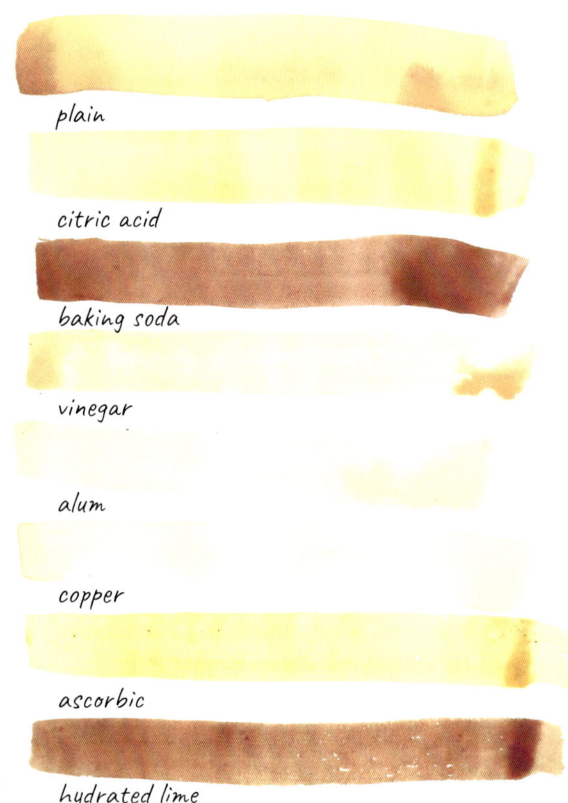

COLORS CREATED	red, yellow, orange
PARTS USED FOR PIGMENT	root (fresh, dried, or powdered from the grocery store)
PLANT TYPE	perennial
HARDINESS ZONE	8

1. Simmer for 30 minutes to make pigment or dye. Strain.
2. Simmer again to reduce liquid to desired color strength.

Verbena Species

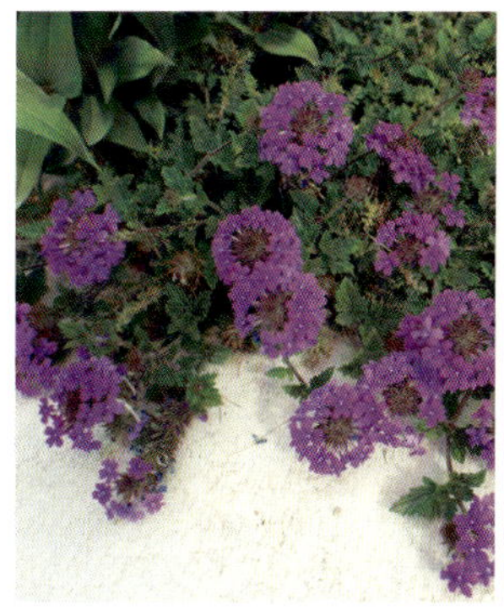

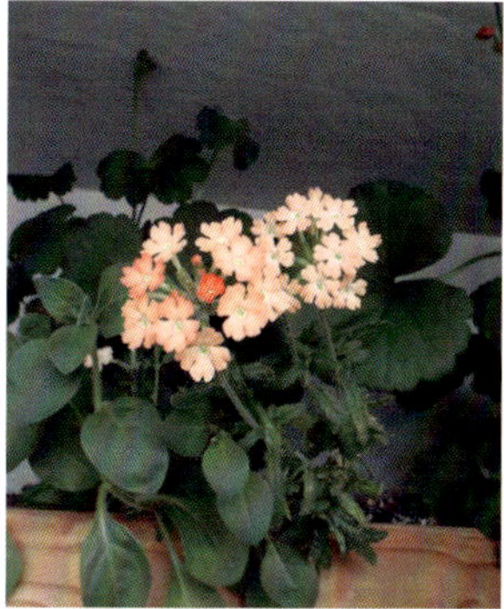

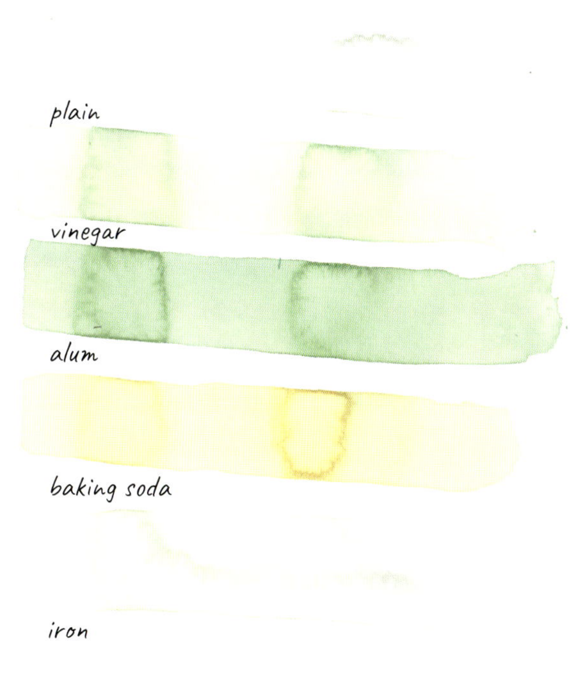

PAINT

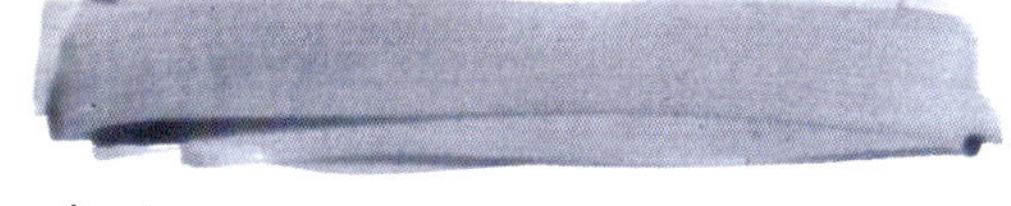

COLORS CREATED	blue when mulling fresh red flowers into the Yolk Tempera Base Paint (see page 77); green with alum and yellow with baking soda from cooked purple flowers
PARTS USED FOR PIGMENT	flowers
PLANT TYPE	landscape flower
HARDINESS ZONE	7
SEEDING	Seeds available at SeedRenaissance.com.

1. Simmer for 20 minutes to make pigment or dye. Strain.
2. Simmer again to reduce liquid to desired color strength.

VICIA AMERICANA

Vetch

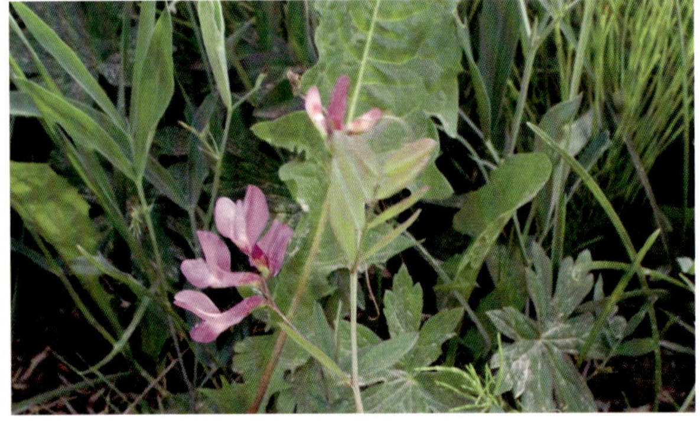

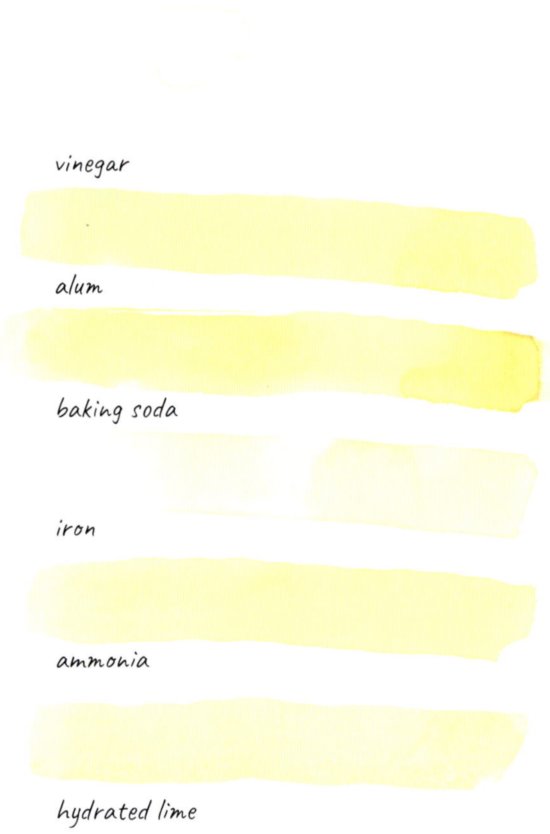

COLORS CREATED	yellow
PARTS USED FOR PIGMENT	purple flowering spikes
PLANT TYPE	perennial
HARDINESS ZONE	4

1. Simmer for 20 minutes to make pigment or dye. Strain.
2. Simmer again to reduce liquid to desired color strength.

Notes: Flowers need to be at peak bloom, otherwise the yellow color produced becomes pale.

CATHARANTHUS ROSEUS AND HYBRIDS

Vinca

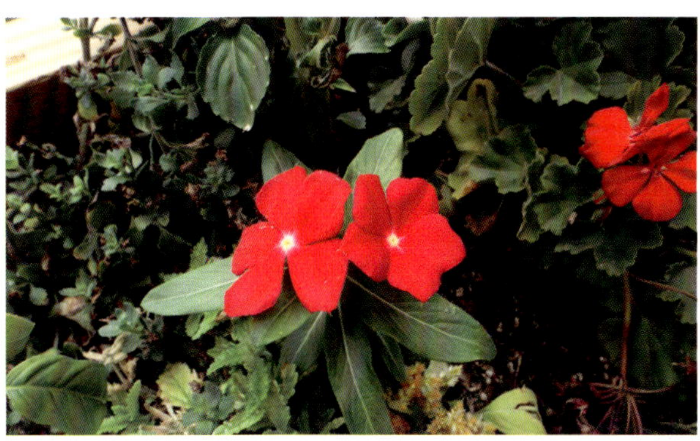

COLORS CREATED	greens, blue
PARTS USED FOR PIGMENT	petals
PLANT TYPE	tropical perennial
HARDINESS ZONE	10

1. Vinca flowers make only pale and highly unstable colors when cooked, but when pressed fresh, they shine. Blue/purple vinca makes blue eco-prints with no mordant, and green with vinegar of copper.

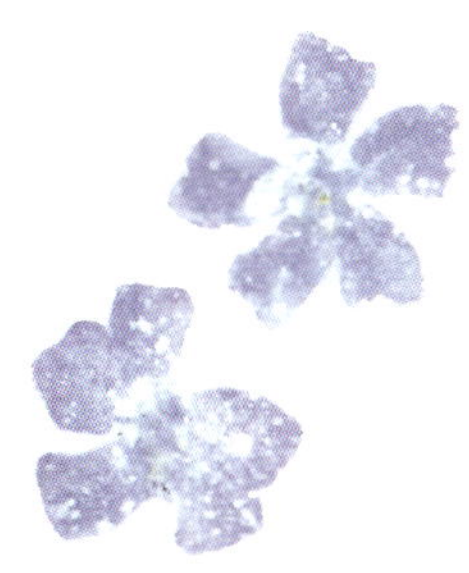

VIOLA SPECIES

Violets

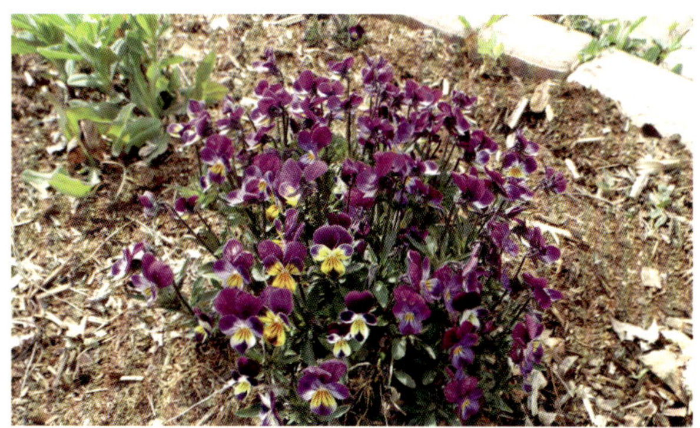

COLORS CREATED	turquoise, blue, green
PARTS USED FOR PIGMENT	fresh flowers
PLANT TYPE	self-seeding annual

1. These flowers are only used fresh for eco-prints or pigment.

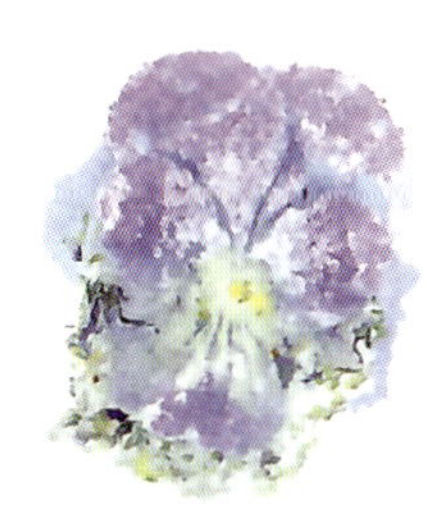

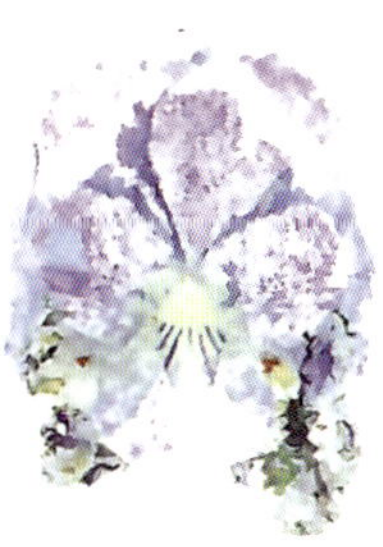

PARTHENOCISSUS QUINQUEFOLIA

Virginia Creeper

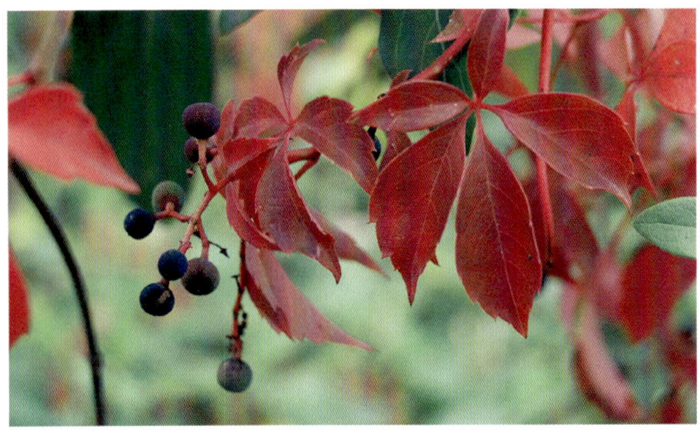

COLORS CREATED	blue, green, gray
PARTS USED FOR PIGMENT	mashed ripe berries
PLANT TYPE	perennial vine
HARDINESS ZONE	3

1. Simmer for 10 minutes to make pigment or dye. Strain.
2. Simmer again to reduce liquid to desired color strength.

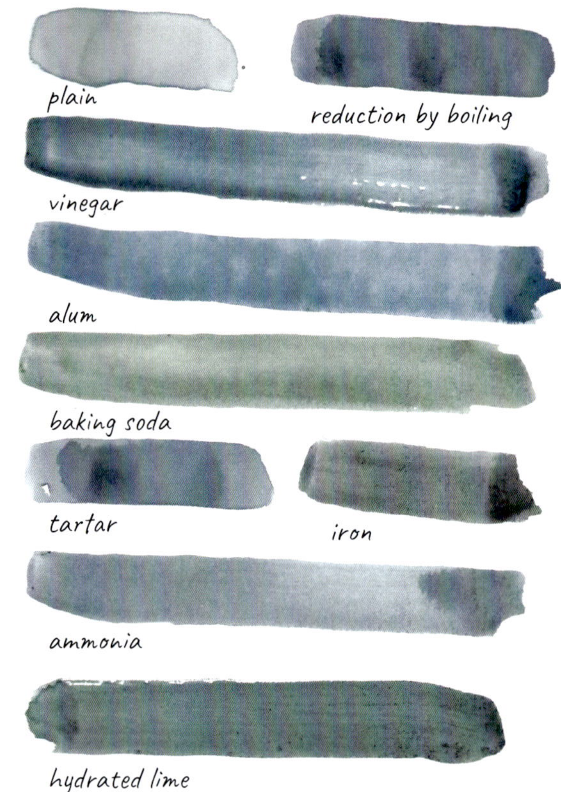

VIRGINIA CREEPER WITH VINEGAR

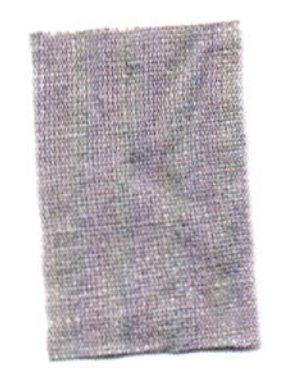
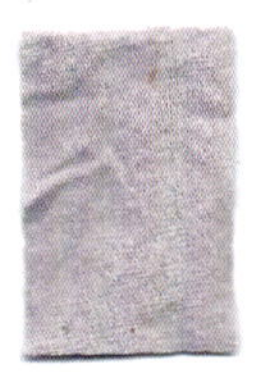
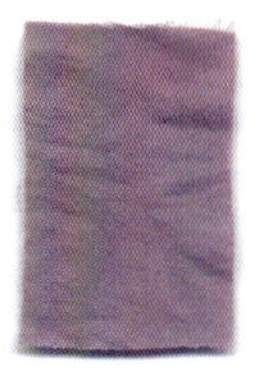
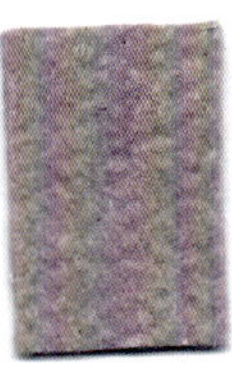

linen cotton silk wool

VIRGINIA CREEPER WITH LIME

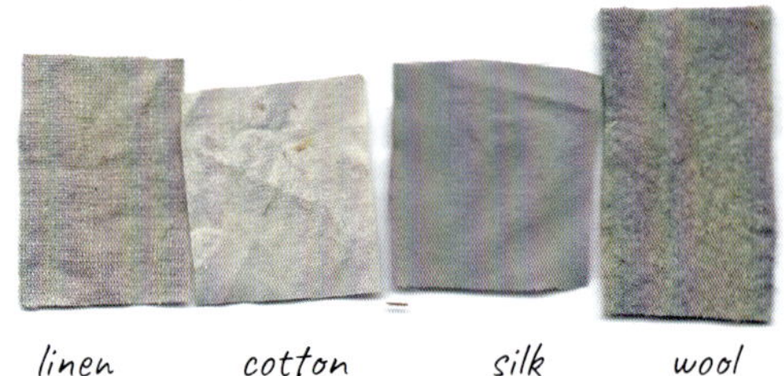

linen cotton silk wool

VIRGINIA CREEPER WITH ALUM

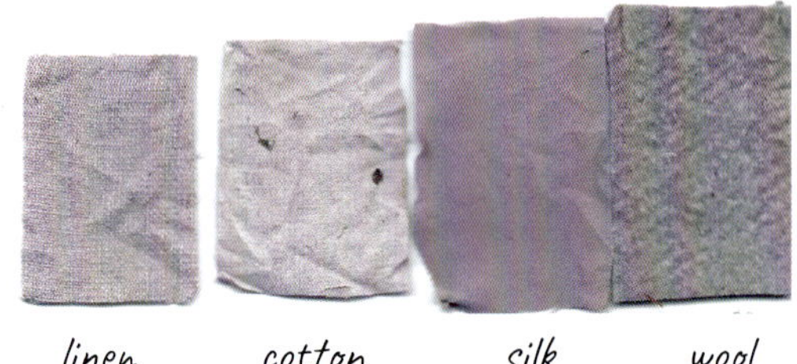

linen cotton silk wool

ERYSIMUM CHEIRI

Wallflower

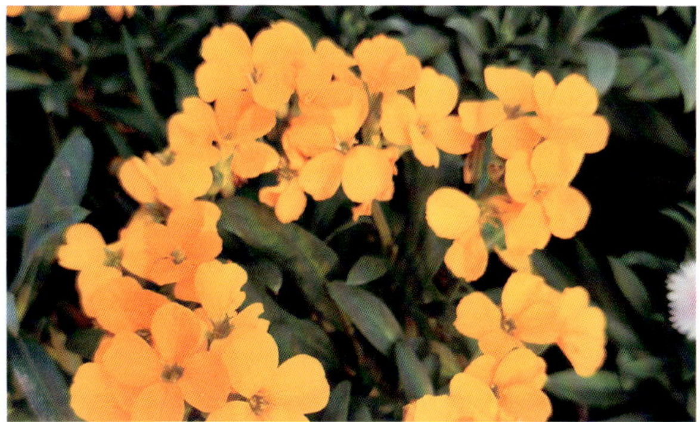

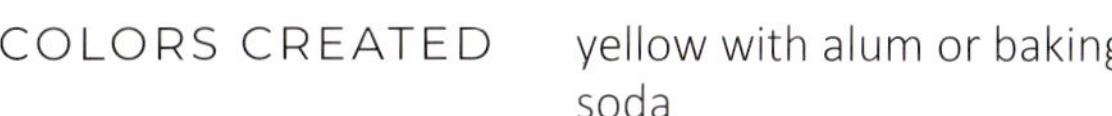

COLORS CREATED yellow with alum or baking soda

1. Simmer for 10 minutes to make pigment or dye. Strain.
2. Simmer again to reduce liquid to desired color strength.

JUGLANS SPECIES

Walnut

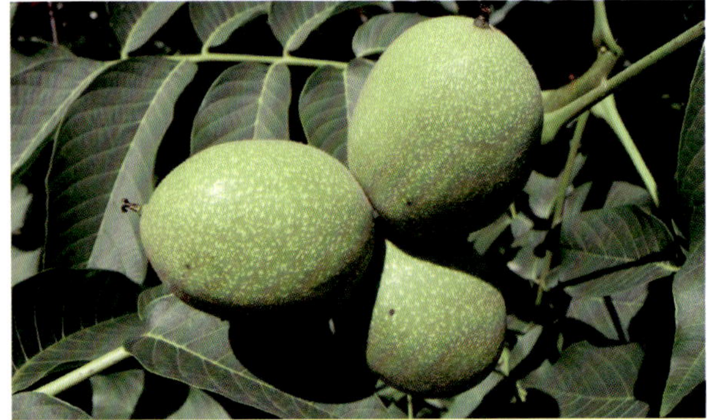

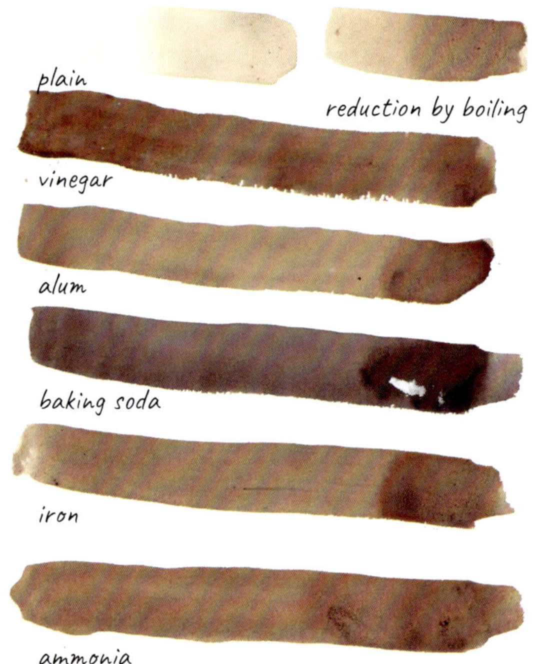

COLORS CREATED	brown
PARTS USED FOR PIGMENT	hulls
PLANT TYPE	nut tree
HARDINESS ZONE	4

1. Immature walnuts resemble hard green pears. The green flesh is thin around the large immature seed. Slice the flesh from the seed and boil the flesh and seed in water for 20 minutes to create tan. Strain.
2. Simmer again to reduce liquid to desired color strength.

Notes: The boiling water had a strange pattern of tiny sizzling bubbles. The finished liquid had an oily sheen on top.

RESEDA LUTEOLA

Weld

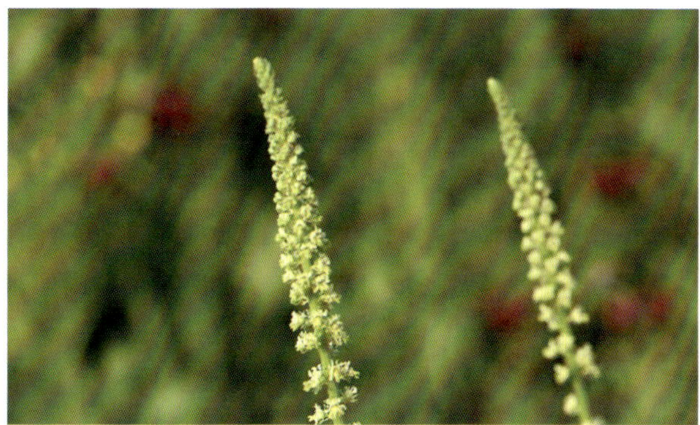

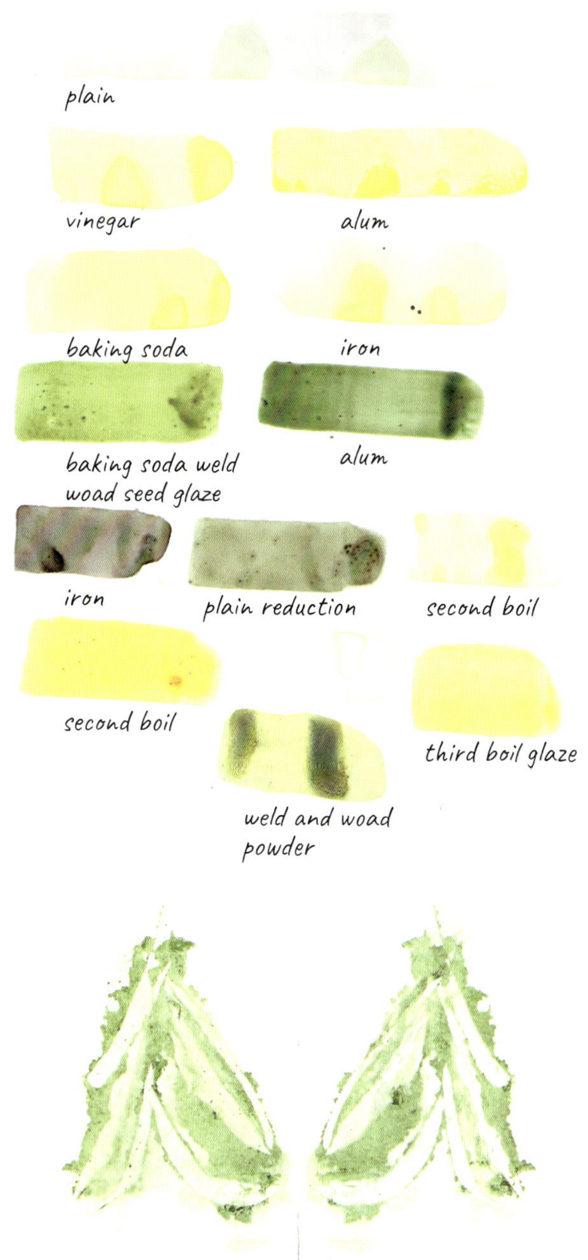

COLORS CREATED	yellows, green
PARTS USED FOR PIGMENT	flower spikes (fresh or dried from fresh)
PLANT TYPE	biennial
HARDINESS ZONE	5

1. Simmering for 15 minutes produces a pale to medium yellow. When the liquid is reduced by simmering, a fluorescent yellow is created. Vinegar creates invisible yellow ink—the vinegar mordant appears to destroy the color, but within hours, a pale to medium yellow appears. Alum makes strong canary yellow. Baking soda makes a bright almost fluorescent yellow.

Notes: A second boil of the same flowering stems in fresh water produced a color the same as the first boil. A third boil, fully reduced, produced a strong yellow that was not quite as bright as the first two batches. The color becomes green after the third boil. Mixing weld and woad leaf with a mordant of baking soda makes a grass green. Mixing weld and woad leaf with alum makes a strong forest green. Mixing weld and woad leaf with iron makes gray and black, depending on saturation. Mixing weld and woad leaf with no mordant makes a gray-green that verges on black when concentrated. Weld is a true primary pigment that can be mixed with other primary colors to make new colors.

LACTUCA VIROSA AND *LACTUCA SERRIOLA*

Wild Lettuce

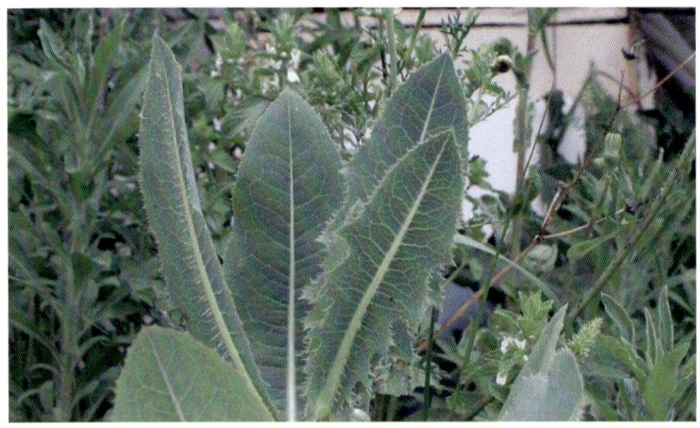

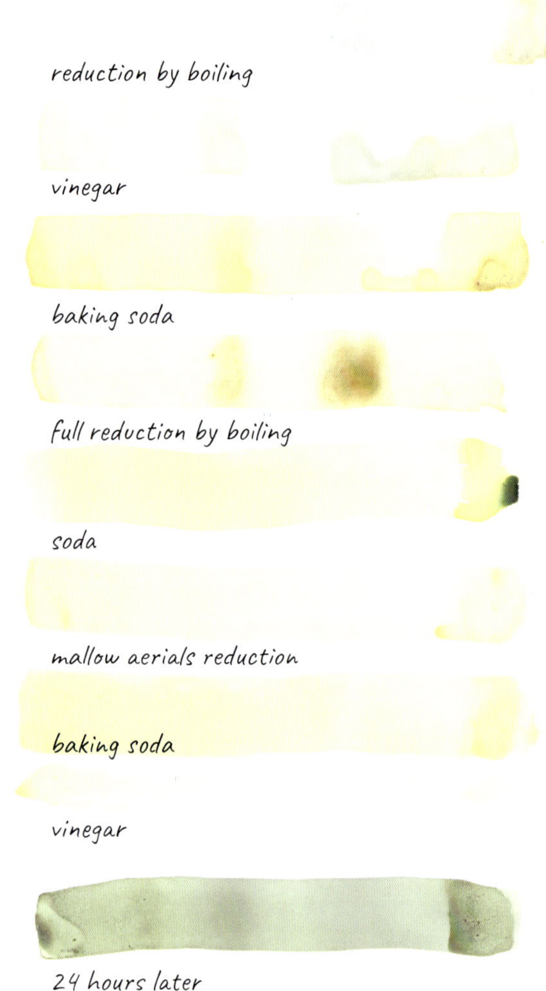

COLORS CREATED	yellow, green
PARTS USED FOR PIGMENT	leaves, stems
PLANT TYPE	weed and important medicinal herb
HARDINESS ZONE	annual
SEEDING	Seeds available at SeedRenaissance.com.

1. Simmer for 10 minutes to make pigment or dye. Strain.
2. Simmer again to reduce liquid to desired color strength.

Notes: If the yellow color is hot when applied, it will dry as yellow. But if you allow the yellow color to dry and then try to use it as pigment, it turns green.

SALIX SPECIES

Willow

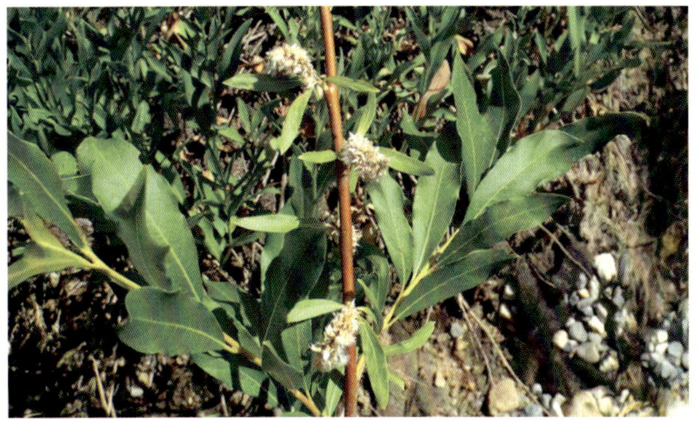

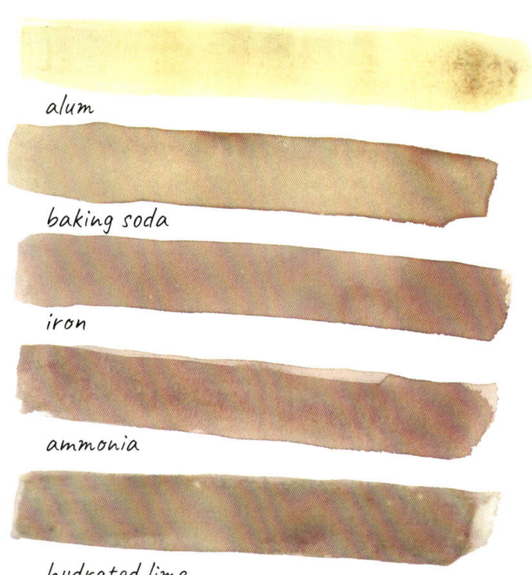

COLORS CREATED	brown
PARTS USED FOR PIGMENT	catkins
PLANT TYPE	perennial

1. Simmer for 15 minutes to make pigment or dye. Strain.
2. Simmer again to reduce liquid to desired color strength.

Notes: The liquid mysteriously seemed slow to boil and reduce with all mordants and without.

ISATIS TINCTORIA

Woad

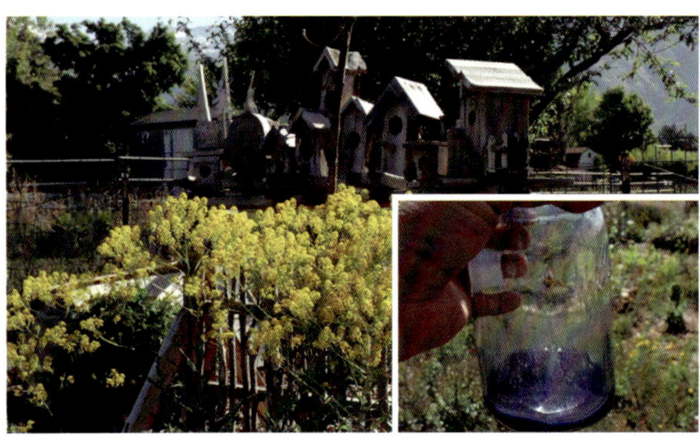

COLORS CREATED	blue, green, pink, yellow
PARTS USED FOR PIGMENT	leaves before flowering, fresh or dried
PLANT TYPE	perennial
HARDINESS ZONE	4
SEEDING	Plant directly outside in spring or autumn.

Notes: Tolerant of drought and alkaline soils. One of the first plants to flower in spring. Taproot grows several feet deep. The blue hue is a true primary pigment that can be used to make other colors. Mixing blue woad pigment with the yellow pigment of dandelion or dyer's chamomile both produce a true green, for example. Blue pigment is created by processing the leaves. Green comes from the fresh leaves. Pink is created by reusing the leaves after processing the blue dye.

FRESH PRESSED WOAD LEAF

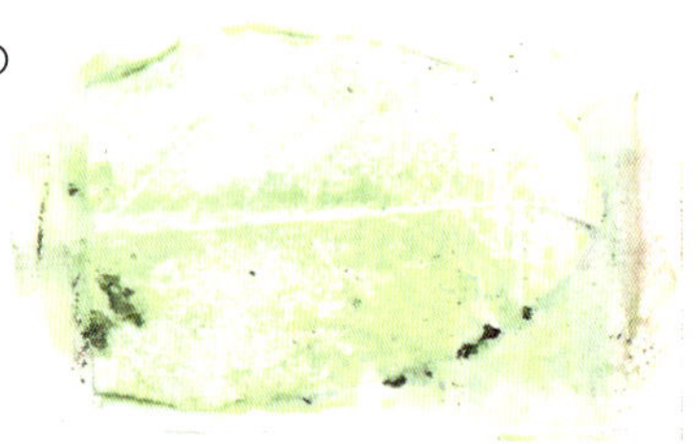

copper

GREEN BABY WOAD SEED

baking soda

WOAD SEED
(painted on purple when hot but dried green)

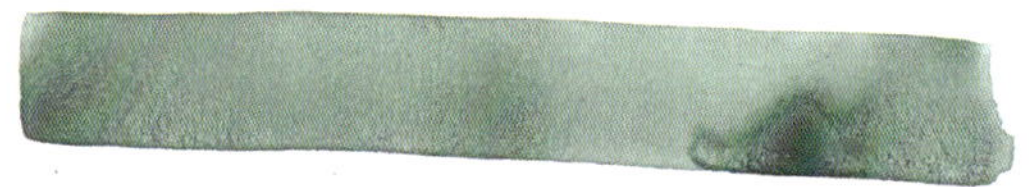

WOAD CITRIC CELANDINE

powdered woad leaf with citric acid

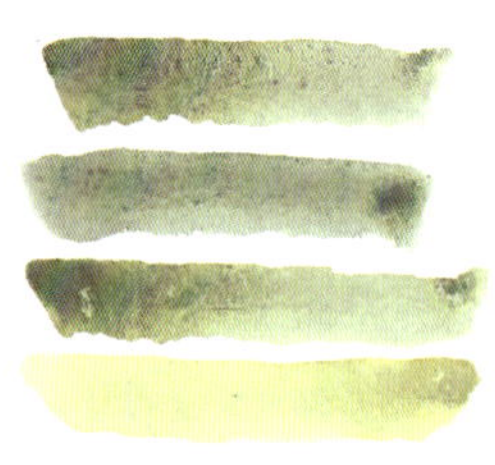

powdered woad leaf with various amounts of celandine

OIL PAINT MADE WITH DRIED WOAD LEAF JUICE, SUNFLOWER OIL, GLAIR, AND WATER

DRIED WOAD BALL MILK PAINT

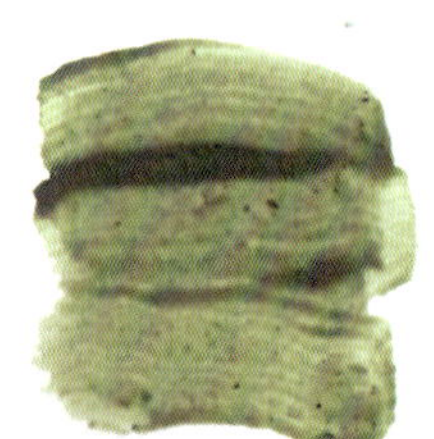

DRIED WOAD SEEDS

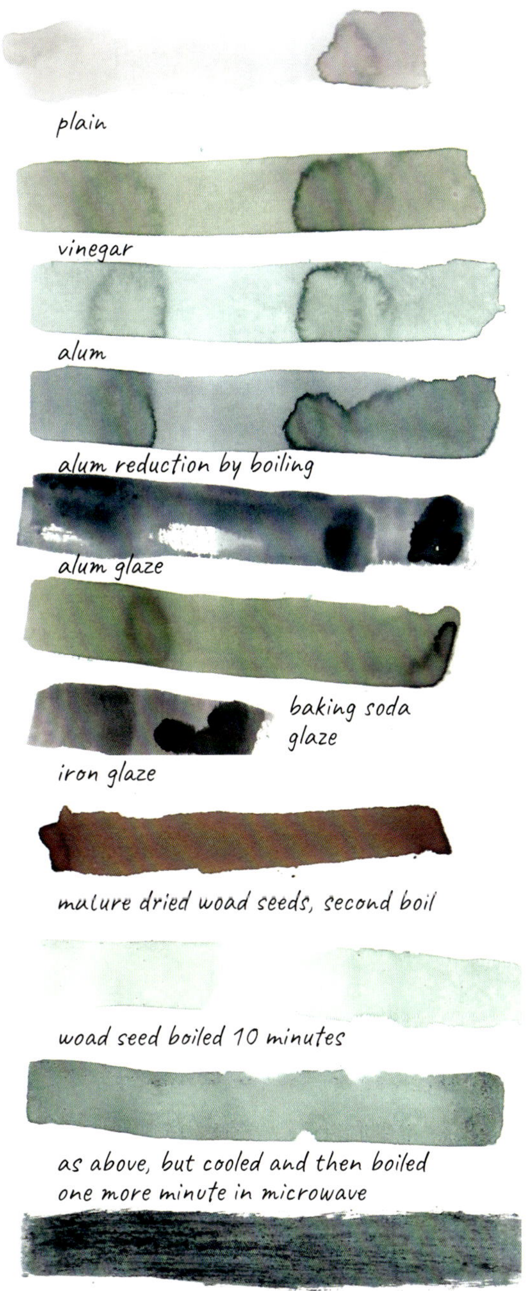

FRESH SQUEEZED WOAD LEAVES JUICE

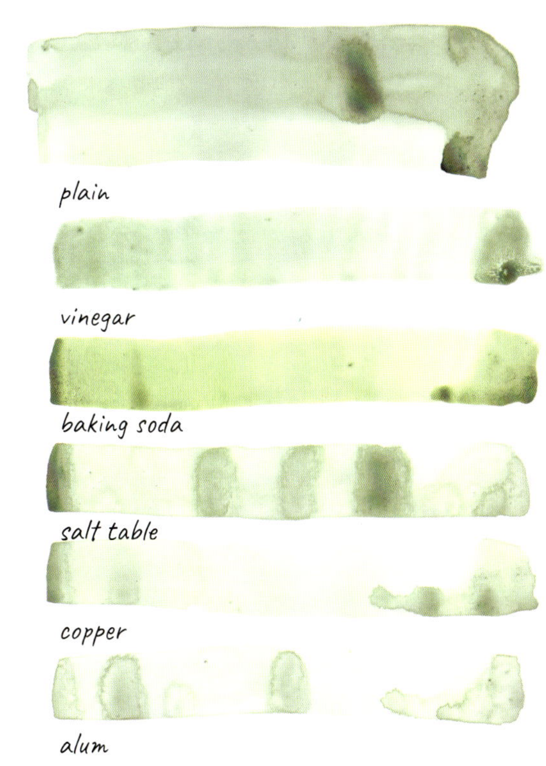

GREEN LEAVES BLENDED WITH WATER, THEN BOILED WITH CITRIC ACID

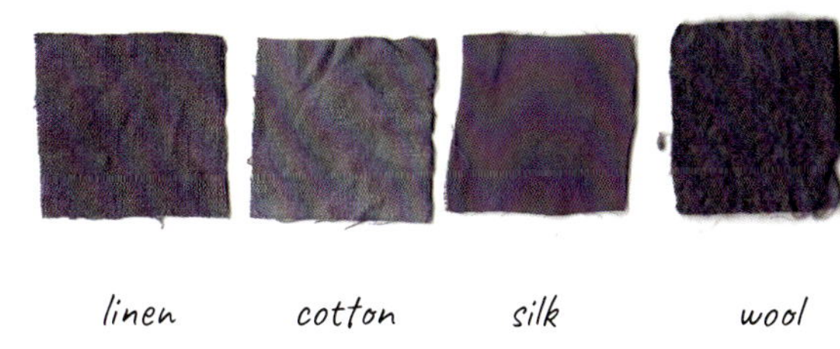

PROCESSED BLUE WOAD PIGMENT FROM FRESH LEAVES, DRIED ON A COFFEE FILTER

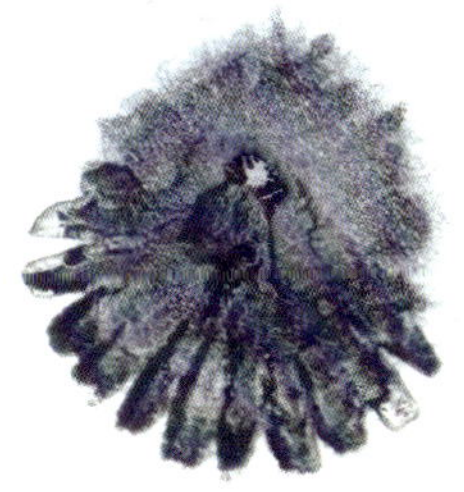

Woad Recipes

Woad Balls

Woad leaves contain the highest amount of blue pigment before they go to flower, and they may contain little or no blue pigment if processed when the leaves are too old after flowering. For this reason, woad leaves were historically sold as dried balls that people could use to make paint and dye. This allowed the leaves to be processed and preserved at their peak pigment levels for later use. Making woad balls preserves the blue dye for later use but also releases a green pigment that is used for ink and paint.

To make woad balls:

Wood leaves from plants that not yet flowered (harvest in spring or autumn)

Scrap board

Bucket

Disposable gloves

Baking sheet

1. Rinse leaves in water to remove dirt and dust.
2. Put a short scrap board in a bucket and crush the leaves on the board with another small piece of lumber or a rock. Let the crushed leaves fall into the bucket. If the weather is warm, green woad dye will begin running down the board into the bucket as you crush the leaves. If the weather is cool, the plants will not release dye yet, which is fine, because it will come out in the next steps.
3. Once all the leaves are crushed, let them sit in the bucket for 5–10 minutes. They will darken in color considerably as they begin to oxidize.
4. Wear gloves for this step or else your hands will be stained green! Take a handful at a time of bruised, darkened leaves from the bucket and squeeze into a tight ball. (As you squeeze, a foamy green dye will release from the leaves; capture this dye in the bucket.) Set the balls on a baking sheet and let them air dry for a couple of weeks in a shed before putting them in a container with a lid for later use. Once dried, the woad balls can be preserved for several years.
5. Strain the liquid green dye left over from squeezing the woad balls. This can be used immediately as green ink or air dried or simmered dry for preservation. The best method of making green paint from this liquid is to let it dry, mull the dried green dye, and then heat with a little water and a tiny bit of gum arabic.

Be sure to cut off all flower stems, otherwise you will not get a blue color.

Rinsing the leaves is easier if you leave the root on the plant.

To submerge the leaves, I use a piece of rabbit wire fencing that I cut into a circle with wire cutters. I push this down to hold the leaves underwater. Other people use bricks or stones.

I don't measure the weight of my woad—and neither did all the people who used this method for thousands of years—but if you are a stickler for modernity, you want to ferment woad leaves weighing twice the weight of the garment or yarn you intend to dye.

Most dyers say you need to tear up the leaves, but I promise you this is completely unnecessary. You can simply put the whole plant in the water.

Woad Leaf Salt Dye

Makes green and sometimes blue.

2–3 woad plants

Bucket

½ cup sea salt (not table salt)

Garment or yarn

1. Cut the flower stems off the woad plants and rinse the leaves.
2. Roughly tear the leaves in half and put them in a bucket with the sea salt.
3. Knead the leaves and salt together.
4. Let them macerate for at least 10–15 minutes at least, or up to several hours. They will begin to expel their juice. As they macerate, mash the wilted, salted leaves.
5. Knead your garment or yarn gently in this liquid.
6. Remove the garment or yarn from the liquid. Let the garment or yarn air dry. The color will quickly change from green to green-blue as the air oxides the color.
7. Rinse the garment and wash in pH-neutral soap.
8. The leftover liquid of your spent dye bath is very salty. You can pour the water someplace where you want to scorch the soil, like a weedy spot in your driveway, or you can simply leave the liquid in the sun to dry out, using it as green paint or—when dried and ground in a mortar—green pigment. Wherever you put this liquid, it will stink for a couple days until dried. Scrub your hands with soda ash and water to get the smell off your skin.

Woad Leaf Solar Dye

Makes baby blue. Overdye to make it darker.

2–3 woad plants

2 buckets

Water

Sieve

1 tablespoon soda ash (see page 59)

White garment or yarn

1. Cut the flower stems off the woad plants and rinse the leaves.
2. Immerse the leaves in a bucket of water and put something over them to keep them under the water.
3. Let the bucket of leaves and water sit in a hot sunny place for at least three days, until all the leaves are completely wilted and a metallic sheen has appeared on the top of the water. The water will stink. The color of the water may be brown, tan, green, or blue. Woad is famous for being unpredictable in color at this stage, but don't worry—the color does not matter right now.
4. Pour the water and leaves through a sieve into another clean bucket to filter out the dead leaves. The water does not have to be perfectly clean, but most of the dead leaf material should be removed. If you want it completely clean, strain the water through a cloth. Don't get the smelly water on you or your shoes.
5. Add soda ash to the bucket of stinky water. The soda ash will likely turn blue when it hits the water. This is a good sign. You can substitute any strong alkali–like ammonia, hydrated lime, or urea–for soda ash.
6. Pour the stinky water between the two buckets a couple times.
7. Add your garment or yarn and pour the water between the buckets one hundred times.
8. Remove the garment or yarn, rinse, dry, and wash with pH-neutral soap.
9. The leftover liquid of your spent dye bath is very alkali. You can pour the water someplace where you want to scorch the soil, like a weedy spot in your driveway, or you can simply leave the liquid in the sun to dry out. You can then use the resulting powder as pigment. Wherever you put this liquid, that place will stink for a couple days until totally dried. Scrub your hands with soda ash and water to get the smell off your skin.

Woad Leaf Solar Dye Pigment

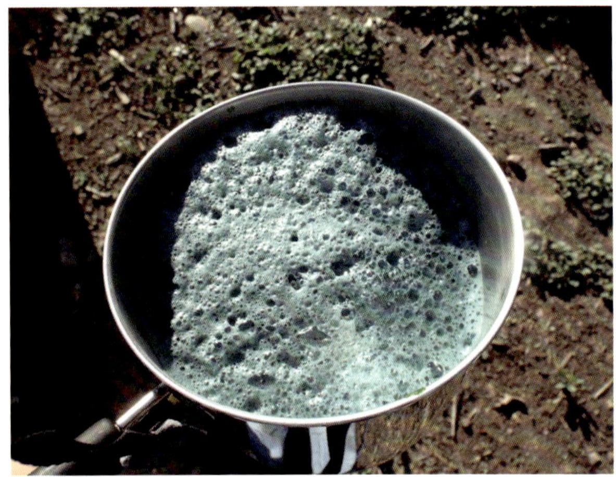

Makes baby blue; overdye to make darker.

This process was traditionally used to dye silk.

10 first-year woad leaves

1 quart soft water or rain water

Ice

1 teaspoon soda ash (see page 59)

2 buckets

1. Cut first year leaves before a flower stock begins to arise. Tear or chop leaves. Keep cool until ready to process (best to process immediately).
2. Add water to a saucepan and heat to 194 degrees. Do not boil.
3. Add leaves, remove from heat, and steep for 10 minutes until temperature reduces to 176 degrees. (If you do not have a thermometer, put the leaves in the pan and heat until the water at the edges of the pan just begins to boil. Turn the heat off immediately.)
4. Cool by adding ice to the pan until liquid reaches 130 degrees within 5 minutes. If the temperature drops below 130 during this 5 minutes, pigment may not form.
5. Steep for 10 minutes, stirring occasionally.
6. Strain and press the leaves. Put the liquid back in the pan. The leaves will still be very green but will not make another batch of blue; they can be composted.
7. Fill a mug with boiling water; add soda ash to the mug and stir. Add this to the dye liquid. The temperature of the woad liquid must be under 155 degrees when soda ash is added. The color of the water may or may not turn blue, it's fine either way. Do not substitute baking soda or ammonia for soda ash; it will not work.
8. Aerate by pouring woad liquid between two buckets one hundred times. Blue foam will begin to show up within a minute or two in most cases. The liquid may or may not turn blue, or maybe you will only see blue foam. If using plastic buckets, you will begin to see blue pigment sticking to the sides. Let the liquid and foam settle for 2–3 hours.
9. Carefully pour off liquid while keeping the sediment at the bottom. If the liquid is green, keep it for ink or dye. If it is brown, discard it.
10. Rinse sediment with water. You should see a visibly blue pigment. Let it settle, rinse, and repeat a couple times. Do not try to use a coffee filter to sieve the blue pigment because it will attach to the filter and be impossible to get most of it off.

Woad Leaf Solar Pigment Extraction

Makes blue pigment.

2–3 woad plants

2 buckets

Water

Cloth

1 tablespoon soda ash (see page 59)

Coffee filter or craft felt

1. Cut the flower stems off the woad plants and rinse the leaves.

2. Immerse the leaves in a bucket of water and put something over them to keep them under the water. The leaves should be about 4 inches underwater.

3. Let the bucket of leaves and water sit in a hot sunny place for at least three days, until all the leaves are completely wilted and a metallic sheen has appeared on the top of the water. The water will stink. The color of the water may be brown, tan, green, or blue.

4. Pour the water and leaves through a cloth into a clean bucket to strain out the leaves. Discard the leaves in the compost pile.

5. Add about 1 tablespoon of soda ash per gallon of sieved stinky water. You can substitute any strong alkali—like ammonia, hydrated lime, or urea–for soda ash.

6. Pour the stinky water between the two buckets one hundred times.

7. Let the bucket sit for at least 1 hour so the pigment can settle to the bottom. You can leave it overnight or even several days.

8. Pour off the top water. Do not allow any of the settled sediment to escape. Pour the sediment water into a coffee filter or scrap of craft felt and leave it to dry for a couple days. Scrape the pigment off and store for later use

9. The leftover liquid of your spent dye bath is very alkali. You can pour the water someplace where you want to scorch the soil, like a weedy spot in your driveway, or you can simply leave the liquid in the sun to dry out, using it as green paint or—when dried and ground in a mortar—green pigment. Wherever you put this liquid, it will stink for a couple days until totally dried. Scrub your hands with soda ash and water to get the smell off your skin.

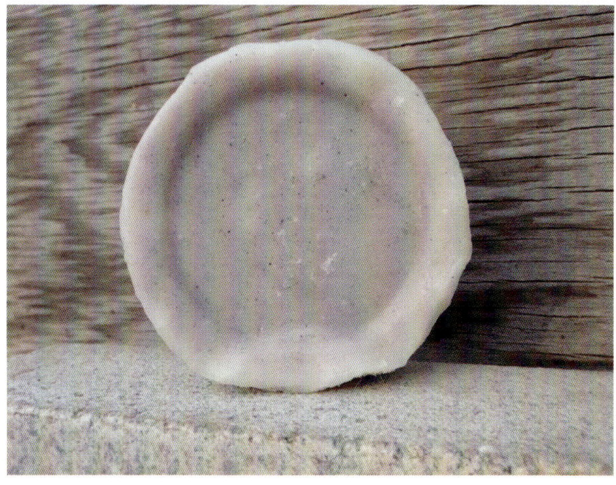

Homemade olive oil lye soap colored with blue woad powder.

ACHILLEA MILLEFOLIUM

Yarrow

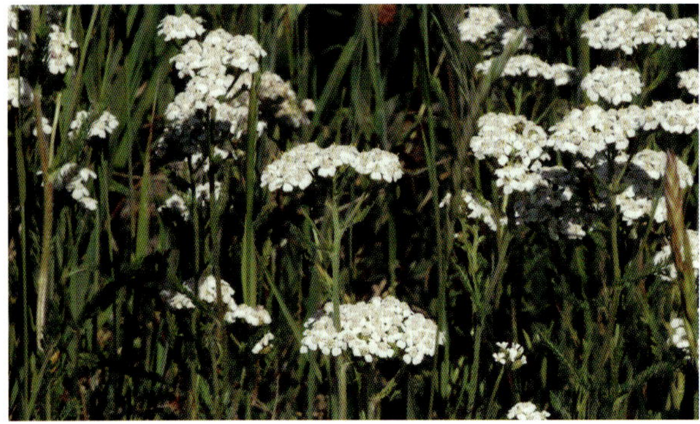

COLORS CREATED	yellow from flowers, brown from leaves
PLANT TYPE	perennial
HARDINESS ZONE	5
SEEDING	Seeds available at SeedRenaissance.com.

1. Simmer for 10 minutes to make pigment or dye. Strain.
2. Simmer again to reduce liquid to desired color strength.

Notes: The used flowers can be boiled again with new water up to four times to produce more batches of color.

YARROW FLOWERS

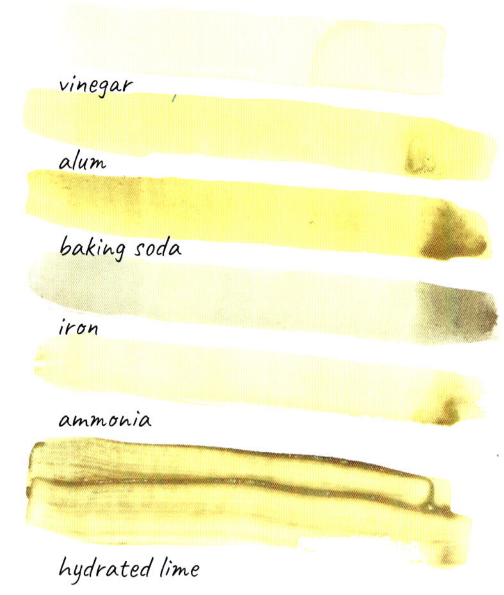

PINK PURPLE WILD YARROW

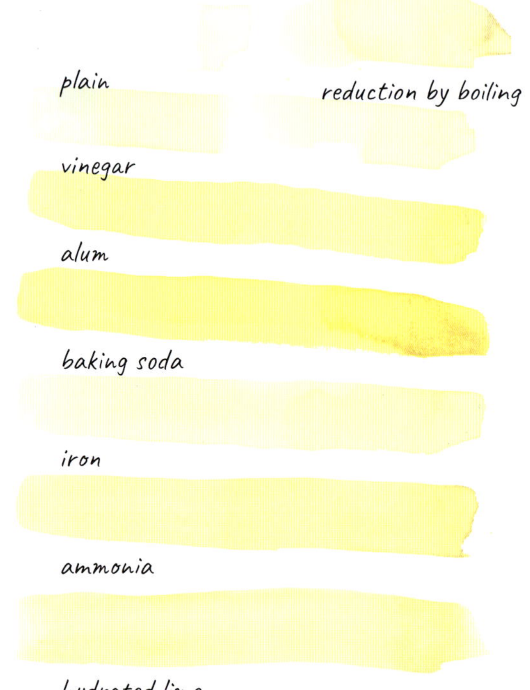

Zinnia (Various Species)

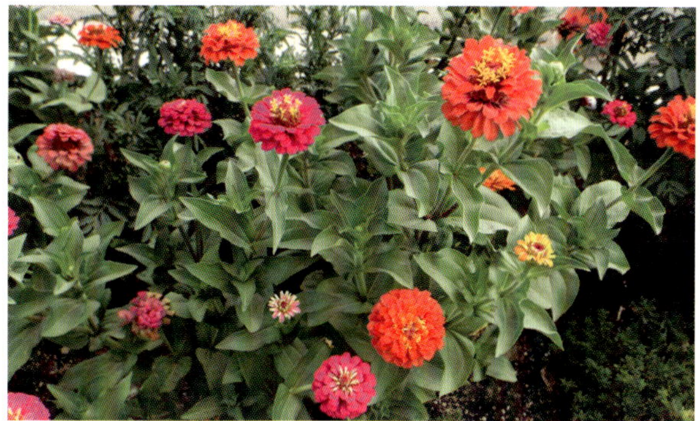

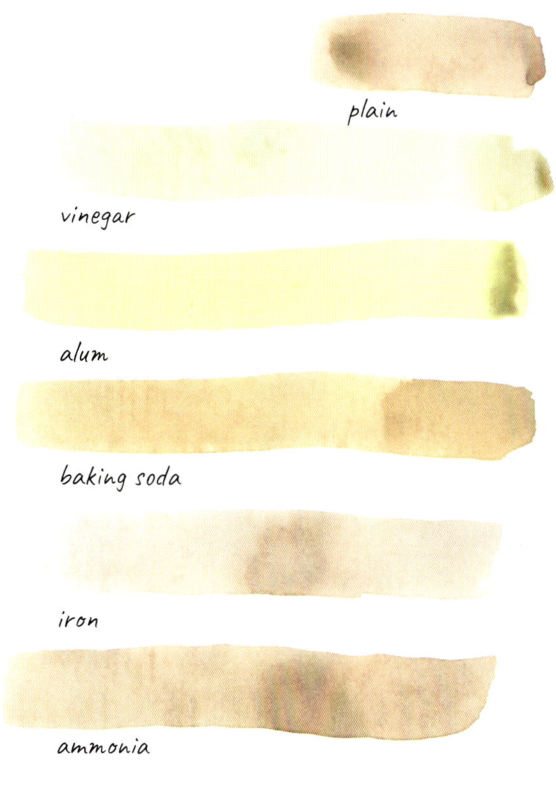

COLORS CREATED	yellow, brown
PARTS USED FOR PIGMENT	flower heads, fresh or dried at peak bloom)
PLANT TYPE	annual
SEEDING	Seeds available at SeedRenaissance.com.

1. Simmer for 10 minutes with the lid on to create a parchment color. Reduce the liquid to create orange or burnt orange.
2. Vinegar creates pale green. Alum creates a pale to medium greenish orange. Baking soda or ammonia creates a medium burnt orange. Iron creates a pale burnt orange.

Notes: I know. It's disappointing. Yellow and brown. Even with citric acid. But what can we do? Just leave the zinnias for looking at and make pigment from other flowers.

PAINT

ZINNIA WITH HYDRATED LIME

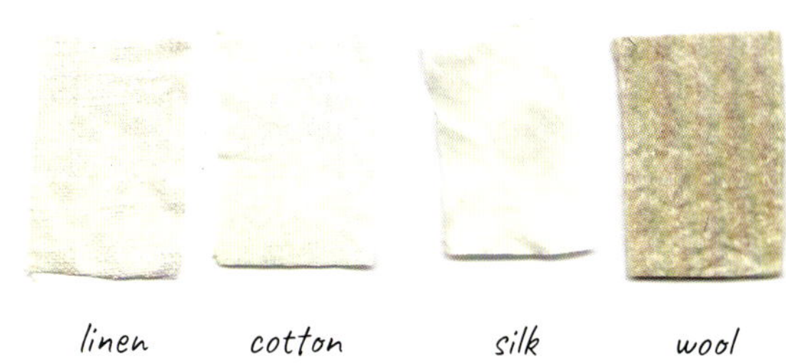

Color Blocks and Botanical Art

Color Block A

All fresh and uncooked, rubbed directly on the paper, no mordants.

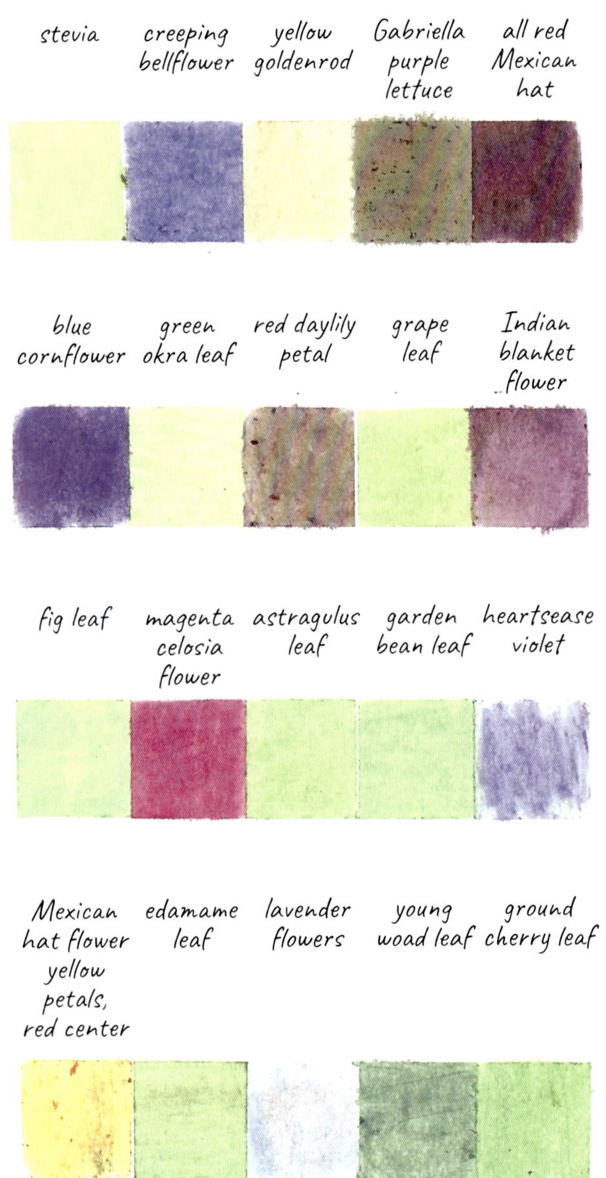

Color Block B

All fresh and uncooked, on paper premordanted with baking soda, citric acid, alum, and vinegar of copper.

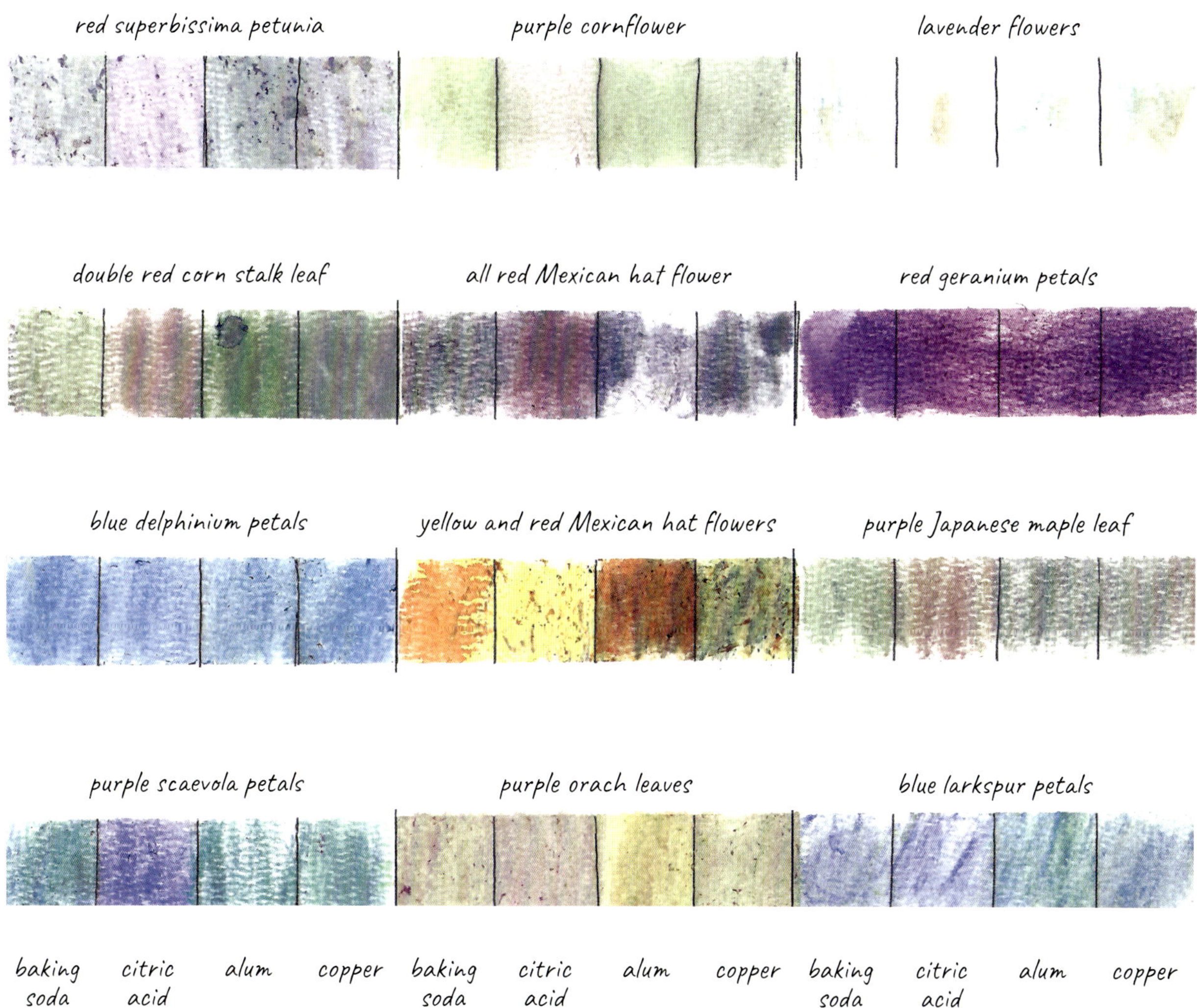

Color Block C

Mulled fresh with water, the first column with no mordant, then premordanted with baking soda in the second column, and then premordanted with citric acid in the third column.

Color Block D

All fresh and uncooked, rubbed directly on the paper, no mordants.

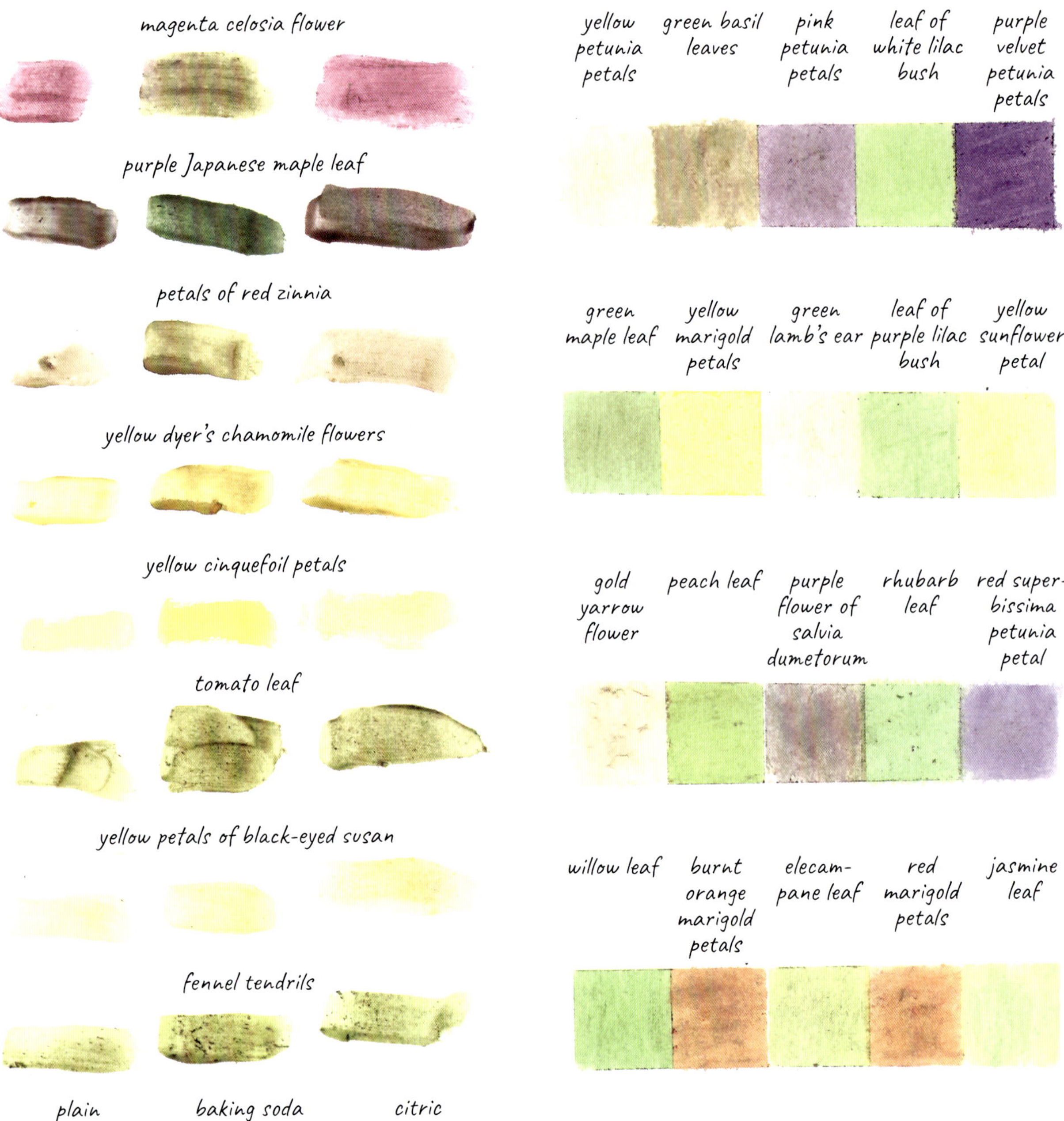

Color Block E

All cooked, painted directly on premordanted paper (first column plain (no mordant), second column alum, third column citric acid, fourth column baking soda, fifth column vinegar of copper).

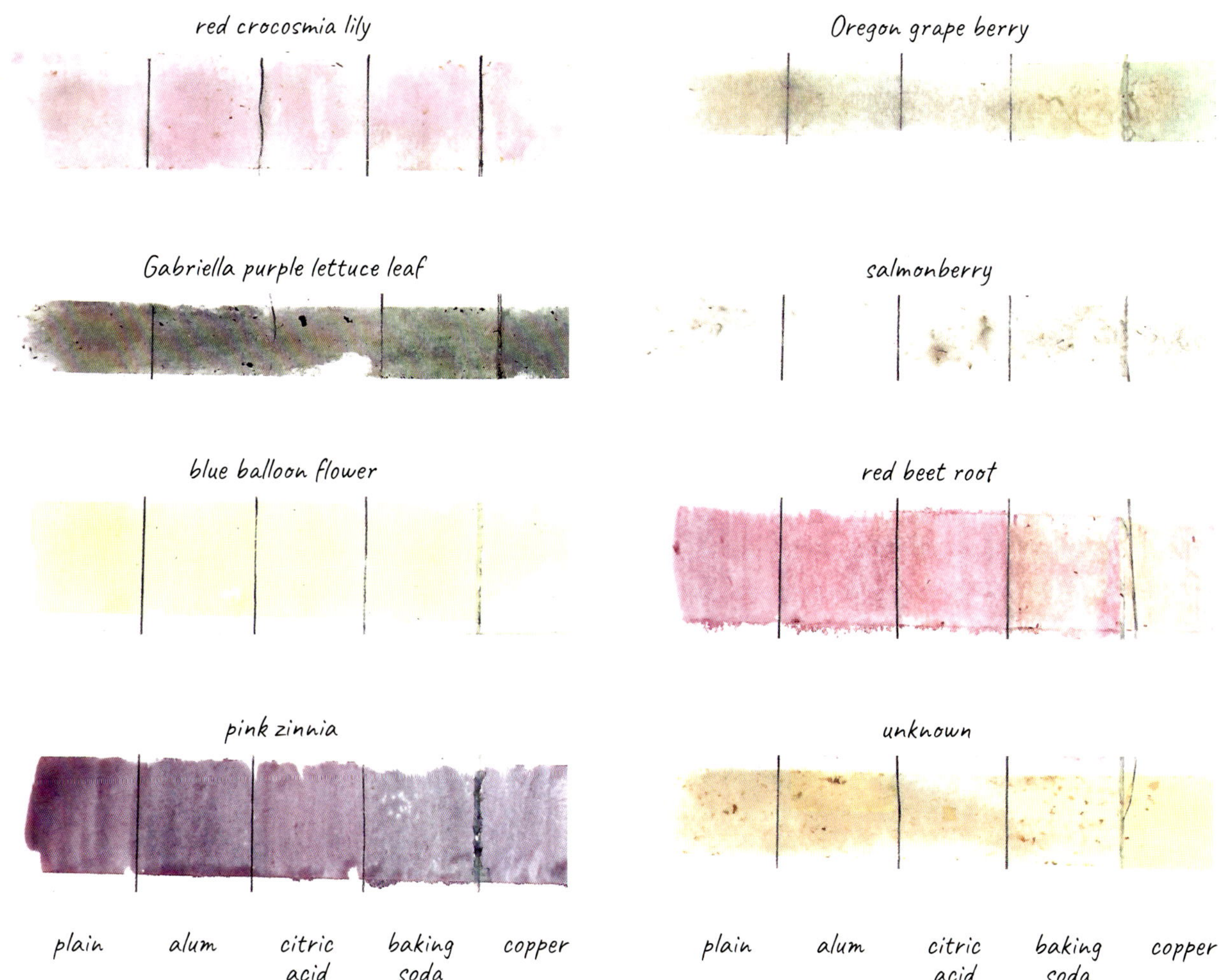

Color Block F

All fresh and uncooked, rubbed directly on premordanted paper in columns with baking soda, citric acid, alum, and copper.

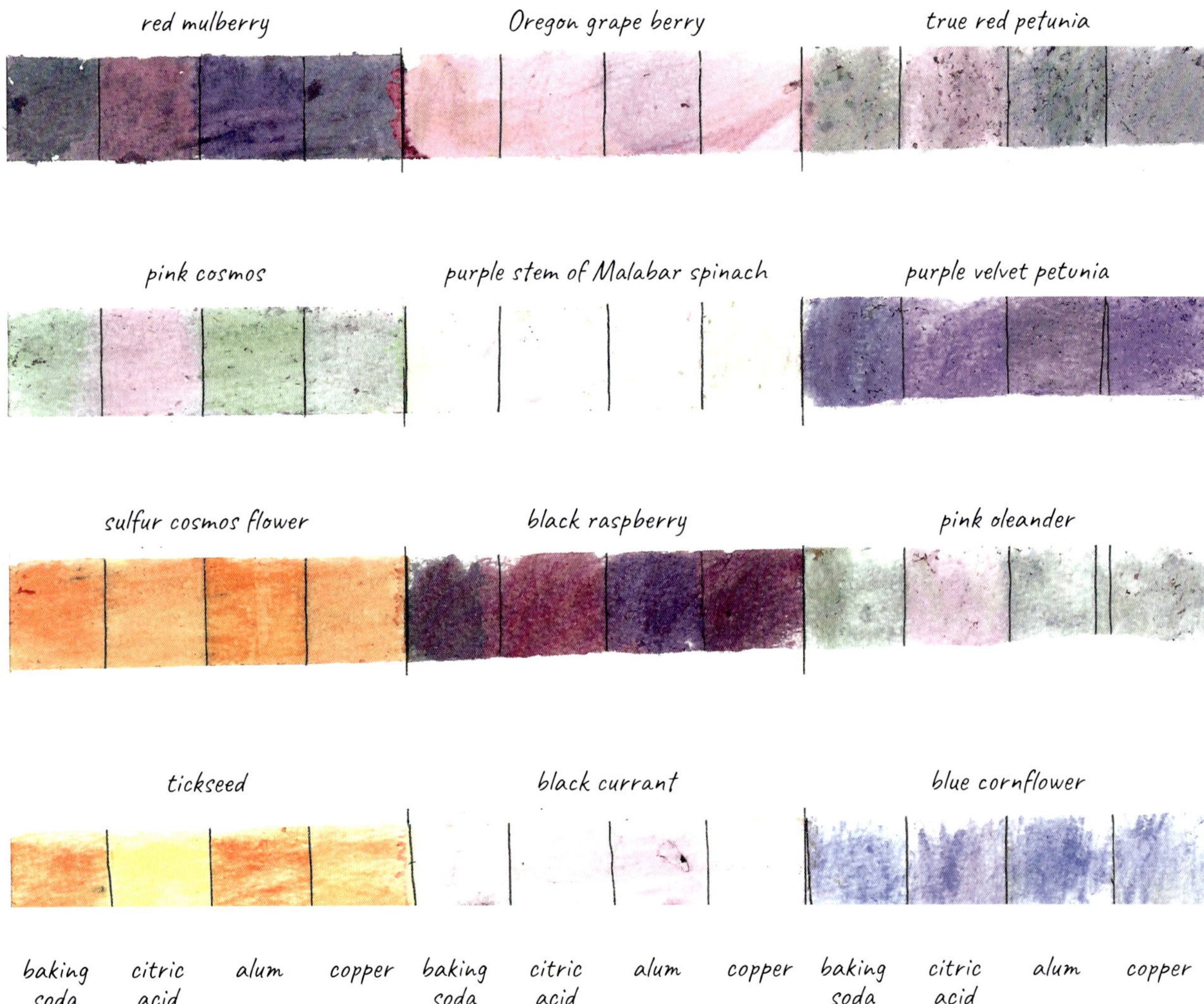

Color Block G

All fresh and uncooked, rubbed directly on unmordanted paper.

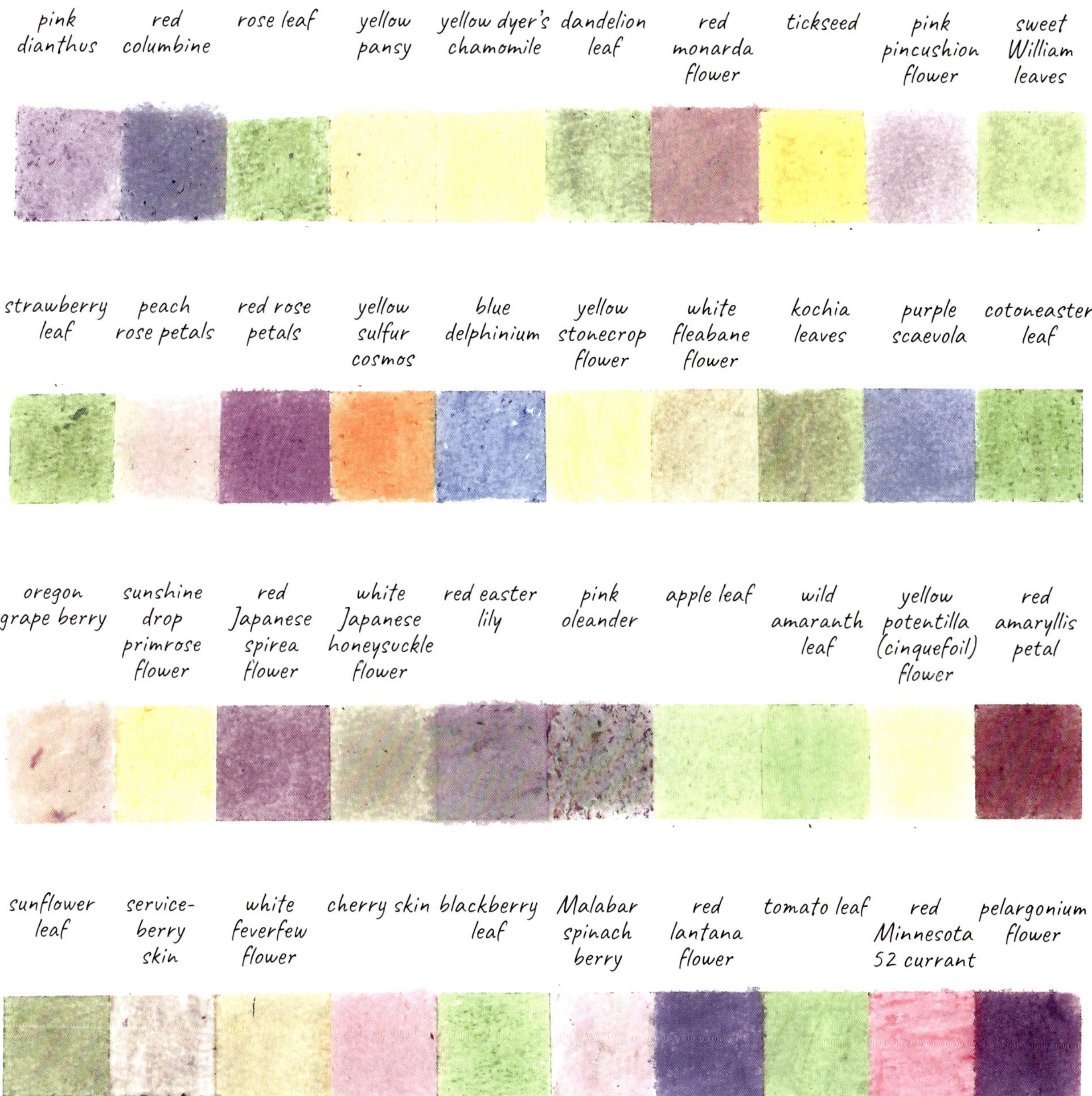

FRESH MULLED ALLIUM PURPLE PETALS

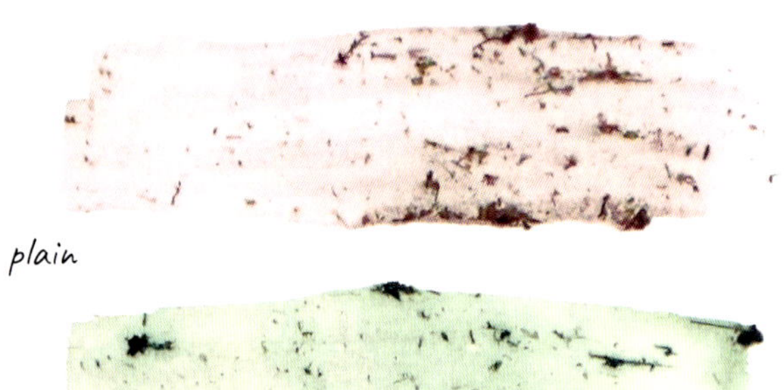

plain

potassium bicarbonate

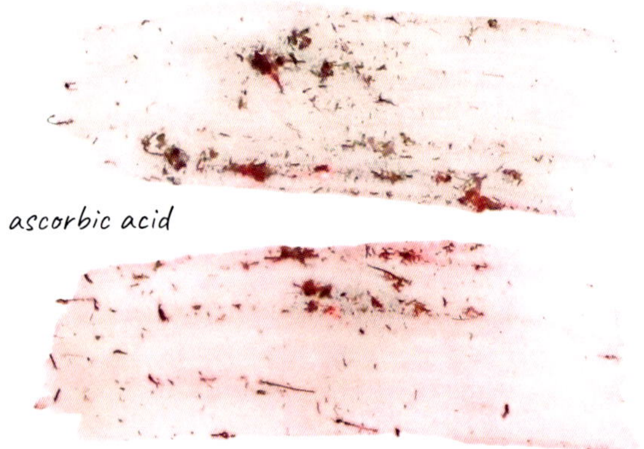

ascorbic acid

citric acid

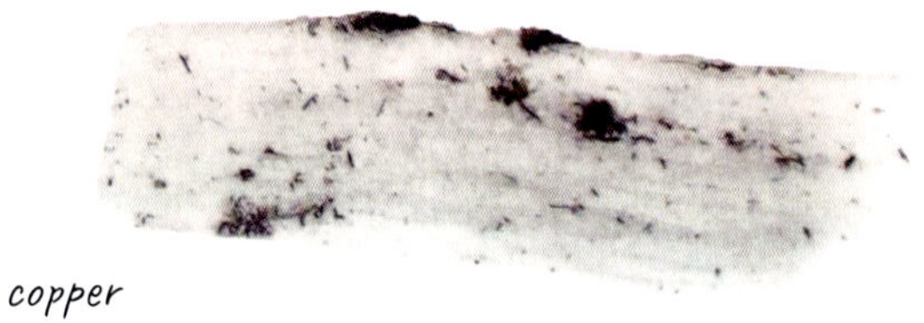

copper

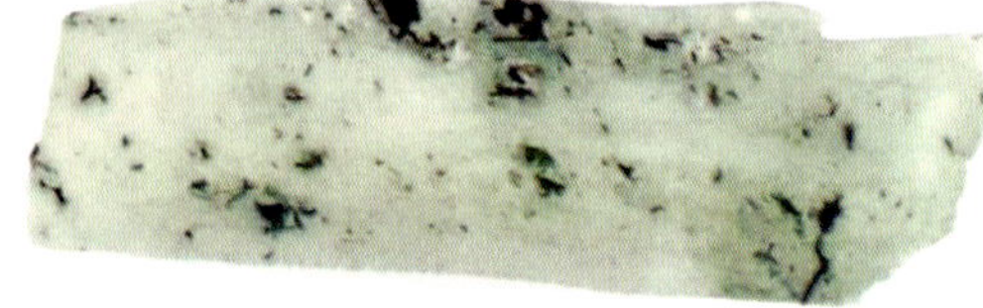

alum

INDIGO

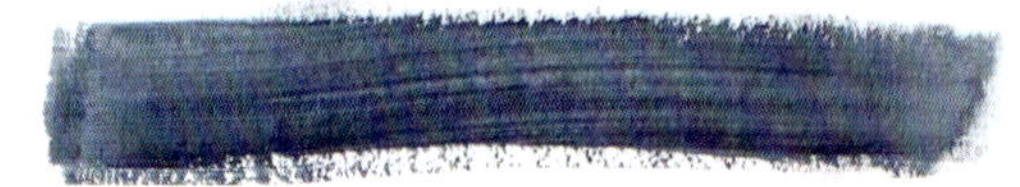

Glair and micellar casein paint with indigo

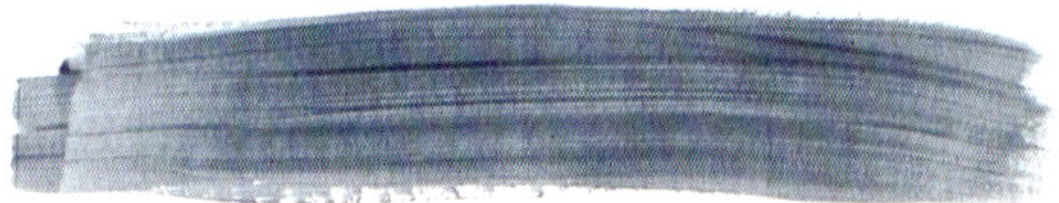

Equal parts glair and quark mulled and tinted with indigo

Equal parts glair and micellar casein mulled with a half-part kaolin clay, tinted with fresh oregon grape berries

Glair "acrylic" paint made with the leftover water of a madder lake

Glair "acrylic" paint made with madder lake water and a single drop of micellar casein powder

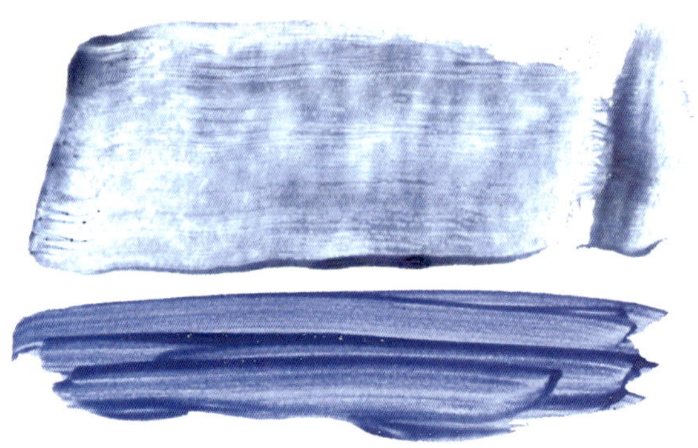

Milk paint made from ground cobalt smalt glass. The lower swatch used twice as much glass as the upper swatch. Cobalt smalt glass for use as pigment is sold by some pigment suppliers, including Kremer Pigments.

VARIOUS

Baking soda micellar casein paint tinted with fresh tickseed flowers with washing soda

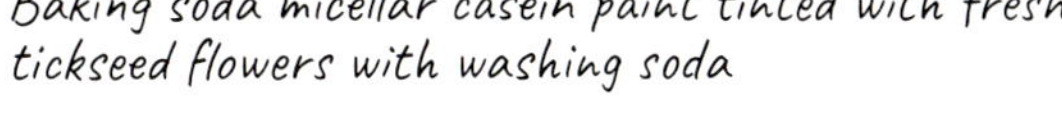

Baking soda micellar casein paint tinted with fresh tickseed flowers with ascorbic acid (vitamin c)

Baking soda micellar casein paint tinted with red zinnia petals and ascorbic acid

Egg yolk tempera paint tinted with oregon grape berries

Egg yolk tempera paint tinted with petals of fresh red verbena flowers

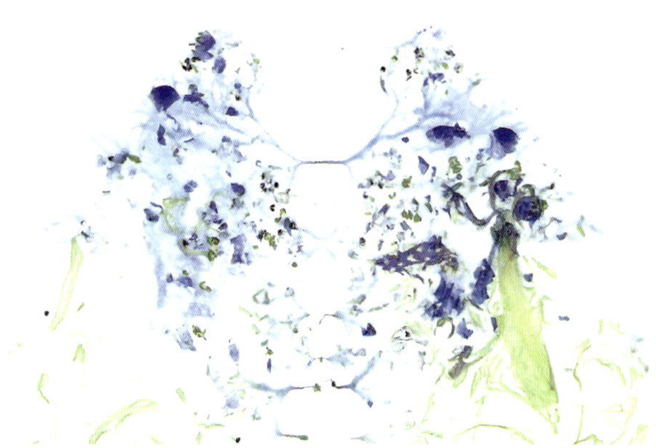

Grape hyacinth fresh press

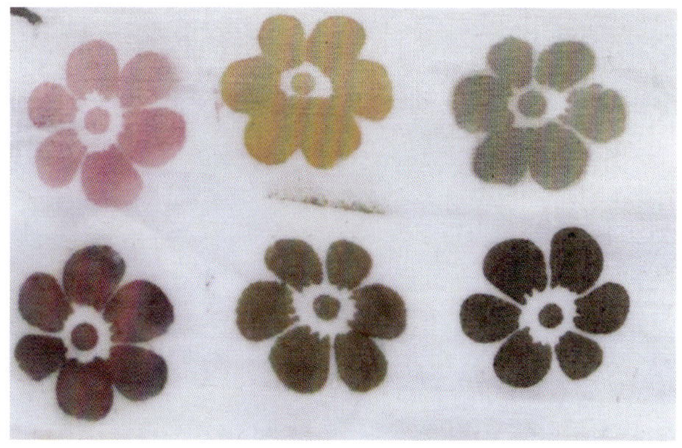

Flowers stenciled with various botanical paints

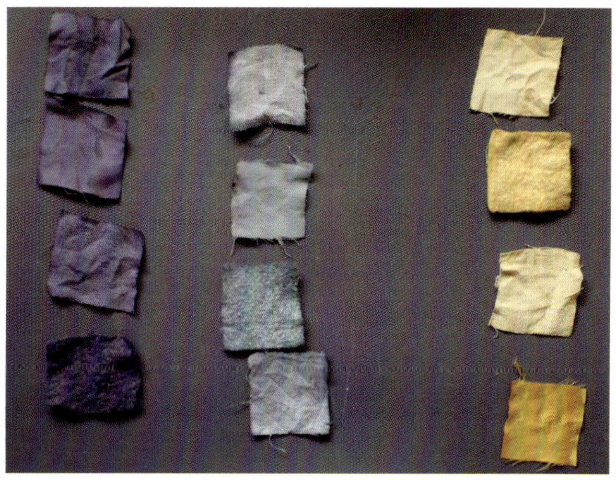

Left column: boiled mature woad seed on; top to bottom cotton, silk, linen, wool.
Middle column: boiled purple clematis flowers on; top to bottom linen, silk, wool, cotton.
Right column: boiled greater celandine flowers on: top to bottom cotton, wool, linen, silk

Stars stamped with gum arabic (left) and no gum arabic (right)

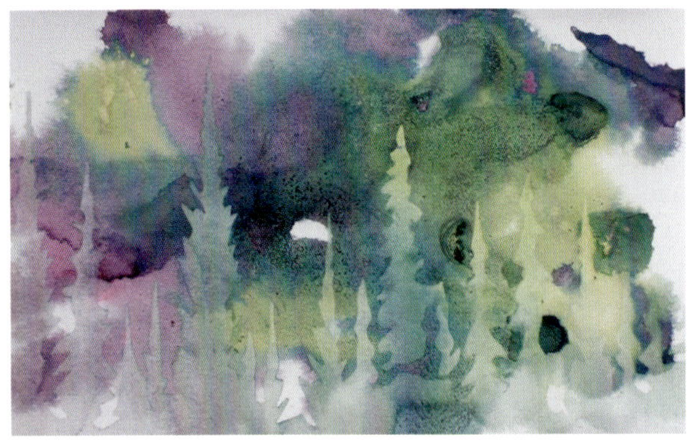

Reverse stencil art with various botanical paints

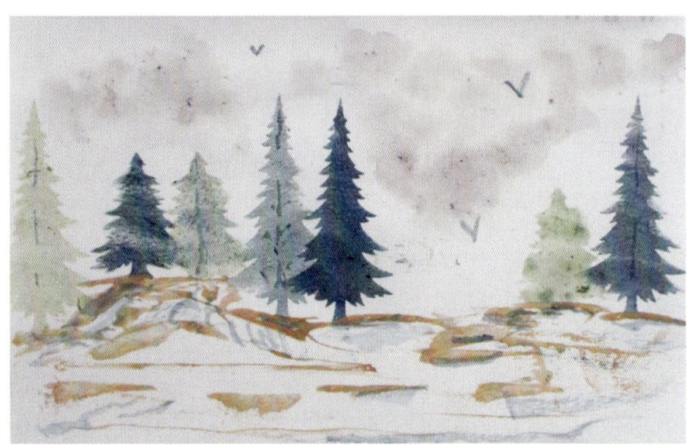

Forest scene stenciled with various botanical paints

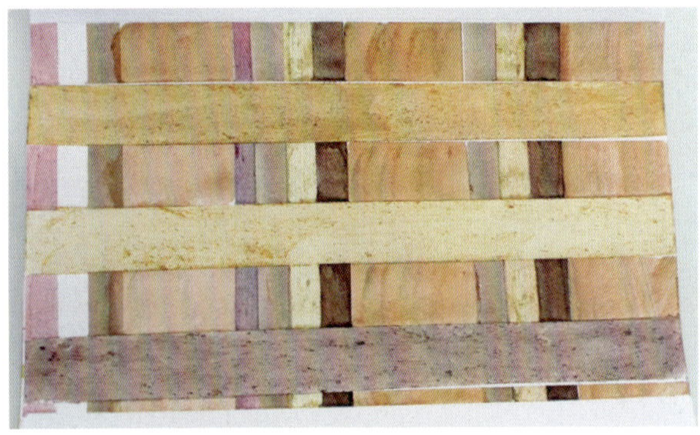

Color block art made with various botanical paints

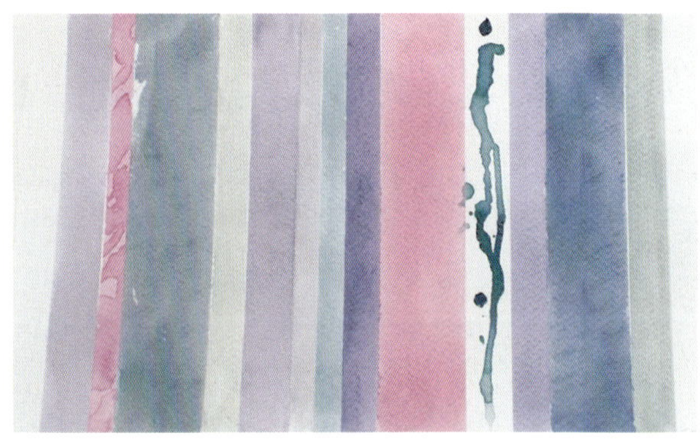

Mordanted colors of purple cabbage leaf

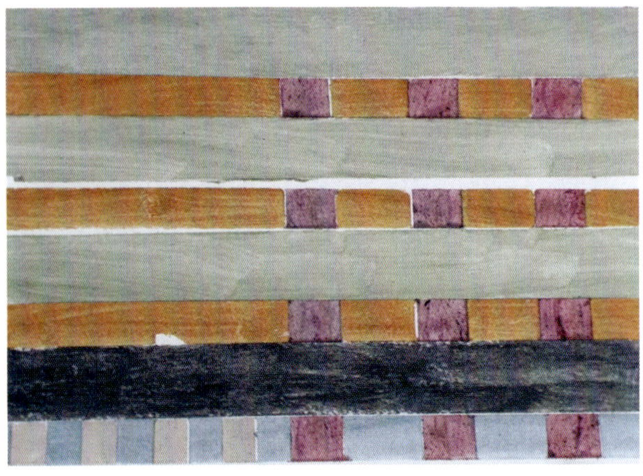

Art made with indigo, rust, vine black, Italian green clay, poinsettia leaf

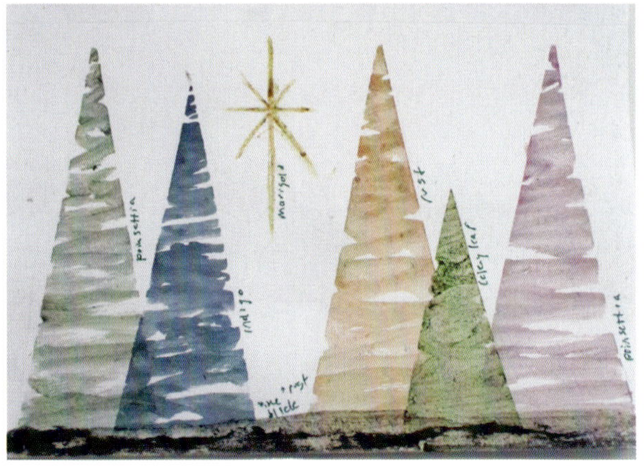

Christmas trees made with masking tape and poinsettia leaf, indigo, vine black, rust, marigold and celery leaf

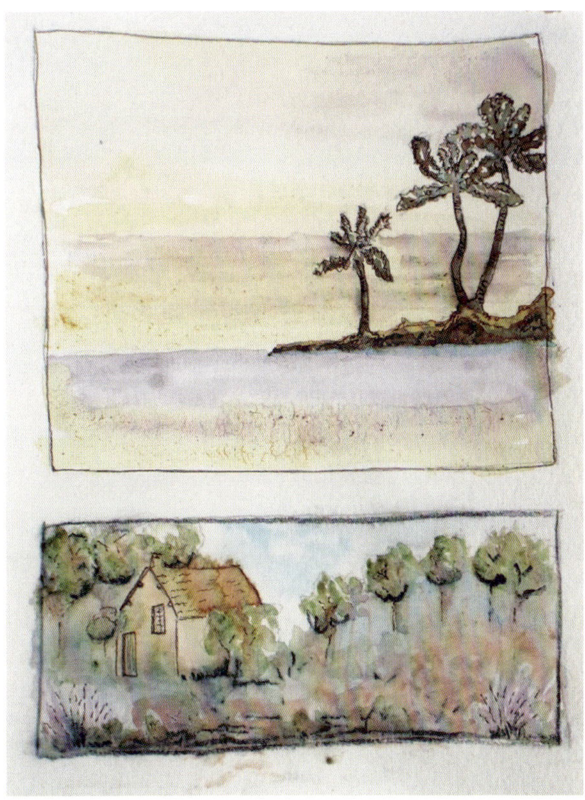

Made with all botanical watercolors

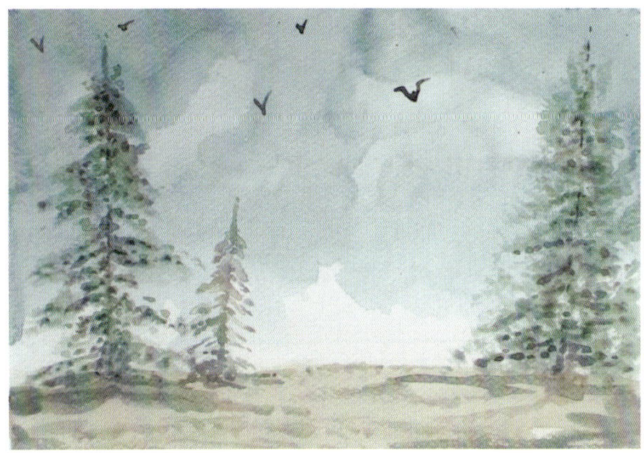

Made from only the mordanted colors of a single hyacinth

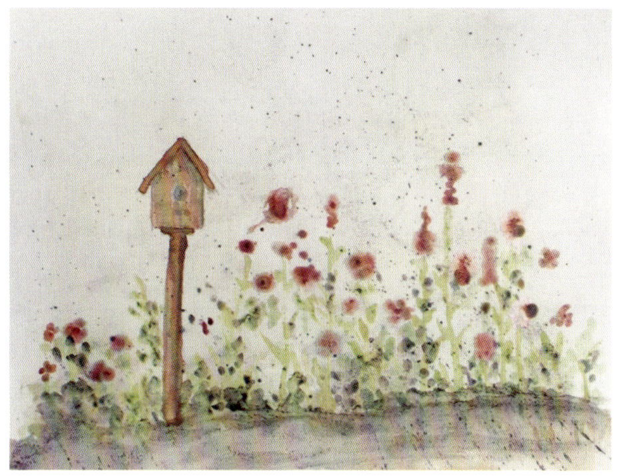

Made with all botanical watercolors

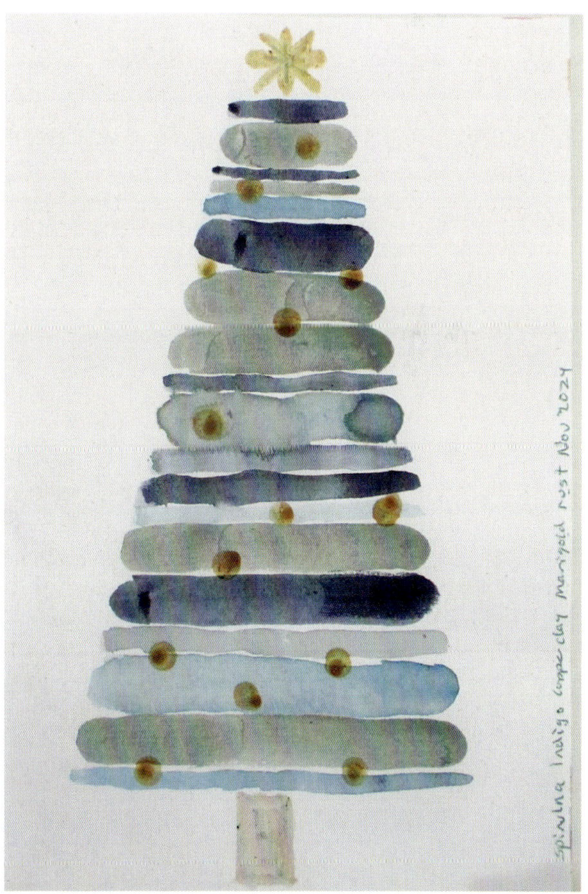

Watercolor Christmas tree made with spirulina, indigo, copper clay, marigold and rust

Image References

Ceanothus: Changku88, CC BY-SA 4.0 <https://creativecommons.org/licenses/by-sa/4.0>, via Wikimedia Commons

Celosia: Hanna Zelenko, CC BY-SA 4.0 <https://creativecommons.org/licenses/by-sa/4.0>, via Wikimedia Commons

Brazilwood: Carlo Brescia, CC BY-SA 4.0 <https://creativecommons.org/licenses/by-sa/4.0>, via Wikimedia Commons

Buttercup: Zeynel Cebeci, CC BY-SA 4.0 <https://creativecommons.org/licenses/by-sa/4.0>, via Wikimedia Commons

Campanula: Humoyun Mehridinov, CC BY-SA 4.0 <https://creativecommons.org/licenses/by-sa/4.0>, via Wikimedia Commons

Cochineal: Thelmadatter, CC BY-SA 4.0 <https://creativecommons.org/licenses/by-sa/4.0>

Cotoneaster: Agnieszka Kwiecień, Nova, CC BY-SA 4.0 <https://creativecommons.org/licenses/by-sa/4.0>, via Wikimedia Commons

Cranberries: Photo by Keith Weller, Public domain, via Wikimedia Commons

Datura: © El Grafo / CC-BY-SA-4.0, CC BY-SA 4.0 <https://creativecommons.org/licenses/by-sa/4.0>, via Wikimedia Commons

Docks and Sorrels: Michel Langeveld, CC BY-SA 4.0 <https://creativecommons.org/licenses/by-sa/4.0>, via Wikimedia Commons

Easter Lily: UpstateNYer, CC BY-SA 3.0 <https://creativecommons.org/licenses/by-sa/3.0>, via Wikimedia Commons

Eggshell: TeWeBs, CC BY-SA 4.0 <https://creativecommons.org/licenses/by-sa/4.0>, via Wikimedia Commons

Forsythia Branch: Ввласенко, CC BY-SA 4.0 <https://creativecommons.org/licenses/by-sa/4.0>, via Wikimedia Commons

Fustic: Maša Sinreih in Valentina Vivod, CC BY-SA 3.0 <https://creativecommons.org/licenses/by-sa/3.0>, via Wikimedia Commons

Gardenia: Storeye, CC BY-SA 4.0 <https://creativecommons.org/licenses/by-sa/4.0>, via Wikimedia Commons

Hawthorn: Davidbena, CC BY-SA 4.0 <https://creativecommons.org/licenses/by-sa/4.0>, via Wikimedia Commons

Lac: Jeffrey W. Lotz, CC BY 3.0 <https://creativecommons.org/licenses/by/3.0>, via Wikimedia Commons

Lobelia: Maciej Opaliński, CC BY-SA 4.0 <https://creativecommons.org/licenses/by-sa/4.0>, via Wikimedia Commons

Logwood: Yakshitha, CC BY-SA 4.0 <https://creativecommons.org/licenses/by-sa/4.0>, via Wikimedia Commons

Magenta Plant: 阿橋 HQ, CC BY-SA 2.0 <https://creativecommons.org/licenses/by-sa/2.0>, via Wikimedia Commons

Malabar Spinach: Shizhao2005年摄于诸暨乡间, ,, CC BY-SA 3.0 <https://creativecommons.org/licenses/by-sa/3.0>, via Wikimedia Commons

Mexican Honeysuckle: Photo by David J. Stang, CC BY-SA 4.0 <https://creativecommons.org/licenses/by-sa/4.0>, via Wikimedia Commons

Mexican Sunflower: Tim Green, CC BY 2.0 <https://creativecommons.org/licenses/by/2.0>, via Wikimedia Commons

Monarda: Tfbybyhf, CC0, via Wikimedia Commons

Mulberry: Zeynel Cebeci, CC BY-SA 4.0 <https://creativecommons.org/licenses/by-sa/4.0>, via Wikimedia Commons

Ninebark Purple: Photo by David J. Stang, CC BY-SA 4.0 <https://creativecommons.org/licenses/by-sa/4.0>, via Wikimedia Commons

Osage Orange: Plant Image Library from Boston, USA, CC BY-SA 2.0 <https://creativecommons.org/licenses/by-sa/2.0>, via Wikimedia Commons

Pink Cotton Flower: Science and Industry Museum, <https://blog.scienceandindustrymuseum.org.uk/worlds-first-synthetic-dye/#:~:text=Perkin%20took%20out%20a%20patent,first%20mass%2Dproduced%20chemical%20dyes>

Poinsettia: Vengolis, CC BY-SA 4.0 <https://creativecommons.org/licenses/by-sa/4.0>, via Wikimedia Commons

Pomegranate: H. Zell, CC BY-SA 3.0 <https://creativecommons.org/licenses/by-sa/3.0>, via Wikimedia Commons

Quebracho: Valerio Pillar, CC BY SA 2.0 <https://creativecommons.org/licenses/by-sa/2.0>, via Wikimedia Commons

Raspberry: GT1976, CC BY-SA 4.0 <https://creativecommons.org/licenses/by-sa/4.0>, via Wikimedia Commons

Rooibos: Winfried Bruenken (Amrum), CC BY-SA 2.5 <https://creativecommons.org/licenses/by-sa/2.5>, via Wikimedia Commons

Salsify: GT1976, CC BY-SA 4.0 <https://creativecommons.org/licenses/by-sa/4.0>, via Wikimedia Commons

Sandalwood: Forestowlet, CC0, via Wikimedia Commons

Spirea: Paul Hermans, CC BY-SA 3.0 <https://creativecommons.org/licenses/by-sa/3.0>, via Wikimedia Commons

Stonecrops: Mount Rainier National Park from Ashford, WA, United States, CC BY 2.0 <https://creativecommons.org/licenses/by/2.0>, via Wikimedia Commons

Sumac: Aleks.milo, CC BY-SA 4.0 <https://creativecommons.org/licenses/by-sa/4.0>, via Wikimedia Commons

Teasel: AnemoneProjectors, CC BY-SA 2.0 <https://creativecommons.org/licenses/by-sa/2.0>, via Wikimedia Commons

Thistle: Niranjan Arminius, CC BY-SA 4.0 <https://creativecommons.org/licenses/by-sa/4.0>, via Wikimedia Commons

Virginia Creeper: Cbaile19, CC0, via Wikimedia Commons

Wallflower: পাপৰি বৰা, CC BY-SA 4.0 <https://creativecommons.org/licenses/by-sa/4.0>, via Wikimedia Commons

Walnut: George Chernilevsky, Public domain, via Wikimedia Commons

Weld: Krzysztof Ziarnek, Kenraiz, CC BY-SA 4.0 <https://creativecommons.org/licenses/by-sa/4.0>, via Wikimedia Commons

Wild Lettuce: Luis Nunes Alberto, CC BY 3.0 <https://creativecommons.org/licenses/by/3.0>, via Wikimedia Commons

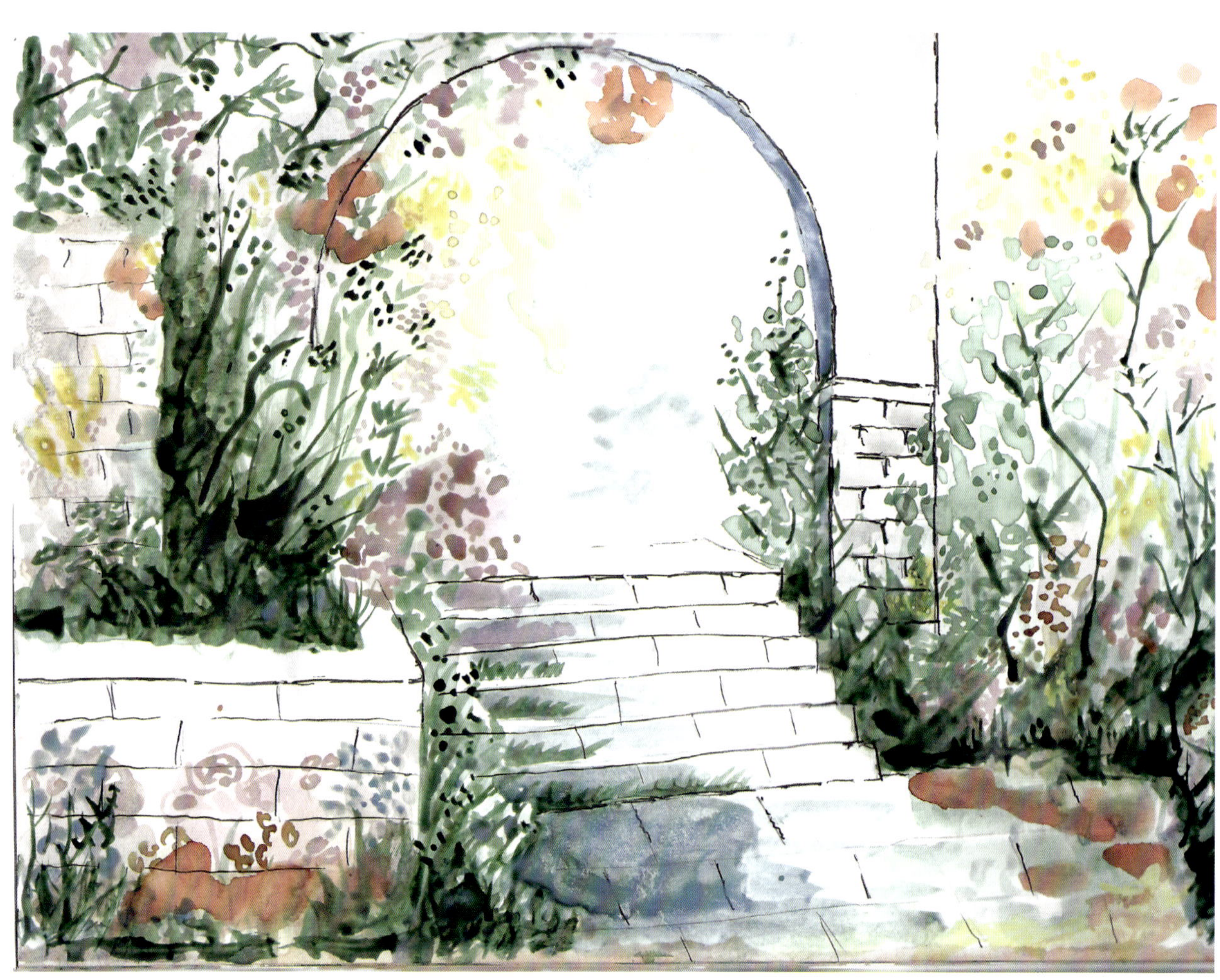

About the Author

Caleb Warnock is a *USA Today*–bestselling author of 24 nonfiction books, including *437 Edible Wild Plants of the Rocky Mountain West*. He is an expert on gardening and self-reliant living and has taught gardening classes for more than 25 years.

Other books by
Caleb Warnock

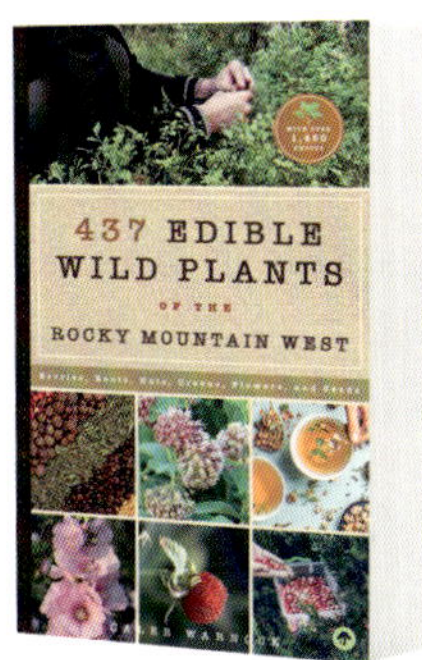

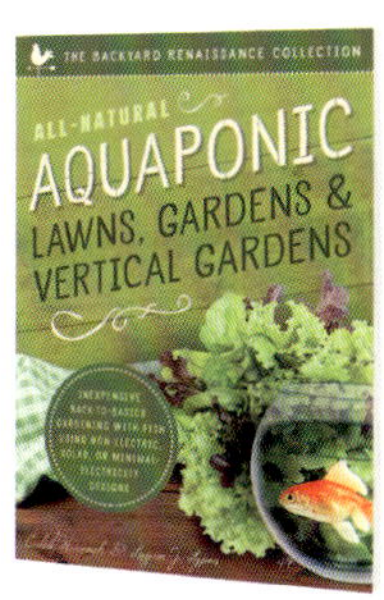

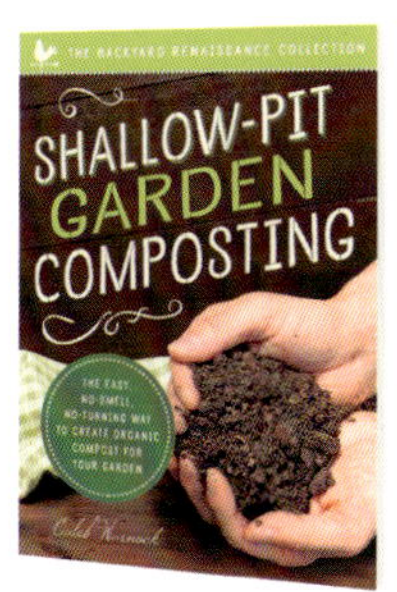

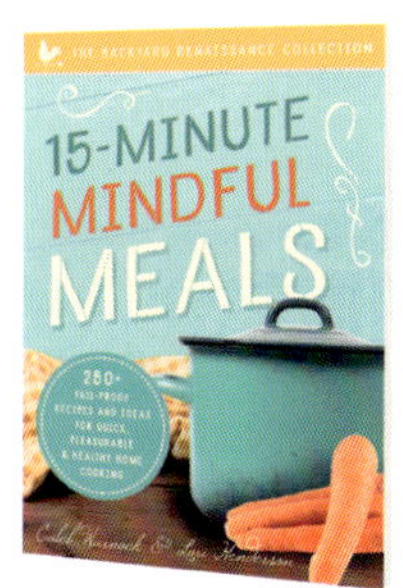

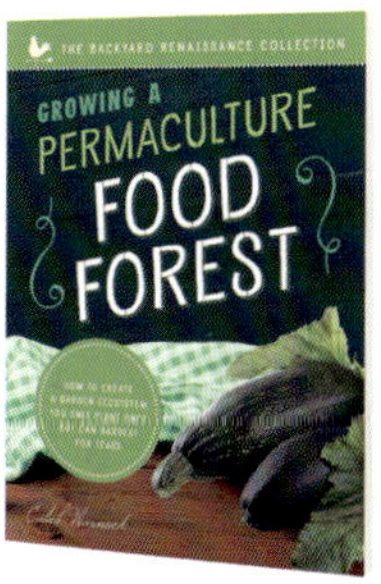

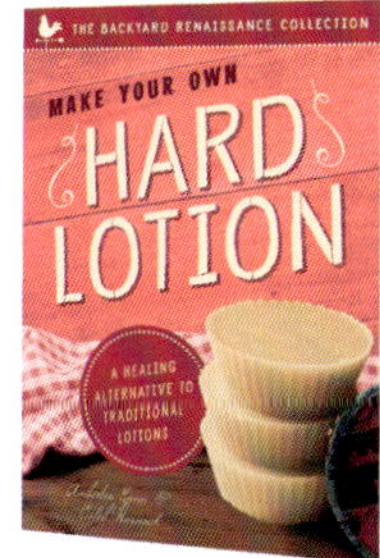

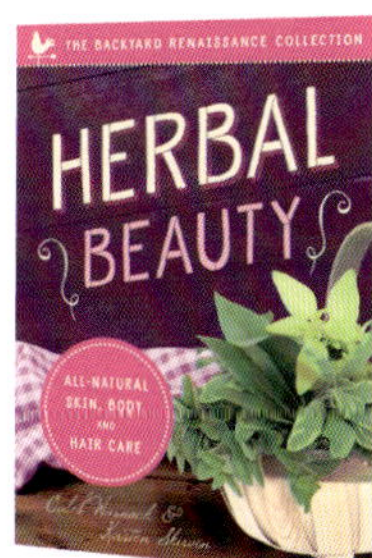

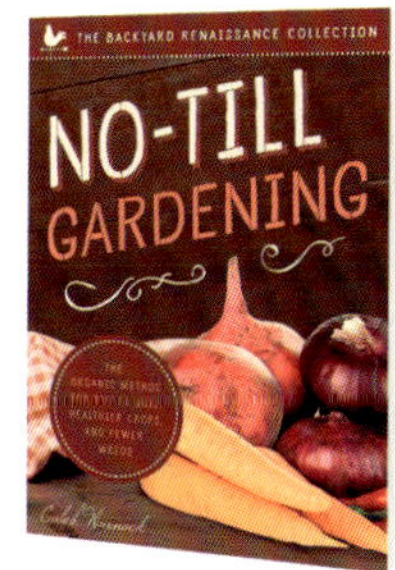

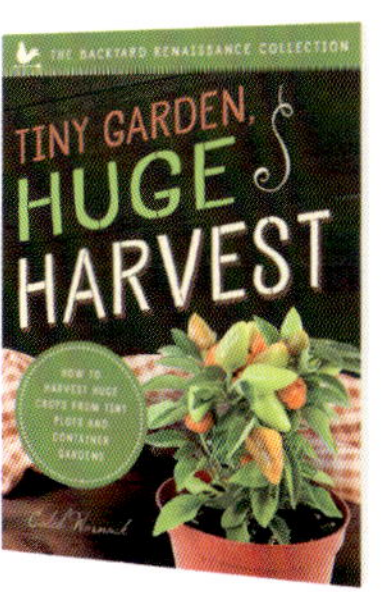

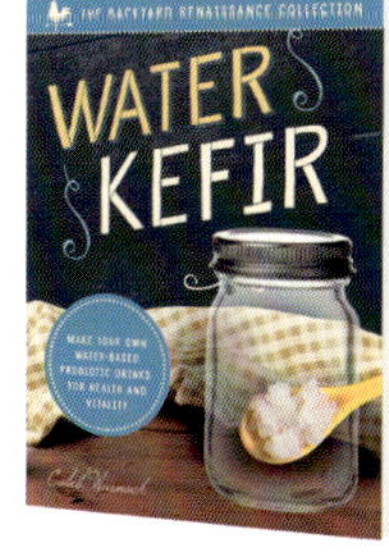

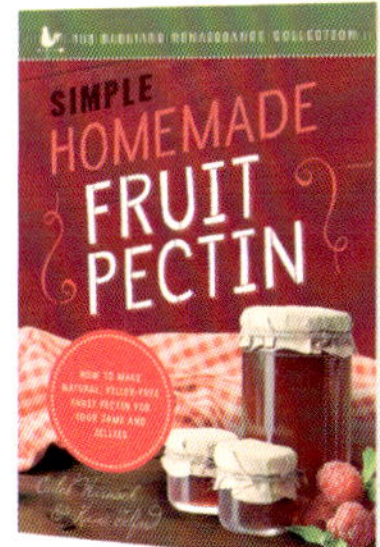

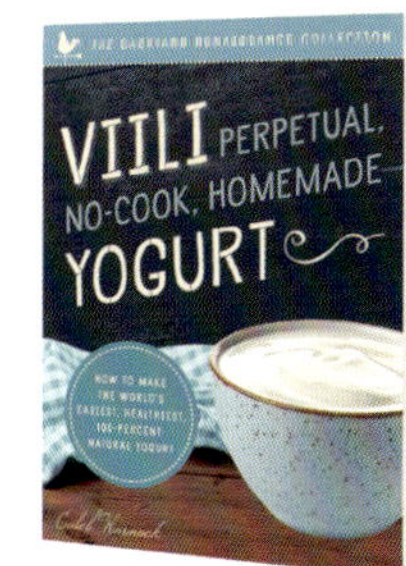

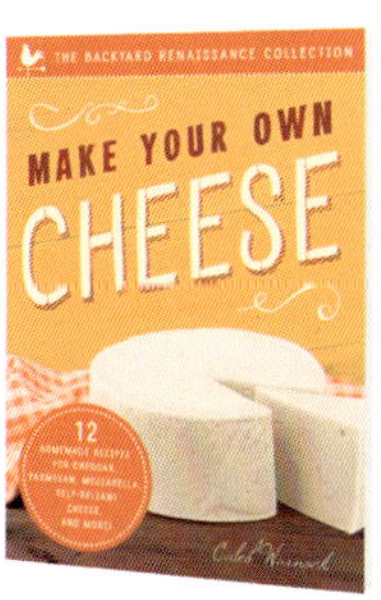

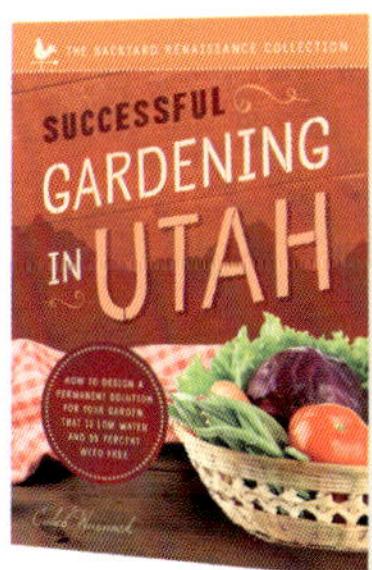

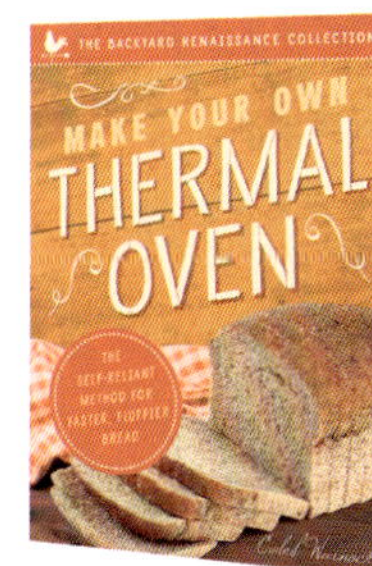

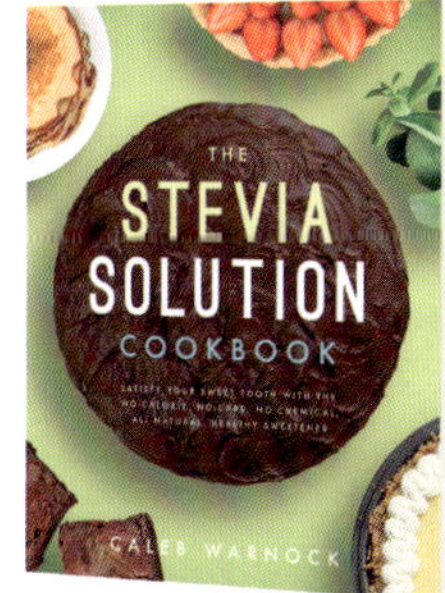

About Familius

Visit Our Website: www.familius.com

Familius is a global trade publishing company that publishes books and other content to help families be happy. We believe that happy families are key to a better society and the foundation of a happy life. The greatest work anyone will ever do will be within the walls of his or her own home. And we don't mean vacuuming! We recognize that every family looks different and passionately believe in helping all families find greater joy, whatever their situation. To that end, we publish beautiful books that help families live our 10 Habits of Happy Family Life: *love together, play together, learn together, work together, talk together, heal together, read together, eat together, give together,* and *laugh together*. Further, Familius does not discriminate on the basis of race, color, religion, gender, age, nationality, disability, caste, or sexual orientation in any of its activities or operations. Founded in 2012, Familius is located in Sanger, California.

CONNECT

Facebook: www.facebook.com/familiusbooks
Pinterest: www.pinterest.com/familiusbooks
Instagram: @FamiliusBooks
TikTok: @FamiliusBooks

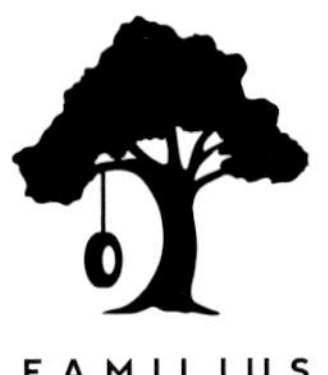

FAMILIUS

The most important work you ever do will be within the walls of your own home.

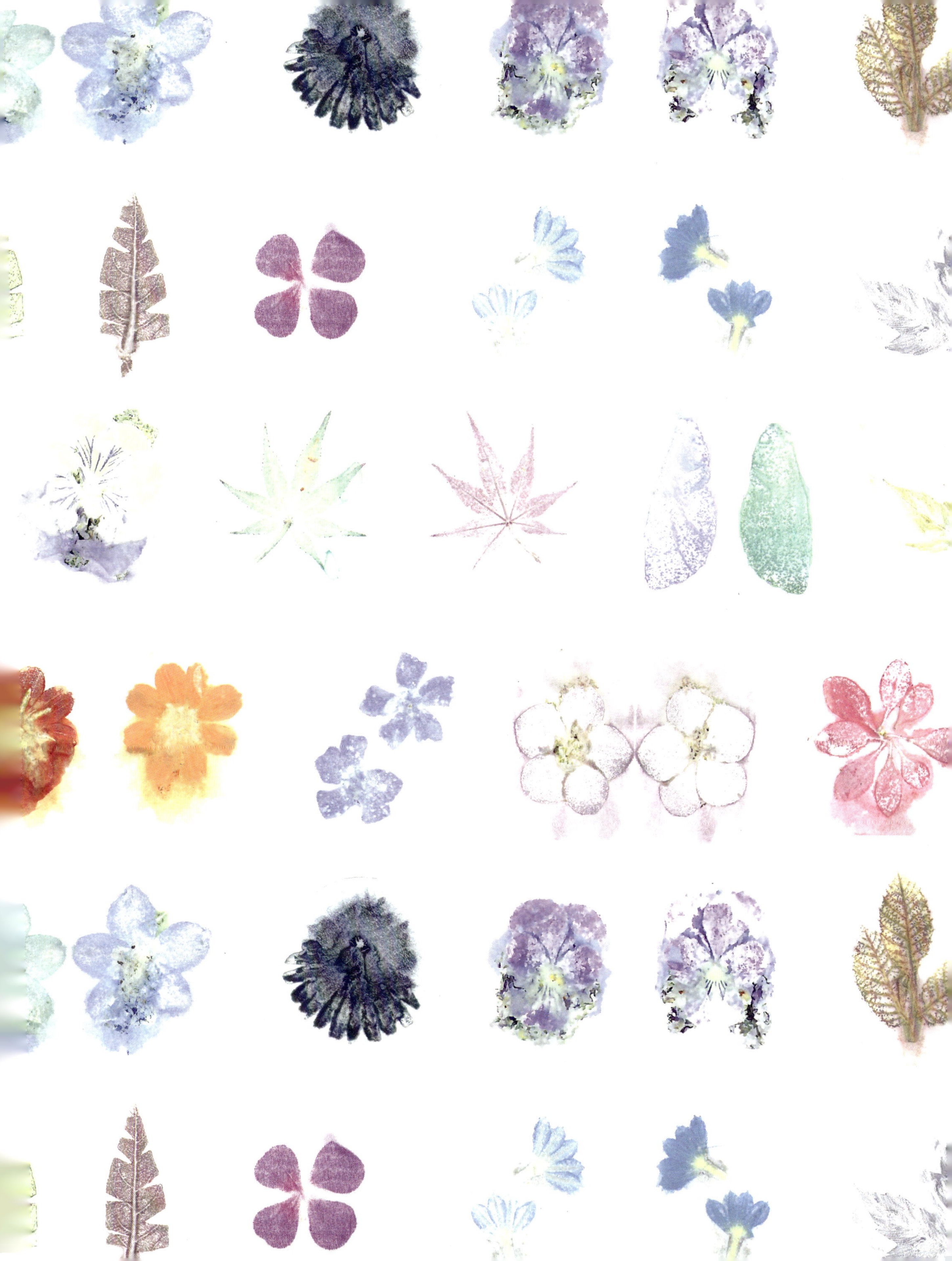

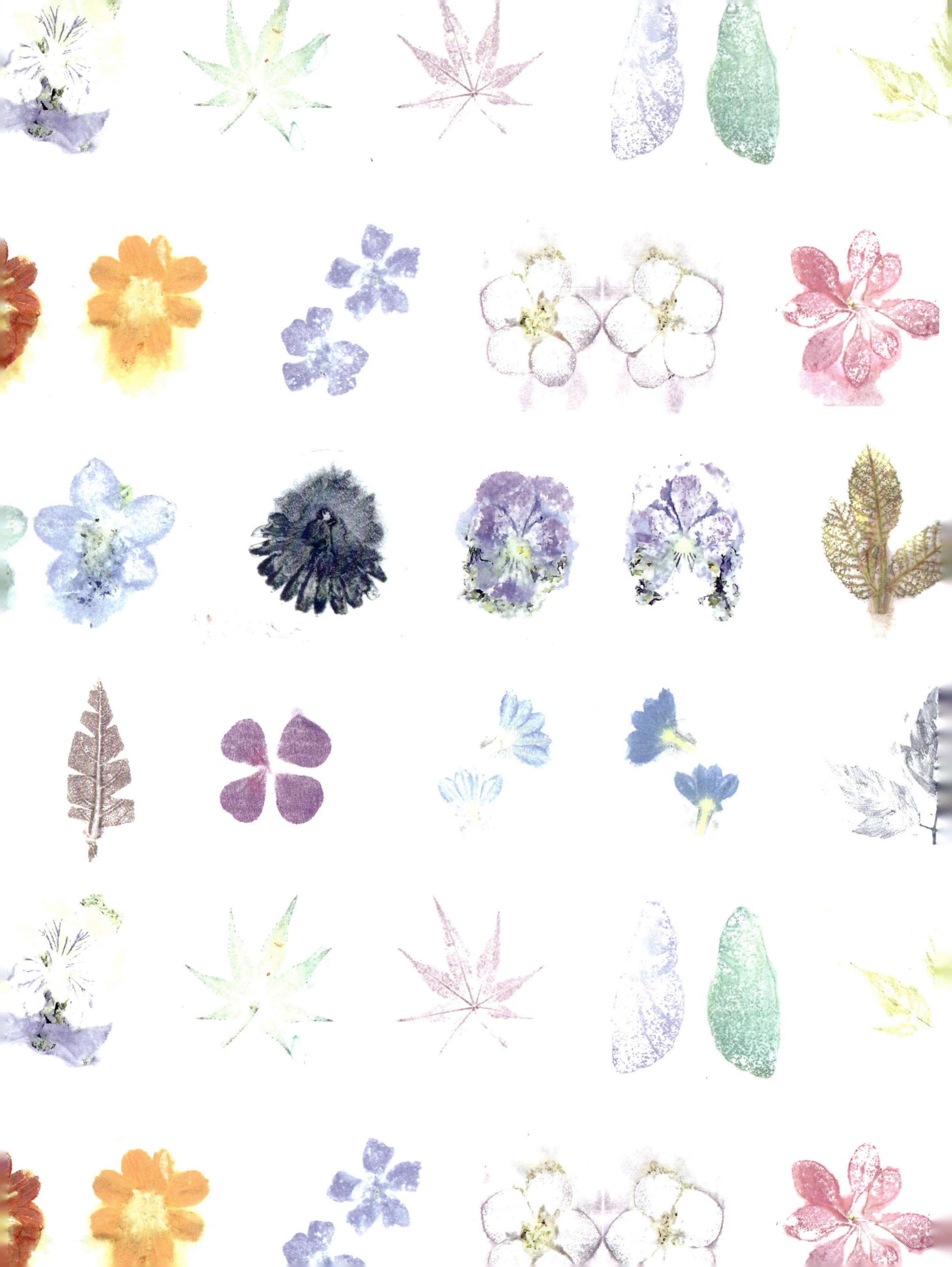